KU-289-276

For the Love of Dance

Dame Beryl Grey DBE

For the Love of Dance

OBERON BOOKS
LONDON

WWW.OBERONBOOKS.COM

First published in 2017 by Oberon Books Ltd
521 Caledonian Road, London N7 9RH
Tel: +44 (0) 20 7607 3637 / Fax: +44 (0) 20 7607 3629
e-mail: info@oberonbooks.com
www.oberonbooks.com

A catalogue record for this book is available from the British Library.

HB ISBN: 9781786820976
E ISBN: 9781786820983

Front cover: ©UNKOWN; Back cover: ©UNKOWN; Author image: ©VIVIENNE; Endpapers: ©S.G. SVENSON

Printed, bound and converted by CPI Group (UK) Limited, Croydon, CR0 4YY

Contents

Part Two – As Director

"What then is dancing but the soul's call to the body?"

RICHARD BURNS

To Sven – my loving and supportive husband of 58 years.

ACKNOWLEDGEMENTS

Mike Dixon for putting me on the correct path and editing my first drafts.

Jane Pritchard for supplying all LFB's performances from1967 – 1979, the venues, theatres and ballets performed.

Heather Knight my assistant at LFB and John Travis soloist and first archivist LFB, for their helpful memories.

Lesley Veal my hard-working, long-suffering secretary.

List of Illustrations

Part One – As a Dancer

29. Discussing *Checkmate* for BBC Television, July, 1963, with Robert Helpmann and Dame Ninette de Valois (Choreographer) (©ROYAL ACADEMY OF DANCE/ARENAPAL)
30. *Checkmate* with Ian Hamilton (©ROYAL ACADEMY OF DANCE/ARENAPAL)
31. *Checkmate,* with Philip Chatfield and Ronald Hynd, Covent Garden, 1948 (©FRANK SHARMAN/ROYAL OPERA HOUSE/ARENAPAL)
32. 1956 Bulganin, Khrushchev and Sir Anthony Eden after the Covent Garden performance of *Lady and the Fool,* Covent Garden (©ASSOCIATED PRESS)
33. My farewell performance as a member of the Royal Ballet, on stage at Covent Garden, 1957 (©S.G. SVENSON)
34. Outside the Bolshoi, 1957 (©S.G. SVENSON)
35. With Yuri Kondratov, my partner in Russia 1957 / 58; (©S.G. SVENSON)
36. Asaf Messerer giving class to the Bolshoi dancers and me (©S.G. SVENSON)
37. With Chinese dancer in the *Theatre of Heavenly Bridges, 1964;* (©S.G. SVENSON)
38. With Wang Shao Pen in *Swan Lake* (©S.G. SVENSON)
39. With Shanghai School of Dance (©S.G. SVENSON)
40. The Queen with Svetlana Berisova, Anya Linden and me (©UNKNOWN)
41. The three Sylvias, Violetta Elvin, Dame Margot Fonteyn and me (PHOTOGRAPH BY GEORGE VARJAS ©REFLEX)
42. Dame Ninette de Valois backstage at the Rome Opera House (©UNKNOWN)
43. Princess Grace of Monaco and Lady Irene Astor after the Sunshine Gala Matinee at Drury Lane, 1965 (©UNKNOWN)
44. Wedding Day, Weybridge, July 1950 (©R. SVENSON)
45. Ingvar with Sven and me 1958 (©VIVIENNE)
46. On holiday in Sweden with Ingvar 1964 (©UNKNOWN)
47. Sven and me feted in China (©UNKNOWN)

Part Two – As Director

48. With Lord Max Rayne at the announcement of my takeover of Festival Ballet (©UNKNOWN)
49. With Dame Alicia Markova and Sir Anton Dolin, 1977 (©MIKE HUMPHREY)
50. With HRH Princess Margaret at the Gala, London Coliseum June 1969 (©UNKNOWN)
51. Office in Athens, Greece (©JOE BANGAY/ARENAPAL)
52. Sunshine Gala, All England Dance Competition – The Beryl Grey Award, Drury Lane, July 1970 (©KEYSTONE/HULTON ARCHIVE/GETTY IMAGES)
53. *Sleeping Beauty*; Galina Samsova and Andre Provkovsky, The London Festival Ballet at the Festival Hall, London, August 1967 (PHOTOGRAPHED BY GBL. WILSON © ROYAL ACADEMY OF DANCE/ARENAPAL)
54. Witold Borkowski rehearsing Patrice Bart and Elisabetta Terrabust in *Don Quixote* 1975 (©ANTHONY CRICKMAY/VICTORIA AND ALBERT MUSEUM, LONDON)
55. Carmen Mathé as the Coquette and John Gilpin as the Poet in George Balanchine's *Night Shadow* 1967 (©ANTHONY CRICKMAY/VICTORIA AND ALBERT MUSEUM, LONDON)
56. Ballet Mistress, Joan Potter and Ballet Master, Vassilie Trunoff (©ZOË DOMINIC)
57. With Wilfred Stiff (©UNIVERSITY OF DUNDEE THE PETO COLLECTION)

58. With Peter Brownlee, General Manager (©JOE BANGAY/ARENAPAL)

59. Frano Jelencic, Ballet Master (©UNKNOWN)

60. With David Rees *(left)* & Paul Findlay *(right)* (©UNKNOWN)

61. Taking Rehearsal with Galina Samsova & Andre Prokovsky with Donald Barclay ballet master looking on (©ANTHONY CRICKMAY/VICTORIA AND ALBERT MUSEUM, LONDON)

62. *Sleeping Beauty*; with John Gilpin, Noella Pontois, Galina Samsova and Andre Prokovsky; Curtain Call; The London Festival Ballet at the Festival Hall, London, UK; August 1967 (PHOTOGRAPHED BY GBL. WILSON © ROYAL ACADEMY OF DANCE/ARENAPAL)

63. London Festival Ballet's 21st Anniversary Gala at the London Coliseum with Terrance Kern, John Gilpin, Terry Hayworth, André Prokovsky and Edward Villella, 1971 (©ROSEMARY WINCKLEY)

64. Ronald Hynd rehearsing Paul Clarke and Patricia Ruanne in his ballet, *The Sanguine Fan* 1976 (©ANTHONY CRICKMAY/VICTORIA AND ALBERT MUSEUM, LONDON)

65. With Sir Adrian Boult (©UNKNOWN)

66. Rehearsing *Parade* (©ALAN CUNLIFFE)

67. With Massine (©UNKNOWN)

68. With Dame Margot Fonteyn (©UNKNOWN)

69. Maina Gielgud in Maurice Béjart's *Forme et ligne* 1971 (©ANTHONY CRICKMAY/VICTORIA AND ALBERT MUSEUM, LONDON)

70. Patricia Ruanne at a rehearsal of *Giselle* (©UNKNOWN)

71. With Paco Pena, Sir Andre Previn and Peter Maxwell Davies (©STEVE WOOD/HULTON ARCHIVE/GETTY IMAGES)

72. Eva Evdokimova (©UNKNOWN)

73. Barry Moreland rehearsing Paul Clarke and Patricia Ruanne *Prodigal Son (in Ragtime)*, 1974; (©ANTHONY CRICKMAY/VICTORIA AND ALBERT MUSEUM, LONDON)

74. With Nureyev (©THE TIMES/NEWS SYNDICATION)

75. Rudolf Nureyev and Beryl Grey with President and Mrs Carter at the White House June 1978 (©JIMMY CARTER LIBRARY AND MUSEUM)

76. With ballerinas from London Festival Ballet, China, 1979 (©UNKNOWN)

77. In China (©UNKNOWN)

78. With Chinese Embassy Official (©UNKNOWN)

79. With Sir John and Anya (Linden) Lord & Lady Sainsbury (©UNKNOWN)

80. With Dame Gillian Lynne (©UNKNOWN)

81. Receiving London University doctorate from HRH Princess Anne, 1996 (©JEREMY MAKINSON)

82. *Swan Lake* Royal Gala; meeting Queen Elizabeth II backstage; Royal Opera House, 1996; (©KEITH SAUNDERS/ARENAPAL)

83. Meeting Princess Diana, Pamela Crouch (Sunshine Homes secretary) (©UNKNOWN)

84. With Sven & Ingvar, 1988 with DBE award (©UNKNOWN)

85. Marcela Goicoechea, Irek Mukhamedov, Dr Wayne Sleep, Galina Samsova & Agnes Oaks, A Dance Gala To Celebrate The 75th Birthday Year Of Dame Beryl Grey DBE, At Sadler's Wells, London (©DAVE BENETT/HULTON ARCHIVE/GETTY IMAGES)

86. With Esteban Berlanga 2006 (©UNKNOWN)

Foreword

It has been my great good fortune to have seen much of the range of Beryl Grey's career, from the dancing of an extraordinarily gifted young girl who shone so delightfully in war-time performances – with the then Sadler's Wells Ballet – to the grand achievements of the ballerina of that same Company, but now installed at Covent Garden as our National Ballet and honoured with a Royal Charter, and then as the director (and rescuer, because of her wise leadership) of another fine but ill-starred ballet troupe. As the terrible scars of war began to fade, what had become our Royal Ballet gained in world acclaim, as did its dancers, and so, most certainly, did Beryl Grey. Her career as the wonderfully talented young artist who had appeared as Giselle and as Odette/Odile in *Swan Lake* as a teen-ager, and then became a leading dancer admired both at Covent Garden and on the world-wide tours by her parent Company; as the first British ballerina to dance as a guest with the Moscow Bolshoi and Leningrad Kirov companies, and then in China; as an educator directing a major school, and finally as artistic director of London Festival (now English National) Ballet, has shown us Dame Beryl as a discreetly astonishing figure in the dance-history of our time.

What was extraordinarily appealing about Beryl Grey's stage appearances was the sense that she was not only in command of her interpretations - nothing fudged or blurred; nothing uncertain; the choreography understood, the choreographer honoured, and her companion artists respected – but that pleasure in her performance was both ours as audience and hers as dancer. It amounted, everywhere, to her integrity as a performer, to her respect for her choreography and for her public. Neither must ever be let down. This may seem a commonplace of theatrical life, but Dame Beryl's communication with her audiences – as with her choreography and her fellow artists – had an honesty, a directness born of her sense of duty and her character itself, which has surely been central to her artistry as it has been her career. Certain dancers rely at moments on a stage-persona which the audience recognises: the joyous look, the oh-so-clever technical trick, the appealing curtain-call ("she should take a bow carrying a doggie with a bandaged paw" observed one cynic), and the public reaction is automatic cheers. Beryl Grey in performance – the grand span of her dancing; the clarity of the interpretation; the radiant grace (her Lilac Fairy) or the inexorable evil (her Black Queen in *Checkmate*) – gave the grand value of her artistry and intelligence to a role, and it lived splendidly for us.

It was, unsurprisingly, these qualities of integrity and sensitivity which were to illuminate her later career, as Artistic Director of London Festival Ballet. Born of the theatrical wisdom and illustrious talents of Alicia Markova and Anton Dolin, the Company had done marvels in taking great dancers and certain grand relics of the Ballets Russes repertory for regional tours and happy London seasons, replete with honourable revivals of choreographic masterpieces, with a gifted ensemble and the irresistible presences of certain great and still potent artists of the Ballets Russes tradition. But hard box-office times, the retirement of illustrious names, less than happy renewals of the repertory, meant that the troupe was heading toward the rocks. Beryl Grey accepted the challenge to rescue it – and despite all the hazards and hurdles and inadequacies and devious politics that, unexpected, awaited her and added to the problems, she made the Company a strong and honourable troupe again. At what cost, and with what integrity on her part, these pages fascinatingly, illuminatingly show. We find here both bizarre insights into the history and inadequacies of British ballet's artistic policies and a very touching and inspiring portrait of Dame Beryl's gifts as woman and artist and Director, and learn of the ever-sustaining joys of her family life.

Today, she remains for me – as she must do for all those who have known her, worked with her, been involved with her good causes – an illuminating presence, a joy, an example of how it should be done! As a critic, I always applauded her performances and her directoral skills with a sense of great gratitude. I applaud her still, admire her still, honour her still, treasure her still.

Clement Crisp OBE. R. is ballet-critic of *The Financial Times*

Preface

Dame Beryl Grey, Empress of British Ballet.

To view the dancer in stillness or in motion is to see the human body in its most crystalline and life-affirming light. Dancers prostrate themselves at beauty's altar, and, all too soon, they are fed into its all-consuming flames. But in their brief iridescence, they are the artists most lightly kissed by God.

Dame Beryl Grey was a unique Prima Ballerina, who radiantly transformed herself into a blazing sundial of humankind that enlightened the lives of those fortunate enough to have seen her dance. When she danced, she was indeed kissed by God.

I was one of the lucky ones who saw her dance. The first time was in 1949, at the old Metropolitan Opera House in New York City, where she danced the Lilac Fairy to Margot Fonteyn's Princess Aurora in Ninette de Valois's legendary production of *The Sleeping Beauty*. Now sixty-eight years later, I still vividly recall her majestic and magnificent expression of the role. Only an artist of a rare gift can touch the viewer so deeply that the passage of time cannot dim the memory of such extraordinary beauty. Such an artist was Dame Beryl Grey.

In 1953 I saw her dance again, this time in London. I watched her approach a more contemporary classical choreographic language with an emphatic and embattled angularity in the dramatic ballet, *Checkmate*. At one moment she crouched down in an angular, deep knee bend on pointe, an extreme dance movement unusual for the time. She was a wonderful interpreter of not only the classical roles but also the contemporary roles of the era. Dame Beryl embodied superb technique combined with eloquent expressiveness.

Through the decades she has been, and still is, an inspiration to the public who love ballet, a muse for all those who will follow in her illustrious path.

Dame Beryl Grey has spent her life exploring the outer reaches of her potential in order to achieve continuous personal and artistic development. As such the echo of her dancing still reverberates through space and time, now given renewed life in this memoir.

Adam Darius, Dancer, Mime Artist, Choreographer, Teacher, Author, 2017

Part One – As A Dancer

Prologue

In writing these memoirs I realise how much dance has encircled and enriched my life. I was an only child and my parents were determined not to spoil me, to encourage me to have faith in God, to listen, obey and respect authority and always to work hard – invaluable lessons for life, as well as for a career in the theatre.

My dancing took me across the world from the Royal Opera House, Covent Garden, to the Bolshoi Theatre in Moscow and to many other renowned theatres. I met numerous prominent people and worked with the greats of the ballet world. This book traces my progress from a young child, working under Ninette de Valois; touring with the Sadler's Wells Ballet during the war, sometimes stepping in for Margot Fonteyn; appearing worldwide as a freelance ballerina; directing and touring internationally with London Festival Ballet (now English National Ballet).

I hope I reveal to the reader the excitement and transience of theatre life with all its ups and downs; the thrill of dancing for an audience; the tingling moments of anticipation on hearing the orchestra warm up before the curtain rises; alighting alone on stage, bathed in a sea of lights, the power of the music lifting me into another world.

Performing is a unique and divine experience which I will always see as a joy and privilege, communicating to an audience through the beauty of ballet and the love of dance.

My life has encompassed many dramatic situations, both on-stage and off, so I suppose it was appropriate that the circumstances of my birth on 11 June 1927 were full of danger for me and my mother. In the private London nursing home at the bottom of Highgate Hill the surgeon said to my father: 'Mr Groom, I have to warn you that either your wife or your baby will die, they cannot both survive this confinement, even though I am planning to give Mrs Groom "Twilight Sleep".'

But survive we both did, and my mother lived for a further twenty-five years to see me established as a leading ballerina at the Royal Opera House, Covent Garden. Her courage and love remain my inspiration to this day, together with my father's faith and deep love for us both.

Neither of my parents had an easy start in life; my mother, Annie, was brought up by her uncle and step-mother in less than affluent circumstances, and my father, Arthur Groom, who everyone called Bob, the last of six children, had rickets as a child. Both knew poverty, and suffered as a result, yet both overcame those disadvantages through hard work and determination. They were childhood sweethearts, who attended the same school in Hackney, London, where they met and fell in love, and remained sweethearts throughout their lives.

The First World War separated them; my father was in the thick of the fighting and blinded for several weeks by mustard gas. Despite my mother's longing to leave her unhappy home at the cessation of war, my father would not contemplate marriage until he could provide for her adequately and offer her a decent home. After two years of saving they were married in November 1920.

Due to my mother's poor health they were advised to wait a few years before thinking of having a child, and what a harrowing time my arrival caused them. Yet whatever trials accosted them, they were always so loving and close throughout their marriage to the time my mother died in 1952. They would go everywhere together and were never seen apart. This devotion and loyalty was the background of my childhood, a living example of faith and true love.

December 1952 saw the worst pea-soup fog London ever experienced, causing many deaths, and it is as if in a haze I recall the events leading up to this, my first deeply personal loss. My mother's operation was at 4.30pm on 19 December, and that very evening I was to dance in a Royal Gala at Covent Garden. It was the only Royal Gala I was ever given at Covent Garden, dancing the lead in a full-length ballet, *Swan Lake*. I was dancing my favourite role, Odette / Odile in a production newly designed by Leslie Hurry about which there was much interest and excitement.

Neither of my parents could be at the Opera House, as they would have been normally – my mother on the operating table, my father by her bedside until the hospital assured him that the operation had gone well.

After the Gala, with the nervous strain and excitement of the performance over, my father gave me encouraging news. But at daybreak the next day, happiness was soon swept away. I cannot describe the awfulness – I had always had a very powerful bond with my mother. She had been a constant reassuring presence, and had guided, encouraged and supervised all my early training. Then, suddenly, she was no longer there.

How blessed I had been by her love and sacrifices which I always took for granted. How fortunate I was now, to have Sven, a wonderfully compassionate husband, to support me, as well as my father, during those frantic days searching for a burial place near Coulsdon where our family enjoyed so many happy years together.

The one uplifting event at this sad time was the totally unexpected arrival of a telegram from the Queen Mother expressing her sympathy at my loss. It was like a magical star dropping from the heavens, and I will always treasure this comforting message from our gracious Queen Mother.

How terrible it was for my father when the light of his life was taken from him, and for the next thirty years he faced life alone, faithful to his Annie to the end. He died peacefully in Sussex, January 1973 and was laid to rest on a bright winter's morning beside my mother in the cemetery on Epsom Downs.

2 *Early Blossoms, The Beginnings*

In writing this autobiography it becomes clear to me that so much that happened in my life just fell into place, as if an unknown power was looking after me, directing and controlling everything.

My parents held no ambition for me to become a dancer. As an only child I joined my two cousins in dancing classes once a week at Sherborne Preparatory School, which we three attended. The dance teacher, Madeleine Sharp, was unusually gifted and destined to become the foremost dance teacher of young children in this country. It was she who spotted my talent and gave me such a remarkably sound early training, watching my every move. Even today I meet those whose childhood and adult life has been enriched by her teaching.

Madeleine Sharp was a striking personality, always impeccably dressed, with gorgeous hats and matching gloves. Her strong features and radiant, confident smile brought out the best in her pupils, combining strictness with encouragement. After only a few months she asked my mother if I could undertake more frequent training, suggesting that I take part in her more advanced classes in Bromley. This is where I first met Gillian Lynne, now famous for her choreography, including the Lloyd Webber musicals, *Cats* and *Phantom of the Opera*. We struck up a lasting friendship, which we still hold dear today.

We both benefited from the all-round training we were given by Madeleine – ballet, Greek, national dances, musical comedy, tap, ballroom dancing, even mime, and I recall dancing with skipping ropes, too – an astonishing range. Madeleine had a gift for imaginative, simple dance arrangements for her young pupils for whom she designed all the costumes herself. Her annual shows at the Rudolf Steiner Theatre in London were of an exceptionally high standard, and I used to look forward to these occasions with great excitement. Our make-up was carefully plastered on us, the only aspect I strongly disliked.

My mother took my training very seriously and followed Madeleine's instructions to the letter. Overseeing my exercises every morning before school and every afternoon on my return home, she always referred to the detailed notes she made. As well as running our home and tending the garden she was a very gifted needlewoman, making all our clothes. I cannot help but wonder at the preparation and care with which my mother supervised my practice routines at home and rehearsed me in my solos. She played the piano well and had a beautiful voice. I would listen to her and my father singing together, songs from operettas, so popular pre-war.

My father arranged a mirror behind a barre, which he installed in our lounge, and there I worked very hard every day of the week including Sundays. I didn't mind all that training; in fact I was so much in love with dance that I wanted to be the best in my class and outshine everyone. It did not bother me that I missed many children's parties and other children's activities. 'Miss Sharp' took a keen interest in me, and I wanted her and my parents to be pleased.

My first ever public appearance, at the age of three, was with my father on New Year's Eve in our local, large public house The Red Lion, in Coulsdon, the village we moved to from London. The upstairs ballroom was packed with revellers wearing paper hats amid a sea of multi-coloured balloons, and as a clock struck loud and long, I danced in the New Year while my father, disguised as the Old Year, limped sadly away from the scene, pushed out by the lithe New Year. I loved that experience, although I disliked being woken from sleep in a warm bed, to be dressed in a pretty but thin frock, with a little make-up applied to my face. My mother was very strict about my getting sufficient rest and sleep and for years insisted that I lie down before an event, something that I have done all through my life. How invaluable that little rest is, always.

Today, after eighty years or so, the spot where I made my public debut is almost unrecognisable. The nice old Red Lion has been pulled down to make way for a wide main road leading uphill past our church, transforming the formerly quiet Woodcote Grove Road into a main thoroughfare. At the northern approach more buildings have been demolished to accommodate a fast new highway uphill and away to the south from Coulsdon towards the M25. It is quite bewildering, as are so many other changes one encounters today.

Many changes are inevitable with the tremendous increase in road traffic, but some remain questionable. Although I am sad that the Red Lion pub in Coulsdon has vanished, I realise that it is also a question of fashion and finance. Pubs with baronial ballrooms on the first floor are almost non-existent. Guilds and merchants no longer dine in the ornate splendour of these banqueting rooms, only echoes of past Masonic meetings remain, drifting like cobwebs on the breeze. In the past in these grand halls many a young ballet dancer struggled to remain upright on a shiny, slippery floor with sliding chairs masquerading as barres. Now we have specially designed dance studios with nonslip, well sprung floors, barres, mirrors and all the accessories expected in today's safety-conscious society. Dancing is no longer taught in a teacher's own sitting room or in makeshift back rooms, as was often the case in the twenties and thirties when there was far less money about and far less interest in dance as a serious art.

When I reached six, Miss Sharp advised my parents to send me for elocution, piano and singing lessons, all of which I thoroughly enjoyed. I had little time or interest for play, but I resented having to practise on Sundays. That was the day I went to church with my father in the morning while my mother was cooking the Sunday roast. Lunch over, I was off to Sunday school in the early afternoon. Once back home, I loved to open my dolls house, unpack my farmyard animals, carefully arranging my tin hedges and trees. This was my regular special Sunday treat. As I grew older I was given a train set of which I was extremely proud, and I kept it neatly packed in a wooden box my father had made for me.

My teddy bear lived on my bed, sleeping with me each night. Yet even with him beside me I was frightened of the dark, and my parents always kept a light on outside my bedroom on the landing until I fell asleep. I had a few small dolls, including a lovely velvety black doll with large gold earrings, named Belinda. Another favourite was made of white porcelain and called Ethel; her eyes rolled whenever she was moved. She had a pristine white cotton dress edged with lace, a plain cotton petticoat plus pantaloons, and I enjoyed dressing and undressing her, for she possessed a little voice when she was tipped upside down!

On my sixth birthday my father's senior manager, Mr Bond, and his wife gave me a large beautifully dressed doll. We were the same height: I was a small child until growing taller by fourteen. My parents thought I should give it away as I already had some dolls. I was broken-hearted and have never forgotten how fine and big the doll was and how much I longed to keep her. But my parents wanted me to realise that some children had no toys or dolls and that I must learn to give, even if it hurt, which it most certainly did!

Two years later, that same manager gave me an invaluable opportunity – to speak in public. He and his wife were very fond of my parents and invited all three of us to join his party to see the Crazy Gang at the London Palladium. It was my first grown-up evening out, and was followed by dinner at the Florence restaurant in Rupert Street, Soho. At the end of the meal Mr Bond asked me to get up and tell all those present at his birthday table, in my own words, that they were now permitted to smoke. I was so surprised and used to obeying my elders without question that I stood up and apparently pleased all those present. That experience remained with me, giving me confidence through many a nerve-racking occasion.

I know that many families thought dance a very dubious activity for a child. That was certainly true of my first headmistress at Sherborne Preparatory School, Miss Constance Horsey. Although permitting once-a-week dance classes as a way of achieving good deportment, she was horrified when my father informed her that I had been offered a scholarship to the Vic Wells Ballet School, which he thought I should accept. Miss Horsey saw a dance career as a stupid waste of an intelligent girl, wishing me instead to study at a grammar school before going on to university. Thank goodness the writer, Arnold Haskell, pronounced intelligence as a necessary element for a successful career in dance.

I was fortunate that my prep school training was sound, with a careful balance of all general subjects, together with painting, singing and sports. We had a marvellous art teacher who encouraged me to enter my watercolour of an iris flower in a competition for young people at the Royal Academy of Arts. I was nine when it was sent in, and I was one of the fortunate children whose paintings were hung there for a short time. The previous year I had became the proud possessor of a certificate of merit from the Royal Society for the Prevention of Cruelty to Animals for an essay on 'Kindness to Animals'. I have always loved animals and dogs in particular.

My favourite dog was a beautiful black Scots terrier who I promptly christened Boo-Boo. She and I became firm friends. She used to watch me practise at home and join in; trying to catch my feet when I was learning to master 'beats' (jumping in the air and switching the front foot to the back before landing!). As I battled to master a pirouette (a complete turn on one foot) she would mimic me by also turning round in circles. This used to make me laugh and laugh as I continued to pirouette, so perhaps it is Boo-Boo I should thank for helping me to eventually attain good pirouettes!

I missed her so much after she died a few years later. She had been my confidante for many years, sharing my ups and downs, and I was forlorn without her.

3 *The Big Change*

The Summer of 1937. My parents, after much discussion and soul searching, decided to return to live in London, so that I could attend daily dance classes at the Vic-Wells School in the Sadler's Wells Theatre at the Angel in Islington.

Ninette de Valois and Lilian Baylis offered me a quite unique scholarship, and my parents were determined I should not lose this incredible opportunity. They realised that it would be too much of a strain to travel to London every day as well as continuing my schooling. With the Spanish Civil War ongoing and the threat of a major world war looming, 1937 was a bad time to put a house on the market. Eventually my parents sold our lovely 'Rothgate' at a far lower price than they had originally paid, six years earlier, with all their hard-earned savings. This was the most selfless action parents could take for their child. It must have been a terrible wrench for my mother to leave the garden she spent so many hours planning, planting and tending; even the kitchen garden was bordered by lavender and arches of climbing roses. It was a picture of loveliness and is still clearly imprinted on my mind.

So many life-shaping events flowed through those precious years. A host of memories crowd in, and strangely they are all sunny. Every Boxing Day my parents and I would go to see the annual pantomime. We always sat in a box, enjoying in the intervals oranges, chocolates and ice cream! But the highlight was the magical dancing of fairies and elves. This must have ignited in me the first flame of love for dance which was to light my path through life.

At school I thoroughly enjoyed sports, particularly netball, but found rounders dull. I wanted to take part in everything and waited expectantly for the weekly list of sports teams to be posted onto the notice board on Monday mornings. I would rush home at midday to tell my mother all that I was involved with and whether or not I obtained a gold star for my school work.

Dance was always very much to the fore, the thrice-daily practice periods were religiously adhered to, regardless of whatever else was happening. In term time, my ten-minute walk, or rather run, to school after my morning practice meant I was forever tumbling over fearful of being late. I would rush down a gravel incline, a short-cut, arriving breathless in the classroom with grazed, bleeding knees. These soon stiffened and were agony when exercising.

I was taking the short-cut one day when I was approached by a man who exposed himself. This so distressed me that I couldn't even bring myself to tell my parents. I felt curiously ashamed of the shocking experience, but could confide in no one.

Perhaps my happiest and most precious times came when the bluebells were in flower. Between morning and afternoon school my mother would drive us up into the hills nearby for a simple picnic amongst bluebell covered woods. The hills are now all smothered under endless rows of houses. The fragrant sweet-smelling flowers are gone, crushed to death, replaced by concrete roads and evil-smelling exhaust fumes pouring from the lines of vehicles streaming through. The precious countryside of England, still being eroded by man's ever growing and insatiable demands.

Looking back at my childhood, I am both humbled and overwhelmed by the tremendous generosity and loving care with which Miss Sharp oversaw my development, laying a sound foundation for my future career. How intelligently she paced my exams, competitions and public performances, never over-exposing me – she was indeed my "Fairy Godmother".

After my first grade exam, taken with the British Ballet Organisation (BBO) in 1932, she switched her allegiance to the Association of Operatic Dancing, later to become known as the Royal Academy of Dancing (RAD). She entered me for Grade Two in 1933, Grades Three and Four in 1934, and Grade Five the following year – all of which I passed with honours. At that time the syllabus included a national dance in each grade – Scottish, Irish and even the sailor's hornpipe.

She entered me for my first senior RAD exam, the Elementary, at the early age of eight. When I passed, she set about training me for the demanding Intermediate exam, which included a little pointe work for the first time. I was thrilled at this development. She cautiously instructed me how to hold the back and tighten the buttocks, totally straightening the knees. All this I did with the help of a barre to raise and steady myself on pointe. It is hard to master the art of dancing correctly on one's toes and can take something like three months to achieve. Nine is an unusually early age to put a child on pointe as the body is not fully developed nor bones completely formed. I was therefore only permitted by Miss Sharp to undertake just those steps stipulated for the exam and no others. Her careful training was rewarded by my passing the Intermediate exam with honours in July 1936, at the age of nine. My adjudicators were Grace Cone and Mr D.G. MacLennan, neither renowned for their leniency!

Miss Sharp was selective in the number of competitions for which she entered me. Pushy teachers entered their pupils for as many competitions as possible in order to promote their own school, thereby often overtaxing the pupils. But Miss Sharp planned my development intelligently, never entering me for more than two competitions a year – generally the Beckenham Festival and the All England Sunshine Dancing Competition.

There was one exception: when I was six and entered for the Streatham Festival. The adjudicator was the great Danish prima-ballerina Adeline Genée, then President of the Association of Operatic Dancing. I wonder if this was to bring me to her attention, as all my exams were taken with the RAD except for the very first, taken with the BBO.

Edouard Espinosa, another famous dancer, headed the BBO. He sat me on his knee at the end of the test, foretelling a successful future for me in dance, providing I worked hard. His distinguished dance family spanned several generations. Six years previously he had been one of the founders of the RAD, from which in 1925 he broke away to form his own dance society, the British Ballet Organisation. Now, over eighty years on, I am their President, as well as a Vice President of the RAD, so feel that life has come full circle, for I am also president of the All England Competition.

The idea of an all-England competition grew out of the Sunshine Matinees first staged in 1919, the brain-child of the eminent PJS Richardson and Mrs D Claremont organiser of The Sunshine Homes for Blind Babies. In 1923 they successfully launched the first All England Sunshine Dancing Competition, which became an annual highlight in the dance calendar. It ran Preliminary Heats, Quarter-finals in four cities, Semi-finals in two major cities, with the Finals at the Scala Theatre off Tottenham Court Road, London.

I was an established ballerina by the end of the war, but still very young, when to my surprise Lady Irene Astor, the President of the Sunshine Homes for Blind Babies, asked if I would agree to be Chairman of the Competitions. I felt honoured at being invited to take this on – I was only in my early twenties. It allowed me to work with distinguished teachers of whom I was still very much in awe. To work with stalwarts of the teaching profession – Grandison Clarke, Olive Ripman, Grace Cone, Victor Leopold, Noreen Bush (then all on the board of the Imperial Society of Teachers of Dancing), and Edouard Espinosa, Chairman of the British Ballet Organisation – was an education. All great teachers, these remarkable people laid the foundations of ballet and dance in this country between the two world wars. Pioneers, they developed a British style and a new confidence in their teaching.

In pre-war years the adjudicators for the Sunshine Competitions included such eminent artists as Alicia Markova and Anton Dolin, then leading their own company; Ursula Moreton, teacher, and a principal dancer of the Vic-Wells; Phyllis Bedells, the first English ballerina of the pre-First World War period, running her own school in Maida Vale; and Ninette de Valois, at that time battling to establish the major English ballet company at the Sadler's Wells Theatre in Islington. The chairman was none other than PJS Richardson, director and editor of the monthly magazine *Dancing Times*, co-founder of the RAD in 1920 as well as the Camargo Society in 1930. An impressive group together with many renowned teachers, all of whom were giving up their own precious time to encourage and guide the aspiring dancers and teachers of this country. And the Camargo Society, although only existing for three years, helped keep ballet alive in England following the tragic death of Diaghilev in 1929.

For financial reasons the Sunshine Homes for Blind Babies Competition was brought to an end in the late 1960s. The competition, however, was so keenly missed that a similar one has now been established, titled the All England – no longer linked to The Sunshine Homes, but fulfilling a big demand. Once again I am involved. This revival came about in 1983, through the passion and dedication of several distinguished teachers, including Brenda Last, a former principal of the Royal Ballet's touring company, with Dame Alicia Markova as President. The motivation a good competition brings to both teacher and young dancer is invaluable. Competition teaches how to embrace success and failure, situations artists must face whether amateur or professional.

The annual galas at the Scala Theatre were revived, and we also reintroduced the original Sunshine Galas, held at a large, West End venue. These were a public showcase for the best of the competition winners to perform on the same stage as professional dancers. Lady Irene would invite a member of the royal family as guest of honour. My last-ever London performance was in a Sunshine Gala matinee at Drury Lane Theatre, when Princess Margaret delighted everyone with her presence.

4 *Auditions*

It was the Easter that I was nine when I first became aware of the unpredictability of life. Miss Sharp entered me for the RAD Scholarship audition, and I had been working diligently. The scholarship offered once-a-week training in London with notable teachers. The all-important day came, but I awoke with a severe outbreak of mumps. I insisted I could manage to take the exam, but as this would have been together with other children, the RAD would not permit me to take part. I lost this wonderful opportunity and, inconsolable, wept for two days. My darling father brought me my favourite cream cake from Zeetas, a popular tea shop, but even that failed to cheer me! I thought all my hopes were dashed as I realised that I would have to wait a whole year before I could try again for the scholarship.

Fate, however, was taking a hand and steering me into an even more exciting venture, one which shaped my entire future. Since I was seven, Miss Sharp had arranged for me to have six private lessons twice a year from her own teacher, Phyllis Bedells, one of England's first ballerinas. These private lessons were a generous gift from Madeleine, whose endless kindness to me I could never repay.

Going to the Bedells' studio in Maida Vale was an education in itself: to watch established dancers training, sweating, all hard at work. How touched my parents were by Miss Sharp's further generosity when she decided that I should also take Spanish dance classes there with the celebrated Spanish dancer and teacher, Elsa Brunelleschi. Thrilled by her presence and deportment, I enjoyed every moment of her classes. She showed me how to play the castanets, which I struggled to master at home, practising over and over again. Once, badly frustrated, I lost my temper, banged one castanet on the stone kitchen floor and broke it, much to my distress and shame – not to mention my mother's anger. But it all proved worthwhile – a great value to me later in my career.

Miss Sharp determined that my training should now be with more experienced teachers and, undaunted by my mumps setback, unbeknown to me, in 1937 she arranged an audition at the Vic-Wells School. On that day, there seemed nothing unusual when she took me to London, my practice clothes neatly packed in a little bag ready for a private lesson.

When we arrived at the Sadler's Wells Theatre, we were shown along a dark passage and into a long dressing room stuffed with costumes, headdresses and shoes. Amidst the bustle of students, I changed into my practice clothes and joined them in a studio for class. This was taken by Ursula Moreton, both ballet mistress and a principal dancer of the Vic-Wells Company. I found it enjoyable, although many of the *enchaînements* (a sequence of steps) were new to me. As I was told later, it was an audition, unexpected and bewildering. Afterwards Miss Sharp and I indulged in my favourite cream pastries at Lyons Tea House on the corner of the Angel Islington. Served by smartly dressed waitresses with white aprons and frilled head bands amidst the mirrored grandeur of the first floor, it was an exciting end to an exciting day.

My parents were soon informed that I passed the audition and would be accepted into the school in September. What joy. I could hardly take it in. But thrilled as Miss Sharp and my parents were, when they added up all the costs, my parents found they had insufficient income to meet the fees, together with the required ongoing costs of dance apparel, tunic, headbands, shoes, socks and so on.

A bitter blow, but the indefatigable Miss Sharp proposed that I be re-auditioned for a scholarship. It was marvellous of her to have arranged this, and once again she took me to the Sadler's Wells Theatre, this time to be seen by Ninette de Valois herself. I realised this time that this was something important, crucial for both Miss Sharp and me. I determined to do my very best, no matter how difficult the audition might be or how many intricate steps I might be asked to perform.

It was, however, a very strange audition and not at all what Miss Sharp and I envisaged. De Valois seemed interested to judge the height to which I might grow. She asked me to stand, stretch my arms and hands to touch the sides of my knees and inspected the length of my hands and feet. She then asked me to point my feet in front, then raise one leg in a grand battement to the front, back and side. She enquired if I knew a little dance I could perform for her. My teacher proffered me her elegant big straw hat as a prop for a birdcage, and with Miss Sharp humming the music I danced a solo about a bird which had escaped. Miss Sharp had arranged it especially for me, and I had danced it on several occasions before.

That was all I was asked to do. De Valois had obviously been given all the information she needed about my technical standard from Ursula Moreton, but wanted to see for herself my personality and judge my future potential. This 'performance' took place in the Wells Room where all school and company classes were conducted. Although it is much changed, I never enter that room without thinking back to my first encounter there with the now legendary Dame Ninette de Valois, who influenced so much of my career.

I cannot now recall how many days we all waited to know the outcome of that somewhat unconventional appraisal, but what a remarkable response it was when it eventually arrived. Ninette de Valois, together with Lilian Baylis, offered an eight-year agreement. A scholarship to begin that September with four years free tuition at the Vic-Wells school, followed by a further four years in the Company, providing I developed as predicted. An unique contract of which I am extremely proud, signed by the stalwart Lilian Baylis, restorer of the historic Sadler's Wells Theatre.

An indomitable woman, ahead of her time, Lilian Baylis believed in making opera, drama and ballet available to the poor at affordable prices, both at the Old Vic Theatre in Waterloo Road from the mid twenties and later at Sadler's Wells from 1931. I met her once on the staircase at the Wells, and in passing I heard de Valois say 'this is the scholarship child I was telling you about.' Lilian Baylis scrutinised me and said a few kind words before continuing down the stairs as I dropped a curtsy. I shall never forget the impact she made on me. She was a big woman, round and homely like a grandmother, grey hair scraped back into a bun, but I was perturbed by the appearance of her mouth, twisted and dropped to one side. I realise now she must have had a stroke at some time, which left her face one-sided, but for me, a child, her disfigurement was a shock, despite her kind, if somewhat austere, manner. But, above all, I am so grateful for her farsightedness in agreeing to that scholarship which completely changed my life.

5 *London Living*

So, entirely for my sake, my parents and I came back to live in London, the city they had been glad to leave. What faith they had in Miss Sharp's foresight. What tremendous support and confidence my parents gave me, unstintingly, with no thought for themselves – true love. I will be forever in their debt, and my love and admiration for them is immeasurable. Similarly, my gratitude to Madeleine Sharp as without her keen eye and financial support I doubt there would have been a 'Beryl Grey'.

That was to become my name, changed from Groom to Grey by de Valois during a company class. I had only just joined the Vic Wells Company and was still feeling self-conscious among all the professional dancers and totally in awe of de Valois. I had no option but to agree, for that was the power of Madam (as de Valois was called by her Company).

Having found a flat in Highbury Crescent, my parents pursued the question of schooling. Close to the Wells Theatre was Dame Alice Owen's, a grammar school supported by the Worshipful Company of Brewers. It was a little outside my parent's orbit financially, so the sympathetic headmistress, Miss Bozman, suggested I apply for a supplementary County Scholarship, which I was awarded. She also consented to my leaving school at three thirty each day, half an hour early, so that I could be ready in time for my classes at the Wells, which began at four pm and ended by seven in the evening. Miss Bozman was an unusually understanding headmistress; few would have permitted this arrangement. Once again fate stepped in, and I became a very happy member of that school community, whilst also following my heart's desire at the Vic-Wells School.

It was marvellous to have daily ballet classes, and I was in my element as we had several notable teachers. Having learned from my mother, I wrote down everything we were taught, together with all my corrections, which proved to be invaluable. Sheila McCarthy taught the youngest in the school, whilst fulfilling her appearances in the Company in demi-caractère roles. Sheila was a very 'English' teacher, clear and precise in her aims to instil in us a clean and sound technique. This grounding has remained with me throughout my career. She was never perturbed, but kind and understanding, with a special sense of humour in which we all shared.

Ursula Moreton, like Sheila McCarthy, was English and had danced in the Company since its humble beginnings in 1931, developing into a most beautiful and sensitive leading artist. I recall with awe her poetic gracefulness dancing the prelude in *Les Sylphides*, and whenever I hear the mazurka by Delibes from *Coppélia* I still see her dignified deportment as she led the company in this Polish dance. Ursula not only taught us Checcetti classical ballet, but also gave special character and mime classes held every Saturday morning in the Finsbury Town Hall. These were a joy. She was such a romantic artist and managed to convey this quality to us through her teaching.

Once a year Ursula took a small group of students to dance at her local garden fête near Leighton Buzzard to which I greatly looked forward. She and her husband would give us a delicious cold lunch before the afternoon's activities. Two vivid memories remain: their colourful tame parrot, which flew about freely, chattering nonstop; and cold potatoes which I had never eaten before and found rather unappetising! I also remember her telling me not to get so excited as I waited in the bushes (wings), talking too loudly! Although she could be strict, she was a wonderful person, a most accomplished artist who remained the greatest inspiration to me even after her death in 1973. Her husband asked me to speak at her memorial service, but to my distress I could not because I was on the other side of the world – on tour leading London Festival Ballet. This has remained a great sadness for I admired her so much and have retained a special love for her.

Nicholas Sergeyev, the Russian émigré, whose classes were very demanding, also taught us at Sadler's Wells. He carried a little cane which he did not hesitate to use as he walked up and down, inspecting our barre work, flicking our knees if they were not tight or slapping his cane onto our thighs if our legs were not held high enough for our développés. He made us hold each développé in front, at the side, at the back, and again at the side, for a full eight bars of slow music. It was torturous. He insisted on giving his enchaînements not sixteen but thirty-two times.

A perfectionist, he would not suffer any shirking. Despite this we all loved this man with his dapper little moustache and beady eyes, doing our best to please him. He had a wry sense of humour and would often tease me by calling me not Beryl, but Barrel, much to everyone's amusement and my embarrassment.

He certainly drove us hard, providing a little insight into the Maryinsky training at St Petersburg. After watching class one day, de Valois reduced the number of times I performed certain steps. She had already forbidden me to do any pointe work for a year, aware of the abnormal strain on my as yet undeveloped body. At the time I did not appreciate her careful attention and was not pleased to be left watching other, older students battling on, when I so much wanted to continue working, too.

In 1918 Sergeyev had smuggled out of Russia twenty-one books of Stepanov notation. These included the notations for the Petipa ballet classics, five of which he mounted for the Vic-Wells company. He had escaped together with his own accompanist, Ippolit Motchaloff, who played for all his classes.

Motchaloff was a most cultured musician, who in the thirties, as well as becoming a much sought-after recitalist, founded the Gramophone Society. We developed a special friendship, and he gave me weekly piano lessons during which he delighted in explaining to me the magic of Chopin's music, exploring its delicacy, its power and why one should never tamper with the prescribed tempi. He played inspirationally and tried to help me do likewise. I was never able to get anywhere near what he wanted, but it has left me with a lifelong love and understanding of Chopin's divine works. Even after the war I continued to take piano lessons from him during our London seasons.

Motchaloff lived in Chesham Bois, where I gave my first truly professional solo appearance at one of his recitals. I danced the 'Mirlitons' solo from the *Nutcracker* ballet. I will never forget this unique artist, truly a gentleman. Before the Russian Revolution, Motchaloff had taught music to the daughters of the Tsar. He even spent time with the family on their royal yacht. When the West investigated the identity of Anastasia, Ippolit Motchaloff was one of those whose opinion was sought. He was convinced that Anna Anderson was Anastasia, the Russian princess whom he had taught.

Soon after I joined the School, de Valois asked my parents to see our dentist about getting my front teeth straightened, as they were slightly crossed. This meant wearing plates with complicated wires, which I disliked intensely. De Valois was also concerned about my lower back and sent me to a physiotherapist, Celia Sparger, who gave me special exercises that I carried out religiously every day. In order to counteract my hammer toes, she instructed me to wrap cotton wool around my two little toes and to use match sticks as splints. These I fastened with cotton every night before going to bed. How relieved I was to remove them next morning. This actually worked: after two years the toes straightened. Looking back now and reflecting on the remarkable insight and care showed by de Valois, I realise how fortunate I was to have had such attention. She oversaw my development not only as a student but later too as a Company member. What I never recognised was that she was really fond of me.

We students were very much in awe of Madam and frightened by her outbursts of rage. She would sometimes explode in class on some unfortunate student who displeased her, either by her work or her apparel. The poor girl would then run out of the room sobbing. We did not understand that Madam did not enjoy good health, suffering bad migraines. Aside from the migraines she would disappear from time to time into hospital to undergo an operation, returning as energetic and omnipotent as ever.

I retain many memories from those student days at the Wells, including the spellbinding visits we made to the hallowed Royal Opera House in Covent Garden. It was an enormous thrill to sit in the gallery watching great Russian dancers performing with the famous de Basil company. Hoping to collect the dancers' autographs after a performance, we would rush down the gallery steps to wait outside the stage door. I have saved every one.

There were two notable events for me during those formative years at the Wells. Queen Elizabeth (our future Queen Mother) honoured by her presence the British premiere of Ninette de Valois's ballet *Checkmate* in 1938. As the youngest member of the school, I presented Her Royal Highness with a bouquet of flowers. Amongst the excitement backstage, in a dressing room packed with nervous dancers, I was made up and fastened into a small white tutu with a matching white organdie headband. Pink satin ballet shoes over white socks completed the outfit.

I was then guided to the front of house foyer, packed with important dignitaries, all waiting to greet the Queen. Upon Her Majesty's arrival, I was ushered forward and, curtseying, presented her with the flowers. A magical moment I will never forget as Her Majesty, with a most beautiful smile, said to me, 'Thank you. I hope to see you dance one day.' Just a dream for me then, it was to come true and on more than one occasion. The Queen, floating amidst a sea of sparkling pink tulle, moved on to enchant all those lined up to welcome her.

As if that was not sufficient for one childhood, another exciting event followed in February 1939. The Company was once more honoured, this time by the visit of Her Majesty Queen Mary, widow of King George V, attending the first performance of *The Sleeping Princess*. Once again as the youngest member of the school I presented a bouquet to this great lady, and had the honour of curtseying for a brief moment to this royal personage. Queen Mary stood tall and upright, and to me it looked as if thick white makeup encased her face. Several important-looking men wearing white tie and tails, adorned with decorations, accompanied her. They swept Her Majesty down the receiving line, on out of sight, to the waiting audience.

This wonderful encounter helped offset my big disappointment at being too young to go on stage in the production. Several of the older students appeared as pages or in other minor roles, and I watched with yearning as many rehearsals as possible. The ballet mesmerised me, and I would lie awake at night dreaming that Margot Fonteyn had been taken ill and I took her place as the fairy tale princess! Little did I know that in three years' time that is what would actually happen, except that the ballet would be *Swan Lake*. Sadly for the Princess Aurora, she would soon be disturbed by the advent of World War Two.

6 *1939: War*

Visiting a relative of my mother's in the little village of Tickhill, near Doncaster, we heard on the radio the dreaded news that war had been declared. It was Sunday morning the 2nd September 1939. I was terribly frightened and escaped to the outside lavatory to be on my own. I sobbed, thinking the world was coming to an end. We packed quickly and left for London with father driving our small Ford unusually fast. The Vic-Wells School and the Company closed and children across the capital were summoned back to their schools, given gas masks and told they would be evacuated outside London to avoid predicted air raids.

On learning that Owen's girls school was being evacuated to Kettering, Northamptonshire, my parents set about finding a nearby property to rent. On the outskirts of a village named Little Harrowden six miles from Kettering they found a recently built two-up, two-down house. The long garden was still wild like the field it backed onto. It seemed exciting and was far enough from London for my mother and me to feel safe, but where my father could visit us on weekends.

Within three weeks of the outbreak of war my parents, however, received a card from the Wells secretary. The school was to reopen at Sadler's Wells on September 25th and I was expected to attend daily. As I had no wish to miss out, my parents took a flat in Highbury New Park to allow me to recommence my training.

With Owen's evacuated to Kettering, my education was the next problem. Many children had remained in London, so the government reopened some secondary schools and I began to attend my local school. It was, though, a horrible experience; the children were for the most part unkempt, ill mannered and poorly spoken. Every morning our heads were combed with disinfectant to kill off nits. Never having mixed with this type of child before, it was a big shock to me, and I implored my parents to take me away. They needed no persuading and an alternative was found – a convent in a square behind Sadler's Wells. I attended this school, but was miserable there, too. The house was dark and cramped and I disliked the nuns, the children and the lessons. I dreaded going through the door each day.

We all carried our gas masks with us wherever we went and in some ways London adopted a more normal atmosphere, except for the strictly adhered to blackout. The avid air raid wardens pounced on any chink of light showing between or through curtains or doorways, and there was absolutely no lighting in the streets. The lamps on all motor vehicles were completely covered, save for a permitted pin-hole through which a miniscule glimmer of light would guide drivers on their way.

The dreaded air raids gradually started the following summer of 1940 and sirens began their wailing in earnest, no longer for practice. By September the raids became terrifyingly heavy. People took refuge in public air raid shelters or Anderson huts dug in their back gardens. Many people took shelter in the underground stations, their mattresses and belongings strewn across the platform, a hazard for daytime travellers. If people were caught down in the underground during the day when the siren sounded, the entrance gates to the station were shut. I was caught several times and found it quite frightening, unable to determine what was happening in the streets above.

As an air raid warden my father was kept busy on duty most nights, as well as working in the day at Gosletts, a family furniture firm at Old Street in the city. He had started there at the age of fourteen as an office boy, earning five shillings a week, and through the years had worked his way up to the positions of office and factory manager, as well as becoming front of house manager. The staff greatly loved him, admiring his commitment and loyalty to the firm. His cockney sense of humour endeared him to workmen and customers alike, as it did to the police. When break-ins occurred, he was the one called out in the middle of the night, which always scared me.

During the First World War he had been in charge of a concert party in which he sang and danced, and I can imagine how popular he must have been. Like my mother, he loved music and singing, following his own father, who particularly enjoyed Gilbert and Sullivan.

My father had four married brothers, all with children, and one unmarried sister – Edith – who lived with their mother. She was left bereft in the war. A lorry mounted the pavement pinning my grandmother to iron railings. Grandma Groom died almost immediately, saying, 'What have I done?'.

Grandma was the kindest and most gentle of women. My poor father took her death badly, coming as it did during the heavy bombing in November 1941. He was her last born, and they had always shared a special relationship. I was away on tour when I received the news by phone from my mother who, too, was terribly upset, for we all loved Grandma deeply.

Whenever we visited her she would ask me to brush her hair and then pin it up into a tiny bun. She made the most delicious roast potatoes in a black lead range with chrome fittings, fixed to the side of an open fire which appeared to be always burning, rather like an Aga. But it would burn no more with Grandma gone at the age of 81. My canary, Joey, had not gone with us to Kettering and had become a quaint companion to

Grandma. Joey sang beautifully, but he ceased his warbling when the bombs began to fall. He died soon after Grandma, and eventually the family house was sold.

The war for me became a time of opportunities. Once the air raids began in earnest, Sadler's Wells Theatre was shut and bombed-out families housed there. With the Vic-Wells School closed once more, my mother and I retreated to Little Harrowden. I resumed my education with Owen's in Kettering, cycling six miles there and back twice a day, which I enjoyed tremendously. Each Friday on my way home I would stop at a large nursery to buy my mother some flowers – her favourites were lilac-coloured chrysanthemums which I so much loved giving her. I somehow managed to transport them on my bike without either them, my satchel or me coming to grief, despite the hills I climbed, pushing down hard on the pedals.

The outskirts of the major town, Kettering, boasted a large park – Wickstead – which my mother and I sometimes visited with our neighbour when he had sufficient petrol to drive us there. Occasionally he took me boating on the lake whilst mother did a little shopping in the town. The lake was beautiful, encircled by graceful birch and willow trees.

My parents found a piano teacher for me in Kettering, Cyril Butlin, so I was able to continue my lessons. He was a good tutor, entering me for several exams in which he and his wife Sybil took a keen interest. Even after the war we kept in touch.

I took a few classes with a dance teacher in Wellingborough but found she could teach me little after the advanced training I had received at the Wells. Although I continued to practise my ballet exercises daily, I began to believe that the war meant all my aspirations of becoming a professional dancer were over and I must decide upon another career. Medicine always intrigued me and was an area that I thought would be most interesting. It would be wonderful to be a doctor and be able to help others. But this was not what fate had in store!

Early in 1940 after unsuccessfully pursuing the purchase of a country property, the Vic-Wells School settled for sharing part of the re-opened RAD's London premises. Despite the bombing I was asked to return to continue my training, and I longed to resume my dancing. A scheme was eventually agreed between all concerned to continue my education with Owen's in Kettering Monday to Thursday and my dance training Friday and Saturday in London. This worked remarkably well. I took an early morning train on Fridays and felt very grown-up travelling on my own to bomb-scarred London. When petrol was available, and the car working, my father would drive us back to my mother in Little Harrowden late Saturday. Otherwise we took a blacked-out train from St Pancras.

One Friday morning, June 20th 1941, I was handed a letter for my parents from de Valois, requesting I remain in London for rehearsals to appear in the forthcoming London season. This was scheduled to commence on the 21st July at the New Theatre in St Martin's Lane (now the Noël Coward Theatre). As school holidays were approaching, my understanding headmistress Miss Bozman raised no objection, so I left school for London straightaway. As the season drew near, my excitement mounted.

This was my first opportunity to dance with a professional ballet company; moreover, it was in the heart of the West End of London. I would be dancing in the corps de ballet of *Giselle* on the opening night. I already knew the choreography, learnt in Miss Moreton's classes. I was given my place in the first act as a peasant girl and in the second act as a Wili at the end of the row.

What I had not been taught, however, was how to apply make-up. I did my best to copy what the other dancers were doing, but not well enough. Half an hour before the curtain was due to go up the ballet mistress, Joy Newton came to check us. She took one horrified look at me, slapped a handful of removing grease on my face and told me to start again, this time under her eagle eye. It was nerve-racking as the quarter of an hour had already been called.

I was only just ready in time, putting on my costume, when the call-boy returned, shouting 'Beginners please'. My heart sank. How did he know I was a beginner? Everyone would now know. It was, of course, the routine last call to get everybody on stage in time to begin the show, but I did not know that then. I was totally unprepared, a real greenhorn.

Once down on stage, the sea of strange faces bewildered me. I found it hard to recognise anyone as the heavy make-up transformed all the dancers. With the bright lights from the wings shining on them they looked magnificent in their period costumes. Suddenly, we were cleared off stage into the wings beyond the free-standing strong lights, the orchestra began playing and, after what seemed an eternity, the curtain rose and we went on. A most marvellous dream which finished all too soon, as dreams do.

We rushed up three flights of stairs to change into our white net costumes after applying wet-white onto our arms and shoulders. This enhanced the unearthly effect of the Wilis who inhabit the forest night scene of the second act of *Giselle*. That evening, 21st July 1941, was my first step into the truly professional, magical world of ballet, of which I will never tire – the sound of the orchestra and the bright lights on stage – such a memory.

I had never danced to a live orchestra before, and I found extraordinary the power with which it swept me into the atmosphere of the drama. Music is an intrinsic part of dance and has always inspired me. For a dancer to be accompanied by an orchestra is the most uplifting experience, particularly when the conductor is sympathetic to the needs of the dancers.

Once on stage, a dancer is totally subject to the conductor's baton. It is so important that a conductor understands a dancer's idiosyncrasies, style, strengths and responses. A principal needs to have total trust in a conductor who knows when to push or restrain the artist and who is on the same wavelength. Later, when I danced in Russia, my conductor at the Bolshoi, Yuri Faier, came to all my rehearsals and even watched me in class. He was able to evaluate my response to music so that by the performance we were both together, as one, and I was lifted into another world.

Music has been very important to me throughout my life. I adore the opera, but it was ballet which led me to opera and introduced me to the kaleidoscope of music the world has to offer. I find, too, that music recalls so many events that have enriched my life.

Specific scents can also evoke a special memory, like flowers presented on stage at the end of a performance. The fragrance of a sweet william reminds me of the very first flowers I received, at the age of nine. They were from Miss Sharp when I was lying ill in bed with mumps, broken-hearted at missing the Royal Academy of Dancing audition. The pungent smell of rotting vegetables always carries me back to Covent Garden and the market, arriving for performances, butterflies in the stomach.

But the old fruit, flower and vegetable market has now vanished, swept away to Nine Elms. With it has gone so much that was Covent Garden with its cheeky barrow-boys and stall-holders, whistling and good humouredly flirting with dancers, singers and musicians alike, as we went on our way to perform. I suppose today it would be deemed sexual harassment, but it was just high spirits and jolly good fun: English qualities that helped to get England successfully through the war. A sense of fun and humour have taken me through many a difficult situation.

That first exciting season as a student with the Company lasted just three weeks, after which I returned with my mother to Little Harrowden. Back down to earth, I prepared to rejoin my school, Owen's, away from air raids. It had been wonderful to dance every night in London with the Sadler's Wells Company, but all too soon the memory began to fade like a dream. It was an important experience for me which strangely coincided with a big change in my father's life.

Two months previously, Gosletts had been bombed, burnt to the ground and totally destroyed. All the staff lost their jobs, and he too was bade farewell. My father had devoted his life to the firm, but was abandoned with only a month's pay and left to find other employment. This despite Goslett's ownership of another branch in the West End, which sold bathroom furnishings and remained unscathed. It was a heartless farewell which deeply hurt my father. He had always been faithful to the owners, who he served well.

My father immediately searched for another position, and happily his application to the Ministry of Works was successful. It turned out to be fascinating work in overall charge of the furnishings at government establishments, such as Hampton Court Palace, Lambeth Palace and numerous other historic buildings in and around London. It meant he travelled a lot, always by bus, meeting many interesting people and in a way his own master. I know he came to enjoy the work very much and was sorry when the time came for him to retire. He again became much loved and was given a touching farewell party where, to my surprise, I was asked to say a few words. I have since felt remorse that I was unprepared and did not do justice to all my father's gifts, but at least I spoke spontaneously from my heart.

8 *Out On The Road, 1941*

Less than a week after the end of the London season came an astonishing summons from Ninette de Valois to join the company in Burnley the very next Sunday, 17th August. There was an emergency: a dancer off with appendicitis, and I would be required to tour and dance for approximately three months, until her return. It was all so sudden. There was hardly time for me to get suitable, grown-up clothes. My father rushed to make arrangements for me to have a cheque book, as well as informing the long suffering, understanding Miss Bozman at Dame Alice Owens.

My parents came to Rugby station to see me safely onto a train taking me to Burnley, where I was to be met. Alighting at the station I could find nobody waiting, so I went off with my luggage in search of the theatre which I eventually found, but could not find a way in. Looking all around the building I discovered an iron staircase winding its way to an upper floor with a door at the top. On opening it I found myself in the wardrobe area, engulfed by costumes.

Amidst the colourful haze of tulle stood the ballet mistress, Joy Newton, who had been so shocked at my attempts to make up only a short time before. Again she looked at me in horror, this time realising she had forgotten I was coming and due to be met by her. She emerged from the labyrinth of fabrics, boots and exotic headgear and escorted me to my digs where she informed me I was to share a bed with a corps de ballet girl, June Vincent. The modest charge of 35 shillings a week included breakfast and supper after the show. Despite the strict rationing in progress, the food was not at all bad and quite filling.

They were the cheapest digs I was ever to encounter, possibly because there was only the one bed. It was not a great success with June, however, who insisted on laying a bolster down the centre of the bed every night! Not too demoralised by this embarrassment, I tried to fit in with the rest of the Company. I concentrated all my efforts on learning the corps de ballet work in six ballets as quickly as I could so as not to waste the other dancers' time. I loved every minute on stage during performances. I learnt to adapt to different sized stages, some raked, some flat and some very uneven and splintery.

The largest theatre we visited on my first tour was the Manchester Opera House, with a beautiful flat stage, a theatre for which I have held a special affection ever since. It was in this very theatre that, a few years later, de Valois pushed me forward during curtain calls after the closing performance. I cannot remember her ever giving such a display of satisfaction at any other time. It must have been a very special occasion at the end of that two-week season.

On that first tour we also performed in another fine old Opera House, the Grand Theatre, in Leeds, which had a raked stage and appeared to me very grand indeed. In complete contrast was the tiny theatre in Harrogate attached to the Spa. I recall the overwhelming smell of sulphur that met us and which we endured all night as six of us were put up in the Spa itself; sufficient digs being unavailable for the Company in the city.

One of the soloists, Joan Sheldon, toured with a gramophone, and it was there in the romantic setting of the Harrogate Spa that after performances we sat and listened every evening to her records. The piece I loved most was the haunting Tchaikovsky Piano Concerto Number One. Whenever I hear it I am transported back to that wondrous week with the music drifting through the dark, empty rooms. I began to feel very grown-up and proud to be one of the six. Deep down, however, I still felt an outsider, a student, and very conscious of being the youngest. De Valois would detail different dancers each week to keep an eye on me, which I did not mind, but I doubt if they appreciated the added responsibility.

Totally focused, we all worked hard within a tight schedule, getting into the theatre each morning by 9.30 in time to change and warm up for our 10 o'clock class on stage. Being war-time, theatres were not well heated, if at all, and even the lighting for our class and rehearsals was invariably dim. I often wondered how our pianists managed to play so well in the cold and poor light. Madam generally took class as well as most of the rehearsals on stage, ably aided by the ballet mistress. I enjoyed those daily rehearsals, which began directly after class and ran through until the half hour call at 6.55pm when the stage had to be swept and the scenery set for the evening's show. I watched every rehearsal I could, sometimes missing lunch, absorbing more than I realised, learning and loving every minute.

The memory of being a ghost in de Valois's ballet *The Haunted Ballroom* lingers strangely still. I recall the grey chiffon arm drapes floating across our faces as we performed to Geoffrey Toye's eerie music. Infected by another dancer, Joan Sheldon, it was not unusual for some of us to get the giggles on stage, swathed within these restless cobwebs.

I learnt all the corps de ballet work in every act of each classic we gave. In *Sleeping Princess* (now titled *The Sleeping Beauty*) I danced a lilac fairy attendant, a garland dancer, hunting lady, nymph and finally in the last act, a mazurka courtier. In *Swan Lake* I became a peasant girl in Act One, a swan in Acts Two and Four, and one of the four mazurka girls in Act Three. A demanding schedule for a fourteen-year-old.

The Vic-Wells was a relatively small company to undertake full-length classics, so we appeared in every scene. Making a rapid change from the Act Two Hunting Scene into a nymph in the Vision Scene was particularly frantic. Just off-stage, in cramped wings, in semi-darkness and in a few seconds we changed from a tight-fitting hunt dress into a balletic nymph dress, knee-length, decorated with large water lilies.

At one performance I realised everyone on stage was laughing. In the rush of changing I had inadvertently hooked up my brassiere onto a lily and to everyone's amusement it was cheerfully dangling as I danced, unaware. Was I embarrassed! Fortunately there were no other incidents like that on the tour, in either *Swan Lake*, *Coppélia* or *Nutcracker* where off-stage quick changes were less fraught.

My first ever tour of six weeks flew by. We travelled under war-time conditions at night, in blacked-out trains, wandering through unlit streets to search for digs. On arrival in each new city every Sunday we perused lists of addresses pinned to the theatre notice-board, and the search began. Handing over to the landlady precious weekly food coupons we prayed that the digs would not be too cold or damp and hoped there would be sufficient hot water for the regulation five inches of bath water. After a day and evening's physical activities a bath was vital as the theatres rarely had hot water or showers.

During that tour the Germans began their air raids on the Midlands, attacking our big cities, including Northampton and Bedford for the first time. The gunfire could be seen and heard at Little Harrowden, which made my mother very nervous. My father tried to join her at weekends but petrol coupons were getting harder to obtain and our car became increasingly unreliable. Night driving continued to be a major hazard with only a pin-point of light allowed and air raids often in progress.

During the week, my father continued his duties as an air raid warden in London, and these nights were now becoming much more arduous and harrowing with regular wailing sirens and bombings. My mother constantly worried about his safety and, with my absence on tour, felt vulnerable and isolated in Little Harrowden. As well as making all my clothes including my overcoat, my mother took on a little sewing locally to supplement my father's income. I did not realise my parents' finances had been running low until I read her diaries years later. I was doing my best to help, sending home one pound each week – the most I could muster from my weekly four pound salary. From this I paid for my digs, usually two pounds a week, quite often a bit more. I lived as frugally as I could, without losing face among the other dancers.

We had to buy our own stage and body make-up, silk tights (which wrinkled horribly at the knees when we perspired) as well as satin ribbons for sewing on our pointe shoes. These were rationed to one pair a fortnight, although we usually gave nine performances a week – three matinees and six evenings. To make the shoes last, we darned around the toe of each shoe using strong thread to stop the satin fraying and filled the block inside the shoe with straw hat dye, hardening it for a longer life. The rock hard cotton lining frequently rucked, causing blisters which burst and left our toes red raw. I found that surgical spirit was the best way to harden my toes, although it stung terribly on open skin. I carried a bottle of my magical medication with me, together with a store of elastoplasts squeezed in with my lucky rabbit's foot.

I soon learnt to pack swiftly when we were moving on from one theatre to another at the end of each week. Every dancer supplied his or her own wicker basket (laundry basket size) for transporting practice clothes, tights, shoes, make up, talcum powder, toiletries and medications, dressing gown, slippers, towels, soap and make-up towels used to remove the then heavy stage make-up. The small towels we left at the stage door Monday mornings for collection by the local laundry, which we usually got back in a day or two, nice and clean for more make-up removal. This was quite expensive, depending on how many towels one used. There is a story that a famous Russian dancer was known to slip his soiled towels into other dancers' laundry, thus avoiding the laundry bill!

Immediately after our tour, that November of 1941, a London season started. Because of the increasing number of air raids, performance times were readjusted to help the public; matinees began at 1.30pm with evening shows starting at 5.30pm. It was marvellous to be dancing in London again, staying with my father at Grandmother's. I began to wonder though how much longer it would be before I was sent back to school and my time with the Company be over.

As the four-week season drew to a close, my parents were asked to meet Madam's assistant, Ursula Moreton. She informed them that de Valois had decided that in future I was to alternate with another student, Lorna Mossford, for a spell of three months at school and then three months with the Company, rather like a pendulum. Not what I wanted to hear, but de Valois's word was law, and I knew there was no possibility of changing her mind. This arrangement, however, was never to be. Destiny determined that I should become a full-time member of the Company.

9 *Fate Steps In*

It was the last night of my second London season. We were performing the newly revived *Sleeping Princess,* made possible since the welcome reinstatement of the orchestra. In the Prologue Pamela May, dancing the Lilac Fairy, strained her knee badly, crumbling to the floor in agony. The orchestra stopped momentarily as she was helped off stage. Immediately Mary Honer, the Violet Fairy, came forward, Constant Lambert raised his baton, the orchestra resumed, and she danced the Lilac Fairy's variation to everyone's relief. Luckily for me, with one dancer out of action, I was needed after all to stay for the forthcoming six-week tour, along with Lorna Mossford.

Taking us to Christmas 1941 the tour went to Edinburgh and Glasgow, for two weeks in each city. I had never been to Scotland before, and Edinburgh thrilled me with its fairy-tale castle perched high on the rocky tor. There was more food available there, too – even cream cakes in the elegant restaurants and delicious soups in the digs. It seemed a far cry from the bomb-stricken South, and I was determined if possible to bring my mother on my next visit to Edinburgh.

Whilst I was away on tour my parents went through a sad time. My father became exhausted and dreadfully run down, travelling to the Midlands every weekend now by bus or train, which was not easy in the war. Coupled with his nightly ARP duties, his hazardous journeys for work in and around London were beginning to take their toll.

He became ill, developing a serious carbuncle on his neck and was unable to work for four weeks. Normally lively, he hated not being at work, but his doctor was adamant that he rest. This enforced absence from the Ministry of Works meant his pay for the month was stopped, so he could not afford to visit his wife at Little Harrowden for some time. She was very lonely.

It was during my father's recovery that his mother was killed in the road accident. The shock was terrible, and it was after the coroner's inquest, amidst all the bombing, that the funeral took place. My mother came to London to help with the arrangements. It has always been my regret that I was not able to be with them during that tragic period, nor to attend my much loved Grandmother's burial.

But I was able to send them some good news. I was to dance as one of the four skaters in *Les Patineurs*, which was a big step forward. At this time Robert Helpmann was creating his first ballet *Comus,* and cast me to understudy not only Moyra Fraser as Sabrina, the second lead, but also Margot Fonteyn as The Lady. It was unbelievably thrilling.

I began attending every rehearsal, avidly watching and writing down everything as the ballet developed. I danced in the corps as a water nymph attendant to Sabrina, Goddess of Water, in which all eight of us entered, moving forward on our knees, wafting along with us a long sheath of blue floating chiffon material representing water. Once again the irrepressible Joan Sheldon would have us all giggling helplessly, imitating a frog croaking as we desperately tried to control our mirth.

We had some memorable moments on tour, and I was beginning at last to feel a tiny part of the Company. We were working hard and, despite the war, giving an average of nine performances a week as well as travelling from one city to another most weekends: an exhausting but exhilarating timetable.

The bombing continued to increase as we travelled across the country. Links between trains could be problematical and sometimes we slept overnight in a compartment, lying rather like sardines, crisscross over uneven, unyielding large suitcases packed between the seats. I came to prefer the strong net luggage racks above the seats – at least you could stretch out full-length without disturbing a sleeping mass of exhausted dancers. There was one large junction at the station where we invariably changed trains (it might have been Crewe), where on the bridge was a tiny shop like no other – it always had supplies of chocolate on sale. This was curious, as chocolate was very hard to come by. We used to charge up the steps to buy the precious sweetmeat, praying we would not miss our connection.

Never for one moment did we feel hard done by. We were fortunate to be dancing for our ever-growing audiences, with numbers increasing from the armed forces. We were engaged in something we loved, which we believed helped to cheer people and raise their spirits.

Looking back now, it seems miraculous that de Valois managed to keep the Company running. Male dancers were being called-up, with those few remaining taking on extra work. The Company suffered injuries and illness through the incessant touring, but that gave me a splendid chance early in 1942 after I had been with the Company six months.

We were in Cambridge that February during the first week of a month's tour, performing *The Nutcracker*, when Moyra Fraser slipped and twisted her foot dancing a solo in the last act, the Kingdom of Sweets. The ballet mistress hissed at me from the wings to go forward and complete her solo, and I did not have to be told twice!

Madam must have been pleased. Before the tour finished I was told to learn the Lilac Fairy in *The Sleeping Princess* – the second leading role. I was overjoyed and determined to make a success of such an important role. I began practising the tricky solo at every available moment. Madam was busy reviving her ballet *The Gods Go A-Begging*, and I was thrilled that she chose Lithuanian-born Alexis Rassine with me for the leading roles. This was a big honour as I was a comparative newcomer to the Company and, at fourteen, still very young.

The next incredible opportunity came when, arriving for our week at the New Theatre, Oxford, I was told by the stage door man to go immediately to Madam's office. She told me that Margot Fonteyn was unwell, and I was to replace her that night in *Les Sylphides* and remain on stage after class to rehearse with Robert Helpmann who would be partnering me. I had never danced with him before and was still very much in awe of this great artist. I was already cast to dance the revival of *The Gods Go A-Begging* that evening so it became a very exciting one indeed.

Dancing in *Les Sylphides* was my idea of heaven. I have always loved Chopin's music and to have the opportunity to perform the Mazurka solo with its soaring leaps across the stage was wonderful. In addition, to be lifted by Robert Helpmann to such poetic music in the pas de deux; I felt I was in a dream. I had not been trained in double work (dancing with a partner) so being lifted on high and supported in pirouettes was a new experience. I was very fortunate to have, for my first major debut, such an experienced partner as Helpmann.

Even more exciting developments followed, with Margot Fonteyn too ill to dance for the rest of the week and both Julia Farron and Mary Honer also away sick. As I walked in at the stage door next morning I was summoned to Madam's office. She informed me that I was to stay behind after class again, this time to rehearse *Swan Lake*. As I had begun to grow quite tall I presumed it was to dance one of the two Big Swans and politely enquired of Madam which side I was to dance. She exploded, saying, 'Don't be so silly, girl, you are to dance the Swan Princess!' I was to learn and rehearse the lead with Helpmann for that evening's performance.

I was stunned but determined to make the most of this unbelievable opportunity. Today I still cannot believe it happened – I was still only fourteen, had been in the company only nine months, and had just begun to be given some solo parts as well as dancing all the corps de ballet work. Madam must have had enormous faith in me. I did my utmost not to disappoint her, nor those who had come to see Margot as the Princess.

I rang my mother in great excitement asking her to come to Oxford that day to see my performance. Despite the difficulties of war-time journeys, she arrived in time, as thrilled and disbelieving as I. My darling mother had managed to be present at most of my performances in the corps de ballet in London but this performance was beyond our wildest dreams and one she was determined not to miss.

My first ballerina role went well up to the very end of the pas de deux when, on full pointe, I was supposed to execute first one then two turns holding the finger of my partner overhead. When it came to the last three turns I mistakenly let go too soon as I was pirouetting. Had it not been for the quick reaction of Helpmann I would have fallen off pointe, flat onto my back. I'm told there was a gasp of horror from the corps as, unperturbed, he gallantly caught me in his arms, and the audience were none the wiser – thanks to Robert Helpmann.

We were a tightly knit company, travelling the length and breadth of the country, miraculously escaping injury from the bombing in each city we visited. After my amazing week in Oxford, we arrived in Bath Sunday morning following the first, totally unexpected 'Baedeker Raid' (as it came to be called) to find many digs and hotels bombed or destroyed.

Five members of the company thought they had found refuge in the beautiful little theatre where we were to open the next day. The German planes returned that Sunday night dropping incendiaries across the city and hitting the Victorian theatre. Miraculously, our five – which included our music director, Constant Lambert, and our stage manager, Robbie – fought the flames, extinguished the fire and saved the theatre from burning down. It was too damaged for us to open on the Monday, so sadly we were forced to return to London. Much to my disappointment I lost a second scheduled week deputising for Fonteyn.

I had experienced a most remarkable seven days – partnered by the Company's leading dancer, Helpmann, actually dancing Fonteyn's roles in *Les Sylphides,* Odette in *Le Lac des Cygnes,* the Lady in *Comus,* the saucy solo from *Façade,* as well as Madam's planned revival for me of *The Gods Go A-Begging* – all in one week! It was like a fairy tale, which I look back upon now with total disbelief and incredulity. Sadly we had all to be transported back to London for classes and rehearsals (such a disappointment for me), prior to the summer season at the New Theatre, which opened the following week.

On the opening night, Tuesday 5th May, I had the thrill of performing the Maid in *The Gods Go A-Begging* with Rassine as my partner, and to my delight received several little bouquets from well-wishers. Some of these fans have become life-time supporters from whom I still receive Christmas cards or meet at ballet events.

My fairy tale had not ended. Madam was pleased and said she wanted me to learn the rest of *Swan Lake*, Acts Three and Four. I was astonished and found myself being taught by Madam herself – rather terrifying but wonderful. She was a very clear teacher and producer, although impatient and intolerant of anything which displeased her, so one had to pick up quickly her directives. She was insistent that the two characters, Odette and Odile, be clearly defined both in movement and facial expression. It was a very precious time for me, being so carefully rehearsed by Madam, and I worked hard to please her. These sessions were squeezed in during the London season's daily performances, and six weeks on came my next great opportunity.

My fifteenth birthday was fast approaching, and it coincided with the matinee scheduled for my debut in the full-length *Swan Lake* at the New Theatre. It was tremendously exciting, and all my energies were focused on the performance. It was unusual for my shy mother to stay with me in the lower dressing room together with the nine other occupants. This time she remained by my side up to the half-hour call when all visitors must leave. She was deeply concerned because my menstruation chose to start for the very first time that morning. Even so, I was determined that nothing should upset or distract me from this thrilling opportunity.

I clearly remember waiting impatiently in the wings, looking at the brown lino as Tchaikovsky's inspirational music led me towards my entrance. Following in the hallowed paths of the great ballerinas, I could hardly believe that I had been given the chance to dance such a dramatic classical role. Constant Lambert was the conductor, and I instinctively felt he would lead me carefully through my performance. Likewise my experienced partner Robert Helpmann, who I knew would support me come what may. At last, the first act over, chords rang out from the orchestra to herald the entrance of the Swan Queen Odette, and I was on. The performance just flowed; I enjoyed every moment and coped determinedly with the interval metamorphosis into Odile, the changing of tights, shoes, costume and headdress.

Most tricky of all was putting up one's hair into rolls of formal curls before pinning round the heavily ornate headdress. In that production, with Hugh Stevenson's designs, Odile's costume was a stunning red velvet bejewelled tutu with headdress to match, and it was exhilarating to wear. This was an important factor in the mental change from the pure, innocent Odette into the scheming, flashy Odile. All this had to be accomplished during a 15-minute interval, plus adding rouge to the cheeks and a powdering cover up of body wet-white from the white swan.

In those days we managed all this ourselves with the exception of wet-whiting our bodies. This was done by a dresser who then fastened us securely into our costumes. As these were often also worn by other dancers, they could have up to three rows of hooks and eyes to accommodate all sizes, becoming unpleasantly stiff and smelly from perspiration! That day I was wearing Fonteyn's old costumes, refitted for me, so I felt comfortable in them, though disappointed that the tutus were droopy.

How long ago in retrospect, yet it all still feels so real – the encouragement between the acts from the ballet mistress, Joy Newton, Madam's approval after the show, which meant so much to me, and the many who came round to see me afterwards. What kindness and praise. How thrilled I was to be taken out to tea later by Arnold Haskell, the esteemed ballet critic and historian, together with my parents and Madam herself. We gathered in an informal restaurant in the Strand called The Curb. There one could relax on settees and eat quite substantial meals. That day remains imprinted on me, although little did I realise that it was the start of my long journey through the wonderful world of dance and theatre, one which has never ceased to attract and fascinate me.

It was that day that I met for the first time GBL Wilson, who always said it was me who made him fall in love with the ballet, ably encouraged no doubt by his school friend, dance historian and lawyer Ivor Guest. GB was a passionate photographer, and it is to him I owe the photographic record of my progress over the ensuing years until his untimely death in 1973. He was present at all my debuts, during and after the war, soon becoming a close friend as well as a keen balletomane.

His dictionary of ballet, dedicated to me, first published in 1950, remains my preferred and most helpful dictionary. Like many others, I miss him to this day. A Wykhamist, he was a quiet unassuming person with a formidably retentive mind and could give the correct answer to any question on almost any subject from engineering to the history of dance. He left his vast collection of photos to the RAD, a unique history of the development of English ballet through and after the war, for future dance students and teachers to appreciate.

My career-shaping summer season of 1942 at the New Theatre was a longer one than usual and ran for ten weeks. On stage at the close Madam brought forward Jack Hart, one of my partners. He had been called up to join the Royal Air Force and to everyone's dismay was having to depart. He had taken over many leading roles from other dancers, as they were called up to join the forces, and had himself achieved a big success and gained many appreciative fans, who gave him a great reception. He offered me his large blue suitcase at a next-to-nothing price as he had noticed mine was really too small and flimsy for touring, and I took advantage of his kind offer.

Following my successful debut in *Swan Lake,* I was usually given the leading role in matinee performances. I was still cast to dance in the corps in the evenings, however: Madam did not encourage any swollen heads. It was an exciting and demanding season as both David Paltenghi and John Field began to partner me. To be seen and assessed in London dancing some of Fonteyn's roles was an incredible opportunity.

There was also the challenge of *The Gods Go A-Begging,* revived especially for Alexis Rassine and me. I came to love this ballet with its delicate Handel music and deceptively simple costumes by Hugh Stevenson. How I used to enjoy wearing the pink rose atop my piled-up hair! I began to receive flowers after my performances and realised that I was acquiring a loyal following in the gallery. This was a new experience, encouraging me to dance better and better. I was always conscious of how hard I needed to work if I was to achieve a truly high standard, and felt a responsibility not to let down those who had faith in and expectations of me.

During the season Robert Helpmann staged his second ballet, *Hamlet,* which he worked on during the spring tour. I was one of six court ladies, yet again he chose me to understudy Fonteyn's sensitive and emotional role as Ophelia. I found Helpmann's work so theatrical and different, and was mesmerised by his rehearsals.

The ballet was well received, subsequently enjoying a big success on tour. Robert Helpmann had persuaded the artist Leslie Hurry to design the sets and costumes. The decor was striking, almost overwhelming with its strong colours and bold sweeping lines. This was the first time that Leslie Hurry had worked in theatre, yet he produced such exciting results. The dancers were delighted with his costumes, rich and swirling, somehow different from any we had previously worn. This helped steep us in the brooding atmospheric mood of this dramatic work encapsulated within Tchaikovsky's great overture.

The right sets and costumes are vital for a successful production. Dancers should not be dwarfed or overshadowed by heavy sets and care must be taken that thrones (as is *Swan Lake* and *The Sleeping Beauty*), cottages (as in *Giselle*) or flights of steps do not encroach too much within the performing area. Costumes, whilst depicting period or atmosphere, need to be as lightweight as possible so as not to weigh down or impede the dancers. Sleeves have to be carefully judged so as not to restrict arm movements above the head. Oliver Messel's original, delicate sleeves for the Princess Aurora Act I costume presented a problem and had to be rethought to enable freedom of movement for the arms.

Only one week after the close of our London season the Company performed for the first time in the open air: at Victoria Park, in Bethnal Green. I believe the season was presented by the London County Council with low-priced tickets. It was a big success with our new public, and the programme was perfect for me: *Les Sylphides*, which I danced with Helpmann, *The Gods Go A-Begging,* and *Façade* in which I delighted performing the cheeky Polka solo. All these works we had just given during the ten-week season in the West End, so it required little extra rehearsal.

It was a surprisingly different experience for everyone, being close to the audience seated below the high, specially built stage, which had no footlights. There was the constant fear of dancing too near the front and falling off into someone's lap! We spaced ourselves cautiously. What thunderous applause we received, even on days when it rained and the audience sat under their own umbrellas. Mercifully, the stage was covered.

11 Win Some, Lose Some, 1942

Once I became a member of the Vic-Wells Company, my parents decided to relinquish the cottage in Little Harrowden and search for a house outside the area of heavy bombing. They settled on a house in Sanderstead, to which amidst snow and freezing conditions our belongings were moved at the beginning of March. It was reassuring to have my parents living within reach of London again as I was able to live at home whenever the Company was in the capital.

I was on tour dancing in Manchester when I reached them by phone to tell them my wonderful news. Madam told me I was to dance the Lilac Fairy in the *Sleeping Princess.* The Lilac Fairy is a big role, the second lead, appearing in every act. It requires a strong technique for the difficult solo in the Prologue and then clear, convincing mime in the successive scenes. I was stunned by this totally unexpected opportunity and began practising the solo whenever and wherever I could. Over the years, I have become closely associated with this role, the 'Good Fairy' protecting and guiding the princess to safety and ultimate happiness.

With its many mime scenes, one can continue to develop and imbue the role with tenderness and love together with the quiet dignity and authority it demands. It is a magical role to portray. At only fifteen, however, when I first took on the role, I was more concerned with remembering every detail, fitting the mime scenes to the music correctly as well as conquering the demanding fouetté relevés near the end of the variation in the all-important Prologue.

An amazing Autumn 1942 followed. From the Victoria Park week, we were off on tour again, this time for seven weeks. Two weeks in Newcastle, two weeks in Liverpool, one week each in Manchester, Leeds and Cambridge, returning to open in London at the New Theatre again two days later. We certainly worked hard in those wartime years – I wonder if the dancers today would have the stamina or whether unions would even permit this? We all lived to perform. I was completely immersed in performances, rehearsals, classes, learning all I possibly could while being backed by loving parents.

I certainly needed their loving support for there were times when I felt very alone. As a relatively successful newcomer in the Company I felt I was not really welcome among the corps or soloists and most certainly not within the top hierarchy. Such a new young member given unheard-of opportunities must have been hard for some to accept. Without my realising, I must have caused envy and resentment in my fellow dancers.

Still young, enthusiastic and trusting as I was, an unpleasant shock was awaiting me. We were in Newcastle when I was summoned to the ballet mistress Joy Newton's dressing room one morning. She severely reprimanded me for something I was supposed to have said: that I would be sharing Margot Fonteyn's dressing room from now on. I was astonished and absolutely flabbergasted for I most certainly had never uttered those words nor even contemplated such an idea.

I was still very much in the corps, appearing only in the leading role of the full length *Swan Lake* at matinees, when I was temporarily put in Fonteyn's star dressing room. This was closer to the stage but I returned to the corps de ballet room as normal in the evening. I fervently protested my innocence, and thank goodness Miss Newton eventually believed me and accepted my word. But not before she had told me off harshly, saying how shocked she was and how cross and disappointed Madam was with me.

The episode shook me terribly, and I have never forgotten it. In those few unhappy minutes I suddenly grew up, awakening to the realisation that I could not trust everyone as I had always done. I was still very naïve, completely absorbed in performing. I had a lot to learn about life in the theatre: its undercurrents, its little cliques, the jealousies, ambitions and resentments that abound (albeit hidden), as well as the sexual permutations. I was blissfully unaware of homosexuality around me, of which I knew nothing, and I did not grasp the implications of such relationships for several years.

In many ways I was still very much a child, always happy, smiling and keen to please, very much in awe of my elders and respectful of authority of any kind. One of my partners, John Field, nicknamed me 'rose-bud' which upset and embarrassed me.

Most certainly I was made to feel very much the young dancer, especially when I was under the wing of an older dancer. De Valois thought it was a good idea to have an older person chaperoning me. Sometimes it was a member of the corps – June Vincent or Jean Bedells –and sometimes a soloist – Celia Franca or her husband Leo Kersley, who was perhaps not the best influence as he invariably came in late for make-up! Poor things – they were to make sure I was coping, and I only hope they did not mind too much!

At fourteen, I had been thrust into a complex group of ambitious young dancers, many of whom must have greatly resented me. I so much wanted to be a part of all their offstage lives but felt I was kept at arm's length, with the exception of one or two.

After the Newcastle experience I determined to make friendships outside the Company whenever possible. This turned out well for it encouraged me to search out other arts and artists and gave me an awareness of life outside the confines of a touring ballet company, thereby broadening my horizons.

I was blessed with a few friends in the Company, like Moyra Fraser with whom I sometimes used to stay overnight at her home with her parents near Victoria Station. She adored them, calling her mother Moth and her father Tua, and was enormous fun to be with, kind and generous. She was a born comedienne and became a great friend of Helpmann, who appreciated her wit and cast her as the amusing Hen in *The Birds*, his third creation. He also chose me to star in this ballet as the Nightingale, opposite Rassine as the Dove.

This was my first ever created role in the Company: a new and testing challenge. I had the joy of interpreting the descriptive Respighi music and the satisfaction of being fitted for my very own costume, designed on me. What a breathtaking moment it was when we first saw the delicate scenery designed by Chiang Lee. During the war *The Birds* was to become one of the most popular and frequently performed ballets.

Helpmann worked on the ballet with us during the late Autumn season and I loved all the rehearsals with him; we all did. He was so professional, confident and knowing exactly what he wished to achieve and how to go about it. He had a wicked sense of humour, which at first I found disconcerting until I got to understand him better. An incredibly versatile Australian artist, a rare mixture of kindness and bitchiness and always up to some kind of mischief. With Helpmann there was never a dull moment on or off stage, and we had to keep our wits about us.

We were all excited when we finally saw the amazing bird costumes and headdresses and impatient to see it all work out in performance. An enchanting little ballet, it was well liked. On the first night, to everyone's astonishment, we took 15 curtain calls, and I received three bouquets and a box of all too rare chocolates. How pleased I felt that the first role created for me should be in such a well received ballet.

As the months slipped past I was still growing and, problematically, I was really now too tall for Helpmann. Madam then looked for other partners of a more suitable height. John Field, before joining the company in 1939, trained in Liverpool with a brilliant teacher, Sheila Elliot-Clarke. John was a very good height for me: tall and well built with an amazing ballon (the ability to look suspended in a jump) and an effortless technique. He was a romantic dancer and appeared almost laid-back in his approach to some roles.

I felt, though, a certain reluctance on his part to accompany such a new, young girl. John was a good partner, nonetheless, and we did many *Swan Lakes* together before he too was called up the following spring. Fortunately there was Rassine who already partnered me in *Les Sylphides, The Birds* and *The Gods Go A-Begging*. He was, however, neither strong nor tall enough to support me adequately in the big lifts the choreography demands in *Swan Lake.*

For this classic Madam chose David Paltenghi as my Prince. He was Swiss, so not liable for conscription, and had begun learning ballet far later than most men. Although lacking an advanced technique and not as tall as John, he was strong and supportive. Handsome, every girl's heart-throb, he was very much a man of the theatre, revelling in the dramatic roles in which he excelled. I, too, enjoyed dramatic parts, and we got on well together. He would give me books of poetry, essays and biographies all of which helped educate me in the arts, and I greatly valued his friendship.

I think David was almost as surprised as I was when Robert Helpmann invited me to meet Laurence Olivier. This was between shows on Saturday 24th April at the New Theatre during our 1942 spring season. Nervously entering Helpmann's dressing room, I was thrilled to be meeting Olivier, this great star of the theatre and films. They were obviously very good friends, and chatted with me about my dancing. Eventually Olivier asked me if I would be interested in playing the role of the French princess in his forthcoming film *Henry V*. I was completely taken aback, swept off my feet and immediately stammered my keen interest. Olivier went on to explain that I would need to learn Princess Katherine's lines by heart and then to have a screen test. To my enquiries about Madam's reaction to all this, Helpmann assured me that he would make all necessary arrangements.

I confided in David who at once undertook to help me learn and perfect the part in readiness for the test. We worked on it for several weeks before Madam informed me that on no account could she allow me to even consider auditioning for the role as I was still so young; moreover, she needed me. That was the end of that particular dream.

The actress Renee Asherson played the role – and with great charm, too, but I have always regretted not having even been allowed to audition. The film was to enjoy such a great success. The little princess was an endearing, delightful role, which I would have adored playing opposite the romantic and quite wonderful Laurence Olivier! Recounting the great British victory in France at Agincourt, I believe that the film also acted as a boost to public morale, arriving on the screens as the Allies were retaking Europe. William Walton wrote the dramatic score and the music is still enjoyed to this day. The film received many accolades with its cast of distinguished actors. Olivier himself was the recipient of an Academy Award for his outstanding achievement as actor, producer and director. Lose some, gain some.

A few months later Madam created for me a delightful part in a new ballet, *Promenade,* a lightweight work to Haydn's music. Gordon Hamilton, an Australian dancer who joined the company in the same year as I, played the leading role of a lepidopterist. Madam arranged for me a romantic pas de deux with David Paltenghi amidst a number of other short divertissements. The setting for these was a French park, and they finished with a unique finale based on Breton dances. *Promenade* premiered in Edinburgh in October 1943, but unfortunately I was taken ill so Fonteyn kindly stepped in and took over my role instead. By the time we were back in London I had recovered well enough to dance my original role.

I continued to have occasional trouble with my health, and my parents were always on hand to support me. As a child I suffered from a weak chest and anaemia, for which I was prescribed Guinness and boiled cabbage water. Ugh, how I detested both, and have retained a lifetime dislike of beer and boiled greens. I made regular visits to our family doctor for vital checkups and medicine.

As well as being watchful of my physical development, my parents were concerned about my general demeanour. I received a very stiff letter from my father during one Autumn tour after I went with some of the Company to a fun-fair on the Sabbath. My parents were truly shocked and upset by my lack of respect for the holy day even though I had attended church that Sunday morning, a ritual I tried always to maintain wherever we were.

I had left school at such an early age and my parents were naturally concerned that I did not neglect reading the books recommended by my uncle, the headmaster. They cared deeply for me, my health and safety in those dangerous war years. In return I wanted to please them.

We were a very loving family, respectful of authority and religion. My deeply held belief in God and prayer has always been my anchor and has helped me throughout my entire career. When in London, I used to go into St Martin-in-the-Fields church before my performances for a few calming minutes of prayer.

When I appeared in London, my father always met me at South Croydon railway station from the last train home. After the performance I would run down St Martin's Lane to Charing Cross station in full make-up to catch the 10.20pm train and, gasping for breath, tear along the platform to the last carriage – the LADIES ONLY compartment. Thank goodness it was still in use and rigorously respected. Once safely aboard the moving train I would proceed to smother my face in make-up removal cream, transforming quickly into a clean faced young girl!

Sometimes the bombings were so bad that the line was damaged and men with megaphones would clearly direct passengers off the train onto a waiting bus. This would take us to another train waiting further along the line to continue our journey. It was remarkable how difficulties were overcome and everyone went about their life and daily work. Despite day and night bombing there was an immense swell of camaraderie amongst the population. Today I look back in amazement at the efficiency and perfect calm in which obstacles and destruction were dealt with and defeated – no wonder we won the war.

13 1942, My First Christmas Away, And Onwards

After such an exciting London season we were off immediately for a short run in York over Christmas. This was the first time I had ever been away from home over the festive season, and I felt very homesick, even though we had but one day free: Christmas Day itself. I still see in my mind's eye a small, rather dingy room with tired-looking hanging festoons, where a number of us gathered to celebrate Christmas. It must have been a private room in a pub, but I did not enjoy either the food or the drink – I was missing my parents so much. I still like to be with my loved ones at this special time. For me it is a thanksgiving for having been blessed with family and friends – sadly there are many who have neither and to whom Christmas must become a long, lonely time.

The stage in York was small, raked and covered by a nasty, black, tar-like surface. During one performance of *The Birds*, travelling downstage in a series of pirouettes, I should have been caught by Rassine on the last double fouetté. Somehow to his horror (not to mention mine), he managed to miss me. I fell flat on my back, sliding forward a few more inches before I could get myself up gracefully and continue as if nothing untoward had happened. But my precious silk tights and pointe shoes were covered in the black tar, a clear give-away!

York was followed by performances in Bradford and then back to London preparing for our first 1943 season at the New Theatre. It opened with Fonteyn dancing Swanhilda in *Coppélia* on 25th January to a sold out house. The following our company had built up both on tour and in London was incredible. By spring the box office restricted their London sales to four seats per person for each performance.

I performed all the time – at both matinees and evenings, dancing leads as well as corps. I continued to be given new parts – the devout solo, Prayer, in the last act of *Coppélia* and, to my delight, the elegant leading role in Ashton's ballet *Les Rendezvous*, created for Alicia Markova in 1933. The opportunity to follow in the divine Markova's footsteps thrilled me. The role has the most enchanting, delicate head, body and hand movements in which Markova excelled. I was so happy when, after my first performance, the ballet mistress said she was pleased with me.

All through the first week of the season I had felt distinctly unwell but would not give in, dancing leads in *Les Sylphides* Tuesday, *The Birds* Wednesday, the full length *Swan Lake* Thursday matinee, the opening ballet *Comus* on Friday, before *Les Rendezvous* on Saturday matinee with *Comus* at night. On Monday of the second week *Apparitions* was presented to an enthralled public. What a glorious, romantic work. It was heaven dancing to Liszt's glorious music, dressed in Cecil Beaton's exquisite ball gowns; Ashton was surely a genius. To my disappointment, he never chose me to understudy Fonteyn in this beautiful ballet; nevertheless I felt fortunate to be dancing in the corps, swirling amidst beautifully costumed dancers.

The third week brought two exciting events. I was scheduled to dance *Swan Lake* with Paltenghi on the Wednesday matinee, but we were replaced at the last moment by Fonteyn and Helpmann because the Queen and the two Princesses came unexpectedly to the performance. It was a great honour for the Company to have the interest and support of the Royal Family amidst the dangers of war. I was thrilled by their presence and did not mind forgoing my performance to Fonteyn as, the following evening, I was given her *Swan Lake* instead.

Then on Saturday I was rehearsed in *Les Rendezvous* by Frederick Ashton himself for three quarters of an hour before the matinee. My diary simply records 'wonderful', and so it was. He was so inspiring and enthusiastic, so elegant as he demonstrated the body movements he wanted. He was a true artist and used to enthrall us all with his expositions of Pavlova. We never tired of watching him.

That spring tour began with two weeks in Bournemouth, where I gave my first performance as Ophelia in Helpmann's *Hamlet.* The mad scene, where she twists her fingers round her interlocked hands, distraught and broken-hearted, was a new dimension for me, and I found this compelling. Perhaps my interpretation of this role encouraged Madam the following year to give me the chance to play Giselle. But that was something I had not yet envisaged.

To everyone's delight Ashton had been granted three months' leave from the RAF to create a new ballet, *The Quest*, based on an episode from Spenser's *Faerie Queen.* He began work that last week in London before we left for the tour, during which Ashton worked persistently every day. He eagerly awaited the arrival of newly composed music from William Walton, whom he had chosen to write the score. Ashton gave Walton detailed instructions for each of the five scenes, but as Walton was out of the country the score took time to arrive. Ashton pounced on each sheet the moment it caught up with us during our six-week tour. It must have been a nightmare for him. He was working under great pressure, against time.

The tour took us to Hanley, Coventry, Derby and Oxford, and watching the renowned master creating this work enthralled me. I remember a nail-biting week in Coventry, the broad stage completely cleared after class and Ashton pacing nervously awaiting the arrival of music for the fifth and last scene of the ballet. We ran through all that Ashton had completed, and he then proceeded to create the final act without the precious music, guided only by the directions he had given Walton. I am still astonished how such a musically driven choreographer as Ashton managed to create without music, but he did. Thanks to his professionalism, when the music eventually arrived it all fitted perfectly, to everyone's astonishment and joy!

The tour finished on Saturday, and we opened the following Tuesday in London at the New Theatre. Within a week, on April 6th, there was a Gala premiere of *The Quest.*

It was an exciting evening with the money raised going to Lady Cripps' Aid to China Fund. I can still visualise Robert Helpmann's bold white costume with its symbolic red St George Cross emblazoned on his chest, in contrast to Fonteyn's delicate raiment as Una, embodying Truth.

Ashton entrusted me with an exciting role as the seductress Duessa: a challenging character for me to develop. My own costume was a strong purple satin, body-clinging dress with generously padded out bust, to help portray a much more mature woman, Duessa – Falsehood. Three Saracen knights, David Paltenghi, Peter Franklin White and Alexis Rassine, partnered me, which gave me some complex double work. Equally complicated was my scene with 'Bobby' Helpmann, seducing him while I lay back on his shield dancing on full pointe. I loved the challenging drama of the part, William Walton's music and John Piper's costumes. I only wish it had remained far longer in the repertoire.

14 *Nourishing Support – 1943*

I find something soothing and inspiring about trees. When dancing in *Les Sylphides* I imagined myself as a sylph flying amongst tree branches, being carried by gentle breezes up and over the tree-tops. I found holding a pictorial image particularly helpful in abstract works. It also helped me to use my imagination for such dramatic roles as Giselle.

My strongest motivation comes from music, and there was much wonderful music in our repertoire. During our ten-week London season in 1942, I danced to Auber, Chopin, Handel, Respighi, Tchaikovsky and Walton! What variety, what an education. Encouraged by our remarkable conductor, Constant Lambert, I also endeavoured to read a conductor's score. Lambert took upon himself the added role of an unofficial ballet master, insuring the corps were in line, costumes and headgear correctly worn, no 'pig's ears' (untidy ends of shoe ribbons), and that we were in time with the music. He truly loved the ballet and a certain ballerina (Fonteyn!) and gave his all to improving the Company in every aspect.

In the Spring of 1943 with so many ongoing performances he took on an associate conductor, Julian Clifford; then in the autumn Alec Sherman. But neither was in the same league as Lambert. He also thrilled audiences with his infectious compering of *Wedding Bouquet.* Mary Honer was so entertaining in this ballet as the Bride: she was born a soubrette dancer, outstanding in such roles as Swanhilda in *Coppélia* and the Blue Girl in *Les Patineurs*.

To my disappointment she chose to leave the Company during the long 1942 season to become an actress. Since childhood I had adored her scintillating performances partnered by Harold Turner. They excelled together in many roles, including *The*

Nutcracker pas de deux which my father applauded wholeheartedly. He was not particularly enamoured of the ballet, often sleeping through an entire matinee, but for these two dancers he was always wide awake and enthusiastic! Mary Honer was to be sadly missed in the many roles which she had made her own, such as the Betrayed Girl in *The Rake's Progress.*

De Valois's dramatic ballet had been restored after its tragic loss in 1940, when the Company had been in Eindhoven and forced to flee the invading German army, leaving behind six ballets, their costumes, décor and music. So it was an emotional evening when *The Rake's Progress* came back into the repertoire, gloriously alive, to Gavin Gordon's descriptive music. One appreciated all the more the cleverly drawn characters portrayed throughout the dramatic scenes. It is still enjoyed today, almost a century on from its premiere. What a great choreographer we had in de Valois, and what a tragedy that she had so little time in which to create more works. Creative choreographers are all too rare.

I was unusually fortunate to have been given so much at such a young age. Looking back now over my dancing career, my big regret is not having had more roles created for me. I realise that my height was a problem for some choreographers, as was finding a suitably tall, reliable partner, although, at five foot six inches, I have never felt myself particularly tall. After the war there were fewer new works created, possibly due to rising costs and the risks incurred as a resident company in a large opera house with more leading dancers.

My parents came to as many of my London performances as they could manage, and I was so happy when I knew they were out front. What confidence and encouragement they gave. I know money was short, yet they paid to be in the audience; no free seats then. There were also train fares from South Croydon station to Charing Cross and back.

The Company were once again at Sadler's Wells for rehearsals as it was no longer being used to house bombed-out families, despite it too having received a little bomb damage. When I was not rehearsing, my mother and I would meet in London and go to a film after snatching a tasty lunch together at our all-time favourite – the wonderful Lyons Corner Houses. It was our special treat. My mother and I would sometimes go back to the Corner House at the Angel, close by Sadler's Wells Theatre, where Miss Sharp had taken me after my audition with de Valois in 1937. From the first floor, one could look out through the gracious long windows onto the busy street corner below.

There were other branches in the West End: in the Strand and another frequented by us in Leicester Square, each superior to the numerous local Lyons Tea Houses dotted around the capital. After a Saturday matinee dancing *Swan Lake,* my parents would take me to the Leicester Square one to enjoy their special salads – one shilling and five pence with spam (a ham substitute) or one shilling and seven pence with tinned fish. It was excellent value for money, attractively displayed on a large oblong plate and served by smartly uniformed, welcoming waitresses – Nippies, they were called.

Money was short, however, and despite all my work in the Company I was still receiving only four pounds ten shillings a week. My feeling remained that perhaps it was wrong to receive money for doing what I most loved. But perhaps not quite as strongly as when I received my first pay packet of four pounds from de Valois's own hands in 1941! She ran almost everything: taking classes and rehearsals, acting as a manager paying all the company each Friday, seeing to the general overall running of the Company, as well as planning ahead. She was phenomenal. Shortly after I joined, Donald Albery, aghast at seeing de Valois's workload, took over as Company manager, and it was he from then on who would pay the dancers each Friday. I was not to know then how many times our paths would cross in the future.

A few days after my sixteenth birthday, during our summer season at the New, we were honoured by an informal visit from the Queen. I was fortunate that this time it was a triple-bill programme in which I appeared as Duessa in *The Quest* and the leading dancer in *Les Rendezvous.* What a great occasion; I was so excited, dancing in front of the Queen at last. Ever since I had presented her with a bouquet in 1937 I had dreamt of this happening, her gentle words, 'perhaps one day I shall see you dancing', still in my mind.

The next week was the last in that season during which Margot was sometimes indisposed, and I had the opportunity to dance her *Swan Lake* in the evenings, too. My number of fans increased and to my surprise I began to receive quite a few more bouquets, especially after *Swan Lake*, often tied with satin ribbon. One fan in particular, a Miss Georgina Dudt, frequently sent me a large bouquet, always bound by the most extravagant amount of wide red satin ribbon, completed by a beautiful big bow. Little packets of food would be left for me between shows on a Saturday, a portion of cheese, two – sometimes even three – eggs, packets of sugar, chocolate and, on rare occasions, a small piece of steak.

As food was severely rationed, these generous offerings were obviously the fans' own precious rations, and I was deeply touched that they would sacrifice their food to help me keep up my strength. Madam was also aware of the need to keep her dancers fit and from time to time would bring us packets of glucose –almost impossible to come by, but which her doctor husband Arthur acquired for us. I was always enquiring at different chemists for blackcurrant puree, unrationed but hard to obtain, likewise tinned grapefruit marmalade. One's coupons allocated only one jar of jam or marmalade a fortnight, which was all too little for a hungry dancer. To this day, I harbour a love for toast and marmalade. From time to time parcels would arrive for the Company from American Ballet Theatre. Ballet shoe ribbons, dried foods and bars of chocolate were distributed to us and much appreciated, as we were all working extremely hard with little respite.

At the end of June 1943, as soon as the New Theatre season was over, we were immediately dancing once again in London's Victoria Park. By midweek Madam sent me to a specialist about my knee, which had been paining me, and I was told to rest for the remainder of the week. I was not happy to do this, but it helped and I was back dancing with the Company again the following week in Manchester. I used to look forward to a weekend there because Sheila McCarthy (my first teacher at the Wells school) now lived outside the city with her doctor husband, Arthur. She would invite two or three of us to spend Sunday with them, giving us a happy relaxing time and lots of good food! She retired at the outbreak of war when the school shut and devoted herself to helping her husband and his patients in and around Manchester.

15 A Welcome Break – And My Beaux

After two more weeks in Leeds we were treated to a fortnight's 'holiday', certainly much needed and much enjoyed – our first real break since I joined the Company two years earlier. After I had relaxed for a few days at home, I accepted GB Wilson's invitation to Trowbridge, where he lived with his mother. He was now a kind family friend who frequently visited us in Sanderstead, often staying the night. For the next week I was well looked after and thoroughly spoilt by his mother.

Each day GB organised an interesting outing, either to Wells Cathedral, Glastonbury, Weston-Super-Mare or Bath. At Bristol Theatre Royal we saw a performance by Ballet Rambert of de Valois's ballet *Bar aux Folies-Bergère*, which I thoroughly enjoyed. Madam choreographed it in 1934, and it was the only work she ever created for the Rambert company. Some days GB and I cycled and went swimming as the weather was glorious. We also visited the gas works he managed nearby in Warminster; I was fascinated to learn about the way it all worked.

One day he drove me to the breathtakingly beautiful Cheddar Gorge. It was my first ever sight of this amazing area, but what I had not known was that he had arranged a visit to a cave in the Mendips. We were met by two professional pot-holers who brought appropriate overalls for me to don, together with a miner's lamp which they fixed securely on my head. We descended into the mouth of the cave and, not wanting to appear nervous, I expressed great interest in how much further we were to proceed. And proceed we did, right down to the very bottom of the cave – the sump. It was scaring, crawling along narrow corridors of rock, and finally clambering perilously high up along the side of a huge, vaulted chamber.

Once safely below, we could appreciate the unbelievably beautiful setting, almost like a cathedral. With water gently dripping around us we rested in readiness for the frightening (for me) return crawl. This seemed like an eternity. Never have I been so relieved to see daylight. I now know what it feels like to be underground and understand how terrible it must be to be trapped in the earth in utter darkness. I feel sure Madam would have been outraged had she known about that particular excursion! In retrospect I am glad to have been pot-holing, but I would never choose to repeat the experience!

Refreshed, the Company was soon back at the New Theatre. I was given many *Swan Lakes* to perform, mostly matinees, but to my surprise some evening shows, too. I was glad that despite the war, many of my parents' friends managed to come, including my dear Madeleine Sharp and her marvellous pianist Mary Cook. Mary had watched my progress as a child in class, whilst accompanying us with great feeling. She also taught us tap dancing, which I revelled in and was surprised when later de Valois forbade tap dancing in the school as she believed that it weakened the ankles. Mary Cook was now a full time professional at the London Hippodrome with the show *This is the Army*. What a bubbly, fun person she was, a real joy to be with, how we had loved her.

It made me so happy when those who played such an important part in my early years came to one of my performances. I recall in particular the unexpected and touching letter my father received from Miss Horsey, my primary school Headmistress, saying how pleased she was by my achievement and could I arrange a ticket for her at a Wednesday or Saturday matinee. She came to a midweek matinee, and it was wonderful to see how happy and proud of me she was. I owe her a tremendous amount. Her superb teaching, high standards and discipline played an important part in my development.

While I was still a schoolgirl the son of one of my father's business friends became very attracted to me. Reginald Barr was a keen musician, and I would often listen to him practising the organ at our local church in Clissold Park, appreciating and absorbing some great organ music. He won a music scholarship to Trinity College, Oxford, where he took me to my first grown-up dinner and dance for the undergraduates.

For this my mother made me a full-length, pale blue evening dress – my first ever – complemented by the beautiful corsage I had been given to wear. I was fifteen and, although already touring the provinces with the ballet, I found this a most memorable occasion. More importantly it was there he introduced me to another undergraduate, Michael Meyer, who was to become one of my lifetime friends and also a devotee of my mother. Michael learnt to speak Norwegian, Danish and Swedish fluently and was later to achieve fame for his translations of Ibsen and Strindberg. Many years after he was a great help when he verified the intentions of Sven, my Swedish husband-to-be!

Reg, like so many young men, was conscripted and sent out to India. By his return after the war I had accumulated a number of other admirers and sadly had to dash his hopes and those of others. Most certainly I enjoyed their attention, their gifts and flowers and grew very fond of them. I appreciated being taken to lovely restaurants like the May Fair with ballroom dancing, dining at the Savoy or at the famous theatrical restaurant in West Street, The Ivy. But at that time I never felt a desire to marry; dancing was my life and everything else came second.

My mother was much loved and admired for her gentleness and generosity, and sometimes my invitations would include her as well. She had a very special admirer in Michael Meyer, who found in her the love and attention his own rich but busy parents were unable to give him. He often presented her with beautiful gifts, which she greatly appreciated. Occasionally my mother would join me on tour for a week, when between rehearsals we would hop on a bus and leave the city behind for the hills and dales. We would often be accompanied by one of the orchestral players who, like us, appreciated the beauty of the English countryside.

I first danced the lead as Giselle on the 1st March 1944 in Derby. I was sixteen. It had been planned that my debut was to have been a week previously but my old weakness, my chest, was giving me trouble and I had developed a bad cough. Madam sensibly postponed my debut for a week, which saddened me, but it was obviously right to make me wait until I was fitter.

The delay also gave me extra time to prepare for such a dramatic role. The simple peasant girl in love, driven to madness and death through her lover's infidelity, returns in the second act as a spirit. It calls for powerful acting and an effortless technique, including a soaring jump. This ballet holds a special place in my heart since it was aged fourteen in *Giselle* that I took my first steps in the corps de ballet. The Adolphe Adam score perfectly portrays the story, and as Giselle I was led by the music. I found my technique must be subservient to the interpretation and development of the role – one of the greatest in classical ballet. Giselle is often equated to Hamlet in the straight theatre and is most certainly one of the great highlights of a dancer's career. I was very aware of this and determined to give of my absolute best.

At that first performance my partner was Alexis Rassine. Like me, he excelled in romantic roles, and we were well suited temperamentally. He was not tall, but he managed me well in the ballet and we built up a sympathetic relationship. Relieved that I had recovered, my mother came up to Derby to watch my debut. Many friends, including GB with his camera, travelled to Derby, and it was quite an occasion. Madam and the ballet mistress were pleased with me, but I knew I had a long way to go to do justice to such a famous role.

I was given several more performances as Giselle during the northern tour and to my delight also one evening performance. This was invaluable as it helped build up my strength and develop a closer understanding of the role before performing it in London. The first performances were in Hammersmith at the old King's Theatre (now pulled down to make way for financially more rewarding premises), where I danced two performances on the same day, the 11th May. I performed the matinee with Alexis and the evening with Robert Helpmann, who once again supported me wonderfully in every way. His incredible acting as well as his partnering made the difficult, delicate lifts in Act II appear effortless.

It was a great honour and experience to have performed with such a talented artist, and I realise now how much Helpmann has inspired, influenced and helped me in my career. If only I had not grown too tall for him to partner me on a regular basis. By watching him at work in the Company I learnt so much about stagecraft. His partnership with Margot Fonteyn has become legendry. How fortunate she was to have found such a unique personality and charismatic artist.

As our tour continued on to Hanley, Bolton and Blackpool I was given more performances of Giselle, including the opening night of our week in Hanley, which helped bolster my confidence, developing the character at each performance. I would lie awake at night going through every moment of the role, examining her character and temperament, trying to decide whether she would have stabbed herself to death or died of a broken heart.

Meanwhile in the South the frequency of the air raids was increasing. On January 15th Alders, the big store, and the nearby Davis Theatre in Croydon where as a young child I watched the pantomime, were both hit by new mystery bombs. On Friday the 24th March a bomb exploded in our garden, and it was a miracle that it was not a direct hit on the house, where my father was home alone. Although our house was damaged, no one was hurt. The Company were having a two-week break and my mother and I were staying in the country just outside Sheffield with Michael Bonavia, a great lover of the arts and an ardent admirer of mine. When my mother and I received the news of our bomb we returned home immediately, cutting our stay very short.

I spent the second free week with GB and his mother in Trowbridge. She insisted I breakfast in bed each morning before being taken out and about in the surrounding countryside. An eventful week which saw me accidentally drive his car into a tree! I returned refreshed for a week of rehearsals at the Wells, relieved that there was little damage to either the car or our friendship.

After the bomb fell so close to the house, my parents decided that we should return to live in London where they rented part of one of the beautiful old houses in Lloyd Square. Close to Sadler's Wells Theatre, a part of the last Welsh settlement in London, it still boasted a dairy.

When in London, I took extra classes with Vera Volkova at the West Street studios, taking an occasional private lesson with her when I could afford it. Volkova was Russian and trained under the great teacher, Vaganova, later appearing with the Kirov Ballet before leaving Russia in 1929. She came to London in 1936 after several years as dancer and teacher in Shanghai and running her own school in Hong Kong. She always arrived a good five minutes late to take her ten o'clock morning class, giving us all time to warm up. The exception amongst the students was Diana Gould (later to become Mrs Yehudi Menuhin), who preferred to drape herself, albeit artistically, along the barre.

Volkova was an exotic woman, a fine teacher and also Fonteyn's coach. After a while I felt that perhaps I should go to a teacher who would take a closer interest in me. I chose Anna Northcote, also teaching in the West Street Studios. She had been a dancer in the de Basil Ballet Russe company and became a distinguished teacher. Her two-hour classes were heavy but strengthening, and I got more individual attention and private coaching from her which helped to develop my technique, expression and confidence.

There were several dancers in the Company who took outside classes, even though Madam was not happy about this. She had appointed Volkova as Company teacher, but Volkova only remained for six months during which period I particularly valued her help with my Giselle. She also taught in the Vic Wells school for quite some time, which was a wonderful bonus for the students. In 1950 she left London for La Scala, Milan and a year later settled in Copenhagen where for over twenty years she gave inspiration and direction to their ballet dancers as well as guesting with other companies.

I was unexpectedly given the opening night of the London season on the 30th May with Paltenghi in *Swan Lake* due to Fonteyn missing performances with a strained foot. I was thrilled, but also very nervous for now, at sixteen, I was becoming aware of a growing responsibility. It turned out to be a superb evening, ending with much applause and many bouquets, and by midnight we were reading good press reviews, too. I always looked at reviews, avidly taking them very much to heart. We were so fortunate in those days to have reviews published within a few hours of performances. I only wish this still happened today.

17 — 1944: Allied Invasion

A week later, 5th June 1944 saw the invasion of Europe by the Allies, which gave a terrific upsurge of hope and excitement across the country. Like so many, I wanted to give of my very best at every performance. We felt revitalised as the Company continued the heavy touring schedule through 1944, with an occasional let-up for a few days mid autumn. Towards the end of the year we had another London season, this time at the Princes Theatre, which had a larger auditorium and stage than the New Theatre. The Princes seemed alien to me after the familiar intimacy of the New, feeling a lot larger and loftier, with an uncomfortably steeply raked stage. Somehow the ambience was wrong for ballet.

During the war, however, the Princes theatre served us well. It was a time of the German 'doodle bugs', the V1 flying bombs, launched from occupied France, targeting our capital. They came undetected and unannounced and were a source of great fear. Barrage balloons were floated over London's skies to trap and explode them mid air. But many got through and did a lot of damage.

During a performance of Act III of *Swan Lake* a doodle bug landed while I was completing a series of double pirouettes finishing backwards in my partner's arms. As the orchestra reached the climax the bomb exploded. The timing could not have been better, the explosion adding extra drama to the scene. There was a hushed second of silence, then the performance continued; nobody stirred or left the theatre. People were truly stoic during the war and carried on as well as they could despite the frightening destruction going on all around.

During that same season Helpmann created *Miracle in the Gorbals*, in which he played a modern, Christ-like figure, coming to the aid of a prostitute, brilliantly portrayed by Celia Franca. Both roles were highly emotional, dramatic and superbly performed. I was not in the ballet but found it an arresting work to watch and very thought-provoking.

I danced a variety of roles during this period, including the poetic Chiarina in Fokine's romantic ballet *Le Carnaval* set to Schumann's music. Another favourite solo of mine, featuring many bourrées, was Prayer, in the last act of *Coppélia*. My second performance of this solo surprisingly received four curtain calls and several bouquets. My growing number of fans were tremendously kind and supportive, and I received flowers and little letters of appreciation with congratulations after almost all my appearances. I danced leading roles in *Les Rendezvous, Promenade, The Birds* and my much revered *Les Sylphides.*

I had strained my left foot in class, and it was giving me increasing pain, having previously stumbled down a few steps in Piccadilly tube station, hurting it the day before we opened at the Princes. When we were ill or injured Madam sent us to St Bartholomew's Hospital (Barts) where we were well looked after, but it was often to a Mr Dempster in Manchester Square that we were dispatched with specific injuries. One never wanted to complain for fear of being off, consequently we were invariably in a bad state by the time we admitted to Madam that we had a problem. After an evening's performance of *Swan Lake* my foot was so painful I had to have a few days off. This happened to coincide with an encouraging raise of £1 a week, which took my salary to £5 10 shillings a week.

I was soon back performing one-acts and the full-length ballets *Swan Lake* and *Giselle.* To everyone's delight just before the end of the season Frederick Ashton was given one week's leave from the RAF. Arriving in time to take final rehearsals of his ballet *Nocturne*, he made an unexpected appearance in his original role as the darkly cloaked Spectator.

A five-week tour followed covering another Christmas and New Year in York. With the successful invasion of Europe by the Allies the rumoured possibility of a tour to France and Belgium to perform for our troops and a foreign public materialised. With the war still in progress, and being under eighteen, much to my dismay I was left behind. I anxiously awaited news of the Company and was thrilled to learn of the great successes they were enjoying wherever they performed.

I was expected to continue training, however, and found myself working with Michael Somes. Madam thought he would make an excellent partner for me as he was tall, strong and handsomely broad-shouldered. His potential as a leading dancer with his effortless ballon had already been recognised pre-war. Following a bad injury and subsequent operation he had been invalided out of the army, gradually getting back into training. We met each day to practise, starting with slow, careful warm-ups, and we got on well together. I looked forward to the future with confidence, little knowing that this good relationship would not last.

18 1945: Danseurs Returning

Mid April 1945 saw the entire Company in London preparing for the start of another long season at the New Theatre. It was a rather special time as the male dancers were gradually returning from the war, receiving a marvellous welcome from the gallery. By the end of April we learnt that Frederick Ashton had definitely been released from the RAF so was in evidence again in the theatre, at rehearsals and performances.

I was thrilled, too, that Harold Turner returned, dancing the Blue Skater in *Les Patineurs* again. This leading role, in which he remained supreme, was created for him by Ashton in 1937. Michael Somes's return was the opening night of *Carnaval*, and as the season progressed he began partnering me in *Swan Lake*. Vera Volkova was the company's ballet mistress at the time, and she gave us some remarkable two and three-hour rehearsals of this great Russian classic. Having trained under the renowned Vaganova, she passed on to us her unique style.

I felt, however, that Michael's heart was not truly in it. Our rehearsals together did not go at all well. Now back on form, his ambition was to partner Margot Fonteyn. He began to adopt an indifferent attitude to our performances, and I was really scared he would let me fall. I was terribly worried and lost all my confidence. After many sleepless nights and ever increasing nervousness, eventually I became dreadfully depressed.

Witnessing this, my father took matters into his own hands and went to see Madam about my unhappiness and increasing unease. She promised to speak to Somes and to take our rehearsals herself, which she did and things improved. It did not develop, however, into a happy relationship. I believe, moreover, that Ashton had not liked the complaint made on my behalf about one of his most talented protégés. After this, there were no more leading roles for me in his ballets. I realised that he did not enjoy working with tall dancers, which may have been the reason, but during the war this had not appeared to be a problem.

Eventually John Field took over from Michael Somes and became my most frequent partner in the classics. This was the start of a long and successful partnership. John was tall, a really good dancer with the most amazing beats and effortless elevation.

We still rehearsed spasmodically at the National Gallery where Myra Hess continued to give her popular, inspirational lunchtime concerts to packed and appreciative audiences. It seemed very strange going through the empty galleries to our designated area, fading outlines being the only reminder of the great paintings that previously hung on the walls. At the start of the war they were removed for safety to caves in the Welsh mountains. One felt terribly shut in, rehearsing there, with no windows to let in light or sound, feeling divorced from reality and the outside world.

The Gallery was conveniently near the New, and I found it exciting to pass the large area when Myra Hess was playing. She gave so much pleasure and always looked elegant, dressed with such grandeur and good taste despite the restrictions of coupon rationing. She was an inspiration and a great encouragement for many hundreds through those frightening war years.

As our season progressed, the war was drawing to a close, but on VE Day itself I was ill in bed feeling dreadfully sick, so missed all the excitement and celebrations going on everywhere. The Company's performance of *Coppélia* was hilarious with Helpmann as

Dr Coppelius having great fun decorating the balcony on stage with flags during the first act and goodness knows what else by the close of that celebratory performance!

The assistant conductor Alec Sherman left, to be replaced by Geoffrey Corbett. Before his war service in the Royal Naval Volunteer Reserve, Geoffrey had been chorus master and assistant conductor at Sadler's Wells. By July we were all back at our old home, after a popular week at the Finsbury Park open air theatre.

With the growing interest in ballet through the war, the New Theatre could no longer meet all the ballet company's requirements. There were exciting rumours of enlarging the Company and housing us elsewhere. One of my partners, Tony Burke, accompanied me to a front of house party on the 15th September – he had become a good friend and an ardent admirer. This party was great fun until we tried to leave and found ourselves locked in; it took some time trying to get out into the street!

The next day the Company left for an eight-week provincial tour, beginning with three weeks in Manchester. It was during this season that we were addressed by a distinguished looking man called David Webster who informed us that in the new year the Company was to have a new home at the Royal Opera House, Covent Garden. He explained that we were to be the resident ballet company together with an opera company. We would be reopening the theatre in February with a new production of the *Sleeping Beauty* with him, David Webster, as the administrator, together with Madam as our Artistic Director.

We were thrilled and overwhelmed by this confirmation of the rumours which had been circulating. We dancers were elated as the tour continued up to Scotland, and finished with a fortnight in Newcastle. We could be sure of full audiences there, enthusiastic and supportive. I knew some of the medical students at the local hospital, and they would sometimes smuggle me in to observe operations. Medicine always interested me so I would look forward to our Newcastle visits.

19 *My First Foreign Tour, 1945*

We had a brief three days in London, much of it spent at Drury Lane Theatre for injections prior to the Company's tour to Germany. I was tremendously excited because this time I was included. I had never been abroad before but, with both the European and Far Eastern wars now thankfully over, I was allowed to go.

At 6pm we gathered for our passports at Drury Lane. Within an hour, all dressed in smart ENSA uniforms, we were off to Victoria station, en route for Dover. After clearing customs and passport control we boarded a small, diesel-powered ship leaving Dover at midnight bound for Belgium. We were given sandwiches before climbing into cramped bunks, but it was too uncomfortable to get much sleep. I went up on deck in the darkness, enjoying the wonder of the sea in the chilly but invigorating night air.

A friend of GB's, Major Maurice Cockburn, was there to meet me in Ostend and kindly gave a few of us a delicious meal there. After lunch we clambered up onto lorries taking us to a waiting train.

It was an amazing journey for me, a newcomer to mainland Europe. It was still very much war-scarred yet functioning, and I could hardly contain my anticipation and curiosity. After two days travel, we alighted in Hamburg to find battered coaches waiting to drive us to the centre, where we were billeted in a reasonably comfortable hostel, fell into comfortable beds, and slept well until late morning.

It seemed unreal to be waking up in Germany, the country we had been fighting for six years. I found it hard to comprehend. When I went out into the streets and saw the awful ruins everywhere I realised the futility and the cruelty of war. Hamburg had obviously been a beautiful city, with its flowing river and fine buildings, and this somehow made the destruction all the more terrible and pointless. There were people wandering in the streets, bandaged, without limbs, without sight, and we saw men, women and children searching for shelter in the shells of bombed-out buildings – such destruction of property and human life. Yet, as visiting artists we had been found somewhere comfortable to sleep and were being well looked after. Britain had caused this damage – but had we? We had not wanted this war and we, too, had suffered greatly. But not, it appeared, quite as badly as our opponents.

Despite the Germans having lost the war, certain things were already functioning surprisingly well. That first afternoon we were escorted by British officers to a fine concert given by the Hamburg Philharmonic Orchestra and State Singers. I had heard of the Germans' love of music, and the impressive performance certainly confirmed this. It was an unexpected introduction to our five-week tour for the Allied troops.

In our ENSA uniforms, we had access to the officers' club at The Atlantic Hotel, near our hostel, which had been requisitioned for all the exhausted service men who won the war. They were thrilled to see us and gave us a huge welcome.

Just as we left on our European tour, my foot had started to give me great pain after I strained it one day when particularly exhausted. I therefore had a car and chauffeur at my disposal which took me daily to a local hospital for treatment. I expected miracles, so was bitterly dismayed when on my first day in class I found my poor foot still hopelessly restricted. I was forced to be off for a good part of the tour, which disappointed me terribly. Ironically, it was in Hamburg that I saw my name up in lights for the very first time which, thrilling as it was, also made me feel a bit of a fraud. The theatre was still standing, well appointed and well heated – amazing, a total contrast to the chilly theatres to which we had become accustomed in Britain. We were also astonished at the delicious food we were served, the likes of which we had not enjoyed at home for years. How could that be?

Moira Shearer and I took advantage of the car, and one day the driver drove us out to the countryside and through the villages around Hamburg. We had become good friends since she joined the Company the previous year, sharing the same rehearsals and digs. Moira was breathtakingly beautiful with her glowing chestnut-coloured hair and always smartly dressed. She was a great success with the army officers who gathered excitedly around her. All the dancers enjoyed the officers' attentions, and they were most courteous. In our free time they took us to lunch in the officers' mess, to the cinema or to a concert.

This warm welcome was also extended to us while in Hanover, our next city. The troops poured in, and the Company enjoyed a rapturous reception as in Hamburg. Still unable to dance, I was driven in an open army jeep to a nearby hospital twice a day for treatment kindly organised by the Officer in Charge.

Once again I witnessed appalling destruction, so it was a welcome contrast when Moira and I were driven through beautiful woods on the outskirts of the city. Travelling in an open jeep we were guarded carefully by two officers, Hugh and George, both armed, on the alert for snipers. It was a highly enjoyable week for us all, thanks to several charming young officers. There were four in particular, Brucie, George, Bip and Hugh – the latter I particularly liked and rather fell for! With promises of meeting up again soon, we bade them a fond farewell by the coach which was to take us on to Berlin.

I felt a nervous frisson on crossing the Russian barrier before reaching Berlin. What appalling destruction met us as we got closer to the capital, now divided between the four victorious powers. Everywhere, nothing but ruins of great buildings littering the streets, people looking as if they were past caring, the famous Brandenburg Gate pitted with gunshot and now guarded by Soviet soldiers.

The great capital, Berlin. We were there amidst a sea of devastation, ruined edifices, crumbled houses and only the shell remaining of the all-important centre of control – the Reichstag. It was hard to take it all in, and what it represented: the complete collapse of what had been such a formidable and frightening power. I brought back a small piece of the huge glass chandelier which was lying smashed on the central floor of the Reichstag. Had Hitler really committed suicide there in the bomb-proof bunker beneath or was he still at large, escaped to another country – no one knew, it was all very macabre. How much misery, destitution and death he had brought to his people and the world before he was defeated.

In Berlin I found myself sharing a room with Jean Bedells, Moira Shearer and Mavis Jackson, which was fun, although I was frustrated at not being able to perform but merely seeing the others dance. Tony Burke was an understanding, good friend, and throughout the trip we often went on expeditions together. In the evening I would sit out front with our wonderful company pianist, Edna, watching the performance, observing the amazing enthusiasm shown by our troops absorbing ballet.

On my continuing visits to German hospitals, I always saw severely injured people. In Berlin I was duly collected at 11am from our very first morning onwards – such organisation. It was all laid on, and I was taken in an open lorry, together this time with Gillian Lynne and Audrey Bowman, both now also requiring treatment. It took half an hour to reach our destination driving through suburbs and industrial areas, all smashed and destroyed, so once again one was shaken by the stupidity and harshness of war.

Late Wednesday afternoon Gillie and I decided to go to the Savoy hotel where Madam was staying. We needed to tell her that the masseur had advised us not to dance for at least another week. As this, to our deep disappointment, meant we would not be able to appear again on the tour we wondered if we should return home to England. Madam was most sympathetic, but the next afternoon she told us that it would not be permitted for us to travel back on our own so would have to wait to return with the Company. Quite understandable, but we felt it had been worth asking, and Madam appreciated our doing so.

Our twice-daily hospital trips for massage and physiotherapy continued, as did our visits to the YWCA where, as well as eating, we could buy eau de cologne and other luxuries. Towards the end of the week we were invited to the Military Governor's mess for lunch after which we were driven back in an imposing black car visiting the hugely impressive Berlin Stadium and Arena. Realising that this was where Hitler had held all his great parades, displaying his strength and power, the emptiness was somewhat eerie and thought-provoking.

It was in Berlin that I saw my first transvestite revue, which I found distinctly disturbing. I was taken by several members of the Company who were all perfectly aware that the shabby cafés housed these strange shows. They were very amused at my shocked reaction of horror and disbelief on realising these crudely made-up figures in evening dress were, in fact, female impersonators. I took care never to be caught up again in such visits.

There was often a reception and dinner to attend, and I was impressed by de Valois's incredible assurance. On these formal occasions she would reply to the speeches of the military hierarchies with effortless charm and authority and without any notes whatsoever. Watching her I learnt so much and felt very proud of her.

Madam did not allow me, unlike the rest of the company, to attend all of the informal late-night parties, which lasted until the early hours of the morning. I hated missing so much fun, but now realise she acted in my best interest because I was only eighteen. By the end of our week's season at a miraculously unscathed Theater des Westens, I was not sorry to leave Berlin. The broken capital, with its four military controlled zones, was both divisive and unsettling.

The journey to Düsseldorf was very long and cold. The journey took two days in all, across frozen, flat landscapes. After leaving the Russian border control our first stop was at one o'clock that Sunday afternoon when we were given welcome hot tea and cakes.

To my joy on arrival at Minden, our night's stop, Moira and I found our two officer friends from Hanover, Hugh and George, waiting to welcome us. They had kept in touch with us regularly by phone during our week in Berlin, which was rather touching. This was now au revoir until back in Britain where we planned to resume contact. We felt proud and happy to have met these and many other valiant young soldiers and only hoped our performances to the troops might have sparked a future interest in ballet.

Düsseldorf, yet another devastated city in the midst of Germany's industrial heartland. What, I asked myself, would it have been like to have suffered those onslaughts. In Britain we were terribly bombed, too, but the resulting devastation was not as extensive as that we witnessed in Germany.

That last week of the tour I was again sharing a room with Moira, Jean and Mavis. As in Berlin, they stayed out very late every night having fun whilst, rather like Cinderella, I had to go to bed. Madam was very strict about this, and I would not have dared to disobey her.

The last Sunday in Düsseldorf, as we had at the start of the tour, Tony Burke and I set off early in search of the garrison church. After catching a tram, followed by quite a trek, we found it in a room at the garrison headquarters. Here the priest was giving a special celebration which was a rather wonderful end to the tour. Those two services were a poignant and meaningful start and end to the tour, which was a heartrending experience, never to be forgotten.

Arriving at Victoria at the end of the tour, it was so good to be back home safe and sound with my parents – and in time for Christmas. How much more we appreciated that festive season, with peace at last.

20 *Royal Opera House, 1946*

Rehearsals of *The Sleeping Beauty* commenced in earnest in January 1946 for the reopening of Covent Garden in February. We had only six weeks in which to prepare. The first rehearsals were at Sadler's Wells Theatre with Madam in complete control, supervising the entire production.

The largest and longest of all the classical works, it has a number of demanding solos which expose the classical standard of the performer. As the Lilac Fairy I appeared in every act, with most of the dancing performed in the Prologue and a fiendishly tricky solo which I worked on for weeks. I was required to attend many rehearsals taken by Madam, who was undecided about how the Lilac Fairy should travel during her many mime scenes. Should she bourrée on full pointe across and around the stage or should she walk? We worked on both possibilities until finally Madam decided that I should walk all my entrances and mime scenes.

This was just as well, for it transpired that in Act I the designer Oliver Messel had created a sweeping flight of steps on one side of the stage, down which I was to descend. It was tricky enough stepping elegantly without looking down at the stairs, but to have done this on pointe would have been an even greater challenge! Madam, however, decided that I should bourrée for the closing scene of Act I. This is when the Lilac Fairy casts a spell, sending everyone in the palace to sleep for one hundred years whilst a forest magically grows, entwining the castle and all within.

At Madam's request, Frederick Ashton choreographed a new Garland Dance in Act I, with men back once again partnering the girls in an intricate and beautiful six minutes of garland interweaving. His distinctive style could be found in several other numbers, too, which Madam wished to be updated. How fortunate she was to have such a sensitive choreographer to enrich this classical creation.

Madam was intent on getting the highest possible standard from everyone to make our opening a spectacular success, thus silencing those critics who did not believe we were able to take on the majesty, size and history of the Royal Opera House. The numbers of the Company, dancers and orchestra, were doubled, and Madam engaged some interesting and talented young dancers, including a very beautiful Russian called Violetta Prokhorova. I was most intrigued by her Russian style of dancing, the way she held her body, her glorious moon-shaped arabesques and the amazing height to which her legs stretched, with such apparent ease. Madam did not approve of the height, however, and was forever telling her to keep her leg lower to retain a straight-line arabesque.

Violetta was born in Moscow and studied under Pavel Gerdt at the Bolshoi School, from which she graduated into the Bolshoi company as a soloist in 1942. In Moscow with the Bolshoi company at the end of the war, her friendship with an Englishman at the British Embassy flourished and by 1946 she married him. As Mrs Elvin, with a British passport, she was permitted to leave for England where amidst the Wells dancers her beauty, exotic style and authoritative attack shone through her every performance. We became good friends, often sharing rooms on foreign tours and talking late through the night.

I will never forget the excitement of actually going into the Royal Opera House, former venue of the great Russian dancers of Diaghilev's company. It was like entering the mystique of a cathedral, a hallowed ground now in our care – a British ballet company. Would we succeed? We must; we could not let ourselves and all who believed in us down.

Once in practice clothes on stage we realised just how enormous the area was which we were expected to cover – we had never before appeared on a stage as vast. Madam was forever calling to us to project more and more and to use all of our bodies in movement and in repose, while not forgetting the value of facial expression. We had to aim to reach everyone in the theatre, consciously projecting to the very back of the lofty gallery (amphitheatre).

Our latter rehearsals took place amidst the on-going restoration of the theatre from the Mecca dance hall it had been in the war to the opulent, gracious Royal Opera House of pre-war days. The big dance floor which had covered the stalls was removed and ageing seats, retrieved from the basement, reinstated in their rightful positions. Carpenters repaired them, and workmen were still securing them to the floor right up to the last minute before the opening night, whilst artisans applied the final touches of gold paint onto the mouldings adorning the boxes and fascias around all five tiers. It was such an exciting time. As the costume parades proceeded on stage, with the magnificent wine velvet curtains drawn up, we observed the tremendous front of house activities taking place at the same time.

What a lot of work went into awakening the *Sleeping Beauty*. The recently assembled stagehands were faced with setting up the most elaborate scenery, and the stage managers with working some very complicated scene changes, in particular the magical transformation scenes which Messel so cleverly devised. For instance, at the close of Act I the Lilac Fairy drew up trees from below, the stage growing in front of one's eyes, as more foliage descended from the flies. This all gradually enveloped the castle and the sleeping courtiers as the Lilac Fairy was gradually lost to view, gently spinning on pointe, magically controlling nature itself.

Messel's creativity also embraced the most ravishing period costumes and headdresses, exquisitely decorated, in the most tasteful array of colours. The small wardrobe staff were completely overwhelmed with the amount of detail demanded for each and every costume, of which there were no fewer than 248. So we, the dancers, sewed extra pieces onto our costumes as the overture played and throughout all three intervals on that remarkable wonderful opening night, February the 24th 1946.

What tensions, what excitement and what nerves we experienced that evening as the theatre filled with women in full-length evening dress, men in white tie and tails, wearing their medals, while from the orchestra pit we heard the stirrings of the musicians tuning up. What a great privilege it was to be a part of such an historic occasion and to be performing in front of the entire Royal family. Sitting in the newly appointed Royal Box, where the audience could see them, were King George VI, Queen Elizabeth, Princess Elizabeth and Princess Margaret, and the dowager Queen Mary.

My excitement intensified when, in the second interval, Madam, Margot Fonteyn, Robert Helpmann and I were shepherded to the Royal Box retiring room where each in turn was presented to the Royal family, who were charming and complimentary. All too soon it was time to return backstage, and we curtsied and backed our way out of the room towards a fearful downward flight of stairs. As if in a dream I continued my performance as the Lilac Fairy that evening.

A truly magical occasion, the gala reopening of the illustrious Royal Opera House after the horrors of the war. What an enthusiastic and long ovation we received at the close, the *Beauty* indeed had re-awakened the great theatre and recreated something truly beautiful and uplifting. To the astonishment of many sceptics, the Company proved that they could follow in the Russian dancers' footsteps, receiving a remarkably good press.

We gave *Beauty* every day, bar Sundays, until mid March, with Margot and Pamela May alternating as Princess Aurora, a role I so longed to dance. Madam told me I could never dance this as I was far too tall to manage the attitude balances (balancing unsupported on pointe on one foot) in Act I. But I was determined to prove her wrong, and each evening I would practise all the Aurora entrances, solos and above all the Rose Adagio at the side of the stage, grabbing any available male dancer or stagehand on whom to balance. I learnt it all from watching in the wings, but was devastated when early in March, Moira Shearer was given the role to perform along with Margot and Pamela. I persevered with the balances, however, hoping and believing my chance would come one day.

After all the opportunities and adventures of war time, in 1946 I began to worry about my place in the Company. In the list of ballerinas reading down (as opposed to across), my name was listed fourth in the programmes. As expected, Margot was at the top, Pamela May (her knee now better after her accident in the war) next and – much to my dismay – Moira was given the third place although she had not been with the company as long as I nor taken on ballerina status until 1944. By March, with the return of June Brae, I was listed fifth and became so alarmed that I summoned up courage to speak to Madam and tell her how upset I was.

Madam, however, had a way of wheedling her way out of an answer, assuring me that I was not to worry as there were more leading dancers now and she tried to be fair to each one of us. I came away as despondent as ever. By April, however, Margot was lifted up out of the list to have separate, top, larger-print billing along with Helpmann, so I was once again fourth. Quite clever juggling.

By May there were further adjustments to the billing – the vertical listing replaced by horizontal lines which was much fairer. Under the heavier typed Helpmann and Fonteyn, it read across: Pamela, June, Moira and me. I felt slightly placated and a little less worried about my position in the Company. By the end of May, June Brae had left and so to my relief there were just our three names across the top under Margot and Bobby – Pamela, Moira and me. As ballet is such a hierarchical art form I am afraid billing order matters very much!

After completing weeks of *Sleeping Beauty*, in mid-March the Company gave our very first triple bill at Covent Garden, which went well with houses continuing to be full and enthusiastic. An interesting programme, it showed works by the Company's three choreographers: De Valois – *The Rake's Progress*, Ashton – *Nocturne*, and Helpmann – *Miracle in the Gorbals.*

As I was second cast as the Rich Girl in *Nocturne* I did not appear on the first night, nor was I on for the next triple bill first night, which included Ashton's meaningful wartime *Dante Sonata* and his pre-war, exuberant *Les Patineurs*. In *Dante* I was both third cast Child of Light as well as second cast Child of Darkness. It was particularly disappointing for me when I learnt for the first performance of *Les Patineurs,* the White Skater, a role I particularly loved, was being given to Moira Shearer. A romantic, short pas de deux, it is a perfect expression of Meyerbeer's delightful, flowing music.

The programme also included the premiere of Helpmann's *Adam Zero,* his first and sadly his last creation at Covent Garden. It used all the new technical mechanics available at the Garden including a vast cyclorama which moved in front of one's eyes, a novelty at that time. The whole ballet also was given on an open stage to the fascination of the audience. Bobby's ballets were all totally different, very theatrical and never without impact.

It certainly seemed I was not being given as many important roles as in the war, now that there was an increased number of principals less tall than me from whom to draw. I began to realise that the transition from baby ballerina to ballerina was not an easy one;

roles I looked forward to performing now evaded me. After all the relentless touring in the war under less than ideal conditions, performing even when unwell, I was now too often second cast and sometimes third cast. This even though Rassine and I had led the company successfully for ten weeks whilst Margot was absent. Now at Covent Garden it appeared I was being overlooked in favour of other newcomers. Perhaps I expected too much.

All I could do was to work as hard as I possibly could and study all my roles in greater depth. I wanted to bring out their meaning and the beauty of movement, expressing its relationship with the music. To help me achieve this I found the most wonderful teacher, Audrey de Vos. She helped restore my shaken confidence, taking the time and trouble to strengthen, re-train and produce me in all my roles. I had also a truly remarkable group of fans, ballet lovers who followed my progress with love and enthusiasm, supporting and encouraging me. Believing in me as they did, I did not want to disappoint them; I had to battle on and give of my very best at every performance. In return they left flowers carefully tied with shining ribbons to be presented to me on stage. They waited outside the stage door for me to autograph their programmes and to congratulate me on my performance.

There was one particularly devoted fan, a Miss Jay Norman, a teacher, who followed my every step and after every performance wrote me screeds of constructive criticism with countless suggestions. These were amazingly sharp observations from a non-dancer, which I found most helpful and greatly appreciated.

I was deeply upset that Ashton did not cast me in his beautiful new abstract ballet *Symphonic Variations*, which was premiered a month later. I realised my height was possibly the reason, although I hoped he might have made me second cast to Margot. This was not to be.

One of my regrets is that I have never danced in this ageless masterpiece, which was to receive such acclaim when premiered in our third triple bill, a week later. Ashton successfully translated music into dance, the clarity, purity and simple beauty of César Franck's music reflected in the movements. The women's costumes, designed by Sophie Fedorovich, soon became a much favoured basic pattern for both amateur and professional dancers, for either practice or performance – a short skirt comprising tiny pleats hanging from the hips, a fitting, sleeveless top, simple and graceful, giving complete freedom of movement.

Les Sylphides, which I danced with Helpmann in the war as young as fifteen, has always been one of my most cherished ballets. I was stunned when it came into the triple bill programme in May and I was excluded from dancing in it on the first night. But worse was to follow with the newly costumed *Giselle.*

I had danced this leading role since I was sixteen, and now Madam told me that only Margot was to dance it over the next two years as I was too immature to play this role in the Opera House. I was heartbroken, consoling myself that at least I was to dance the Queen of the Wilis in Act II, the secondary role. This turned out to be a wonderful challenge dramatically as well as technically, and on the vast Opera House stage I enjoyed leaping through the air in the elevation steps. In this new production, designed by James Bailey, the Wili Queen appeared out of the ground, which I found intriguing as I had to go under the stage and stand on a trap door. This unsteadily took me up to stage level, just off-centre, whereupon I would step onto full pointe and bourrée right around the stage, returning near the then closed trap door.

At one performance, however, the trap door had not been replaced by the piece of flooring which normally slid back in place over the gap, and to everyone's horror I came within inches of falling through to the basement. I was bourréeing backwards, impervious towards the impending danger!

Another problem with the technical pyrotechnics in *Giselle* occurred when dancers, strapped into harnesses to simulate flying Wilis, were left haplessly swinging backwards and forwards. One Wili collided with the leading man, Albrecht, kneeling in sorrow at the grave of his dead love. After this the dancers relied on their classical training to suggest flight and were no longer assisted by wires. It was a pity as it had looked magical, although the dancers did not enjoy wearing the iron harnesses. In that second act the long white ballet skirts were exquisitely decorated with shiny leaves which, like the many layered skirts, were perhaps too heavy when turning on full pointe but looked wonderful from out front.

Only two weeks after her heartbreaking statement that I was too immature to perform *Giselle* at Covent Garden, Madam called me into her office. I was completely dumbfounded when she proceeded to tell me that, as I was now more mature, she and Bobby had decided I was to play Hamlet's mother Gertrude in Helpmann's ballet. This highly dramatic, sensual role was created on Celia Franca in the war and was a role I had never contemplated playing. Perhaps, I reasoned, my luck was changing. Patience, Beryl.

I always had great faith in God, which gave me strength and a certain resolve. I believed that if one worked hard and always did one's very best, one would be rewarded and a chance would come. And so it turned out.

Before the season was over Madam finally agreed to let me dance Aurora at a matinee of *Sleeping Beauty*. As it happened, unexpectedly all three Auroras went off ill and I was thrown on at both the Thursday and Friday evening performances as well as the scheduled mid-June Saturday matinee, just a week after my nineteenth birthday.

At long last I danced the Princess, but for the first time in my life I was most dreadfully nervous – nervous about the Rose Adagio which Madam had told me was beyond the capabilities of a tall dancer. But manage it I did at every performance, although I was truly scared of this section, a phobia I was never able to completely overcome.

22 *On To Vienna, 1946*

After such an eventful and extended season, lasting a little over eighteen weeks, we were more than ready for a holiday. During that first ever season as the resident company of Covent Garden, the dancers had enjoyed unexpected success – over a quarter of a million people came to watch us perform.

Wonderfully encouraging, but it was felt that there was a long road ahead to secure our place as a major contender amongst the established ballet companies in the world. This was brought home to us that summer by the first post-war visit of a foreign ballet company to London: Les Ballets des Champs-Elysées. Their dancers were brilliant, in particular Jean Babilée who showed just how compelling male dancing could be. A strong personality with an equally strong technique, he acted a range of different roles with total conviction and was mesmerising to watch.

Mid-July saw the American Ballet Theatre company occupying Covent Garden following on from our first season. Their contemporary works were in a style quite different from anything we had seen before, incorporating realistic movements. The dancers' attack and vitality was stunning. Once again the standard and ability of the male dancers was way above ours, leaving one breathless at their astonishing technique, fast spinning turns and high supple leaps. The three men in *Fancy Free* – Harold Lang, John Kriza and the choreographer himself, Jerome Robbins – brought the house down. It was Robbins' first ballet: brilliant, saucy and slick, amusing and very American. He adapted the jitterbug and other contemporary dance hall styles into ballet, which later inspired both the popular film *On the Town* and other musicals.

The ABT presented so many wonderful dancers, which made the 1946 season thrilling for the London ballet world. We saw for the first time Alicia Alonso, Rosella Hightower, Eugine Loring, Eric Bruhn, Michael Kidd, André Eglevsky and Herbert Ross, who later became a distinguished film director and married the American ballerina Nora Kaye. The two most memorable dancers for me were Nora Kaye, born of Russian parents, and the Cuban-born Alicia Alonso.

Another of their outstanding works to make a great impact on me was *Pillar of Fire*. Highly dramatic and deeply disturbing, this was Antony Tudor's first major work, to Schönberg's *Verklarte Nacht*. This ballet established Nora Kaye as a great dramatic artist and was also to become one of Tudor's masterpieces, and what a master he was himself. In later years I was to watch him at work with my Festival Ballet dancers, marvelling at his extraordinary talent.

A couple of years later, Alonso was to return to Cuba to create a school and ballet company within her communist country. Despite her age and her blindness, she still directs the Cuban Ballet: truly mind over matter, an example of dedication and determination. Today the school is renowned for producing outstanding male dancers.

After our well deserved holiday there was a short rehearsal period before we were off on a UK tour again. With another visit to the Continent planned, we rehearsed with ardour and soon found ourselves flying to romantic Vienna. I was tremendously excited and determined to see all I could. We went under the auspices of the British Council with permission to use the British officers' mess, of which we took full advantage. Each evening after our performance a group of us would visit the Redoutensaal in the Hofburg Palace, eating and dancing in the small but beautiful ballroom where a string orchestra played Viennese waltzes. Despite the recently ended war, one was still expected to dress formally and we girls wore our full-length evening dresses. This added to the romantic ethos of the beautiful palace, taking one back to a much happier, elegant period in the city's history.

I still have vivid memories of Harjis Plucis, our Latvian ballet master, spinning me round and round as the musicians played one Strauss waltz after another. Plucis was a superb ballroom dancer, the best I have ever known, and these were magical evenings, especially as the waltz has always been my favourite dance. It was a wonderful nine days, much of it spent sightseeing amidst the overpowering yet glorious, baroque architecture of Vienna.

The Company was invited en masse to the Habsburgs' country palace, Schönbrunn, where we were treated to a most delicious tea – all the royal silverware brought out in our honour. Later that day Madam called us together on stage with a very grim visage. One of the silver teaspoons was missing. Madam was understandably most dreadfully upset and angry, for it reflected badly on her dancers. The miscreant owned up, explaining he had taken it as a memento of the occasion. After facing the fury of Madam and witnessing the embarrassment it caused her and the rest of the Company, I doubt he was ever tempted to take a keepsake again.

I was privileged to be present at Elizabeth Schwarzkopf's first performance in Vienna since the end of the war in the Richard Strauss opera *Der Rosenkavalier*. Despite rumours that she had been a member of the Nazi Party, she had the most tremendous reception, an outpouring of understanding, love and admiration for their great soprano. I will always remember this moving occasion, with its unforgettable production – dazzlingly beautiful, an escape into an enchanted realm of white and silver.

After flying home, we began rehearsals on Madam's new production of *Coppélia*. Ashton was also starting work on a new ballet to be titled *Les Sirènes* with music specially written by Lord Berners. I was cast as skittish Lady Kitty, partnered by Michael Somes, as hearty Captain Bay Vavaseur. The frivolous costumes by Cecil Beaton reflecting the Edwardian period were beautiful, but what I remember most are the wooden waves, behind which we all had to emulate swimming, and Bobby coming down from the flies in a hot air balloon. It did not receive rave reviews and all too soon deflated, disappearing from our repertoire.

In December 1946 *Swan Lake* received its first showing at the Royal Opera House with Margot and Bobby dancing the opening night in Leslie Hurry's original sets and costumes. My turn came shortly afterwards, dancing with Michael Somes. As in Ivanov's original choreography from 1895 we had a third character: Benno, the prince's friend, who in Act II took part in the pas de deux. According to legend, Benno was created to aid Pavel Gerdt, the originator of the prince's role, then fifty-one years old and still one of the greatest danseurs nobles of his time. By the mid 1960s, only the Prince partnered the Princess as the age and strength of male principal dancers had apparently improved!

The famous pas de deux of the third act was not then known as the '*Black Swan pas de deux*'. The 1946 Odile of Sadler's Wells did not wear black but appeared boldly attired in red – a luscious red velvet bodice complementing a dazzling red tutu, and a ruby-studded tiara. It certainly suggested Odile's allure and seductiveness. Dancing the role I appreciated the freedom the large stage at Covent Garden offered, and I was determined to make the best possible use of this. I felt reasonably confident in the production, which I knew well, and so happy to receive a good press.

23 *The Dawn Of The Opera Company*

We prepared to stage Purcell's *Fairy-Queen,* Constant Lambert's long-held ambition. It was an interesting combination of acting, dancing and singing, but it never truly worked and did not satisfy as a unified whole. The three different groups – singers, actors and dancers – had not rehearsed together until the dress rehearsal, which may have been why the production was uneven.

The singers were forerunners of the Opera company, and I enjoyed much of the singing and music. Moira Shearer, I recall, hated playing opposite a singer whose spittle landed on her face as he sang. I was one of three *Echoes*, the front and tallest one, with Gillian Lynne behind me and Margaret Dale, the smallest, behind her. It was a clever idea of Ashton's but his masterly choreography was impeded by swathes of grey stockinette cascading from our heads to toes. Bobby, with his high-pitched voice, played the Oberon opposite a deep-toned Margaret Rawlings – which was ill-matched. I liked Michael Ayrton's sets, especially the fountain in the first act which flowed continually, descending into the basin beneath. Apparently it had a disastrous effect on some of the artists but happily never disturbed me.

To my joy the New Year 1947 ushered in a complete change of heart from Madam, who decided to let me perform *Giselle* again despite her earlier diktat that I must wait another two years. She instructed the wardrobe, however, to add long sleeves to my first act costume to help disguise my long arms. This did not give me much confidence. I worried that my arms were not suitable for this romantic role and determined to work very carefully with them.

Madam certainly had been critical of my hands, which she said I used too obviously and flamboyantly, so I had been on my guard to use them with discretion and purpose. My private teacher, Audrey de Vos, had taught me to realise that my hands were the final statement of my arm movements, which helped me considerably. I felt elated to be allowed to dance *Giselle* again as it was such an important and dramatic role on which to work. I took private lessons every day with both Anna Northcote and Audrey de Vos to study and develop this role of which I had become so enamoured during the war years.

Except for my London debut on my sixteenth birthday with the dynamic Helpmann, my regular partner as Albrecht had been Rassine. Now my Albrecht was to be Michael Somes, and to my relief it turned out rather well. Somes now partnered Margot in some ballets and was more relaxed about our partnership. He was yet to dance with Margot in *Giselle*; that was to materialise the following year. Meantime Somes was a perfect height for me, and we gave our first performance together at Covent Garden on Saturday matinee January 11th 1947. He partnered me well, the difficult lifts in Act II went effortlessly, and I felt there was a definite harmony on stage between us for the first time.

It was quite a hectic month as the following Monday I danced Odette / Odile in *Swan Lake* which was followed the next day, Tuesday 14th January, by the much awaited opening night of the newly formed Covent Garden Opera Company with *Carmen.* Because of my early training by Elsa Brunselleschi in Spanish dance and my ability to play the castanets I was chosen to perform a solo in the last act of the opera. The dynamic Brunselleschi, by now regarded as the foremost teacher of Spanish dancing, was engaged as choreographer for the dances in the opera. To my great delight we worked together again and successfully too – my solo got the biggest applause of the entire evening – a point referred to in Montague Haltrecht's biography of David Webster, *The Quiet Showman.*

At the end of the show Leslie Boosey came backstage and congratulated me, adding 'That's the last opera of mine you will appear in!' Queen Mary graced this opening night, as well as several cabinet ministers, and afterwards there was a big party at the Savoy. I was thrilled to be introduced to the distinguished statesman Sir Stafford Cripps.

Before the week ended, Moira Shearer celebrated her 21st birthday, and the Canadian dancer Norman Thompson also held a big party for his birthday. Norman was at this time my partner for *Les Sylphides*, and we were both astounded to find our photograph from the ballet featuring on a biscuit tin! *Les Sylphides* suited his style and ballon well, and it was a pity that he was a little short for me in the classics. I was very sorry when he left the Royal to choreograph and dance in musicals in Vienna, Budapest and other European capitals.

The move into the Opera House saw many changes in the Company. With the number of leading dancers now increased to eight, I felt more than ever the need for extra outside tuition and guidance. Watching Audrey de Vos teach was a revelation. Not only did she relate exercises to steps, guiding each student's body into the most helpful position for achievement, but she also trained the dancers' minds to understand their own physical problems and their body's capabilities.

Audrey had a working knowledge of anatomy from her hobby as a sculptress and an eye for any physical defect or weakness which she would then work on with her student. This was exactly the help I needed, for after the demanding schedule during those war years my health and body were not in good condition. I was often going over on my ankles in the street, and on Anna Northcote's advice I already attended osteopath Edward Hall for this and recurring back trouble. Mr Hall strapped both my lower legs in a roman sandal pattern to help strengthen my calf muscles. Madam's husband was a doctor and she did not approve of any alternative healing outside his medical profession, so I kept my strapping well hidden from her. That well placed support, however, along with the enlightened teaching of de Vos, gave my ankles just the help needed.

Audrey began each class by warming up the body with free natural movements, as opposed to commencing the abnormal ballet turn-out without any previous muscular easing. She would sometimes include floor exercises. This was quite unique at that time and frowned upon by Madam, but I began to feel in better control of my body and more confident overall. De Vos was a charming woman with a great deal of patience and a wonderful way of encouraging all her students. As well as dancers, she attracted many artists from the theatre as well as the professional ice-skater Belita, shaping their exercises to their specific needs.

Gradually more dancers from Covent Garden began to come to Audrey de Vos, including the South African ballerina, Nadia Nerina, with whom I alternated early-morning private lessons at 8.00 and 9.00 o'clock. We then dashed to Covent Garden to take the 10.30 Company class in order not to upset Madam by our absence. Company dancers were expected to attend at least four of the five Company classes a week.

We all knew that Madam did not approve of her dancers taking outside classes, fearing, I suspect, that they might lose some of the Company style. She was horrified to hear that de Vos was such an unorthodox teacher, believing this would harm classical control and schooling, and she did not want me to continue to go to her.

For the first time, I stood up to Madam, explaining that I felt de Vos's teaching was in fact helping my classical dancing and that I was certainly not willing to cease my lessons with her. I am afraid Madam thought me very foolish and was honestly worried by my decision. I knew, however, that de Vos had restored my confidence and my health, which had become very problematic. I had such faith in her I could not contemplate leaving her expert teaching. I had found an understanding, artistic and intelligent friend. We spent hours discussing my roles and my approach to them as well as the importance of interpreting the music through movement. I can honestly say that I believe she saved my dancing career.

There was great excitement in the company at Massine's arrival in January 1947. This famous character dancer trained in Moscow before the Russian Revolution before joining Diaghilev's company as a dancer, later becoming choreographer. He staged for us two of his successes: *La Boutique Fantasque* and *Le Tricorne* with its sensational Piccasso designs. He had created both ballets as long ago as 1919 for Diaghilev's London season.

Moira Shearer and I were the two Jota Girls in *Le Tricorne* (*The Three Cornered Hat*), leading the finale lifted onto our partners' shoulder and whirled round and round until the music stopped. Our hooped skirts completely enveloped the poor men beneath, my partner being diminutive Alex Grant dancing as the Dandy. Although really too short for me, Alex never ceased recalling proudly how he had been my partner in this ballet, carrying me across the stage to the footlights at the very front.

Although Margot initially danced the Miller's Wife opposite Massine as the Miller, both Violetta Elvin and I were also cast in this role, and to our great delight we soon performed it. I found the De Falla music wonderfully exciting, and it was the most exhilarating role to dance – full of fiery temperament and womanly guiles. I had watched Massine's dynamic performance as the Miller, and to be taught and rehearsed by him was both an honour and an inspiration. I used to enjoy wearing the Miller's Wife costume: a gorgeous bright pink satin over a big hooped skirt, which was quite heavy to manipulate. It was a challenging role based on Spanish dancing, which I loved. Dancing backwards around the stage, it was tricky jumping in heeled shoes whilst tantalizingly shaking a handful of skirt at the Miller in hot pursuit.

Massine's next work, *La Boutique Fantasque*, was presented about three weeks later, at the end of February but by then I was ill and forced to miss the first night. I should have been dancing Queen of Clubs, but my recurring health problem reared its ugly head again, and my doctor ordered me to rest in bed for a week. Whenever I became unduly exhausted the glands under my arms and in the groin would swell up, severely inhibiting movement. But I returned as soon as it was bearable, usually against my doctor's advice. Dancers hate to be off sick and invariably want to race back too soon after either illness or injury, fearful of losing their roles to others. Today the importance of a carefully measured return to performance is better understood, and for some, Pilates offers a helpful, safe road to recovery.

By February, during our second season at Covent Garden, Robert Helpmann was away temporarily appearing in two plays at the Duchess Theatre: *He Who Gets Slapped* and *The White Devil*, which he and Michael Benthall directed. My mother and I saw the latter and were amazed by Helpmann's performance – I had not realised that he was such an accomplished actor as well as such a charismatic 'danseur noble'.

24 *Friendships*

As a prima-ballerina I was thinking always of the next performance, eager to improve on the last, and intent on pleasing the audience. One's own next performance becomes of such overriding importance that all thoughts and energies are directed towards that end. I would become totally preoccupied with my diet, how much sleep I needed and how much rehearsal I required. My free hours in town, more often than not, were spent with either my mother or a friend outside the ballet world. I was very careful not to do anything unnecessary – like going for walks or staying late at parties. As in wartime, I found a visit to a play, film or concert the best way to relax.

During the war years when the New Theatre had been our home we were able to watch the most powerful plays given there: *Uncle Vanya* starring Ralph Richardson, *Arms and the Man* which starred the tall, gracious Margaret Leighton, tiny ebullient Joyce Redman, mighty Ralph Richardson and the handsome Laurence Olivier – what an opportunity and education. They were already great actors, possibly in their heyday, but I did not appreciate that at the time. Neither had I pondered the value and help friendships in the theatre could prove to be. Olivier and Helpmann often appeared in the same films and plays, and I believe it was Margaret Rawlings who, many years before, had written the letter introducing Bobby (Helpmann) to Lilian Baylis and De Valois.

True friendships in the theatre are usually strong and lasting. I treasure mine with Gillian Lynne, Pamela May and Moira Shearer, and of course my dance partners. On retiring from dancing, some settled abroad, like Bryan Ashbridge. He became a television producer, returning to Australia and taking his newly acquired skill to assist in the work of the Australian Ballet. Tony Burke, my faithful friend and admirer, became a successful artist and taught painting at a top boys' school outside Melbourne. Philip Chatfield, my very last partner at Covent Garden, and possibly my favourite, married my friend the ballerina Rowena Jackson. They eventually returned to New Zealand where they ran the Ballet Company and School in Wellington for many years. We have never lost touch, keeping close nowadays by email. These friendships become more precious as the years roll by, slowly but surely taking away our friends to another unknown stage, leaving us with only treasured, unique memories.

One precious memory I have is of Moira Shearer. She had been interviewed by Michael Powell and offered the leading part in a forthcoming film about a ballet dancer. Moira began at once to go on a strict diet, as well as vigorously massaging the top of her legs with a rubber roller after every shower and bath. I was full of admiration for her self discipline when I watched this regular and very amusing procedure. She really set her mind to achieving the required weight and shape to become the star of the now internationally famous and much admired film *The Red Shoes*. There had of course been rumours and speculation for several months in the Company until it was confirmed that both she and Bobby were to be filming during our summer holiday.

I was surprised that Madam had actually agreed to Moira doing this, after the way she had reacted a few years earlier when I had wished to accept Laurence Olivier's invitation to play the French Princess in his film *Henry V*. It was only after reading Robert Helpmann's account of what took place between Madam and Moira that I understood what agonies Moira must have gone through before accepting. The filming ran on well into the Autumn so they missed the Company's season at the first ever Edinburgh Festival. There was such excitement in the Scottish air with so many interesting performances and concerts taking place around the city. We gave two weeks of *Beauty*, having already performed the same full-length work for two weeks in Manchester. Straight after Edinburgh we left for a long European tour, still without Moira and Bobby. Towards the end of the tour Madam had to return to London to prepare for the forthcoming season and Frederick Ashton then joined us. Ashton had been busy staging a new ballet: *Valses Nobles et Sentimentales* for the Sadler's Wells Theatre Ballet. This was now the resident company at Sadler's Wells, formed by Madam to maintain a foothold in upkeeping the tradition of ballet in that theatre.

I believe in fate, but also in being prepared. On the 21st March 1947 I was given the opportunity of dancing the Swan Princess in *Swan Lake* at a special performance for a 'Visit of the Delegates of the Supreme Soviet of the U.S.S.R.' On such an important occasion Margot unquestionably would have starred in the leading role, so presumably she was away ill. This was a most thrilling windfall for me, and I revelled in the opportunity, enjoying every moment on stage amidst my special friends: David Paltenghi my partner, Leslie Edwards as Benno, David Davenport as Von Rothbart and Gillian Lynne performing the Spanish Dance. Everything went well, and a most successful evening flew by, many compliments being exchanged before everyone departed in good spirits.

Fortune shone on me again that same season when on my birthday, June 11th, our King and Queen unexpectedly attended the performance. It was a triple bill in which I was dancing the leading roles in both *Les Sylphides* and *Hamlet* in addition to a secondary role in *La Boutique Fantasque*. I was elated when I was taken to be presented to their Majesties during the second interval. This great privilege was the most wonderful birthday gift I could have wished for.

We assembled at Victoria Station on September 9th and left England to dance in five different countries: Belgium, Czechoslovakia, Poland, Sweden and Norway. The whole tour was a tremendously exciting prospect for me. Our first venue was Brussels, which I was eager to see. The Company had danced there whilst the Allies were freeing Europe from the Nazi occupation but, as I was under 18, I had not been allowed to go. After our visit to Vienna in the Autumn of 1946, news of our Company's success had now spread and our arrival was eagerly awaited in six cities. This was partly helped by the pre-publicity work, handled this time by the British Council.

It was a notably successful tour of amazing contrasts. I was moved to see the dazed suffering of the people of Prague. Deeply disturbing too were the devastated streets of Warsaw, where hardly a building was left standing and wounded inhabitants wandered aimlessly. Both were an enormous contrast to the peace and normality of Sweden where no physical battles had been fought. Yet even here there had been vital political talks and exchanges, undercover bribery, blackmail and espionage which had been pivotal to the outcome of the war.

Our journey across war-torn Europe was by sleeper train, which inevitably took not hours but days. Our second venue was the Velka Theatre in Prague, where we were greeted by overwhelming expressions of kindness and enthusiasm, so freely given after their terrible years of subjugation. The people flocked to our every performance, revelling in the beauty of the music and dance; it was truly gratifying to see how much pleasure we gave them. Overshadowing this was the ongoing threat of the Russians walking into Czechoslovakia again and taking control of everything. Just a few days after our departure, the Russians invaded.

Before the next train journey, the Company were allowed to buy foodstuffs from British military stores in Prague. We stocked up with provisions for the next three days' train travel. Because of the difficulty in obtaining safe drinking water I bought a huge tin of tomato juice which Moira and I proceeded to enjoy during the journey. There was still some left in the tin when we reached Warsaw. In our hotel room we finished the juice, not realising the awful stomach upset that would result after consuming fluid from a tin open for three days. Our ensuing sickness seemed to reflect the awfulness around us.

There was nothing but ruins to be seen for miles and miles. One wondered how any human being could emerge alive from such appalling devastation. Miraculously they had, and we witnessed the first two bulldozers that arrived to begin the horrific task of clearing away the bodies and remains of a capital city almost totally destroyed by the Nazis. For the people of Warsaw, however, it seemed that the annihilation of the much treasured, time-honoured city distressed them the most. As they tried to rebuild their lives as well as their city, the theatre was included in their priorities, which revealed the vital role it played for them.

Amidst the devastation stood the partially rebuilt, re-equipped theatre, waiting for our performances. Helpmann's ballet *Hamlet* was very well received in Czechoslovakia but what a shock it was in Warsaw, when, at the end of the ballet, the audience did not applaud at all but simply got up and walked out. We were later reassured when we heard that a performance ending in death was never applauded but in accordance with their tradition people quietly left the theatre.

In almost all the cities in which we performed we were treated to a civic reception, and Warsaw was no exception. There we were treated to the most amazing spread of delicious foods and drink, specially flown in for the occasion. Having seen the shortage of food elsewhere, I felt it was somehow wrong to be given such a repast, but being hungry dancers, we enjoyed it. A group of dancers are like locusts, clearing a table laden with food in a remarkably short time!

Our performances were of such importance to the Polish people that they would stop us in the streets, shake our hands, thank us over and over again for coming and beg, not for food, but for tickets. It was an extraordinary humbling experience. We also gave performances in another important Polish city, Poznan, where we were once again rapturously greeted and deeply appreciated.

What a contrast lay ahead in Sweden which we reached by boat from Gdynia, landing just across the Baltic at the Swedish port of Trelleborg. Here we were halted by tough customs men. After having found and confiscated bottles of vodka which some dancers – including Margot and Bobby – optimistically tried to smuggle through in their theatre baskets, customs went through absolutely everything. Eventually we were allowed to leave the port and were driven by coach to Malmo. After the austerities of war-torn Europe, we basked in the luxury of a modern hotel amidst a city of normality, devoid of devastation.

We were totally unprepared for the ultra-modern theatre in which we were to appear. At first none of us could find the stage door, and we wandered round and round this white circular building before being rescued and welcomed inside. It remains in my memory as a theatre in the round, the stage in the middle, surrounded by rows of seats ascending to a low roof. We had a big success and were feted by everyone. Little did I think then that, three years later, I would marry a Swede: a partnership that would grow and develop idyllically for almost sixty years.

During our week in Malmo a friend of mine, Michael Meyer, came south from Uppsala to visit me. He was professor of English at the University of Uppsala and spoke perfect Swedish. As I had a night off, he suggested we took the ferry across to Copenhagen to hear Paul Robeson sing in *Porgy and Bess* at the Danish Royal Opera House. It was a sensational evening, and the ovation he received for this his first visit since the war was incredible. Many years later I was to meet Paul Robeson when he signed his book for me with a delightful inscription that I still cherish.

Oslo was our last venue. What a beautiful journey it was by train along the Southern coast of Sweden to Norway, with its towering mountains, waterfalls and fjords. It was hard to believe that a Norwegian – Quisling – had betrayed his fellow countrymen during the Nazi occupation.

On arrival in the capital we were met by Louise Brown, a former musical comedy actress and dancer who had set up her own dance studio in Oslo after marrying a Norwegian. She was excited by our visit and asked us to give a demonstration class in order to help, guide and inspire the local dancers and teachers. It was agreed that Margot, Pamela and I, with Bobby, Somes and Harold Turner, would take part in a class given by Ashton. This was much appreciated and we were all taken out to a huge lunch later that afternoon to celebrate!

Once again all our performances were packed out and rapturously applauded, with Ashton's *Symphonic Variations* the most admired ballet. We were thrilled when Norway's King Haakon honoured us with his presence at a performance, which made an important and exciting finale to our six-week European tour.

During our return journey by train through Sweden we stopped in Malmo to enjoy a marvellous farewell party. Dancers came from four Scandinavian companies – Copenhagen, Oslo, Malmo and Stockholm – which was a totally unexpected opportunity to meet with so many Scandinavian performers. The Royal Stockholm Theatre had not invited us to perform in their capital, and we were told this was because the director feared that his wife, the leading ballerina, would be compared unfavourably to the visiting ballerinas. It was an historic gathering and a great get-together. A lovely end to a multi-faceted tour.

After our return to England, rehearsals began for the Covent Garden season – the first with Robert Helpmann billed as Guest Artist and without Constant Lambert as our Music Director. We were told he had retired from the Company to concentrate on composing. I felt sad that we had lost this wonderful man who had been such an integral part of the Company for sixteen years, from its earliest beginnings. He helped so many of us. His love for ballet coupled with his musical expertise and faith in the future of the Company made him irreplaceable. Hugo Rignold was brought in as second conductor to Geoffrey Corbett, already assistant conductor since the move to Covent Garden two years previously.

We opened with *Giselle* on November 12th. I danced the Queen of the Wilis to Margot's Giselle and, according to my mother's diary, I had a fall. Strangely enough I do not remember – it would have happened so suddenly that I must have instinctively got myself swiftly up and continued as if nothing untoward had happened. I know, nevertheless, that I would have been troubled for several days. Every performance was so important to me that I could not bear anything to go wrong.

I was very excited about the revival of *Checkmate* as I was to alternate the leading role of Black Queen with Pamela May, who was the first cast. All rehearsals were with Madam who, as usual, was very clear in her directives. She was emphatic about every little detail – that the role was properly understood and the choreography faithfully adhered to and correctly executed. It was a wonderful opportunity to be trained by her in her own ballet, even though she was sometimes impatient and most intimidating. I worked terribly hard on the role, which demands a strong technique: dramatic ability together with a certain sensuality overriding the powerful evilness of the character.

My opponent as the Red Knight was Michael Somes. Since he had partnered Margot successfully in *Giselle* and other works during Bobby's absence he was now easier and more pleasant to work with. It was an exhausting part but thrilling to perform. To everyone's relief *Checkmate* was well received, without any suggestion that it was dated, even though it had been created in 1937 specifically for the French exhibition in Paris.

In the world outside, preparations were being made for the wedding of Princess Elizabeth to Phillip Mountbatten on 20th November, the day after my first *Checkmate*. There was a tremendous fervour across the country over this Royal event: the beautiful young heiress to the throne marrying a handsome, youthful Naval Lieutenant. We certainly felt the frisson in the theatre. That evening the opera company gave *Carmen*, in which I was dancing my Spanish solo and also singing surreptitiously with the chorus!

Afterwards I went with my parents to our favourite Greek restaurant, the Acropolis, with Kenneth Neate, the leading tenor in that production. He was a great admirer, and we became close friends in a remarkably short time. It was through his friendship that

I came to know many of the young singers including Geraint Evans, just embarking on his great career, and Constance Shacklock, the beautiful soprano, with whom I remained in touch until her death in 1999. I also saw quite a lot of the much maligned conductor, Karl Rankl. He was a very serious person who kept his cards close to his chest, yet someone for whom I felt a certain empathy and admiration.

As a ballerina in the Royal Opera House I was in a position to watch rehearsals and performances of both the ballet and opera companies, and I witnessed the gradual development of both. I had inherited from my parents a strong love of opera, and my blossoming friendship with Ken meant I saw all the operas as they entered the repertoire, as well as the visiting artists engaged by David Webster. As the General Administrator, Webster was not given an easy ride and his every move appeared to be criticised. Despite this he pressed on determinedly, building from scratch a resident English opera company for the first time ever in the history of the Royal Opera House. Ninette de Valois had already led a ballet company, formed in 1931, from which to expand as the first ever resident dance company when the Opera House re-opened in 1945. David did not have that luxury. How fortunate and privileged I was to have played a part in this memorable period.

To my joy I was at last dancing Princess Aurora, working hard on the role, as well as continuing to appear as the Lilac Fairy to Margot's Princess Aurora. Much as I loved the Lilac Fairy, to which I gave deep thought and affectionate care, I also wanted to develop the role of Aurora. I still did not feel totally confident in the Rose Adagio and was forever standing on pointe in attitude in the wings, balancing on some poor stage hand's shoulder. I was never able to totally overcome my nervousness of these balances as I was never able to forget Madam's earlier diktat.

The 1947/ 48 season saw Constant Lambert reassuringly reappointed as Music Director, which was wonderful. But I was a little shaken when Violetta Elvin's name also appeared on 'my top row', making four ballerinas once more. We were all in competition, each of us secretly longing for Margot's position and also longing to be given new roles of our own.

It seemed I would never be able to re-establish the position I had won in the war, namely second to Margot. I looked back on the time when Alexis Rassine and I had led the company for ten weeks, billed as the top artists, while Margot was away ill. I was getting a bit depressed at the way things were progressing since our arrival at Covent Garden. Whenever I summoned up enough courage to challenge Madam about this she was always very clever in pointing out that Margot was the top ballerina who everyone came to see, and she had to build up a team of other ballerinas now we were in a large opera house. My position had not changed, she would say, always managing to dangle a carrot of some sort for me to look forward to. So I would go away but only somewhat reassured.

On the 26th of February 1948, I danced Margot's role in Ashton's *Scènes de Ballet.* It had premiered on 11th February with Shearer as second cast. I had had time to become familiar with the astringent Stravinsky music, written four years earlier for the *Seven Lively Arts* revue in New York. Ashton's choreography was classical yet modern, sharp and brilliant, reflecting the music and showing a new side to Ashton. He might perhaps have been somewhat influenced by the 'French chic' of the Paris Opera Ballet who danced in London the year before.

My partner for this was the reliable, amiable artist John Hart. He became my partner that season for several of my roles. Although *Scènes de Ballet* was challenging and demanding, I found it fascinating to execute – so different from Ashton's other works. But I have always thought it a dancer's ballet more than one that satisfies an audience.

27 *1948 – Spring, Swan Lake And Madam's 'Job'*

A one-week tour had been arranged for the ballet to visit Amsterdam, The Hague and Rotterdam, under the patronage of the Wagner Society and the British Council. This was the Company's first visit to the Netherlands since the Nazi invasion of 1940 when the Company, fleeing for their lives, were forced to leave behind the costumes, music and scenery of seven ballets. The Company's progress since that time had surprised the current audiences who gave us a most marvellous reception in all three cities. We were well looked after by the Dutch people, who took great pleasure in taking us to see dykes and farms where their fine cheeses were made and where families slept one floor above their animals. My strongest recollection, however, is of seeing dead bodies still floating in the canals – horrible.

We were safely back home by 19th March. Until this, our third season, in the great opera house we had presented two much loved classics: *The Sleeping Beauty* and *Giselle*. Now we prepared for the return of *Swan Lake* to the repertoire. There were several choreographic changes made by Madam and Ashton and some by our ballet master from Latvia, Harjis Plucis, who added authentic touches to the national dances.

Plucis was a strong personality, entirely concerned with ballet, its teaching and performance. He was a truly dedicated wonderful person to have amongst us, and we all benefitted from his presence, his enthusiasm and his patience. He treated us all fairly and was of particular help in pas de deux work, where his experience partnering ballerinas was invaluable.

We began to have double work classes for the first time, giving us added control and poise on stage. He would watch every performance and would come to our dressing rooms immediately after the show to give us his notes and corrections. I found this invaluable and followed the same procedure when I was to direct London Festival Ballet years later. His classes were sometimes heavy but strengthening, while his rehearsals were confidence-building: strict though very enjoyable. He had a great sense of humour, too, as well as a deep respect and love for the art of ballet.

There was not long to prepare for my first *Swan Lake* at the Garden, which came on Friday 16th April 1948. I was tremendously excited to be dancing this my favourite role and in the historic opera house where so many famous ballerinas had enthralled audiences with their individual interpretations of this role. I was conscious of the responsibility I had to continue in this great tradition. Would I make full use of the large stage? Could I bourrée fast enough, as the evil magician tears me away from the Prince? I was determined to give all I could to bring the tragic Odette to life and then dazzle as the evil Odile in the third act.

Not being first cast, I did not enjoy the advantage of a dress and orchestral rehearsal, thus losing the opportunity of familiarising and interpreting the sounds of the different instruments in relation to the steps. Once on stage, my reliable partner John Hart, the magic of the ballet itself, the expressiveness of the orchestration, lit a fire inside me. I was carried through to the moving and triumphant last act where good eventually triumphs over evil. I lived and loved every minute, receiving a marvellous reception at the end with ten huge bouquets and, unusually, the sweetest posy also being brought to me on stage. I feel I was fortunate to have lived at this time as I received many corsages from admirers, presents of jewellery and, on one occasion, a brace of pheasants after a performance as the Black Queen in *Checkmate*.

The revival of Madam's ballet *Job*, created in 1931, was celebrated on 20th May 1950 with a gala in aid of the Sadler's Wells Ballet Benevolent Fund, which was founded by Arnold Haskell in 1936. Originally the brainchild of Ninette de Valois, it was created to help members of her Company and their dependents in times of need. It has grown to become, today, the Royal Ballet Benevolent Fund, helping those not only in the Royal Companies but in other dance companies as well. I was later to serve as one of its trustees for twenty-eight years and as chairman for twenty. A humbling position demanding an awareness of the Fund's history, as well as bearing an enormous responsibility to others. This, however, would be a long time ahead.

Sir Adrian Boult conducted in the gala for Alicia Markova and Anton Dolin, who were appearing in England for the first time since the war. There was enormous interest to see their progress since their years dancing with American Ballet Theatre in the States and in other countries. They were engaged as guest artists while Margot was in Paris dancing with Roland Petit, and their artistry and expertise shone through all their performances.

I had the privilege of being on stage with Markova and Dolin in *Sleeping Beauty* as the Lilac Fairy, as well as in their *Giselle* as the Queen of the Wilis. It was a most inspiring experience as I could see at close hand both Dolin's superb partnering and Markova's ethereal lightness and apparent effortless technique, which enthralled audiences. Their partnership achieved overwhelming admiration and enormous success.

As a young girl before the war I had seen them dancing at Sadler's Wells and also in the big arena at Wembley. I still retain the magical memory of meeting Markova in her dressing room after a performance. She lay gracefully on a chaise longue. A lady, who I later learnt was her sister, Doris Barry, covered Markova's shoulders artistically with a beautiful wrap, as if wrapping the magic of her performance so that it would linger for her many admirers.

If only today something of the mystery and magic created so painstakingly on stage could be retained by artists offstage after their performances. We are no longer in that age. Rather we are accustomed to our leading dancers leaving the theatre dressed casually in jeans and anorak, the magic immediately dispelled. I think it is a pity. None of us, especially Margot, would have dreamt of leaving the stage door unless well groomed and with a certain hint of glamour to reward and indulge our faithful followers.

My last performance in our third season was with John Hart in *Swan Lake*, when I received fourteen bouquets and a heartwarming ovation. Since dancers occupied the same dressing rooms as the opera singers, we had to clear out our belongings after every performance. Once again I packed my make-up, practice clothes and paraphernalia, including my lucky charms, into my theatre basket. This time it would stay shut for a month while we all disappeared on holiday. This much needed break was soon over, and the roller coaster of dancing life began once again.

28 *Friends And Guest Artists*

Although the life of a dancer is very demanding, I still found time and made special effort to make friends outside the ballet world. Soon after joining the Company I had been introduced to the secretary of the Cavalry Club at 127 Piccadilly: Major Guy Horne. He took a great interest in everything I did, ensuring I was eating enough nutritious food, especially during the war. He frequently invited me for a delicious meal at his club, somehow procuring my favourite anchovies or potted shrimps. He used to compare dancers to horses in their eating requirements, believing both needed oats. Genial, authoritative, an important figure, he was highly regarded by everyone there. As the war progressed, Guy had been put in charge of the barrage balloon in Hyde Park, just opposite his Club. After having fought in the First World War on the harsh Russian front, he was proud to be of service again to his country.

I went to many parties, including the Vic Wells Ball, an event much looked forward to by all the artists. With Kenneth Neate, I met many personalities in the music and opera worlds. He had become fond of me and often stayed the night with my parents after a party or late performance. We began to see a lot of each other and not only at the Opera House, often going together to the coast or to Glyndebourne where we saw many performances including the new Benjamin Britten operas. It was about this time that John Christie, founder of Glyndebourne Opera House, asked me if I would be interested in arranging the choreography for some of the operas at Glyndebourne. Although flattered, I did not feel I had sufficient experience to take on such a responsibility, so reluctantly declined.

During the war my mother and I went regularly to films, concerts and plays. I believe it was how one survived those dramatic, frightening times – a form of escapism which took us into another world for a few blissful hours. What a valuable service the world of entertainment provides. I adored the Fred Astaire and Ginger Rogers films; their elegant dancing lit in me the wish to dance. They influenced me greatly as a child, as did Shirley

Temple with her slick tap dancing and gorgeous curls reflecting her bubbly personality. Every night for four years, at Madeleine Sharpe's request, my mother painstakingly rolled up my hair in curlers before I went to bed. We both endured this until mercifully Ninette de Valois called an end to the Shirley Temple curls and insisted on my having straight hair. I suppose the curls had a certain childish charm!

I enjoyed romantic films the most. I recall dashing between rehearsals across to the Odeon Leicester Square to see *Gone With The Wind*, delighting in the handsome Clark Gable and the exquisite Vivien Leigh. So many great films were created at that time; *49th Parallel* in 1941 packed with great British stars who included Eric Portman, Glynis Johns, Raymond Massey and my particular heart-throb, Leslie Howard. We saw *Dangerous Moonlight* with Richard Addinsell's haunting background music. The following year brought *One of Our Aircraft is Missing*, in which Robert Helpmann appeared with Godfrey Tearle, Bernard Miles (who I got to know years later) and Pamela Brown who was introduced to me by Kenneth Neate. That film presented an amazing number of outstanding actors. We were fortunate that the film companies engaged so many great artists – Wendy Hiller, Peter Ustinov, Merle Oberon, Googie Withers and Esmond Knight, as well as Margaret Lockwood as the *The Wicked Lady* in 1945.

The films were not all masterpieces. In May '45, having seen *The Sign of the Cross*, I wrote in my diary – 'awful' – but there are many that I still remember, like *The Sky's the Limit, Now Voyager, In Which We Serve*. And I will never forget *Blithe Spirit* with the incomparable Rex Harrison.

The autumn of 1948 developed into a rather disappointing one. As the touring week in Croydon was drawing to a close I hurt my foot in rehearsal, thereby missing the imminent three-week foreign tour to Paris, Düsseldorf and Hamburg. This was a blow as I was curious to revisit Hamburg and Düsseldorf to see the progress made after all the destruction. I disliked missing any performances – let alone a foreign tour which included Paris. By the time the Company returned, though, I was sufficiently recovered to dance both *Giselle* and *Swan Lake*, once again at the Davis cinema.

A new work by Ashton – *Don Juan* – opened our fourth season at Covent Garden in the late November of 1947. Despite the glorious Richard Strauss music I never cared much for the ballet. Sadly for Margot, she slipped and fell on the first night, and was consequently off for three months with a bad strain, so Violetta Elvin and I alternated in her role. But I never felt at home in *Don Juan*. It is the only ballet in which I have ever blacked out for a few seconds, travelling on a diagonal downstage, unable to remember the choreography.

Margot's absence gave Moira Shearer an enviable opportunity to take her place in the new three-act ballet *Cinderella*. Fred had designed it for Margot, but postponement was out of the question as it was to be presented over the Christmas season. So, with Helpmann back full time in the Company and Constant Lambert returned, sharing the artistic direction with de Valois and Ashton, everything proceeded well. *Cinderella*, Ashton's first full-length ballet, achieved an overwhelming success, as did Moira. In Act II she looked every inch a fairytale princess, in the elegant ballroom scene dancing with the precision, grace and delicacy which were her forte. Ashton and Helpmann also appeared in this ballet, as the two ugly sisters. Helpmann was the bossy one of the duo, whilst Ashton was the pathetic one. Their hilarious performances have never been bettered, at no time overstepping the line into crude comedy but showing great artistic restraint.

I found my costume as the Winter Fairy unbearably uncomfortable. The shiny, prickly icicles hanging from my arms scratched me with every movement. It may have looked effective, but the designer Jean-Denis Maclès could not have visualised the discomfort his design and choice of harsh material would cause the wearer. I certainly enjoyed the solo Fred created for me, with its low sweeping ronds de jambes across the stage. But naturally I would have preferred to have danced Cinderella.

There was much anticipation about the visit in March of Alexandra Danilova with Freddie Franklin. I still held memories of her gorgeous performances at the Royal Opera House before the war and queuing up outside the stage door to obtain her autograph. I was just an eager, adoring ten-year-old student, yet I still have her signature and those memories of her scintillating performances imprinted on my mind. It seemed unbelievable that she was coming not only to dance here again but also to give us classes. She was to perform Swanhilda, the joyous soubrette role in *Coppélia*, with Franklin as her Franz. We all watched their dress rehearsal, their energy and assurance, with delight.

At her first performance, however, this vitality and confidence evaporated. Cruelly, Danilova's nerves took over, and she was not the same ballerina we had seen the day before. I was most terribly disappointed for her, particularly as I was on in the last act and could see that all was not going well. I was dancing the solo 'Prayer' which I am told stopped the show, and at the final curtain Danilova and Franklin generously brought me forward to receive applause for my short appearance. This touched me very much – no wonder she was such a generous teacher. For the short time she was with us I tried hard to absorb all I could from her teaching and as always wrote everything down. It was then I realised that I must not go on dancing for too long. I decided I would stop when I was forty. I have met many kind people throughout my career and always felt deeply touched and humbled by appreciation for my performances. I realise that I am very blessed to have been able to follow a career which I love and enjoy. Working hard at something I adored was no hardship. Only failure to dance at the highest possible standard is frightening. I determined to be remembered dancing at my peak, having seen Danilova and later Toumanova giving disappointingly declining performances. To me it has always seemed tragic to see great stars waning.

In the same month Ashton revived his romantic ballet *Apparitions.* I adored dancing in one of Cecil Beaton's ravishing ball gowns to Liszt's haunting music, even though I never danced the main role. Constant Lambert returned to conduct this work and received a most wonderful ovation after his absence. It was not only the dancers who loved and appreciated him.

I was excited about my first ever visit to Italy, which came in May 1949. The Company were invited to appear at the prestigious Florence Festival: a wonderful introduction to magnificent art. We were fêted and taken all over Tuscany, to art galleries and to the surrounding countryside. On our last evening, Warwick Braithwaite and Robert Irving came up to my hotel room with Ken Neate, who had arrived for a few days to celebrate the success of the season. This was the first time that Robert Irving had been with our Company, having been snatched from the Sadler's Wells ballet to which he had been appointed at the beginning of the year. I liked his conducting and felt particularly confident in performance with him.

Once back in England our minds ran ahead with thoughts of the forthcoming autumn tour to America. We must all have realised that this would be the biggest challenge the Company ever faced with preparations already going ahead.

Madam commanded all the girls to lose weight to be in line with the slender American women pictured in fashion publications. We were to be on show everywhere, ambassadors of British fashion. British dancers under a microscope, as it were. I started dieting seriously, swallowing fresh lemon juice first thing in the morning which eventually put my teeth so much on edge that my dentist forbade me to continue. I took great care not to eat cakes, biscuits and other sweet foods.

Madam also instructed the girls to have short hair in the current fashion, so precious locks were condemned to the hairdresser's waste bin. I regretted having my hair cut short as it did not suit my small head. It also made it difficult to style for performances with little hair on which to fasten headdresses. But once it was cut there was nothing one could do except wait for it to grow long again. Mine refused to do so, retaliating by returning to only half its original length. The cut, however, certainly helped to show off the fashionable hats and clothes in which we were outfitted for the tour.

The tour was seen as an opportune time to display British costume design to the wide American public. The five leading ballerinas (Fonteyn, May, Shearer, Elvin and me) were dressed by the twelve top couturiers of the day. We did not choose our designers; it was decided by a draw. It was my good fortune to win not only Hartnell, the Queen's dressmaker, for my cocktail dress, but also Victor Stiebel, a great lover of the ballet who designed both my evening dress and winter coat.

Hartnell chose for me a charcoal-coloured satin cocktail dress with a heavily ruched skirt drawn back into a sort of fish tail. It was dramatic, but I did not ever feel quite comfortable in it, nor with the mock diamond studded sculptured hat designed to perch at an angle on my head. This was created by Madam Verbier who also made me some other more fetching hats. Together with its matching steel grey, high heeled shoes, a chic matching satin clutch bag and long gloves, I felt Hartnell's outfit, glamorous as it was, was too sophisticated for me.

Stiebel, however, designed for me a most romantic ball gown in which I felt more comfortable. It was an unusual coffee-colour satin with a V-neck on a beautifully fitted bodice, from which flowed a long full skirt, a swirling mass of exquisite satin, which I adored wearing. Stiebel was also the one drawn to make my winter coat. This was cut from a grey, warm wool material, lined with grey and yellow plaid, long and with a high neck. To wear under this, Stiebel also gave me a timeless matching fitted suit together with two exquisite blouses which I loved – one a patterned yellow silk, the other white sharkskin, both close fitting, hugging the body. To all this, he added a little matching grey velour hat.

I have them all to this day with the exception of the two blouses, having worn the coat and suit for many years as I could not bear to part with them. They are an example of the perfect craftsmanship of the skilled staff in Stiebel's workrooms at Jaeger. The clothes are also a memory of when on that first American tour I met the man of my dreams who later I was to marry.

Preparations were now well underway for the American tour, and an underlying excitement crept in to our activities. I went for two fittings at Hartnell's premises where everything went smoothly and swiftly. I went many times to Stiebel as he was giving me so many clothes including an unexpected present – a beautiful blue cocktail dress enhanced by a modest cluster of small red cherries nestling in the V of the neckline. He took a very close interest in the styling of every garment, supervising each fitting himself. He took great delight in choosing the artificial corsages for the evening and cocktail dresses, placing them in exactly the most attractive position. I was overwhelmed by his generosity and his courtesy in inviting my mother to join me for the fittings, and realised how much he loved the ballet and what delight it gave him to supervise my attire for America. It was the beginning of a long-lasting and much treasured friendship.

I made another lovely friendship from that remarkable period: Madge Chard in South Moulton Street, who made the most captivating hats for me from then on. As well as all the thrill of new outfits, we were also fitted out with gloves, shoes, stockings, handkerchiefs and scarves.

Despite these lovely distractions, I was preoccupied with my calibre of dancing. I had daily lessons with de Vos, from whom I was beginning to benefit and learn so much. We studied all my roles in depth, together making copious notes after every session, which I took with me across America. Her fee was a guinea for an hour's private lesson or one pound and six shillings for a half hour longer. Her classes, which occasionally I also attended, cost five shillings and could last up to two hours.

Our month's season at Covent Garden was a pre-run of the repertoire we were taking to the States. I danced *Swan Lake* with John Field for the first time, which went well – a good forerunner for future American performances. We all assembled at Northolt Airport in our stylish new outfits on the morning of Monday the 3rd October, photographers recording the historic moment for posterity. Mary Clarke, the editor of the monthly dance magazine *The Dancing Times*, had asked me to write an account of our tour of the States for the magazine, which I enjoyed undertaking. This was the first time I had been asked to do something like this professionally, and I found it quite rewarding to focus my mind on such varied and interesting events. I was an avid letter-writer in those days, sending a report almost daily to my parents, so I did not find this commission onerous.

There was a mêlée of well wishers, relatives and friends to see us all off. I began to realise that I would not see my parents for two and a half months, and a sadness welled up inside me. There was no time to say goodbye properly, however, as suddenly we were being swept out of the VIP room onto the airfield and walking up into a Super Constellation with a smiling BOAC crew waiting to welcome us. We took off for Reykjavik, Iceland where we stayed for only a short time and were soon on our way to the second stop, Keflavik, Greenland. At both airports we were served a delicious breakfast of eggs and bacon, seeming unbelievably extravagant with food still on ration in Britain.

Finally we landed at Idlewild Airport, New York City, unprepared for all the entry regulations to be encountered, including individual interviews, which took time. Then a great welcome awaited us. The press clamoured for photos, and for the first time we experienced the persistent demand to show more leg! So we lifted our skirts and smiled bravely before being whisked off into the centre of New York to our respective hotels. We five principals were all at the St Moritz, very glitzy and busy. Violetta and I shared a room on the twenty-second floor, with a lovely view over Central Park.

The five of us agreed to meet downstairs for a snack in the hotel café, but were soon to be dreadfully embarrassed by an American woman who came up to our table and enquired, 'Are you with the Moira Shearer company? I just adored *The Red Shoes*.' It must have been awful for Moira, with Margot sitting there, and even worse for Margot to realise she was virtually unknown to the American theatre-goer. Perhaps that is what made her so determined to give such a great performance a few days later on Sunday 10th October – our opening night at the Metropolitan Opera House.

That day Margot came to our ten o'clock class as normal, not leaving off half way through, but working on to the end of class at 11.30am. She was still in the theatre when I went up to the wardrobe an hour later and found her checking her costumes and headdresses for the evening's performance. She was always such a reserved and disciplined person, and I was lost in admiration at her no-nonsense approach to what must have been the most crucial performance of her career. For that evening was to make or break her internationally, with the American critics and countless foreign media all sharpening their pencils in anticipation.

As we now know, Margot, a radiant Princess Aurora, conquered everyone in the audience that night: politicians, famous stage and film stars, directors, dancers and other dignitaries. Margot led the Company in the *Sleeping Beauty* to an incredible success, and I felt so proud to have played my part as the Lilac Fairy. My abiding memory from that evening is of the terrific heat as we made our way to the Metropolitan Opera House, at that time far down Broadway between 39th and 40th Street, and being hit by the stifling heat once inside the theatre. Our make-up melted as we tried to put it on because the small dressing rooms, packed with our theatre baskets and tutus, were airless. There was no air conditioning in the theatre but at least our muscles were kept wonderfully warm and supple, which must have aided our performance. We were all nervous and tense, unsure what the sophisticated, high profile American audience would make of us, the British Sadler's Wells Ballet, nor indeed whether they would enjoy sitting through a full length, three-act ballet, hitherto unknown in the States.

The first appearance of Lilac Fairy is in the Prologue and my heart pounded as the curtain rose to the glorious strains of Tchaikovsky's music. At this came an unexpected burst of applause for Oliver Messel's magical setting. As each fairy entered she too was met with applause, so by the time of my entrance as the last and senior fairy I was filled with excitement and optimism, hoping that I would not let the Company down. I was always worried about the fiendishly difficult fouettés at the end of the lovely Lilac solo and prayed that all the pirouettes would go well which, by a miracle, that evening they did. What a comfort it was to know Constant Lambert was there in the orchestra pit.

All I can now remember of the evening is the uplifting, thrilling atmosphere coming from the audience as I walked and bourréed through all my later mime scenes. As if in a dream, with every act I felt a rapport building with the audience. Then, as the curtains came sweeping down at the end of the finale, we heard the most rapturous applause from out front. The applause went on and on and on as flowers showered onto the stage, with Margot and Bobby applauded again and again – it seemed the audience did not want to lose sight of Margot; she had won their hearts. We all began to realise that we had succeeded in winning over the American public.

The relief was intoxicating as we were driven away in coaches with police escort through New York's busy streets, sirens wailing all the way to Mayor O'Dwyer's Gracie Mansion. This was an official reception with many notable persons present from whom it was rather wonderful to be receiving so many compliments.

From the moment the Company flew into New York people were in contact to meet and entertain us, to offer lunch or coffee, or to invite us to cocktail or evening parties. The hospitality was quite overwhelming, but I did not feel able to accept every invitation, as I was afraid of becoming over-tired. I was careful to get sufficient rest, concerned about rehearsals, determined to excel and be successful. I knew instinctively that I had to conserve my energy for those future performances from which nerves would take a good part of one's strength. The flight had been long and, with the time change, I needed to recover and not waste my strength unnecessarily.

I relied a lot on Harjis Plucis, taking confidence from his encouraging, careful rehearsals. I always felt that my dancing wasn't good enough and that I must work harder and harder to constantly improve. As our tour proceeded to new venues, a strong bond developed between us. We would often eat out together after the show and Mr Plucis, as I always called him, saw me safely back to my hotel, which I so much appreciated.

Food in the States was very different to the boring, rationed food to which we had become accustomed in England. I fell for the delicious waffles with maple syrup and bacon on the side! In New York there was a multitude of little bars open to the streets where, to my amazement, one could eat at any hour of the day or night. But it was shocking to see the waste of food – precious food, like a fried egg being thrown away, uneaten, yet still wholesome. Adjacent to our hotel was a very smart coffee shop called Rumplemeyers where newly acquired friends frequently invited me to enjoy a splendid choice of delicacies.

All the Americans I met were kind and friendly, easy to get on with, eager to show one around and be truly helpful. I had numerous press interviews as well as sessions with the popular dance photographer Walter Owen and others. I was approached to feature in an advertisement for Schweppes tonic water for which I had to get permission from Madam. Several photos were taken of me standing elegantly in a balletic pose, wearing a white tutu, beside a tall man with a white beard holding a glass of Schweppes. It did not take long, but I found it most enjoyable and was delighted to receive a respectable payment for the session.

Quite early on during our four week New York season I felt honoured to be invited to lunch with Anatole Chujoy, the influential founder and editor of the much-read American magazine *Dance News*. It was at the Russian Tea Rooms, one of the most celebrated of New York restaurants, renowned for its Russian blinis filled with black caviar and sour cream. Chujoy was a most interesting person and time spent in his company was both enjoyable and informative. He had persuaded the writer and dance critic P W Manchester to leave England and co-edit with him the *Dance Encyclopedia 2nd Edition*. I was thrilled when they signed a copy of this huge volume for me in the year it was published. I had missed Bill Manchester, as she was known, since she left England where I frequently saw her with Audrey de Vos, with whom she enjoyed a long friendship.

One of many highlights was attending classes given by the lovely Russian dancer and teacher Felia Doubrovska. Her flowing style and encouraging manner were inspirational. As were the classes given by Balanchine, who was a hard taskmaster, accepting only the highest of classical ballet standards from his students, but terrific to work for. It was incredible to have the experience of these two great artists from Russia, here in New York, watching them pass on their unique, invaluable training and knowledge to eager young American dancers.

I felt waves of energy in the dance studios I visited, which was exceedingly contagious. I think this vibrant energy marks out American dancers. I have always been conscious of the importance of saving my strength and energy for my dancing, whether it be for training in class, rehearsals or performances, even for lectures. Since I can remember I have been afraid of disappointing people through exhaustion, so I am incredulous when people remark upon my boundless energy.

The memories of that first time in New York – the bustling, vibrant city of so many hues, the skyscrapers so astounding and intimidating to ascend, the amazing art galleries to assimilate and museums too numerous to encompass in those few fleeting weeks. I met many fascinating people and developed interesting new friendships. Ken Neate flew out to see me and at the same time transact business in connection with his singing career. It was in New York, through Ken, that I first met Peter Pears and Benjamin Britten, who I found to be charming, witty and intelligent.

I was especially pleased to find Charles Gunderson, my wonderful GI friend from the war years, waiting to welcome me. Whilst based in London and being a theatre lover, he had introduced me to several English stars, including Beatrice Lillie and Vic Oliver to whose flat we often returned after seeing a show. Vic would play the piano, entertaining us for hours. Now back in his home country, Charles with his wartime bride Barbara (who hailed from Cornwall), drove me out to their home in New Jersey each Sunday evening after the two shows Saturday and two Sunday. It seemed strange to perform on a Sunday, still not normally permitted in England. As Monday was our day off in America, I was able to stay Sunday night with them and their children.

They loved sailing and had built their home on the waterside, so it was a wonderful change to relax in a homely atmosphere away from the high profile, high society whirl of parties at which the Company were constantly being kindly entertained. Charles would leave Manhattan through a deep underpass which went below the Hudson River. Then we were up onto an elevated highway driving rapidly along fast, wide lanes, which to me was quite frightening with so many huge cars, all speeding along.

Those weeks in New York passed all too soon, and Violetta and I were already repacking our suitcases prior to our departure for Washington. On the 6th November, the last night in New York, Hurok gave the Company a celebratory party, a sweeping finale to the close of our historic season. Violetta and I were so afraid of oversleeping that we did not even go to bed, instead staying up and ordering an early breakfast. In what we thought to be good time, we rang for a porter to take down to the lobby all our considerable luggage. Clutching armfuls of flowers, we waited and waited for him to come, but unfortunately many others were checking out at the same time. We became more and more agitated as the time for our departure from the hotel passed, seriously afraid we would be left behind and miss the Company train to Washington.

Eventually, after an interminable wait, the porter came, and we descended to the ground floor to find an irate Ninette de Valois awaiting us. The rest of the dancers were already seated in a coach outside, engine ticking over, waiting to take us to our special train. This apparently comprised six baggage cars, seven Pullmans and a diner. Violetta and I were severely reprimanded, and Madam would not accept our explanations that we had not overslept and it was not our fault.

The outcome was Violetta's non-appearance that evening in Washington for the opening performance. I was not due to appear anyway but poor Violetta was taken out of *The Rake's Progress*, Ninette's own ballet, and replaced by Pauline Clayden, far less experienced in that leading role. In the dark backstage of old Constitution Hall Violetta cried her eyes out upon receiving the devastating news from Ninette, just before class. The stage was highly polished and very slippery, so at least we two did not go through the agony of endeavouring to stand up in front of President Truman and other politicians. On her first entrance in *Swan Lake*, Margot fell flat on her bottom, an event so unusual that it was gleefully picked up by most newspapers.

Chicago will remain imprinted in my heart forever, for it is there that I met and fell in love with Sven Svenson. It was a busy week – not only with performances but also with press and radio interviews, photographic sessions, receptions and parties. It was also terribly cold and windy – even to open the stage door was a heavy battle. As the week progressed, a fog descended upon the city, blocking out familiar landmarks.

I had become used to messages being left for me to ring people and, unless they were known to me, I did not always ring back; there were just too many and never enough time. But after three messages to ring a certain Sven Svenson, my curiosity got the better of me, and I rang the number. The moment I heard his voice I recognised it as belonging to the osteopath who had treated me twice, two years previously in London, when my regular osteopath Edward Hall was taken ill. We agreed to meet for tea the next day, Thursday, but because of the fog I was half an hour late, having completely forgotten the name of the hotel, even though that was where I was currently staying! I had been opening an art exhibition miles away, and my taxi driver became more bewildered as he drew up at one large hotel after another before, despite the fog, finally discovering the right one.

I recognised Sven Svenson at once, patiently waiting in the foyer – a handsome, broad-shouldered man. While I stammered out my apologies and explanations he escorted me into the hotel tea-room. So it all began…

We met again on Friday for dinner after the performance and by Saturday between the shows I confided to Pamela May that I had met someone I wanted to marry, but it could never happen. He was Swedish, 20 years older than me, and moreover was planning to set up a practice in Stockholm as the first osteopath in Sweden.

Red roses arrived for my next two performances. Observing them, Mr Plucis smiled and said, 'someone is serious!' After both shows Saturday and Sunday, I had a marvellous time with Sven. Along with his doctor friends and families we had great fun, first at a barn dance, which I had never experienced before, then returning exhausted to their homes where we were treated to some good food and delicious homemade milkshakes, a novelty for me.

We met up again the following evening, but I had to leave for a compulsory Company reception held about two or three in the morning. Sven came with me. We stayed for some considerable time, unable to bear to part from each other, then found an all-night restaurant, The Lobster Pot, where we sat for a couple of hours talking, whilst picking abstractedly at our lobsters! Dawn beckoned us outside along Lake Michigan's shore, which we followed quite a way, walking to the Lakeshore Hotel. We waited in an empty foyer until we were served an early breakfast. I can never forget those precious hours together; they are forever imprinted on my heart.

That Monday morning the Company was leaving Chicago, and Sven came to see me off on our train to East Lancing. Detroit followed, but my heart was trapped and I found myself missing Sven and just longing to see him again.

Madam returned to Covent Garden following the Chicago season with eight dancers who were not needed for the smaller one-act ballets we were now to give. Once home, Madam started work on a new ballet, *Don Quixote*. She was to have given a talk in Toronto to the Drama Club but in her absence Mary Skeaping and I deputised for her. I felt very proud to have been chosen to do this and was most relieved when it went well. On our return to London Mary asked me to give a big lecture at the Friends Meeting House opposite Euston Station which was well attended.

During our ten days in Toronto I made several long lasting friendships. For the first time ever I saw the sea actually frozen on the shore, a scene of glacial beauty. A party of us went to Niagara Falls; the might and majesty of the roaring water was beautiful yet also strangely disturbing. I was surprised and a little disappointed that the whole area was so built up and commercialised, directing visitors to walk along wooden structures alongside special viewing points. I imagined it to be out in the wilds untouched by man; how wrong I was.

For the final five days of the tour we found ourselves in an equally frozen Montreal. All the buildings, though, were wonderfully warm, defying the snow and ice outside. We were warmed, too, by the rapturous reception for all our shows. I danced the full length *Swan Lake*, as well as *Checkmate* in the triple bill programme.

To my great joy Sven flew up to Montreal to see me again, asking me to marry him before I returned to England. At that time Sven was working in Florida for three months, treating the owner of a large hotel. This wealthy, romantic man wanted to see us married in the splendour of his palatial hotel. I was sorely tempted, but felt we should take a little more time to get to know each other, for Sven to meet my parents and for us to plan our future together. We parted reluctantly in Canada just before Christmas, and I waited impatiently to see him again.

My parents were eager to hear about the tour and, of course, Sven! They were, I think, intrigued that he was Swedish. I thought my father might not be happy about this as he was such a keen Londoner, proudly British, but he did not appear to mind at all. I was relieved. I felt they were much more concerned about the age gap, particularly my mother, but they could see that I was so much in love with this man. As a colleague of Edward Hall, they felt Sven must be trustworthy; Edward held very high standards.

I had already written about Sven to my good friend, Michael Meyer, who was a professor at the University of Uppsala, Sweden. As he was living and working with Swedish people I thought he would be the right person to contact Sven. I was keen to know what Michael would think of him. Within a month I received the most reassuring reply, praising Sven, and congratulating me on my good fortune and good taste! This news I passed to my parents, which I know helped put to rest any doubts they might have been harbouring.

But well before this, as January came, it was necessary for me to speak to Ken Neate and break the news to him, telling him of my encounter on the American tour. This was not easy, as Ken had always hoped that I would marry him one day. He had been my most ardent companion and good friend for four years, and I was genuinely fond of him. It saddened me having to hurt him in this way, but we cannot control Cupid's darts, and there was no doubt in my heart of Cupid's accuracy. Time is a great healer. Years later when Ken was married to a designer milliner and was himself teaching in Germany, he visited Sven and me whenever he was in England.

The opening at Covent Garden on Boxing Day with *Cinderella* was rather a let-down after the adulation the Company had received everywhere across the water. *The Sleeping Beauty* would have been the ideal ballet to galvanise the audience on our return, but the scenery had been badly damaged on its journey back from Chicago, so *Cinderella* replaced it. *Beauty*, however, was soon restored and took its place back in the repertoire to everyone's delight.

I was glad to be back dancing once more at Covent Garden, especially being fussed over occasionally by dear Beatie, the dresser for the Number One dressing room. This only happened when I was dancing a full-length role and was promoted into Margot's dressing room for the performance. I appreciated the quietness and luxury of having greater space and one's own dresser for the entire evening. Beatie was really Margot's dresser, who she adored, but when Margot was not there, she took care of whichever dancer occupied Number One, the star dressing room. The rest of us shared: two, three or five to a room.

Covent Garden backstage may have been old but it was packed full of atmosphere – one could sense all the legendary dancers and singers of the past who had appeared there, willing one, I liked to think, to perform better and better. I felt so fortunate to be there and to have become a tiny part of that great tradition. But this euphoria was not to last long.

32 *After-Effects*

1950 did not start well. After all the romance and excitement of the American tour, I was exhausted. It resulted in my going down with suspected flu towards the end of January, just before one of my performances of *Beauty*. After two days, both Edward Hall and our local Doctor Doran were called in because I felt awful. I got worse, feeling sick and developing a temperature with awful pains across the diaphragm. At mid-week, by which time my upper back had become agonisingly painful, Dr Doran diagnosed hepatitis. Edward Hall came regularly to correct the upper spine which was giving me such pain. He ordered hot mustard baths, which certainly helped, as did all the flowers kindly delivered by fans and friends. Even Madam rang to enquire about my progress, informing us that Alexander Grant and Leslie Edwards had also contracted hepatitis. I was not to worry about returning until fit and strong.

There was also another phone call from Covent Garden: my most regular partner John Field, concerned for my wellbeing and sending lots of 'get better soon' wishes, which meant a lot to me. I was confined to bed for almost three weeks, unable to eat for the greater part of that time. Gradually I was tempted with grapes and allowed potato-in-its-jacket – but without any additional salt, pepper or seasoning! It was the only time that I have ever been so ill, while desperately anxious to recover sufficiently in time to work with Balanchine who was soon due at Covent Garden to stage one of his most popular works.

By the 19th February I was well enough to stay up all day, so following our doctor's advice my mother took me the very next morning by train to Brighton. This was the day of the premiere of de Valois's *Don Quixote*, the first work she had created at Covent Garden, and I was sorry to be absent. We stayed in Brighton for a week in a pleasant hotel, The Bedford, on the seafront, going out for little walks each day, gradually recovering and carefully building up my strength. The infection had left me weak, and when we arrived I could hardly walk. But by the time we returned to London eight days later I was able to get back into training in time for Balanchine's arrival, initially under Hall's watchful eye. Within four weeks I was back dancing at Covent Garden.

Part of me of course was thinking of Sven, counting the days to his arrival in England. He had already laid plans to open his own surgery, but now we had met, all this changed, and he had to cancel his arrangements in Stockholm. Sven was intent on setting up home here with me and opening a practice in London instead. He came just before Easter, so on Good Friday, April the 8th 1950, we made our engagement known to the public. My parents, friends and relatives were thrilled, but not the visiting Balanchine who said I would be throwing away a good career if I married. Needless to say I did not heed his admonition.

Together Sven and I went to Regent Street to the famous jewellers Mappin & Webb where we chose my engagement ring, a trilogy of diamonds. It is so beautiful, a reminder to this day of Sven's love for me. When on the tube or a train for many years I felt that everybody must be admiring the ring. In return I insisted on giving him a gold signet ring bearing his initials, which I have worn ever since his death, helping me to feel his love still with me. Against all odds, our marriage was to last happily for almost sixty years. The difference between our ages was the reason Sven was reluctant to propose marriage to me – in fact I had to propose to him!

My parents became very fond of Sven: his gentleness, openness and innate good manners plus his own special Swedish charm. He soon became part of our family, driving us to the country on weekends, which pleased my parents. Sven managed to rent rooms at a medical practice in Charles Street, Mayfair so he could continue his work building up a practice whilst searching for our future home. Flats were difficult to come by after the war but he was eventually successful through the help of a friend, Margaret MacInnes. Born on the Isle of Skye, she was a distinguished physiotherapist, much loved and sought after. She lived at Claridge House in Davis Street, knew of a flat there becoming vacant that autumn, and put in an application on our behalf, which was accepted.

During those months before my wedding I worked harder than ever, taking private dance lessons daily with Audrey de Vos, building up my strength again. The spring of 1950 Balanchine staged for our Company his magnificent work, *Ballet Imperial*, with stunning designs by Eugene Berman. He chose me to dance the ballerina secunda. Margot was the leading ballerina in a shimmering golden tutu partnered by Michael Somes. I wore a striking black velvet bodice over a grey and black tutu, partnered by John Field and Kenneth MacMillan. I adored this role with its broad sweeping movements and a wealth of elevation embracing the entire stage, being completely transported by Tchaikovsky's inspirational Piano Concerto No 2.

It was a privilege to work with this great master, himself a product of the famous Maryinsky in St Petersburg, a dancer and choreographer with Diaghilev and subsequently co-founder of New York City Ballet. He was strict and demanding and knew exactly what he wanted. I would have so liked the chance to dance in more of his ballets, for he liked to use tall dancers and I felt confident in his choreography. I was thrilled by my success in *Ballet Imperial* as the Ballerina in Black, an exhilarating but exhausting role to dance. We used to say that Balanchine dancers would die young from the tremendous strain of performing his long dance sequences! Even so this role was something quite wonderful with the glorious Tchaikovsky music embellishing the choreography's true classicism. There were many performances scheduled in that season, so I was able to become at one with the role. I look back now and see it played an invaluable part in my overall development. Balanchine, alas, never returned in my time to stage another work at Covent Garden.

There was one notable distraction; a performance at Sadler's Wells in May to mark the Company's 21st Anniversary. It was great fun, with almost all the former dancers of the Company appearing on stage again in one or other of the three ballets given: *The Rake's Progress*, *Façade* and *A Wedding Bouquet*. Remarkable to see these artists, now in middle age, back on stage still able to perform. The programme was well chosen, giving just the right flavour to the celebration, which became uproariously enjoyable but never completely out of control. De Valois was so happy, and rightly so when you think of her amazing achievement in that comparatively short time. I felt so proud to be photographed with her and a group of early dancers after the final curtain. I cannot remember a more happy and relaxed Ninette as on that particular occasion.

I was keen for Sven to see me dancing at the Royal Opera House as soon as possible and arranged a ticket for him to watch me in Madam's new ballet *Don Quixote*. I danced as I had never done before to impress him. After the show I was eager to get his reaction. But he didn't utter a word, so I just had to ask what he thought. To my great disappointment he had missed my appearance on stage because a woman in the audience had been taken ill, and being a doctor he had attended to her, thereby missing my entire performance! But there was our lifetime of performances ahead when Sven would be watching, advising and supporting me. It is only now that I realise how much he helped me in my career through his medical knowledge and keen interest in movement. He was an excellent antidote to Madam, who did not build up one's confidence, being always highly critical. I found it unnerving and distracting to know that she watched closely every performance from the box nearest the stage.

33 *Wedding Bells*

The four months after Sven's arrival flashed past with my parents making all the arrangements for the wedding, which Sven and I wanted to be held quietly in the country. One of my uncles and his family lived in a beautiful house in Weybridge, where they kindly offered to hold the reception.

I decided to have four bridesmaids: my three cousins and Sven's sister from Stockholm. Sven chose his brother Ruben to be his best man. Ruben and their sister Greta arrived from Sweden several days before the wedding, our first meeting. She accompanied me to my hairdresser in Regent Street who fell for her Scandinavian beauty and was soon styling her hair. My mother made all four bridesmaid dresses and was needlessly anxious about Greta's, awaiting her arrival to fit and alter if necessary. The full-length dresses were of lemon tulle, with fitted bodices, nipped in at the waist, exploding into voluminous skirts, with which they wore romantic wide brimmed hats adorned with lemon roses to match their bouquets.

After enjoying the beautiful clothes that Victor Stiebel made for me for the first American tour, I knew he would be just the person to design my wedding dress, and so he was. Once again he took particular delight in overseeing my fittings, when inevitably our conversation turned to the ballet. He designed for me the most romantic white wedding dress with a tightly fitted satin bodice above a skirt of 65 yards of pleated tulle edged with satin ribbon. The clinging long sleek sleeves were finished with tiny buttons matching those on the bodice. A small dove was placed amidst the flowers on my headdress, from which cascaded a full-length veil. My mother was in her element, coming to all my fittings; at one session we were photographed for the popular weekly magazine *Picture Post*.

Victor Stiebel also insisted on making and giving me my going away outfit, a beautiful navy blue grosgrain coat and coordinating floral dress with a balletic flared skirt. To go with this outfit, Madge Chard designed a dramatic, large, navy blue and white hat, under which no groom could comfortably kiss his bride!

During those last weeks of that London season there still seemed to be so many things to put in place for our wedding. The banns to be read in London and Weybridge, meetings with the local Vicar, flowers to choose, cars booked, caterers engaged, lists drawn up, invitations sent out and, most pleasurably, choosing with my mother her outfit for the great day. My father hired his morning suit from Moss Bros as was the custom. I wanted a week after the close of the London season to do last-minute shopping, prepare myself, and finalise many loose ends. This included driving to Weybridge to rehearse the ceremony as soon as Ruben and Greta arrived by boat from Gothenburg.

My Uncle Sydney officiated at the service, together with Sven's great friend, Gunnar Dahmen. Gunnar was the Swedish priest in Great Britain throughout the war, first in Scotland and later in the East End docks area of London, for the support of the Swedish seamen. Sven got to know him well whilst practising in Glasgow and later became godfather to his son David. I had already become very fond of him and his big Swedish family whom I began visiting quite frequently with Sven following our engagement.

Gunnar came from the South of Sweden and had a very distinct attractive brogue, with a strong, clear voice enunciating every word with clarity and meaning. Even I was able to follow what he was saying when he spoke Swedish. I was trying to learn a little of the language before going to Sweden on our honeymoon. I thought it important to be able to speak a few words to Sven's parents in their native tongue when meeting them for the first time. To our disappointment, they had felt that they were not up to the long journey by boat all the way to far-off England, so sadly were not present on our special day.

The day of the wedding dawned. My parents and I left home in Islington, where I was still living with them, at eight in the morning, collecting loads of canapés and petit fours from the Marble Arch Lyons Corner House. Truth to tell, we got rather lost around Hampton Court on the way to Weybridge, which was a bit worrying, but my father made it through eventually. When we arrived, everything was underway for the sit-down wedding breakfast which was to follow the welcoming reception. It was exciting, with everyone dressing upstairs for the occasion, the delicate bridesmaids' dresses at last adorning their wearers, and the men struggling into their hired morning suits – my Uncle Fred panicking when he found his waistcoat far too big, until my father pointed out it was double-breasted, and order was restored!

How delighted my father was when I appeared at last in my exquisite dress. Suddenly the house emptied, everyone left for the church which was a quarter of an hour away, and my father and I were left awaiting the arrival of the wedding car to take us to the church. But the minutes ticked by and no car came. We remained calm, expecting it had been delayed somewhere and would soon roll up. But it didn't and my father, now seriously concerned, rang the firm providing the Rolls Royce. They had just heard from their driver that it had broken down and were in the process of sending another car to take its place. After an agonizing wait, another Rolls rolled up and we got in as fast as my long train would allow. I was beside myself with worry whilst my father did his best to calm me down before we arrived – a whole half-hour late – at the church.

To our surprise, there were crowds outside, a large number of whom were my fans who had come down from London specially to wish us well, which helped restore my equanimity. It was with tremendous relief we entered the church filled with people and flowers. The organ began playing Tchaikovsky's *Panorama* music as we walked down the aisle to stand next to Sven. I learnt later that my mother had reassured a worried Sven, saying that I always had a tendency to cut things fine, but would most certainly arrive!

Our wedding was all I could have wished for. It did not rain, and our guests were able to enjoy the lovely garden where the all-important wedding photos were taken. The rest of the day passed as if in a dream, and all too soon it was time for me to change from my fairytale gown into my Stiebel going-away outfit. Sven and I were waved off amidst showers of rose petals, confetti and rice, which we had trouble getting out of our clothes at the spacious country club in Cobham where Sven had arranged for us, through a patient's kindness, to spend the next two nights. Our suite was large, filled with fabulous flowers that Sven had ordered, and it overlooked well kept grounds, which we enjoyed together in the sunshine the next day. We were loath to leave this peaceful setting on the Monday but had to drive to Tilbury to catch the boat for Sweden.

The most intriguing part of the trip was the way in which our car was winched onto the boat, hanging in a strong hemp net. It was then lifted by crane onto a fine old boat called the The Suesia. Once safely manoeuvred above the rear of the boat, it was gently lowered onto the deck. There it was chained for the voyage alongside a few other cars. There were not many travelling to Sweden in 1950. The Suesia boasted mahogany fittings throughout, including a restful library and writing room. Ruben was also on the same boat, travelling back to Sweden and getting up to mischief so that everyone on board knew Sven and I were on our honeymoon. I felt so very proud to be Mrs Svenson and have remained so to this day. Greta chose to remain in London for a few days, staying with my parents who were pleased to have the opportunity to get to know her and take her sightseeing.

34 *Swedish Honeymoon*

Sven was keen to show me around Gothenburg, where we landed – a well-ordered city with canals and tree-lined streets. We stayed overnight in one of their oldest and best hotels and next morning drove the four hours to Sven's home town, Vadstena, where his parents lived. I received a most loving and wonderful welcome. Using my new Swedish dictionary, I had been practising a line in Swedish, to say how happy I was to meet my new parents. Sven's father burst out laughing, saying 'we are not so "fresh" but quite elderly.' I had chosen the wrong word for new! This brought about much merriment and broke down any barriers that there could have been. Sven's mother was so kind and motherly and his father courteous and caring in his upright manner, and I was at once put at ease and taken into their hearts.

We stayed with them for about 10 days, during which time they went to so much trouble, producing the most delicious meals and giving us so much of their time. I felt spoilt, touched and happy. They often accompanied Sven and me in the car visiting many relatives in the outlying farms who naturally expected to meet the new English bride. Each welcoming family produced coffee and cream with the customary seven offerings – 'scorpa', (rusks) spiced breads, 'bullar' (cinnamon spiced buns) 'vienna brod' (like a Danish pastry), a variety of homemade biscuits (which usually included ginger ones), a kind of cheesecake (served from a bowl) and finally the 'piece de resistance', a cream gateau. One was expected to enjoy all seven delicacies; all were home baked and absolutely delicious. As we sometimes fitted in two or three visits a day, my weight, surprisingly, went up rather fast!

I met many of Sven's childhood friends with whom we enjoyed many a jolly evening al fresco dancing to the accompaniment of accordions which were played brilliantly. Sven was eager to show me Vadstena, his home town, which is beautiful – very old and steeped in history. It lies on the shores of the deepest lake in Sweden, Lake Vättern, whose waters feed the moat around its castle, which was built as a fortress in 1500 by Gustav I. The castle today guards the town's historical documents. It can only be entered by way of the drawbridge under a portcullis to a huge inner courtyard from where some of the rooms are open to the public. During the summer months, when people flock to visit the ancient, picturesque town, concerts are held regularly in the vast music salon on the first floor.

It would take an entire book to describe all the treasures of Vadstena; suffice to record that on every succeeding summer holiday there Sven would tell me more of its history, some only recently discovered. As a boy, Sven was involved with one of the many archaeological digs around what had been the monastery and church, which unearthed former royal chambers. The magnificent, cathedral-sized church is the resting place of St Birgitta, the much revered mystic saint of Sweden, famous throughout Europe. Her celebrity makes Vadstena a place of pilgrimage to this day.

Stockholm was sheer delight. It is such a beautiful capital, the sea inlets lapping unexpectedly alongside leafy avenues, flowing under its many impressive bridges, revealing a bustling city of many hues. It has an outstanding town hall, and large modern shops, arcades, galleries, cafes and restaurants are scattered everywhere. Across a bridge, in complete contrast, lies the picturesque old town, packed with shops selling just about everything from the very old to the very new. Close by looms the imposing royal palace built of grey stone, whilst across the water on another granite hill stands the historic opera house. At that time I had no inkling that I was to dance there.

I loved Skanson, the amusement park, where Sven and I wandered one evening before watching a scintillating, open air performance of the Oscar Strauss operetta *The Chocolate Soldier*. The whole area is enchanting and romantic, especially when experienced during the light Scandinavian nights. Sven's sister Greta insisted we stay in her attractive flat from where we were able to visit much of Stockholm during our all-too-brief stay.

It was a long, interesting drive to Dalarna, a picture-book county in the middle of Sweden, a long way north of Stockholm. There we were met with great warmth by Sven's friend Joseph Strindberg (cousin of the famous writer August Strindberg), Joseph's wife Elise and daughter Amy, with whom we were to stay for a few days joining other friends already there. In the grounds of their enormous farm Sven and I slept in a hydda, a small wooden barn-like hut which was surprisingly warm and cosy.

Being far north the daylight hardly seems to fade for more than half an hour and sleep comes unwillingly where there is no darkness.

One morning I crept out into the early daylight and untied a rowing boat moored at the side of their vast lake – only I couldn't somehow get going properly, battling with the oars until Sven appeared to rescue me. Knowing nothing of boats I had been rowing with the back of the boat at the front, all the wrong way around. No wonder I could not travel to any advantage! It was a big joke with the family and friends after we all gathered in the hot morning sunshine, so dear Elise strung together wild strawberries on grass stems for me as a consolation. She then produced a huge, delicious breakfast for everybody, and my incompetence was soon forgotten.

Sven had booked us a little cottage on the west coast where we spent a week enjoying the strong sunshine all day. We were incredibly lucky with the weather and have never since enjoyed such uninterrupted sunshine on any of our annual trips to the west coast. We sailed every day out to the many islands which are dotted along this glorious coast. The sea is so clear – like crystal – and we had such fun diving off the side of the boat, swimming, without seeing a single soul. It was a perfect dream. We sunbathed on the hot granite rocks, devouring a delicious picnic of raspberries and cream with our coffee.

A month later I was back in London and brought down to earth, preparing at Covent Garden for the Company's return visit to America. But this time it was to be an extremely long tour of nineteen weeks. The works chosen to go were *Swan Lake, Sleeping Beauty*, *Giselle* and several one-act ballets: *Les Patineurs*, *Façade*, *Checkmate*, *Dante Sonata*, *Symphonic Variations* and Madam's new *Don Quixote*.

I was dreading leaving my Sven so soon after our marriage, but my dancing took priority, which Sven understood and accepted. In those days dancers had no choice but to go, however long the tour, regardless of the upheaval to personal lives.

35 *The Second American Visit*

With Sven and my parents, I arrived at Heathrow airport along with the other principals on the morning of the 5th September 1950. The vast majority of the Company had assembled early at the Royal Opera House to be cheered and seen off in coaches by a huge crowd of enthusiastic, loyal fans. Eventually we bid long and loving farewells to husbands and family in the customs shed before walking to board the plane – a Stratocruiser – from which I was able to see my three darlings from a window on the right hand side. They saw me holding a small white pillow and waved as the plane took off. Mr Plucis had secured me a seat next to him but my heart was very heavy at leaving all my dear ones behind for such a long time. I was grateful for his quiet understanding.

At Idlewild airport the press and photographers were as friendly, enquiring and demanding as before, and many photos were taken, some with our impresario Sol Hurok. I found it comforting to be back in the familiar surroundings of the St Moritz Hotel as I unpacked my fine new clothes. Although I was glad to be alone in a single room, number 917, I felt a deep emptiness and longing for Sven and was already aching to return home to him. The pain of separation remained throughout the tour, fascinating as the whole experience would turn out to be. Fortunately there was plenty of writing paper and envelopes in the room for my letters home and my account of our current tour for *The Dancing Times*.

Sven insisted I take a rather battered-looking diary to record my progress in America and as I opened it at the correct date I found the sweetest message written from him to me: 'Good luck my darling and a safe return.' I knew then that Sven truly loved and cared for me as he demonstrated throughout our long and happy marriage.

Sven arranged that I meet his Danish friend, Marius Zwiller, a chiropractor married to an American woman, Violet, whom Marius adored in his matter-of-fact, direct, Danish manner. Marius phoned me at the hotel soon after I arrived, informing me that Vi would collect me at 7.30 that evening to have dinner with them. Vi made the most sensational Orange Blossom cocktails, which she always produced whenever I had supper there.

Marius gave me regular treatments during our time in New York, which were a big help to me, although different in approach to the osteopathic ones to which I had become accustomed from Sven and Edward Hall. To my surprise and relief they were equally beneficial. Marius held some interesting beliefs about life and reincarnation and because of his brilliant, enquiring mind I found our sessions together stimulating and enriching. No wonder he and Sven were lifelong friends.

Next day I was already rehearsing with John Field at the Met, where the staff greeted us with a big cheery welcome. We were scheduled to appear in *Swan Lake* within a week, and determined to be on our best form, despite the Company having less time to recover than on our first visit. Once back in New York, moreover, invitations began to pile up, and it was most heartening to have so many acquaintances from the previous visit eager to renew friendships.

Arthur Todd arranged for me to meet and to have dinner with Ruth St Denis, a meeting I found very inspiring. Violetta Elvin and Alexis Rassine were also keen to meet her, so, after rehearsals the following day, Arthur organised for us to be photographed standing with her outside the theatre. I still treasure this photo.

Ruth was such a beautiful and gracious lady, standing regally erect, already over eighty, yet still thrilling audiences with her recitals. I was deeply moved at her performance, her refined composure and the spiritual manner in which she moved across the stage engaging her audience by the intensity and sheer artistry of her movement. A dancer, choreographer and teacher, she was married for many years to another famous dancer, Ted Shawn. Together they established the renowned Denishawn Dance School, which produced many of America's early modern dancers, including Charles Weidman, Doris Humphrey and the remarkable Martha Graham.

In the Spring of 1954, Martha Graham was to stun the London public when she appeared for the first time at the Saville Theatre with her own company, which embraced her unique style. Modern and expressive, the dancers, barefoot and supple, performed a range of totally controlled, intriguing movements unlike any we had seen before and raised many an eyebrow. On their opening night her company caused a sensation amongst the ballet audience, which included Ninette de Valois. Madam was renowned for always looking ahead and appreciated this innovative, creative technique which stunned the few who attended. Surprisingly, no one else from our Company appeared to be there, not even Ashton.

This time in America I determined to experience some of the contemporary dance training myself, so took classes whenever possible with some of their outstanding teachers. I believe I gained most from Hanya Holm and Eugene Loring, very different yet both riveting. Their contemporary dance styles helped and extended my own dance movements.

To everyone's relief our three-week season in New York was once more a huge success. I am sure we all felt a certain apprehension that this return might not be quite as well received as our first visit. But it was – as the ecstatic applause proved at the end of *Swan Lake* on our opening night. The stage was strewn with flowers by the final curtain calls and even when the front of house lights came up, people refused to go away, continuing to clap Margot, Somes, and in fact all the dancers. So the curtain was raised again revealing to all those on stage the magical sight of the golden semicircular tiers of the old Metropolitan Opera House, each circle packed with an applauding, beautifully dressed audience.

I was disappointed, however, that Madam gave me so many matinee performances of the classics in preference to my friend Moira Shearer, who was given the evenings. There was nothing I could do about it except to press on and work hard to improve on each of my performances. With the world-wide success of her film *The Red Shoes*, I realised that Moira was a great draw. She was, moreover, such an attractive dancer and a remarkably lovely person, always taking great care over her appearance. I thought she was under great strain, overwhelmed by her movie fame, which she seemed to shun.

Being so famous in America, she was bracketed with Margot and frequently photographed with her. A sort of friendship developed between them and she became accepted into Margot's exclusive circle – Fred, Ninette, Bobby, Robert Irving (our Music Director) and Pamela May, Margot's closest friend. Success certainly never altered Moira. She met new people in the same way as she would old friends; however famous, always the straightforward Scottish lass. I always admired her – her artistry and her incredible allure, with that lovely lustrous chestnut hair – and often felt rather ordinary in comparison to her outstanding beauty.

I am rather hazy about the long, fascinating tour the 120-strong Company undertook following our successful New York season. My diary reminds me of some of the 1001 incidents. The unions insisted that for each staff member there was an American counterpart, which increased our numbers. These included an American conductor, Robert Zeller, augmenting our own two, John Hollingsworth and Robert Irving. The

Company – dancers, conductors, orchestra, artistic and administrative staff, stagehands, plus all the costumes, scenery, lighting equipment and lighting technicians – travelled 21,000 miles across America, finally finishing in Canada, all transported in a special train named The Ballet Special. When we had one-night stands or were off for a long haul across several States, we generally steamed off about two o'clock in the morning after the eight o'clock evening show, which was invariably followed by either a public reception or a special party, which Madam expected us to attend. Every so often we were fortunate enough to have a relaxed late-night meal on our own, away from public scrutiny, before boarding, when I would wearily clamber into my bunk for a restless sleep on the rocking, creaking train.

36 *The Long Haul*

I was always scared I would miss our special mobile home and be left stranded miles from the Company. With all our clothes stuffed into suitcases piled high at the ends of the carriages, the train invariably covered a good 400 to 500 miles a night. On arrival in the early hours, our train would be shunted noisily into a convenient siding. It was only then that we were able to snatch some much-needed sleep!

The astute organiser of all six Pullman coaches was our company manager, Herbert Hughes. Herbert arranged one coach for stage staff, two for the orchestra, three for dancers, of which two were for the more exuberant members of the Company. The third was designated for those seeking a more peaceful time and requiring as much rest as possible, which included the principals. Six more coaches contained the scenery and props needed for the long tour. The two biggest classics, *Swan Lake* and *Sleeping Beauty*, could only be given in large theatres whereas the scenery for *Giselle, Les Patineurs, Don Quixote, Checkmate, Façade* and *A Wedding Bouquet* could be hung in smaller, less well-equipped venues.

For engagements of two nights or longer, often with an odd matinee thrown in, we were able to go to hotels. This was blissful, with the luxury of a hot bath, in which I would soak for a good half hour, diligently following the advice of Mr Plucis. He was concerned with our welfare and our bodies' capability to cope with climate changes and the many strange, unsuitable stages on which we were expected to perform. He made sure that, just before a show, Moira and I drank a mixture of raw egg yolk beaten together with brown sugar, to give us an energy boost. Following Sven's advice I sought osteopathic treatment whenever an opportunity presented itself. I often wonder how I would have completed the tour successfully without this therapy.

In 1950 not all the cities in which we were scheduled to appear boasted a theatre. So it was usual for Hurok to have booked us into what was termed the Municipal Auditorium. This would be a huge building, holding a large central floor area surrounded by seating on the same level, as well as a higher tier of seats. The entire structure could be divided into two separate areas by an iron shutter. This meant that we were frequently performing back to back with another show. Every so often we were booked to follow the *Roller Skating Vanities* who, unknowingly, would leave the stage dangerously slippery. Invariably the stage crew would have all too little time to set up and light, let alone restore the stage surface before the public came pouring in. This meant principals rarely had a chance to try out the stage before a performance. The corps were also challenged when there was no time for them to be positioned on a new stage, as each one offered its own different dimensions, entrances and exits.

Changing room space was sometimes very confined, with two shows running simultaneously. In St Louis we found ourselves sharing the building with a circus, which was rather unpleasant with the animal smells and general hurly burly of the circus way of life. But even that was an interesting experience! As was finding ourselves dancing on a stage which covered an ice rink! Small wonder we were cold when not dancing.

We dancers quickly learnt to adapt to endless new stages, to have classes and rehearsals taken in unconventional quarters, whilst new audiences waited eagerly for the performance and later to entertain the Company. Life took on an unreal whirl of performances, parties and receptions as we travelled hundreds of miles from one city to another, crisscrossing the vast American continent. I can still recall the underlying excitement, knowing we were undertaking such a huge voyage, dancing in cities whose names summoned up, certainly in my imagination, films about the Wild West. There was also the understanding that even off stage we were representing our country, so were always under scrutiny.

One of the highlights was our two-week stop in Los Angeles. We stayed in the fabulous Ambassador Hotel on Wilshire Boulevard with its alluring array of shops. I fell for a beautiful black, thin wool dress with diamante straps worn over bare shoulders and a diamante belt. Wearing it I felt a million dollars! Many of the most famous stars of the time attended the opening night at the Shrine Auditorium, so there was much tension and nervousness backstage before the curtain rose. As it went up, one felt a warmth of good will emanating from the audience, and we were able to give our all. After the show Hurok gave a big party for the entire Company. Amongst those present were a galaxy of film stars: Charlie Chaplin, Gene Kelly and Danny Kaye, the latter two afterwards coming almost every night of our season. I was particularly thrilled to meet Greer Garson, having fallen in love with her in the film *Mrs Miniver,* although I was somewhat disappointed to find her plumper than she appeared to be in that film!

After two weeks in the luxury of the Ambassadors, it was a wrench to leave LA. I had enjoyed swimming in the huge pool, which each day was decked with dancers absorbing the glorious Californian sunshine. We had a nine-hour train journey to San Francisco, transported this time on a regular deluxe train to which three extra carriages were attached to take the Company. We passed along the coast enjoying magnificent views of the Pacific rollers crashing onto the shores, while appreciating the comfort of the public train with its elegant dining, lounge and observation cars.

In San Francisco we had the joy of being in an opera house with an impressive facade and well-equipped interior. But the first night audience was very stiff, unlike the friendly atmosphere encountered in LA. This was a society first night house who paid to be seen and sat waiting to observe what we could give them for their money. We were apparently worth it, and the initial, polite applause became a full-hearted roar of approval by the finale.

There was one big blot on our time in San Francisco. In the theatre one day I heard raised, angry voices. It was Madam and Bobby engaged in a fierce dispute, audible to all. At the end of that tour, to my deep sorrow, Bobby announced his resignation from the Company and gave his last performance with Margot in *Beauty*. Theirs had been the perfect partnership since 1935, and it was tragic that it ended abroad and so abruptly. I learnt so much from watching Bobby through the years: his acting, partnering, charisma and the confidence that he gave to those on stage. His wit and wicked sense of humour would be greatly missed, too.

I realised what a great artist he was and wondered how Margot felt about losing such a long-term partnership. Margot rarely showed her feelings to anyone, and in any case would probably not have confided in me. She was always very kind and polite, but we were never close. It was only after she retired from dancing that I felt she was more friendly and relaxed. Poignantly, I remember a formal dinner at the Chinese Embassy in London one evening, which we both attended. Margot and I were seated together and, as I now felt more comfortable with her, we both enjoyed ourselves, laughing and chatting together for the first time.

37 *Living Back On The Train*

After our closing night in San Francisco, the Company train took us to Sacramento for performances that evening and the next, after which we hurriedly boarded the train for Denver, Colorado. When the train eventually climbed the west side of the Rockies to Denver we were in for a shock: it is a mile above sea level and dancing was going to be a strain. I recall the amazing help of the oxygen masks when coming off stage gasping for breath, an unknown hand having placed a mask firmly over one's face, and the sheer relief of being able to breathe again. Not only was Denver the highest point on the tour but it was also the halfway point, and the Company was determined to celebrate. It was a fancy dress party with absolutely no outsiders, lasting for hours – the night saw some amazing creations.

I spent much of the time on the train reading and writing letters. As one city followed another, we slept mostly on the Company's special train as we had done for far shorter periods on the previous tour. When our steam engine stopped we would jump out to stretch and fool about between the railway sleepers, then leap back on as it began to steam off on its travels again. Moira Shearer and I would alternate between the upper and lower bunks, each night changing the inconvenience of one for the other.

The tour was terribly exhausting, yet I enjoyed seeing so many new places, albeit briefly, meeting interesting people, experiencing different venues with contrasting audiences. Our unscheduled train meandered from one famous city to another on an almost daily basis, so that we rarely experienced the comforting relaxation of a hotel. We travelled over 14,000 miles and performed in 15 different cities over five weeks. To every new audience we were expected to give outstanding performances, often in less than ideal conditions on a variety of stages. I doubt the unions would allow this today, but I would not have missed the entire tour for the world; neither I feel sure would the others, even though it put an enormous strain on our bodies and general health.

Back in London, Sven was staying with my parents while he organised our new home: the top floor flat at 32 Davis Street, which had been the home of the film actress Deborah Kerr. Her housekeeper appeared to have paid more attention to the country house than the Mayfair flat. This meant my poor mother spending many hours eradicating the dirt and making it spotless, ready for us to live in. Moreover, as Sven decided to open his own practice there, using the larger part of the flat for his surgery and waiting rooms, it had to be scrupulously clean and attractively decorated.

I know my mother took great pride in preparing my new home, as well as pleasure in helping Sven during spasmodic shopping expeditions for furnishings and basic essentials. Sven chose furniture from Waring & Gillow, an especially firm bed Sven prescribed from Heals, and lovely curtain materials from Sandersons and Fortnum & Mason. My mother wrote to me of her joy in watching Sven choose with such loving care everything needed for our first home – from carpets to crockery – and of his exceptionally good taste. For his part, Sven took wonderful care of my parents, taking them to the theatre, the cinema, as well as to our favourite restaurant, the Acropolis in Charlotte Street, to which Michael Meyer had introduced us during the war. The restaurant proprietor always took special care of me in those bleak years, sometimes slipping me a little rationed food to take away discreetly in a newspaper.

Sven left London to spend Christmas in Sweden. Meanwhile, we were in Chicago opening at the Opera House with *The Sleeping Beauty*, which we could only perform in large theatres because of the tricky scene changes and large number of elaborate costumes. All of the costumes needed freshening up, ironing and often repairing after travelling squashed tightly together, many packed still wet from perspiration. Our long-suffering wardrobe created incredible transformations in no time at all under less than ideal conditions. *The Sleeping Beauty* also opened our seasons in Los Angeles, San Francisco and Boston, where this magical full-length classic delighted and enthralled our audiences.

On our second visit to New York it had been decided to open with *Swan Lake*; a popular choice and well received everywhere. As it was less problematical to stage, we gave something like 50 performances of this production across America, which was wonderful for me; dancing Odette / Odile has always been my favourite role. Our American audiences were warmly enthusiastic so that however stiff and tired one felt they were a magical medicine. They helped lift me out of the personal stress and strain encountered on the tour.

Much as I enjoyed being back in Chicago, with its special memories of our romantic tryst, I was already growing impatient to be back with Sven. At last I could begin to visualise the end of the tour – not too far off now – with the New Year taking us into Canada: Winnipeg, Ottawa, Quebec and Toronto; Boston; White Plains, New York, then back to Toronto from where we would be flying home to England.

Boston could have been a disaster. The train was late, with an exhausted group arriving nine hours behind schedule on the same morning of the opening night with all too little time to settle in at a hotel and grab a few hours much needed sleep. This presented the technical director and his stage staff with a near impossible task to have *The Sleeping Beauty* staged in time. They had to unlock the scenery trucks, unload and, with all the costumes, travel right across town to the theatre. Once delivered there was little time in which to unpack, hang the mass of intricate scenery as well as placing the special lighting equipment needed for *Beauty*.

Amidst this pressure one of the most crucial technicians was called away for two hours to resolve some legal problem. The last straw was when the authorities threatened to put a 24-hour embargo on the playing of all the musical instruments, having thought they had not been declared on leaving Winnipeg for Boston. Eventually they were persuaded otherwise, withdrawing the threat with time fast running out. Finally with all the problems successfully resolved, and dedicated, determined hard work by the stage and wardrobe staff, the show was, miraculously, just ready to go up on time.

The extraordinary result was that despite all the nervous tension and desperate struggle to stage the gigantic production that evening, this was possibly the best performance of *Beauty* given on the entire tour. To finish that remarkable evening, the Company were taken by bus over snow-covered roads to a magnificent house. There our host prepared for us the most lavish array of food accompanied by champagne. It was such a pleasure to renew the acquaintance of the British Ambassador to America and his wife, Sir Oliver and Lady Franks.

After the closing night in Boston the entire production of *Beauty* was shipped back to England for restoration. The Company performed in White Plains before returning to enchant Canadian audiences in Toronto, Ottawa and Quebec. There, to mark the end of the tour, Hurok gave a tremendous party for the Company and staff. Delighted with the success of the whole tour he made a fulsome speech, to which Herbert Hughes responded wittily, in Madam's absence. One of the dancers then praised and thanked Margot for having led the Company so well, which we all applauded. Margot answering graciously with a few simple words.

Little did we then realise the demands the tour had made on us, going down like nine pins on our return to London. The incessant travelling; constant changes of venue, audiences and climate had taken its toll. We were always expected to give quality performances, however tired we might be feeling. But a wonderful team spirit emerged, enabling us to blindly keep going. Mary Drage, who was a leading dancer on that tour, wrote to me only recently reminiscing: 'I still have nightmares about that US tour, can't find the theatre, or my costume, and the music is almost up to my cue, Oh dear!'

I will never forget how stiff and uncooperative my body felt, going into an unknown venue to dance a full-length classic after little or no sleep, sometimes with only a basic warm-up through lack of time or space. We were totally at the mercy of the stage crew who would be struggling to get a set up in time for opening. No one who has not experienced a Hurok train tour can possibly understand what it was truly like and what it did to one's body.

Finally, our direct flight to Heathrow landed safely at 3.15 in the morning. I could see men rushing around outside the plane, which we were all so eager to leave after months of travelling. I felt almost sick with impatience to get off and see Sven again. We walked through to the waiting crowd, to be enveloped in the welcoming arms of our loved ones.

38 *The Start Of Married Life, 1951*

That end of January was the beginning of a new life with Sven in our first home together in Davis Street. Everything was in place, the long hall with its polished parquet flooring partially covered by a soft, cherry-coloured carpet, welcoming and warm for the patients Sven saw in his consulting room in the front area of the flat. Sven picked me up and carried me over the threshold – one of the most romantic moments of my life. The next few days were like a dream and passed all too quickly.

The Company were given a fortnight's break to rest and recover before recommencing work for our return to Covent Garden on Wednesday 21st February. Princess Margaret's presence added glamour and excitement to our performance of *The Sleeping Beauty*, which despite repairs and work on the scenery and costumes, was not looking its pristine best after the rigours of the tour. Margot was once again impeccable as Princess Aurora with Somes as her Prince, while I watched over them both with love and pride as the Lilac Fairy. The Company received an ecstatic welcome from the audience, flowers showering down from fans in the gallery. Madam stepped forward and acknowledged this welcome saying we were much more nervous appearing in London than abroad, for there we were a novelty and here a habit!

This began, however, a period of deep uncertainty and worry for me: for the first time Moira had been billed in the programmes on the same line as Margot, which shook me profoundly. All too soon, however, the Hurok tour began taking its toll. Moira was the first principal to fall ill, after only one performance, and I followed shortly afterwards. There was an outbreak of flu to which Pamela May succumbed and like me was unable to return for the rest of the season. There were countless numbers of injuries through over-tiredness.

This was remarked upon by the press and picked up by *Punch* who printed the following triolet:

Miss May and Miss Grey are still away
And Miss Lind was ill.
Ah woe is me and alack-a-day
Miss May and Miss Grey are still away.
Though Fonteyn and Shearer were there today
And the company danced with a will
Miss May and Miss Grey are still away
And Miss Lind was ill.

As well as rehearsing revivals for a part of the 1951 Festival of Britain, Fred was working on a new ballet: *Daphnis and Chloe*. The premiere was scheduled for April 5th, just a month after our season opening, but I was still off. Physically and mentally we gave everything over those nineteen weeks acting as ambassadors for Britain. Madam expected a full attendance at all official receptions in America and Canada and would put up a list of those to attend smaller occasions. She would be incensed if someone chickened out, giving the culprit a severe dressing down next day. Often I was so tired that I had to go back to my bunk between 2 and 3 o'clock in the morning, long before the others returned. No wonder we were now feeling the after-effects: a wretched time; so it was a relief to escape on holiday for a month's blissful oblivion.

This meant a happy return to Sweden, this time with my parents. Sven was anxious for his elderly parents to meet mine and arranged bookings on the Swedish Lloyd Line from Tilbury to Gothenburg. My parents adored Sweden and were charmed by Sven's parents, who went out of their way to make them welcome. I often wonder how they all got on so well as my parents did not speak a word of Swedish and my in-laws spoke very little English! Sven wanted my parents to see Stockholm, with its numerous bridges over the sea inlets and its imposing palace seated high up over the old town.

There was still time to visit the West coast, where we found Ruben awaiting our arrival with his wife Gunborg and son Hasse. The weather was glorious; we were able to go out on fishing boats, swim and explore some of the hundreds of little islands. These islands are mostly austere granite rocks supporting a minimum of grassland and wild flowers, clear sea water swirling at their edges. The time came around for my parents' departure and two weeks later Sven and I sailed home from Gothenburg – sunburnt and so very happy.

Preparations for a brief London season were underway, but I was still not quite recovered from acute anaemia so I began gentle lessons with de Vos at her studio in Linden Gardens. I also needed to lose the weight I had gained in Sweden even though I swam a lot in the freezing Lake Vättern. Ashton was working on a new ballet, *Tiresias*, especially commissioned for the Festival of Britain. Constant Lambert composed the music with designs by his wife Isabel. Fonteyn and Somes took the leading roles, but the ballet was not a success as the scenario was found unpleasant and too long.

Margot had just received the CBE in the Queen's Birthday honours, and this caused great excitement amongst us. We were so pleased for her, and she gave a party that evening to celebrate. Madam had been created a Dame at the beginning of the year before we returned from the States. This was a tremendous boost for the entire Company. It was deeply satisfying to feel that Madam's long and brilliant leadership, since 1931, had at last been recognised, and we all felt so proud of her.

On 21st August the sad news came of the death of Constant Lambert, which I found hard to take in. He had always been there, a part of the Company. I thought back to the war years when he was like a ballet master to us, keeping his eyes on our appearance and performances on stage; he was a friend to so many, as well as the close colleague of de Valois, Ashton and Fonteyn. Although he had not, in recent years, been prominent as our conductor, he was still an important part of the triumvirate, and his loyalty to the Company never wavered. Everyone realised this was a terrible loss.

39 *Working With Massine, 1951*

All ballerinas yearn for new roles upon which they can put their own stamp, which can be both challenging and exhilarating. To have a new role of one's own to interpret and develop had been all too rare an experience for me. Second and third casts are inevitably compared to the creator of the new role, generally unfavourably, because it will have been built around that artist's particular talents and personality. But at last I was to be given a role of my own by the great Russian dancer Leonide Massine in *Donald of the Burthens.*

Massine had already staged several of his works for the Company. From our very first rehearsal his personality bewitched me, which ignited the moment he was involved in creating. Working with him was one of the most fulfilling experiences of my career. For my role as Death he would explain what he wished me to convey through new, strange movements. We would work on them together until they developed into what he had conceived. Our rehearsals began on Monday 10th September 1951 at 5pm, and were so enthralling that my admiration for his creativity increased at every session. I could not but hold him in the greatest esteem and awe.

Alexander Grant soon joined the rehearsals to play a wood-cutter to whom, as Death, I gave magical healing powers, providing he always acted as Death dictated. Alex was shorter than me and, once again, Massine instructed him to lift and carry me around the stage, as he had done in Massine's Spanish ballet *Le Tricorne.* This was not exactly comfortable for either Alex or me, which we both found hilarious! Massine obviously appreciated Alex's gifts as a character artist and enjoyed creating for him. Our rehearsals ran smoothly, but there was little time given to rehearse with the entire cast because the Company had new corps dancers to be taught the repertoire. There was also a short season away from the Garden, which interfered with rehearsals.

Our rehearsals generally took place at the Upper Ballet School in Barons Court or at the Hammersmith Town Hall, where one always felt horribly exposed since other people in the building were able to walk through. Orson Welles often wandered through on his way to make recordings. With few full calls I wonder that Massine was able to stage this new work, and I felt that Alex and I had little connection to the action in the rest of the ballet.

As part of the production we were taught authentic Scottish steps by an expert. These were all on half pointe and our feet got very sore with blisters. The Scottish dancing was performed to the accompaniment of a bagpiper on stage amongst us. It was the second ballet in which I was appearing as Death (*Checkmate* had been the first) and in both works Death wins, as it does in life. I enjoyed dramatic roles, and for this one I was dressed in daring, bright red body tights.

Donald of the Burthens premiered at Covent Garden December 12th with striking scenery and costumes designed by Robert MacBryde and Robert Colquhoun. The music composed by Ian Whyte did not inspire me and, to my great disappointment, like the ballet was not well received. But that period of working with Massine will remain one of my most valuable experiences.

Despite resting during the summer, I still tired very easily. I saw various doctors before Sven finally succeeded in diagnosing the cause – my thyroid gland had ceased to function. Overwork, and the swift return to dancing after my bout of hepatitis, was the obvious cause. My doctors refused to believe it until the results from tests at the thyroid clinic in Hampstead proved Sven correct. Persisting in his research, it was Sven who gave me back my dancing career. I could not have continued much longer – hardly eating in an effort to stay thin and having to push myself to work every day, constantly feeling inexplicably tired.

From then on I came under the care of the distinguished thyroid specialist, Raymond Greene. I went regularly to his Harley Street practice where pictures of his mountain-climbing expeditions were displayed in his consulting room. His was an interesting and famous family: Graham Greene the author was his brother, as was Hugh Greene, the BBC Director General; Felix Greene, writer of many books on China, who Sven and I later got to know very well, was his cousin.

My autumn was busier than usual with rehearsals and performances. I returned as Myrtha, Queen of the Wilis, in *Giselle* at a Gala on September 13th, the same week my rehearsals with Massine began. I was soon hard at work on *Swan Lake* and *Les Sylphides,* both favourite roles of mine. As the weeks went by, Madam began reviving *Beauty* to which there were some new additions. The music for the ballerina's solo in the Vision Scene was changed, and Fred was charged with choreographing it. As Margot was still away he chose to create it on me, to my great joy.

At our rehearsals at Hammersmith Town Hall I tried out many steps based on his inspired suggestions before Fred finally decided upon the most expressive movements. If only he had choreographed a whole ballet on me, too. I suspect he did not feel so comfortable with tall dancers, and there was the problem of finding a tall enough partner for me. He had his perfect muse in Margot, so in a way I understood – but I so admired Ashton's creations and appreciated the time and care he took at rehearsals when working on one of his ballets.

He would put his hands on my shoulders, pulling them down into the small of my back whilst yelling, 'Use your head and neck much more, free it up, so it goes further back.' Fred looked for a full use of épaulement (shoulder positioning) complemented by an equally expressive use of hands and arms. He often talked at length about Pavlova, getting up from his chair to demonstrate her bourrées and body movements: like most Russian ballerinas she obviously held nothing back but imbued her every movement with feeling and emotion. She died in 1931, on tour in The Hague, and I have always regretted not being old enough to have seen her.

Despite the wonderful opportunity of helping make a new ballet with Massine, I recognised that I was deeply upset and hurt by the billing of Moira alongside Margot after that last tour. I was even more disturbed that, when Margot was away for three or four months in the autumn, having strained her foot badly, Moira's name replaced hers at the top, just as mine had in the war. This was dreadfully worrying for me and impacted on my health. I knew nonetheless that the *Red Shoes* film had made Moira a great star so that her name was of more value to the Company, particularly during Margot's absence.

Then in November something strange happened. Neither Moira nor her position on the billing were to be found in the Royal Opera House. My name and Violetta Elvin's topped the list, without any explanation from Webster or Madam! Moira later told me that Michael Wood, our press officer, informed her that Madam no longer wished her to appear with the Company. Moira was indignant that, for whatever reason, Madam did not tell her herself, but allowed Michael Wood to do so. One was rarely told anything. Looking back to those twenty precious years working under Madam, I realise one was treated more as a child than an artist, and any questioning by a dancer was not tolerated. How times have changed.

Margot's continued absence meant Madam entrusted me to dance the lead on the first night of her revised *Sleeping Beauty* on the 9th January. This gave me renewed hope, and I was determined to make it a success. According to the press and management it undoubtedly was a big success, to my joy and relief. I had been terribly nervous about the Rose Adagio which follows almost immediately after the first entrance. But my four princes – John Hart, Kenneth Macmillan, Philip Chatfield and Bryan Ashbridge – partnered me superbly, and the dreaded balances went well. After that first ordeal I was able to really enjoy the performance, with John Field as my Prince Florimund.

We also had the inspired conducting of Robert Irving, who could be relied upon to follow a dancer's every move. He was the best conductor we ever had, following the demise of Constant Lambert. He understood each dancer's quirks, weaknesses and strengths and knew instinctively when to push the performer or to pull back a little. He was absolutely the right man to take up Lambert's baton as music director for he had the required experience as well as the respect of both dancers and musicians. Not only a marvellous ballet conductor (sadly there are so few) he was also a good ambassador for the Company, and it was a sad day when he left in 1958 to join the New York City Ballet as their music director.

Running my own home, I found I had all too little time to see my parents, although we made a point of trying to give them dinner in our flat most weekends. I always applied for tickets for them to see my performances when they were free to come. But my mother was not in good health, missing me very much and becoming depressed, which was worrying.

King George VI died unexpectedly on February 6th 1952, just before Margot's return on the 9th after her long absence. I was dancing in *Donald* that evening, and Guy Horne was to have given a dinner party at the Savoy after the show but, in view of the nation's loss, he instead only asked Sven and me back to the Cavalry Club for a quiet dinner. The following Friday he arranged for us to watch from his club the late King's funeral procession as it passed along Piccadilly. That moving event made a deep impression on me: the solemnity and respect shown by everybody along the route and the dignity and magnificent orderliness of the procession as it filed past. People loved and held King George in high respect for the courageous way he and the Queen behaved throughout the war, touring amidst the ruins and meeting and inspiring the homeless and bereaved.

40 *3D Film, 1952*

Peter Brinson, the eminent writer and lecturer on ballet, planned the first ever three-dimensional ballet film: *The Black Swan*. He obtained Madam's permission for me to feature in this famous ballet excerpt, with John Field as my Prince and David Paltenghi as the Evil Magician. We were told it would be about 16 minutes long and take three or four days to shoot at Elstree Studios in April.

It was all new and exciting: costume fittings and attending the orchestra's rehearsals of the Black Swan divertissement from the third act of *Swan Lake*. Brinson chose Charles Mackerras as the conductor, as he was experienced in understanding dancers' demands. As this was to be filmed to recorded music it was essential we were present to ensure exactly the right tempo for each sequence. We had no problems with such a cooperative and skilled conductor, and we were comfortable with the finished recording when filming.

We arrived at the studios by 6am to be made up, hair and headdress arranged, by 7am. Audrey de Vos kindly came to give me a good warm-up – barre and centre work – on the set, sensing what I most needed in order to give my best throughout the day. Once cooled down I would get into my pink tights, pointe shoes and lastly be fitted into my black and gold costume, bedecked with necklace and earrings in time to commence shooting at 8am.

For this new Stereoscopic filming two cameras were employed, so there were a number of cameramen and many other technicians about, all of whom were fully committed and a joy to work with. John Field was always easy-going and like David Paltenghi made friends effortlessly. Peter Brinson, in costume, appeared as commentator, walking through the ruins of the ballroom and finding a white feather which reminded him of the scene about to be re-enacted. It ended with the destruction of the palace and the death of the hero.

Although there was no audience out front, I had become adjusted to dancing in small studios for television, without an audience present. We all became good friends in the studio, working until 5pm each day when John and I would make a quick dash for Covent Garden where we were dancing each evening. It was a busy but happy time. We thought that we were successfully finished by the end of the third afternoon but, as we were leaving, it was discovered that the second camera had not been working that day, so we would need to return next day to re-shoot the finale. This is the most technically demanding part containing the famous thirty-two fouettés. These had to be completed on the same spot without any travelling because of the limited space in the studio. Thankfully, I managed to accomplish this satisfactorily all over again, and on Thursday afternoon we bade a fond and thankful farewell as we left for Covent Garden and my appearance in *Donald*.

41 *Sylvia – Its Creation – And Laughing Legs!*

In 1952 Violetta and I began to learn the title role in Ashton's new full-length ballet *Sylvia*. Fred was creating it on Margot, so I was pleasantly surprised when he altered some steps especially for me. This helped me to receive some good notices when it was finally presented in September. Violetta was second cast and I was third, partnered this time by a relative newcomer in principal roles, Philip Chatfield. It was the first time we danced as a partnership, and we suited each other well.

There was one accident during a rehearsal when we were learning the lovely third act pas de deux. I was to run across the front of the stage, leaping backwards into my partner's arms after suddenly turning in the air. Philip almost dropped me, but just managed to catch me round the chest, winding me and bruising my ribs so I could hardly breathe. Philip was dreadfully upset, but it was the only time in our long partnership that he failed me. We were to dance together with success for many years to come, and he became my favourite and most trusted partner.

1952 was a very interesting year for me, and I received many exciting invitations: I not only danced on television but also compered some BBC concerts of ballet music on the radio, which I greatly enjoyed. I opened a photographic exhibition at the National Portrait Gallery, which I found interesting. It was also during that spring that I spoke at the Critics' Circle Luncheon, together with many distinguished artists of the theatre. Other speakers I remember included Flora Robson, one of the actresses I most admired, and the sparkling Mary Martin whose performance I had so enjoyed on Broadway in *South Pacific*. This was the first time that ballet had been recognised by the Critics' Circle, and I felt truly honoured to be there representing my art.

The stereoscopic film which I made at the beginning of April was screened at the Riverside Theatre in May as part of the reopening celebrations of Battersea's Festival Gardens and was reported to have been seen by a hundred thousand people over a six-month period. To obtain the desired 3D effect, glasses were provided for each member of the audience. It remains today as the only stereoscopic dance film made.

In mid autumn, Sadler's Wells was invited to take part in the International Art Festival in Berlin. This was an interesting return for those of us who were there in 1945 at the end of hostilities. We were amazed at the way Berlin had rebuilt much of its city since that period, when it was still divided into four sectors. I loved what one German critic wrote about me: 'There are some legs that have more laughter and intelligence in them than some heads,' and I gained the nickname 'Laughing legs' which I took as a great compliment.

It was in the autumn of 1952 that my biography by Pigeon Crowle was published, and my parents were tremendously thrilled and proud. My mother was to die just before Christmas, but with the knowledge that all the care and love she bestowed on me as a child had successfully shaped my destiny.

That December – a month of such major events with their deeply conflicting emotions. The weather was generally rather foggy, and my mother was enduring more and more pain although, puzzlingly, tests showed nothing at first. By the second week of December, however, another test showed a small growth in the abdomen, which her doctor said would need to be immediately removed. My mother was seen at University College Hospital on Monday 15th and taken in next day. The prospect was frightening for her as she had lost one of her best friends after an operation when a swab was left inside.

Meantime I was working hard as there was to be a Royal Gala on the 18th with a new production of *Swan Lake*. I was to be given the rare opportunity of dancing the lead in place of Margot, who was still away recovering from diphtheria. That week I was busy with rehearsals and fittings and photographs and only found time to visit my mother on Wednesday, the night before her operation, when I took her a tiny posy of violets. As Sven and I left her, she sat up in bed in the hospital ward bravely waving.

I did not go to see my mother on Thursday before her afternoon operation as I was concerned to rest all morning before class, in preparation for my big night. Sven came to see me at the theatre before the performance, having called in to the hospital en route. He had been assured that although the operation was delayed by two hours, it had gone well. What a relief. I was soon lost in *Swan Lake*, my first ever opportunity to lead the Company at a Royal Gala and moreover in a new production. The beautiful costumes and scenery by Leslie Hurry were wonderfully dramatic, and I was swept along by Tchaikovsky's inspiring music. I was further elated when at the end of the performance I was taken to the Royal Receiving Room to meet the royal party, which included Queen Elizabeth the Queen Mother and Princess Margaret. The Company were given a party following the performance after which Sven and I slipped away to The Savoy where Guy Horne was waiting to give us a celebratory late dinner.

My darling father had not come to my performance but went directly to the hospital after work, to be by my mother's bedside until he was told to leave that night. My father woke Sven and me early next morning, saying he received a call that my mother had taken a turn for the worse. He was leaving at once for the hospital. It was then barely 7am, and although we threw on clothes and drove immediately to the hospital we were too late. My darling mother died at 7.20 am…

The grief I felt was something quite new to me, and I broke down and cried and cried in the hospital – the shock of losing her. I was bewildered: she was always there for me, she patiently helped me to ballerina status and suddenly she had been taken away from us. It was too painful to take in and the rest of that day – in fact the entire weekend

– became a blur of misery. This was my first great loss, my first encounter with death, the death of one I loved deeply. There was, though, one ray of light in that bleak weekend – a telegram arrived from the Queen Mother expressing her sympathy at my great loss – how did she know of my mother's death, and how incredibly kind and gracious of Her Royal Highness to send her condolences. I found this helped me so much – my mother would have been overwhelmed, too. What a remarkably caring Sovereign this country had in our beautiful Queen Mother.

On Friday morning Sven rang Guy, who was absolutely marvellous, driving us across London, assisting with all the necessary requirements that go with a hospital death and arranging for my mother to be taken home to be with my father until her funeral. There was the most terrible pea-soup fog that Friday, which made getting about a nightmare. The fog caused many deaths which, together with Christmas the following week made the task of finding a cemetery able to take my mother a real challenge. She had always expressed a wish to be buried near to Coulsdon, in the countryside, where we had been so happy. We eventually found that Epsom cemetery could arrange for her burial before Christmas. The family grave was dug, and one cold, misty Tuesday morning we laid my dear mother to rest.

Yuletide that year was terribly sad; opening my mother's pre-wrapped presents, including a lovely nightdress she had made as a surprise for me. I stained it with tears – I still have it to this day. I suppose it is sentimental of me but it is something of her, the incredibly kind and loving person she was – loved by all and so greatly by my poor father who was now devastated by his terrible loss.

I determined not to give in and danced my scheduled performances into the New Year, when eventually I fell ill with the flu – a sort of delayed shock, I have since thought. It meant being in bed for quite a few days. After I recovered, my father returned to live alone in his flat. He would only stay a short time with us after the funeral, although we tried to persuade him to stay longer. He, too, determined not to give in to grief but to endeavour to return to as normal a life as possible, as soon as he could. We made sure he came over to see and have a meal with us every week, and he began visiting his brother and family on weekends.

43 *First Guesting*

1953 became an exciting year as I was invited to guest away from the Sadler's Wells Company in my own right for the first time. Mary Skeaping, the Company's ballet mistress for several years, had become the director of the Swedish Royal Ballet. This is one of the oldest ballet companies in Europe, dating back to 1773 when it was founded by the art-loving King Gustav III, upon whom the opera *The Masked Ball* is based. It was in the Royal Opera House in Stockholm that he was assassinated, during a ball taking place there. I was immensely moved to be allowed to handle the finely embroidered waistcoat bearing the hole made by the bullet which killed him. This is kept safely in the huge wardrobe department of the theatre, a testament to their knowledge of and respect for their history.

It was quite an event, too, for them to invite an English ballerina to dance in their Opera House – a point not overlooked by Madam as she gave her consent for me to be absent for two weeks. Mary also asked that John Field partner me, to which Madam agreed. Together with Sven, we left in mid March for Sven's homeland – a country for which I had developed a strong feeling of affiliation.

Rehearsals in the Opera House went well with the company who had already performed *Swan Lake* with four of their own ballerinas as Odette / Odile. John and I, though, needed to become used to their production as well as to the extreme stage rake – reproduced exactly in the huge rehearsal room in which we worked. This took some effort after the flat stage of Covent Garden. The floor sloped quite considerably towards the footlights, so one had to counterbalance by leaning back slightly. All the stages of the old European Opera Houses were raked to ensure the public could see everything that was happening on stage. So, too, the provincial theatres where we toured during the war, so it was not altogether a new experience. We rehearsed happily albeit cautiously with Mary and the company, together with their chief conductor.

Our first performance went wonderfully well, resulting in eighteen curtain calls. In the interval we had the huge privilege of being presented to the King and Queen of Sweden in the gilded receiving room. I was told later that the Queen stood applauding for fifteen of those amazing curtain calls.

I felt quite anxious knowing that some of Sven's relatives were coming to see his foreign wife's performance. I think this must have added an incentive to excel in my favourite role. It was a delight to meet them afterwards, especially seeing how much they enjoyed the whole evening. For me not to let Sven down was the greatest reward. John and I gave more performances in Stockholm, and whilst in the capital I met many interesting artists including Sweden's most renowned contemporary dancer, Birgit Cullberg. She invited us to her home where we saw her two young sons, Niklas aged ten and Mats two years younger, dashing about the house. Both destined to become internationally known as dancers, and Mats later also a choreographer. I think back with amusement to my first glimpse of them playing so happily, unaware of the future ahead of them.

Amongst other notables from the Swedish ballet scene I was thrilled to meet Jenny Hasselquist. Born in 1892, an admired European ballerina, she was renowned for her interpretation of Fokine's works. She moved on to become a film and stage actress and later a much respected teacher back in her home city, Stockholm. She had left the Swedish Royal Ballet in 1920 to become a leading ballerina of Ralph de Marie's *Ballets Suedois*.

Whilst in Stockholm I also met and got to know Bengt Hager, one of the most respected and knowledgeable ballet personalities in Sweden. He was widely known as the director of the Museum of Dance, which he founded in 1950, but had also enjoyed the most amazing experiences as an author, impresario, manager of touring ballet companies, President of the Swedish Dance Association, General Secretary of the Parisian les Archives de la Danse, sitting on UNESCO boards, and was founder director of the Swedish State Dance School. He was very proud to show me around his wonderfully arranged Museum.

On a later visit I gave a lecture there, which to my surprise Birgit Cullberg attended. I felt very honoured that she should have spared the time to come and listen to me. My friendship with Bengt grew over the years right up to his death. I learnt so much about my art from him – how introvert and narrow was my own knowledge of European ballet and how much still I have to learn.

Returning home to Covent Garden after two weeks of being treated as a prima ballerina I was somewhat brought down to earth by a letter in the News Chronicle, written by David Webster, stating categorically that Margot Fonteyn was 'the prima ballerina assoluta and shares a position with no one. The Company enjoys the services of three ballerinas. We place them in alphabetical order – Violetta Elvin, Beryl Grey and Nadia Nerina'. This did nothing for my confidence and only served to make me realise that as long as Margot remained at Covent Garden I could only hope to be number two, at best. I wondered how much longer I could bear this.

To my joy, however, another invitation came to dance abroad, this time in Belgium in May – a Gala performance in Mons for King Baudoin of Belgium, again with my partner John Field. His wife was Belgian so she (like Sven) came with us, and our performance was a big success. We celebrated in a little café before attending what John thought would be a short, informal gathering. To our horror and embarrassment we arrived to find a sit-down dinner – everyone already seated awaiting our arrival. We were nonetheless warmly greeted and enjoyed a magnificent banquet which extended late into the night.

On our return to our sleeping hotel we crept in quietly, Sven carrying my numerous bouquets. Once in our room I looked around for him and, hearing an almighty crash at our open window, found him outside clinging on to the window sill, clutching a bouquet of red roses which he was merrily proffering to me! His feet had obviously met a glass roof a little below. He was grinning with amusement and joy but all my energies were engaged in pulling him up into our bedroom. He said he was playing Romeo to me, his Juliet. Dear loving, adoring Sven. As we departed next morning, the hotel's owner remarked that a pane of his glass roof had been mysteriously broken in the night – had we heard a noise at all?!

Once back from Belgium, John and I were plunged into Ashton's new work which was to celebrate the young Queen Elizabeth's Coronation in June. It was well titled *Homage to the Queen* as it was just that, presented rather like a masque. Margot and Michael with we 'three other ballerinas' and our respective partners, each pair representing one of four elements. It was gorgeously designed by Oliver Messel, whose exquisite programmes for the audience added richly to the occasion, as did the lavishly decorated tiers, all festooned with fresh flowers. Fred's choreography meant that each dancer's talents were fully displayed, and I felt that we dancers appreciated Malcolm Arnold's specially composed music, which was melodious and rhythmical.

All four couples had a train of followers so that every member of the Company took part in honouring our lovely new Queen on the evening of June 2nd. The programme began with Margot and Bobby (back as a guest) appearing in the second act of *Swan Lake*, followed by the Queen's speech relayed throughout the Opera House. After which came

Fred's personal offering. An historical and rather wonderful evening, in which I felt proud to have played a part.

I had no idea, at the close of this season late in June, that this was to be my last appearance at the Opera House for sixteen months. It had been a busy year packed with engagements outside the company, including my piano lessons with Ippolit Motchalof, which we had continued whenever possible since my early days as a student at Sadler's Wells. I enjoyed appearances on television, viewing and opening exhibitions, seeing the opening of Parliament, going to hear the fabulous Maurice Chevalier sing at the Café de Paris (site of such tragedy in the war), meeting interesting people and visiting a number of hospitals and community centres to help cheer and entertain both the elderly and the young. Still worrying me, however, was my father's loneliness, and I was so pleased when Sven and I were able to take him to see *South Pacific* in May. We thoroughly enjoyed the show and watching it all together was a tonic for my father.

There were also numerous photo sessions to attend at the studios of Hans Wilde, Derek Allen and many others, including Gordon Antony (Ninette's half brother). He had been the first one ever to photograph me in his studio when I was still only fourteen. We got on well from the word go, and a real bond sprung up between us.

Gorki, as he was known by friends, often used to give me unusual, tiny, antique jewellery pieces, which I have kept to this day. Romantically staged photos were the fashion during the war, and in those early post-war days he would take inordinate trouble setting up the background and arranging the lighting. Sessions could sometimes last the best part of a day, especially on a Saturday. He took the best studio photos of me, not only dancing shots but also portraits.

44 *Summer Holiday, 1953*

Sven and I left Tilbury for our annual holiday in Sweden at the beginning of July, taking my father with us. Sven always tried to make our journeys in Sweden as interesting and enjoyable as he could. After driving off the boat at Gothenburg we would stop at the town market of Borås, and later at a café in Ulricehamn which specialised in my favourite Mazarines, a delicious small almond pastry, similar to a frangipane, which could vary considerably depending on where it was made. After four hours' driving we arrived at our destination in Borghamn where we received a wonderful welcome from the owners of the little hotel.

We liked to stay there every year as it was close to the lake in which we enjoyed swimming before breakfast each morning. This was a magical time to slip into the water with no-one about. Only the occasional solitary fishing boat on the horizon stopped the sky falling into the vast expanse of crystal clear waters of this, the deepest lake in Sweden, which holds so many mysteries as the myths which abound suggest.

Omberg, referred to locally as 'the mountain', is a nature reserve, housing rare plants, flowers, trees and general flora, as well as a refuge for many rare and interesting birds. These nest on the rocky, windswept mountainside, high above the granite rocks, the shingle embellishing the shore far below. Sven took great pride in this strange geological phenomenon, which rises above the flat, extensive expanse of Östergötland. He delighted in driving me across Omberg every holiday, and it became a much anticipated annual pilgrimage. One can walk for miles, finding untramelled areas of ancient forests and historic areas where an early queen is said to have taken refuge from marauding invaders many hundreds of years ago.

The days sped by all too fast and the time came for us to leave for a week on the rugged west coast of Sweden, which I adored. After sun-baked days, my father was whisked off to stay with Ruben and his wife Gumborg and son Hasse for a few days at their summer house in the south. From there they saw my father safely onto the Swedish Lloyd ship taking him back home to England.

I had not been feeling too well, experiencing bouts of nausea most days. Sven took me to the local hospital, where tests announced that I was pregnant. This was something I had never thought seriously about. Suddenly faced with the prospect of having a child of my own was both wonderful and rather daunting. Sven and I were far North, in the famous county of Dalarna, when, with mixed emotions, I wrote to Madam telling her my news. I explained that I would not now be able to go on the next tour to America scheduled for the coming autumn. Although I had regrets at letting her down, as it were, at the same time I felt a certain relief at not having to face another long separation from Sven. He was overjoyed at my pregnancy and from then on took even greater care of me, deciding to get me home as soon as our bookings could be rescheduled on a Swedish Lloyd ship.

45 *Lady In Waiting*

Once back in England I felt a lot better as my sickness became less severe, so we decided to visit the West Country, which Sven had never seen. As in Sweden we were blessed with hot sun, which enticed Sven into the surf at St Ives and even me to the edge of the big waves, as they rolled in and collapsed into a million sparkling diamonds dropping onto the gleaming foreshore. Back in London, Sven arranged an appointment for me with the gynaecologist Douglas Macleod to ensure care during my pregnancy. I liked him straight away, and he gave me great confidence for the time ahead, seeing me on a regular basis.

I was also regularly seeing Raymond Greene, the great thyroid specialist, who now kept a strict check on my thyroid condition, which had been correctly diagnosed by Sven. That nightmare is well behind me now, although I remain on thyroid tablets –

except when I was carrying my baby. Incredibly, the baby took over the working of my thyroid until birth, after which the gland needed supplementing again.

From the time I learnt of my pregnancy I felt an hitherto unknown sense of freedom, a realisation that I had many months ahead without the incessant strain of performances. I would not have to endure the continual battle for position within the Company with the conflicting emotions this engendered. I was free to go where and when I chose, and more importantly to spend more time with Sven as a real wife, not just as a dancer concerned about her next performance with all the restrictions this imposed.

Lord and Lady Wakehurst were avid lovers of the ballet, and he was at that time the Governor of Northern Ireland and one of the directors of the Royal Opera House. As keen followers of my performances, they learned of my pregnancy and kindly invited me to stay with them for ten days at Government House in Northern Ireland. It was an invitation I could not resist.

In early October John, Lord Wakehurst, was waiting to greet me at the foot of the plane steps before sweeping me away in a splendid chauffeur-driven Daimler. A lovely welcome awaited me at Government House where Peggy, Lady Wakehurst, embraced me warmly before leading me into the large, beautiful house and showing me around. John had commissioned a huge mural of *Swan Lake* in their bathroom, which she proudly showed me. This large and beautiful tableau was of the second act, portraying me with my prince surrounded by a corps de ballet of swans. I was amazed and felt flattered that they should have chosen me as their swan princess.

Despite their daily, sometimes quite heavy, duties the Wakehursts included me whenever possible in both their social and formal engagements. They both commanded much love and respect. I was particularly thrilled when early on the Sunday morning we all went aboard an aircraft carrier where we were received in great state.

On most evenings there were important guests to be entertained and it was always formal attire – dinner suits for men and full-length dresses for the ladies. I was most interested to meet all these people, although I have to admit finding one or two rather heavy-going! It was a privilege to stay at Government House, and each day I rang Sven to tell him of all the wonderful things we had done. I loved the soft rolling countryside with its narrow lanes and the picturesque harbours, sheltering scores of tiny fishing boats. Possibly the most breathtaking sight was the Mountains of Morne, their granite rocks shining in the sun reaching down to the sea in the most romantic way.

On the rare evenings when there were no VIPs to entertain, we would sit around the fire and John would show some of his many films. On such an evening, Peggy and I dangled my wedding ring on a piece of string to forecast the sex of the baby: a boy was predicted. How I hoped this was true, for I knew how much this would mean to Sven. Peggy agreed to be Godmother to my baby, which made me especially happy knowing the care and love she would bestow on the infant.

Although not performing, I continued to be in the public eye, and was happy not to have been forgotten. I accepted invitations to open exhibitions, visit schools and give talks to such contrasting centres as The Rose Bruford College for Acting and the St Pancras Library! Sven and I saw many plays, went to musicals, as well as sharing the emotional inspiration of concerts at the Royal Albert Hall and recitals at the Wigmore Hall.

It was at Wigmore Hall that I often took my piano lessons with Ippollit Motchaloff, who continued to tutor me. I valued these times spent with him which nurtured my appreciation and love of music. Invariably, however, I was drawn back to my magnificent Royal Opera House with its great tradition and rich offerings. As well as the ballet, I adore the opera, which presents such a perfect synthesis of the arts – music, singing, dance, drama and design. It seemed very strange, however, to sit with Sven out front at the Garden watching my Company dancing and not being on stage myself.

For the premiere of her revival of *Coppélia* I was invited by Madam to join her in her box, which was a privilege. Alongside us were Mr Plucis and Ailne Phillips. I had not realised how clearly one saw everything happening on stage. I am certain that nothing ever escaped Madam's eagle eyes and that is what maintained the standard of her Company.

We dancers could sense her presence, overlooking the stage and all that was happening on it. There could be no slacking; we dreaded falling below her expectations and receiving a reprimand. For me there was always the wish to please, together with the fear of disappointing. Whilst in the Company I was always in awe of Madam, never feeling completely at ease. Those of us who witnessed her outbursts before the war were intimidated by her very presence, fearful of her mood changes and temper. She was very Irish, beautiful and mesmerising, strong willed and commanding, so that one both admired and feared her. I was not alone. Even one of her oldest leading members of the Company, Leslie Edwards, had the same feeling of awe.

During those months of waiting, Sven and I travelled around the country visiting friends. Whenever we stayed with my teacher Audrey de Vos at her retreat near Henley on Thames, we fell into deep discussions on art and dance. What an inspiring woman she was and what a wonderful help to me. As well as having danced herself she was also a keen sculptress, which explained her sharp eye for any body misplacements in her students. How fortunate I was to have found her for, together with Sven, she helped restore my strained, overworked body by her patient, loving guidance.

The sculptress Dora Gordine invited Sven and me to her home overlooking Richmond Park to meet her husband, Richard Hare, a titled MP. His quiet, very English gentlemanly manner was in complete contrast to her exuberant Russian temperament. Born in St Petersburg she grew up in Estonia, finding fame in Paris in the twenties. It was a surprise to discover that they had together designed their unique, eclectic house. Named Dorich House, a combination of their names, it provided a comfortable home, with studios, a gallery for sculpture and a study for literary work. They both took enormous pleasure in showing us their collection of Russian art, which was truly breathtaking, as was her suggestion that I sit for her.

This was a completely new experience for me, and I felt very flattered that she should wish to make a bust of me. I would arrive at 9.30am by when she would have finished cleaning the shining parquet floors, using a special electric machine. After donning a compulsory pair of soft shoes from the line-up of slippers kept for all visitors, we would go straight upstairs to her large, bright studio where she would begin work at once. She was an exciting personality – strong, forceful but kind – and I used to look forward to the hours spent with her each week. She was once described as the finest, feistiest female artist of her time, and it is such a joy to know she will go on 'living' through her work.

Perhaps the most novel experience for me came when I was already eight months pregnant. One of Sven's patients, Denise Fitzpatrick, repeatedly invited us to stay with her whenever she was at her house in Gstaad, Switzerland. So it was all arranged that Sven and I would fly out and stay with her for two weeks.

We had the most wondrous time in Gstaad, rarely reading newspapers or listening to the radio. As there was less snow than usual for February, the town was not crowded and remarkably peaceful. Some days the weather was glorious – blue skies with the sun shining so strongly that sitting high up in the mountains I got quite a tan. Sven and Denise skied every day while I sat in the sun sipping the most delicious hot chocolate.

They insisted I tried to skate, something I had never before contemplated. I went on the ice supported by Sven on one side and an instructor on the other. I have to admit to being very scared and out of kilter. To skate I needed to place my weight forward, the exact opposite to ballet where one is trained to stand very upright. I got over my initial nervousness, however, and skated almost every day following my handsome husband and friend Denise onto the ice, gingerly, after their inspiring exhibitions.

Once home again, life became busier than ever preparing for our new arrival. I even endeavoured to knit a little jacket, which sadly did not turn out at all well! Sven was once more busy looking after his patients in whom he took such interest and care. To our surprise he was approached to treat some of the Martha Graham dancers appearing at the Sadler's Wells theatre. One morning Pearl Lang, one of Graham's finest leading dancers, was waiting for treatment in our flat, and we had the most illuminating and wonderful talk together. She explained to me much of Graham's thoughts behind her ballets, not readily understood at first viewings. Having attended the company's first night and been thrilled by their performance, this was an added bonus. I could now comprehend and appreciate even more the ensuing performances I was to watch. I was also able to go backstage with Sven after performances to meet and talk with some of Martha Graham's other disciples, all outstanding dancers.

It was wonderful to witness the development of the opera at Covent Garden and the increased interest of its audiences, whilst the ballet was steadily building a most loyal and appreciative following. Sven and I also greatly enjoyed the brilliant performances of Antonio, the dynamic Spanish dancer, who so fired the London public's imagination. Antonio was sensational and the talk of London at that time. What an exciting era.

47 New Arrival

Before leaving for our Swiss holiday we had chosen, from quite a few interviewees, a Norland's Nurse who we believed would fit in well to our little household and be the perfect person to look after our baby. On our return, however, she was obliged reluctantly to cancel her agreement with us because of her uncertain health. There seemed to be no one else available at such short notice who we felt we would want in our home, looking after our newborn child.

Time was slipping by fast and we were feeling desperate when our good friend Margaret MacInnes came to our rescue. She knew of a first class nurse, unhappy in her present position who, if she could be persuaded to leave, would in her opinion be suitable. We met, and we liked her instantly. She was an elegant, slender woman with breeding, and showed at once an intelligent, firm yet loving approach to the welfare of babies and young children. She had served in several distinguished houses, with servants to wait on her, so I was a little fearful that our homely, modest flat would be too great a contrast. But she agreed to come when baby arrived and straightaway gave in her notice to her current employers. It was such a relief. Sven and I were now able to enjoy the remaining time together, confident that everything was falling into place.

Friends and acquaintances started to send me good wishes and little gifts for the baby, and it was becoming all very exciting. I couldn't help feeling, however, rather apprehensive about this hitherto unknown world of motherhood soon opening up before me; I knew nothing about caring for a baby.

To my delight there was also press interest and interviews, which was surprising coming so soon after Moira Shearer's recent confinement and the publicity that attracted. A friend kindly gave a lovely shower party for me at the Savoy to celebrate the awaited little stranger. Amongst my many friends there were Svetlana Beriosova and Margaret Dale who managed to come in-between rehearsals from just up the hill at the Garden. This was also reported by the press, which was encouraging as I was intent on continuing my career after the safe delivery of my baby. That was why it was so important to have someone who could be relied upon and totally trusted at home when I returned to the theatre.

One afternoon I went to visit one of my friends from the Company, Thekla Russell, who had recently had a baby. I hoped to learn some tips about basics – I wanted so much for Sven to be proud of me and was determined not to let him down when I became a mother. We were enjoying tea and cake when my first pains began.

As the contractions increased, Thekla summoned a taxi to take me home to Davis Street. Unfortunately there was the most dreadful traffic jam and we sat there not moving for a good five minutes. I became really worried, so leant forward and asked the driver if he could somehow get out of the hold-up, explaining that I was about to have a baby. That did the trick: I have never seen a driver react so fast and successfully – he managed to get out of all the solid, static traffic, turning left down towards Marylebone, right around the back streets to Marble Arch, and eventually to number 32 Davies Street. I do not know who was the most relieved, but it was certainly comforting to fall into Sven's strong, loving arms, home safely at 6.15pm.

He immediately rang Doctor Macleod, who said not to rush to hospital. It would be many hours before the baby arrived, and we were to have dinner before leaving. Meat was still rationed in 1954, and the pork roasting in the oven did not go to waste, although I preferred to eat only potatoes and cauliflower before gathering my things hastily together to leave with Sven. He rang Margaret MacInnes in the flat below, who instantly appeared with her cleaner, Mrs Costa, both bearing little bunches of heather for me. I felt so touched and encouraged.

Our other neighbour below, Miss Chapman, also came up and unexpectedly insisted on driving us to hospital herself, which – as it was raining – we very much appreciated. It seemed incredible that she would do this as she had complained about my singing in the bath and my playing castanets when practising my Spanish dancing, with its accompanying foot stamps. It is remarkable what a baby's imminent birth can achieve!

Once welcomed into the Lindo Wing at St Mary's Hospital about 8.30pm, things seemed to go very fast. I was given an enema, followed by a lovely hot bath, and within an hour was sitting down with Sven, writing my diary. But I began to feel rather weary so climbed into bed. The pains began to get stronger and my lower back ached terribly, which Sven was able to alleviate miraculously by making a gentle, specific adjustment to the sacroiliac followed by a gentle massage. Soon I was in the second stage being told to push, to push and to push harder, but it was much more painful than I expected. I squeezed Sven's hand very hard.

Miraculously, our baby son, Ingvar, arrived at 10.20pm without Macleod being present. He arrived a little later, astonished to find baby safely delivered, and immediately set about clearing the afterbirth. He was upset at having been absent, saying, 'but I left in the second interval missing the last part'. He had been watching the brilliant Spanish dancer Antonio, appearing at the Stoll Theatre in the Kingsway (now sadly torn down), who Sven and I had also enjoyed only a week before.

The happiest day of my life will always be my wedding day. The next most life-changing event was the birth of our son. This filled me with such joy but also with wonder at the miracle of nature and of life itself. Having a child puts a different perspective on life and changed my outlook considerably. I felt a different person, one with a clearer sense of purpose. Those months away from performing gave me time for reflection, as well as a brush with life outside the ballet. I realised I was very blessed – to have a son, a wonderful husband, and my dancing career still ahead.

After the long absence from performing I felt more keen and confident than before my confinement. After a month of maternity leave, dancers received no payment whatsoever as there was no agreement then in place for this event. I was more determined than ever to continue my career, but not at the expense of my dear husband and precious son. They were my real life. The theatre was a beautiful background in a world of make-believe.

Loving his work as he did, Sven understood the love I had for mine. We were able to continue in our careers whilst enjoying the love and companionship of a very real marriage. As long as Sven was content for me to continue dancing, I was happy. I was so fortunate that he respected my talent, was proud of what I achieved and encouraged me to pursue my career.

But where should that be? Margot still remained supreme in the Company, and I wondered for how much longer I should – indeed could – remain in the second eleven? I was feeling restless and contemplated leaving the Sadler's Wells Company to explore other fields. I had the support and understanding of a remarkably loving husband who cared deeply for my wellbeing and would, I knew, always give me support and advice.

48 *My Return To The Stage, 1954/55*

Within three weeks of my confinement, I began exercising again under Sven's supervision, slowly getting back into practice. I soon resumed lessons with Audrey de Vos, and it felt good to be in the studio once more under her careful eye. I was determined not to race back to the Garden to be seen in just a minor role but rather to slowly build up my strength in order to return to the Opera House on top form in a full-length classic. In the late autumn I readily accepted an invitation to dance *Swan Lake* in Helsinki with the resident ballet company at the Helsinki Opera House and their leading dancer, Klaus Salin. He was a powerfully built man who would have no trouble in supporting me if I tired in performance. All was well, rehearsals ran smoothly and our performances earned us high praise.

With the close proximity to Russia Soviet ballet exercised a strong influence on the Finns, so it was quite a responsibility to be the first British dancer to appear there since the war. The beautiful Bolshoi ballerina Tikhormirnova, moreover, had only recently danced Odette/ Odile in the same production there with tremendous success. The comparison, however, was very favourable, and the Sunday Times wrote that I had done much 'to redress the balance between East and West in this meeting place of competing cultural influences'. I fell in love with their beautiful Opera House, a replica on a smaller scale of Moscow's Bolshoi Theatre where three years later I was to appear. At that time I could never have envisaged so great an honour.

My return to Covent Garden in *Swan Lake* was finalised for the first day of the New Year, Saturday evening 1st January 1955. I was not given a stage call but rehearsed with my partner John Field at the Hammersmith Town Hall. During my absence there had been some interesting changes. The Lower Ballet School moved from Colet Gardens and was now housed at White Lodge in Richmond Park, releasing more space for the Upper

School in Colet Gardens. This also allowed the Company to rehearse there, which was of great benefit not only for the Company but also for senior students of the school, some of whom would be taking part in performances.

It took time for me to adjust to the change in venue after so long at the Hammersmith Town Hall where the spacious first floor dimensions were surprisingly suitable for large company classes and rehearsals. I think that John and I were probably the last dancers in the Company to ever work there. Whenever I pass the old Victorian building, still boldly surviving the changes at the busy Hammersmith intersection, it conjures up many precious memories.

How to describe that return to Covent Garden? I had thought about it for so long and was full of mounting excitement as well as apprehension and worry that I might not come up to expectations. For my arrival at the stage door my fans hung a red and gold banner reading 'WELCOME BACK'. I was stunned, but it gave me just the encouragement I needed. Later after the show they presented me with a small glass swan on a plinth, engraved 'BERYL GREY ON HER RETURN TO COVENT GARDEN Le Lac des Cygnes 1ST JANUARY 1955, FROM THE GALLERY'. No words can describe what this meant to me and still does. It is kept in a glass cabinet with other treasures and is possibly the most treasured of all.

From my dressing room, which looked out onto the street below, I heard Sven calling to me as I was making up. I unfastened the window to see him smiling up at me, wishing me good luck. It did so much to boost my confidence, and I joyously blew him a kiss. Now was the time to go on stage and warm up for what I prayed would be a good performance, and miraculously it became so.

From the moment I came on stage as Odette in Act II it is recorded in the Times newspaper that 'stalls, boxes and gallery thundered their welcome that evening'. To be so welcomed inspired my whole performance. As the final curtain came down, the most tremendous applause arose from around the house which did not cease until Madam, who came on stage and embraced me, pushed me forward to say a few words. This was exceptional as ballerinas are rarely if ever given permission to speak.

All I could say was 'thank you for not forgetting me' after having expressed my happiness at being back. I was showered with bunches of roses and anemones while 'anachronistic silver-wigged flunkies' heaved mountains of flowers on stage at my feet. Those floral tributes seemed to envelop me with love. What an unbelievable comeback, followed by a host of good reviews. Arnold Haskell finished his authoritative, detailed review with: 'It seems clear to me that in the mature Beryl Grey we have a classical ballerina at the beginning of a new and spectacular career.' And so it proved to be.

The spring season in 1955 was a busy one, soon engaged in numerous rehearsals for *Sylvia*, which Fred was reviving. Returning to the repertoire also were Madam's dramatic *Checkmate* and Balanchine's glorious *Ballet Imperial.* To my delight our music director engaged distinguished guest conductors – Anatole Fistoulari, Sir Adrian Boult, Sir Arthur Bliss and Malcolm Arnold – to conduct specific ballets. This did wonders for the orchestral players and served to inspire us dancers. In *Checkmate* Sir Arthur Bliss drew from the orchestra the most fascinating resonance and exciting tempi. Under his baton I know I gave some of my very best performances, for he observed carefully our rehearsals of *Checkmate*, all with Madam shouting out her corrections.

49 *Guest Invitations*

I was often asked to provide commentary for concerts, and the BBC engaged me also to give a series of broadcasts from Bush House, introducing ballet music to overseas listeners. I looked forward to, and thoroughly enjoyed, these sessions, as I was always treated with such respect and kindness. In fact, shortly after the war I did a lot of work with the BBC, from television to radio broadcasts, thus witnessing the rapid development of television in this country, from the early days at Alexandra Palace where I so often danced with John Field, to today's highly developed entertainment industry.

One of the perks of dancing at the Royal Opera House was that I had the opportunity of watching the opera in rehearsal and at performance. I adore opera and made the most of this chance when I could. Having danced in their very first opera production of *Carmen* in 1946 I felt a kind of bond and watched the company's progress with a certain pride. It was amazing to see how well some of the original chorus singers developed, like Geraint Evans, a baritone who became an international star and later received a knighthood.

On the 27th January Sven and I attended the premiere of Michael Tippett's new opera *Midsummer Marriage*. As the conductor John Prichard brought to life the three-act work, I recall sitting close by Tippett in the grand tier, his gaunt face appearing more strained than usual. What a great achievement to compose such an opera, and what emotions a composer must endure to watch the presentation of his creation. I never cease to wonder at the mystery of creative talent.

In March 1956 John and I were given permission to guest in Sweden again with the Royal Swedish Ballet. We led their fine company in *Sleeping Beauty* as well as in *Swan Lake*, slipping in to their productions remarkably easily, as Mary Skeaping's productions were fairly similar, but not exactly like, those we performed in London. One expects productions of the classics to differ from company to company depending on the tradition of the theatre as well as the taste of the artistic director. This adds to the interest and challenge of guesting abroad where not only tradition but also the director determines style and choreography.

Once more we were honoured by the presence of the King and Queen of Sweden and were again privileged to meet them during the second interval. Following that performance a farewell dinner was given in the Opera House for the retiring Artistic Director, at which we met Ingrid Bergman and her second husband Roberto Rossellini. To my surprise she was remarkably modest with a great amount of feminine charm, and it made my evening to have met with such a great film star, who was friendly and disarming.

Once back in London we had only two days before taking the train to Blackpool where John and I had been invited to appear in the Royal Command performance, dancing the Aurora pas de deux, solos and coda. This was a big honour and something quite new to us. I loved being amongst such a mixture of stars from the world of variety and being on stage with them in the finale, alongside the Crazy Gang and Brian Lucky, all of us singing '*There's no business like show business*' to the accompaniment of Jack Hylton's band.

Afterwards we all caught the sleeper from Blackpool Station at 3am, together with the Crazy Gang, who kept banging on the door of each compartment, waking everybody. So eventually I decided to get up and go to the dining car at the centre of the furore, which the Crazy Gang took over. What chaos they caused, but what fun we had until our arrival at Kings Cross Station, promptly on time at 8 o'clock in the morning, rather bleary-eyed.

By 12.30 that same day I was back working hard with de Vos, prior to a rehearsal with Ashton for *Sylvia,* my first performance in this new ballet scheduled a few days later. How I enjoyed that role, leaping to the exhilarating woodwind playing for Sylvia's first entrance. I never lost the thrill of performing Fred's choreography, which perfectly captured the character of Sylvia, the huntress. Margot had the first night, as expected, while Violetta Elvin and I were given the second and third performances.

Since my return at the start of the year I had been unhappy about the billing in the programmes: there were now four ballerinas listed under Margot, with Elvin's name preceding mine, followed by Rowena Jackson and then Nadia Nerina. As the season progressed I finally complained about this to Madam, who as always had a ready answer. 'This has nothing to do with position in the Company,' she explained, 'it was done alphabetically; you must realise that there are other dancers coming to the fore who have to be billed, and this was the fairest way to do it.' I tried to stammer 'length of service surely should count also' but was immediately shot down and told not to be silly but concentrate on my performances. I went away feeling more downcast than ever.

Unbelievably, at long last a ballet was to enter the repertoire in which I would take the first night lead: *Lady and the Fool.* The choreographer John Cranko revived his ballet for our Company, having successfully created it for the Sadler's Wells Theatre Company a year before, with Patricia Miller in the leading role. Now I had the inspiring experience of working with Cranko as he recreated the role of the Lady, La Capricciosa, on me, with Philip Chatfield as my partner.

What a joy it was rehearsing with Cranko. He just loved dance. His enthusiasm and great sense of fun made it a shared and much treasured time. How I loved working with him, exploring new lifts with Philip and playing out the touching mime scenes with the two clowns – Philip and Ray Powell as his companion. This comes at the opening of the ballet, when the Lady meets with two destitute clowns, Moondog and Bootface, falling in love with the taller of the two, despite the ardent attentions later of three affluent young men at a glamorous ball.

Cranko chose to use Verdi's music, which John Lanchberry arranged brilliantly, using excerpts from several of Verdi's lesser-known operas. Verdi's music is wonderfully inspiring, and the resulting score was perfect for dancing with its glorious melodies and compelling rhythms. I enjoyed every performance, finding it fantastically rousing. The love duet between the clown and the Lady is deeply emotional, whilst the finale with the entire cast truly thrilling.

During that time I was asked to introduce on television the beautiful Indian dancer, Shanta Rao, to whom Arnold Haskell had previously introduced me. He knew of my interest and love of Indian dance as well as my role, with Yehudi Menuhin, as vice-patrons of the Anglo-Indian Society. The rehearsal with Shanta Rao in the television studios began at 4 o'clock with the transmission starting at 9.30 in the evening. Everything ran smoothly at rehearsal with the time limit fully explained and understood by us both. But once Shanta Rao began her dance she became totally immersed in it and could not stop. The cameras switched away from us at the agreed moment, but it was as if she was in a trance. She went on dancing, oblivious to those all around her. Although I stayed on for a long time I finally had to depart, leaving her still dancing, lost in the hypnotic mystery of movement.

50 *To America Again, 1955*

A two-week London season preceded the Company's fourth (my third) American tour. This one was to be for fifteen weeks, to everyone's relief, with longer seasons in fewer cities.

I was terribly disappointed by the casting, however, and thought that once again I was not being given a fair exposure with all too few performances. I felt I was being pushed down. Even though the billing under Margot had been changed, putting me first, ahead of Elvin, there were now several ballerinas coming up, filling the ranks, also giving lead performances. An increased number of leading dancers emerging meant fewer performances for me.

The opera company were also increasing their number of weekly performances, causing a reduction in the number of ballet performances given at Covent Garden. It worked out that I was given only one full-length role a month, which – at the age of twenty eight – worried me very much. I was brought up performing every night, but now found myself getting terribly nervous with so few appearances in London. I wanted to dance, to give performances and have the opportunity to develop my roles. I even considered employing an agent to get me more guest engagements – I knew some of the dancers had agents, who also ensured personal publicity. The Covent Garden press office did not promote anyone other than Margot, and I believed my career was standing still.

After much heart-searching it seemed to me that the time had come to leave the Company and branch out on my own. I finally made up my mind to see Madam one Thursday morning and hand in my resignation. She refused to accept it, saying I would be making a great mistake, and that I must think it over and see her again at the beginning of the next week. She said she had plans to create a ballet for me, *Joan of Arc,* which would be a great role. With that carrot dangled I went off to discuss this with Sven.

On Monday I spoke with her again and eventually agreed to stay. I would see what changes, if any, might come out of those two, for me, awful meetings. I hoped that Madam now understood the frustration and disappointment I was enduring; my unhappiness had greatly increased over the last year. After Moira left I expected a more prominent status but Violetta Elvin had been promoted while my position remained the same.

With renewed optimism I left for America with the Company on the 5th September for our opening in New York on Sunday the 11th with *Sleeping Beauty*. Once again I was Margot's Lilac Fairy, a role with which I had become increasingly identified. Much as I loved the Lilac Fairy role, I naturally wanted to be seen also as Princess Aurora, but it wasn't until the third week of our five-week season that I had this opportunity. By then I had become so nervous about the Rose Adagio that this was noted by one critic who otherwise gave me a good review. During that long season I was given only three Auroras and three Swan Princesses. Small wonder I felt so depressed. Thank goodness I had my *Lady and the Fool* in which to shine.

After leaving New York and touring the US, we returned to New York for a week to film *Sleeping Beauty* for relay on television across the country. It was to be shot for NBC in colour and in comparatively short takes. We all looked forward to this immensely, and it turned out to be a riveting experience, particularly for me. As the Lilac Fairy I was on in every act! It was the first cast throughout, with Fonteyn and Somes leading the Company. As we were paid on a time basis, I benefitted financially – and I like to think artistically, too. We were told that the film was seen by thirty million viewers. It was the first time a full-length ballet had ever been televised, as well as being the Company's first exposure on American television.

I was glad to have this extra money as I was still poorly paid at the Opera House despite seeking interviews with first Webster, then Madam. Moira and I received £14 10 shillings a week for the first couple of years and, after struggling between the two directors for well over twelve months, had eventually been rewarded with a rise to £18 a week. When touring America my pay was much better and with money allocated also for food – a 'living allowance'. I tried to save as much of this as I could to take back home to England. This extra was a welcome bonus, and I hoped it would help to make up a little for those fifteen weeks away from my beloved Sven and little Ingvar.

Home in time for Christmas, surrounded by such joy and love. I was soon busy not only dancing but also being interviewed on BBC and at Bush House for their overseas programmes. New Year's Eve saw the Company reopen at the Garden with a triple bill in which I danced in *Les Sylphides*.

Following the exciting news that Margot had been made a Dame in the 1956 New Year's Honours, there was a party on stage after her performance of *Swan Lake* on the 2nd January, after which she invited some of us (my one and only visit) to her house, there to continue the celebrations.

A week later I flew to Helsinki to appear in both the *Sleeping Beauty* and *Swan Lake* and once again to dance with Klaus Salin. He was such a strong and sympathetic partner and a fine dancer. I felt relaxed and confident with him on stage, particularly in *Swan Lake* which we had performed two years earlier. I took much pleasure in our dancing together once more, as well as renewing my friendship with the delightful director and his wife.

A Midnight Gala was held at the Stoll Theatre a few days after my return from Finland. It was arranged as a tribute to the memory of Anna Pavlova, a legend and inspiration worldwide. Dancers from many companies across Europe took part, including some from Sadler's Wells. I was happy to find myself dancing in the beautiful *Les Sylphides* as my tribute to such a great artist.

Alicia Markova performed an intricate Spanish solo on full pointe with such grace and lightness, her high jumps seemingly effortless. She appeared hardly to touch the ground; what style and aplomb she brought to this solo. The other precious memory is of the orchestra playing Saint Saen's *Dying Swan* to a stage, empty save for a moving white spotlight, bringing Pavlova's quintessential interpretation of a dying swan to life again. It brought tears to my eyes. I somehow wish nobody else ever danced it.

A week of *Sleeping Beauty* celebrated the tenth anniversary of the reopening of the Royal Opera House. As in 1946, I was the first cast Lilac Fairy to Margot's Princess Aurora, but only third cast Princess Aurora. Obviously there had been little advancement for me over those ten years.

I decided now was the time to engage an established agent, Ian Hunter, who was recommended by John Steele, a good friend of ours and then press officer for the May Fair hotel. Ian was one of the top people at Boosey and Hawkes, and said that he would do his best for me in a rather limited field. I explained that I longed to dance abroad in opera houses with other companies, a ballerina in my own right and not in Margot's shadow, as all we ballerinas most certainly were at the Garden.

I continued to be engaged regularly by the BBC for radio and television broadcasts and went quite frequently to Lime Grove, the TV centre. I appeared that March in the same programme as Richard Attenborough who I found most considerate and gentlemanly. Earlier the same week I danced on TV's *Music for You*, a popular weekly programme, with the infallible Eric Robinson conducting the BBC Orchestra. We got on well, and he was a most considerate conductor under whose baton I never felt worried during the numerous times we worked together. The very next evening there was a Royal Gala at Covent Garden when, much to my delight, I was presented to the Royal Family after dancing the lead in *The Lady and the Fool.*

Despite my numerous engagements Sven and I managed to have a very happy home life, too. I met and dined with Sven's friends as he did with mine, enjoying much fun together. In particular we loved our visits to Caryl Brahms, the brilliant authoress of *A Bullet in the Ballet* and several other dance-linked novels, who was enormous fun. She was also quite a serious, deep-thinking person who one could not help but admire and adore.

Evenings spent in the company of Philip Richardson, editor of *The Dancing Times* magazine, further educated me in the history of my art. I greatly respected this tall, distinguished historian in whose home we were royally dined, spending many interesting hours with him. He had such a modest, dignified manner which it was hard to equate with the important contribution he had made to the founding and development of ballet and ballroom dancing in Great Britain. I was honoured to be counted amongst his friends and greatly valued the hours spent in his company.

Before March ended I was back at Lime Grove again to televise *Swan Lake* Act II with the Ballet Rambert, which in 1956 was still very much a classical ballet company. We were allocated Studio E, one of the larger studios, but even so were quite limited for space. Philip Chatfield had begun to partner me in the classics since John Field's imminent departure to run the Sadler's Well's touring company had been announced. This for Field was an interesting and important shift in his career.

It was the beginning of yet another partnership which truly blossomed, for Philip and I were well suited temperamentally. We were perfectly matched height-wise, breathing the music as one, which is something intangible but essential if a true partnership is to develop. Ours became a most happy and successful one. Philip was later to marry my best friend Rowena Jackson, and I was their matron of honour in February 1958. It was wonderful for me to see how Philip and Rowena's hard work and talent had put them now in the top stream of leading dancers at the Garden.

With the slight thaw in East-West relations in 1956, Britain welcomed the Soviet leaders, Krushchev and Bulganin, to London in April, and the visit included a Gala performance at Covent Garden. It was a triple bill programme: Margot danced the second act of *Swan Lake* which followed *Les Patineurs*, and then I danced in *The Lady and the Fool.* This ballet had at the last moment, inexplicably, replaced *Checkmate*. Perhaps *The Lady and the Fool* was thought more acceptable, highlighting to a certain extent the rise of the proletariat?

Immediately after the last curtain, Prime Minister Sir Anthony Eden brought the two leaders on stage to meet the dancers. When my turn came to be introduced, Krushchev was full of smiles, squeezing my hands warmly and through an interpreter expressed his enjoyment of my dancing. The more serious Bulganin was less exuberant but pressed a small bottle of perfume into my hands. The performance was obviously a success, and I went on to a dinner at the Swedish Embassy feeling unusually elated.

Krushchev announced that there was to be an exchange of companies – the Bolshoi appearing at the Garden in late summer and the Royal Ballet dancing in Moscow in the Autumn. We were all extremely excited at the thought of performing in the famous Bolshoi Theatre and very disappointed when, because of growing political tensions following the invasion of Hungary, our visit was later peremptorily cancelled. So the thaw, which did bring the incomparable Ulanova to London with the Bolshoi ballet, sadly soon froze again.

The London Palladium is the largest non-lyric theatre in London, and I was thrilled when asked to take part in a special midnight matinee to raise money for the Artists Benevolent Fund. I found it fascinating to be amongst individual entertainers, all very professional and extremely confident. It was highly enjoyable, and I was surprised at the ease with which one could communicate across the footlights to the audience at the Palladium. This theatre has a special atmosphere – even the dressing rooms feel alive with the spirits of great performers long since vanished.

Another Anniversary came around for the Royal to celebrate on Saturday May 5th. It was 25 years since the Sadler's Wells Ballet had been created and therefore an historic stage to have reached, crowned with unbelievable achievements in such a comparatively short time. It had become Britain's national company now residing at the Royal Opera House, Covent Garden.

To mark the occasion, Ashton created a special work titled *Birthday Offering*, set to a selection of Glazunov's romantic music, in which he gave solos to all six top ballerinas and their partners, led by the ubiquitous Margot Fonteyn and her partner Michael Somes. It was a joy dancing to such melodic, flowing rhythms, adorned in Levasseur's ravishing costumes with glittering necklaces to which the costumes were attached in a complicated manner. The ballet was so well received that it is still revived from time to time. It is interesting now to see other dancers tackling dances arranged specifically around the talents of Elvin, Nerina, Beriosova, Jackson, Fifield and me, and Chatfield, Blair, Grant, Ashbridge, Doyle and Shaw.

To be involved in a completely new ballet is food for a dancer – one always craves something created on oneself. To be a part of that process of creation is very special indeed: an unique experience to have Fred create a solo exploiting one's particular gifts. The creation of a ballet around so many different artists in the same work clearly displayed the genius of Ashton. The rehearsals, eventually joining up with the other participants, then working all together until the full stage rehearsal, were thrilling. Weaknesses and strengths were worked on up to the full orchestral call with every dancer on stage. Hearing the players warming up, trying out new passages from the score (unfamiliar sounds as yet to the dancer), and then the marriage of music and dance. What exhilaration, what a magical experience. How fortunate I am to be a dancer.

If only I had had more leading roles created for me. Margot was Fred's muse, so there is little hope that he would ever create a major role for me. I wondered if Madam would ever find time to choreograph again as she wished? I was getting restless despite frequent engagements on TV and radio, invitations to dance for ballet societies, clubs and other such events, including talks, which I took time to prepare in depth. Violetta decided to give up and retire, giving us a charming farewell party before the end of the season, and I felt very sad and somewhat isolated at her departure.

After a holiday I returned to rehearse a small group of dancers from the Company who I picked to perform for a week at the Tor and Torridge Festival. I had by now engaged Ian Hunter as my agent, and it was he who booked this week in early August. I received the necessary permission from the Garden, who offered no objection as it fell within the Company's rehearsal period. I found it rewarding to organise the programme, the pianist and the music, costumes and so on. The advance publicity, plus the travel and hotel arrangements, were handled by Ian Hunter.

We numbered eight altogether: six dancers, a pianist and a wardrobe mistress. We travelled by train to Exeter on the first Sunday in August, opening the next night with excerpts from the classics. We gave four performances – three evenings and a midweek matinee – travelling on to Barnstable on Thursday morning, where we gave three more evening shows and a Saturday matinee. I gave a class each day before our rehearsals, and it all went amazingly well. We thoroughly enjoyed our West of England venture which I named 'The Beryl Grey Ballet Group', a straightforward and truthful title! And, although I had no thought of it at the time, it gave me a taste of the directing and producing I would undertake at Festival Ballet many years later.

52 *Arrival Of The Bolshoi*

The Bolshoi company arrived in London for their opening night, Wednesday the 3rd October 1956. What interest and excitement their arrival brought. Ballet fans queued for three days and nights with their sixpenny stools, which only guaranteed a seat in the gallery. The excitement and curiosity was immense and the build-up tremendous.

No one could have envisaged the impact these Russian dancers were to make. Their dancing exceeded all expectations; London was spellbound and enraptured. Never had we seen such a display of talent, such superb dancing, with such breathtaking partnering by the men, whose technique went beyond anything we believed possible.

The Bolshoi opened with *Romeo and Juliet*, a three-act masterpiece, with music written by Prokoviev and choreography by Leonid Lavrovsky. Their leading ballerina, Galina Ulanova as Juliet, gave the most moving, utterly breathtaking performance which to this day stands out in my memory as the greatest interpretation I have ever had the good fortune to see. Already in her forties, the youthfulness and innocence she brought to the role were totally convincing – she danced fluently and acted with a most touching demeanor.

The company brought a galaxy of outstanding stars – Struchkova, Kondratieva, Fadeyechev, Timofeyova, Karelskya and Plisetskya, who was to become Russia's principal dancer when Ulanova retired from that exalted position in 1960. It was inspiring to see their *Swan Lake* and also *Giselle*, in which Ulanova gave an equally great performance in another of Larovsky's beautifully crafted productions. The company also presented *The Fountain of Bakchisarai*, an exotic ballet based on a poem by Pushkin and choreographed by Zakharoff in 1934 which showed to advantage the male dancers' high leaps and brilliant number of controlled turns, whilst the women's supple bodies produced staggering backbends and unbelievably high extensions.

We, the Wells Company, during the Bolshoi visit were playing two weeks at the Davis Theatre in Croydon. Those of us not always on stage were eager to stay in town to watch the Bolshoi. We were amazed and inspired by what we saw and just could not go often enough. We were generously invited to watch or join in their classes, which we did on the rare occasions our schedules permitted.

The disappointing news that our pending season in Russia was cancelled meant that our scenery and costumes – already en route to Leningrad – would have to be shipped back, at Covent Garden's expense, adding an unwelcome drain on finances. There was, however, the encouraging news of the Royal Charter bestowed upon our Company. Webster, informing us, said: 'In future you will hold the title of Royal Ballet together with the Royal Opera', news that elated all who were connected with the Opera House. But proud as I felt for our Company it did not change my position in it. Despite working conscientiously each day I began to feel dispirited and discouraged, seeing little point in remaining. Should I leave or just hang on, trying to find as many outside engagements as possible, I kept asking myself. But the decision to leave was really made for me.

53 *Striking Out On My Own, 1957*

Ian Hunter procured for me a ten-week engagement – dancing across South America and finishing in Mexico. This was a most prestigious tour and, on Friday the18th January, I went apprehensively to ask Madam for a leave of absence, having worked out that on average I was appearing only once every six weeks. She was in St Bartholomew's Hospital where I had a 4 o'clock appointment to see her.

We talked for some time but, as I feared, she said emphatically, 'No, I cannot possibly spare you for ten weeks,' to which I replied, 'Madam, I so want to do this marvellous tour.' But she would not change her mind or even suggest a compromise. Finally I said, 'Madam, I am very sorry but I want to accept this invitation even though, as you have explained, this means I will have to leave the Company. You must realise that I am terribly reluctant to do this.' Madam smiled wryly and kissed me, acknowledging the parting of our ways but expressing the hope that I would return to 'my home' periodically, to dance with the Company as a guest.

I went home with a melee of mixed emotions: upset to have had to cut the umbilical thread yet at the same time excited by the challenge lying ahead. But doubts began to assail me. Would I succeed? Sven was such a comfort at that time. Year by year my confidence had been gradually eroded and my thoughts of giving up altogether grew stronger day by day, but he encouraged me to continue my dancing, saying, 'My darling, try. Of course you can become a successful artist on your own now, but if you don't attempt this you will never know.'

It was while I was away dancing with Gerard Ohn in Brussels and Wiesbaden that the news of my imminent departure from the Royal was given out. This produced quite a flood of press observations which gave me fresh hope and confidence.

On the 6th February I went into a private clinic to have my appendix taken out. During the operation it was found that an ovary was entwined with the appendix which needed to be removed, too. This was the reason for the increasing pain I had suffered when dancing over the past years. I remember coming out of the anaesthetic, looking up and seeing the surgeon and Sven, standing there together. This was such a big comfort as I found I was in great pain, but all went well. A week later I was allowed home to recuperate and build up strength for my farewell performance at the Royal Opera House before venturing into unknown territory: a new world on my own.

I was soon back at the Garden, with Plucis rehearsing Philip and me in *Sylvia* and *Swan Lake*. I resumed my private lessons which Babs Philips occasionally gave a chosen few from time to time, while Tchernicheva continued to give classes to the Company which I rarely attended as I gained little from them. The press and media were now to show a definite interest in me. I found I was in demand on TV, being interviewed and photographed by various press and press organisations including South American and South African ones.

Ian Hunter also arranged an engagement for Oleg Briansky and me in South Africa and Rhodesia (as it was then named) to follow a fortnight after our return to England from the other Southern Continent. All tremendously exciting – although my conscience was beginning to trouble me about Ingvar. Should I leave him for such long periods, I asked myself. He knew me as a Mother who was sometimes there and sometimes away, but I always came back. Importantly, Sven was always around at some time in the day, and the loving au-pair, Gunilla, was ever present. I told myself that I had to wake up to the fact that I was a career girl and that I would be torn, inevitably, between career, home and my loved ones. Sven came into all these deliberations, and we made decisions together.

It was now up to me to decide what to do, when and for how long. Like me, Sven adored Ingvar and understood the tussle I had between home and career. He reminded me that I had put so much time, energy and hard work into my dancing that I could not now throw it away. Life had to be a compromise. Even so, how fortunate I was that my Sven was a mature, forward thinker and an understanding husband, else I might well have finished my career at that point.

54 *Leaving The Royal Ballet*

My final performance as a member of the Royal Ballet came on Wednesday the 18th April 1957, two days before Easter – almost sixteen years since I first stepped onto the New Theatre stage during the war, as a peasant girl in *Giselle* with the Sadler's Wells Company. How excited I was then, but this my last night at the Royal Opera House brought a very different kind of excitement with many conflicting emotions.

I put everything I could into my rendering of Odette / Odile, revelling in a new sense of freedom, untroubled by what the powers that be might think, but giving my all to my loyal public and devoted fans. At the end of the performance the stage filled with bouquets and baskets of flowers as more and more flowers and little posies came streaming down from the gallery amidst deafening applause. It was like a wonderful dream, especially when Madam pushed me forward to say a few words.

When I finally emerged at the stage door, where a large banner was hanging saying 'HAIL and FAREWELL', I was presented with a most beautiful silver tray from the gallery together with a magnificent glass swan on an ebony stand engraved 'BERYL GREY ON HER RESIGNATION FROM THE ROYAL BALLET, 18TH APRIL 1957', below which were inscribed the first names of nine of my most ardent supporters. What a touching, precious gift to be treasured for all time. As too is the tray, which is in constant use – an everlasting reminder of the overwhelming kindness of all those in the gallery who believed in me and helped shape my career.

The three weeks which followed that incredible evening were packed with preparation. As Sven was to accompany me to South America, at home Gunilla would have absolute responsibility for Ingvar, although I knew that Margaret MacInnes our close friend and neighbour in Claridge House would be popping in to keep her experienced eye on them and their activities. My father also would be calling in often to make a fuss of his grandson and check on his wellbeing. I was very fortunate in having a most reliable cleaner, Hettie, who came to us daily after cleaning Margaret's consulting rooms one floor below, and I knew I could rely on her diligence.

Much of my time was now spent rehearsing with Oleg under Audrey's guiding hand, and there was so much to think about. David Tidbold, a young, emerging conductor who had enjoyed a recent success with his Wigmore Hall recital, agreed to be my conductor and pianist for the South American tour. He was a lover of ballet, short in stature but not in temper. He was a most sympathetic and enthusiastic musician, someone I knew would come through all trials and tribulations unperturbed.

I had invited Oleg Briansky to be my partner. Tall, dark haired with a fine agile body he was extremely handsome. I admired his performances with the London Festival Ballet Company where his striking personality and strong technique gained him an enthusiastic following. Born in Belgium, his parents were both Russian, and Oleg retained the temperament and feeling for theatre which seems inherent in Russians. Moreover, he was known internationally, having successfully partnered several great ballerinas including Markova and Toumonova.

With de Vos we set about planning the repertoire, deciding upon excerpts from the classics for our concert recitals. This included the *Black Swan* pas de deux, the *Aurora* pas de deux, *Les Sylphides* and *Sylvia* – and of course the ever popular *Don Quixote*, without which no recital would somehow ever be complete!

On learning I was leaving the Company, John Cranko offered to create a romantic pas de deux on a Scottish theme for Oleg and me. He chose a Prelude by John Field on which we had such an exciting time working together, creating a little cameo, titled *Ecosse*. A designer patient of my husband, much in demand by the opera, offered to design our Scottish costumes. Oleg looked terrific in the gaily coloured kilt, and I loved my costume with its flowing ribbons and dainty skirt. Oleg had a favourite solo he wished to be included, a Chinese Ribbon dance to music by Khatchaturian, which was tricky but sensational.

De Vos had created a romantic solo, *Reverie* to the Liszt Prelude, Number Three for a television programme. I decided this had to be included in our repertoire, as well as another solo she had created for me. This was in a contemporary style on pointe set to Delius's haunting Irmeline which we titled *Ondine*, as it portrayed a mermaid torn between land and sea. One year later Ashton was to produce the three-act ballet *Ondine,* a perfect role for Margot in which he exploited her appealingly whimsical character through some beautiful free movements and which became one of her most memorable interpretations.

De Vos choreographed two more works for Oleg and me: an opening pas de deux, very formal and classical, befitting the majestic Handel *Water Music* to which it was set, and also a light-hearted number for us both, to a piece by Schubert. Our costumes were made by Mr Roth, who knew me well from Covent Garden but was now working freelance with an assistant in Soho. Slender, with an earnest gaunt face, he was a great perfectionist and no detail was too small to be left unfinished.

Not knowing if I could procure any suitable pointe shoes in the Southern hemisphere I ordered two hundred pairs from Victor Gamba, my regular shoe-maker. Dancers' feet differ considerably, and each one chooses a firm whose style is best for her, a shoe which fits the foot snugly and gives the necessary degree of support on pointe. There were several different firms: Porselli, who also sold the then famous Niccolini pointe shoes, lightweight with a long vamp, suitable for feet with high insteps (as I have) and which invariably need extra support; Freeds, with a wide choice of fairly lightweight shoes; and Gamba, whose reputation was for a strong shoe. I danced my way through all the types available and eventually settled with a splendid maker at Gamba who was able to make me exactly the strong, supple and light shoe I felt happy and confident to wear.

For my headdresses I went to Hugh Skillen just off the King's Road, Chelsea whose work for the Garden – particularly for Oliver Messel's *Sleeping Beauty* – I so greatly admired. His cherubic face was inevitably wreathed in smiles as he sketched his designs – a great artist and a lovely person. David Tidbold acquired all the music we chose – orchestral parts and piano scores. There were various props to be packed in large laundry baskets, together with makeup, tights, practice clothes and other necessities, including large lumps of rosin to help civilise the slippery surfaces we were bound to encounter. This was all to travel with us on the plane.

A week before we were due to leave, the Russian Embassy invited Sven and me to discuss the possibility of my dancing in Russia towards the end of the year. I was tremendously excited and could hardly believe what I was hearing. There had been some subtle feelers before, but now we were actually talking about roles I would dance: *Swan Lake* and *Giselle*, even perhaps at the Bolshoi in Moscow and the Kirov in Leningrad. I went away quite optimistic, hoping that it would all come to pass but realising it might never happen.

55 *Spreading My Wings – South America 1957*

Ian Hunter assured me that all the necessary travel arrangements to and across South and Central America had been arranged, including finances and all hotel bookings. It was agreed that Oleg's attractive wife Mireille and Sven would accompany us for the initial four weeks, to see us safely underway.

Sven and his secretary, Hazel Moutrie, planned his absence from his practice. Hazel was wonderful with Sven's patients, her warm brown eyes shining friendliness and confidence. She was also becoming a great help to me, checking the itinerary of the impending tour and all my boxes of costumes now arriving at Claridge House, while attending to a thousand-and-one queries before the day of departure, Wednesday 15th May.

We flew to Paris on Air France before boarding a Lufthansa plane flight number LH502 at 4pm, landing at Dakar in North Africa and then Pernambuco, also known as Recife, on the East Coast of Brazil. I reflected on Pavlova and her travels. In the twenties she would have landed by boat further north on this same coast in order to travel up the Amazon River to dance in Manaus with its classical European opera house, built in the 1880s for the entertainment of the rubber barons during the rubber boom, and nestled eerily amongst the jungle vegetation. I wondered how Pavlova survived the mosquitoes and all the other difficulties she must have encountered performing in such an isolated area and enchant such an unusual audience. What dedication, courage and determination she must have possessed to dance in the overwhelming heat and humidity.

At last we reached Montevideo, our destination. To my surprise and delight we were met by a large welcoming party, led by the second secretary at the British Embassy, the British Council representative, their wives and a grinning, well built Mr Uhlfelder, the business partner of Mr Frischer, our South American agent. A group of artists and young dancers were all eager to meet and welcome us to Uruguay whilst Lufthansa personnel presented me with a bouquet of flowers and served us drinks amidst a lot of noise and commotion. I felt overwhelmed and excited at this beginning of my new role as a freelance ballerina as we set off for our modern hotel. There were flowers in our room to brighten the unpacking, and it all seemed to augur well for the forthcoming tour.

I felt excited when Mr Uhlfelder took us to see the theatre where we were to give our first recitals and were met by its enthusiastic director. But I was somewhat taken aback to find it was in fact an Odeon cinema – although larger by far than our British ones. Everything actually worked out all right as it offered us plenty of space for dancing, with a cyclorama and simple black legs (wings) and good lighting equipment. I found it hard to work in the heat, but I was responsible for getting the show on and lighting it despite all the dust and humidity.

Oleg had to be reminded to appear in good time for the press conference planned by Mr Uhlfelder. As Ian Hunter's representative, we were expecting to see quite a lot of Uhlfelder over the coming weeks. We had two press conferences on our first day, one after rehearsals in the theatre and the other later at the hotel. We were bombarded with questions and flashbulbs but it was all rather enjoyable, with a lot of shared goodwill and broken English.

Monday 20th May saw our first performance of the tour, and I felt exceedingly nervous about all the quick changes. David was completely satisfied with the piano and played beautifully for us throughout, including his solo interludes when we were changing our costumes and getting our breath back between numbers. Despite our careful rehearsals the curtains went up and down at the wrong times and the lighting was completely wrong for Oleg's solo, which greatly annoyed him. The audience did not seem to notice the technical problems, and we felt they were in complete empathy with our dancing. I felt buoyant after my first experience of giving an entire evening's entertainment only with a partner.

I was very stiff the next day, however, and thankful to have Sven give me osteopathic treatment and a strong massage. His loving presence gave me the confidence I needed to run my own foreign tours. I welcomed the freedom to express myself in dance without the restrictions of Company directives.

The different programme on our second evening was better than the first and well received, after which we packed all our belongings before socialising at a convivial Anglo-Uruguay Society reception. During the party the theatre director asked if we would consider returning to give some more performances later on our tour, and we promised to try to fit this in. We felt we had also built up a good rapport at the local ballet school where we enjoyed giving two classes to enthusiastic young hopefuls.

A seaplane took us over the Rio de la Plata to land in Buenos Aires an hour later. I dimly remember feeling rather nervous, sick and ill as the journey became bumpier and bumpier, and I swore never to board a seaplane again! Waiting on the quayside were representatives from the British Embassy and the British Council, so I had to pull myself together pretty quickly.

We met Uhlfelder's colleague, Mr Wagner, a little man who accompanied us to our hotel to discuss finance. I was longing to see the famous Colon opera house, a beautiful theatre with a vast stage. We met an attentive staff before I proceeded with the lighting rehearsal, after which Oleg and I found a studio where we commenced our daily practice. A press conference was scheduled for 6pm in the theatre, but before this we received a nasty shock: the orchestra of the Colon was on strike, meaning we would only have piano accompaniment for our recitals.

This was terribly upsetting. I had dreamt of dancing in this great theatre, famed for its wonderful acoustics and rated as one of the five best orchestral venues in the world. We were all devastated, especially poor David, his aspiration of conducting the orchestra at the Colon shattered. The building had been erected in 1908 on the site of an earlier one constructed as long ago as 1857. Here we three were – exactly one hundred years later – faced with filling this enormous theatre without the inspiration of its orchestra. But we had no option: our performances were fully booked, and we would not condone any cancellation, as we made clear at our press conference.

Stepping out onto the stage of the Colon for the first time to rehearse, Oleg and I felt like tiny fishes in a huge bowl looking out into the glorious auditorium with its six glowing golden tiers. With only a piano to accompany us, we realised what a challenge dancing there was going to be. We needed a helping pair of eyes to place us correctly for our first ballet, so we asked Sven to act as ballet master. He was indispensable: strict and precise, the accuracy and care of the doctor coming to our help!

David thundered away on a fine grand piano trying hard to substitute for a full orchestra while Oleg and I were doing our best to engage and delight our audience. At the press conference I expressed my dismay at the musicians' strike with the optimistic hope that it might be called off at the last minute, but unfortunately it was not, a sad fact picked up by the critics who remarked on 'the lack of orchestral support for the two inspiring dancers alone on the empty stage,' though they praised David's 'heroic playing.' It was a disappointing and worrying start to our Argentinian visit. The orchestra had not settled its grievances even by the time we left. We were cheered when the director asked if we would return on our way back from Chile to Uruguay to appear once more at the Colon.

We arrived in Santiago at 1 o'clock local time to be met by charming, 'very English' officials from the British Embassy and British Council and driven in the pouring rain to a fine hotel. We lunched and rested before being taken to the Opera House: we were to take part in its centenary celebrations. A radio interview took longer than expected so we were half an hour late for a press conference, which did not go as well as our previous interviews in South America. Some awkward questions were thrown at us by two tricky English reporters, but the rest of the press were friendly, especially the photographers. To my surprise Oleg was able to speak a little Spanish, which helped break the tension considerably in what turned out to be a two-hour session.

Next morning we were driven to Vina del Mar. We stopped for lunch at an attractive hacienda and, whilst waiting on a vine-covered terrace for our meal, Oleg and I began to practice the Schumann piece with David humming the music, much to the amusement of the restaurant owners. At our destination, we were met by yet another friendly British Council man who took us to the University which, in 1957, was the largest in South America. Their theatre seated 1,200, but the stage, though wide, had little depth. Disappointingly, their lighting technician failed to appear, but there were other willing hands to help with unpacking our costumes and props.

It was a lovely sunny day in Vina del Mar when I was called at 10.30am to do the lighting with an experienced man specially sent from Santiago. I only had to tell him everything I wanted and left, entrusting him to arrange it all, while I rehearsed with Oleg and then sorted out all my ballet shoes – quite a long job. The audience that evening was mostly made up of enthusiastic students who mobbed us afterwards and presented me with some colourful flowers. We returned to our hotel for food and a good night's sleep, before travelling back next morning to the capital, Santiago.

Early that afternoon we were disappointed to find Santiago shrouded in mist and the snowcapped mountains, which form such an imposing background to the capital, lost to view. We were shocked to find the theatre ice cold. The re-opening of the opera house was to be celebrated with a gala where we were to perform with their ballet company but, being South America, the restoration was not complete.

We rehearsed in a good-sized rehearsal room in the theatre: David with their orchestra, Oleg and I with the company. We were allotted two days of rehearsals and discovered the dancers well trained, professional and friendly. On the opening night we found ourselves looking up at the sky from our dressing rooms through the unfinished roof. It was winter, and an electric heater was placed in our chilly quarters. As the Gala progressed, the cold night air began to permeate our rooms, making it essential to exercise immediately prior to resuming our performances after the two forty-minute intervals. Oleg, after the second interval, foolishly went on stage insufficiently warmed up and in consequence pulled a muscle in his calf while dancing. Although he had it treated next day, the injury continued to plague him for the rest of our tour.

The performance was a big success. The South American public was always wonderfully responsive, and we had many joyous hours in cafés watching their spontaneous explosions into song and dance in which we were almost always encouraged to participate.

Despite the cold, I enjoyed dancing in Santiago as the ballet company was enthusiastic and good. This was not surprising as they had competition from a strong modern dance company also based there. It had been founded by the German dancer and choreographer Ernst Uthoff and included several leading dancers from the former Kurt Jooss company. I saw them perform at Hammersmith during the war and was fascinated to see Laban's influence on their style. The two works I most enjoyed were *Big City* and his much acclaimed *The Green Table*, both created in 1932, one year before Nazi pressures forced Jooss to leave his homeland and take up residence in England. *The Green Table* can still be seen and appreciated by audiences today with its prophetic message.

The Jooss company split up at the end of the war, a number of dancers remaining in Chile following a season there. Sven saw a performance of the company's *Carmina Burana*, which greatly impressed him. I was delighted when Ernst Uthoff and his wife Lola Botka invited us for a meal at which we met several of the company, including the well known Hans Zulich. I only wish I had been able to see them perform but my timetable did not allow it.

I needed a replacement for my red *Don Quixote* fan, broken in performance, but found the shops so poorly stocked I couldn't even find a pair of stockings. A Swedish school friend of Sven's, Erna, now living in Santiago solved the problem by finding not one but two fans: a strong one for performance and a gorgeous, large white lace and ivory one, presented in an ivory box.

Oleg and I were scheduled to give two recitals in Concepción in their University theatre. On landing, we were astonished to find much of the city in ruins. The west coast of Chile is subject to earthquakes, and one had hit Concepción the previous week. Many of the concrete roads were sticking up in the air, split in two, with a number of buildings demolished. It was a horrific sight with rubble everywhere, yet the people accept earthquakes as a natural phenomenon and life appeared to be going on, including our performances. The theatre, miraculously, remained intact as its director informed us over our lunch together.

It was on June 7th during our second programme that I had to give an encore. It was the first time this ever happened to me, and I was overwhelmed. It made up for the disappointing lighting due to the slow, manual changes, though the staff did their best. After the show there was a farewell sit-down dinner, with haunting music and passionate singing, which continued into the early hours of the morning revealing the musicality and fantastic energy of the Chilean people. It was a wrench to leave such special people and return to Santiago.

For our last performance in Chile on the 9th June we danced with their ballet company in both *Swan Lake* and *Les Sylphides* as well as giving the *Don Quixote* pas de deux. After this, our final show, many people crowded into our dressing rooms to thank us and wish us well, including the Ambassador's wife, Lady Empson. She brought a group of cheerful Americans who all wanted autographs, so it took some time before we could commence our packing and make our way to a dinner party specially laid on for us at the Chilean Place Municipality. There we enjoyed singing and dancing to the compelling rhythms and intoxicating sounds of their instruments, which included lute-like guitars called charangos, pan-pipes and a variety of flutes. It was an evocative experience, like so many other wonderful occasions in that colourful country.

The fascinating feature of Santiago is the proximity of mountains and sea shore depending whether one is going east or west, both reached within a half hour's drive. This particular afternoon we drove to the mountains, where we were privileged to meet David Montgomery, son of the famous 'Monty', Lord Montgomery of Alamein. David was utterly charming and a first-rate host who invited us for tea in his hideaway high up in the mountains. Showing some of his father's fortitude, he insisted on driving Sven and me to the highest point of the mountains on snow-covered roads which we both found quite terrifying, although the view was breathtaking. From his chalet we were able to appreciate the most glorious sunset before setting off in convoy back to Santiago. The convoy was just as well – the car Sven and I were in managed to slide into a snowdrift, despite the brilliant moonlight, much to everyone's amusement. Fortunately David and his friends in the other two jeeps were able to pull us out unharmed. We arrived safely back in time for a large party for over two hundred people, given by the British Council, after which a champagne dinner had been arranged at midnight to celebrate my 30th birthday. There were candles and cake as many people came to wish me well, including critics, musicians and the whole host of friends we had made during our time in Chile.

Before leaving for the airport I was presented with a lovely ceramic vase and a bouquet of flowers. The vase somehow survived the rest of the tour and journey home and is sitting on my table as I write – a reminder of the attention and help I received from the British Council throughout that challenging ten-week tour of South and Central America. I was also given stacks of photos to sign, which I managed to complete over a breakfast of champagne, which came with the compliments of the hotel manager. At the airport we were given a rousing farewell before enjoying an excellent flight to Buenos Aires. We made the most of our last view of the Andes, ice crowning their peaks glittering like diamonds.

57 *Return To Buenos Aires*

Once back in Buenos Aires on the 11th June for our final performances, I realised with a sinking heart that Sven would be flying home in just four days' time. His four weeks with me in South America had gone by so quickly, and I knew I would miss him terribly. I would also miss his treatments which had helped me, this far, to dance really well. I was strengthened by his very presence, inspired by his patient love. He had seen me recognised as an artist in my own right at last, capable of taking care of myself, managing to cope despite all the problems that never ceased to emerge. Moreover, he saw that David, Oleg, Mireille and I got on well together and that he could leave us with every confidence.

The dreaded Thursday came but Sven's departure for the airport at two o'clock was thankfully somehow softened: the rest of us were concerned with catching a train to Rosario an hour later, so there was no time to brood. I had been prevailed upon to squeeze in a recital for the Music Society in Rosario, a port on the river Ibicuy where, after a five-hour journey with our all-important paraphernalia, we arrived late in the evening.

I was surprised to see Uhlfelder present for our afternoon run-through next day in the theatre, but to my annoyance there was no sign of a lighting technician. I fumed at Uhlfelder for not having arranged this, nor having any photos placed around the premises. He had also failed to book dressers for Oleg and me – so necessary with all our quick changes. He had, moreover, muddled up the press conference so that two reporters arrived an hour early and just a few about an hour or so later; no one was sure of the correct time.

Poor David, meanwhile, was also annoyed with Uhlfelder, having found the piano badly out of tune that afternoon. He was told it would be put into perfect condition by the next morning. Next day in the theatre for our warm-up, however, the piano tuner had still not materialised, nor was he there later that afternoon. David was assured nevertheless that the tuner would most certainly arrive before the show. Needless to say 9.30pm came and went, and we found ourselves dancing happily on a good-sized stage to an out-of-tune piano in an enormous hall, packed with enthusiastic music lovers.

The evening had been due to commence at 9.30pm but the curtain did not rise until 10.15pm. Despite this late start our performance turned out to be a huge success. Next morning, laden with presents and flowers at the railway station, our attention was called to a radiant official who came dashing up to David to tell him that the piano tuner had arrived and was tuning the piano at that very moment. It was then that I began to fully appreciate the word 'mañana'!

The British Embassy gave a cocktail party in my honour on our return to the capital. Three hundred and fifty smartly dressed guests were received by the Ambassador and me at the top of a grand staircase, before the party entered the beautifully decorated ballroom. After two hours my right hand felt as if it might fall off.

Oleg and I had a long photo session with the capital's famous photographer Anne Marie Heinrich. She was extremely professional, exceptionally well organised and totally unrushed, which resulted in many excellent photos of Oleg and me, alone and together. More press and radio interviews were lined up for our return, and we were pleased by the ongoing interest.

Our last performance at the Colon was a happy one. Because of the huge gap between the extremely wealthy and terribly poor people of Buenos Aires, I was keen to give a recital for the needy children of the city before we departed. I managed to persuade the stagehands at the Colon to give their services free for a charity performance, and we were given permission to go ahead. It was a most wonderful afternoon – the theatre packed, every box overflowing, with hundreds of well behaved, neatly attired children of all ages, sitting transfixed by our dancing. By the end of the show, the applause that broke out was deafening and went on for a long, long time, which pulled at our heart-strings. Everyone in the theatre was so happy and enthusiastic. It was the only theatre in South America we had so far encountered where the curtain was raised punctually at the advertised time. The staff, clad in immaculate white linen coats, were warmhearted and considerate, in particular my dresser. Everybody expressed their sadness when the time came for us to leave. The children's matinee was the most evocative finish to our time in the Argentine.

It was just a short return flight that evening to Montevideo where we were upset that neither Uhlfelder nor Frischer was to be seen, nor any of their deputies, so we were left to pay the excess baggage ourselves. Several of our friends were waiting patiently to welcome us back and to warn us of the riots that were taking place. Fortunately we were able to avoid them during the few days there, and the theatre was not touched. From my hotel bedroom window that evening I watched the police confronting the student rioters, both sides convinced of their rights. I spent a fitful night pondering the complexity of social behaviour.

I was invited next day to watch a performance by the internationally famous French actor and mime, Marcel Marceau, at the Solice Theatre. His rendering of Bip the Clown was touching, and it was fascinating to see how much he could portray without speaking one word. It must have taken many years of concentrated practice to have reached such perfection. Four years older than me, he had managed somehow to survive the awful Nazi occupation and succeeded in rescuing many Jewish children during the war. I knew I was most fortunate to meet such a superb artist and fine person. In 2001 he became the 11th recipient of the Wallenberg Medal, awarded for humanitarian acts of courage during World War II.

It felt good to be back in Montevideo, in the lovely, 100-year-old Solice Theatre, where I was warmly welcomed. I was, however, totally unprepared for the invitation I was to receive from the director. He wished me to consider becoming the artistic director of their ballet company. I felt immensely flattered but it was out of the question: I could not accept such an invitation at this stage of my career.

58 Brazil, June 1957, And Central America Travel Troubles

We landed in Sao Paulo, Brazil in the last week of June. Press and dancers welcomed us with glorious flowers. Not for the first time, a tiresome scene with Uhlfelder unfolded over a dreadful muddle about dates, and I was again vexed by the inefficiency of our agents. To our dismay he admitted that we were not to

Top Left: With my Mother (©UNKNOWN); *Top Right:* Shanklin – Isle of Wight with parents – early 1933 (©UNKNOWN); *Bottom Left:* First Tutu age 5, 1932 (©UNKNOWN); *Bottom Right:* Spanish solo with castanets, 1938 (©UNKNOWN)

Top Left: My first dance teacher, Madeleine Sharp (©UNKNOWN); *Top Right:* Spanish dance teacher, Elsa Brunellschi, 1937 (©UNKNOWN); *Bottom:* First time en pointe age 9, 1936 (©UNKNOWN)

Top: Presenting bouquet to Queen Elizabeth at Sadler's Wells Theatre at the English premiere of Dame Ninette de Valois's ballet *Checkmate*, 1938 (©WORLDWIDE PHOTOS); *Bottom Left:* En pointe (©TOPFOTO/ARENAPAL); *Bottom:* Practising in the garden (PHOTOGRAPHED BY GBL. WILSON © ROYAL ACADEMY OF DANCE/ARENAPAL)

As Duessa in *The Quest*, choreographer Frederick Ashton, 1943 (©GORDON ANTHONY/VICTORIA AND ALBERT MUSEUM, LONDON)

Top: With Mary Skeaping, far left, and Harijs Plucis, far right (©NATIONAL FILM BOARD OF CANADA);
Bottom: One of many visits to the wounded in hospitals (©UNKNOWN)

Top Left and Right: The Lilac Fairy, 1946 – a role I danced frequently from 1942 (©UNKNOWN);
Bottom Left and Right: Princess Aurora (LEFT: ©VIVIENNE; RIGHT: ©UNKNOWN)

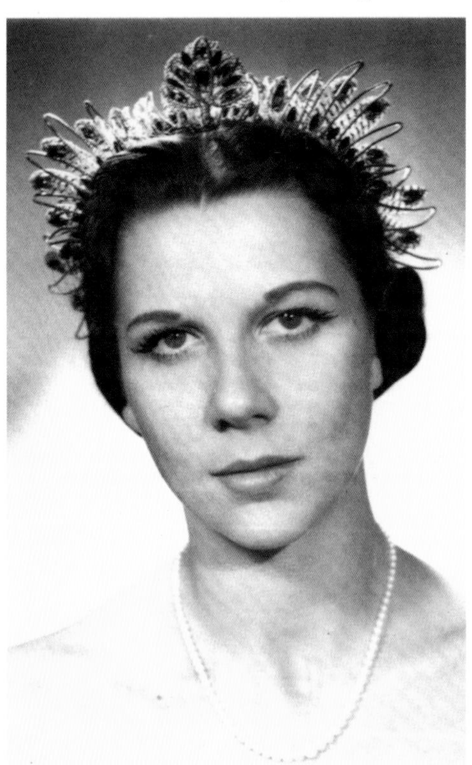

Top Left: As Death in Massine's *Donald of the Burthens* with Alexander Grant, 1951 (©UNKNOWN); *Top Right:* As Giselle, Buenos Aires, 1944 (©ANNEMARIE HEINRICH); *Bottom:* Royal Opera House Stockholm 1953 with John Field in mirror. Mary Skeaping on bench. Also seated, Sven (©MERKEL RYDBERG)

Top: From left to right, Dame Margot Fonteyn, Svetlana Beriosova, me in class (©TED STRESHINSKY); *Bottom Left:* with Charlie Chaplin (©ASSOCIATED PRESS); *Bottom Right:* Sadler's Wells first visit to New York, 1949 (©UNKNOWN)

Top Left: Swan Lake Act III with John Field (©CARL PERUTZ); *Top Right: Swan Lake* Act II (©HOUSTON ROGERS/VICTORIA AND ALBERT MUSEUM, LONDON); *Bottom: Swan Lake* Act II as Odette; John Field as Prince Siegfried; Bryan Ashbridge as Von Rothbart; Sadler's Wells Ballet at the Royal Opera House, Covent Garden, London, 1950 (©ROGER WOOD/ROYAL OPERA HOUSE/ARENAPAL)

Top Left: Swan Lake Act III with Yuri Kondratov (©S.G. SVENSON); *Top Right:* Princess Aurora with Caj Selling, Covent Garden, 1959 (©HOUSTON ROGERS/VICTORIA AND ALBERT MUSEUM, LONDON); *Bottom Left:* With Bryan Ashbridge, 1966 (©HOUSTON ROGERS/VICTORIA AND ALBERT MUSEUM, LONDON); *Bottom Right: Swan Lake* Act III with Gerard Ohn (©ZOË DOMINIC)

Top Left: Discussing *Checkmate* for BBC Television, July, 1963, with Robert Helpmann and Dame Ninette de Valois (Choreographer) (©ROYAL ACADEMY OF DANCE/ARENAPAL); *Top Right: Checkmate* with Ian Hamilton (©ROYAL ACADEMY OF DANCE/ARENAPAL); *Bottom: Checkmate,* with Philip Chatfield and Ronald Hynd, Covent Garden, 1948 (©FRANK SHARMAN/ROYAL OPERA HOUSE/ARENAPAL)

Top: 1956 Bulganin, Khrushchev and Sir Anthony Eden after the Covent Garden performance of *Lady and the Fool*, Covent Garden (©ASSOCIATED PRESS); *Bottom:* My farewell performance as a member of the Royal Ballet, on stage at Covent Garden, 1957 (©S.G. SVENSON)

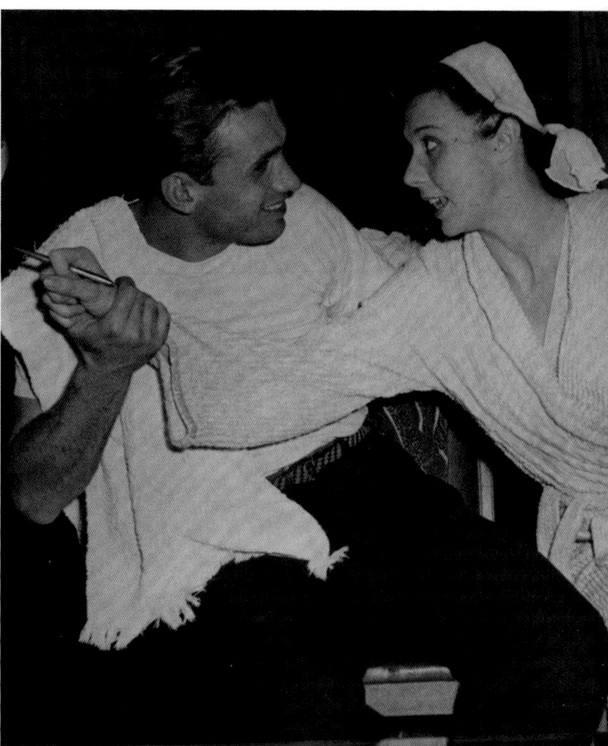

Top Left: Outside the Bolshoi, 1957 (©S.G. SVENSON); *Top Right:* With Yuri Kondratov, my partner in Russia 1957 / 58; (©S.G. SVENSON); *Bottom:* Asaf Messerer giving class to the Bolshoi dancers and me (©S.G. SVENSON)

Top: With Chinese dancer in the Theatre of Heavenly Bridges, 1964; (©S.G. SVENSON); *Bottom Left:* With Wang Shao Pen in *Swan Lake* (©S.G. SVENSON); *Bottom Right:* With Shanghai School of Dance (©S.G. SVENSON)

Top Left: The Queen with Svetlana Berisova, Anya Linden and me (©UNKNOWN); *Top Right:* The three Sylvias, Violetta Elvin, Dame Margot Fonteyn and me (PHOTOGRAPH BY GEORGE VARJAS ©REFLEX); *Bottom Left:* Dame Ninette de Valois backstage at the Rome Opera House (©UNKNOWN); *Bottom Right:* Princess Grace of Monaco and Lady Irene Astor after the Sunshine Gala Matinee at Drury Lane, 1965 (©UNKNOWN)

Top Left: Wedding Day, Weybridge, July 1950 (©R. SVENSON); *Top Right:* Ingvar with Sven and me 1958 (©VIVIENNE); *Bottom:* On holiday in Sweden with Ingvar 1964 (©UNKNOWN); *Bottom Right:* Sven and me feted in China (©UNKNOWN)

appear in Rio as agreed because of conflicting plane bookings for our two performances in Recife.

To placate us, however, he arranged for us to appear on television in Sao Paulo with their ballet company in *Swan Lake.* This would be our first opportunity to dance in a South American television studio, and we were keen to see their set up. It proved to be nothing out of the ordinary and, despite a certain unhurried approach combined with vague camera work, everything proceeded surprisingly well. The setting was beautiful with plenty of space for dancing amidst the sorrowing swans of the second act of *Swan Lake.* Despite rehearsals having commenced half an hour late, ample rehearsal time was accorded us before the transmission, which we were told was well received.

We found ourselves comfortably entertained during our week's stay in Sao Paulo and particularly enjoyed our time with the small ballet company, which was remarkably good. David was also very satisfied with the orchestra. Oleg and I, however, were less pleased with the theatre, which we found rather cold, the stage cramped and with little wing space. Moreover, there were no dressers for our quick changes, which made me nervous. Miraculously, things went splendidly, and we were given a terrific reception for all our numbers. Afterwards at a party thrown for us at a big popular club I was given a flow of Portuguese '*hurrahs*', all most thrilling.

Our tour became even more complicated due in part to the appalling mix-up of performance dates and travel bookings. Our two agents were generally to be found in Buenos Aires, and we were now bound for Central America where they had representatives who we were advised to contact if need be! Infuriatingly our Central American agent, Wagner, had not turned up as agreed in Sao Paulo, and we were beginning to feel very much on our own. The intricate flight schedules meant David and I spent almost two hours at a travel bureau trying to work out and book three seats to Guatemala. We also needed to see if we could fly from Recife to Rio for one performance the forthcoming Friday, as the director of the Municipal Ballet there insisted that we appear.. To our disappointment it proved impossible because of the complex plane connections and bookings already in place for our later recitals in Central America.

After a mere three hours sleep following our last performance in Sao Paulo we boarded an early morning plane. The flight was delayed owing to a Braniff airline cancellation; we did not arrive in Recife until 6pm and were expected to give a recital at 9pm. With only a smattering of English spoken by anyone at the airport and with no agent present, there was all our luggage and music to be collected and paid for. We deposited our suitcases at the hotel en route before heading to the theatre. Even so it was 7.15pm before we arrived amidst the most tremendous heat.

Multi-tasking, I immediately unpacked the costumes for ironing, changed into my practice clothes and commenced lighting the stage with a helpful technician who then watched fascinated as Oleg and I did our barre work and a minimal rehearsal. The stage was unpleasantly raked and not very big, our dressing rooms airless, cramped and infested by mosquitoes. Yet somehow we were ready to perform almost on time, our make-up melting on our faces. The audience seemed strangely unreceptive but, by the end of the show, appeared to have come to life and showed their appreciation by clapping earnestly.

After the performance we realised that we had not eaten properly all day and now at midnight felt ravenous. To our dismay we could find nowhere open. A kind ballet enthusiast offered to give us a light snack in his tiny flat before helping us find our hotel. We had not bargained for the endless noise coming from the airless, mosquito-infested hotel itself and the streets below, which seemed to increase as the night progressed. We got little sleep.

At 7am I knocked despairingly at David's door asking him to accompany me to the local travel bureau. Like me he was wide awake and equally concerned about our itinerary, which remained unconfirmed for the rest of our tour. We were shaken to find there was no plane via Belize to Honduras as we had been promised. Our only option was not to fly north as expected, but south – back again to Rio. Worryingly, there was no guarantee of acquiring ongoing reservations from there. Very perturbed, we realised there was nothing further we could organise from Recife and that we had to wait until we were in Rio before any further bookings could be made. So we retreated to our hotel, hoping in vain for a good sleep before our second programme that evening. But it seemed that the people of Recife never slept, so neither could we.

At our second show, once again, the audience appeared apathetic amidst the stifling heat, but at the end roused themselves to applaud warmly. We were promised a lift back to our hotel and, still dripping with perspiration, we had to pack everything as quickly as we could. To our surprise we found food laid on in our rooms despite all the heat – just as well as the coming day was a manic one.

On arriving at Recife airport early next morning we were devastated to find our baggage from the theatre had not arrived. No one spoke English, the phone lines were out of order, there was nobody to see us off and the plane was about to leave. Witnessing our distress, a man with only limited English offered to help, promising to see all our theatre baggage safely on board the next plane to Rio. Due to bad weather our flight landed late in Rio but was followed shortly afterwards by the plane carrying our precious theatre equipment. We were overwhelmingly relieved that our saviour had been able to keep his promise and truly heartened by his act of kindness.

It was no surprise that the new agent, Frischer, was not around to pay the excess on all our theatrical paraphernalia nor to escort us to a hotel. We were left to find one for ourselves, and once installed David and I went off in search of a reliable travel firm. To our consternation it appeared there was little chance of passages to Honduras as everything was booked. After several hours of haggling – and with a financial goodwill gesture – three bookings were miraculously put in place. Although David and I stayed up until midnight anxiously awaiting final confirmation by telephone, it never came, and we understood why next day.

We were back at the travel bureau at 8am to find that no seats were booked. So we started all over again, finally managing – after hours of wrangling and another financial enticement – to obtain two first class and one second class ticket. Back at the hotel we were relieved to find the British Council representative, with his wife and secretary, waiting to help us in the absence of our agent. Our theatre luggage had gone astray but was eventually traced to another airport. We stayed just one night in Rio with little time to admire Sugar Loaf mountain and the gigantic figure of Christ, nor to enjoy the Copacabana beach.

Just before boarding the overnight flight to Caracas we were overjoyed to be reunited with our luggage. The plane fortuitously was delayed by one and a half hours, and so all our luggage travelled safely with us. Landing at Caracas at 10.15am we had only 15 minutes in which to catch another plane for Panama. To our immense relief, the flight was held for us, so we just made it, luggage and all. I tried to sleep a little before landing safely around 4pm in Panama, the strange land bridge between North and South America. Exhausted as we felt, none of us was able to sleep in the sticky heat and humidity of Panama, even in air-conditioned rooms. The smart hotel in which we found ourselves had been built on posts, to allow air to circulate below and around the building – but you could have fooled me!

Thankfully it was only a short night as our next flight left Panama City at 6.30 in the morning, en route for the capital of Honduras – Tegucigalpa. This was our first time in a small plane, and to our consternation it appeared to be flying extremely low. We then realised that this was not meant to scare us but to allow us to enjoy the landscape of undulating hills as we left the uncomfortable climate of Panama. We flew northwest across Costa Rica, on over Nicaragua, where the hills were higher. We had a wonderful, birds-eye view of the far less known, unexplored West Indies, separated by the Caribbean Sea from the host of popular islands to the east of the Caribbean.

After seven hours, we flew in on a rather short runway, disembarking at the modest little airport for Tegucigalpa, to be greeted warmly by the British Consul, Mr Jackson, a good looking man, and his equally attractive wife. Another man in some way connected with music, who I presumed to be our agent, was there to meet us too and pay our excess, so our luggage was released. We were relieved to hear that because of our delayed arrival, our performance that evening was postponed until tomorrow (Tuesday) and the second performance switched to Wednesday. It was hoped we would not mind this change in schedule. Mind! We could not have been more thankful and did our best to show our appreciation for their forethought. En route to our hotel Mr Jackson pointed out the theatre, where our scheduled performances were already provoking enormous interest.

Exhausted by the heat, we were relieved to find a good hotel with an unusual central atrium. I found my room opened out onto a sun-roof, revealing a dramatic view of hills and mountains. Mr Jackson had arranged an informal dinner party at his home but we explained that first we needed a rest before going to the theatre to unpack, exercise and try out the stage. He collected us for the theatre, and later took us for a relaxed evening at his home. Next day, refreshed and revitalised, I sorted out the lighting at the theatre. The ambient heat was helpful in exercising and rehearsing for our opening. The stage was small but had excellent surface and wing space, enabling us to enjoy dancing for a wildly enthusiastic audience. This despite wrenching my left foot during my fouettés, on a tiny patch of water sprinkled on the stage in place of rosin. There was no real damage, and after tending it carefully during the interval I was able to continue without too much pain.

On waking early the next morning I thought I must be going mad. The sandy streets were packed with people enjoying a huge carnival. There were bonfires everywhere and fireworks going off at regular intervals. I was surprised our recital that evening was to go ahead at all. The excitement and jollification in the streets seemed to permeate into our evening show, which went with a swing, followed by a most enjoyable party given for us by the hospitable Jacksons. I sensed an unusually happy community in Tegucigalpa, which appeared to be more of a big village than a capital city. Before leaving we took time out to wander along its unmade streets amidst friendly, smiling people.

All too soon we boarded our flight to Guatemala. The increasing altitude began to have an effect on our breathing. We had noticed it in Tegucigalpa but now, as we flew north, the hills became higher, which was to present more of a problem.

Landing midday in Guatemala City (yet another capital in another Central American country), to our horror we could not find our orchestral music, which travelled separately in its own box. The British Legation reassured us all would be well, driving us to see and explore the lovely old capital Antigua.

We were booked for only one recital in Guatemala City – in a cinema the following evening – and I was beginning to be affected by the increased altitude. Dreadfully tired the next morning I dragged myself to the Mexican consul to arrange our visas, before going to the cinema and finding no one to help with the lighting. The British Council, in the absence of any agent, not only arranged for more photos to secure our visas but also our plane tickets for Mexico.

Oleg and I danced carefully that night to avoid extreme breathlessness as we certainly felt the effects of the five thousand five hundred feet altitude. My foot was good at the start of the performance but jammed again whilst dancing the pas de deux of the Black Queen and Red Knight from *Checkmate*, but I was able to finish the performance. Despite persistent entreaties for another performance, it was not possible as we were booked to fly next morning to Mexico. Just as well – a revolution began the day after our departure!

59 *Mexico*

Saturday 13th July was quite the most exasperating of our tour. Landing 15 minutes early in Mexico City we were then held up for two hours over visas and passports. We felt we had already wasted enough time applying for visas in South and Central America, sitting in legations, filling out forms whilst securing scores of unflattering photos. I became so irritated at one point that in answer to a question 'What languages do you speak?' I filled in 'English, Swedish, French and Chinese', so somewhere in those regions I am registered as speaking Mandarin!

We were now terribly worried about our orchestral scores, which had been put on the plane with us in Rio but had not surfaced since. David and I had made inquiries to little avail, while for the past week the British Council also was trying hard to hunt them down. Having reached Mexico, we needed the music for all our performances over the next two weeks in both the theatre and the big arena where we were contracted to appear. It seemed that the music was lost and no amount of cajoling or show of temperament made the slightest difference. I had lost my temper for the first time in my life in Buenos Aires with our thoroughly incompetent agents, but found it a useful weapon for many impossible situations during the tour, until now… our precious cargo had definitely vanished.

Poor David made a desperate search of music shops in the city as well as combing the Opera House music library for orchestral scores and sheet music for our recital programmes. Despite his best efforts he could not find all that we required, so our repertoire changed to include excerpts from *Coppélia* and *The Nutcracker.* Our hotel reservations had gone astray but eventually Franco, the local agent, arrived and sorted out our bookings. He handed me a letter from Wagner who was refusing to pay the outstanding 895 dollars which I had been charged for the excess baggage. I was absolutely fuming. From 6pm to 10pm David and I sent cables, while trying to work out what best to do – we had no more money.

Totally worn out by worry, I slept soundly through the night in the first quiet hotel we had encountered in something like two weeks. But on waking I felt rather unwell and unutterably tired. I was still very worried about the money and the stiff letter we had composed to Wagner the previous night over dinner. Franco turned up before 1 o'clock and handed me just 20 dollars! We talked business for some time, after which I could hardly bear to walk out to buy some much needed soap flakes. I felt distinctly sick on the way back to our smart, modern hotel. With David, I worked out our new programmes from the orchestral material available, but I had to return to bed that afternoon, realising how much the eight thousand feet altitude was in fact affecting me. I recovered enough to unpack and wash before going to church. On returning to the hotel I found Franco waiting for more discussions which lasted a further hour and a half, ending inconclusively.

I awoke next morning, 15th July, feeling terribly sad to be away from Sven on our seventh wedding anniversary. I longed for the tour to be over so I could be back with him and Ingvar. I was curious to see the theatre in Mexico City, which was, it was claimed, rather like the Tower of Pisa, slowly sinking into the soft spongy subsoil. I gasped as we approached the Palacio De Bellas Artes to see the most impressive building, the exterior in the Art Nouveau style in glimmering white marble. This had been imported from Italy, making it the most important opera house in Latin America. We were equally thrilled on entering to find a wondrously large stage. We unpacked and tried a little gentle limbering but soon had to stop: the altitude was taking its toll and we returned to the hotel to rest.

Oleg and I decided to rehearse our new repertoire in the morning from ten o'clock for two hours when yet again the altitude affected us. We recovered in time to enjoy a splendid late lunch at the British Embassy, hosted by Lady Noble. Back at the hotel we were given the good news that the music had surfaced at last, in Caracas, discovered by the British Council! Tracing it gave us hope; there was no means of knowing how or when it would reach us in Mexico, but it somehow felt a good omen.

As the week progressed, our bodies became better acclimatised to the high altitude. I loathed feeling nauseous as it took away all energy, and dance requires energy. With the help of oxygen on our opening recital – Friday 19th July in the beautiful Palacio De Bellas Artes – we achieved an overwhelming success. It was quite a heavy programme with excerpts from *Les Sylphides, The Nutcracker, Swan Lake* Act *II, Sylvia* and *Don Quixote.* The orchestra played superbly, and I felt I danced better than at any of our other performances to date, even though the dresser was pretty hopeless, not even having the foresight to bring me a towel after my shower. The majority of dressers I encountered on our trip were quite fazed by the number of quick changes. I presumed they had never had to cope with anything like this before!

I found our second performance at the opera house much more of a strain, despite having had a day in between to recuperate. The dreaded feeling of sickness coupled with extreme lethargy returned, and my legs felt distinctly wobbly. Throughout the day I prayed hard that I would be all right for the show, and by the evening a miracle occurred: I felt strong enough to tackle our performance at 9.30pm. This included the demanding *Black Swan* divertissement and the exhausting *Checkmate* excerpts. As on our first night we had a rapturous reception with more flowers and more people than ever crowding into the dressing rooms to congratulate and thank us.

Throughout our tour I was astonished by the number of people who had seen Pavlova dance, and thirty years later still spoke with such fervour about her wondrous performances. It helped me understand the great impact she had also made on Frederick Ashton as a young boy in Peru. Inspired by watching her dance, he became a dancer and the great choreographer of Sadler's Wells, his ballets becoming the anchor of the now titled Royal Ballet. The spirit of Pavlova seemed to have accompanied me throughout our tour ever since alighting in Recife. Once again I marvelled not only at her dedication but also at her unique magnetism, which remained with these people over so many years.

We gave two performances in a huge auditorium on the Wednesday and Friday nights – an amazing experience. Situated in a beautiful park, the auditorium was vast, seating 10,000 people of which 7,000 seats were on sale for our first night. As these were all sold, the number of seats was increased by another 2,000 for the second performance. After our recitals in the Opera House we were by now accustomed to the oxygen masks placed over our faces the moment we reached the wings. We certainly could not have coped with such a demanding programme at that altitude without oxygen.

Oleg and I were at first troubled by the number of strong lights dazzling us on stage, but I really loved dancing in the auditorium, the distance from the public giving a feeling of unlimited space, making it a magical experience. After both shows the audience gave us a great reception. At the end of our final performance the orchestra played a Mexican farewell, which brought tears to my eyes as the staff and audience all joined in, singing together.

To my despair, I was still haggling up to the last day with the agent over our excess baggage charges. Neither Wagner nor his local agents were prepared to pay. It fell to my agent Ian Hunter to straighten things out and reimburse me once back in London.

With all our luggage taken to the airport after the show we had but a short sleep before flying Air France out of Mexico City at 8 o'clock next morning, Saturday 27th July. Everything seemed strangely still: no dogs barking, no birds flying, the sky overcast and a heaviness in the air. We heard later that two hours after our departure Mexico City suffered an earthquake and our beautiful hotel had split in half. How blessed we were to have escaped!

60 *Russian Murmurs*

We finally arrived safely back in London, only half an hour behind time. The thrill to see my Sven waiting for me as I came through customs! Nothing to pay this time as Ian Hunter was there.

There was a gathering of press reporters because the news of my possible appearance in Russia at the Bolshoi had somehow been leaked and the press were agog. I could not give them, however, any news other than that it had been discussed. In fact Sven and I had been invited to the Russian Embassy in order to discuss my appearing that December in Russia. The Embassy had been sent a possible itinerary by the Ministry of Culture, to include Moscow, Leningrad and Kiev. I felt this indicated a firm invitation and tried not to get too excited at the thought of being the first British dancer to step onto the hallowed Bolshoi stage.

Sven drove me home where we found Ingvar at the door. He put both arms around me, hugging me from side to side, saying softly 'Mummy, Mummy'. I am afraid I cried. My father was there, but our au pair Monica was on holiday. For a few days I was happy knowing I would have my family to myself.

All the worries of the tour soon faded into the background with exciting horizons in view. Within a few days of my homecoming I was on a train to Kings Lynn where Oleg and I were to give two performances in the Festival. During this period I was invited to escort Queen Elizabeth the Queen Mother with Edward Seago around an exhibition of his paintings. Her Majesty charmed all she met and was curious to know about my invitation to dance in Russia. It was a relaxed, informal afternoon with Her Majesty and Seago, whose paintings she greatly admired.

This was the first time I had met Seago, and I instantly felt a rapport, which was the beginning of a long and precious friendship. He was a very special man: sensitive, kind and generous with a deep love for the ballet. He had collaborated with the Poet Laureate, John Masefield, to produce a beautifully illustrated book printed just before World War Two in 1938. The book is titled *Tribute to Ballet in Poems by John Masefield and Pictures by Edward Seago*. I have a much treasured copy of this book given to me and signed by the Poet Laureate himself. On the first page it reads:

In grateful Tribute to a very beautiful Prelude, April 25th 1943. John Masefield.

After one of Sadler's Wells Ballet's regular visits to Oxford, Masefield sent me the most exquisite poem, which he wrote after watching me dance the Prelude solo in *Les Sylphides.* Thrilled and quite overwhelmed, I naturally wrote to thank him for such a surprising accolade, which was followed by Sven and me being invited to his home in Abingdon for tea. This meeting was the first of many happy hours spent there with this great man of whom I grew incredibly fond. He was powerfully built, erect, grey haired with handsome features. His deep warm smile was all-enveloping. Like all truly great artists that I have met he was extremely modest and always went out of his way to ensure that Sven and I were comfortable.

Masefield was a classic English gentleman, and I treasure all his letters, of which I have a great number, written in a superb hand with sincerity and affection. He would generally send us home with a gift: a little wooden Chinese boat for Ingvar, a special book either for Sven or for me, always containing some hand-written kind words. Our visit was always followed by a charming poetic letter of thanks for visiting him. What courtesy; he was most certainly the kindest person you could ever imagine. How honoured and enriched we were to know such a fine man.

Sven, Ingvar and de Vos drove to the market town of Kings Lynn in time to watch Oleg and me rehearse with David. My little boy was more interested in the seats than in my dancing, but was quite excited when allowed on stage after our run-through, rushing around in little circles until he got dizzy and too worn out to be taken to that evening's show.

Next day he watched the second half of our recital, sitting quietly on Hazel's knee. It was one of the proudest moments of my life, knowing he was there watching his mother for the first time, dancing to a live audience. Afterwards nothing could keep him from trying to dance on the stage, and he had a marvellous time, becoming so exhausted that he slept soundly all the way to London. As on the previous evening, scores of my loyal fans came to see our performances, which I found most encouraging. It was a big help to have Audrey in front and later to hear her observations and criticisms during our journey home from Kings Lynn.

Sven organised a necessary brief holiday for us in Corfe Castle before my next foreign tour. In London I had just a few days to prepare for my first ever tour to South Africa. Hugh Skillen devised a green shimmering wig, while poor Mr Roth went through agonies with a mermaid costume he was making for the new solo de Vos had created for me – *Ondine.* It was about a mermaid marooned on a shore, dreaming of returning to the sea, to the Delius music *Irmelin.* The solo was to become a popular inclusion in my programme. The dress with a mermaid tail was ready just in time to be sent ahead together with the costumes, head-dresses, shoes and other requirements for the nine-week tour of South Africa.

Exactly a year previously, on August 18th 1956, I was packing to go to Edinburgh as a member of the Royal Ballet, but now my luggage was packed ready to fly with me to Johannesburg as a star in my own right with my pianist/conductor David and partner Oleg. But on that Sunday afternoon my heart was terribly heavy as I kissed Sven goodbye, holding him tightly. As the BOAC plane began to taxi along the runway my eyes swelled with tears as I spotted Sven holding our son close, both waving madly. I envied Oleg who once again had his wife Mireille accompanying him, flying from Paris, arriving several hours after David and me in Johannesburg.

I wonder at the miracle of flying. We could pick out vast banks of orange-tinged soil bathed in the sunshine below, deposits from the gold mines I mused. I felt buoyant to see South Africa, praying our performances would be well received. I was already dressed, with hair done and make-up carefully applied ready for landing in Johannesburg, but nothing prepared me for the romantic archway of floral garlands through which I walked, to be greeted by an excited group of young dancers and their teachers – all falling over themselves to welcome me with tiny posies of flowers. That precious memory is tucked away in my special, expanding memento box.

Amongst the welcoming crowd were no fewer than five people from African Consolidated Theatre Management who were responsible for our stay in South Africa, presenting and organising everything. I liked them immediately, and they gave me a reassuring feeling of confidence. There was Jim Stodel, the managing director who, with his wife Joyce, were to become firm friends. Jim introduced me to his assistants Levard, Cherniasky and Desmond. Their press man, McKenzie, had certainly done good work already as there was a mass of reporters, photographers and a film crew, and a man from the local radio station who interviewed me before we left the airport. I realised that a lot was expected of me and was determined to make the most of this opportunity.

After the excitement calmed, the press finally satisfied, David and I were driven to a smart hotel, The Carlton, in the centre of a clean, modern city buzzing with activity. The high altitude only affected me later when we returned to perform. I was told it was about 8,000 feet but I did not see it as a problem. After the South American fiasco, it was wonderful to realise that we were being handled by professionals.

I had a pleasant surprise the following morning to find that the Johannesburg cinema where we were due to appear later in our tour was a really good theatre with a large stage and intelligent stage staff. I met the crew who were to tour with us, as well as the quintet who would be playing under David's baton for the next few weeks. We chose curtains and various pieces of equipment, in discussion with the crew, and made a lighting plan so the lamps could be sent ahead to Durban in time for our opening the following Monday.

What efficiency – I felt better able to concentrate on rehearsals to which, to our amazement, a number of press and photographers were invited. McKenzie certainly knew his business: our rehearsals were photographed, a long session in a photographic studio arranged, two radio interviews recorded and a charity signing in a big store. Altogether those few days were a forerunner of what turned out to be a remarkably happy and well organised tour.

After the early morning flight to Durban we landed safely to find a banner strung across the reception area saying in large letters *WELCOME BERYL GREY.* What a fabulous surprise and how wonderful to be so greeted. Several charming teachers enquired if I would give a class, but reluctantly I had to refuse, knowing how much our recitals took out of me. Oleg gave two classes instead during our week in Durban, for I knew I had to save my strength whenever possible for our demanding shows.

The theatre was well equipped, and it was a joy to have 'my' Vic and Leslie with me to set up our lighting, scenery and drapes as planned in Johannesburg. David chose to take the train from that bustling city along the picturesque coastal route. On arrival in Durban he had been driven through an Indian market which captured his imagination and which he could not stop talking about. I was certainly glad to see him in time to rehearse with Oleg and me for our opening two days ahead.

On stage that afternoon we were treated to a huge party given by the local dance teachers and their pupils. It was enjoyable because they were so sincere, natural and friendly. South Africa has produced some extraordinarily talented teachers highly regarded worldwide within the balletic sphere.

My first performance on a new continent. The first night audience was appreciative and enthusiastic, clapping louder and louder as the performance progressed, showering us with flowers at the end. The management gave a big party in the front of house, crowning the excitement of the evening. Next day, to my relief, we picked up ecstatic reviews, all of which I sent home to Sven who had cabled me in time for the first show. It meant so much to know he was thinking of me all those miles away. As on all my other tours we wrote most days to each other. Just before the show I received a letter from both Sven and my father, so felt buoyed up by their loving support.

After the success of our debut I felt anxious that our second programme might be an anticlimax, but it was also greatly enjoyed by both audience and press, who went out of their way to heap praise upon Oleg and me. Before our return to Johannesburg, McKenzie lined up a press conference which was notable for its good will and merriment. He insisted on celebrating our first week of success in South Africa with champagne and fruit! We had a smooth flight back to Johannesburg to prepare for our debut in the city on Tuesday 3rd September.

To my consternation I felt breathless during that first evening, together with a feeling of weakness in my legs which was quite unnerving. I feared I might not be able to get through the entire programme. I knew I was unable to give the standard I aimed for, moreover the audience was rather cold and far less responsive than in Durban. But to my relief and surprise we had a burst of overwhelming applause at the final curtain calls, from which we could tell that the whole evening had been well received.

By the second performance my body was beginning to cope much better with the altitude, and I did not get as exhausted or feel that our programme was such a strain. I received lots of flowers – a sign that Oleg and I had won over the very stiff, discerning audience. It was vital to have this success in Johannesburg, and it made me happy to see the pleasure and satisfaction it gave Stodel and Cherniasky.

During our two-week season in Johannesburg I had daily massages from Sam Busa, who was highly recommended. He was a superb masseur who counted many sportsmen among his patients, thereby understanding the demands ballet makes upon the body. Sam was also a very spiritual person. After losing his sister, who drowned herself in the sea, Sam searched for a meaning to life and found it in an Indian-based philosophy. I became very interested in this: the more I learnt the more I was drawn to its moral precepts which answered so many of my own questions about man's existence. I have studied Sant Mat and have remained a firm devotee ever since, trying to live up to its teachings and guidance, but not always succeeding, particularly with meditation. Sam introduced me to several followers of the philosophy, including an ex-military officer, Sir Colin Garbett who, when serving in India, met the Sant Mat Master. Sir Colin became a dedicated follower, and I found him both enlightening and convincing.

Oleg and I left Johannesburg on Sunday morning 15th September to fly south west to Cape Town. During the flight I fell into a deep sleep. Just as well for, refreshed, I was able to fully appreciate the wonderful welcome awaiting us. Dancers were arrayed in sparkling white tutus with their teachers cradling glowing bouquets of flowers. It was truly heartwarming and a good omen for what turned out to be a successful and enjoyable week in this picturesque city. Its beauty, embracing the Atlantic Ocean on the west coast and the Indian Ocean on the east, was thrilling – such a miraculous canvas of Nature, with the unforgettable majesty of Table Mountain rising high into the sky.

I was booked into a small, enchanting hotel, perched above a little sandy cove where the sea, incessantly roaring upon the shore, lulled me into a dreamy state of relaxation for my tired, aching body. The recitals took their toll, and I often got cramp in my legs during performances, even though I took care to exercise sensibly each day.

Throughout the tour I kept a record after each of my performances, criticising and listing what had and had not gone well. Sven and de Vos had given me helpful observations after the King's Lynn performances, so I had much to work on and improve. For a true artist there is an overwhelming desire to be better, and since my earliest debut I always turned to God for guidance. Once on stage, curtain up, an audience out front, the leading dancer is alone to express as the moment calls. How blessed I am as an artist to feel a greater power take over and carry me through a performance. It is an incredible experience which comes all too rarely, but happen it most certainly does, lifting one onto another plain for a short moment in time.

Leaving for Rhodesia (now Zimbabwe), we were given the most heartwarming send off from South Africa: all the friends we made were there to say au revoir. We experienced an unnerving, bumpy flight to Bulawayo where we were held up for ages by immigration. Eventually we met the theatre manager Mr Charles and his wife holding some flowers which had begun to droop in the heat of the airport. They drove us to the hotel along sandy roads lined with blossoming trees to the little theatre where we unpacked among a notably languid staff.

Later that evening a frightening storm with thunder, lightning and torrential rain turned the sandy roads into rivers of gushing water. I had never seen anything like this and, terrified, rang Oleg and Mireille, asking to join them in their room. There I stayed until the worst was over, returning to my room for an all too rare early night.

A sunny morning invited me to go for a little walk between colourful bougainvillea, luscious jacarandas and silver oaks. The air was fresh, filled with a most delicate fragrance, and at that moment I fell in love with Rhodesia. I could now understand how those I knew who had visited the country had fallen under its spell. Our performance in Bulawayo that evening was to a friendly audience. Although the stage was not large, it was flat with a good surface, and to my surprise we were well served by the local stage crew. I had an exceptionally good dresser, which made the entire evening a pleasure for us, particularly as there was no excessive altitude or heat to combat.

Our last performances were to be in Salisbury, and I awoke in the morning exhilarated at the prospect of flying there in a small private aircraft via the Victoria Falls. At eight in the morning a charming Mr Skinner collected me. He was an informative, pleasant companion, as was the pilot of the one-engine plane. A magical day ensued, flying low over the bush, spotting wildebeest and giraffes and, as we drew near to the great sprawling Zambezi River, it became sensational. We flew over Victoria Falls, which were much greater and wider than I expected. The waters of the Zambezi seemed to go on, cascading and falling, forever. When we landed close by, the great roar of the waterfalls was almost deafening. What immense power. I was overwhelmed by it: the breathtaking beauty of the untouched jungle, the trees drenched from the water's incessant spray.

On arrival in Salisbury I had little time to unpack and change for a cocktail and dinner party hosted by the local dance teachers. There were some important people present, including representatives from the government. The formality of the occasion was in complete contrast to the raw natural beauty I had so recently enjoyed and which I could still visualise – the great shallow Zambezi peacefully meandering its way across the vast stretches of uninhabited jungle of Mozambique, emptying itself into the Indian Ocean through the sprawling delta near Chinde.

The last two days in Salisbury with our three remaining performances passed swiftly and victoriously. Although the stage was small and the heat stifling, we had another fine pianist together with David inspiring us, and an audience that was with us all the way. I knew it to be one of our most successful performances, which made it a happy finale to the smoothly run tour.

On the first leg of our flight home to England I was astonished to be treated to the luxury of the State room on the plane. Stops in Nairobi, Khartoum, Rome and Frankfurt before finally arriving at Heathrow on Saturday October 5th at 1.30pm. It was with the greatest happiness that I was reunited with my darling Sven, falling into his loving arms once more. Once clear of customs with all my paraphernalia we drove home with my father. There, a waiting, excited Ingvar who went quite red in the face before squeezing and hugging me tightly as if he would never let me go. It tore at my heartstrings knowing there would be other tours taking me away from home.

November 10th, just over a month later, saw me airborne once more, this time heading North to Norway's capital city Oslo for a short engagement. The theatre director was awaiting my arrival at the airport, together with Peggy van Praagh and a British Council representative. I was handed a beautiful bouquet and driven straightaway to the theatre to begin rehearsing with the Norwegian dancer Werner Klausen.

The theatre was attractive, modern in design, but although the stage was large I found it rather hard. I was very pleased that my partner, Werner, was tall, strong, and easy to get on with. We worked carefully together and, by the time the company joined us later for placing and a run-through of *Swan Lake* Act II and *Les Sylphides*, I felt we had begun a sound partnership. The next two evenings proved this, and I found him on stage both calm and confident which allowed me to savour our performances together.

My Norwegian visit was only fleeting, but a happy and satisfactory one, and I was stunned and thrilled to be asked to give an encore both evenings. A short sightseeing trip the next day to the splendour and silence of the Olsofjord and forests, then home again to London.

63 *To Russia, 1957-58*

I was soon busy preparing for my forthcoming performances in Russia, becoming increasingly excited and not a little nervous at the prospect of being the first Western ballerina to perform there. With de Vos, I worked carefully on my weakest points, my arms, my shoulders, my back in arabesques and generally strengthening my overall technique. We studied carefully my interpretation of the two major classical roles I was to perform.

On general release there was a film of Ulanova in *Giselle* taken at a live performance during the Bolshoi's first visit to Covent Garden in 1956. I went to watch it several times in an attempt to spot the differences in choreography between their version and ours at the Garden. For differences there certainly were, both in *Giselle* and *Swan Lake.* I only hoped that I would pick them up swiftly once rehearsing at the Bolshoi.

I managed to take some special double work classes with the Russian trained Hungarian teacher Maria Fay, who taught me some of the Soviet-style big lifts with one of her male students, which was very helpful. I found them difficult to master at first and was glad to be trained in holding my back a certain way for the lifts, which would be required in Russia. I was also studying at a language school, endeavouring to learn sufficient Russian to cope with my forthcoming time in that country.

There was a great deal of press interest in my engagement – the first Western ballerina ever to guest with the famous Bolshoi Ballet. Sessions were held with a number of photographers, including Barry Swaebe, Houston Rogers, Mike Davies and Douglas Glass who, like his wife, was very cheery and friendly. Douglas spent a lot of time setting up the best possible lighting for head and shoulder shots, one of which appeared a week later in the Sunday Times Portrait Gallery, complete with a splendid article about me. I had a long radio interview on BBC Overseas Service which I thoroughly enjoyed and an interview with Reuters. At home a reporter from The Christian Science magazine visited, whose interview was published at the same time as a photograph of John Field and me appeared on the cover of their journal.

I gave a talk to the Royal Academy of Dance on my recent tours, as well as one to the Critics Circle, about which I was very apprehensive. It was silly of me to have worried so much as it went down well.

There were many other engagements but the most unexpected was an invitation from Michael Powell at the beginning of December. He came to our flat to enquire if I would be interested in taking the lead in a film he was to make in Spain with the famous dancer Antonio. I would have to both dance and speak and would need to take a film test on my return from Russia. I was thrilled at the idea, of course – to work with such a famous producer (he had made the successful film about ballet, *The Red Shoes*). In 1950 he had asked me to appear in the film he was to make, *Tales of Hoffman*. As it would have meant shooting during the month of my honeymoon, regretfully I had turned down the offer. This time I would be available if the screen test was satisfactory, and it would be a marvellous opportunity to appear with so great an artist as Antonio. I was able to thank and tell Michael Powell that indeed I would be most interested.

All the while costume fittings for *Swan Lake* and *Giselle* were underway, with Roth working rather slowly but carefully, while Sven and I hunted for warm apparel for the cold Siberian winter. Sven chose for me a beautiful mink hat which even today is as good as when it was delivered. We were perturbed that our visas had not arrived despite having applied for them several months before. Our numerous enquiries at the Russian Embassy met only a polite, phlegmatic response, and the visas did not come until two days before we were due to leave.

The Sunday Times approached me to write a weekly account of my activities in Russia, which was to be collected by their representative in Moscow at the end of each week for publication in England. I thought I could do this as I was used to writing a daily diary since I married Sven. Some twelve years previously I had been asked by the editor of the *Dancing Times*, Mary Clark, to write about the tours in America in which I had been dancing with Sadler's Wells Company. As these accounts had all appeared in her magazine I felt I had enough experience to undertake the Sunday Times suggestion. With the increasing interest in representing Britain in Russia I began to realise my enormous responsibility. I became increasingly excited at the prospect of actually dancing with the Russians, and grew impatient for the time to come.

By 9.30 on the evening of 5th December I was completely packed ready for our 7.30 departure next morning. My loving father was with us by a quarter past seven and, with sweet Ingvar, helped take all our luggage into the lift and down to the waiting hired car. Once more the dreadful tug leaving Ingvar behind. I knew he would be wonderfully cared for by Gunilla, Hazel and Margaret MacInnes, but the pain stayed. I was fortunate, however, in having my ever-supportive Sven with me for what I knew would be a fascinating, but difficult, tour.

After a hurried connection in Paris, I drank a symbolic glass of vodka proffered me immediately after take-off. I felt we were now under Soviet jurisdiction and tried to enjoy the food served. But I was very apprehensive, realising the great challenge lying ahead. All eyes would be on this British visitor not only in comparison with the greatest dancers in the world but also as a representative of her country.

On our descent towards Moscow airport I got the most awful pain in my ears –much worse than I had experienced on other flights – and thought they would burst. I feared this might be a bad omen but the pain eased as we came in to land. I was mesmerised by a huge glowing red star illuminating the airport and snow-covered tarmac.

At the foot of the plane steps, waiting to welcome us, was the first secretary at the British Embassy and also a man from the Ministry of Culture, together with a small young woman introduced as Jhana, who was to be my interpreter for my month in Russia. I was a little disappointed that there was no one from the Bolshoi there to meet us too but, to my surprise, waiting for interviews inside the building were men from the press, including the Daily Worker and Reuters. The British Embassy had a car ready for us which, however, we were not allowed to take, being escorted instead by two large Russian men to their waiting vehicle.

The twenty-mile drive to the centre of Moscow seemed endless, past hundreds of birch trees on both sides of the snow-cleared road which was remarkably void of cars. Around and beyond lay a vast landscape of snow extending as far as the eye could see, broken only by a few little homesteads, their lights twinkling eerily. Soon the flat, frozen expanses gave way to blocks of flats, high buildings – a new scheme we were told to house up to 2,000,000 people. As the lights of Moscow beckoned us, the red stars on the Kremlin came into view and, with Red Square lit up rather like a stage set, it made a dramatic impact. The Turkish-looking St Basil's cathedral was beautifully floodlit as was the magnificent Bolshoi Theatre, which we passed.

It was then my heart began pounding as I thought of my great challenge ahead. Before I realised it, we were drawing up outside a huge, old-fashioned looking hotel, the Metropole, which was across Sverdlov Square, almost opposite the Bolshoi Theatre. Once in the hotel foyer with our luggage, we found ourselves surrounded by a mass of rather poor looking people seemingly just hanging about. With the strict formalities of signing in completed, we were at last taken up one floor over drugget-covered carpets to a suite at the far end of a long corridor. It was very Edwardian, with heavy velvet maroon curtains and a large dining table, more curtains concealing a recess with a double bed and a bathroom annexe beyond.

I noticed a large woman sitting by a table at the other end of the corridor, noting everyone's comings and goings. It was only then that I became aware that we were in a country where one was under constant observation. So different from our easy-going nation, where freedom is taken for granted and perhaps insufficiently valued or cherished.

Fruit and Russian tea with lemon were brought to the room, and I was given the shattering news that my Leningrad performances had been cancelled and switched instead to Tblisi, the home city of my future partner, the famous Chaboukiani. Interesting as a visit there might be, I felt outraged and insisted that my agreement with the Russian authorities in London be upheld.

I was told this would be difficult as the French ballerina Liane Daydé had also been engaged to appear in Leningrad with her own French partner, so it was felt that three visiting artists around the same time might be too much. I stood my ground forcefully, and it was agreed that the Ministry would be informed of the unfortunate situation and that it might possibly be reconsidered. I remained determined and optimistic whilst also waiting for the expected day-to-day schedule.

Meanwhile Terence Lancaster, the Daily Express man, was waiting downstairs in the lobby so Sven and I went to meet him. We liked him immediately, his cheerful no nonsense manner, finding him most knowledgeable and helpful about the present Soviet Union. He apologised for being unable to be at the airport when we arrived (just as well, as we had landed almost an hour late at 10 o'clock Russian time) because of his attending a reception where Krushchev had made an important speech. With Terry giving such a clear, first-hand picture of what to expect in this unfamiliar, state-controlled country, I felt a little more confident about the whole undertaking.

My stomach was still tight with nerves as the reality of actually being close to the Bolshoi and all that it stood for in the world began to sink in. I could not even relax in a hot bath as the water would only run tepid. Thank goodness we had taken the precaution of bringing our own bath plug which miraculously fitted the big old bath, so we could at least have an overall wash after our long and tiring journey.

Moscow time is three hours ahead of London, and we slept well up to 11 o'clock. Jhana the interpreter arrived at midday to take us sightseeing, but first I insisted upon contacting Mr Bone at the Ministry to find out what was being done about Leningrad. Nobody seemed to know anything, so we went off with Jhana, Sven equipped with his camera and I hidden amidst a sea of woollen scarves in a determined effort to keep out the bitter cold. I was intent on staying fit and well despite the bitter wind and frozen snow everywhere. Later that afternoon we endured an unbelievably long wait in the Metropole restaurant just for a light snack of coffee and caviar before being at last escorted to the Bolshoi.

We arrived at the appointed time of 3.45 to a great welcome from the director, Mr Chulaki, who we knew from his time in London with the Bolshoi in 1956. He took us on a guided tour through the huge, richly decorated red and gold theatre, introducing us to staff and artists. They seemed delighted that I was to work with them, and I began to feel more relaxed. I was surprised to see dust sheets over almost everything, rather like the Metropole, as if to be kept in top condition for special occasions. I was tremendously excited by the enormous stage, gently raked, flattening out nearer the footlights, which nevertheless offered an intimacy out to the auditorium, and knew I would enjoy dancing in this vast, beautiful theatre.

64 *Bolshoi: Coaching And Rehearsing*

Sunday 8th December was my very first day working at the Bolshoi, and what a marvellous experience to be so welcomed and cared for. To my delight I was rehearsed by two of their most famous artists: Marina Semeyonova and Asaf Messerer. In the morning Jhana accompanied Sven and me to watch a senior class led by Messerer himself, in which I spotted many of the male dancers we had seen during their London season – Serge Koren whose performance as Mercutio in Lavrovsky's *Romeo and Juliet* I had so much admired, as I had Lapauri's sensational partnering of his wife Struchkova in *Walpurgis Night*. To my surprise Messerer gave no corrections to those in his class, instead inspiring them with wonderfully travelling enchaînements. This was followed by the soloist class where I noticed that the lovely Bogomolova was a lot thinner than I had remembered her in London, still full of promise and dancing divinely.

I was given a studio in which to do my own barre and warm-up exercises, watched with curiosity by a number of other dancers. I explained that initially I would prefer to do my own workout and not take on a different training as yet, which was readily understood.

My chosen partner, Vakhtang Chaboukiani, arrived early for our first rehearsal of *Swan Lake*, which was good as it gave us time to get to know each other. We began to walk through the second act pas de deux which differed quite a lot from my version, but happily the pianist soon arrived together with the great Semeyonova. What a joy and privilege it was to have her keen eye and experience in creating the best synthesis. Chaboukiani was not as tall as I expected, but he was the most marvellous partner and such pleasure to be with: patient, kind and a true artist. By the time we had worked out both pas de deux's from the second and third acts I was quite tired and ready to hand over the studio to Struchkova for her four o'clock rehearsal of *Sleeping Beauty*.

That evening we were invited by Chulaki to watch *Swan Lake* from his director's box, together with his family. Maya Plisetsya was dancing the Swan Queen Odette/Odile with Yuri Kondratov as her prince and Levashev as the magician. They gave a dynamic performance, and I watched closely every move and the choreography. The fourth act was totally different – longer, with additional music, involving more dancing and acting with the prince and also the magician. This made it dramatically exciting, moving and beautifully emotive. I hoped that I would learn, remember and express the deep emotions expected in time for my Friday performance.

When the curtain came down Mr Chulaki took us backstage to introduce me to all the swans, one of whom made the most delightful speech in broken English to welcome me, which was warm and touching giving me much needed encouragement for what lay ahead. I then met Plisetskya and Kondratov and the chief conductor, Yuri Faier, who were all charming and surprisingly modest. What an impressive large stage and what magnificent grand scenery, it made me long to be a part of it and impatient for my first night. On leaving by the stage door I was approached by a gathering of fans wishing me well as they presented me with a copy of a book about Plisetskya. What a lovely end to my first working day in Moscow.

The next few days were taken up with learning and perfecting all the new entrances and exits and the various little changes as well as being coached with considerable care by Semeyonova, matching my line with Chaboukiani's and finding the way to make us move as one. It was truly wonderful to receive this attention from such an inspiring and gifted artist, giving me the confidence I never found during my twenty years with the Royal Ballet.

I also received invaluable instruction from Messerer himself, the choreographer of Act Four, which he taught with absolute clarity and enthusiasm – in particular the difficult Russian lifts. He showed me how and where to hold my body and was a most sympathetic teacher, like Semeyonova, whilst Chaboukiani taught me so much about the art of stance and from where to take one's strength. I worked really hard and was thankful that my body was coping so well with the different way of approaching certain movements. With my toes getting sore and my legs and back beginning to ache I was thankful that Sven was with me to give me a good massage later in the hotel after many hours of rehearsal.

I particularly enjoyed working on the mime scenes with the company as the dancers always went full-out in rehearsal without a trace of embarrassment, which I found profoundly helpful. Some of the company would stay to watch my rehearsals, bursting into applause one day when I performed the thirty-two fouettés! The renowned, much loved Ulanova herself watched some rehearsals, too, after most warmly greeting first Sven and then me. I saw how much the art of ballet meant to the dancers at the Bolshoi – ballet was their life.

By day three I was scheduled to actually rehearse on the mighty Bolshoi stage and was feeling very excited coming into the theatre. Tragedy struck, however, with the news from Chulaki's own lips that Chaboukiani had injured his knee in class that morning so would be unable to partner me. It came as a big blow after all the hard work we had put into creating a good partnership. Poor Chulaki and Tomski, the artistic director of the Bolshoi, looked so grave and upset that, despite my heart sinking, I smiled and went forward to greet Kondratov, who was already on stage waiting to take over and partner me.

Taller than Chaboukiani and nearer my own age, Kondratov was adaptable and easy to work with. He was Semyonova's pupil and we three got on splendidly. We worked fast and well so that, after two hours of more wonderful coaching from Semeyonova, we found that Kondratov and I were well suited, musically and temperamentally.

Fortunately, he knew the fourth act intimately. This was a big help as Chabukiani had never performed Messerer's version and we both had been struggling to remember it all. Now, my first rehearsal ever on this stage, with a partner I had not worked with before and a number of the company, there was a lot to discover. But with the presence of Faier conducting the pianist we finally pulled everything together much to everyone's relief and satisfaction.

There were people including Plisetskya out front watching the rehearsal, which was rather unnerving, but I soon forgot them as I became totally immersed in working with my new Prince. After each day's rehearsal I wrote down all that I had learnt, and today was no exception. This time Kondratov helped me, along with the ever willing Messerer, in readiness for the full company run-through next evening on stage.

Back in the hotel, Terence was waiting to write a piece to wire through to London about my change of partner and eager for any photos Sven might have taken at rehearsal. Later that evening Chulaki collected Sven and me for dinner at his home with his family – his wife and two sons, and quite a few from the company; Plisetskya, Kondratov, Fadeyechev (another leading male dancer), Semeyonova, Faier and Tomski.

It was a big, happy party, with the most amazing amount of food – some strange and new to us, some Georgian specialties and several other Russian delicacies, with plenty of vodka, which I would not drink so near to my performance. It was a truly jolly evening with music and singing and marvellous speeches, reminiscent of Swedish parties. On our departure, snow was falling thickly and everyone except me felt it was the time to drive through the Moscow snow-shrouded streets. They understood my need to rest, so reluctantly I left Sven to join them in experiencing the bewitching Moscow night.

For my run-through on stage next evening, Wednesday, I began to feel unusually lethargic and listless, so much so that I omitted my two solos on the advice of Semeyonova and Messerer who were intent on safeguarding my strength and wellbeing. But once back in the hotel I started to feel sick and by morning I was actually terribly ill. With my stomach in complete disarray I managed to get across to the Bolshoi for the ten o'clock full call on stage. All the stage lights were on as I was introduced to the entire company, on stage and out front, and Faier then introduced me to the hundred-strong orchestra. I had not felt well enough to do my usual barre work, thinking it better to put what strength I had into this, the final rehearsal before my first performance next day.

I did my best but, as it was a straight run-through without stopping, by the end of Act Two I was terribly sick, my hands and face vibrating and almost numb. I was unable to continue and hardly managed to return to the dressing room. Very soon it became filled with people anxious to know how I felt, including Ulanova, who held my hand saying, 'Do not worry about tomorrow, another date for the performance will be arranged and I will dance yours tomorrow'. She continued holding my hand for ten minutes until a doctor and nurse arrived. They gave me a quick examination and pronounced severe food poisoning as the cause.

I hardly remember being driven back to the hotel, given tablets to swallow and put to bed with a hot water bottle, which was a real comfort. But I was sick again in the afternoon and again in the evening and felt awful. The doctor came twice more that day and again the following morning, Friday 13th, the date for my debut at the Bolshoi. Was it perhaps an unlucky date? I was by then terribly weak and in no condition to get up, let alone dance that night.

Chulaki was deeply concerned that it might have been something in the Metropole that had caused my illness and so ordered nutritious food to be cooked and brought over from the Bolshoi kitchens in a continual stream of thermos flasks. As if in a haze, I remember Kondratov coming to see me, and the Minister of Culture himself ringing to say they had arranged after all for me to perform in Leningrad and kindly enquiring after my health. I was told that Ulanova had generously offered to give up her performance of *Giselle* later in the coming week to substitute my missed performance. In the end it was arranged that my time in Russia be extended a few days and that I would return to Moscow at the end of my tour to dance my lost performance on 1st January.

Saturday dawned and the doctor returned to find me feeling more normal so he agreed to my walking over to the theatre in order to do some careful rehearsing for my performance scheduled for the following evening, Sunday 15th – a performance I was determined to give. After a gentle warm-up, Semeyonova and Messerer took Kondratov and me carefully through everything, and I found my strength miraculously returning as we progressed. I returned to the Metropole late in the afternoon and, after a light meal, retired early to bed very thankful to have got through the rehearsal with no ill effects, praying for renewed energy next evening, my debut in Russia.

65 *Bolshoi Debut And On To Kiev*

The great day arrived, throughout which I managed to keep remarkably calm in readiness for the evening. Chulaki arranged for the stream of food he had ordered on Friday to be continued. Such concern and kindness I could only repay by giving the finest performance ever. Sven gave me treatment before we set off across the frozen Sverdlov Square, almost sliding our way to the theatre. As was the custom there were no quick run-throughs with a partner before the show. As Kondratov told me, 'Everything completed by the last rehearsal should not need any more work, all energy must go into the actual performance so that you are longing to go on stage.'

I was in the theatre well before six, doing a thorough barre and warm-up. To my astonishment the dressing room soon began to fill with well-wishers. The first to enter was Semeyonova with a very precious gift which she herself had been given and now wished me to have – the most exquisite vase, which I have kept proudly, safe and unharmed to this day. Then Struchkova came with a present and many others arrived including Tomski and Chulaki. Baskets of flowers began filling the room – from

Ulanova, Kondratov, Levashev, the Bolshoi Theatre and the British Ambassador, Sir Patrick Riley, who with his wife had already shown us kind hospitality.

I felt overwhelmed by such generosity and wrestled with my nerves, as even the rustling of paper was starting to disturb me. Nevertheless, I was just ready in time and eager to begin. Thankfully without my heart banging with nervousness, but feeling a certain tension and determination, I prayed that my strength would carry me through to the end of the performance. My prayers were answered and, with all the wonderful goodwill and support I had from the company and stage staff, everything went well. Semeyonova and the stage prompter were in the wings throughout, guiding me each time towards the correct entrance and exit – of which there were a bewildering number. How grateful I was for their directions and continual encouragement.

On my first entrance I was dazzled momentarily by the glare of the strong lights and somewhat shaken, too, by the noise of film cameras, which continued whirling throughout the entire performance. It was being filmed and shown live on television. I knew that Mrs Krushchev headed the dignitaries out front in the packed house from whom I was given a warm round of applause as I appeared and held my first swan position. Kondratov entered and from then on I was swept into our lakeside idyll, together with the magnificent Bolshoi corps de ballet. The exhilaration of performing with a 120-strong orchestra, led by their conductor Yuri Faier, carried and uplifted me into a magical world. Whenever I hear that soul-rending Tchaikovsky music now it takes me instantly back to Russia and my incredible time with those wonderful artists.

With Act II successfully over, though everyone was very happy with my performance, I knew how much better I could have been had I felt stronger. I wanted to use my arms in a more expressive and powerful manner and to travel faster on full pointe encompassing the stage with more agility. I was determined to dazzle in the next act. And so I did, aided by the superb partnering of Kondratov backed up by the complete involvement of everybody on stage. The company lived the dramatic events as they unfolded, so it was up to me to dance brilliantly. As I danced I felt all my strength miraculously return, and I enjoyed every second on stage.

In the euphoria in the interval, Semeyonova gave us a quick run-through of the last act. I finished that dramatic act without a mistake or tripping up a single swan, but only through the guidance of my prince and my evil magician. When the performance ended I could hardly believe it had all happened and gone so well – and neither can I believe it today. It was a huge success with the encouragement of a very warm and enthusiastic audience and the cushioning by the company who were willing me on throughout.

After the seemingly endless curtain calls, everyone gathered waiting on stage to congratulate me, and one of the dancers gave a heartwarming speech. Amidst another outburst of clapping I was handed a wonderfully worked hunting horn decorated with tiny ivory swans and also a lovely, hand-painted box. I had only been with the company for eight days yet I felt a great wave of love and friendship coming from them. I was extremely touched, shedding tears on returning to my dressing room. Amongst the professional photographers on stage Sven, too, was busy taking photographs, deliberately fading into the background. More photos were taken in the green room, where we also gave press and radio interviews.

After a quick shower, ably scrubbed down by a woman attendant, my own dresser then helped me dress for the British Embassy. Chulaki was waiting to take Sven and me and already gathered at the Embassy were many of my other friends from the Bolshoi – Ulanova, Semeyonova, Kondratov, Plisetskaya, Messerer, Levashev, Struchkova and her husband Lapauri, Mr Bone and other representatives from the Ministry of Culture together with ambassadors from other Western countries. The Embassy was decorated for Christmas adding a festive note as we sat down to a delicious Christmas dinner.

The Rileys told us it was the first time that anyone from the Bolshoi hierarchy had ever accepted an invitation to the British Embassy and that this was a breakthrough in relations between our two countries – a chink of light through the Iron Curtain. There were over sixty seated at the candle-lit dinner, and I could not help marvelling at the incredible kindness and understanding of Sir Patrick and Lady Riley in having transferred this magnificent party from Friday to Sunday, to celebrate my first night. They had already been very helpful since our arrival, showing much interest in my Bolshoi interlude, and I valued their continued support during our stay.

We were about to fly to Kiev, and waves of anxiety flooded in. I found it difficult to sleep after all the nervous excitement and tensions of Sunday. I was up early Monday morning to start packing in the hotel, after which I had to undertake the same task in my theatre dressing room. There was my article to finish for the Times and Jhana was late arriving – as was the case on several other occasions when she was delayed working on our behalf at one of the ministries. All business seemed to take ages in Russia.

Once again, Sven took me across the frozen square to the stage door where we were met by an equally frozen doorman refusing to let me enter. It was Monday, when shops and theatres were mostly shut, so it took time to find the right person to allow me in, even though it was only twenty-four hours since I had filled the theatre. I was beginning to learn that life was not too easy in Russia.

Once I had cleared and packed my things from the dressing room, we hurried back to the hotel to be interviewed by waiting press people. It was by now getting chaotic, and Jhana was being sought by both Mrs Chulaki and Kondratov. She eventually arrived at 2.30 with our all-important plane tickets for Kiev. With our departure due in less than an hour we crammed into the waiting car which drove at break-neck speed, skidding frighteningly over frozen roads and swerving violently to avoid huge lorries. Somehow we made it in one piece to find the 3.20 plane held, waiting for us. Sven, Kondratov, Jhana and I were waved off to the Ukraine on the next leg of the tour.

Landing in Kiev at 6pm we were met by the director of the Opera House, V.P. Gontar, who introduced four of his principals from the ballet company: two charming ballerinas smothered beneath fur coats and two leading men equally warmly dressed and partially hidden by huge fur hats. They presented me with a beautiful bouquet of white chrysanthemums and azaleas, a rarity in the freezing cold. Sven and I were bundled swiftly off to our hotel which, to my delight, was extremely comfortable and peaceful after the restlessness of the Moscow scene. And wonder of wonders there was a bath which ran hot water so that I was able to bask in the first bath I'd been able to take since leaving home, retiring immediately to bed, and soon drifting into the arms of Morpheus.

Meanwhile, Kondratov went with the welcoming party directly to the theatre to rehearse in their production of *Swan Lake,* preparing it for me. The stage of the Kiev Opera House was not as immense as the Bolshoi, narrower and nearer the size of Covent Garden, although fairly steeply raked, with a surprisingly poor surface. When I came on stage the next day the company and orchestra greeted me most warmly, and I soon felt at ease as we began working together. I was pleased to see quite a few tall dancers in the company, who performed with acrobatic ease and assurance.

One of the two soloists dancing in the Act I pas de trois was Galina Samsova. I was to come to know her well many years later when she became the principal ballerina of London Festival Ballet. Kondratov prepared me for the changes in this production, which was nearer to the version I grew up with in England. Even the fourth act was not as different as I feared, shorter than the Bolshoi version and using the more familiar passages of Tchaikovsky music. That evening I chose to stay quietly in the hotel, mending my silk tights and darning the tops of my pointe shoes while Sven was treated to a performance of *Aïda* in the theatre, which he thoroughly enjoyed.

Those hours of tranquility enabled me to give what I knew to be a good performance of *Swan Lake* the following evening, with Kondratov discreetly guiding me through the last act! Both the public and the company gave me a great reception at the end of each act, the company lining the corridors clapping whenever I went to my dressing room. At the end they presented me with a reproduction of a group of Ukrainian dancers in porcelain, engraved in Russian "from the dancers of Kiev". Their leading ballerina herself had made a white practice slip, especially for me. The conductor was remarkable, following superbly, almost as if we had always worked together. Along with the fine playing of his orchestra this was sublime, and without the strain of the vast Bolshoi with its great history I was far less tense.

I was also more in tune with Kondratov throughout this, our second performance together. He was an amazingly strong partner, lifting me overhead in the marvellous Russian lifts of which I was now fearless. I was able to dance or hold a position at an angle off balance in a way I had never known before. I found it thrilling to dance with such a fine partner on whom I knew I could utterly rely.

The next afternoon Kondratov and I began to rehearse our versions of *Giselle* in readiness for our appearances in Georgia and Leningrad. After two hours we needed a rest before meeting again later in the theatre. At the director's invitation we watched *Carmen* from his box, sung by the visiting American mezzo-soprano Blanche Thebom. She had a glorious voice and gave a great performance. In the second act on picking up a pot of flowers to throw at Don Jose she found she was holding an entire row of flower pots all secured to the same board! The Ukrainian audience roared with laughter while, unperturbed, she gallantly replaced the board of flowers on its window ledge, still singing and glowering at her lover throughout!

At the end of the evening Gontar gave me a present of a book about Kiev which pleased me – I was told he was Krushchev's brother-in-law. I felt particularly honoured when, after my third and last performance, he presented me with a pair of Ukrainian red leather boots which he was pleased to point out were my exact size. I proudly brought them home to England but, fearful of soiling them, it was years before I actually dared wear them out of doors. Kondratov and I received an ovation with many curtain calls to finish our happy time with the Kiev company.

As on our opening night, many fans gathered. A man stepped forward from the crowd to give me two loaves of bread, a gesture so meaningful and kind in a city where the people were obviously very poor, I wanted to burst into tears. The entire crowd then escorted us down the hill, a short walk to our hotel where, together with Kondratov and Jhana, we bade them a fond farewell, retiring for a little celebration in our room where we talked and laughed for many hours – Kondratov's sense of humour would prove invaluable as our tour developed. Finally, happy that the first appearances had so far gone extremely well, we all drank to the future.

It was nearing Christmas, but for us, in this friendly capital of the Ukraine, December 23rd was to be a day of relaxation and sightseeing. First, a broadcast was to be recorded at midday for transmission to Britain from Russia. I thought this connection over the airwaves rather wonderful. I was struck, on our drive, by the drabness of the shops, mostly without any window-dressing, though some sported small Christmas trees with a little tinsel: for their New Year I presumed. But I was wrong; we were in the middle of the Independence celebrations. It was the 40th anniversary of the Bolshevik victory in the Ukraine, and people were out celebrating. I went early to bed, listening to the singing and music in the streets but to my relief it only lasted a short time. The previous night a woman's voice had been relayed over loudspeakers across the city until well after midnight. The streets were decorated with red stars, red lights and flags and opposite us, the Academy of Science was all lit up with photos of Lenin and the reigning Praesidium (somewhat like the British cabinet) by day as well as by night. I also noticed many military vehicles and personnel in the streets, all happily celebrating.

It did not seem at all like Christmas Eve, and I was beginning to feel homesick. We waited from six in the morning until half past two in the afternoon for a plane to fly us to Tblisi. We were told repeatedly that no plane had been able to take off since the previous day because of fog, and they could not say when flying would recommence. Jhana wanted to send a telegram to Tblisi about our delay but I thought it wiser to wait. By 5pm it was obvious we would not be taking off until the next day so we asked Jhana to send a telegram cancelling our first performance on the 25th. Neither of us was prepared to travel and dance on the same day. She was loath to cancel, but Kondratov and I were adamant and the message was reluctantly dispatched.

That evening was spent in our room, with Kondratov and me practicing sections of *Giselle* and *Swan Lake*. He was as keen as I to perfect our performances and was only too pleased to do this. Before retiring to bed we were told by Jhana that we would definitely be flying to Tblisi in the morning and must be dressed and prepared to leave at short notice before eight o'clock. We were ready and lying on our beds fully dressed when Jhana rang at eight to say the airport had not yet opened! At 9.30am an agitated Jhana rang from the airport telling us the plane was about to take off and we must come at once. On arrival at the airport we were told that we could not have a direct flight to Tblisi, but would have to change planes at Vladivostok after a six-hour flight and then face another five-hour flight. I was furious but that cuts no ice in Russia, where one has just to accept the authorities' decision.

Inside the airport we found a charming man from the opera house sitting with a drooping bouquet of flowers: he had been waiting for over twenty-four hours to wish us a happy send-off. He explained there had been numerous people with him from the opera house waiting there all day to see us off. What patience, and how disappointing for everyone.

66 *Tblisi And Moscow*

The Ilyushin eventually took off at 11.15 on Christmas morning. The safety straps did not function, the springs of the seats had long since given way, and we found the toilets absolutely filthy. There were no refreshments once airborne so a cup of Russian tea at Dnepropetrovsk and Stalingrad airports – cities at which we landed en route – was nectar indeed. Finally alighting at Rostov we were met with the news that there would be no plane to Tblisi until the morrow – just that, no explanation – and that we would be housed for the night in the airport hotel along the passage. In fact Sven and I were given a comfortable room with more modern, coloured furniture than expected, but with a failing light bulb and no hot water.

We spent our Christmas evening in the restaurant eating strange Christmas fare. Kondratov and Jhana insisted we celebrate with champagne and turkey. But I thought the turkey tough and more like roasted cat might have tasted, and the alcoholic drink was an unusual red colour. I wondered if it was a Georgian champagne. Anyhow, we were determined to make the best of what the evening could offer, and Kondratov kept us well entertained. He played the piano and sang a lot of Russian songs amidst much joking and laughter. We relaxed, for we had been assured that there would be a plane to Tblisi next morning, leaving at seven o'clock. Optimistic, we retired to our rooms.

This time we were not disappointed for, although the plane did not leave until nearly eight o'clock, we were thankful to be on our way. As seemed the norm in Russia we were left standing out on the airfield, shivering from the icy cold while a flight of steps was eventually found and brought to the plane for us to clamber into the cabin. There were no refreshments as usual, the seats were worse than before and my head, neck and back ached. Without warning, I found myself sobbing inside my winter coat; it had all got too much. I felt terribly homesick, sad and annoyed by the endless problems arising from our endeavour to reach Tblisi.

The flight over the Caucasian mountains, however, was so spectacular and beautiful that my equilibrium was restored by the time we landed at our destination in bright sunshine and crisp pure air. But – horror of horrors – once inside the airport Sven was taken away by two men, and I was beside myself with terror. After a seemingly endless quarter of an hour he reappeared, smiling. The air hostess on our plane had reported Sven filming whilst flying over the glorious mountains, which was apparently forbidden, and so his offending cine-camera was confiscated until the film inside was developed. Unfortunately, Sven did not think to tell the authorities that it was a colour film, and it was developed as black and white. On the camera's return, we found the film had been ruined. There were many apologies, but it was a bitter disappointment after all the care Sven had taken with his filming at the Bolshoi and Kiev theatres – all those historic moments lost.

After this trauma, disappointingly there was absolutely no one to meet us and no messages for us either. Jhana was beside herself trying to reach somebody in the theatre, and we waited impatiently, feeling all the omens were growing bleaker by the minute. But the long wait was eventually rewarded with not one but two cars pulling up, brakes screeching, to take us into Tblisi itself. After half an hour's driving we were halted by two big black cars coming from the opposite direction. Out hopped a man from the theatre, one from Intourist and another from the Ministry of Culture. They were deeply apologetic, warm and friendly: apparently, no one knew of our whereabouts until we landed, and so they had been unable to welcome us to Georgia as planned. We were completely mollified and began to appreciate the very real problems faced when travelling across an area as vast as the Soviet Union.

At our hotel everyone seemed very curious about us as we were shown to nice rooms with high vaulted ceilings and velvet drapes. There was, however, an appalling smell of disinfectant permeating along the corridors, which seemed like a threatening health hazard. Sitting downstairs in the restaurant for a much appreciated good meal, I was surprised to see that two flags – one British and one Russian – were placed on our table. It was symbolic of the respect, interest and I can say affection that was shown to us throughout our time in Tblisi. The people were very pro-British, alive with temperament, strong-featured, with long aquiline noses, shiny black hair and physically well built. Whenever we were out in a restaurant or café people would toast us, sing and come up and shake our hands. It was wonderful to experience such goodwill.

By three o'clock Kondratov and I were in the theatre rehearsing *Giselle* with the company for a full two hours, during which time Chaboukiani arrived to welcome us. He had telegraphed to Moscow for permission to partner me here with his own company but the message had not arrived in time and rehearsals were now too advanced for me to change partners and no doubt some of the choreography. I felt pleased, though, that he still wished to dance with me after the disappointing fiasco in Moscow.

I began to realise what a great hero Chaboukiani was in his homeland. Having been Ulanova's partner in Moscow for many years he had returned to lead his own company in Georgia for the last six years. That evening – the 26th December – we watched him perform the role of Othello in his own ballet version of the play. It was a full-length work with three intervals, absolutely riveting and highly dramatic. Chaboukiani gave a great portrayal of Othello which was both thrilling and deeply disturbing. Both the décor and the music fitted perfectly the unfolding tragedy. Georgians are reportedly staunch admirers of Shakespeare, as one could sense from their rapt attention throughout the evening's ballet and the ecstatic reception accorded the company at the end. During his many curtain calls Chaboukiani bowed several times to me, sitting in the director's box, which was most heartwarming and generous of him as all eyes were then focused on me.

I worried, after seeing the superb acting in *Othello*, that my mime scenes in the first act of *Giselle* the following evening might not match their high standard of portrayal. I need not have for with the committed response of the company I was thrust into the role of Giselle from the time I stepped onto the stage, encouraged by a ripple of applause. I lived every moment as Giselle, along with the company's gifted artists, to the satisfaction of the audience who gave me the most rapturous reception at the end.

After the show I was asked to give an extra performance the very next day. I so much wanted to agree, as I was now feeling a lot better and stronger after the awful food-poisoning in Moscow. With the pain in my liver almost gone, I believed I could manage this. But Sven was adamant that I should keep one day free between performances, and so I regretfully turned down their request. Next morning, however, the director again asked if I would reconsider and dance that evening. I was very torn but knew it would be foolish to dance such a demanding role three days in succession. I was able therefore to stay in bed and rest all morning prior to a one o'clock press interview.

That evening I was interviewed at the local TV station. To reach it, we took a funicular to the mountain top where I was royally received in the one and only studio. Jhana interpreted, which she did splendidly despite being terribly nervous. There was no make-up room, and it seemed rather quaint. We sat on Victorian-style chairs around a Victorian table, covered by a heavy lace cloth. There was a friendly atmosphere and the interview, which lasted a good quarter of an hour, went well. On departing, I was presented with an exquisite basket containing little jars of mistletoe and other beautiful, colourful berries.

Once safely back down the funicular, a waiting car drove us through Stalin Park to an attractive restaurant for dinner. It was full of Georgians enjoying their Saturday evening to the exhilarating sounds of a small band. On seeing us enter, the musicians broke into several outdated English tunes, including *No Johnny, No!* and *I'll Be Loving You Always* which everyone at their tables sang with great gusto. Those at the table next to us would get up from time to time giving little speeches of welcome and goodwill in very broken English, interspersed with showers of floating kisses. Georgian songs were much in favour, too, in which we tried to join – and soon chocolates, fruit and liqueurs were arriving at our table. It was the most incredible show of friendliness I have ever known from strangers, and the big-hearted generosity of this strong and ancient race remains. The evening finished with a remarkably good rendering of *Auld Lang Syne*, which can never have been surpassed anywhere in the world.

My last performance in Tblisi next evening was televised, and I thought the interval longer than ever. The production demanded all kinds of contraptions for Act II. For instance, as Giselle, I had to climb a ladder in the wings to lie on a waving branch of a tree, high off the ground: worrying but doubtless effective. I rather enjoyed flying across the backcloth at speed, perched on a wheeled wagon (the latter well camouflaged, of course!). As on my first night, there were baskets of flowers: one from the director again and, to my surprise, one from their skillful and supportive conductor Mirtzhulava.

My dressing room filled with well-wishers after the show, many of whom brought flowers and little gifts, but to my disappointment none of the theatre people or company principals appeared. Back in the hotel we found a wonderful party had been arranged as a surprise for me with all our theatre friends waiting to greet us: the theatre director, three theatre governors, Chaboukiani, Kikaleishavili (who had played Iago) and the beautiful ballerina Tsignadze (Desdemona) with the producer and composer of *Othello* also present.

The spicy food was colourfully laid out on a huge table. There were many exotic Georgian specialties and amidst much merry drinking a succession of speeches, all sincerely spoken in a curious mixture of Russian, English and Georgian. By the time our party was drawing to a close the men were imbibing from ancient Georgian drinking horns. Finally, a huge bowl was passed round in turn to everyone present, the contents having to be completely emptied, and not just once either! It was a fantastic memory of Georgia to take away with me – the most foreign and the friendliest country I had ever visited.

At seven o'clock next morning, even after the late night revels, the theatre director, the governors, the Intourist person and several others were at the airport to offer us a little breakfast. On departure they handed both Kondratov and me the most lovely posies of flowers. We were scheduled to stop at Rostov and three other places before coming in to land at Moscow. But to our surprise the plane, which was far comfier than before, was diverted (due to bad weather in Rostov) to a watering place on the Caspian Sea. There we stayed for a good hour, wondering what on earth we were doing in such a deserted spot and worrying about the future flight plans. Abruptly taken back onto the plane, we proceeded to fly directly to Moscow, where we landed in the middle of a snowstorm. Whatever happened to the poor passengers waiting for our plane in Rostov and the other three towns, we wondered. In Russia flight schedules were not adhered to, which must have accounted for the scores of people always found lying on the concourse floors, waiting patiently with all their luggage for transportation by air to some outlandish post.

On landing, I was told we were booked into another hotel which I refused to accept, and poor Jhana had to battle on the phone to get us relocated back to the Metropole which was only walking distance from the Bolshoi. To our astonishment we were given a four-room suite and, wonder of wonders, hot water actually came through the taps. So I was able to soak in a hot bath after our day of travel and have an early night in preparation for my return to the Bolshoi next day. There a very warm welcome awaited me, not only from the dancers and répétiteurs, but also from Tomski and Chulaki, which was very reassuring.

Kondratov and I were soon being coached by Semeyonova once again. She made some readjustments to our Act II pas de deux, bringing it closer to the Bolshoi version. Happily, however, she did not want to change any part of our third act. I knew I needed to go through the fourth act: the work with the magician was tricky, full of what were to me alien lifts with highly dramatic effects. During our time away, my memory of it had become a little hazy. There had been the Kiev version of *Swan Lake* to learn, then *Giselle* to fit into the Tblisi version, all in a short space of time. Ulanova told me that she thought I had been given too tight a schedule but, as I was used to touring, it had appeared acceptable to me. After rehearsal, I had a radio interview with the BBC for relay to England followed by an interview for the Bolshoi's own newspaper.

That evening Sven gave me a strong massage before he went to see a performance of *Eugene Onegin* at the Bolshoi. Despite the excellent singing and impressive staging he said that the audience was rather unresponsive. He was back in time to see in the New Year with me before we drifted off in a deep slumber.

New Year's day 1958 at the Bolshoi was celebrated with a gala as it coincided with the 800th performance of *Swan Lake* in that theatre. It had fallen to me, a foreigner from England, to be dancing the lead on such an important occasion. I was determined it should be my best ever performance, and I know it was, through God's help. I was truly inspired and lived every minute on stage, uplifted by the great acting of the other dancers and the playing of the huge orchestra. With the guidance of Plisetskaya in the wings for every entrance and exit, I could not make a mistake. No one could have been more helpful. Plisetskaya was the most wonderful support throughout the entire evening, even instructing me from where in my back to take my strength to aid my breathing. To cover the enormous area of the stage was extremely taxing, and I was so grateful for her wonderful help to me as a fellow artist.

At the end, in front of the rich red curtains embellished with gold political symbols, I curtseyed low then walked first to one side and across to the other, acknowledging the applause which went on and on. Embracing onlookers in every part of the house, this Russian tradition of taking curtain calls offers artist and public a closer intimacy.

There was a remarkable gathering on stage after the curtain calls, which was both touching and thrilling. Semeyonova, Faier who had conducted for me so responsively, Messerer with his sister Sulamith, just returned from Europe, Plisetskaya who had given up her evening for me, the ever gracious Ulanova as encouraging as ever, Struchkova, Lepishinskya, Chulaki, Tomski, all the dancers and countless others – with Sven standing unobtrusively in the wings taking photos. What an incredibly warm and friendly farewell. Later, as we left the stage door, Sven and I were besieged by fans, some of whom escorted us cheerfully back in the gently falling snow to the Metropole, where they gave me an album of photos of Plisetskaya they had made themselves. What thoughtfulness and generosity.

Our next evening was spent at the Stanislavsky and Nemirovitch-Danchenko Lyric Theatre watching that company's new production – *Joan of Arc*. It was their second performance of this work by Bourmeister, and we found it enthralling and theatrically effective with plenty of corps de ballet addition. There were some battle scenes with exciting, realistic fights. The role of Joan, originally intended for Ulanova, was finally given to Violetta Bovt to create. She gave a sensitive, appealing interpretation. I was puzzled, though, by the Dauphin's role in the ballet: he was portrayed as a man seemingly frightened of people, who hid from the interrogating Joan. It was an interesting conception and made a splendid finale to our stay in Moscow.

After the show, it was back to the Metropole for the last time. Again we found fans waiting to see us before we left for a scrupulously clean Moscow railway station. We were to take the midnight train to Leningrad with Kondratov and Jhana. To everyone's surprise, more fans were waiting there too – obviously mostly Kondratov's – to wish us well on our journey through the night. Though excited, I slept well in my single bunk opposite Sven's while, to my amazement, Kondratov and Jhana shared the next door cabin without any qualms!

Arriving in Leningrad at 9.20 we were disappointed that there was no one to meet us at the station. We waited until ten when Jhana made a telephone call, which miraculously produced a car. We were not expected for two more days – revealing the appalling muddles of the organisations in Russia. Once in the elegant Hotel Astoria we breakfasted together in the restaurant which, like the hotel itself, had a more Western atmosphere.

Kondratov yearned to take the midday class at the famous Imperial Theatre School in Rossi Street (now the Vaganova Academy), which has produced some of the most famous dancers of the 19th and 20th centuries – including Pavlova, Nijinsky, Karsarvina and Nureyev. The school was founded by a Frenchman, Jean Baptiste Landé, in 1738 under the auspices of the Empress Anne and was first housed in the Winter Palace. The Empress herself chose the first pupils, twelve girls and twelve boys, from amongst the children of her staff.

After leaving Kondratov at the famous school, on our short tour of the breathtakingly beautiful city we drove on to the great Maryinsky Theatre – then known as the Kirov. It was clear that no one there was expecting us, and astonishingly I was billed to be dancing *Swan Lake*! I put my balletic foot down firmly at this mistake and insisted to the theatre director that I dance in *Giselle* with the company, as agreed months earlier in London. He was not pleased, and although he invited us to that evening's performance at the theatre he did not offer us any refreshment during the interval. That evening, two leading French dancers from the Paris Opera Ballet – Liane Daydé and her partner Michel Renault – were guesting in *Giselle*. I preferred her dancing to her acting, while Renault danced well but appeared lightweight in comparison to his more virile Russian counterparts.

It proved very helpful for me to see the production and to observe the Kirov dancers, who to me lacked the spontaneity of the Bolshoi artists and their beautiful use of arms. At rehearsal next day I did not sense a happy atmosphere in the company, and the dancers seemed morose. There was no warm welcome as I had received elsewhere in Russia, other than from a few of the dancers. The ballet master, ballet mistress and the former ballerina, Elena Lukom, now a répétiteur, however, were all amenable, as was their attentive conductor.

Lukom, a great Giselle herself half a century ago and a contemporary of Karsarvina, now appeared very fragile and old. She was transformed, however, when demonstrating certain passages and would suddenly get up and leap across the stage like a young girl. She rehearsed me with care and understanding as there were a number of new moves which I had to work out, particularly in the mime scenes as well as the mechanical tricks in Act II. How thankful I was to have the support of Kondratov, who managed every situation with calmness and good humour. Coming from Moscow, he received sly remarks about his condescending to dance on the Kirov's old wooden stage. I gathered there was much resentment as the Bolshoi were renowned for taking their best dancers – the most notable being Ulanova.

Beautiful as I found the Kirov-Maryinsky with its lovely blue, white and gold auditorium, its big raked stage narrower than the Bolshoi's, I felt much more comfortable on the expanse of the Bolshoi with its more gentle, unobtrusive rake. The city of Leningrad-St Petersburg, however, was a joy to behold. I was determined to see the Hermitage, housing its world-famous collection, but we had only two hours to wander through an opulent maze of rooms. On display were precious objets d'art, fine furniture and great masterpieces of painting, too numerous to appreciate fully on a first visit. It was the biggest and finest collection I had ever set eyes upon. I could not help but speculate about the hordes of poorly clad Russian visitors pouring through the palace of their last Tsar and his family, ignobly murdered by the Bolsheviks.

On the day of my last performance in Russia, Sven unsuccessfully tried to buy a toy for Ingvar and some caviar to take home with us. Thank goodness the Astoria came to our rescue by supplying us with six small jars. We could hardly have returned from Russia without their famous delicacy, and fortunately, after my performance Lukom proudly gave me a little toy to take home for my son. I was most moved by this; she had been very kind and helpful to me throughout our rehearsals. It had been so wonderful to have been coached by a famous Giselle, herself so modest and self-effacing. I tried to remember all she had shown me, and our performance in the famous theatre was an enormous success, everyone congratulating us as the audience continued clapping and expressing their enjoyment of our *Giselle.* There were speeches and flowers with the curtain still raised, and I could hardly believe it all, particularly after the initial coolness shown us upon our arrival. But I was now eager to get changed and packed in time to catch the night train back to Moscow and was even ready before Yuri!

I was perplexed by Jhana's absence during most of the show for, after giving me an exquisite white porcelain figure of Ulanova as the Swan Queen, she was nowhere to be found. All was explained as we boarded the train with our stack of luggage to be met by a smiling Jhana in our compartment. It was entirely decorated for Christmas with a feast laid out for us to tuck into on our return journey together.

She had been busy arranging this surprise party and had coerced the train crew into agreeing. As we enjoyed the chicken, caviar, cheese, bread and butter, Jhana proudly handed around what she termed English buns! It was a very merry party with plenty to drink: wine, vodka and lemonade followed by tea and chocolate, finishing with fresh fruit. I do not understand how she was able to acquire so much tasty food. She must have grown very fond of us, as we had of her. I was too excited thinking of our return home to sleep much. As we stepped off the train in the morning, ahead of time, we found it was bitterly cold – 25 degrees below zero.

Jhana had somehow found us tickets that very afternoon for London via Prague, so we were bundled into cars for a big send-off at the airport. There was Kondratov, his lovely young wife, a TV producer, Mr Tomski, Mrs Chulaki (on her own as her husband was ill in bed) and of course Jhana, all coming out to the airport to wave us goodbye. I could hardly believe my eyes and was deeply moved by such a demonstration of friendship. We did not have long to wait in the airport lounge as our luggage was put on the plane without customs formalities, whilst I prayed that the plane would take off despite the snow and freezing conditions.

The call to board came over the loudspeaker and everyone followed us onto the frozen field. Having obtained special permission, they were allowed to come with us right up to the boarding steps. Kondratov was unusually silent, Jhana was in tears and so almost was I. It was hard to part with these dear, kind people with whom we had forged such a special bond, and I wished we could have brought them back to England with us. Like them, I hoped with all my heart that we would meet again and that I would be able to return to Russia some day to dance with such true artists. I knew nothing could ever be as inspiring as dancing at the Bolshoi and that I would miss them all terribly.

Back at Heathrow, there was a crowd of press reporters eager for news, as well as BBC and ITV crews wanting interviews. I longed to get home, but by the time everybody was accommodated we did not arrive back in Davis Street until 10.30pm. To my bitter disappointment, darling Ingvar was sound asleep in bed. Gunilla told us he had just developed a bad cough but, as we crept into his room, he woke up and was so very, very happy to see us and was so sweet, hugging and kissing us over and over again.

What boundless joy it was to be back safely home with him. I have always suffered the agony of separation throughout my career, which from the early age of fourteen has torn me in two, growing more harrowing as the years have passed. That pull between the rapacious demands of my career and the patient love of those at home tugged at my conscience, and I have never been able to stifle this pain when away from those I love.

68 *1958: Multi-Tasking*

Once safely back in England that January of 1958 I began to fully appreciate the freedom we enjoy and take for granted here in the West – freedom of movement and of speech. Despite all the kindness and friendship I was shown in Russia I never felt totally at ease. We had been warned that the hotel rooms were bugged and that we should be guarded in our conversation in our bedroom. All comings and goings in hotels were routinely observed and reported by a forbidding, large woman stationed at the end of the corridor. One felt under constant surveillance in the Soviet

Union even though generally accompanied by an interpreter. It was my first experience of life under a totalitarian regime and in 57/58 the Communist empire was strongly policed, with every activity reported to members of the Party, who held absolute power. Violetta Elvin, nee Prokhorova, told me: 'It was normal for people to spy and report on one another,' and she had grown up accepting this as usual behaviour.

Our first day back, Tuesday, was manic. Not only was the phone ringing continually with colleagues welcoming us home, interested to hear all about our experiences, but I also gave a long interview in our flat for the television news. I was shown giving Ingvar his presents from well-wishers in Russia, which many viewers found very touching. There was my last instalment for the Sunday Times to be concluded and as luck would have it John Allen, a schools inspector and writer, called in just as I was finishing it and to my relief helped me with the final sentences. After that we went off to the Acropolis restaurant to celebrate.

During those first weeks at home I had many other press and television interviews for both the UK and abroad and managed two broadcasts at Bush House, one even in Swedish and another in French, as well as making recordings for the Canadian and the North American services. There were also a number of requests to give talks about my time in Russia. These included one to speak at the Holborn Town Hall to 500 members of the Association of Ballet Clubs, of which I was president.

There was also an invitation from the Women's Institute to give a talk at the Royal Albert Hall on the subject of 'having a career and bringing up a child'. I accepted but became very nervous on learning it was to be in front of six thousand women! I had danced at the Albert Hall with the Royal Ballet on one occasion and also judged ballroom dancing there, but never before had I taken to the stage alone in that vast arena. Apparently my talk went down well – what it is to be young. A number of less daunting but interesting challenges flooded in, including school prize-givings. At these I had the opportunity to speak briefly to each recipient before giving the main address. I always wrote my own speeches, memorising them prior to the engagement, be it the opening of an exhibition, fete or bazaar, or simply an after-dinner speech.

The most wonderful surprise on our return home was to find that Ingvar's cot had been moved into our bedroom by a painter redecorating his nursery. And there his cot and its incumbent remained for several days, until the strong odour of paint vanished from his newly decorated bedroom.

Peggy van Praagh, a former leading dancer and ballet mistress with Sadler's Wells, pressed me to dance at the Edinburgh Festival in a new work being created by Andre Howard. Although I had told her I was not interested in doing this, she was persistent! Michael Powell was still chasing me to appear in a film he was to make featuring Antonio, the famous Spanish flamenco artist; though wary, I was much more interested in this. Powell had left the script with me before the Russian engagement and was now eager to know what I thought of it. The film was to be shot mostly in Spain, and the thought of playing opposite Antonio was attractive. To my inquiry about our respective heights he explained the differences would be disguised through raised platforms.

The date was set for my film test, with two days for rehearsal before. On the first day I was coached by David Oxley – where to move, how and when. He was quite young, self-assured, assertive and very helpful. The second day was with Helen Ross who was also kind and constructive. Next morning – 5th February – a car arrived to take me to Elstree GM studios, stage 5. There I met Massine's daughter for the first time, so gathered that her father was also involved in some way with the film. It took one and a half hours for make-up and hair to be completed but once dressed and on the set I enjoyed playing the role. David Oxley was most helpful, and to my relief Michael Powell was delighted. I felt it had all gone well and hoped so much I would get the part.

I knew, however, that Tcherina was testing for the role next day, and later that week, on seeing the rushes, I realised she gave a far more polished performance than I could have done. This was not surprising as she had already acted in the film as the other leading ballerina in the *Red Shoes* opposite Moira Shearer. I waited for a week before I was put out of my agony. Through the morning post a charming letter came from Powell regretting that he could not offer me the part as it was felt my personality was 'too strong' for the role. Although I had already begun to fear I would not get it, nevertheless when the news eventually came I was terribly disappointed.

But it was a day of contrasts and conflicting emotions, as I joined Prince Philip in the Royal party at a film premiere that same evening at the Empire Theatre, Leicester Square. Although rather nervous about the whole event, I felt elated to be chosen to be part of such a distinguished group. At 7.30pm I was collected by a respectful Stephen Mitchell and driven to the theatre where I met the Prince, who was absolutely charming and courteous, asking me questions about my time in the Soviet Union. I also delighted in the company of those in the Royal party and returned home at 2.30am on a cloud of happiness, escorted once again by the chivalrous Stephen Mitchell.

I met another small group of fascinating people including Roy Plomley the very next day at the BBC. We were taking part in a radio programme titled *These Foolish Things* which was great fun as we all got on well together. Then the following morning (Friday) I again met Roy Plomley at Broadcasting House, this time to prepare and record a *Desert Island Discs* programme with him.

At first I found it tricky to decide on the precise section from my chosen pieces for recording and then the moment at which to fade out the music. But with such sympathetic help from Roy I soon found myself engrossed and fascinated by the skill of the technicians. Once the programme was being recorded I felt relaxed and comfortable in the way Roy talked on air with me, drawing out all sorts of anecdotes and memories. What a warm, deep voice he had. He was a perfect presenter as well as being a lovely person. I am glad that we were later to record another *Desert Island Discs* programme together, this time for the purpose of advertising the BBC Overseas Service.

To my great surprise I was approached by the publishers Secker & Warburg to consider extending my newspaper articles for the Sunday Times into a book. I didn't know what to answer and wondered if I could write well enough for such an undertaking. I spoke with Terence Lancaster, the Daily Express journalist who had been in Moscow when I was there and who was entrusted with relaying my articles back to London. We had become good friends, and he had been very helpful, so I knew I could rely on his opinion. After deliberation and consultation I finally agreed to 'have a go', for the idea appealed to me; I believed it was an opportunity to share with others my unique time in Russia.

My continuing poor health since the food poisoning incident in Moscow was another factor in my decision to go ahead and write. Taking time away from the theatre I could concentrate on the book whilst remaining in training. Everything was an effort and I was still losing blood daily. Our family doctor was puzzled and sent me to see several specialists who were equally baffled. Nothing I did or swallowed made any difference, and I was warned not to take on any dancing engagements until it cleared. This was my husband's wish, too, and resulted in my turning down a number of performances, invitations I was loath to miss and which upset me at the time, although I knew it to be wise. After some months of little improvement I was sent to the Hospital for Tropical Diseases who, after numerous tests, were also perplexed and unable to identify the problem.

I began writing the book and found I enjoyed sitting down for hours. Guy Horne encouraged me to go to his 'barn', close by the river near Abingdon, ensuring absolute peace whenever possible. By late spring whatever it was that was affecting my health seemed to be less debilitating, and it was agreed I should attempt some performances abroad. I was beginning to feel like myself again, with more energy and enthusiasm. With sporadic periods in the country at Guy's lovely old 'barn', away from town, the book came on well and was near completion. Wondrously, I finally finished the text in time for publication by the end of the year.

Sven was of great assistance with the book, reading through my writing in the evenings, filleting and sometimes taking it to pieces – much to my disappointment and annoyance. It was the only time in our married life that we argued, and I would become furious. My precious darling – without his input the book might never have been accepted. Sven had taken masses of photos when we were in Russia and those in the book were all his, with the exception of seven which the Soviet authorities kindly supplied.

In the meantime, the end of May saw me dancing again on stage in *Giselle*, this time with the Munich ballet company directed by Alan Carter. Alan had been a prominent soloist at Sadler's Wells before the war, returning to the Sadler's Wells Company after serving in the forces during hostilities, when he began to choreograph for the Company. This talent encouraged him to leave the Wells to become artistic director of several companies in Europe where his choreographic skill was in demand. Alan was also a most gifted painter, a talent he developed during his latter years, and I was to have the honour of officially opening one of his future exhibitions in London.

During my visit to Munich I gave press and radio interviews and a talk to the Munich Ballet Circle, which was well received, as was my Giselle. It was truly wonderful to be back dancing on stage again, particularly in a role I so loved. I saw for the first time ever a Cuban ballerina dancing an exciting *Don Quixote* pas de deux – her name sounded like Dulcie Aragya. She was a sweet person but suffered the same hapless partnering from

Heino Hallhuber, their leading dancer, as I did in *Giselle*. It proved to be a most happy week in Munich despite the poor partnering of the good-looking, somewhat conceited Hallhuber.

That summer, among several highlights, for the first time Sven and I attended a Royal Garden Party at Buckingham Palace. We took Ingvar as far as the gates of the Palace, for he was extremely excited at the thought of us seeing the Queen. Margaret McInnes also accompanied us in order to take Ingvar safely back home after waving farewell to us in our splendid outfits. He told everyone, 'Daddy was in morning suit and a funny (top) hat and Mummy in a lilac chiffon dress and pretty hat.'

I could not refuse Julian Braunsweg's pressing invitation to dance with London Festival Ballet during their 1958 summer season at the Royal Festival Hall in July and August. As my first London appearance since I danced in Russia it provoked an enormous amount of interest from the press, and I knew a lot would be expected of me from fans, critics, colleagues and management. My partner was to be Oleg Briansky with whom I had by now established a sound partnership, and it was agreed that we would dance with the Company in their productions of *Les Sylphides, Giselle, Swan Lake* Act II*, Don Quixote* and *Black Swan* pas de deux, as well as giving two of our favourite solos.

We enjoyed rehearsals taken by Anton Dolin who was kindness itself, encouraging and helpful. I absorbed a lot from his coaching, particularly his mime. I rather fear mime is an art in danger of being lost. Although I remained calm on the day of my opening, by the time the performance came my heart was beating fast, and I felt terribly nervous. Once on stage, all went without mishap and everyone was thrilled with our performance, with the exception of Sven and my teacher, de Vos. She and I knew it could have been better and – sure enough – not all the reviews next day were good, which was disappointing. I had so hoped they would all have seen a strong improvement since my time in Russia but knew in my heart that my Odette could have been more moving and expressive.

After that first night on the shallow stage of Festival Hall, however, I was able to relax into the roles, dance with more confidence and portray more emotion. My first season with Festival Ballet became a success with public and critics alike. Dolin invited me to dance the first two nights in each city during the company's forthcoming autumn provincial tour. As I was no stranger to touring in the UK, this appealed to me and I accepted. I liked the company, their enthusiasm, friendliness and maturity, confirming Violetta's impression when she guested with them earlier.

After my London appearances, Sven, Ingvar and I sailed away to Sweden on the lovely old boat Britannia, sister ship of the Suesia, my father following a few days later. He so looked forward to our holidays together, playing with little Ingvar by the Swedish lakes and visiting Sven's brothers dotted around the south of the country. I was quite exhausted but uplifted by all that had happened over the past, remarkable year. I had left the Royal, danced across South America and South Africa, performed at the Bolshoi and Maryinsky with Russian companies and finally experienced the pleasure of dancing with another major British ballet company.

After four weeks reminiscing and relaxing in the Swedish sunshine and sailing and swimming on the dramatic west coast, I became impatient to return home as new horizons beckoned. I had continued my daily lessons with de Vos on my return from Russia, despite being unwell. I love movement and feel the need for it, as I do even today. Careful exercise under a knowledgeable teacher can always help the body recover.

I heard that the Bolshoi were due to appear in Paris in the autumn and I determined to go to renew our friendship, take class with them and enjoy their incomparable dancing. I joined Messerer's class with most of their principals and brought back some lovely large photos of the time spent there – truly inspirational. I loved working with them, their high respect for their art and constant endeavour to perfect their own work.

There was plenty to attend to after our holiday. The most important event was Ingvar's first day at preparatory school near Sloane Square. He was very excited, dressed in a blue blazer, cap and tie. I felt a motherly pride in his good looks. I left him outside Miss de Brissac's School for his first step alone into another world amongst many other children. When I collected him later he was full of all the things they experienced that morning and already looking forward to the next day.

It was a relief to know Ingvar was happy there, but Sven was taken violently ill early that morning. At 5am I woke Margaret in her flat below for help. She came at once and found Sven's heart was not functioning normally. She sat with him whilst I took Ingvar to school. I was back before the doctor arrived and confirmed Margaret's findings. Sven's secretary cancelled all his patients for two weeks. A heart specialist arrived early evening, confirmed fibrillation of the heart and gave Sven tablets, while I prayed his heart would soon return to normal. The cause was food poisoning from cooked oysters he ate the evening before at the Mirabelle, where we had been the guests of Sir Victor Sassoon. Sven remained in bed for a couple of days, sleeping peacefully most of the time. On Monday morning our doctor returned to find further improvement in Sven's pulse, and two days later he was up, insisting on seeing a few of his patients.

The two-month engagement with Festival Ballet (now English National Ballet) took me across England to eight cities I knew well from wartime touring with the Sadler's Wells Company. Festival Ballet spent a week in each venue, beginning in Coventry, a city badly bombed in the war. The start of the building of its new cathedral alongside the war-torn ruins of the former great structure was a stark reminder. To celebrate, Ninette de Valois had organised for Sadler's Wells to dance excerpts from her ballet *Job*. It had been the perfect choice – we performed beneath the great Graham Sutherland tapestry of Christ the King; my first experience of dancing in a church or cathedral.

The start of each week for touring companies generally has the lowest box office returns, as audiences wait for reviews. My appearances on Mondays and Tuesdays boosted sales, and gave me the rest of the week for training in London and fulfilling other engagements.

I worked in Paris with the strong Belgian dancer Gerard Ohn and with the composer Victor Gsovsky, learning from him his famous *Grand pas Classique*, a piece created for Chauviré and Skouratoff and beloved by French ballerinas for its dazzling virtuosity. It was a great experience to be taught by Gsovsky, a big genial personality, and I valued the time spent with him. Gerard and I were proud to perform *Grand pas Classique* on *Sunday Night at the London Palladium*. We had great fun working amongst other variety performers in two run-through rehearsals on the same day. With only one orchestral call, the players managed the Auber music surprisingly well.

Negotiations were taking place between Ian Hunter and Covent Garden for my return as guest artist in the early spring. I suggested inviting Kondratov to partner me, which Madam thought a good idea. I wrote him a note enquiring if he thought this a possibility, and he immediately answered yes. So the Garden proceeded through the diplomatic route to officially invite Kondratov while I held my breath! Ian Hunter also discussed fees with Webster, who finally agreed to pay me £150 a performance. I appeared on BBC television and on radio promoting my book, *Red Curtain Up*, as well as giving more talks and interviews for the press and women's magazines. During this busy time I took a flight to Brussels to dance in a gala at the Monnaie, which saw a wonderful mix of artists, including Alicia Markova.

The highlight of the Festival Ballet tour was the opportunity it gave me to be partnered by Anton Dolin in *Giselle*. He was the most sympathetic of partners, the difference in our heights presenting him with no obvious problems. With Kondratov, too, it was the same. My height was no problem for either of these accomplished artists. Dolin always presented his partner with a modest showmanship, making the ballerina his priority. His manners on stage were impeccable. I felt safe with him even in the most hazardous lifts, whilst being truly inspired and locked into his convincing mime. It was an honour to dance with such a great artist, whose partnership with Alicia Markova has become a legend.

The Festival Ballet tour was followed by two engagements: the first in Copenhagen with Frank Schaufuss and the second in Stockholm with Caj Selling. Departing from Heathrow I was filmed by ITV and was met by more photographers and press on landing at Copenhagen. Caj was permitted to come from Sweden to rehearse with me in Copenhagen prior to our forthcoming appearances with the Swedish Royal Ballet. I was particularly touched that he came to the airport and greeted me with some lovely flowers – a happy omen for this new partnership.

Frank Schaufuss, the leading dancer of the Royal Danish company, was an elegant, tall man: an ideal partner for me, and I only wish there had been more opportunities for us to dance together. At our first rehearsal, however, he seemed somewhat distracted. I later learnt the company had gone on strike in protest at Harold Landers' possible reinstatement as director after an absence of seven years. The day before our performance Frank actually tendered his resignation. No wonder he was a little preoccupied and in fact was soon to leave the company. It was a strange time to be there but interesting to be working with two new partners: Frank in the *Black Swan* divertissement and Caj in the full *Swan Lake* ballet.

There was a good orchestral rehearsal next afternoon for the following day's Gala, after which I had a long rehearsal with Caj on *Swan Lake*. I was overjoyed that Vera Volkova was the company's resident teacher at that time, so I was able to benefit from her classes whilst in Copenhagen. The Christmas gala put on by the newspaper *Politiken* was a brilliant affair followed by a superb dinner at which I was asked to say a few words. I met Frank Schaufuss's talented wife, the leading ballerina Mona Vangsaa, and their son, Peter, whose dancing I was to admire and appreciate years later when he joined my company.

After the short stay in Copenhagen, a city festooned with Christmas decorations, to my husband's great joy we flew to Stockholm where there was a truly festive atmosphere and the streets were ablaze with Christmas lights. I gave two performances of *Swan Lake* with the company in the Royal Opera House, Stockholm, having had a 'general run-through' with the company in the afternoon and evening on the day of my arrival. It was good to be back with this company again, but I had completely forgotten the splintery, uneven stage surface! After our performances together I felt sure Caj would be a splendid partner for me. He was a good dancer, the right height, with empathy and a charming manner. We seemed to breathe and feel the music in the same way, something difficult to explain but important in a partnership.

Several of Sven's family and friends came to my performances. At my last performance I was honoured by the presence of the two Princesses, Sybella and Margaretta, who sat in the Royal box. I knew it was my best performance to date as the Swan Queen and even Sven, my toughest critic, was pleased. All the press reports were full of praise – for the very first time in my career there was not one carping critic. I was still feeling disappointed with some adverse criticisms I had picked up in London on my return after dancing in Russia. But at last my dancing was winning all-round approval. It had been a long, uphill struggle to get this far, and I found it immensely reassuring.

Sven and I left Stockholm by train for Vadstena where Sven's father was waiting at the station to welcome and drive us to 'Heleneborg', the family home. At the door stood his mother, arms out to embrace us. The flag was flying above the snow-filled garden and there was much excitement at the bevy of flowers we brought from my performances. Dear Farmor, Sven's mother, prepared a traditional meal which we thoroughly enjoyed, candle-lit, by the Christmas tree. The windows glowed with the traditional four candlesticks which light up the windows of almost every house across the Swedish countryside at this time. The candles represent the four Sundays of Advent: as each Sunday arrives a candle is lit, so by Christmas all four are alight. The 'Tomter', the mischievous leprechaun-like creature, was naughtily ringing the Christmas bells on the table. I loved Sven's parents, particularly Farmor who helped fill the void left by my own dear mother's death, eight years ago already.

70 1959: Covent Garden, Bucharest And Christmas

My return to Covent Garden was not all plain-sailing. To my great disappointment, after enquiring about fees, the Soviet authorities said they were unable to release Kondratov. After further discussions with Madam, David Webster rang Bronstad, director of the company in Copenhagen to enquire whether Frank Schaufuss might be permitted to guest with me for a month in London. Sadly Bronstad replied that it was not possible for him to be away for such a long period. So Madam and I discussed Eglevsky, who was keen to dance with me and had invited me to join his small company in America, an invitation I did not follow through.

Finally it was agreed the most practical way forward was for me to contact Caj Selling in Stockholm directly, to enquire about the possibility of his availability. He was thrilled to be asked, but doubted that the Stockholm company would allow him a month's leave. I was in an agony of suspense until Michael Wood rang on Friday January 23rd to tell me that the director, Hilton, had agreed to his coming and it was all finally settled. What relief I felt as I went to Svetlana Beriosova's wedding and witnessing her radiant happiness.

Sven and I met Caj at Heathrow on the evening of Sunday 15th February and rehearsals began next morning at Colet Gardens. It felt strange to be back in the school-like atmosphere where, after almost two years, nothing appeared to have changed. Everyone was welcoming, but I was pleased that we were left to ourselves during our first few days and covered all the repertoire we were to perform. By the end of the week we were hard at work in the Opera House with Emanuel Young who was to be our conductor. Enthusiastic and cooperative, he was guesting at the same time as Richard Arnell. The music director was Hugo Rignold and associate conductor Kenneth Alwyn.

Friday was memorable for my first meeting with the great soprano Joan Sutherland in number five dressing room, the one always used by leading artists. We were occupying it at different times, but she came in unexpectedly early that afternoon. I was completely overcome by her friendly, natural charm.

The following Monday I rehearsed *Checkmate* with David Blair and Caj at Colet Gardens under the eagle eye of Jack Hart, now the company's ballet master, who was delighted with how well Caj worked with the other knights. Ninette took all the rehearsals on stage, and I found her supportive and encouraging. We had a totally different relationship now that I was no longer a member of the Company.

At the end of the fortnight's rehearsal we had an orchestral full company call for *Swan Lake*, which marked my return to the stage of the Royal Opera House. I experienced a tense weekend, but what a wonderful reception we were given at Monday's performance.

Feeling surrounded by goodwill I received 18 bouquets, lots of telegrams and cards. I knew the performance had gone well, my faith in God seeing me safely through another challenge. It was two years since I had appeared at Covent Garden, and there were many critical eyes watching closely.

I was happy when the time came to go home with a pleased Sven, de Vos, Caj and other close friends. Surrounded by flowers we celebrated with champagne, and it was well after 3am by the time I checked the cards attached to all the glorious flowers and arranged them in suitable vases. It made me realise how kind and supportive were my faithful fans. I went to bed feeling blessed and much loved.

There were further orchestral full company calls for *Sleeping Beauty* and *Giselle*, a luxury one was never granted as a Company member. Only Margot as first cast was entitled to have them, which certainly placed other casts at a disadvantage. There was also a Gala at Covent Garden at which Caj and I had hoped to dance an excerpt from *Raymonda*, but through some misunderstanding with Stockholm regarding performing rights we settled for the *Aurora* pas de deux instead. Those performances during March meant so much to me, and I found it wonderful to be dancing at the Royal Opera House again.

Margot was on a tour of New Zealand and Australia with a small group of dancers from the company while I was at Covent Garden. I thought that this might partly explain Madam's continued interest in my returning as guest artist on an annual basis. I was delighted when in July she suggested more performances in the autumn as well as at the beginning of the next year to lead the second company on their South African tour. At the same time, Braunsweg was pressing me to dance with Festival Ballet on their forthcoming autumn tour, but I turned down his invitation.

I asked my agent to discuss fees with Webster but what he suggested was so little (£75 a performance) that we felt I should not accept it. We presumed that the recent decline in the ballet audience attendances at the Garden influenced Webster's low offer. In August Madam and I had lunch together, during which I felt embarrassed having to discuss money, but to my relief she was understanding. Although the autumn tour would not now happen, for financial reasons, we left the South African tour open for further discussion. Madam indicated she would seek better remuneration for that tour, so I lived in hope. Madam did agree to release Bryan Ashbridge to partner me in Bucharest in the autumn, although not at Covent Garden as initially hoped.

Our arrival in Bucharest was filmed as we descended from the plane, with floodlights, cameras and a host of people, three interpreters, and dancers to greet us on the tarmac. We were to dance the full-length *Swan Lake*, and it became a joy to work with their big, national ballet company. The company was of a high standard, professional in every way and, most importantly, very friendly. Long rehearsals began next morning and were essential, for the production differed considerably to those we knew, lasted four hours, and there was much to learn. Their leading ballerina, trained in the Russian style, was superb, with eloquent arms which she used to great effect in *Swan Lake*: I realised I had real competition.

Gelu Barbu, as the magician Von Rothbart, was a fantastic partner and actor who helped me through our many scenes. We became good friends and remained in touch even after he left Bucharest for Las Palmas where, for many decades, he has run his own successful school and company. Recently he has been invited to return to his country as a guest teacher, which has given him much pleasure.

The conductor came especially from Moscow to conduct our *Swan Lake* performances. He was experienced and accommodating as our tempi were different. After hours of rehearsal, learning so much new choreography, my toes became raw and my body very stiff and sore, and I was glad that Sven had been able to come. The successful opening was followed with a party at the British Embassy attended by the dancers and VIPs from the opera house.

Bryan and I also gave recitals in the older, smaller Savoy Theatre which had a good-sized stage, and another recital in the opera house. We had the accompaniment of a fine pianist and these advertised recitals were well attended. We were given numerous receptions including by the Minister of Culture and the British Legation. Another day we visited the large ballet school filled with its exceptional students, training in the Soviet style.

My memory of Bucharest is not only of its magnificent buildings but also the feeling of being watched all the time. In some ways it felt like Russia, with whom it was closely linked: one distinctly felt the communist stranglehold on the population. In a corridor on my first day in the theatre I was secretly warned by a dancer that my dressing room was under surveillance from a window in the opposite building and that every room was bugged. How sad that this was all too true.

As we flew away from Romania on the first stage of our journey home I experienced the same feeling of relief which I felt on leaving Russia. Yet the people we met were so warm and kind, as was our wonderful send-off at the airport. Gathered there was a host of dancers mingling with British Embassy personnel, a man from the Ministry of Culture and our interpreters, Nina and Margit, both in tears. We were showered with flowers and chocolates, and with so much affection and goodwill that it was hard to leave them behind. I wondered if perhaps they were stifling a longing to go with us. One does not realise what it must be like to grow up in a society where everything one says and does is under scrutiny.

When in London I always continued my daily training with de Vos in my quest for the elusive perfection – an artist's constant goal. I enjoyed partaking in radio interviews, and I also enjoyed dancing on the comedian Arthur Askey's television programme. I was pleased to be rehearsing again at Covent Garden with Bryan, preparing for the South African tour in the New Year, which was apparently going ahead.

It was not straightforward, however, and I had to see both Michael Wood and Madam about the unsatisfactory billing for the three-month tour. I was also displeased with the proposed performance dates – I was expected to dance but not offered both the opening and closing nights – so there was further wrangling. I gathered that the problem lay with Beriosova and the South African ballerina Nadia Nerina. It was eventually agreed that I would arrive a week after the opening and would dance the final night of the tour in Cape Town. Disappointed at still being dictated to, I sadly realised that there would always be a battle at the Garden. Nonetheless, I felt reassured that the decision I had made to leave the Company as a permanent member was the right one. Now it was for me to map out my future without the restrictions of a resident company.

There was great excitement on Boxing Day when we went with my father to see *Aladdin* at the Coliseum: Ingvar's first pantomime. He sat mesmerised, whispering eager questions to Sven and behaving beautifully. When a scene changed to reveal rows of fountains showering water on girls beneath, however, Ingvar enquired in a loud voice: 'But where is the soap, Mummy?' to the amusement of the audience around us! That family Christmas of 1959 was a particularly happy time.

71 *1960: Flying South*

A few days into the New Year, however, we suffered a big shock. Returning from rehearsals at the ITV studios I found a very worried husband and Ingvar ill in bed, his glands and body very painful but with no cold or cough. All I could do was to try and get him interested in his favourite book, so I read to him from *The Water Babies*. Next day I was off to class and rehearsal as usual, hoping Ingvar would get better.

Sven called our doctor who came at 2pm and was puzzled. Another doctor was contacted who came at 6pm. Sven then took Ingvar to hospital where he was operated on two hours later for appendicitis, with a gland also removed. Oblivious to all this, Bryan and I were dancing the *Don Quixote* divertissement on ITV. It was only after leaving the studios soon after 10pm that I was given a message from my father, telling me what was happening and to go straightaway to the hospital. I did – scared, but praying hard. I was in the waiting room by 10.45, when Sven came through to tell me that all had gone well. With Margaret MacInnes (Ingvar's godmother) we were allowed to creep in and see our precious child sleeping peacefully.

That was Tuesday night but the next day – and for several more to come – he was in agony, asking me to pray to God to take away the awful pain. He kept being sick, unable to keep down even milk and water. Sven and I were at his bedside for the next three days because his temperature would not go down. By Sunday morning we found him much brighter but to everyone's consternation his temperature rose again. I couldn't sleep for worrying; it seemed inhuman to leave him in the hospital, seeing him so ill, even though we always said prayers with him last thing before departing. Tuesday evening, however, his two doctors thought things were beginning to improve and that he might be well enough to go home by the end of the week. Sven and I collected Ingvar on Friday afternoon, finding him waiting, fully dressed and excited. We experienced such happiness being at home together again.

I made meatballs for the homecoming. It did my heart good to see Ingvar's pleasure at being served his absolute favourite and also a special chocolate dessert, even though he became too tired to finish it and was happy to be back in his own bed again. It was wonderful next morning to hear him in his bedroom chirping away happily to himself. How grateful and relieved we were. By Monday he was allowed his first bath since the operation when Sven carefully removed the plaster over his wound. Ingvar stood this well, reminding me how, despite his terrible pain in hospital, he never cried, determined to be brave.

The time was creeping towards the South African tour, and my heart began to sink at the thought of leaving Ingvar and Sven for such a long time. Less than two weeks later, on February 6th, with a very heavy heart I flew to South Africa again – this time not to give recitals but to dance with the Royal Ballet. The tour started in Johannesburg, and I joined the Company a week after the opening, finishing three months later in Cape Town on the last day of April. It was an interesting tour, not without incident. My overriding memory is of the incredible kindness and consideration given me by both the Stodels and the Mackenzies who looked after me as if I were their own child.

South Africa was still without television, so live theatre was popular and well attended. With certain exceptions the performances were 'for whites only' but, through Equity's insistence, our Company gave special performances for the coloured population in Johannesburg and Cape Town, where the audiences engaged immediately with the dancing and were very responsive. In Petermaritzburg, blacks were allowed to watch from the gallery, both races under the same roof. These shows followed our six weeks in Johannesburg where the Company won much acclamation.

I was interested to see the changes in the Company since I had left and was impressed one evening watching a young dancer's debut as Giselle. She was obviously talented and gave a compelling interpretation of this great role, which demands strong acting ability and a good elevation. She gave a touching performance, and I felt sure she had a great future ahead. I was not wrong: Antoinette Sibley's partnership with Antony Dowell was to become a ballet legend and, with him, she went on to lead the Royal Ballet for many successful years.

The day after we left Johannesburg there was an uprising in the nearby shantytown of Sharpeville. We later learnt of the tragic massacre that had taken place. Once in Durban we faced an all-out strike and sensed an undercurrent of unrest. We heard that black locals were massing behind the hills, and the hotel staff were warned not to return home. There were also demonstrators outside the theatre who tried to get in, and three men were shot dead. All of this was disturbing in this normally idyllic spot. Our performances nevertheless went ahead as planned and were well attended.

Mercifully, by the time we reached Cape Town the volatile situation appeared to have settled, and we were able to enjoy the famous scenery. Our conductor John (Jack) Lanchbery hired a Vespa and one morning insisted on taking me up the mountain to the furthermost point from which we could appreciate the Cape's wondrous position between the Atlantic and Indian Oceans. Holding on like a limpet, I managed to enjoy not only the glorious scenery but also the sweet clear air. All around were wild flowers, fragrant smelling shrubs and exotic proteas, the national flower of South Africa. What I had not expected was to see zebras, springbok and baboons roaming wild. When we stopped, to my consternation the baboons attempted to climb onto the Vespa so we quickly made off as I clung madly to Jack's waist! In our escape a stray bee left a rather painful sting on my face. But the pain was soon forgotten through the sheer beauty of our surroundings. Jack was always such fun to be with, but what an outing!

Our final night in Cape Town proved exciting. I was dancing my favourite role Odette/Odile and as *Swan Lake* was much loved in South Africa, there was a feeling of goodwill from the audience, mixed with a general frisson of excitement within the Company. When the performance ended, Stodel came on stage to make a speech congratulating and thanking the Company while balloons and streamers showered down on performers and audience alike – a glittering end to the tour.

72 *Southern Hemispehere, 1960*

True to her word, Ninette allocated to me a few performances at the Garden on our return from South Africa. Bryan and I rehearsed next day for *Swan Lake* the following week. Plans were now being finalised for my tour to New Zealand, Australia and the Lebanon, organized by James Laurie, a young Australian impresario. With the conductor Dudley Simpson, Bryan and I were to lead a small group of dancers from Sadler's Wells. Pamela Moncur, Donald Britton and Dudley were to fly two days ahead of Bryan and me. They were delayed 24 hours en route so had little opportunity to adapt to the twelve-hour time change in New Zealand.

Bryan and I left London after our last performance, *Giselle,* on Saturday night 28th May. Travelling that far in those days took a long time, as Bryan and I were to discover. We left Heathrow on Sunday at 3.30 on a BA flight, finally reaching our destination Auckland on Tuesday evening at 7.30, having stopped at a wet Düsseldorf, a hot Beirut, a sweltering Calcutta, and made two shorter stops in Karachi and Bangkok. On landing in Sydney we were met by several dance celebrities before being ushered onto a plane onwards to New Zealand.

After only one night's sleep, we dealt with the local press who were already in the lobby agog with questions. Eventually we were able to escape to a formal morning reception given by the representatives of the Festival. We were pleasantly surprised to find the theatre had a generous sized stage with a good surface, albeit hard and raked. With only one afternoon in which to prepare we ran through the entire first programme, acclimatising ourselves to the overall lay-out and, surprisingly, not getting too exhausted.

I still had to oversee the unpacking of all our props, costumes and their much needed resurrecting and ironing. It was a pleasure supervising the lighting with the technicians who, like all the staff, were willing and helpful. My doubts about James Laurie's capabilities were assuaged as I was driven to the television studios where I was interviewed live: the very first person to be so honoured by the newly opened New Zealand Television service. Fifty years on, I was contacted here in England to speak again for the service's 50th Anniversary.

It must have been wonderful for Bryan to be back dancing in his country of birth and with his family out front. He had left for England in 1947 to attend the Sadler's Wells school, joining the Company a year later in 1948. It was a pleasure to meet his parents who welcomed our little troupe warmly and were obviously proud of Bryan's achievements.

We gave four performances in the first three days. On the second night I was terribly upset when the interval music was cut by mistake, leaving me little time in which to change costume and shoes for the *Black Swan* divertissement. This caused me to fluff my last few fouettés, something I had never done before, and I covered up with fast piqué turns to the corner to finish on the music. Fortunately, few would have been aware of the change, but I was dreadfully disappointed in myself and wanted to cry. My one consolation was that the house was not full, which we thought might have been due to the many other Festival entertainments in progress. Our remaining four performances over three days passed swiftly as the audiences grew and by the time came to leave we enjoyed a full and enthusiastic house.

Exhausted after the Saturday evening show, we left to recuperate at the Hot Springs Hotel. Arriving at 2am, we immediately slipped into a soothing thermal pool. After revelling in its hot, healing waters for three hours, we returned to our rooms and slept soundly. None of us had spotted a warning notice saying it was dangerous to stay in the hot springs for longer than an hour! Unaffected, we returned to Auckland rejuvenated and refreshed.

In Auckland I met my New Zealand pen-friend Gwen de Leon for the first time. We had corresponded for 23 years, since we were seven years old. In those days, as drinkers of Bournville cocoa, children were encouraged to join the Cocoa Club and write to another member in a foreign country. This was popular in the 1930s and my parents thought it would be a good way to learn about other countries. Gwen would post exciting packages containing all sorts of dried flora, Maori artifacts or special sea-shells she gathered, which would arrive carefully wrapped in tissue paper. This awakened in me a keen interest in the two islands, although I never dreamt that I would visit them nor meet my pen-friend. But here she was in my dressing room having come to a performance, a charming young woman with a beautiful smile and a lovely figure. We arranged to meet next day at her home for a long talk; there I met her genial parents who shared the pleasure of our meeting.

After performances in Palmerston and a long drive to Wellington, the next day – Monday – was nonstop, starting with yet another press conference in the hotel lobby, and a private reception with the city's distinguished Lord Mayor, at which I was expected to say a few words before leaving for the theatre. There was a lot to do prior to a late lunch with Laurie's representative Hayes presiding, followed by a big reception given by the Minister for Internal Relations. I gave another speech there, which seemed to flow quite well. Thank goodness the theatre arranged a masseur for me before our opening that evening which, mercifully, was on a fair-sized stage. Although our dressing rooms were not warm enough we did our best to give our audience a good show and were rewarded by wonderful applause. Once again, however, the house was not quite full, and my doubts as to Laurie's advance advertising began to surface again.

I was thrilled, however, when after the performance a man of striking posture came backstage and introduced himself as Algeranoff, one of Pavlova's most famous partners.

I could hardly believe it; this renowned artist here to see me. What an honour I knew it to be, and managed to mumble nervously something to that effect. I found him such a kind, lovely man, brimming over with life and merriment, and the time with him went all too quickly. His link with the immortal Pavlova was, I felt, a precious endowment for New Zealand and Australia where he made his home, working with the Borovansky company as a teacher as well as with the Australian Children's Theatre. I am now the proud owner of his entertaining book *My Years with Pavlova* which makes for riveting reading. It pleases me to realise that I have danced in many of the theatres, cities and countries in which the greatest ballerina of the last century herself appeared and is still remembered by those who watched her perform.

From Wellington we flew down to Christchurch across the Cook Strait, the body of water separating the north and south islands, extending north west to the Tasman Sea and to the south east the Pacific Ocean. Our two shows there – as in Dunedin which followed – were less well attended than expected, much to our disappointment. This despite the press reviews which continued to be full of praise but came out too late to fill the theatre. I was thankful that we were able to pull out of performing in Melbourne and Sydney as I had no faith in our impresario, who proved to be as incompetent as he was unreliable. Instead we were able to return to England for a much needed few days respite before our next important date in the Lebanon.

On arriving back in London after the long haul with many stops, to my intense joy I found Sven in the customs shed waiting to embrace me, whilst waiting outside were my father with Ingvar, who once again leapt up on me and would not leave my side. I was moved beyond belief. To have such love from those I held so dear meant everything in the world to me.

The next day I thought I detected a slight change in Sven; he seemed to have aged a little, his hair was certainly greyer and his boundless energy curtailed. My conscience troubled me horribly. I had a strong feeling that I had been away too long this time and must be more careful in the planning of my tours in future. It was heaven to be home in our beautiful top floor flat; it was clean and shining although, every so often, smoke from Claridges hotel blew across, delivering filthy hard particles of soot into our home. Sven would ring them to complain and there would be the most polite apology that something had gone wrong with their boilers but was being attended to!

There was but a week and a half before flying to Beirut and I spent as much time as I could with Ingvar between my rehearsals and TV recordings, taking him to and collecting him from school. These were his last days at his pre-prep school, run so well by the principal Miss de Brissac. Sven and I were now looking at and deciding on the most suitable prep school for him to attend next.

The dreaded morning arrived. I awoke with a heavy heart and was whisked away by taxi at 7am to meet Bryan Ashbridge and his wife Dolly (Dorothy Zaymes) at London Airport. We were escorted into a private room for coffee before posing for photos on the plane's steps, prior to an excellent flight to the capital of the Lebanon. I felt intensely interested in this country, knowing we were to dance in the ancient temple at Baalbek and curious as to our reception. We were met at Beirut by two enthusiastic, smartly dressed young men who straightaway drove us to a hotel with an air-conditioned suite. An early evening, big press conference saw us seated at a long table and bombarded with searching questions. When this concluded, we were driven to the television studios to be interviewed by a young woman with a pronounced American accent.

Next morning we assembled by 9 o'clock for the drive to Baalbek with Mrs El Said, who was responsible for the festival. This proved a drawn-out affair, stopping first at her friend's house for refreshments before driving for some time in the boiling sun through arid country. The road to Baalbek goes ultimately to Damascus and was busy with cars, trucks, donkeys and many strangely robed people who we presumed were Bedouin.

On arrival at an over-hot hotel, Mrs El Said disappeared. One and a half hours later – the agreed meeting time – no one was about except for a British Embassy official who drove us to the Roman ruins. No one was there either for the 5 o'clock rehearsal; no stage manager or wardrobe mistress. Mrs El Said miraculously reappeared an hour later with the keys for the recording machinery. Once that was unlocked we were able to commence rehearsing on a well built stage within the shadow of ancient, mighty pillars. We practised until after midnight, returning worn-out to our uncomfortable hotels. The next day we left for our final run-through at the sun city of the ancient world, which the Phoenicians christened the temple of the Sun god, Baal Hadad. As the evening light faded, we felt transported back in time.

At our opening performance next evening I was inspired. Surrounded by the great columns, the moon shining upon us, heart and soul encapsulated in dance – I visualised the immense mystical power this setting would have held over its worshippers – for the Romans it was called the temple of Jupiter, and so named by the Greeks, too. The audience that first night was a most distinguished one with the Lebanese Prime Minister, a large number of the diplomatic corps, the Vice President of the University, as well as the British Ambassador, who kindly sent me flowers. It ended in triumph at 1.30 in the morning in mystical moonlight with a thousand stars glittering in the heavens above. An incredible scene.

Once back in the hotel, I tucked into my supper of bread, butter and jam! We went back early the next afternoon to be photographed in this famous setting amidst the imposing pillars. The sun was baking hot and the heat intensified as the photographer set up a huge sheet of silver paper for lighting the shots! Never have I been so uncomfortable, leaning backwards against Bryan's perspiring arms for what seemed an eternity, and I wondered if the worshippers of old ever moved far in the scorching heat, or did they melt into oblivion? We enjoyed another inspired, though exhausting, performance before returning to 20th-century London, going directly to the airport from the ruins.

From Heathrow, on Monday 18th July 1960, I took the airport bus to Victoria and then a taxi which brought me home by 1 o'clock. There on the door was a well-written message in crayon, 'WELCOME HOME MUMMY'. I could hardly believe my eyes. A young body jumped on me with such love and fervor, almost knocking me to the floor! What excitement and joy followed, the sounds bringing Sven out from a patient he was treating. How happy he was to see me home again, and once more I thought I must never leave them again. Ingvar and I had a marvellous afternoon together as he helped me unpack and put things tidily away. He was so thrilled to be allowed to stay up for dinner with us all – my father, Hazel, Sven and me – and when the time came for bed he went into his room singing away contentedly. Little did I know what Sven and he planned for the next morning.

I awoke as they both came in with coffee, Swedish buns and lighted candles – and with another thrilling unexpected surprise present, to celebrate our 10th wedding anniversary. I hastily blinked sleep away from my eyes as I opened the nicely wrapped little box and found the most magnificent pair of long drop diamond earrings nestling inside. I gasped with delight and was so overcome by Sven's exceptional kindness that I burst into tears, which Ingvar rushed to wipe away. It was a precious moment we three had together, happy beyond belief.

74 *Family Matters*

Three days later we were on the high seas, sailing once again to Sweden for our much longed for annual holiday, accompanied by my father. He relished this time with Ingvar who, aged six, was alive with curiosity about everything. The boat was a source of infinite delight and surprise, except when the funnel blew its deafening blast as it passed other ships – then Ingvar was terrified and had difficulty not crying. He behaved well at mealtimes, sitting up straight and eating all the strange Scandinavian food put before him. We anticipated an idyllic three weeks in Sweden, although once we arrived, the weather was poor – disappointingly wet and on the cool side. It did not prevent me from swimming at every opportunity, whenever we spotted a lake close to the roadside. I expected Sven's Lake Vättern, as the deepest lake in Europe, to be cold but I would not allow it to weaken my resolve to swim every day. A holiday has to include at least one swim a day, and I liked to think that the icy dips compensated for the lavish food I was devouring.

Autumn came and, back home, I relished the time with my family. Sven and I went to the Royal Festival Hall to see John Gilpin's farewell with Festival Ballet. The Artistic Director Anton Dolin gave an emotional speech praising Gilpin's contribution to the

Company. I turned down the invitation from Madam to tour the regions with the Wells Company because we could not come to a satisfactory agreement over my billing. I wondered why there was always a battle to be fought at the Garden. I adjusted to the outcome as there were other offers on the cards, including an intriguing proposal from the Chinese Embassy to dance in China, possibly early in the coming year. I relished being free to choose where and when I would dance.

I thoroughly enjoyed my daily training with de Vos in the ongoing battle for improvement. We worked on body placement, use of neck, head, arms, hands, and countless other details, including the all-important personal response to music, paramount for a sensitive performance.

I was happy to dance on television from time to time, thereby keeping in touch with my loyal fans. They must have been surprised at Christmas when I performed a contemporary solo to Bach music. This was commissioned especially for the Max Jaffa Trio programme celebrating Christmas, and Max accompanied me on his violin. A beautiful experience; I gave several shows with Max but none as moving as this one, his fine playing enhancing the special atmosphere that Christmas generates.

Through the late autumn good progress was made in the discussions for me to dance in China with the Peking Ballet Company and with one of their leading male dancers. In anticipation I practiced hard my repertoire, arranging my costumes and having more dancing photos taken. It was agreed that Sven would come with me, but we were worried about leaving Ingvar, a six-year-old, for five weeks so brought up the possibility of him coming too. Plans moved fast and, at the beginning of January, a man from the Foreign Office came to see us and everything appeared to be going well: we had their approval and support.

Earlier I had received another invitation from Ninette which interested me: to lead the Sadler's Wells Company on their forthcoming tour to Japan in late spring. I had to clarify the billing as Margot was to dance initially with the Company, leaving me to finish the engagements in Japan, Hong Kong and the Philippines. This time, discussions concluded to my satisfaction. It was now up to me to decide whether to go or not as it meant being away for seven weeks.

Meanwhile the Chinese came back with the disappointing decision that my son could not accompany us. In the light of this news I suggested a postponement for a couple of years until Ingvar would be boarding at school. The Chinese accepted this proposition with grace, and I was secretly rather relieved – we could not have left Ingvar in the care of an au pair for such a length of time.

The lease on our flat was coming up for renewal, about which Sven had been in touch with our solicitors for some time. We felt that we were beginning to outgrow our lovely flat. Since I became freelance the bedroom areas were now adorned with tutus hanging from the ceilings. So we were considering the possibility of moving to a house, and began the search for a suitable one. I had fallen in love with one nearby – in Park Street – which had been sold, but once more a For Sale board was outside. Sven, always cautious, was hesitant about acquiring it, but finally, after entreaties from Hazel and me, he agreed to pursue this. We also searched for a small weekend cottage and many of our weekends were spent traversing the countryside, often with dear Guy Horne in his lovely old Rolls Royce. What a great friend he was to us both, and how much we appreciated his advice – given so often over a magnificent meal at 'his' Cavalry Club.

As January 1961 drew to a close, I had a terrible shock: news of the death of my former dance partner, David Paltenghi. He had been my friend and partner since 1941, the year we both joined Sadler's Wells Company. During those war years and afterwards, dancing together at Covent Garden, I knew him as someone I could trust. When in 1957 he left to work as choreographer with his former company Ballet Rambert I missed his companionship. He also appeared in straight theatre, films and television, and we had rather lost touch.

On the morning of February 10th, GB Wilson drove me to David's funeral, where I met his wife Pamela for the first time: a very beautiful young doctor who behaved with great dignity. I admired her composure despite her terrible loss after only a few years of marriage. David died young, aged just forty-one. They were blessed with a son, Jake, which I hoped gave her some solace. I was shocked that after his years dancing with Sadler's Wells there were only two present from the Company, both dancers like myself: Leslie Edwards and David Davenport. I am still in contact with Pam, who now lives in the West Country, and also with Jake. He is a talented artist and spends his time painting, either in France or Gloucestershire near his mother.

After much deliberation, Sven agreed that I should go with the Wells to Japan. I had of course to suffer anguish at being away again for a long stretch from the two beings dearest to me in the whole world. It was a hard decision to make, but the tour was one I knew I should undertake. The repertoire was ideal for me: the full length *Swan Lake, Checkmate, Les Sylphides* and *Giselle.* I had never danced in the Far East before, so it offered new fields to conquer with the backing of a big British ballet company.

Ninette suggested the possibility of my also dancing on the tour in Andre Howard's ballet *Fête Étrange*. I liked the atmospheric work immensely – the Fauré music and Sophie Fedovoritch's fabulous costumes – so was disappointed that this did not transpire. Instead I was offered the lead role in *Veneziana*, another Andre Howard ballet but, despite the delightful Donizetti score, this work did not have the same depth and appeal, so I chose not to dance in it.

The first weeks of spring were packed with activity. It was pure joy for me to be able to take Ingvar to school each morning before my lesson with de Vos and to collect him when I was free. Sven was keen that Ingvar should take extra gym lessons, and I took him once a week to a private gym near Sloane Square. He learnt to climb a rope, to balance on a bar, jump over a 'horse' and other daring pursuits. One afternoon when I was watching, somehow he slipped, falling backwards from a height and hitting his head badly as he crashed down onto his back. With the pain and shock he was unable to hold back his tears, and I was terrified that he might have seriously hurt himself. Once safely home Sven immediately checked him over, put my mind at rest and gave him a soothing treatment. By the morning we were relieved to find a brighter, happier young chap only a little the worse for the accident, but still somewhat dazed by the unexpected fall. I had not slept well throughout the night and was so thankful for Sven's reassuring presence and his wonderful, calm handling of the incident.

Most weekends we tried to slip out of London to the peace and loveliness of the countryside. Our favourite hide-away was an old, small pub in Fittleworth, Sussex, appropriately called The Swan. One of Sven's many patients recommended it, and we loved the cosy, friendly atmosphere, the open fires in the winter, the good food and the comfort of a four-poster bed upstairs in an oak-beamed bedroom. It was within easy reach of the sea, too, but we preferred our walks along the banks of the nearby stream, exploring along muddy paths to a maze of forests and fields. Ingvar adored these rambles, which became voyages of exploration and learning: Sven was a keen botanist and very little of the wonders of nature escaped him. They were such happy times, just the three of us. How is it that the power of dance holds such sway over me that I am drawn away from my loved ones again and again? Perhaps one returns wiser from enforced separation, all the more aware of the riches love inspires.

75 *Japan, Hong Kong And The Philippines, 1961*

April was soon upon us and, after numerous rehearsals and fittings at the Garden, I was off once again, this time with the Company on a KLM plane to Tokyo. My last picture of my loved ones was of them standing on the tarmac as a coach took us to the plane. They waved me off as we took to the sky, but they looked so lost and forlorn that I thought my heart would burst with misery. What was I doing?

Apart from Bryan and Dolly Ashbridge, I did not know anyone in the 'second' Company led by John Field. So I was pleased when one morning on the coach going to the theatre, Margot came and sat beside me, chatting in a friendly manner. We agreed on the coldness of Tokyo's Festival Theatre, in which we were now rehearsing daily for our opening on Monday 17th April. We found the unusually wide stage a challenge and the hard, unyielding floor a problem. Perhaps because of its newness, the entire building felt damp with little atmosphere. We had several days in which to rehearse and acclimatise ourselves to these conditions, but were under the scrutiny of press photographers and reporters. I had never seen so many flashbulbs as at our dress rehearsals. I reminded myself Japan was the birthplace of many world famous cameras and cine-cameras, and reckoned they were all assembled there that day!

Margot opened our first two-week season in Tokyo with *Giselle* giving, as always, a superb performance. I was seated out front amidst a distinguished audience who, disappointingly, appeared to be almost as unresponsive and cold as the theatre. After the performance there was a formal, sit-down dinner at the British Embassy. This meant a rather late bedtime for me prior to my first night, about which I already felt quite apprehensive. I need not have worried as *Les Sylphides* and *Checkmate* flowed well under the sympathetic baton of Kenneth Alwyn, and I enjoyed having the extra space afforded by the huge rectangular stage. The next performances were in the Bunkyo Hall where, three days later, I danced *Swan Lake*: my first full-length role for over a year. A host of butterflies invaded my stomach beforehand.

On the evening prior to my performance I managed to fit in a visit to the Takarazuka Theatre. There, spellbound, I watched the Takarazuka Revue, an amazing all-female Japanese group, founded in 1913. It was the most phenomenal musical I had ever witnessed, and its perfection stayed, galvanising my performances for weeks to come.

A two-hour meeting was arranged for the Company to meet selected Japanese dancers and teachers, which I actually found strangely embarrassing as it was all very formal and polite. I began to realise this is the norm in Japan when meeting with strangers, yet we were all in the dance world, meeting in a theatre, with a common bond. I had hoped for a more genial relaxed time with the opportunity to get to know them a little and their outlook and approach to classical ballet.

Our next date was in Osaka and we travelled there on the amazing Bullet Train – very modern, very clean and very punctual. We arrived promptly at 3.30pm. Our hotel was in joyful contrast to those in Tokyo, being ultra-modern, spacious and, mercifully, with larger rooms. With mine, I was thrilled to discover a huge bathroom with a surprisingly big bath in which I could lie full length and soothe my aching limbs.

I found that the New York Philharmonic Orchestra were giving a concert that evening with Leonard Bernstein conducting, and I went on my own, listening to the most magnificent playing. I just had to meet the artists afterwards to thank them, which I was able to do. I had not met Bernstein before and immediately fell under his enigmatic spell.

As I was not performing on our opening next day I had the opportunity to visit, together with the British Vice Consul, a wonderful Zen Buddhist monastery. On meeting their senior monk, a doctor, we became involved in a most interesting debate about the hereafter. He patiently explained that to understand, one had to go within oneself, where all would become clear. I was intrigued and heartened as this was identical with the Sant Mat teaching. After a good debate we left this sacred centre of learning and peace, to return to the bustling industrial city of Osaka and rehearse for *Swan Lake.*

The following evening an enthusiastic audience uplifted me in my performance; Bryan, like me, was quite inspired by Ken's sympathetic conducting. On our closing night at the Osaka Festival I danced *Giselle* to an equally receptive audience. As the curtain fell, the entire Company assembled on stage and, as the curtain rose again, we acknowledged our thanks to the audience, coloured streamers descending upon us amidst deafening applause. Showers of flowers covered the stage, and the orchestra struck up *Auld Lang Syne*, which everybody out front and on stage joined in singing. It was totally unexpected and very moving. Now that Margot had left the tour, I had the privilege of giving both the first and last night performances.

Back in Tokyo, Sunday was the Company's last appearance in Japan, and it turned out to be as wonderful as in Osaka. The orchestra struck up *Auld Lang Syne*, which was immediately enhanced by a sea of voices both on and off stage, while paper streamers of a hundred hues fluttered down, enveloping us. Well aimed bouquets and single flowers flew from the applauding audience, miraculously missing the dancers who showed our appreciation by sweeping forward and back across the now flower drenched stage. A colourful memory to take away from Japan, together with other precious ones like their traditional Kabuki theatre, which I had so enjoyed watching. A land of great traditions – alien to the West, but nonetheless fascinating.

I wished that it had been possible to have made closer friendships with the Japanese we met. I became very fond of my dresser, a charming young woman, always very caring and helpful, but I felt there was always a kind of barrier. Maybe I imagined this, but I do not think so; perhaps it is the differences in our cultures. We continued to correspond for several years and when I returned as a director, eight years later, she came to see me: a tremendous surprise and delight.

The next stop on the Sadler's Wells itinerary was Hong Kong. We held our breath as we landed on a precarious land strip, flanked on either side by the South China Sea. I was agog to witness this famous island and was not to be disappointed. They say New York never sleeps – neither does Hong Kong. Waiting to welcome the Company was the impresario Harry Odell with his wife Sophie, who accompanied us all to the hotel in Kowloon. There was a mix-up over rooms so the Odells insisted I went home with them. There I made a very quick change before attending an important dinner given by a wealthy Chinese sponsor. The Odells took me under their wing for our three-nights stay, which I much appreciated: they were the most understanding hosts, allowing me to sleep in and really relax in their bohemian home.

Sophie was Chinese, warm hearted, comely and great fun. As astute as her husband, she took me to a small dealer specialising in pearls and chose on my behalf each pearl to make up a two-string necklace. The result when strung was perfect, and I have worn them on special occasions ever since.

What a contrast the Hong Kong theatre was after the huge, wide stages of Japan. It was small and felt more like a hall, with a small stage, no orchestra and no air conditioning. We danced to two pianos, which was fine for *Les Sylphides*, but not as appropriate for *Swan Lake*, which I danced both evenings, as well as the *Don Quixote* pas de deux with stoic Bryan. The heat and humidity was oppressive, yet the performances were full and the audiences ecstatic – even for the matinee which was squeezed in on the Wednesday.

The Company was loath to leave this vibrant metropolis early on Thursday morning to go on to Manila – it seemed we had only just arrived. How fast the time sped by and what a fascinating three days they were for us all.

That evening the whole Company were invited to a magnificent party given by a wealthy Pakistani supporter in his modern luxurious house and gardens. The dresses of the women were exquisite and the men wore attractive shirts of embroidered cotton decorated with lace – apparently the accepted attire in Manila. The heat even in the evening was still oppressive, and we were glad to find ourselves outside in the gardens where a huge table made of ice held, within its glistening circular formation, foods and fruits of many kinds. Such a display of wealth I had never seen before and, bearing in mind the poverty of the main population across the island, I found it disturbing.

The Company gave three performances in Manila with a marvellous party after the first night given by the British Ambassador. I found the big theatre a pleasure to dance in, with its air conditioning and splendid flat stage. The Company, too, appreciated the amenities of a large theatre after the cramped, airless conditions in Hong Kong. The rehearsal of *Swan Lake* ran smoothly and throughout the performance everyone was inspired to dance to their full potential.

The great day arrived at last and I could hardly contain myself with excitement: we were set to start the long flight home. I had been counting the months, weeks then days, and now it was just three days before we would be back in England, reunited with our families. Overnighting in Thailand, we were escorted to a hotel in Bangkok for a quick lunch before a performance by young Thai dancers which had been arranged especially for us that afternoon. We learnt that the students are trained in the early hours of the morning to accomplish complete control of their eye and facial muscles. Their telling hand movements, delicate fingers embellishing every gesture, was breathtakingly beautiful. It was different from any other ancient dance form, and impressive to see the grace, dignity and control in such young girls – we came away enthralled.

After stops in Karachi and Rome, I suddenly realised that it was Wednesday 24th May: in only a few hours we should be safely home. It seemed a miracle that we landed on time at Heathrow and, dazed, I waited with the Company for our luggage to appear. Mercifully the customs let us through without further delays, to be engulfed by a huge barrage of hugs, kisses and tears, all of us reunited with our dear ones. After coping with the crowd of press (but surprisingly no television crews), Sven, Ingvar, my father and I drove home. What happiness.

76 *1962: Appearances With Royal And Festival Companies*

I was relieved that my BBC interview for *In Town Today* had been switched to early the next morning, after which I had the most wonderful surprise: Sven drove me to 78 Park Street, unlocked the door and carried me over the threshold into the house. He handed me the keys, kissing me gently and saying, 'This is our future home, my darling.' He knew how much I had longed for this elegant house since it first came on the market, and now my joy knew no bounds. It had delicate linenfold panelling in the front ground floor room, above an ancient stone-worked fireplace, while on the first floor the sitting room was entirely oak-panelled, as was the study. This was the first time I had been inside, and it was more beautiful than I had imagined. Sven was to relocate his practice to our new home, so there were a lot of alterations to be undertaken before we could move in. Over the next months ,between our daily commitments, we happily chose furnishings, finally moving in before Christmas. We lived there contentedly for the next seventeen years.

Within two weeks after the tour I delivered a speech at the Lord Mayor's Banquet, which I struggled to learn by heart. It was well received, but I found it nerve-racking amidst such grandeur, pomp and ceremony. In contrast, I presented an evening of ballet music live on BBC radio at the Royal Festival Hall with the BBC Concert Orchestra. I also made a number of recordings with them at Portland Place for a series of concerts of ballet music, for which I wrote the scripts.

I had the pleasure of returning to Munich to dance with the company in their productions of *Swan Lake* and *Sleeping Beauty*, as well as appearing on German television. On my return to London I was just in time to attend the Kirov (Maryinsky) Ballet opening at Covent Garden and enjoy numerous receptions given in their honour. Their performances differed in style from the more vivacious Bolshoi company, the orchestra playing at a slower pace to the intense, studied interpretation of the dancers.

In mid-July, Lord and Lady Astor invited Sven and me for lunch at their country house, followed by a visit with them to Glyndebourne to hear a Britten opera. This was the beginning of a long friendship with the Astors, which sprung from my work for the Sunshine Homes for Blind Babies. Irene Astor was their President and every so often our paths would cross at meetings. She was a gracious, reserved woman, slender, erect and I suspect a little shy. Gavin was the opposite: outgoing and jovial.

August was on the horizon and Sweden beckoning. Sven, Ingvar and I left for a month's holiday, happy to spend time with Sven's parents and relatives. My father joined us two weeks later and stayed on a further week with Ingvar after Sven and I returned to London. The house took a lot of our time through the autumn, which as usual was filled with numerous other engagements. Regrettably it saw my father's retirement from the Ministry of Works, a post he had really enjoyed.

I worked hard every morning with de Vos and fielded a number of talks which included one to NatWest bankers, another to the Swedish church, school prize-givings, committee meetings – some with the Invalid Children's Association in which I took an ongoing interest. I was President of the Association of Ballet Clubs, and we held regular meetings. Marie Rambert was one of our many guest speakers: dynamic and witty; she was a huge success. I also felt it a great honour that Ninette de Valois gave an interesting account of her life to our members.

I was approached about possibly touring Australia with a small group from the Royal Ballet, including Bryan Ashbridge and Svetlana Beriosova, which would have been ideal. But just before Christmas I was disappointed to be informed that Margot was now to lead the tour instead of me. As I was already rehearsing with Bryan for my performances at the Garden in February in *Swan Lake*, this came as a surprise.

I was better pleased, however, when the Garden allowed Bryan to come with me the following month to dance *Swan Lake* and *Sleeping Beauty* in Oslo. By May I was in Stockholm working with Caj Selling, the tall classical dancer Mary Skeaping had chosen to partner me in her *Swan Lak*e in the Stockholm opera house. He did not compare with Bryan's partnering, needing to be more supportive of his ballerina in pirouettes, although he certainly improved as we got to know better each other's style.

Immediately on my return to London Madam rehearsed me at Barons Court in her *Checkmate.* I valued her stimulating calls; she was clear and informative in her instructions, drawing out the best in one. I felt well prepared for the performances at Covent Garden and then on with the Company to Coventry and Bath to appear in *Swan Lake*.

The end of the season also marked the end of Ingvar's school days at prep school. How quickly the years had sped by – he was now eight and all his school friends were going to boarding school in the autumn. He wanted to be like them and go away, too, but I dreaded this. In mid- September, was with a heavy heart that Sven and I drove him to Gloucestershire, leaving him one Thursday at Beaudesert Boarding School. I cried most of the way home. It was ironic that now I was able to be more at home he would be away. I would miss him terribly – his happy chatter and smiling, loving face.

By the start of October I was occupied with rehearsals at the Garden for *Lady and the Fool.* These were taken by either Michael Somes or Jack Hart, both former partners of mine, now accomplished répétiteurs. Initially we rehearsed the individual pas de deux from the pas de quatre. Three of the four men in the pas de quatre were new to me – Derek Rencher, David Drew and Brian Lawrence – but Ronald Hynd I had known for some time. Also during those weeks of rehearsals I taught *Les Sylphides* to Keith Rosson, another dancer unknown to me. During these calls, standing on full pointe to show Keith a certain hold, I strained my left calf muscle. This meant my being off for a few days and missing performances, which was upsetting even though everyone, including Madam, was understanding. To this day my calf is inclined to cramp.

Towards the end of 1962 I became more involved with teaching. I gave occasional classes at the RAD, which attracted large numbers and which I always enjoyed. From time to time I adjudicated test classes at White Lodge, the Royal Ballet's lower school, where I was impressed by the enthusiasm of the young students. Grace Cone, one of the principals of the Cone Ripman Schools, was also keen that I should judge their end-of-year dance tests and their Markova Award.

I continued to be on radio and TV, but at the back of my mind always was Ingvar. We enjoyed visiting him in Gloucestershire, where he seemed to have settled in well. Our friends Jill and Humphrey Strong lived close by, their two nephews already at the school, which was one of the reasons we chose Beaudesert. The headmaster, Austin Richardson, was a keen ballet enthusiast who we felt would keep a good eye on Ingvar. On Sundays all three boys were allowed to visit Jill and Humphrey's delightful home, and we enjoyed many a happy weekend with them, which continued long after Ingvar's school days in Gloucestershire were over. How wonderful it was when Ingvar came home to us at half term and in the holidays; this became the highlight of our home life. He was so dear to us.

In early 1963 I appeared frequently with London Festival Ballet partnered by Caj Selling. We danced only on the opening nights of their week-long seasons in the major cities of the UK. Over Easter we also appeared with them in Monte Carlo, which was extremely exciting. I felt privileged to dance in the lovely Salle Garnier, where Diaghilev had brought his fabulous Russian dancers every year from 1911 until 1929, creating many of his works there. The stage is small, likewise the theatre, nevertheless this 600-seater retains a great atmosphere with a host of memories, and it was an inspiring setting in which to appear. Whilst in Monte Carlo I watched the company's new ballet, *Peer Gynt*, choregraphed by Orlikovsky. I looked forward to creating the leading role in this work, but was not satisfied, as it evolved, so reluctantly withdrew.

Within a day of my return from the glamour of Monte Carlo, Caj and I danced once more with Festival Ballet at the Hippodrome Theatre Golders Green, another theatre with strong balletic links: Pavlova appeared there and also Anton Dolin. During May we danced the first nights in Brighton, Edinburgh and Newcastle, returning after each performance to London. This allowed me to carry out many other engagements, amongst which I particularly enjoyed presenting BBC concerts. These were generally recorded in advance of transmission. I recall rehearsing one morning at the BBC TV Centre with the Philharmonic Orchestra, whose conductor Laurence Leonard I much admired. It was marvellous being close to the players, listening to their corrections, then returning early evening to the Centre for the live transmission of our programme, titled *Music in Camera*. I so loved these concerts when I felt one with the music and the orchestra, losing myself in all the expressive harmonies.

In mid-June I was dancing with Festival Ballet in Nice at the Lausanne Festival, returning just in time to adjudicate the Sunshine competitions. It was usual for me to give a group of competitors a class before they performed a solo, which I always set. These were talented young teenagers, the best of whom won the Beryl Grey Award. I hoped this would lay the foundations for a successful dancing career.

To the delight of ballet lovers, the Bolshoi Ballet returned to Covent Garden in July for another highly successful season. During the same period I worked once more with Madam on *Checkmate*, which was to be televised by Margaret Dale, one of Madam's former soloists, now a successful television director. After four days of rehearsals with Ninette in a Hammersmith drill hall, on Saturday we arrived at the Television Centre for a day of positioning the cameras. By Sunday all was set for shooting. It was fascinating to watch how Maggie went about filming the ballet, the long-shots and the close-ups, and I loved every single minute.

The Chinese Embassy had not forgotten me, and 1963 saw us discussing plans to dance with the Peking ballet company the following year. I was to dance with one of their leading male dancers, who would also partner me in Shanghai: all very exciting. Ingvar's return from school coincided with the close of the Bolshoi season, after which we left by boat for our Swedish holiday at the end of July. Before the month was out I flew from Sweden to Salisbury Bulawayo to judge the dance competitions held there annually.

The standard was high, as I expected, Rhodesia having sent to England some highly trained dancers such as Merle Park, who became one of the Royal Ballet's leading ballerinas. I had the pleasure of meeting and congratulating her outstanding teacher. It was quite a tiring but enjoyable week, watching dancers of all ages in different dance disciplines. As the competition progressed we saw some innovative and artistic short ballets which greatly impressed me. They certainly had gifted teachers.

The summer sadly saw Madam's retirement as Director of the Royal Ballet, and I thought it wise to have a meeting mid-October with her successor, Frederick Ashton. I was bitterly disappointed when he said he could not offer me any hope or promises of any future performances at Covent Garden. This was a great blow: after all my years serving the Company, twenty-two in total – the past six as a visiting artist – I was deeply hurt.

The next day to my surprise there was a phone call from John Tooley, Assistant General Administrator at the Opera House, telling me of an inquiry for me to dance at the Rome Opera House and who I should contact there. It was arranged that I dance with their company in *Les Sylphides* and *Checkmate* over a four-week period covering January 1964. Claude Newmand was the artistic director of the Rome Opera House Ballet and had been one of Madam's leading dancers in the early days of Sadler's Wells, becoming a successful maître de ballet.

Prior to this engagement I flew to Johannesburg early November – on the same day that Ingvar returned to school after his half term. I was met at the familiar South African airport by Mrs Domisse, director of the Cape Town ballet company, who drove me to my hotel before I met with the company and my future partner, Gary Burne, a South African who had been with the Royal Ballet. He had left the Company in 1961 to lead the Cape Town and Johannesburg company. Rehearsals began immediately with them, the day before Vera Volkova arrived to stage her production of *Swan Lake*.

After so many years, it was curious to work with Volkova again, and I admired her production and the care she took in producing every dancer. The first night of *Swan Lake* a week later was for an audience of non-Europeans and the second night for a charity. The third, the premiere, fell on Thursday 14th November. We played a week in Johannesburg to full houses before going to Pretoria for two further performances.

Our opening at the Aula theatre was on Friday 22nd November 1963 – a date etched in people's memories as the day of President Kennedy's assassination. We had finished Acts I and II when the theatre director came into my dressing room to tell me the horrific news, saying he would have to make an announcement to the audience before the next act. I begged him not to do this but wait until the third act concluded. I presumed with the diplomatic corps in front they would all be obliged to leave and miss the third act, the highlight of the ballet. Delaying the announcement by half an hour, we performed the third act before, as I forecast, the tragic news emptied a large number of seats.

The next evening's performance was my last with the company, having given 19 performances of *Swan Lake* with Gary partnering me. It was a lovely production in which to appear, and it had all gone without a hitch, thanks to Volkova and Mrs Domisse. Back in Johannesburg for my flight home I was feted by all my friends from ACT, who then gave me a great send-off at the airport on Sunday evening.

Over the festive season, Bryan and I worked with de Vos, preparing for our month's season in Rome.

Leaving Sven and Ingvar to enjoy the rest of the Christmas break, we departed on the 6th January 1964. Rehearsals were already underway at the Rome Opera House, and on arrival we found ourselves immediately at work with the company on *Checkmate*. The union rules were strictly adhered to regarding rehearsals so, with only two or three performances a week, Bryan and I had time in which to wander through the city and explore on foot the wonders of its bygone age. It was an ideal month to be in Rome – clear blue skies almost every day. Bryan and I would sit al fresco in the glorious sunshine over coffee between rehearsals and performances, absorbing the atmosphere. It amazed me how this ancient city with its impressive ruins had withstood the onslaught of time, nature and tourists, dwarfing those of us who stood beneath its great colonnades.

After a successful opening night in the Opera House, following a preview press night, Bryan and I flew to Brussels for two days to appear on television in two pas de deux: the *Don Quixote* and *Aurora*. This was to be with recorded music, and it took time finding the correct tempi, but the final transmission went well with all concerned delighted. De Valois came out to Rome for the first night of *Checkmate* and was pleased with the help I gave in its production. I treasure the photo of her with me and Claude, taken just after the final curtain.

77 *China, 1964*

Our Rome engagement finished at the beginning of February, leaving me only three weeks to prepare for China – unknown territory for me. The Chinese Embassy suggested that I might like to give instruction to the dancers as well as dancing with them. I realised this could also include talks on ballet history so I went armed with Arnold Haskell's penguin paperback edition of *Ballet*, a book I have referred to many times.

Sven and I were friends with Felix Greene, one of only a few people who in the fifties were allowed to travel across China. His book *Awakened China*, which he gave me, offered an insight of what to expect. He recommended I read Edgar Snow's authoritative tome, *The Other Side of the River*. Being a slow reader I did not manage to finish it entirely in advance of our departure. Both books were published in America in 1961 and were invaluable, as surprisingly little was known of China at that time.

Before I left England the publishers Collins approached me to write about my visit to China, so I kept a detailed account of my day-to-day activities in that fascinating, awesome country. I wrote in depth of my experiences, and my book *Through the Bamboo Curtain* was published in Great Britain in 1965 and in America in 1966.

From the Tuesday morning in mid February when Sven and I were collected and driven to Heathrow, to our departure from Canton a month later, we were shown great kindness and treated with the utmost respect and consideration. It was a flight into a fascinating continent, divorced from and at that time still behind the rest of the world, a country where physical labour allowed the nation to operate. Men and women still pulled heavy cartloads even in the capital, while old-fashioned factories spilled out foul fumes.

There were signs of modern influences infiltrating, with a few cars amidst the sea of bicycles cramming the streets. Everywhere there was a flood of activity, whilst inside buildings of learning a feverish desire to acquire knowledge and to succeed. In towns and countryside masses of men and trousered women went about their work, diligently and painstakingly – to our astonishment the fields were still tended by hand, as in ages past.

Practising with the dancers and witnessing the speed with which they understood and responded was impressive. They worked extremely hard, and I never had to repeat my instructions, even though working through an interpreter. When I was giving classes it was a joy to sense their rapport and watch their improvement, whilst giving lectures was like talking to a forest of blotting paper. Teachers, dancers and school pupils were all agog to learn, displaying the same enthusiasm to discuss, enquire and debate en masse at the close of every talk.

My partner Wang Shao Pen was courteous and cooperative, and we soon built up a sound partnership. Within a week we performed for the Peking audiences *Swan Lake* and *Les Sylphides* with a smooth confidence. The company had also an internal theatre in their rehearsal building, which I found invaluable, particularly when I helped them stage *Sleeping Beauty.* We gave a special performance there for students and staff before leaving by train for Shanghai. There we danced with the Shanghai Ballet Group, who were outstandingly talented – they became the official Shanghai Ballet Company later that year.

Sven and I were prevailed upon to spend three days of 'recuperation' in Hangchow, the silk capital of China, high in the mountains. It was a glorious setting from where we were taken to many ancient places of interest. Flying on to Canton, we had an enforced landing in Nanchung where we spent a night, giving us a more intimate, off-the-record, glimpse of the old China. We walked through rows of hovel-like dwellings and became modern Pied Pipers, collecting over a hundred poor but well fed children around and behind us, all following with friendly, grinning faces as we strolled along. It was tremendously touching.

I am reminded of a host of wonderful experiences; the old gateways protecting Peking, the Great Wall of China, the incredible Terracotta Army, guardian of the first Emperor of a united China centuries ago, palaces, temples and many other monuments to China's wondrous history, one of the world's earliest civilizations. I found them truly lovely people, even including the occasional political enthusiast we had to endure! It was a pleasure to write about them on returning to London at the end of March, after a brief stop off in India to see our Master at Beas, the centre of the Sant Mat philosophy.

Sven and I managed to be back home just one day before Ingvar and were able to spend the Easter holiday time with him. To our delight, he read the lesson in church for the first time and accompanied us to stay with the Astors at Hever Castle for a weekend. They had moved from their beautiful home nearby to take up residence in the castle when Gavin's father vacated it to live in the south of France. I thought the moated castle magical, with its drawbridge still in working order – an exciting part of its evocative XVIth century architecture – and its romantic link with Henry VIII and Anne Boleyn. I was loath to leave, not knowing then how well we were to come to know and love Hever in the future.

I continued taking daily lessons with de Vos, as well as endeavouring to write a little each day about my China visit. I found the best time to concentrate was in the evenings, after the rush of the day was over. Sometimes I wrote until two in the morning, struggling to report as accurately and tactfully as I could. I was also on radio and television introducing the BBC *Festival of Light Music,* giving talks, taking classes, adjudicating and sitting on various committees. Amongst those I most warmed to were the RAD technical committee, various committees of the Sunshine Homes, including All-England Dance committees, 'my' Dame Alice Owen school board and the Imperial Society of Teachers of Dancing.

The ISTD were fortunate in having Cyril Beaumont as Chairman of the Society with its numerous dance departments represented on the main board. I appreciated his quiet wisdom coercing such luminaries as Victor Sylvester, Noreen Bush, Olive Ripman, Victor Leopold, Grandison Clark, Bill Irvine and Grace Cone, to name but a few, to join that impressive board.

78 *1964, South Africa Revisited*

I had optimistically hoped to have completed my writing by the end of June, and was already dreading leaving my dear ones again for South Africa. It was a month's engagement through ACT, the management I knew and trusted from my previous tours there. Ingvar cried because he was not well enough to come to the airport to see me off, but smiled bravely as I was driven away.

I opened with *Sleeping Beauty*, Wednesday, 1st July, with the Cape Town company, performing the Princess Aurora role on alternate nights with Maryon Lane. A ballerina with the Royal Ballet, she was born and initially trained in South Africa before furthering her tuition in London. Like me she adored performing, and we got on well together. By Friday evening I had a cough, which was keeping me awake at night and worrying me during performance. I contacted a doctor who gave me some medicine, which did not seem to help, and I continued to feel unwell. One of my skinned toes refused to heal, and I was feeling rather sorry for myself as I was expected to fly back to dance in London and present the Sunshine Gala on Tuesday 14th at the Palace Theatre, a show I was responsible for producing.

Amongst those appearing in the Gala were Flemming Flindt and Josette Amiel from the Royal Danish Ballet, Nadia Nerina from the Royal Ballet, Galina Samsova and David Adams from Festival Ballet. Western Theatre Ballet created a lot of interest by presenting Peter Darrell's *Mods and Rockers*, which was danced to music by The Beatles and ecstatically received by the younger members of the audience. Irina Baronova and Anton Dolin judged my 'Beryl Grey Award', the class and solos, announcing the winner near the end of the afternoon.

I was still feeling 'below par' on Tuesday, the day of the Gala matinee, so Lady Irene Astor excused me from lunching with her and Princess Margaret. I saw them before the performance, however, and again just before the end of the show, when the Princess was most kind, understanding and complimentary. She always took a genuine interest in ballet and enjoyed watching the young dancers to whom I gave a demonstration class in performance on stage. Miraculously my artists materialised from Denmark and, despite the rehearsal running late, to my great relief the matinee went smoothly. This was largely thanks to the expert stage management of Eddie Espinosa as well as his encouraging push to get a rather sick me on stage to dance *Don Quixote,* splendidly partnered by Gerard Ohn.

At the end of the gala I had a terrific rush to catch the 7pm plane back to Johannesburg where I landed in time for my performance on Thursday. Small wonder my cough got even worse, and I was forced to spend most of the day in bed to ensure I got through my Johannesburg performances. It was a big strain, not helped by the altitude. My toe had not improved either, so I was grateful that the doctor was able to re-dress it before I left Johannesburg.

On Thursday 23rd July we opened in Pretoria where I danced *Swan Lake* to an enthusiastic audience, which included Prime Minister Verwoerd and his wife. When I was presented to them after the performance he asked me if I would send a signed photograph to his son, which I did next day, from the rather noisy hotel where I was staying, before leaving Pretoria on Saturday following my final performance of the tour. I bade a fond farewell to the marvellous company led by David Poole, their ballet master, who a few years later became their artistic director. I was happy and proud to dance with this company for a second time – the first had been *Swan Lake* and this time in *Sleeping Beauty*. What an achievement for a young company to present these major classics, both demanding works. Their achievement was partly due to the early teaching of Dulcie Howes, who became the company's first director.

At the airport I had a great send-off from all my faithful friends gathered there as the Sabena plane flew me away. But we landed unexpectedly at Leopoldville in the Congo and, after an unexplained delay, were all driven by coach a good twenty miles, to a 'rest house'. But it was no rest. The main door was locked, and a fellow woman passenger and I were put in a tiny room. Later that night there was tremendous banging outside with lots of shouting people trying to break down the doors. I was terrified and certain we would be killed but, by a miracle and after what seemed an age, the frightening noises ceased. We were rescued and returned to our plane, which took off immediately for Madrid, before changing for Brussels and finally London. How thankful I was to be back safely in England after that hair-raising experience, which Sven and I later learnt was part of the Leopoldville uprising.

I was home just before Ingvar broke up from school, in time to put up a welcome home notice for him. We had then only one clear day in which to pack for our annual Swedish holiday. I certainly appreciated every minute of that break. In the evenings I continued writing about my Chinese visit, which I hoped to finish by the time we returned home.

We were able to be present for Sven's father's birthday on 6th August – also the official start of the crayfish fishing season in Sweden, where they are regarded as a great delicacy and jealously safeguarded. They are fished by torchlight, at night, in freshwater streams and brooks. This day ushers in many merry crayfish parties around the country. I loved going to these get-togethers when toast, butter and cheese are also served, as is schnapps and beer to help it all down! Swedes become very jolly and vocal after a few drinks, invariably singing and dancing as the meal progresses, adding to the frivolity of the occasion.

I was still busy tidying the strands of my book after our holiday, but the editor was content to receive it by the end of the year. I had not realised how much time the writing would take. Sven had already sorted out the photographs he thought suitable to be included, all of which he had taken himself. By this time the Astors had kindly arranged for us to have an apartment in Hever Castle, which was wonderful as we could spend our weekends there. The little cottage was the last but one attached to the rear of the castle and was beautifully furnished. It was always kept warm and clean, with a fresh supply of logs cut for use when needed. The Astors were generous in allowing us to enjoy the swimming pool and tennis court when not in use.

During the last months of 1964, the Cone sisters and Olive Ripman pressured me to take over their two schools and teacher training college. The three sisters – Valerie, Lillie and Grace – had founded their school in London in 1919, amalgamating with the Ripman School in 1944. Now all in their seventies, they wished to retire, with the future assured by the Arts Educational Trust Ltd. This would be such a big step into a new world of education and instruction of which I knew comparatively little. I was also not sure if I was ready to give up performing just yet, despite all the agonies it entailed – physically and mentally.

I was interested in the possibility and had many long discussions with Sven about our future. My partners – Field and Hart – were no longer dancing and were now directors. Chatfield was planning to leave England with Rowena to live in New Zealand. Ashbridge would also be hanging up his dance shoes in a few months. He was training to become a television producer, following in the footsteps of Margaret Dale, the talented soloist from Sadler's Wells Company. She had already achieved several successful presentations of ballet on television. I was nearing forty, the age at which I always said I would stop dancing. Perhaps it was now time to leave behind the magic of performing.

In 1965, I was immersed in a host of activities. Flying to Glasgow for a television appearance, I was fortunate to meet one of Scotland's most famous teachers Marjory

Middleton who, the previous year, had received the MBE. We had several talks about dance and the importance of good teaching.

I had so many interesting things going on in London that spring, especially my weekly recordings as presenter of a music programme with the BBC Light Music Orchestra and Vilem Tausky, the fine Czech conductor. He was such a lovely man, a sincere, warm person, inspiring to watch at work and completely in love with the music.

My plans for the Sunshine Gala took up a lot of my time and seemed to be running into endless problems. The French dancer Attilio Labis had agreed to appear that year but wished to dance a solo from *Daphnis and Chloe.* Dudley Simpson, our conductor, deemed this impossible as we had only a small orchestra of thirty-eight players, and the Ravel score required a far larger number. Labis remained obdurate, so I rang Anton Dolin in the south of France asking him to talk to Labis and persuade him to choose another solo instead. Dolin kindly rang him but was also unable to persuade Labis to change his mind. So I set about replacing him, which was worrying with the programme not finalised and the gala on July 14th drawing ever closer.

Fortuitously, the Bolshoi Ballet were in London, opening the night before my gala, and I contacted them. They were tremendously co-operative agreeing to come to my rescue and give me, not a solo, but a pas de deux, along with their Russian conductor Mikhail Bank. They all arrived for rehearsal at Drury Lane half an hour early while Niels Kehlet and Solveig Ostergaard were struggling with Dudley Simpson, the conductor, over an incomplete *Coppélia* score. To my astonishment the Russians had come with four dancers for good measure! Yelena Riabinkina and Alexander Vegok danced the *Raymonda* pas de deux whilst Ludmila Vlasova and Stanislav Vlasov danced a virtually unknown duet – *Swan Princess* – with Vlasova displaying the largest pair of wings imaginable, gracefully undulating them throughout the dance. The Russians not only saved the matinee but added wonderful excitement by their thrilling performances, which delighted everyone.

Lady Astor invited Princess Grace of Monaco to our gala, and she was a most gracious guest of honour, delighting all the artists she met on stage at the close of the show. After leaving the theatre, my happiness at the success of the afternoon was abruptly shattered by the absence of my diamond engagement ring from my finger. I remembered wrapping it in a pale blue tissue and laying it on my dressing table before the performance. In the rush to leave the room free for the cleaners to come in before the evening show I forgot to pick it up.

I returned to the theatre and, to my horror was told that all waste had already been collected and put into three ten-foot high garbage containers standing outside the back of the theatre. My heart sank. Desperate, I found a stagehand who kindly offered to help me rummage through these huge bins. After an agonising search, the tissue was discovered – my ring still safely nestled inside. It was truly a miracle, a thousand-to-one chance. Since then, I have never taken it off my finger. Sven thanked the stagehand profusely and put a little reward in his hand. We then continued on our way to Renée Astor's party, held in her lovely house in Lyle Street.

When should I stop dancing? The issue niggled me. I was being pointed in a new direction and realised that an opportunity like Arts Ed might never come my way again. I would still be involved with dance, helping to train and pass on my experience to another generation of dancers. I would also be helping young actors and singers into the world of theatre and putting my past wrangles with administration to good use. I had many meetings with Grace Cone and Olive Ripman, who ensured that I saw all activities in the schools and college, meeting staff as well as assessing and judging a number of their events. I met the Chairman of the Trust, Sir Stanley Rous, a splendid man, then President of FIFA. He too did his best to persuade me to take over Arts Ed, but I was caught in a dilemma, unable to decide.

Eventually I made up my mind to strike out into new territory and negotiations began, but these were protracted and less than straight forward. There was disagreement on the board as to my exact position, responsibilities and title; a meeting was convened in order for the board members to meet me. Meanwhile Grace Cone and I had disputes over finance as she appeared to be going back on what she had promised. I was fond of her, and it was upsetting for both of us.

There was a strange development over dinner at Ashley Clarke's one evening, when he tried to find out if I was going to take over the Arts Ed. I said, 'Nothing has yet been agreed,' but he continued to probe, warning me against the school and against Grace Cone in particular. He implied that she had stolen the idea of a teacher training college from the RAD, to which I replied, 'Then so has the Royal Ballet school'. I disliked his manner, and wondered how he had heard of the discussions taking place. Ashley had always been a supporter of my dancing and on occasions had left a tiny mascot at the stage door for me, so I was somewhat shaken by this conversation.

After several months of discussion I was finally handed a contract with which I was not at all satisfied. I was so disturbed that I asked our friend David Clayton Stamm to look at it. He took one long look, saying, 'This is like a servant's agreement, the board have far too much power and the salary is peanuts. You can't give up your career for this, they do not appreciate what prestige and value you will bring them.' David took the contract to his top league solicitor who took time and care in producing a more fitting and appropriate contract, giving me overall control.

With all parties finally satisfied, the announcement of my appointment as future Director General of the Arts Educational Trust Ltd was made on 19th October 1965. There was to be a six-month handover period, during which time I would 'get to grips' with the running of the boarding school in Tring and both the day school and teacher training college in London, situated at Hyde Park Corner. It was a vast undertaking: there were two hundred and forty-four boarders at Tring, four hundred day pupils in London and more than sixty mature students taking the three-year teacher training course. A huge responsibility, but I have never shirked a challenge. Fate was taking me on a worthwhile path.

The Board agreed that I could still continue to give performances if I so chose, although in my heart I knew this to be unlikely with the demands of this position. I was determined, however, to continue my daily lessons with de Vos to keep in good shape, mentally as well as physically. Above all, Sven was glad that I was to become involved in education, which he had always considered of paramount importance, and it reassured me to know that I had his total support.

When Bryan was available, we met in the evenings with de Vos at her studio to work chiefly on Cranko's deceptively difficult double work in *Ecossaise.* We decided to perform this at the Harlow Festival, as well as the *Don Quixote* and Aurora pas de deux. The Festival was a week after the Sunshine matinee. We both adored Cranko, and this was a homage to his remarkable talent. The festival was organised by Leo Kersley, former soloist with Sadler's Wells, who had his big school situated close by, so we felt assured of great interest in the four shows we were to give.

Many fans and friends came from London, including the critics Clive Barnes and Peter Williams. Although we did not realise, it was to be the last time that Bryan and I danced together on stage. Looking back now, I am glad that our long and happy partnership ended unplanned and unmarked by anything except success. Neither did I realise that I had just given my penultimate performance in England. The finale of my dancing career turned out to be at the next Sunshine Gala, in the presence of Princess Margaret, in excerpts from *Les Sylphides* with the Belgian Gerard Ohn – but even then I was unaware that this was my swansong.

Towards the end of June 1966, I received an unexpected call from John Gilpin, leading dancer of London Festival Ballet and also, at that stage, its Artistic Director, asking if I would complete their new production of *Swan Lake*. There were ructions between the choreographer Vaslav Orlikovsky and designer John Truscot and also, I gathered, between Orlikovsky and John Gilpin. Orlikovsky walked out, leaving an unfinished *Swan Lake*.

This took me by complete surprise as I had never restaged a classical ballet, and to patch and complete someone else's production seemed extraordinary. I was flattered that he thought I was capable of doing this and trusted me sufficiently to make this request. The costumes and scenery were proving extremely costly and Gilpin was obviously desperate to have the ballet ready for their forthcoming season, due to open at the unsuitable New Victoria cinema a fortnight later.

Much as I would have liked to help Gilpin, I did not think I could manage such an undertaking in the time available. I was already busy rehearsing for a forthcoming festival as well as organising the Sunshine gala. So Gilpin finished the production himself with Joyce Graham overseeing the corps de ballet work. It was not a box office success and sadly the exorbitant costs of the costumes and scenery were not recouped by the end of the four-week season. Debts piled up and, when Equity called a Company meeting, the dancers became aware that their future was in the balance.

The Greater London Council, which had supported Festival Ballet financially since the company's foundation in 1950, now looked for other benefactors to avoid their going bankrupt. They approached Lord Goodman, chairman of the Arts Council, for financial aid, which was promised, depending upon certain conditions. Within a month its then director, Julian Braunsweg, left and at the beginning of September Donald Albery, theatre owner and impresario, was appointed in overall charge, with Norman McDowell as Artistic Director and Jack Carter as resident choreographer.

Part Two – As Director

London Festival Ballet Cities Visited

GREAT BRITAIN
Aberdeen
Bath
Birmingham
Blackpool
Bolton
Bournemouth
Bradford
Brighton
Bristol
Brixton
Cardiff
Coventry
Doncaster
Eastbourne
Edinburgh
Edmonton
Exeter
Glasgow
Golders Green
Hanley
Harrogate
Hull
Ipswich
Llangollen
Leeds
Leicester
Liverpool
London
Manchester
Newcastle
Norwich
Nottingham
Oxford
Paignton
Peterborough
Plymouth
Scarborough
Sheffield
Slough
Southampton
Southend-on-Sea
Southsea
Stockton-on-Tees
Streatham
Sunderland
Sutton
Torquay
Wimbledon
Wolverhampton
Woolwich

AUSTRIA
Vienna

ARGENTINA
Buenos Aires

BELGIUM
Antwerp
Brussels
Ostend

CANADA
Montreal
Ottawa
Quebec
Toronto
Vancouver
Winnipeg

CANARY ISLANDS
Las Palmas
Tenerife

CHILE
Santiago

CYPRUS
Nicosia

CZECHOSLOVAKIA
Kosice
Prague

DENMARK
Copenhagen

EIRE
Dublin

FRANCE
Biarritz
Bordeaux
Cannes
Carcassonne
Grenoble
Lille
Lyons
Marseilles
Nice
Paris
St. Jean de Luz
Vichy

GERMANY
Cologne
Düsseldorf
Frankfurt
Freiburg
Giessen
Hamburg
Lunnen
Munich
Stuttgart
Wetzlar
Wiesbaden

GREECE
Athens

HUNGARY
Budapest

ITALY
Bologna
Brescia
Cagliari
Carpi
Catania
Fano
Ferrara
Florence
Genoa
Macerata
Mantova
Milan
Modena
Monza
Naples
Nervi
Reggio Emilia
Rome
Trieste
Turin
Venice
Verona

ISRAEL
Beersheba
Bethsham
Cesarea
Haifa
Jerusalem
Kiryat Bialik
Natania
Petah Tiqva
Ramat Gan
Tel Aviv

JAPAN
Kawasaki
Kobe
Kyoto
Nagoya
Okoyama
Osaka
Tokyo

MAJORCA
Palma

MALAYSIA
Kuala Lumpur

MEXICO
Mexico City

MONACO
Monte Carlo

NETHERLANDS
Amsterdam
Heerlen
Rotterdam
The Hague

N. IRELAND
Belfast

NORWAY
Oslo

PERU
Lima

POLAND
Lodz
Warsaw

PORTUGAL
Braga
Lisbon
Oporto

RUMANIA
Bucharest

SINGAPORE

S. KOREA
Seoul

SPAIN
Barcelona
Bilbao
Cuidad Real
Granada
La Coruna
Madrid
Santander
San Sebastian
Saragossa
Seville
Vigo

SWEDEN
Malmö
Stockholm

SWITZERLAND
Basle
Geneva
Interlaken
Lausanne
Schaffhausen
Zürich

TURKEY
Ankara
Istanbul
Izmir

URUGUAY
Montevideo

U.S.A.
Atlanta
Augusta
Bakersfield
Baltimore
Berkeley
Birmingham
Bloomington
Boston
Brooklyn
Buffalo
Chicago
Cincinatti
Cleveland
Columbia
Columbus
Davenport
Des Moines
Detroit
East Lancing
Edmonton
El Paso
Fresno
Greenboro
Houston
Huntingdon
Kansas City
Knoxville
Lafayette
Minneapolis
New York
Nottingham
Omaha
Philadelphia
Pittsburg
Portland
Richmond
Rochester
Sacramento
San Francisco
St. Louis
San Antonio
San Diego
Seattle
Spartanburg
Spokane
Washington
Youngstown

VENEZUELA
Caracas

YUGOSLAVIA
Belgrade
Dubrovnik
Ljubijana
Opatija
Split
Zagreb

London Festival Ballet Souvenir Brochure 1974–75

The latter stages of my career were as Artistic Director of London Festival Ballet, now English National Ballet. I took up the appointment as Artistic Director of the Festival Ballet in the spring of 1968. It was an unexpected change of direction because I had planned to become a freelance dancer again. After two years as Director General of the Arts Educational Schools and Teacher Training College, I resigned over a disagreement with the trustees on the future of their teacher training college.

Festival Ballet always had a strong link with the Arts Educational Schools, formerly known as the Cone-Ripman School. The Lowe and the Ripman schools merged in 1927, and it was their pupils who were chosen by Alicia Markova and Anton Dolin in 1949 to form a small professional group to tour with them in Britain. By 1950 that initial, small group had grown to become the Festival Ballet with Anton Dolin as Artistic Director and Julian Braunsweg, the impresario, as their manager. Every year promising young children from the schools danced in the Company's *Nutcracker* performances and with visiting companies such as the Maryinsky and Bolshoi, with whom I also danced.

Following its demise in the summer of 1966, after its collapse, Festival Ballet was re-titled London Festival Ballet. The problematical *Swan Lake* at the New Victoria cinema had failed to meet its costs and, with other heavy debts mounting, Equity called a Company meeting to inform the dancers of Festival's grave situation. The Greater London Council, its financial supporter since the Company's inauguration in 1950, appealed for help to Lord Goodman, Chairman of the Arts Council. This resulted in a complete change of management – Donald Albery, the theatre impresario, replaced Julian Braunsweg as manager and a Trust was formed to ensure the continuity of the ballet Company. Max Rayne, property tycoon, was appointed Chairman and, to my delight, the Arts Council invited me to become one of the members of the Trust. I felt honoured to be asked and delighted by this unexpected privilege. My connection with Festival Ballet resumed – no longer as a dancer but as one of those concerned in ensuring a future for this unique Company.

Donald Albery set about replacing the ill-fated *Swan Lake* with another version by Jack Carter and, as it was reasonably successful, he decided to present another full-length classic *The Sleeping Beauty*. To stage this he approached Ben Stevenson and me. I was excited by the invitation, which came completely out of the blue. Ben was one of my guest teachers at the Arts Ed at that time, and as a dancer himself and a promising young choreographer I was confident we could work well together. We were soon busy in the evenings planning the Prologue and following three acts. We worked out the challenging transformation scene with the set designer Norman McDowell, who I found rather temperamental. Ben created new choreography in several scenes while I set the traditional choreography, as I remembered it, for the rest of the ballet. Ben checked the corps de ballet sequences with one of the Royal Ballet's corps girls and, after agreeing a tentative casting, we were ready to work with the dancers. To accommodate Gilpin's height, the petite French ballerina Noella Pontois from the Paris Opéra was engaged for the initial performances at the Royal Festival Hall, which proved successful.

Unfortunately, I was obliged to miss three weeks of the latter rehearsal period, leaving with Sven for our annual holiday in Sweden with Ingvar and my father. It was a difficult decision to make, but I felt the family must come first. I returned from Sweden before them just a week and a half prior to the opening night. Although I had a warm 'welcome back' from the dancers, I was at once aware of a change in Ben's attitude. He no longer consulted or sat with me at rehearsals. He resented my presence, expecting me to stay in the background. I was surprised at his attitude, which made for an awkward atmosphere in rehearsal. The last week saw orchestral and stage run-throughs at the Royal Festival Hall culminating with a problematic final dress rehearsal.

Despite this, the opening night on the 24th August went well and the production received favourable reviews. As was stipulated by the Arts Educational Board, the programme credited me as Artistic Advisor even though it was a combined effort with Ben. I based the production on Sergeyev's version of *The Sleeping Beauty* which I knew intimately. This entailed a great deal of work, contributing substantially to the overall production. Disappointingly, I felt that the credit for that production all went to Ben Stevenson and was hurt that my considerable input was later denied by both Ben and Donald.

2 *Artistic Director – Festival Ballet*

In the early Spring of 1968, Donald Albery suddenly resigned as director of London Festival Ballet at a Board meeting. He had became so exasperated with the Board's directives, with which he disagreed, that he threw down his papers and walked out, saying he was a man of the theatre, knew best and he was not used to being told what to do. The Board at once began looking for a replacement. John Field was eventually chosen and invited to meet the Board one evening at County Hall. We sat expectantly for a good half hour until a telephone message came from John. He apologised for his absence due to an unexpected rehearsal on stage that evening. As it was impossible for there to be a stage call an hour and a half before curtain rise, it was feared he might have changed his mind. That John no longer wished to become artistic director was confirmed next day. Soon after, the Royal Opera House announced the appointment of John Field and Kenneth MacMillan as joint directors of the Royal Ballet.

The Board was recalled to discuss the situation and arrange advertisements for an artistic director. Sir Louis Gluckstein said, 'There is no need, we have one here at the table'. All eyes looked at me and I blushed, completely stunned. There followed general agreement that I should seriously consider this proposal and that the Chairman meet me shortly for a discussion. A few days later Max Rayne came to talk things over with me at our home in Park Street, meeting Sven for the first time. Max encouraged me to apply, adding, 'the Board's only reservation was that family might take priority.' This problem never arose, as my husband was in favour of my accepting the position. Sven was to back me, wholeheartedly, throughout my years with Festival Ballet, providing the anchor I needed.

My time as Artistic Director completely contrasted to my years as a ballerina, when my overriding concern was always about my next performance. I had never sought nor even contemplated directing a large ballet company. It was only after careful deliberation and persuasion by the Chairman that I undertook this responsibility. A director must care for others, spot and nurture talent, choose repertoire, balance finance and art – a new and exciting challenge

I also knew on taking this role that the Company needed to present well directed performances which would attract the public into the theatre, for it had a huge deficit. There were other major problems to be tackled: London Festival Ballet had no offices, no rehearsal studios, in fact no headquarters; a nomadic company, one completely unused to discipline of any kind. I wanted to improve the quality of the dancers and their training, to provide them with opportunities to work with interesting new choreographers and to have roles made on them, all the while with a clear focus on the financial bottom line.

Although Max Rayne suggested I might like to continue to dance within the Company I declined, not wishing to stand in the way of other dancers struggling to work their way up. I looked forward to running the Company and determined to raise its standard and reputation. I had no idea of the hurdles there were to overcome, nor of the many departments I would have to deal with and all the numerous outside threads which were interlinked. Naïve, yet enthusiastic to get going and to succeed, I began my new career with faith, determination and optimism.

My appointment, together with that of Wilfred Stiff as Administrator, was announced at the Arts Council in Piccadilly on 2nd May. Stiff came from the concert management agency Ibbs and Tillett and was new to the world of ballet. Max Rayne presided at the press conference, giving me confidence for the battery of questions that followed the announcement. The Company were in Manchester so I travelled there by train with Donald Albery and his assistant, Anne Rawsthorne.

While Donald was introducing me to the Company as his successor, I sensed an uneasy atmosphere. It was announced that *The Sleeping Beauty* was to be the only ballet for the entire three-week season at the Royal Festival Hall that August. Donald thought that to give the same ballet for three weeks was foolish and high risk. I could tell that the Company thought likewise and were worried. Donald told them it was now up to their new director to speak to the Board about changing the programme, putting me in a difficult position. It was obvious that Donald delighted in the situation, placing me at a distinct disadvantage. I wondered what other problems the future would hold but, undeterred, I determined to forge ahead.

We stayed to watch the evening show, which I found disappointing. Andre Prokovsky, one of the leading dancers, was off with a bad back, and I thought the triple bill lacklustre. I was however impressed that Donald staged *Bourrée Fantasque* with black drapes in place of scenery, thereby saving money for the impoverished company. This was clever of him – the brightly coloured costumes stood out well against the black surround – but in my opinion the overall standard of dancing was poor.

Once back in London there was a great deal to be undertaken. The nomadic company had no headquarters or rehearsal rooms, no permanent wardrobe accommodation, nor workshop, scenery or costume storage – all were rented and scattered across London. Happily Max Rayne was most helpful in addressing the urgent need for suitable premises to house the administration: Wilfred Stiff, with his assistant and secretary; an accountant; a press officer; the general manager (Peter Brownlee); the music personnel – two pianists, orchestra manager, two conductors (David Taylor and Aubrey Bowman); the production manager (James Duff); the technical staff and stage crew, as well as myself and my secretary Kay Waterman from the Arts Ed – all to be housed centrally. Money was tight but eventually accommodation was found at 48 Welbeck Street, where everybody managed to squeeze into small rooms on three floors, not ideal but it brought the admin together in the same building. To my astonishment, Stiff took the best room for himself, which I thought rather presumptuous.

During Donald's time, the Company rehearsals took place at the Donmar Studio, which was some distance from Welbeck Street. Donald was part owner with Margot Fonteyn of the Donmar premises (now the Donmar Theatre), which were close to the Opera House. An army drill hall between Regent's Park and Camden Town was also used, which meant wasting time rushing between venues. Whenever possible I wanted to be present at Company classes and rehearsals, and I aimed to give at least one class a week in order to familiarise myself with the dancers and observe their strengths and weaknesses.

Meantime Stiff and I had to get to grips with the workings of everything to do with touring, both in this country and abroad. We needed to have a rapport with the agents representing the Company on the continent. Many meetings were held with our admin and technical staff, trying to work out a clear plan of action. We visited our scenery and costume storage warehouses whilst addressing a million other details. It was a voyage of discovery.

I was surprised at the haphazard way the three ballet staff operated. Vassilie Trunoff, an Australian-Russian, and his Australian wife, ballet mistress Joan Potter, had themselves been dancers in Festival Ballet. Vassilie (Vass) had been a leading character dancer, Joanie in the corps, and both cared passionately about 'their' Company. Frano Jelencic, a tall Yugoslavian and the other member of the ballet staff, was married to the Company's petite American ballerina, Dagmar Kessler. I discovered that the principals often decided amongst themselves which performances and which roles they would dance. In addition, over the past few years there had been several artistic directors, each with their own ways of running the nomadic Company, which must have been perplexing and demoralising for the dancers. I was certainly unprepared for the shambolic state in which I found things. This shocked me – I had been brought up under de Valois' direction and the tight control she imposed upon her Company. I determined to alter the way Festival Ballet operated and to tighten things up to a more professional level.

Ian Hamilton, a well-trained, classical dancer from the Royal Ballet, pressed me to take him into Festival Ballet and, after much deliberation, I finally agreed to engage him as a principal. Vass was keen to have him join as the Company was short of leading men – Prokovsky (married to the leading ballerina Galina Samsova) had back trouble, and Gilpin was unpredictable. Peter Brownlee, however, was against engaging Hamilton, saying 'it would cause trouble in the ranks', something Vass refuted. I only hoped I'd made the right decision. After watching performances in Oxford I mentally planned to raise first Alain Dubreuil, and later Dudley von Loggenburg, from senior artist to principal status.

No sooner had I joined than the Company was back off on tour. The mid-week Oxford matinee was a complete sell-out, full of excited youngsters, whilst the evening audiences included many enthusiastic students. Because the season in Paris had fallen through, Donald had replaced it with a ten-day season at the New Theatre, London. During his time with Festival it was from the New Theatre that the Company's business was run by Donald's staff, who now had to be replaced. I was surprised to see both Fonteyn and the former ballerina Baronova present in the theatre for the triple bill dress rehearsal, taking an apparent interest in the Company I was shortly to direct. At the close of the New Theatre season on 22nd June, John Gilpin went on stage and made a long speech, bewailing the loss of Donald as their director, saying how greatly he and his staff would be missed, thanking him profusely and wishing him well. There was no mention of me as Donald's successor, despite the fact that Stiff and I were sitting out front, as was Max Rayne with his wife and family. I heard that Donald was now reluctant to give up his position, criticising Rayne as Chairman, but nevertheless making the hand-over appear friendly. Perhaps this gave Max an inkling of the prevailing under-currents.

The Company were given a fortnight's break before a three-week rehearsal period, while Vass, Joanie and I deliberated on casting three weeks of *Beauty* in London and the following short tour of triple bills to France and Spain. Stiff and I became more and more immersed in meetings, including vital ones with our technical crew. I began to realise just how much I had to learn and prayed I would be a strong director with the ability to make clear and wise decisions. I held an open audition at which over two hundred dancers of every shape and size appeared. I was shocked and disappointed by the low standard and only offered contracts to two women and one man.

During a fascinating visit to the costume storage in Hackney, we found many old costumes which needed discarding. Max advised against asking for more money from either the GLC or the Arts Council for a year, suggesting we source funds from elsewhere. He found the proposed new three-act *Coppélia* beyond the Company's present finances and stipulated that it should be rethought. I contacted the choreographer, Jack Carter, explaining the position, and he took the news surprisingly quietly. We then had meetings with Peter Farmer, the designer, and the assistant conductor Aubrey, exploring how best to present a less expensive production. We eventually decided to give only the first two acts until we could afford to add the third and final act, which was purely a series of divertissements celebrating the happy outcome of the *Coppélia* story.

I first spoke to the entire Company as their Director before morning rehearsals on 8th July. Much to my relief I felt my words were well received. That evening I also had my first Board meeting as Director of Festival Ballet. Stiff and I took our written reports to Max for vetting prior to submission to the Board, and I was pleased that he did not alter mine. There followed three weeks of concentrated rehearsals during which time I began to discern the qualities of each of the dancers and to make changes in procedures.

I decided that every Friday the Company were to be given a detailed call sheet for the entire coming week. Class and rehearsal times for the week were shown, worked out with Vass and Joanie, to replace the old haphazard daily call sheet pinned up the night before. Now the Company could see in advance the schedule for the week ahead and be able to plan their lives accordingly. I was pleased when Frano congratulated me during our third rehearsal week, saying: "the Company is much better disciplined already". One unpleasant task I could not delay though was to tell David Adams, a principal of many years, that I thought his dancing days would soon be drawing to a close. That interview was one occasion when I was glad to have Stiff with me. I worried beforehand and was relieved that David appeared to have understood, although I realised it must have been upsetting for him.

3 *First Weeks*

By the end of July I was away on tour with the Company for the first time in my new role. This was a week's season in Southend – not a town strongly associated with ballet. The theatre was not ideal, the stage had little depth with a hard, un-giving surface. With few photos or billboards around to attract an audience, the attendance was poor. A triple bill programme is hard to sell, and little attempt appeared to have been made to sell this one. It was disappointing to see so many empty seats and particularly demoralising for the dancers. There was worse to come.

On Friday evening I was contacted by the local police informing me of the death of one of the Company's dancers, Adrian Reynolds. He was discovered in his parents' caravan where he had taken an overdose and sadly died. Utterly dreadful. I was completely shaken, never having dealt with anything like this before. The police had informed his parents, but advised me not to tell the dancers that night and to wait until the end of our engagement next evening. But by midday Saturday Adrian's absence had been noticed by his close friends and the assistant company manager, Philip Clive, came to me saying: 'Miss Grey we cannot keep this from the dancers any longer – you will have to tell them now'. So I reluctantly addressed the Company before the matinee. It was horrible breaking the news to them and without doubt they were horrified and saddened. But as professionals, regardless of their feelings, they went on to give the two final performances of that ill-fated week in Southend. I never forgot that tragedy and have wondered how his parents were able to deal with such a terrible loss.

The Festival Hall season loomed and, back in London, I spent Monday morning in the theatre with Carter, Farmer, Duff and Stiff. We checked the sets and costumes for the tour before shipment to Biarritz later that week. Rehearsals of *Beauty* at Donmar began at 3pm, and the dancers worked hard and enthusiastically until 8 o'clock by when I was reasonably pleased and optimistic.

Tuesday was spent at Festival Hall until nearly midnight. The orchestra rehearsed in the morning under their conductor David Taylor with Aubrey on hand, but I longed for a larger orchestra. After the dancers finished at 8pm, the lighting call began but ran behind schedule. This was not surprising as staging and lighting takes time to get right, particularly at Festival Hall, which was built as a concert hall. To transform it into a theatre Benn Toff, Julian Braunsweg's right-hand man, had designed a false proscenium, divorcing the platform from the auditorium. This had to be re-rigged each time the Company returned. Duff and his staff worked painstakingly to satisfy Carter, McDowell and me amidst a harmonious atmosphere.

Wednesday was especially happy as my family returned from their month-long holiday in Sweden. They came directly to the theatre and my heart leapt as Sven walked into the stalls and then took me outside where Ingvar and my father were waiting patiently in the car to embrace me. It was the day before the opening and I was in the theatre from ten in the morning until eleven at night. It began with a morning orchestral call followed by the dancers' stage call for placing. Festival Hall was a challenge for the dancers with its wide, shallow stage, narrow wings and – even more difficult – just off stage three steep steps leading up to the area behind the backcloth which concealed the organ. This also blocked dancers crossing – those needing to reappear on the opposite side of the stage had to exit into the main backstage corridor and rush round to the other side. No one could accuse the dancers of not being adaptable. Since my days dancing with the Company a few shower cubicles had been built into the walls along the corridor outside the dressing rooms. These showers replaced the china bowls filled with hot water that previously were brought in by the dressers.

At the close of the placing call at 2pm, we continued lighting until the dancers returned for a photo call at six thirty, prior to the full dress rehearsal at seven. This was with orchestra, sets and lights, and it was wonderful seeing everything coming together. My family watched this final rehearsal, which went fairly smoothly despite incessant criticisms throughout by Peter (sitting next to me) and the chief electrician. In retrospect this was actually helpful: Peter B, as he was known – an Australian and a former dancer – had a lot of experience, although I found his abrupt manner difficult to get used to.

My secretary, Kay Waterman, was still with me, but did not wish to tour. She was a keen ballroom dancer and had already been in a show on television – so I had to think about a replacement. I knew I would miss her as she was good at taking notes of the corrections I dictated throughout rehearsal, which I gave to the dancers next day. I also took notes at performances during my years with Festival, having learnt this invaluable routine from Plucis during my Royal Ballet days. In Russia, corrections are always given to principal dancers immediately after the performance, on stage, 'in heat'; and this also happens in China, with the entire company present. I found, when I went to the dressing rooms of my hard-working dancers after a show, that it was better to wait until the next day to give notes. They only wanted to go home, eat, drink and go to sleep.

4 *Sleeping Beauty*

The Festival Hall opening night on the 8th August 1968 went smoothly, and I was delighted with the overall performance by the Company. Galina Samsova as Princess Aurora had a great reception, inspiring the others with her technique and artistry, but I only wished that her partner Andre Prokovsky exhibited a more noble stance. I was glad to see quite a number of the audience dressed in evening attire, which always adds to the excitement of a first night, an excitement which is picked up by the dancers. After the show I congratulated the Company, later celebrating with Sven at a small dinner party at the Savoy with family and friends.

I anxiously read the critics when the newspapers came out shortly after midnight. They were favourable, with the exception of A.V. Coton. This disappointed me as he had been keen that I take over Festival Ballet, encouraging me whenever we happened to meet. The second evening saw Dagmar Kessler as the princess with John Gilpin as her prince. She danced beautifully but I thought failed to project her personality sufficiently. I was pleasantly surprised by Robert Bestonso in Act III. An elegant French dancer not renowned for his partnering, he danced the famous *Bluebird* variation magnificently, nonchalantly partnering an ebullient, brilliant Margot Miklosy, one of the top principals. On Saturday we had two shows, at 4pm and 8pm, both sold out. Carmen Mathé took the lead in the afternoon, and Galina once again delighted her fans that evening. A splendid event, despite a few backstage problems such as David Adams refusing to wear Jean-Pierre Alban's suitor costume in Act I, to quote just one little incident! Neither was happy to share the costume, but there was no money for individuals to have their own. Sharing had to be the norm.

So were daily dramas. By Monday evening Gilpin was off with a bad back so Alain Dubreuil partnered Dagmar. He must have been most supportive as she projected better than before. Hamilton made a successful debut as Mathé's prince on the Wednesday, much to my relief. By Thursday Gilpin was back dancing, partnering Lucette Aldous as his princess. A member of the Company until 1967, Lucette had returned as guest artist to appear with Gilpin. She was a perfect height for him but a little colourless. Later that season Miklosy, partnered by Dubreuil, gave an exciting performance as Princess Aurora, remembering all I had shown her.

To the Board's satisfaction the three-week season of *Beauty* at Festival Hall was a sell-out despite the gloomy predictions. Things were not going smoothly though between Wilfred Stiff and me. Although we held joint position as artistic and administrative directors, he had placed his name before mine in the programmes and posters, something I took up with him when I discovered this. He tried to exclude me from vital meetings, not sharing important matters with me. Although we agreed that Aubrey's conducting was not good enough, Stiff gave him notice without first informing me. He told Peter B, however, who then enlightened me. I was speechless.

Across the river at the Coliseum Theatre on Wednesday 24th August, during our Festival Hall season, an historic event took place. The Sadler's Wells Opera company was performing there for the first time, having left their home at Sadler's Wells Theatre for London's West End. This left the London Opera Centre and the London Opera Group to continue the tradition of presenting opera at the Wells. Sven and I went to the opening night at the Coliseum where the company looked good on the large stage, but thought the singing needed to be stronger in such a famous theatre. It was a packed house and amongst many other distinguished colleagues I spoke to our board member Sir Louis Gluckstein, saying I wished that Festival Ballet could perform at the Coliseum one day.

Our three-week season at Festival Hall went fast but with many unsettling moments, up to and including the last night, when Stiff proposed to go on stage at the end to make a speech. I felt too embarrassed to say no, but fortunately Peter B managed to convince him that a speech from the administrative director was not expected. Stiff was persistent, even asking Sven if he thought that as administrator he, Stiff, should take me on stage and introduce me to the audience – as if I was unknown! Following tradition, as artistic director I was brought on stage by Gilpin to say a few words of thanks to the audience.

We left England next day for our first engagement of the tour in France, at the Teatro Naturale in St Jean de Luz. We gave the second act of *Swan Lake, Graduation Ball* and *Bourrée Fantasque* – Balanchine's joyous ballet to Chabrier's colourful music – plus two pas de deux for good measure. The next two performances were in Biarritz at the Casino Municipal with two different programmes which included *Lac* Act II, an extract from Petipa's *Paquita*, Balanchine's ballets *Night Shadow* and *Bourrée Fantasque* and the demanding Danish work *Études* by Harald Lander. I found myself uncomfortable in Biarritz, such a famous resort but a shadow of what it must have been. I could imagine the dignitaries from a past era filling the grand hotels, parading along the boulevards, parasols protecting ladies from the rays of the sun, whilst displaying their wealth for all to see.

Our French agent was a friendly little man: Boris Trailine, obviously no stranger to the Company and always busy bustling about. The casino manager was obviously nervous about presenting the Company, and I noticed Trailine was hopeless with him. We were to appear in a large casino where the stage, a huge boxing ring, was covered with plywood which squeaked and gave gently as the dancers pranced around, much to their amusement. While Vass and I tried to rehearse the Company, a group of men, laughing loudly, went back and forth with trees and trellises for masking, whilst mothballed carpeting was laid by other noisy workmen. Beaten by the commotion, Vass and I called a halt to our rehearsal and sent the dancers away.

I heard the first of two orchestral rehearsals and, with Aubrey struggling to conduct the local players, it sounded awful. It was unfortunate that David Taylor was unavailable as the orchestra was still woefully under-rehearsed by the time David conducted the performance at night, which I found embarrassing. I could not understand how Stiff, coming from the world of music, could endure the sound. Stiff, with us for the entire trip, was more concerned about making a speech on stage but the manager declined the suggestion on Peter B's advice. Nevertheless Stiff asked David Taylor to introduce him to the players before the opening, whereupon Peter B said: 'And what about Beryl? She is the artistic director,' and pushed me forward to also wish them well.

The show was half an hour late starting, with people still stumbling in during the first ballet – *Swan Lake*. The lighting was too bright and the programmes did not arrive until the performance was over. It was pretty dreadful, saved only by the beautiful dancing of Galina. The second night's performance was better but the stage area was not big and I was worried about giving *Études*. This exciting ballet by Harald Lander uses all the Company but it went surprisingly well with no disasters. The poor orchestra was tucked away under the stage and had to be amplified. This was hard on them as the amplification was poor. In retrospect perhaps not such a bad thing – the players were still not comfortable with the scores.

Backstage after the show I had to speak to David Adams as he had not put on the required body make-up for the *Corsaire* pas de deux. His excuse was there was no hot water for washing it off. I told him this was unacceptable but he was belligerent, saying he was following Equity rules. The Company was shocked by his unprofessional attitude: the women had managed to remove their wet-white body makeup, so I knew it was right to speak to him. I was concerned about the production manager, James Duff's, offhand manner when he refused to discuss my queries regarding the lighting and staging. This was frustrating as I was keen that we achieved the best possible standard of presentation, but he resented any interference. I decided I must have a long talk with him as soon as the right opportunity arose. I began to realise what a number of problems were waiting to be resolved – the task of directing a ballet company is fraught with unexpected situations.

I was surprised at the ease with which we were permitted to cross the border between France and Spain for San Sebastian, finding the customs men pleasantly helpful. I fell under the spell of San Sebastian with its regal buildings fronting the streets, and it was a pleasure to find the Victoria Eugenia such a beautiful theatre. Both our triple bill performances were packed even though they started at 7.30pm – surprisingly early for Spain.

Returning to Biarritz for our closing night we once again presented the much loved *Swan Lake.* We gave for the first time *Designs with Strings*, an abstract ballet by John Taras to a Tchaikovsky trio, two pas de deux, finishing an exciting evening with *Graduation Ball.* It was also the end of the Company's year, and I was still busy interviewing the dancers about their new contracts: a good opportunity for me to get to know them a little better. We had to pack and vacate our rooms early in the day as we were booked to fly back to London straight after the show that night. So everyone's luggage was brought to the tiny theatre and stacked all over the place, blocking almost every passageway.

I was quite baffled when Peter B said I must organise a defilé which would be expected by the audience. I had no idea what a defilé was, let alone what it entailed! So Peter B took charge, marshalling the dancers to appointed positions on stage for me to approve. At the end of our evening's performance I realised what an impressive and stirring finale this procession made to the season and felt proud of the Company. There followed a frantic move by the staff and stage crew to get the scenery and costumes loaded onto lorries before we were taken by coaches to board our chartered plane, leaving for London at 2.45am.

Sven and I spent the next two weeks in the south of France relaxing and staying with our good friend Guy Horne. He had a house on three floors looking out onto a magnificent garden which had won him several prizes. The house was situated in the hills above Nice so we were able to go to the plage each day for a swim – an ideal holiday. We met many of Guy's friends including Peter Churchill. As an underground agent during the Second World War, he worked with Odette Hallowes in the French Resistance until they were both captured. After the war, in 1947, they married in London but the marriage did not last. His second wife, Jane, made a great fuss of us whenever we visited their home situated on a nearby hillside. One of the highlights during our times with them was listening to Peter playing the piano with his dog singing (or rather howling) by his feet.

At the end of the week there was tragic news that our closest friend Margaret MacInnes had died in hospital. She had suffered a dreadful driving accident some months earlier while on holiday in Portugal, which left her totally paralysed. It was a sad homecoming with her funeral service in the Scottish church in Knightsbridge on the afternoon of our return, so Sven dashed off in time to attend. I could not accompany him as I had to go to the Company offices to prepare for the start of our new working year. It was a busy few days with meetings and endless discussions, but I still managed to fit in a daily class with de Vos, who was always so understanding and helpful.

After one week's rehearsal with a Company refreshed from the three-week summer holiday we opened the autumn tour in Southampton on 30th September, playing eight performances of *Beauty*. The Gaumont is a splendid theatre for ballet with loyal, appreciative audiences. Despite a grumpy Andre (because I insisted on Galina and him coming to Southampton on Monday in case Gilpin's back trouble recurred), the week got off to a good start. I interviewed our assistant stage manager, Geoffrey McNab, who I was told expressed an interest in becoming my secretary. I liked him and as he knew the ins and outs of the Company, I thought he might be the right person for the position. A week later, on a train to Eastbourne I interviewed Alun Rhys, the husband of Helen Starr, one of the company's leading ballerinas, who wished to take charge of the men's wardrobe. I was impressed by his enthusiasm and believed him to be capable and suitable for the position of supervisor. After more interviews, Stiff and I agreed to engage both Alun and Geoffrey – and what a great help Geoffrey became to me. He was always bright and cheerful and loyal, qualities I was to appreciate in the difficult times to come.

After a successful opening in Southampton I flew to America to search for a not-too-expensive choreographer with a suitable new work for the Company. I watched several performances in New York, meeting many in the dance world, and finally invited a promising young dancer/choreographer, Eliot Feld, to stage a ballet for us early in the new year. I returned jubilant on Sunday morning to be met by Sven and we went directly to spend the day with Ingvar at Eton, which he now attended after finishing at prep school.

After an early lesson on Monday with de Vos, Sven drove me to Eastbourne to rejoin the Company. En route we called in briefly at Hever to see how badly the castle had been damaged by the recent flooding. It was terrible, the water having risen six foot inside the castle, causing havoc. We found the family and staff endeavouring to dry out the rooms whilst trying to restore some order. Saturated precious belongings and historic papers were lying on trestle tables. We realised that, with so much destruction and upheaval, this would in all probability mean the end of our six years there.

Festival was presenting *Sleeping Beauty* for an entire week in Eastbourne, and I arrived in time to join Vass rehearsing the corps where improvements were badly needed. The Congress Theatre was popular with the Company, clean, bright and modern with rehearsal space next door in The Winter Garden, the sea around the corner, as well as an adjoining pub – much enjoyed by the orchestra. Ever since I can remember there has been an enthusiastic audience for ballet in Eastbourne, from their war days of hit-and-run air raids, up to the present day. Now as Director I was to appreciate the interest and cooperation shown us by the local Entertainments and Publicity department.

Galina's Aurora delighted the audience on the opening night and was given rousing applause at the end of the evening. If only Andre could have been as inspiring. I wrote in my diary: 'he is so heavy and dull, just stands and supports, without any effort at magic…' so I decided to talk to him next day. He did not take criticism well and went away in a sulk. I worried that he might leave, taking Galina with him, which would have been a disaster. Fortunately, after three days of gloom, he recovered from my well intentioned talk and certainly tried to improve his bearing.

Some dancers were complaining of tight muscles, and there were a few badly strained tendons due to the hardness of the stage surface. I contacted the appropriate person in the Eastbourne arts department and explained the problem, asking if there was any possibility of their replacing the present stage with a sprung one. I described the complications their hard stage caused a number of our dancers who were unable to appear through injury. I hinted that we might have to reconsider our seasons in Eastbourne in the future. This was received with a promise to look into the matter and the stage was eventually replaced with a sprung floor, to the great relief of the dancers and my delight that they had listened to me.

The next week we were back in London, working hard with Jack Carter on his two-act *Coppélia*. The scenery, designed by Peter Farmer, was still being completed and the wardrobe frantically finishing the costumes and headdresses. Dancers were called out of rehearsals for fittings and there was a mounting air of excitement as our week of rehearsals at Donmar ended at 5.15pm on Saturday. There was no let-up as Sunday saw us in Bournemouth. The stage staff were busy throughout the morning, hanging and setting up the new scenery for the afternoon lighting call. This was followed by a two-hour run through of *Coppélia* from 7.30pm, the dancers trying their best for Carter despite having had no day off. I doubt if this would be allowed today, but Festival Ballet existed to tour, dancing and giving pleasure as often as it could. When the dancers finished at 9.30pm the staff recommenced lighting. We worked with Charles Bristow, the lighting designer, through the night until 7.30 the following morning. It was so interesting and absorbing that I did not feel tired but elated as we left for a well earned breakfast together at the hotel. There were many friends and colleagues from London out front for the morning final dress rehearsal with orchestra. The matinee and evening performances went surprisingly well, with Lifar's ballet *Noir et Blanc* as the closing work, which the mayor mistakenly thought was a part of *Coppélia*. After the performance, all smiles, he remarked: 'what a brilliant idea to have designed the last act in black and white, in contrast to the brilliant colours of the first two acts'. Obviously he had not read the programme!

After only three performances our programme changed to *Sleeping Beauty* which was tough on the Company, dancers and stage staff alike. The stage crew worked all night and next day to hang, set and light by 4pm. This tight schedule was apparently not unusual for Festival Ballet, who changed programmes frequently to attract as many people as possible into the theatre.

I had good news from Stiff: Elliot Feld was arriving at the weekend and had agreed a modest sum for the ballet he was to create for the Company. It was encouraging to see how pleased the dancers were at the news of a new ballet. Every dancer enjoys tackling a new work and finds the challenge stimulating. As a director, one is continually searching for talented, interesting choreographers – even today, there are too few. I believe choreography is a god-given gift. Not only had Feld arrived but also Robert Joffrey, director of the American City Centre company. I spoke with him in New York as I was keen to get one of his or Gerald Arpino's ballets. So I was delighted by their arrival and grateful to Peter B who looked after them during their stay. We were appearing in London the coming week at the Odeon Cinema, Golders Green so our two Americans did not have to travel far to watch the Company in performance. We presented *Sleeping Beauty* which gives the soloists an opportunity to show their classical technique. The opening Monday was poorly attended with only half the stalls full, so it was fortunate they did not come until Tuesday by when the attendance improved.

Feld's ballet was called *Meadow Lark*, and he looked at various designers. He became interested in Rosen Emery but neither Peter B nor I thought him suitable and were relieved when Peter Farmer became Feld's final choice. The casting was not easy as Feld was determined to use certain dancers with whom Vass and I were not in agreement. Feld was also unhappy at the short time allocated for the dress rehearsal in Bristol, which could not possibly be extended. Nor could I agree to his working the dancers on the Sunday prior to opening. Feld understood and said I was not to worry, just to let him do the worrying. To add more problems, two of my soloists were off – one for five days with gastro-enteritis, the other with a poisoned toe – whilst Carmen Mathé, one of my principals, had shingles. I heard also that one of the male soloists, a South African, wanted to leave, but Peter B thought he probably just wanted to grumble and attract attention.

I was given all sorts of advice about forthcoming repertoire. That week the writer and critic Richard Buckle suggested that we put on *Symphonie Fantastique* with new scenery and choreography over which he wished to advise. Peter Williams, however, wanted us to revive Massine's original version of the ballet. I wasn't so sure I even wished to stage the work, fearful that it might look old fashioned. This was debated at our weekly staff meeting along with other suggestions and *Symphonie Fantastique* was left in abeyance. The positive news was that we achieved a full house on Saturday night for the first time that week in Golders Green.

The next week the Company was to perform *Coppélia* for the reopening of the Wimbledon theatre. When Vass, Joanie, Peter B and I arrived early afternoon for rehearsal we found the stage was impossibly slippery and the first act not even hung, let alone lit. We decided that the linoleum must be removed, so it was, carefully, strip by strip, to give the dancers a firmer footing on the wood floor beneath. Although I disliked blaming any one person, the staging was Duff's responsibility. Even though he eventually managed to get the scenery set and lit, it was only just in time leaving only a few minutes to place the company on stage. The curtain rose to a prestigious and highly important audience: among those present were Jenny Lee, the Arts Minister with her powerful friend Lord Goodman. To my amazement and relief the Company put on a beautiful performance despite no rehearsal. With Max Rayne and the Board in attendance, plus representatives from the Arts and British Councils, it was important that the evening was a success, which thankfully it turned out to be.

The next day we had a post mortem in the office – with Stiff, Roy Rosekilly our accountant, Peter B, Vass, myself and Duff – about the previous evening's debacle. Although we were fair to Duff, he had been proved unreliable. He gave in his notice later, which was decent of him. Despite my initial nervousness, the Board meeting next day finished without any awkward questions. Afterwards I reported to Max our previous day's meeting concerning Duff, as well as Aubrey's complaint that I was unkind to him, which I refuted. Max reassured me that these problems were to be expected within a company of hard-working artists.

On arriving at the office Thursday morning I found it in uproar: Stiff had opened everyone's mail, including mine. I did not know why he did this but realised I must speak with him immediately to stop any further escalation, which I did. He agreed not to open any office mail again. To everyone's astonishment on Friday, however, Rosekilly announced that he did not mind having his letters opened by Stiff after all! Quite a turn-around. Perhaps he was feeling benign on hearing that Jenny Lee had come to another performance the previous evening, to watch *Sleeping Beauty* again. Certainly we were surprised by her attendance and hoped this might foretell an improvement to our funding.

7 *Autumn Tour and The Gilpin Dilemma*

Now well into November, the Autumn tour took us North to Bradford where we introduced a touch of the festive season with a week's performances of *The Nutcracker*. Preparing this popular classic meant a tight rehearsal schedule as we also had to give Feld time to teach *Meadow Lark*. The Winnipeg Ballet had premiered it on 3rd October so it was still fresh in his memory and rehearsals went briskly. He used six couples in a pastoral scene, dancing to a Haydn quartet. The musicians were on stage in period costumes, an innovation adding atmosphere to this gentle work.

At the start of the Bradford week, Stiff and I heard that Aubrey was not happy and thinking of resigning. We discussed this with him, saying that he was free to leave. The same day Duff saw us in the Alhambra Theatre to ask if he could stay on for the time being, which suited us as there were still three weeks of the tour to complete. There were many programme changes – except for a week's run at the Theatre Royal, Nottingham where we were only giving *The Nutcracker*. All five leading casts would be performing in preparation for our forthcoming Christmas season in London.

During the week at the Alexandra Theatre Birmingham we gave two programmes: the two act *Coppélia* followed by *Corsaire* pas de deux and *Noir et Blanc*, with a change-over for the four last shows to the full length *Swan Lake*. These demanding mid-week changes were to be repeated in Bristol, where *Meadow Lark* was to be premiered in place of *Noir et Blanc*.

In Birmingham I heard that Andre Prokovsky, who had not been chosen by Feld, was grumbling that he had no new roles, and Carter, adding fuel to the fire, bewailed my choice of an unknown, foreign choreographer. I realised that there would always be grumbles about something from someone. The wardrobe's girl assistant was upset by dancers complaining about ill-fitting swan costumes which were often old and stained and handed on from one dancer to another. She was doing her best, sewing on extra hooks and eyes, and I tried to soothe her injured pride. Mathé was off for another two weeks, which was a blow, and Hamilton was also absent with a strained back. There was no news from an absent Gilpin – not even from his agent, which I thought peculiar and worrying. I found the dancers on edge when I took the *Swan Lake* rehearsal, following a row in class between the ballet master Frano, a soloist (Carol Grant) and a corps de ballet girl (Gillian Price). Over a late lunch with David Taylor I had to tell him that neither Stiff nor I believed he was yet ready to become Music Director. I hated having to say this – even though it was true – but he appeared to take it calmly. I then spent two hours casting with Vass, Joanie and Peter B. As the days went by we were faced with other dancers falling ill, meaning cast changes and extra rehearsals.

In spite of the problems, the radio interviews I gave boosted our box office sales, though adding nothing to our depleted dancer numbers. In London Stiff arranged a meeting with Peter Davis at the British Council about our foreign tours. Once again he had not invited me, although I knew it would be important for me to meet Davis and establish a good working relationship for the future.

Finally the Company arrived in Bristol, the last city of our provincial tour. Sunday became a busy one for those involved with *Meadow Lark*, particularly the stage and lighting crews. It was exciting to see this picturesque ballet come to life on the 9th December. The novelty of four orchestral players on the large stage of the lovely old Hippodrome Theatre added to the idyllic setting. The four principals – Dagmar Kessler, Dudley von Loggenburg, Carol Grant and Alain Dubreuil – were ideally cast, and Feld was delighted with their performance. He had wanted to use Hamilton but his bad back prevented his being in it. Personally I thought it just as well because he was considerably taller than the other three dancers.

Meadow Lark was only tepidly received by the audience that first evening, and I realised would not be a good opener in the future – audiences obviously expected to hear a full orchestra at the start of an evening's show. After this, we made sure that, before *Meadow Lark* began the evening, the full orchestra were in the pit playing the national anthem. We invited the press for the second performance, and I was pleasantly surprised that several came from London, including A.V. Coton, Oleg Kerensky and Peter Williams, who appeared to appreciate the Watteau-style ballet. There were two further performances before Feld bade us a fond farewell to fly home to the States. I enjoyed his presence and his enthusiasm so was sorry to see him go.

On Thursday Gilpin's wife rang to say he was back and would be coming to the theatre in Bristol, but I asked her to send him to the office in London. I rang Max to discuss the situation: Stiff thought we should dismiss Gilpin after all his absences but I could not agree to this. Unfortunately Max was unobtainable and so it was finally agreed with the agent that Gilpin become a guest artist with the Company. Later that day Peter B informed me that Stiff told him that he had given Aubrey a few more performances before leaving as a face-saver. I was furious not to have been consulted – I would not have condoned such a move. That evening in Bristol I was calmed by *Swan Lake* danced beautifully by Dagmar with Alain making his debut as her prince. His performance was so moving that the Company applauded him after the curtain went down, which was unusual and wonderful to hear.

The following evening's leading pair in *Swan Lake* were Helen Starr and Ian Hamilton, who were disappointing, and I had tactfully to tell them so. Helen always appeared to resent any constructive criticism or suggestions I made but, on this occasion knowing it to be true, they blamed their performance on the absence of Vass and myself from their rehearsal, which was taken by Frano. At this time Vass and I had been working out casting and rehearsal schedules for London with Duff, Joanie and Peter B. Peter B mentioned that the Company union member had complained about Frano's classes which did not surprise me. One of the corps asked to see me to discuss her future: she no longer wished to continue dancing and thought she should perhaps finish straight away, a decision I assured her needed careful deliberation. I watched her work carefully and realised perhaps she was right.

Then, to top that, Dagmar came to ask why she was not dancing the Flute solo in *Noir et Blanc*. I'm afraid I exploded! I insisted she came upstairs to our staff room where the cast and rehearsal sheets were laid out, and reminded her of her husband Frano's complaint that we were overworking her. I showed her how we were trying to ease her workload. I felt sad and ashamed afterwards having lost my temper at the end of an awful day and resolved not to let it happen again. I knew I would need the patience of a saint. Whether on tour or in London, most days were packed with incidents – some pleasing, some upsetting, all unpredictable.

Towards the end of the tour I was receiving an encouraging number of replies from choreographers I contacted. It was important for the Company to present a wide range of ballets which would appeal to our audiences but remain within the limitations of our budget whilst challenging the dancers. At the same time it was also important to establish a repertoire different from that of the Royal Ballet, although we could not avoid presenting the same classics – *Swan Lake, Sleeping Beauty, Nutcracker* and *Giselle*. Massine was interested in staging a work for us, but I was uneasy about his rehearsal demands and his fee, neither being within our present resources. Reluctantly this had to be put on hold for the time being, with Stiff unable to make a commitment in writing.

There were other interesting possibilities on the horizon. After seeing the company in Bristol, Robert Joffrey expressed interest in staging a work for us. Another American choreographer, John Taras, was prepared to stage his ballet *Piège de Lumière* despite the limited rehearsal time we could offer. Matching choreographers' availability with the Company's was not easy as we spent more time on tour than resident in London.

Whilst on tour I auditioned several lacklustre dancers who did not interest us. We did see one talented French, male dancer who impressed us but we realised his style was too different so sadly were unable to engage him. The tour ended on the 14th December, and we were in London with only a week before Christmas and the traditional season at the Royal Festival Hall. The Company were given a free Monday while I was busy in the morning auditioning thirty dancers at Donmar. On becoming Artistic Director I had seen a horrifying two hundred dancers in one audition. Now the standard was still disappointingly low and only one dancer really stood out. The girl was French, and our second choice was a talented student from the Royal Ballet School.

Audition over, Vass and I dashed off to the Arts Educational School at the Barbican to select children suitable for our forthcoming *Nutcracker*. The young dancers were lined up and eager and, as we needed two casts, a good number were chosen, including two Claras and two Fritzes. They were beautifully prepared by their teacher, Eve Pettinger, a stalwart of the Arts Educational School, a gifted teacher and dance arranger. From there we went to the Maida Vale studios where Stiff joined us to hear Sir Arthur Bliss' composition *The Lady of Shallot*, which we agreed could make a fine ballet if an appropriate choreographer could be found.

Tuesday morning heralded another appalling group of dancers auditioning, so we sent the French girl an offer of a corps de ballet contract. Stiff and I then interviewed some technicians before joining David Taylor at the office to meet a prospective assistant conductor, Terence Kern, to share David's workload. I aimed to increase the size of the orchestra gradually from forty five musicians and knew another conductor would become necessary. Terence was unassuming with a pleasant personality, interested in ballet and willing to fit in to our ceaseless touring. David believed he would be satisfactory but we would have to gauge the dancers' reaction to his conducting before offering him a contract. A three-hour staff meeting at the office followed, meaning a dash to Donmar for the five o'clock Company call of *Nutcracker* which ended at nine in the evening.

By 7.15am on Wednesday a crew arrived at Donmar from the Inner London Education Authority to set up a video recording at 9.30am. The Company were to be filmed taking class and rehearsing *The Nutcracker*. This was a scheme developed with Dr Briault, chief executive of ILEA, who I knew from my time with the Arts Educational Trust. Children would be shown the video at school prior to the Company's performances at a local theatre. This was to give them some idea of ballet and what it entailed, hopefully creating an interest in our forthcoming season. Vass and I knew it would also benefit our dancers to watch themselves in action, and we were not wrong. In fact the dancers were sorry to miss the end of the viewing because of the rehearsal commencing at 4pm.

Sven, Ingvar and I made our annual quest to Covent Garden market for a fine Christmas tree. We were greeted by our usual market trader proffering a splendid specimen which we purchased together with holly and mistletoe. Armed with a box of glorious chrysanthemums, we returned home for a much needed hearty breakfast. I left to have one more lesson with de Vos prior to Christmas. She had not been well, getting out of breath and tiring quickly, which was unlike her. Yet she still managed – a remarkable woman, a great teacher and an inspiration in every respect. Immediately after my workout I got in a quick visit to the hairdresser before rehearsing *Nutcracker* for three hours at Donmar. This was our final call at the studio as it was hired for a short period by the Royal Ballet's second Company.

On Monday following the orchestra's three-hour call in the shallow pit at the Royal Festival Hall, we held our first stage rehearsal of *The Nutcracker*. The lighting crew followed us in, working through the night, finishing on Christmas Eve. I rehearsed two couples – Helen Starr with Ian Hamilton and Carmen Mathé with Alain Dubreuil – before the full Company came on stage in the afternoon. This, our final dress and orchestra call, was with Galina Samsova and Andre Prokovsky, before many onlookers, including Sven and Ingvar. Once it was over, everyone departed in high spirits with presents and cards to spend Christmas, each in their own way. In Sweden Christmas is celebrated on Christmas Eve and since our marriage, Sven and I always enjoyed both the Swedish and English customs, with presents on both days whilst savouring traditional foods. At midnight we attended the service at the Scottish church in Knightsbridge: a special and perfect way to herald in the English Christmas Day.

Festival Ballet opened with two shows on Boxing Day to start a fortnight of matinee and evening performances. The critics were invited to the evening of the 30th December, and I wrote in my diary that the Company danced superbly, although Gilpin was below par partnering Kessler and Miklosy. There was a small party for the Company after the show when, to my amazement, Gilpin handed a farewell present to Aubrey Bowman and then gave a speech surprisingly praising Aubrey's conducting. With David Taylor standing there having just conducted Gilpin's performance, I found this terribly tactless and felt furious that the party had been arranged at all.

I worried about the reviews, though in the event they were good. I did wish they had remarked on the improved level of dancing by the corps de ballet as everybody had worked so hard to raise the standard. With the end of the Festival Hall season the dancers were able to depart and relax for a week, which they certainly deserved. For me it was a pleasing finish to 1968 and Sven and I celebrated at our favourite Acropolis restaurant. En route home we collected our fourteen-year-old son from his first grown-up dance at Phyllis Haylor's studio where, in the holidays, he had begun to take ballroom dancing lessons. The free week was a welcome opportunity for me to see more of Sven and Ingvar, before driving him to Eton for the new term. On arrival he proudly showed us his room – neat, tidy and well organised.

8 *1969 – New Tours, New Dancers, New Ballets, New Troubles*

After their short break the dancers were back for two weeks at Donmar for their daily classes and to prepare for the forthcoming six-week provincial tour starting in February. At the office we were disappointed to learn that Gerald Arpino would not be able to come after all in the Spring. When Joffrey was over in December we had discussed Arpino, his chief choreographer, staging a work for us. I had counted on this ballet, but it fell through because of our inadequate available rehearsal time. I had to find a new work to present in Italy for the spring tour.

Fortuitously, Stiff received a letter from Jack Carter, the company's resident choreographer since 1966, wishing to stage a new ballet to music by Berlioz, *Les Nuits d'Été*, a ballet later presented as *The Unknown Island*. This answered our problem. It was agreed that Carter could proceed, with Norman McDowell designing the set and costumes. John Taras had already agreed to stage his ballet *Piège de Lumière*, and I met with his agent and his costume designer André Lavasseur whose work I much liked. The one-act ballet – about a group of escaped convicts living in a forest and catching rare butterflies – was cleverly designed. Andre, Galina and the French dancer Bestonso were cast in the three leading roles which suited them to perfection, and I hoped this new role would placate Andre who was always grumbling. There were long meetings with the technical staff now that we had two new ballets coming into the repertoire. The fact they were to be premiered in Italy added complications. I also asked Peter Darrell if he would create a pas de deux for Margot Miklosy and John Gilpin, which he was delighted to undertake. So wardrobe and workshops were working full out.

I was quite looking forward to the season's opening at Hull, a city I had never been to before. Surprisingly, a number of the Company chose not to catch the early morning coach there, preferring to take a train later at their own expense. Once safely assembled on stage at the New Theatre, our class and rehearsals were televised, providing an invaluable preview for our season. With Act II of *Nutcracker* and Carter's two-act *Coppélia* we played successfully for a week in Hull. The good canteen in the basement produced lovely Welsh rarebits and stayed open late throughout the show – a plus for everybody.

Come Sunday, we travelled to Scotland giving one week of *Sleeping Beauty* at The Alhambra, Glasgow, one of its fine old theatres. Our box office takings for the week were low: disappointing as it had a large seating capacity. The orchestra sounded thin, the players sounding as if they needed a good rehearsal. But the dancers were in good heart despite a slippery stage.

Worryingly, the designs for *Piège* had not arrived, leaving the advertised April Venice opening programme in question. Mercifully Peter Farmer had finished his designs for the third act of *Coppélia* which received all-round approval.

In Liverpool *Graduation Ball* replaced *Nutcracker* Act II, its engaging charm a winner with the audience. Terry Hayworth, our foremost character artist, played expertly the humorous headmistress, and the Company danced this ballet with obvious enjoyment. Sadly the attendance was poor (as the mayor himself remarked), and did not improve much during the rest of the week. I wondered if the Royal Court was a suitable theatre for ballet in Liverpool and whether we had sent adequate publicity.

Our penultimate week was in the beautiful city of learning, Oxford. Entering the New Theatre brought back wondrous memories – how Ninette de Valois, director of the Royal Ballet, called me to her room to tell me I was to dance *Swan Lake* that evening with Robert Helpmann. I was only fourteen at the time, and returning twenty-six years later as director of Festival Ballet seemed like a dream. Fate is strange.

Taras began work at the Dance Centre Studios in London with Galina and Andre on *Piège*. I called in to check all was well – it was, although my two principals were late arriving. Taras came to Oxford that afternoon to watch the matinee of an abbreviated *Coppélia* and *Nutcracker* Act II. Next morning, with Vass and me by his side, he cast his ballet. I liked Taras' strength of character, and his forthrightness imbued us with confidence. The work was already taking shape and looking fabulous.

But the many challenges of being director continued. I worried that Andre's leg was troubling him, and cut his solo in *Nutcracker* on opening night. Before the end of the week he was unable to perform. I was relieved to see a talented Spanish girl Maria Guerrero dancing again after being off for five weeks. I had a complaint from a top soloist about being cast in corps work in *Piège*, yet he had only just returned from an injury. Bosser, a stubborn corps man, was unwilling to change his place in *Coppélia* – a situation eventually resolved by Vass. Jean-Pierre Alban, an established principal, who had partnered me as Benno when guesting in *Swan Lake* some years previously, was worrying about growing older. He asked to see me, concerned about how it would affect his future and frightened at the thought of not being able to dance any more. I felt so sorry for him and tried my best to cheer and reassure him.

Alun Rhys called, panicking about the costumes still to be completed, but was eventually mollified by Peter Brownlee. Miklosy returned from guesting in Gothenburg and danced her first *Coppélia*, partnered by Gilpin with panache. At the weekend I phoned the American ballerina Mimi Paul to invite her to guest with the already contracted Peter Martins for our coming London summer season. We were already casting principals for that season as well as completing detailed casting for the European tour in April. Meanwhile I had an appointment with a possible benefactor, introduced to me by the shoe-makers Gamba. John Brenna, their director, had become a good friend of mine during my dancing years, supplying me with shoes for both private and professional appearances. This was my first attempt to seek financial support for the Company and, although I never found it easy to ask for money, I am told I became quite deft at this during my years with Festival Ballet.

The last week was not without its dramas, commencing with Carter accusing Hamilton of making Gilpin so drunk after the closing show in Oxford that he was incapable of rehearsing Carter's new ballet *Nuits d'Été* on Monday. Hamilton said he was not responsible but Carter was maddened by Gilpin's absence at his first call with the designer McDowell present. So far, even without Gilpin, it was looking promising. By Tuesday we heard that Gilpin had a clot in his leg and was in hospital awaiting tests and an operation, which he underwent successfully. It appeared that he had suffered a clot three years previously and was warned against drinking or smoking. To our surprise, the police interviewed Stiff and me at the office to enquire about Gilpin's life-style and work schedules.

As the week progressed, ailments abounded. Duff was not well and in an antagonistic mood for the technical meeting on *Nuits d'Été* with Carter and McDowell. This was a shame – the sets looked splendid and were surely not going to be as difficult to stage as Duff implied. Only a week after her return, Margot Miklosy arrived in a terrible state having been beaten up by her husband. He had had a complete mental breakdown and fought off four policemen before being taken to a psychiatric hospital. He and Margot had experienced terrible times in the past when Hungary was invaded by the Russians. He had been shot as they escaped over the border, Margot carrying her wounded husband on her back. He had never made a complete recovery, and Margot was now horribly shaken. Being a great trouper, she was determined not to give in and insisted on dancing in *Nutcracker* that night. Stiff was not well either, his tonsils troubling him, and was in bed by the weekend. Nevertheless we were both out front on Friday evening at the Odeon to meet the press. I was glad to have the opportunity of talking with Peter Williams and Richard Buckle, the critics whose support and advice I really valued. The audience attendance had greatly improved since our previous visit and, to everyone's surprise, it appeared that *Nutcracker* attracted more families around Golders Green than the *Sleeping Beauty* the previous November.

We continued to work in the Golders Green theatre as it was vacant, allowing us the use of a good stage for rehearsals, which was ideal. The rehearsal schedule was tight and tricky to organise with two new ballets and a pas de deux, each choreographer pushing for more rehearsal time. We also had to prepare *Bourrée Fantasque*, *Noir et Blanc*, *Meadow Lark* and *Witch Boy* for the foreign tour. There were shifting patterns with guest artists. Peter Breuer of the Dusseldorf Ballet was booked for the foreign tour then changed his plans, but we were desperate to present him in Paris in June so negotiations continued. Mimi Paul, having agreed to dance in the London season with Peter Martins, subsequently asked if she might leave us earlier than stipulated to accept an engagement with American Ballet Theatre. With Gilpin ill, Breuer agreed to come to London one Sunday and learn the Taras' *Soirée Musicale* pas de deux with Miklosy, which used music by Rossini arranged by Britten. Eventually the guest appearances were sorted out to suit all parties.

To my dismay the director of the Wiesbaden theatre, Antoine, came to watch rehearsals the week of 7th April when Andre's leg was still troubling him and Juan Sanchez, a leading soloist, was not able to dance full-out either. John Fletcher, an energetic corps dancer, landed wrongly during the *Piège* rehearsal, fracturing the lower base of his fibula and, with Gilpin still away, I was getting worried by the shortage of men. Two top soloists – Loggenberg and Jorge Salavisa – and a corps male dancer (Dalton) came to our rescue, filling the gaps immediately. I was touched and encouraged by their willingness to step in. Ian Hamilton asked for a rise in salary to which we could not agree so he planned to leave in a couple of months. This did not upset me – he was generally difficult, seeming preoccupied with money. I knew that Piers Beaumont from the Royal Ballet touring company was keen to join later in the year and, being tall, I thought would make a good replacement.

The news that the Royal Academy of Dance was suggesting an amalgamation with the Imperial Society of Teachers of Dancing came as a big surprise. Some years past, during Cyril Beaumont's chairmanship, this issue had been under discussion but was dropped when Beaumont thought it the wrong time. As a committee member of the ISTD I hoped that this amalgamation might go ahead. It would benefit both societies and the often perplexed teachers, pupils and parents.

On 11th April, I departed with the Company from Gatwick for Czechoslovakia. Stiff came for the early part of the tour. After long delays through passport control and customs in Kosice, we were welcomed by a few dancers from the local company. The city seemed sad and drab, the inhabitants poorly clad, weary and miserable looking. 'So much for a communist society,' I thought to myself as Stiff and I were driven to a rather shabby hotel. How awful to exist amidst such surroundings.

On arrival at the Diradlo Theatre, to my horror I found Vass rather too drunk to concentrate. I had to quickly work out the calls for the next three days myself before the Company arrived for class and the triple bill rehearsal on stage with the local orchestra. The musicians failed to appear, and we never received an explanation. We feared they had not known of the rehearsal or perhaps had too little time between our call and the opera performance that evening of *Masked Ball.*

Festival Ballet opened next evening with *Nightshadow, Graduation Ball, Spring Waters* and *Prince Igor*. Although we were assured it was a success I had expected more prolonged applause. On our second night, however, the programme of *Bourrée Fantasque*, *Meadow Lark, Spring Waters* and *The Witch Boy* received a terrific reception. Bestonso as the Witch boy had a resounding personal success, even more than Galina. Had it not been for Andre's bad back I know she would have received an ovation for the dynamic *Corsaire* pas de deux. Instead she performed the shorter, less flamboyant *Spring Waters,* in which Andre had only to partner and not dance. As director I was expected to go on stage at the close and say a few words. In fact I was pushed on by the local dancers and uttered a big thank you to the audience, curtsying deeply.

Early next morning we flew to Prague, where we landed safely in a snow storm. This magnificent capital with its myriad spires looked magical under the blanket of glistening snow. The Company were booked into three hotels, ours being refreshingly modern. Leaving Stiff, after a long unsuccessful wait for food Peter B and I went to check up on the Company and their rooms. We took a look at the Kirlin Diavadlo Theatre, where we were to perform, but found it disappointingly uninviting. Early evening there was a big reception for the entire Company given by the British Council, which I enjoyed enormously, although to my surprise Andre and Galina left early. Both Stiff and I stayed until the end and took the opportunity to return to the hotel together. We discussed Company matters, but I continued to feel uneasy about his moves and motives. I could never quite trust him to be totally candid and fully informative.

Our class next day had to be divided into separate sessions as the practice room was too small to take the full Company, but the dancers managed to be ready in time for the stage call which followed. That opening night went beautifully with the Company dancing extremely well having benefitted from the previous day's respite. They had a great reception – though the theatre was not totally full. Not so the next night, our last, when every seat was taken and we were given thunderous applause. Once again Bestonso scored a triumph, and I went on stage to say thank you and goodbye in Czech! I was then presented with a beautiful glass vase by Bassova, the senior interpreter from Prague Concerts with whom I worked closely. She kept asking if I 'truly liked it' and I have indeed cherished their gift, as I have a book of beautiful sepia photographs evocative of the great city. It has the inscription to 'Miss Beryl Grey a little souvenir of her stay in Prague Dr Xujka 21/IX 1947' from when I danced there with Sadler's Wells Ballet.

There was in Prague on this visit an underlying, tense atmosphere. There were rumours of an imminent Russian invasion and our interpreters were in tears on parting. Later that night Peter B and I were advised to warn the Company not to go out of the hotels next morning under any circumstances – the Soviet military were expected to be on the streets of the city. After serious discussion Peter B and I agreed it would be more prudent to say nothing to the Company, other than to be ready to board our coaches by nine o'clock sharp. After the late night, we knew it would be difficult enough to have everyone packed and awake by then. To have forbidden them to go out early would, we thought, make them almost certain to do exactly that. It was a risk and we were worried, but it paid off and we watched our bleary-eyed dancers clambering into the coaches at nine. None too soon we were away, driving through eerily empty streets to the airport which was already surrounded by Soviet tanks. With our hearts in our mouths Peter and I disembarked with the Company and under escort were taken into the airport. This was the second time I had been in Prague with the Russians about to enter. My heart went out to the poor inhabitants, thankful that my home was in England.

We flew to Venice, landing at midday, but had a long wait at the airport for the waterbus booked to take us across the lagoon to our hotels. Never having been there, I had a feeling that I already knew the city from the exquisite paintings of Canaletto but it was even more magical and romantic than he could portray, with little paths and small bridges leading to exciting new vistas. Secret squares hidden behind hugely impressive buildings, fine palaces, the great basilica – all as when they were first erected centuries ago, linked by a maze of canals. Likewise, the lovely La Fenice opera house where we were to perform – full of atmosphere from a thousand bygone performances.

We had the day to ourselves in Venice before an evening rehearsal for our performance next day in Ferrara. The performance was pretty disastrous since we had no orchestra: the agent, Mario Porcile, had decided it was an unnecessary expense in that town. Instead the dancers were accompanied by two pianos played gallantly by our two pianists, Jimmy Slater and Hilary Bell, with our conductor feverishly hitting the spider drums. Nevertheless it was poor, the Haydn and Rossini-Britten arrangements sounding particularly odd and, lacking an overture, the performance did not get off to a good start. The theatre was lovely, the stage large, and the Company danced with feeling despite being short of two principals: Prokovsky was still unable to perform and once again Gilpin was absent. I heard from Peter B that Porcile had not liked our guest artist Breuer, which was a pity. He was a fine dancer, even though his hair flopped about as he whirled around! I thought perhaps he looked too tall with Miklosy in Darrell's pas de deux, which had its first performance in Ferrara. I began to think they would look better together in *Black Swan*, so with Porcile's agreement, we switched to the ever popular *Black Swan* pas de deux for the remainder of the tour.

The next two days in Venice were spent busily preparing *Piège* for our opening programme at the Fenice. I managed to squeeze in to see the Sunday matinee at which the great French prima ballerina Yvette Chauviré was appearing. At the age of fifty she was still divine, partnered by Milorad Miskovitch. Also in the same show was the younger Carla Fracci with her partner Jean-Pierre Bonnefous who spoke to me of his willingness to dance with us later in the year. Our first full stage call for *Piège de Lumière* ran from 6 to 8.30pm. Taras was sitting alongside Lavasseur, whose eyes were glued on his vibrant, exotic costumes. The Labisse decor looked promising, and I hoped the orchestra would do justice to the Damase score.

Next morning I met the administration and the artistic director of the Fenice who gave me the most wonderful tour of the historic theatre. Peter B said that this was unprecedented, and I should feel most privileged. Our rehearsals continued late into the evening, and we prayed for the success of our Continental premiere next evening, Tuesday 22nd April.

A success! Porcile, the administration and the audience were delighted. The artistic director sought me out twice to congratulate me on the programme and the standard of dancing. But there was one awful accident – Breuer fell badly during the *Black Swan* coda, and crawled offstage in agony. Ever resourceful, Alain Dubreuil leapt on stage immediately, concluding the finale with Miklosy. A doctor was called instantly to Breuer's dressing room but Breuer knew he had torn his Achilles tendon and was transported to the cheerless local hospital where we visited him early next morning. He was desperate to contact the famous surgeon in Århus, Denmark, renowned in the dance world for his success in repairing dancers' injuries. Once located, the specialist agreed to operate on Breuer in Århus providing he was there by the next afternoon – time being of utmost importance. Straightaway a flight was arranged to Copenhagen. With Geoffrey escorting him, Breuer travelled by water ambulance and then by road to Milan airport.

Breuer had to be replaced and, after some frantic telephoning across Europe, I managed to get Karl Musil from Vienna for the rest of the tour. He came at once, arriving next day, but could not be free for the Paris and London seasons which were to follow. He arrived in good time to appear the same night and, although his performance was understandably a little untidy, he looked marvellous and Porcile was placated. Surprisingly, Ian Hamilton then expressed his willingness to stay on until September, to which I readily agreed.

Backed this time by a good orchestra, the Company enjoyed dancing for a week in the atmospheric Fenice. The performances were well received, albeit with customary muted applause from the elegant audience. During the day, the Company used the small dusty rehearsal room at the top of the building, where Diaghilev's great dancers had also worked and sweated. When we needed two hours on stage, we had to battle with the stage manager until at last the Fenice's director came to our rescue and the stage call took place.

On departing from Venice, Porcile presented me with a magnificent book of photographs of the city, saying he looked forward to my being able to attract a higher calibre of dancers for the Company in the future. A man with perception and a great deal of charm.

We left Venice on Monday 28th April and endured an uncomfortably long train journey to Rome. I was feeling rotten, having been sick in the night. The next day was dreadfully worrying, too, as there was a mix-up with our wagons. The music had not arrived in time for the orchestra's call, and I felt ashamed as it was obviously the fault of our staff. It was then discovered that the dancers' boxes were also missing so they had no practice clothes in which to rehearse. Everyone was up in arms and chaos reigned, with Carter's new ballet *Les Nuits d'Été* due to be premiered the next night. The awful day was eventually erased by watching a great performance of *Aida* that evening in the Rome opera house: John Barbirolli conducting and Gwyneth Jones singing the title role.

It was a blessing that our opening performance next evening was not due to commence until 9.30pm. This gave us much-needed time to get the complex lighting and scene changes in *Les Nuits d'Été* logged and working smoothly, as well as giving our musicians and dancers a little extra time to rehearse together. *Swan Lake* Act II opened the performance and Galina as Odette justifiably received an ovation. Following this, the new ballet earned tremendous applause for its premiere, much to everyone's relief. Not only McDowell, who designed both the scenery and costumes, but also Carter seemed satisfied. The sensational *Spring Waters* pas de deux and the hilarious *Graduation Ball* made for a successful opening in Rome's Teatro Sistina. We had a finely dressed, enthusiastic audience who added to the atmosphere, despite the presence outside the theatre of some communist protestors.

I was upset next morning to hear that 'Dinks', a corps de ballet girl, was complaining the dancers had been let down. They had been promised time off in lieu after working late the night before the premiere of *Les Nuits d'Été,* and she said they had expected to be given a free day. I tried to explain that rehearsals were vital to produce an acceptable standard for presentation to the public, but that we always considered the dancers. We tried to strike a happy balance, bearing in mind the constant programme changes expected by our audiences. But I felt I had broken faith with the Company, and this saddened me. Duty called and, after a morning's work in the theatre, I was collected by an official car for lunch at the British Embassy.

All three evening performances in Rome were hugely successful but not without dramas. Our wardrobe assistant Liz was hysterical on learning she was to be left in charge, her superior having to return to London to be with her gravely ill mother. My two tall soloists – Freya Dominic and Valerie Aitken – were sick, and we were getting distinctly low on dancers. With money short, however, I dared not ask the Board for a larger Company to allow me to reorganise the casting in emergencies, of which there were many. Under these conditions, the dancers were always amazingly cooperative, soloists stepping down into the corps without complaining, to make up the necessary numbers.

British Council friends found a taxi to take me to the airport as Stiff and his wife had already gone ahead without me, indicative of Stiff's behaviour – putting himself first regardless. He and his wife arrived in Venice during our last day there but missed the party for the Company given by the theatre directorate as they were sightseeing. It fell to Vass to make the necessary introductions next morning. I liked her better than her husband; she was a more straightforward person. Once at the airport the Company had a long wait in overwhelming heat for the flight to Frankfurt, while Norman McDowell and Alun Rhys flew back to London together with our distraught wardrobe mistress.

Once landed at Frankfurt, I persuaded the Stiffs to take a taxi with me to Wiesbaden, ahead of the dancers' coach, arriving at a pleasant hotel late afternoon. We managed a game of clock golf together before dining and grabbing an early night. Next day was my first free one of the tour, and I rang Sven with whom I was in regular contact. He was feeling downcast and lonely which came as a blow for I was feeling happier being in Germany and that much closer to him. I spent a miserable morning sewing and writing, torn between my husband and my Company. Geoffrey rang to tell me the Company were well housed and in a good mood. Stiff actually telephoned to invite me to lunch with him, his wife and Antoine our agent. After lunch Antoine took us for a drive to a pleasant swimming pool for a relaxing hour, and later to watch a not so relaxing German play.

Next morning there was a slip-up by the transport authorities. I was in the theatre listening to the orchestra's ten o'clock rehearsal taken by Taylor when a call was put through to me in the pit from the front of house. It was a frantic plea for help from our stage crew, still waiting in vain for customs personnel to arrive, open up our vehicles and verify their contents. Our lorries eventually arrived at the theatre well behind schedule and swiftly began unloading the scenery and costumes. Despite the hold-up, our stage crew managed to have everything set on stage in time for a brief Company rehearsal prior to the curtain going up.

Stiff, Peter B and I were taken to meet the director of the theatre and the dirigent (music director), who was particularly happy to have been invited to the British Council's party in the salon following our opening night. The evening was thrilling – a terrific atmosphere, almost all the audience smartly attired: men in white jackets and women in beautiful full-length gowns. During our time at the Hessische Staatstheatre we gave three different triple-bill programmes and the dancers were on top form. An official luncheon was organised, at which Stiff told me he was to give a speech which he had had translated into German. He read it well and everyone was impressed. But he was not so pleased when I was then presented with a beautifully bound book, to which I too responded. At the close of our last performance the dirigent came on stage, staying to the final curtain. To our surprise, Nicholas 'Papa' Beriozoff appeared, having travelled across Germany to see the show and spend some time with us. Vass and I took him to dinner and discussed his availability to work with us on the Diaghilev ballets.

After performing in Heerlen at the modern Staatschouburg theatre, well appointed and seating 900 people, an overnight coach drive to Antwerp for a sold-out, final performance, and then home to London early next morning, Sunday 11th May.

The next day we were to reassemble in Manchester – how difficult it was to leave Sven again after less than twenty-four hours at home. At the Opera House I found everybody in a whirl of activity concentrated around the new three-act *Coppélia,* its premiere next day. Class was in progress going straight into a chaotic rehearsal with a demonic Carter. I developed a rash and a headache as had one of my corps girls, Rosemary Dexter, so we both saw my hotel's doctor before the evening orchestral company call at seven thirty. The entire evening was spent on Act III, which looked an awful mess with horrific bright colours, glaring costumes and scenery. Fortunately Charles Bristow decided to relight with blue, instructing Geoffrey Guy our senior scenic artist to re-spray the scenery several shades paler. Rhys, now panicking, was told to dye certain costumes a calmer colour. No wonder I felt peculiar!

Despite the previous day's chaos, the production miraculously came together and *Coppélia* was received by a rapturous audience who cheered vociferously at the end, something not known at the Opera House for years. The manager, Appleby, was delighted with the £5,000 advance at the box office for the week, boosted by the television and radio interviews I had given earlier. He gave drinks in his office in both intervals, and the dancers returned to their digs after the performance with armfuls of flowers. I was worried, however, as once again I had several dancers off ill: Freya and Dexter, but also leading soloists David Long, Nona Telford and Dudley von Loggenburg.

Watching the matinee and evening performances of *Coppélia* on Wednesday gave me the opportunity to see different casts. Whilst in Manchester, Peter B, Vass, our press officer Vivien Wallace and I were able to finish work on the Company's new brochure.

With the layout completed, Stiff returned to London, taking with him the casting for Paris, before I returned on Thursday, happy that the full-length *Coppélia* was such a success. Once in the office I had a reassuring telephone conversation with Le Maitre in Paris: he was pleased for us to present Martins with Miklosy in *Black Swan* during our forthcoming season in June at the Halle de Baltard.

On Friday morning, at Stiff's request, I was at the office by 10 o'clock to ring Peter B in Spain as agreed – there was plenty to be discussed. The Company were booked for a three-week tour following the London season, and he was out there making the final arrangements. I was also on the phone in the afternoon with Vass in Manchester; he said all was going well and there was no need for me to return on Saturday – I should take the opportunity to have a rest.

Sunday's peace was shattered by the arrival midday of Stiff who told me that the Company were unhappy with me personally: they did not like the way I corrected them at rehearsal. I was stunned and said, 'I do not believe it,' but he went on to say he had had delegates from each level of the Company and that three principals wanted to leave. He refused to give me any names, however, and I could only stammer, 'This cannot be true'. I rang Vass and Joanie who came around at once and were surprised and disbelieving. Sven, who was present, suggested I rang my friend David Clayton Stamm for his advice. As Stiff would not disclose names, David said I was not to move or do anything about it, neither was I to go to Max Rayne. I hoped this was the right advice and prayed it would blow over. I just could not understand it and began to wonder who I had unwittingly upset and who my enemies might be. Had this originated when Stiff was on the foreign tour? I remembered having said to him on one occasion, 'Can't you trust me to run the Company?' which was perhaps too outspoken. I was terribly upset and bewildered and could not sleep that night.

I felt uneasy going into the office next day but Stiff said nothing. I felt better after my lesson with de Vos, who had total faith in me, saying: 'I too have been through the same kind of accusations and this you must expect from time to time.' Although I slept better, I awoke at four next morning, worrying again that Stiff would take his accusations to the Board. De Vos said not to worry about what people said as long as the end results were right. I heard nothing more from Stiff, though I felt uneasy when he had a meeting with his assistant Nigel and Peter B in his office for some time, while I was discussing with Carter, McDowell and Duff the staging for *Les Nuits d'Été* at Les Halles. This was proving almost impossible, so we finally agreed we must go there early Friday morning to sort out the technical problems on the spot. Meantime, there was a lot to do both in the office and at Donmar, not only taking rehearsals but also discussing with several dancers their casting for the London season before pinning it up on the notice board. Problematic ones I saw in the office: Kessler and her husband Jellincic were positively abusive because she was not given the first night of *Coppélia* in London. Casting was not easy and although I tried to be fair I had to prioritise the needs of our public, presenting the dancers most suited to specific roles.

On Wednesday evening I met Paul Channon, the spokesman for the Arts in the House of Commons. We had a valuable talk for well over an hour about Festival Ballet and its touring in the regions. Afterwards I attended a reception for Les Grands Ballets Canadiens who were appearing at Sadler's Wells for the first time. I was introduced to their founder, Ludmilla Chiriaeff, who I liked straightaway and who was praying for a successful season.

Back in Donmar there was a long *Sleeping Beauty* call after which I went to the office. I had to disappoint Carol Grant by not giving her the lead in *Coppélia* during the London season. Her partner, Salavisa, took this better than Carol, who was deeply upset. I hated having to do this but as director, one's responsibility is first to the public and then to the dancer. Mimi Paul arrived from the States while I was with Vass going through the challenges of Les Halles, to which he added some helpful suggestions. Mimi had a slow American drawl and seemed a little shy but was charming. Her rehearsals were to start next day for *Sleeping Beauty* and *Night Shadow* which Vass was to oversee, so it was fortuitous they met in advance. I had promised to be home by seven that evening to celebrate Sven's birthday with my father and Clayton Stamms. We toasted Sven over a glass of champagne before going on to the Acropolis for a fine dinner. It was such a lovely evening after the fearful tension I experienced through the week.

Next morning I flew to Paris with Carter, McDowell, Duff and David Mohr (the chief electrician, known as The Prince of Darkness) to see for ourselves the space in the meat market where the Company was to perform as part of the Marais Festival. As expected, the unusual setting of Les Halles presented some insoluble problems, and it appeared to be impossible to hang scenery. Our agent Boris Trailine was present with the French stage director, a genial and helpful man who remained with us for many hours. We hoped our suggestions and requests would be fulfilled. Leaving Duff in Paris, the rest of us were back in London by 3pm realising just how necessary it had been to visit the problematical French location.

On returning to Donmar late afternoon I found Vass worrying about Mimi Paul. She did not appear to know *Les Sylphides* and was a slow learner. He questioned her ability to dance Princess Aurora, even though Peter Martins had expressly requested her to be his ballerina in *Sleeping Beauty*. Vass also mentioned that Carmen Mathé was telling everyone that she would probably be leaving the Company after the Spanish tour. Strange, as only the day before at her interview about the London casting she told me how happy she was and thanked me profusely. What was going on? I went to bed absolutely whacked and totally perplexed.

Saturday brought good news from Duff: the advanced casting list was not required until Tuesday – a relief as it was still not finalised. Mimi Paul had obviously recovered from her flight and remembered what she had been shown of *Les Sylphides* the previous day. She rehearsed *Night Shadow* without a problem and apparently knew most of *Sleeping Beauty.* I took her through the solos, which she told me she had learnt in New York from the famous ballerina Danilova. Mimi was pleasant to work with, and Vass and I were now more confident about her forthcoming performances. Prokovsky's foot was still worrying him and David Adams was ill in bed so I sent his wife Sheila Melvin home to look after him. I spent some time with Alain Dubreuil on his solo in *Noir et Blanc* and was pleasantly surprised when John Gilpin joined us and was most helpful to Alain.

An idyllic Sunday was spent with Sven and Ingvar who we collected from college. At fifteen he was the perfect age to remember the momentous landing on the moon, which we watched on television open-mouthed with disbelief. Sven followed this by showing a film of Ingvar skiing in Norway looking very grown-up. In total contrast we went upstairs to play with Ingvar's trains! Bank holiday Monday was the time for a stream of colourful floats to parade through the streets of the West End. Festival Ballet had accepted an invitation to be a part of this and several of our staff, including Geoffrey, were busy decorating the open lorry, with Stiff and his wife overseeing and helping. After some final touches from the designer Peter Farmer, our float looked marvellous as it left, our dancers perched gracefully – if a little perilously – on high. I felt rather proud of them gallantly advertising our Company.

Meanwhile, I was meeting with Beriozoff, Kern and Taylor in the office, talking through possible future stagings of the Diaghilev ballets and those suited to the size of our orchestra and dancers. Without consulting me, Stiff had told our two conductors to take the week off, but despite this they came to the Monday meeting. Later, discussing with Stiff the problems we were facing in Paris, I had a strange feeling that he was holding something back from me – a trump card perhaps? I was getting jittery again. Next day Jean-Pierre Alban told me how pleased he was that all was well once more with the Company. He was astonished that I was not aware of the Company meetings that had taken place in Manchester, or that he and Peter Williams wanted to take me out to dinner to cheer me. This was not exactly what I expected to hear, and I was disturbed.

At a gala that evening at Sadler's Wells I met Michael Wood, press officer of the Royal Opera House. He told me he'd heard that I was returning to dance again at Covent Garden as I didn't like Stiff's behaviour and was unhappy with the way he was spreading rumours about me to his opposite number, John Tooley, administrator of the Royal Opera House. 'Is this true?' he asked me, 'Of course not,' I replied, 'although things are not running smoothly between us.' This conversation was eclipsed by the pleasure that Sven and I felt at being seated at Princess Margaret's table for the dinner which followed the gala.

My report for the Board, with which I struggled for the past few days, had to be finished and typed by Geoffrey on Wednesday. Stiff's directive was that his report and mine were to be taken by hand to all board members in time for Thursday's meeting. I was relieved to see no mention in Stiff's report about the Company problem.

The Board meeting went smoothly, with John Sainsbury speaking up for me at one point and criticising Stiff's actions. After the meeting however Max Rayne suggested to Stiff and me a little meeting to discuss the Company's allegations. 'So Stiff has passed this on to you,' I said. Max concurred, adding he had also heard from other sources. I suddenly realised that it must have come through Donald Albery and his solicitor Laurence Harbottle, a board member. Peter B and Jean-Pierre had visited them with Anne Rawsthorne the previous Sunday and tongues would have wagged. I felt an innocent in a sea of intrigue, instigated by Stiff, who I had felt all along resented my presence and wished to get me out. Unsure how to proceed, I rang John Sainsbury next day and confided in him. He was most helpful and understanding, suggesting I tell Max of the true position between Stiff and me. I tried to reach Max but he was abroad on business, so sadly I was unable to contact him.

By Saturday life brightened up: I was told by Princess Margaret's lady-in-waiting, Lady Juliet Smith, that HRH would definitely be attending our forthcoming gala at the Coliseum in July. After several attempts to reach Max and pass this good news on before informing Stiff, I eventually managed to get him on the phone in France. He sounded surprised that Stiff had not been contacted by the Palace as he had obviously expected. This confirmed my suspicion that Stiff was playing up to Max. How I mistrusted Stiff and how uneasy I felt about his motives and underhandedness.

On Sunday afternoon I was in Paris rehearsing the principals in Les Halles. What an odd venue for a ballet company and how difficult it proved for our technical staff. During a break, Vass confided in me that Stiff told him that he would be interviewing every dancer in the Company for their views on my directing. What was he up to? Rehearsals did not finish until after eight o'clock, after which I took a taxi with Dolin and Gilpin, leaving them at their smart hotel before going on to my more modest abode which was clean and pleasant with trees astonishingly planted in the dining room!

The 'general repetition' next evening started late and finished late. Vass, Joanie and I worked through the morning planning the casts and ate lunch in the meat market close to our performance venue. Company class began at 2.30, and we then went swiftly into placing calls in the rather uncouth surroundings. After the dinner break the orchestra began to arrive, eventually commencing with *Les Sylphides* half an hour late. We had to cut the Aurora pas de deux rehearsal to concentrate on the new ballet, *Les Nuits d'Été*. We were only able to run through a little of *Piège* after midnight to piano as the orchestra had gone home, and by 12.30 we dismissed the Company, too. But Galina, Andre and Bestonso stayed on a further hour to practise *Piège*. Le Maitre and the Festival Director stayed to the end, determined to persuade me to cancel *Nuits d'Été* and replace it with *Bourrée Fantasque*. They were convinced that *Nuits* was technically too complicated to stage successfully in Les Halles and would be a disaster. Looking at the streamers flapping discontentedly in the wind as it whistled through the now deserted, cold building, I felt inclined to agree with them. I could not admit this though, with an indignant Carter confronting them, and said it would be difficult to change the programme at this late stage. I asked them not to worry: I was optimistic our technicians would be able to resolve the problems in time for a successful performance. They left unconvinced, with Carter and McDowell fuming and feeling insulted.

After a sleepless night, Trailine was on the phone early to say Le Maitre would be at Les Halles by 10.15 so I asked him to collect me there and then. We met Vass and Joanie and tried to decide what best to do. We called our two conductors and although they came at once they were dubious that they could get the orchestra together in time to rehearse *Bourrée* for the evening show. Meanwhile the staff were struggling to hang the *Nuits* flats better and at last appeared to be succeeding. By 1.30 our conductors admitted defeat in reassembling the orchestra, so fate decided for us and *Nuits* was premiered with miraculous success that evening, our soprano's voice ringing out gloriously in Les Halles.

We got a good press next day, and the Company danced a beautiful *Les Sylphides* at night despite the cold wind blowing through Les Halles. Some of the dancers took advantage of being in Paris, taking outside classes with distinguished teachers now domiciled in the city. Harald Lander was reviving his tour de force *Études* and at rehearsal the dancers were keen to be chosen. By Thursday the cold in Les Halles was too intense for the dancers to rehearse, and I had to stop the class after the barre work. Later a group from the Company came to tell me they did not want to dance in such cold conditions, quite understandably. Peter B and I went through our contract with the festival, only to find that we would have to pay them for loss of takings if we cancelled performances. This would mean an immediate ignominious retreat to London. We explained this to the dancers in a warm café; they decided they did not want to return to London, and agreed to go on, in spite of the cold. I was in touch by phone with Stiff who was non-committal and as unhelpful as ever. By Friday afternoon he arrived. I felt uneasy as I watched him in long conversations with some of the Company: Carmen Mathé, David Long, Helen Starr, Terry Hayworth and others.

On Saturday morning, I flew back for Ingvar's Eton celebration day. Despite my plane landing an hour late, Sven and I were met by a patient and excited Ingvar who took us at once to his housemaster's cocktail party. To our delight we were given a good report of Ingvar's progress, making it a red-letter day for us. I had to attend a dinner at the Café Royal given by the ISTD in honour of renowned teacher Anita Heyworth, retiring as Principal of the London Dance Teacher Training College, which she had led for many years with inspiration, dignity and success. Sitting on my right was her successor, Phrosso Phister, and on my left John Allen. It was he who was so helpful in initiating me into the bewildering world of education when I became Director General of the Arts Educational Trust in 1966. We both gave speeches amidst a friendly atmosphere of respect and gratitude.

After the stress of the past week in Paris it was a treat to wake up next morning with Sven by my side, safe at home. I kept in touch with Vass by phone before returning to Paris on Monday for our second week of performances. After rehearsals I had coffee with Vass and Joanie, who told of what they learnt at a party given for the dancers the previous day. Drink apparently was flowing freely and it transpired that the delegation who went to Stiff in Manchester, speaking on behalf of the Company against my direction, consisted of Helen Starr, David Adams and (to my surprise) Jelencic. Now I knew the facts, I was shattered, but my religious faith once again gave me the strength and determination to continue. I began to realise how much the dancers must have resented being criticised as well as the loss of the freedom they had enjoyed within the Company's former haphazard state. During the party, Gilpin had apparently been extremely rude to Lander, while Adams was telling the youngsters how to run a company. As Lander, a strict producer himself, later remarked to me, 'What friends!'

Monday's evening orchestral rehearsal of *Night Shadow, Witch Boy* and *Bourrée Fantasque* went slowly and the orchestra were forbidden to continue after 11.30pm, so our good natured pianists took over, finishing the rehearsal for the dancers. The change of programme was well received and Mimi Paul and Peter Martins enjoyed a success in the *Black Swan* pas de deux. To my joy Sven arrived in Paris while I was busily engaged with Lander, his designer and Duff, working on the effective but complicated lighting design for the forthcoming *Études* at the Coliseum. For my birthday, Sven brought with him two exquisite scarves, plus a well written card from Ingvar. We visited the Louvre and, refreshed by the wondrous art, I went to Les Halles to find that Vass had retired to bed early that afternoon – I feared from too much alcohol. I had noticed he was drinking more than usual since our arrival in Paris, setting the Company a poor example. To my surprise, I had birthday presents from Miklosy and Jean-Pierre as well as good wishes from a number of the Company, which gave me renewed hope.

Next morning Sven and I flew back to London, Sven to his patients, while I had a meeting with Rayne, Stiff and Abernethy. Surprised that there was no mention of the Company's unrest, I wondered later if I should have said something to Max about the situation, although it now seemed to have calmed. Back in Paris next morning, I found several dancers off with a fever and Andre's knee bad. Despite this, the Company pulled off a marvellous performance, after which Trailine took Lander and me to dinner.

Saturday 14th June, the last day of our two-week engagement, was busier than ever auditioning dancers – none of whom was of a high enough standard. There were final discussions with Lander, who I hoped could stage a Bournonville ballet for us in the future; rehearsing Mimi and Martins who turned up late as usual; and farewells to many new friends – before an exciting last night. How glad I was it had worked out, despite the initial glitches, and how happy I was to be first off the plane at Heathrow next morning to be met by Sven.

On returning to London I felt I must call in to the Coliseum to cheer our staff during their Sunday evening 'get in'. It was satisfying to see them unloading our scenery and props, baskets of costumes and shoes ready for the wardrobe to unpack in the morning. Our six-week season was to open on Wednesday, so we had to be ready for the Company dress rehearsal on Tuesday. A late office meeting with Rayne and Abernethy took place on Monday to discuss a possible Far Eastern tour – with no reference to the Company problem. I had to rush away to the last evening call of *Noir et Blanc* at Donmar having already missed *Graduation Ball*. We were installed in the Coliseum next day with a full dress rehearsal, which went surprisingly well – despite the lorry carrying everyone's make-up, wigs, hair pieces, new shoes and tights not having yet arrived from Paris. Nevertheless, the Company were glad to be in a proper theatre with a decent size stage and warm dressing rooms.

Our opening night, Wednesday 18th June, went beautifully, and the Company had a wonderful reception although the house was not full. Max Rayne organised a little party at the Garrick Club for the dancers after the performance, where I noticed David Adams and his wife Sheila Melvin in deep conversation with Laurence Harbottle. I suggested to Vass he join them, which he did. Vass later told me that Harbottle asked him whether Stiff or I should run the Company. Vass explained that there were several departments which should work as one in a combined effort to run the Company. Tactful and truthful.

Next Monday, my first ever gala for Festival Ballet, was graced by Princess Margaret. What a strain it was, awaiting the safe arrival of the guest artists Cyril Atanassoff and Wilfride Piollet from Paris in time for their afternoon orchestral rehearsal. Rayne, Peter B, Stiff and I determined the route which HRH should take to her seat in the centre of the Dress Circle, and to the royal retiring room for the two interval receptions. During the first of these, Stiff pushed himself forward and introduced Carter whose ballet *Les Nuits d'Été* was having its first showing in London that evening, but later the Princess did not seem enamoured with the ballet. The whole gala went smoothly, opening with Lifar's *Noir et Blanc*, which showed the Company in a purely classical style. Carter's new ballet followed, before three popular pas de deux: the *Aurora* with Mimi Paul and Peter Martins, the *Grand Pas Classique* with Wilfride Piollet and Cyril Attanasoff, and *Corsaire* danced by our Galina and Andre. The evening ended with the exhilarating *Prince Igor* led by Patrice Bart. A small dinner party was given by Rayne afterwards at his lovely home in Hampstead, where Princess Margaret delighted in his beautiful objets d'art. Sadly for Carter, the reviews next day were poor: the critics were not taken by his *Nuits d'Été*, and The Times criticised me for having accepting McDowell's costumes. The critic was right. I thought the costumes awful but had refrained from saying so, not wishing to aggravate further the explosive situation.

To my delight, Lynn Seymour agreed to guest with us in the *Sleeping Beauty* two weeks later in the season. A great artist, she was possibly the most dramatic ballerina the

Royal Ballet ever produced. She gave herself completely to every role she undertook and received a great welcome from our audience when dancing Princess Aurora with us at the Coliseum.

9 *My Company, And Being Stiffed*

Charles Bristow, who had been lighting some of our works, was not satisfied with the overall standard of our staff. This was music to my ears for neither was I. At a meeting with Stiff and me, Bristow recommended we replace Duff whose work he considered not of a high enough standard. Stiff disagreed strongly, unexpectedly backing Duff. Bristow told me later that after the meeting Stiff took him aside and belittled me and all I was doing. This confirmed my suspicion that Stiff was doing all he could to get me ousted. This tension continued through the next couple of weeks, and I was tempted to speak to Max. I eventually arranged an appointment with him for 5.30 Monday 7th July, but he was delayed in a meeting for almost an hour so I had but a short time with him before having to rush away to catch the first London performance of Carter's *Coppélia.* Thankfully next day it was given good crits and everyone concerned felt pleased –particularly after Carter's *Les Nuits d'Été* debacle.

Thursday: Max invited me for a discussion at his office at 6pm when I was able to speak frankly to him about the unhappy situation between Stiff and me which had led to the disturbance within the Company. He was so understanding that when I got home I collapsed in tears with relief. Max promised to set up a meeting with himself, Abernethy, Stiff and me at 10.30am the following Monday, which went satisfactorily.

He then arranged for representatives of the Company to come to a meeting, which started unpleasantly with Adams and Melvin gunning for me while Stiff sat by, silent. Next, Jelencic was asked in for his opinion, succeeded by three corps de ballet girls, which astonished and horrified me. Then came the two principals – Starr and Mathé – who complained of certain principal promotions. Ian Hamilton challenged a mistake in his contract, claiming it should run until next spring because he had stayed on after Venice to help out. Stiff was vague about Hamilton's details and salary, which remained unresolved. Vass was in attendance throughout and was marvellous, standing by me on everything. It was not over until after 4pm. I was emotionally drained.

To celebrate our 19th wedding anniversary Sven and I had tickets for the Bolshoi Ballet at Covent Garden, which I was determined not to miss. The men in *Spartacus* were sensational and I felt inspired by their prowess and formidable technique. Next day, 15th July – our actual anniversary – Sven brought me breakfast in bed, which I so much appreciated after the strain of the previous day. It was his love and my faith that gave me the strength to face the challenges I was encountering.

Later at the office, discussing contracts with the dancers, it transpired that Stiff had already told Adams and five corps de ballet girls that I did not wish them to remain in the Company. So they knew what I was to say to them before our interviews. How could Stiff undermine me in this way? I was livid. On Friday evening Max told me of a meeting he and Abernethy had held that afternoon with half the Company and Equity. Was it never going to end, this grumbling? And now Equity was involved. With less than good dancers I could not raise the Company standard, and I believe Rayne must have stated this.

I sat quietly through the evening's performance which was excellent, despite the troubles, and I began to feel proud of my Company. Looking at my diaries today, I realise that at this very time, after two years in post as Artistic Director, I began to use the term 'my Company', rather than 'the Company'. I realise now that I did make a mental shift from being the newcomer, the outsider, to being at the Company's heart, as they were in mine.

On Monday morning I was distressed to hear from Max that there was to be an Arts Council enquiry into my 'administration' that afternoon with Peter Williams, Peter Brinson and John Cruft representing the Arts Council. Also sitting around the big table in Max's first floor office would be Abernethy and Stiff. I wondered if the part Stiff had played would be recognised. It seemed so unfair that my actions were to be questioned. Next day there was a meeting of the Festival Ballet Board at County Hall. Max rang asking if I would go to County Hall at 3pm in case I might be called upon to speak. I waited in Abernethy's room until being called at 3.40. Entering, I was relieved to be greeted warmly but sorry not to see Sainsbury present. I heard later that he left before I came in. Max asked me to tell the Council what I thought had led up to the present situation among the dancers. Succinctly I did, after which he asked me to say what I thought I could do to rectify the position. I replied: 'To invite those who are dissatisfied to leave and go to another company'. I also requested that neither Adams nor Gilpin should come on the imminent Spanish tour.

After I left, the Arts Council apparently agreed to this, and I felt more optimistic about the situation. But the trouble was not past and by Thursday Equity was pushing for an enquiry. Max told me there was a meeting at the Arts Council regarding the Coliseum theatre, after which the Company problem was discussed. That afternoon Max called me to a meeting at which Stiff and Abernethy were trying to reverse the decision made in my favour by the Council the previous day. Sir Louis Gluckstein was strongly opposed to reversing the decision, although not every council member present concurred. It was finally agreed that after the dancers signed their contracts, following the holidays they would work until January with the option to leave then if they so wished. I thought this unsatisfactory but there it was. On Friday afternoon I heard from

Max that there had been a Company meeting after the Thursday performance and the dancers had agreed to accept the Trust's counter-suggestion. I did not feel comfortable about this but as Saturday was the closing night of our season before we flew to Madrid next day, it appeared a realistic compromise. I summoned my courage to go on stage at the end and make the traditional speech to the audience. Sven was backstage during the performance and in the wings to make sure I went on. To my astonishment, Gilpin led me to centre stage with grace and apparent goodwill! Some finale to my first Coliseum season.

Next morning I awoke with a heavy heart, knowing I was to fly with the Company to Madrid, leaving behind once again the two persons in the world dearest to me. On the plane I began to wonder if I should continue as Artistic Director. If the Company really were against me it was pointless totally upsetting my family. Was it worthwhile and was it fair on Sven with my frequent periods away? I did not want to give up the battle but rather to press on to raise the standard of the Company. Career versus home life had taken on a whole new aspect.

10 *Spanish Practices*

There was an hour's wait in the baking hot Madrid airport for the coaches to arrive, and I felt annoyed that David Taylor had left without bothering to get our music out of customs. After booking in with a large number of the Company at a pleasant air-conditioned hotel, our stage manager Colin McIntyre collected Peter B, the Trunoffs and me at 7.30pm. With Boris Trailine we went to the theatre to check things out and watch staff lighting our triple bill in the huge Palacio del Desportes. To our dismay we found work could not begin on the lighting until 9am next day and that the orchestra could only rehearse from mid-afternoon until 7.30pm. Yet we were due to open at 9.30pm! My heart sank. How could we prepare the Company properly?

Although I was able to rehearse a few principals for a short time in another theatre, the Teatro Espagnol, the opening night in Madrid was a near-disaster. Andre was still unable to dance, only partner, so we substituted *Corsaire* with *Spring Waters* which, with Gilpin's absence from the Company, did not please the director. With so few in our one-act version of *Paquita*, I thought the ballet looked dreadfully lost in such a vast arena and, to make matters worse, a corps de ballet girl went horribly, and painfully obviously, wrong. However, the Spanish press next day were all good. But not so the English paper, the Daily Express, which was exceedingly critical of the artistic director… slaughtering me.

Wednesday was a change of programme: *Noir et Blanc, Piège de Lumière* and *Bourrée Fantasque*. The director insisted we also present the *Corsaire* pas de deux, replacing injured Andre with a guest artist. Trailine rang me excitedly early on Wednesday morning to say James Urbain was coming to our rescue that day, via Avignon and Paris. What a relief. I rehearsed Carmen Mathé in preparation for her dancing *Corsaire* with him but sadly Trailine said the director insisted Galina perform with Urbain, not Mathé. I had to ring Mathé and tell her the sad news, but she did not seem unduly upset, which surprised me. I had felt there was an undercurrent during our time in Madrid, and I feared someone was trying to stir up more trouble within the Company. Despite a successful final night on Thursday, I was not sorry to leave Madrid for Vigo.

At Vigo it was a pleasure to find a pretty, open-air theatre situated in a large park where a pathetic band was busy practising. To MacIntyre's dismay, he found the lighting equipment almost non-existent. The staff, however, were most co-operative, busy laying plywood over the stage which creaked throughout the performance later that evening. There was little time to rehearse: the bus bringing the dancers from their hotel arrived half an hour late so the 7.30 class did not get underway until after 8pm. There was then just time before opening to place *Paquita* and *Night Shadow* and run through Urbain's pas de deux. Andre came complaining to me that Galina should not be expected to appear with such poor lighting. This finished me and I exploded, saying: 'We are all doing our best for our only performance in Vigo'.

I was able to enjoy a swim in the Atlantic and an hour on the beach in the sun before leaving Vigo with the Company by coach the following afternoon. Our destination was La Coruña further north along the Spanish coast. My hotel looked out over a harbour filled with pleasure boats and freight. With gulls diving and cawing, it was an idyllic spot reminding me of Sweden – Sven and Ingvar would have loved it. Again I found myself wondering what I was doing there. I felt sad and lonely away from my loved ones and was glad of Margot Miklosy's company that evening. We wandered through the crowded streets before settling in a tiny café for food and a long, friendly chat.

On Sunday Bridget Hearn asked to see me again about her future. I had said in Biarritz I would try to help when she told me she did not want to go on dancing but strike out in a different direction. She wanted to return to England before the tour ended and for us to help financially to retrain her. But, so far as I knew, Festival Ballet had not done this before, and there was no mechanism in place for such assistance. I suggested she might like to work in the wardrobe and perhaps also take on some acting roles in the Company, and she seemed to like this idea. With things as they were I did not want to lose her, it would not look good, and I genuinely wanted to do what was best for her. Undecided, I thought this was something Stiff might like to ponder if I was able to get through to him on the phone.

Although we were to open on Monday evening I gave the dancers the day free while MacIntyre was having difficulties with slow and too few stage staff. The orchestra sounded dreadful. Following class we had a placing call, after which Mathé grumbled at not having been given a rehearsal, adding she didn't want to do *Piège* next night but *Sylphides* and *Corsaire* instead. That evening the Company managed to give an acceptable performance until the last ballet, *Études*, which was the worst performance I had endured: the orchestra completely dried up and all the lighting was wrong. I insisted to Trailine that we had more orchestra and lighting calls next day, to which – at 1.40am – he reluctantly agreed. The next evening's performance went better and was sold out, as was our third and final performance at the Teatro Colone – even though Dagmar went off with a bad foot. That last day Bridget told me she had decided that her future lay in working full-time in the wardrobe department. This was a great relief, and now I did not have to consult Stiff about her future. After the performance Helen Starr asked nicely if in future she could have a different partner in *Études*, as Jean-Pierre Alban was not able to support her properly. Jean-Pierre had already confessed this to me, so I was forewarned and readily agreed to change her partner.

In a way I was sorry to leave the charm of La Coruña with its quaint streets and bustling harbour. We were booked to give three performances in Santander away along the north coast so, when the mist cleared at midday, we flew there on the Spanish airline Spantax. It was a nerve-racking experience. It began badly when Bestonso was helped off the coach at the airport obviously unwell. Inside the building the airport doctor gave him an injection before he was carried onto the plane. Once airborne, the flight was so rough that the air hostess fainted twice and Bestonso was given another injection. The plane plummeted two thousand feet, oxygen masks dropped down and, in a panic, Dagmar clutched hers tightly over her mouth. What she did not realise was that without tugging the cord there would be no flow of oxygen, so she passed out. After an horrific landing, all three casualties were taken off the plane on stretchers! Following this, a slip-up over bookings at our hotel in town meant a shortage of rooms so, to help out, I switched to another hotel a little further out of the town. It was most pleasant there with glorious views but, before I even unpacked, Peter B was waiting to take me to our performance venue: the outdoor Plaza Porticada which lay in a hollow surrounded by a beautiful park. I was met there by an indignant Miklosy who said she would leave if her salary was not increased. I rang Stiff and miraculously got through to him. I explained that she was exceedingly popular with every audience and we could not afford to lose such a brilliant principal. He agreed to raise her weekly salary to twelve pounds five shillings. Placated, Margot agreed to stay, brightening and enhancing the Company's performances.

Friday: we opened in Santander with a weak *Paquita*, chiefly due to understudies replacing those dancers off unwell. Nevertheless I felt it was soon redeemed by a beautiful exposition of *Night Shadow*, Galina's stunning *Corsaire* and an exciting *Études* winding up the evening. But I returned to my hotel disappointed that I had not been able to talk with Max by phone about Gilpin's unresolved future in view of his unpredictable absences. The casting for Japan had to be finalised next day with Vass, Joanie and Peter B, who sulked when he realised I was not including Gilpin in the programme. Peter B was already annoyed that Miklosy had been given a small salary increase and not Mathé. In my opinion Mathé did not warrant an increase as, despite having a strong technique, she lacked personality.

There was also a problem with Trailine about our financial arrangements so Peter B was on the phone to Stiff for a long time before I could discuss this with him. I knew meetings were taking place in the Company, which I suspected were about Gilpin's absence from the current tour. Peter B had probably discussed this with Stiff, worrying what was to happen about the Japanese tour. When I spoke later with Stiff he told me he had talked with Gilpin following his recent remarks quoted in a newspaper. Gilpin, however, insisted he had not resigned and said simply that it was for Max and the Trust to come to a decision about his future with the Company. I agreed with Geoffrey that the only way forward was to sit back and stay firm, which was also akin to Clayton Stamm's advice.

On the Saturday and Sunday we gave two different programmes: the Company danced with zest and were repaid by the audience's enthusiasm. After a delightful Sunday afternoon break I was loath to return because of the problems I knew awaited me at the theatre. There were three dancers off: Freya Dominic, Gillian Shane and the not yet recovered Robert Bestonso. After the performance, Mathé came to me to say she couldn't go to Japan if Gilpin did not go. Oh goodness, would it ever end?

We left Santander next morning and flew to Madrid before transferring in the scorching heat onto two coaches which took us to a superb hotel in Vallecas for some refreshments. I was able to phone the London office where, in Stiff's absence, I was put through to Roy Rosekilly who grumbled at Margot's salary increase, saying it was blackmail. After a three-hour coach ride on narrow, winding roads with hairpin bends and only one stop for cool drinks, the dancers were restless, impatient to reach Cuidad Real. We arrived after five pm for the performance scheduled to start at 11.30pm that night. The Plaza de Toros was a huge bull-ring and in the changing rooms we found two buckets of blood – not a pleasant welcome. It was not possible to give class but only a brief placing run-through, so the dancers had to limber up themselves in the stifling night air. After the show Boris Trailine ran Galina and me back to our hotel insisting she appear next night in *Les Sylphides.* She had not wished to but, being understanding, capitulated.

A long bus ride to Seville after which, although free for the Company, proved one of suspense for me over the on-going Gilpin situation. With all his talent and charm, his behaviour was that of a chameleon. I rang Stiff early and he was as non-committal as ever, before saying Max was to have rung me: the British Council were insisting that Gilpin be included on the imminent Far Eastern tour. I could not reach Sven by phone but got Clayton Stamm who said to stay firm. There was an exchange of cables between

Max and me, his last one – three pages long – explained we had to listen to the British Council for financial reasons because of their involvement in the tour. He asked me to reconsider. Geoffrey and Vass thought I should not agree to Gilpin being with us after the trouble he caused. But when I reached Sven early next morning on the phone he felt I should not hold out any longer going against my Chairman's wishes and in face of the British Council's insistence. As he said, even if Gilpin were not to go on the tour there would still be others, like Starr and Mathé, present in the Company fermenting trouble. So I capitulated and sent another cable to Max saying I felt the situation should be cleared and that I left the decision to him. I nearly cried with frustration that Gilpin and Stiff had won this round, and I was now fearful about the Far Eastern tour. The performance that evening was given in front of a magnificent palace, surrounded by a shimmering moat over which a platform had been erected where the dancers performed. This was a romantic, exotic setting and made for a magical evening. It was also my last night with the Company before our three-week break and I was already packed, ready for my early departure from Seville next morning.

11 *Max Opposes Equity's Demand*

Geoffrey collected me for breakfast at 6.30am, seeing me safely onto a bus to the airport for my long, involved journey via Madrid and Copenhagen to catch a train to Sweden for my holiday. I was so excited to see the lovely forests of Sweden again after a two-year absence – it felt like coming home. My train pulled in to Mjölby station at 8.45pm absolutely on time and there, waiting for me, were my three precious ones: Sven, Ingvar and my father. Driving to our much loved Borghamn it seemed unreal. Only fourteen hours earlier I was in the heat of southern Spain and under great tension. Unbelievably still the same day, here I was surrounded by love and the peaceful beauty of the northern Scandinavian hemisphere. What a contrast.

The holiday sped by, first in Borghamn with Sven's youngest brother Torsten and his son Leif who took Ingvar sailing with them each day on Lake Vättern. Sven's brother Eric and his wife now lived in the family home Heleneborg since the death a year previously of Sven's parents. I missed Farmor and Farfar and found it hard to believe that they had died. Sven took me to the family grave in Vadstena, and I felt deeply moved and especially sad for Sven who wished he had been able to spend more time with them. The last few days of our holiday were spent at my favourite Hoks Herrgård, formerly a royal hunting lodge, in the depths of a forest by a lovely lake. I swam early every morning before rowing across the lake with the family for a few idyllic hours.

I was troubled only once by dear Geoffrey who rang me to say Stiff had received a letter from Ben Stevenson complaining about my treatment of *Sleeping Beauty*. This was odd as it was the production Ben and I created together in '67. It appeared that Stiff was still trying to unsettle me, even on holiday. Loath to return to London and the endless troubles at Festival Ballet, I wished it would clear up, but determined to battle on.

The Company reassembled for rehearsals on Tuesday 9th September 1969, which coincided with the day of a Board meeting at County Hall. Max's office was vague as to whether or not Stiff, Rosekilly and I were to be present but we went along and were obviously expected. Finance was discussed in detail, followed by the Coliseum returns and the theatre's available weeks for the future, after which we were told we would not be detained any longer. Stiff and I met Max later that afternoon in his office when, to my relief, Max told us the Board had decided to refuse Equity's demand to reinstate the six dancers. I thought this must show the Board's trust in me and my judgement. He added, however, that Equity had decided to hold their own enquiry the following Thursday. Anxiety hung over me for the next week during my Company rehearsals, as I wondered what the dancers were going to say. It seemed all so petty, unjust and ultimately wrong. Thursday came and Hugh Willatt, Secretary General of the Arts Council – Dance Section interviewed seventeen dancers amongst whom were all the disgruntled ones. Who, I wondered, had put their names forward for interview? It seemed to me to be unrepresentative of a large company and said so to Willatt, adding that I was not willing to talk with him until he first spoke with all of the dancers. On Friday I heard that the solicitor Laurence Harbottle had resigned from the Board saying he would only return should the dancers need defending. I thought this an odd remark, and began to worry that he anticipated more trouble within the Company. Max seemed to think things were going well, so I felt less worried.

By Monday the atmosphere felt less tense: the Equity enquiry was over and, to my surprise, Dolin turned up at the office to ask me if he could play Drosselmeyer in our forthcoming Christmas season of *The Nutcracker*! I could hardly believe this. Things could not be as black as I feared if Dolin believed I would still be running the Company at Christmas. With the Far Eastern tour imminent I rang Max next day who advised me to call Willatt before leaving. But when I eventually caught up with him by phone he said he could not discuss anything with me until he had sorted out his notes and passed that information to the governors. This was a blow – the situation would hang over me whilst I was abroad.

It was heart-rending to leave Sven at the airport next morning, Wednesday 24th September. As I waved him goodbye for five and a half weeks (our longest separation since taking on Festival Ballet), I prayed that God would take care of him, Ingvar and my father, who was suffering with a painful arm. Sitting on the plane for half an hour before take-off was a bad start. Frankfurt, Rome, Karachi, Bangkok, Hong Kong. Exhausting, but we eventually landed late at Tokyo airport where MacIntyre was waiting to welcome us. He introduced Peter B and me to Mr Nubo, a representative from Nippon, the organisers of our Japanese tour. He was to accompany us to Korea, together with another representative, and observe the Company's performances prior to our Japanese opening. Stiff was not present. Much to his disgust, our numbers had been cut back for the tour so only the most essential staff were included on this long, costly trip. This meant I had no secretary with me, and I knew I would miss the ever helpful, cheery Geoffrey. This lack became evident by the close of the tour when there were many empty pages in my daily diary. I had obviously been too tired to record each day's activities, but wrote to Sven every night, an unbroken habit during our 59 years of marriage.

Astonishingly, thanks to MacIntyre, we had only a short time at the airport as he had arranged for our plane to be parked alongside one scheduled to take us on to South Korea. With everything transferred in record time we flew to Seoul where we were welcomed by a host of smiling Korean faces, cameras and TV crews. As the first Western ballet company to visit Korea there was tremendous interest from the media. Three waiting coaches took us to a luxurious hotel in the centre of the capital. Even on that short journey Terry Kern and I were interviewed en route. Next day – after trying to sleep through a howling gale, which on the 17th floor sounded ominous – we had several television interviews at which I was asked to introduce my leading dancers. The interest was overwhelming, and we were touched by the courtesy and kindness shown us by these gentle people wherever we went, especially in the streets, many of which were still compacted sand. One could not help observing that although poor they carried themselves proudly and happily. In the big Citizens Hall, our performance venue, in the modern TV studios and particularly in the hotel nothing appeared to be too much trouble. We saw Korean women in their colourful national dress, for that Friday the citizens were celebrating the Festival of the Harvest Moon.

We opened with a triple bill on Saturday 28th September to an enthusiastic house seating three thousand. The television company had wished to screen an entire performance but sadly our fee was too high for them. Peter B and I had numerous telephone discussions with Equity who were adamant that we were not to go below £4,000. As this was far beyond the Koreans' budget the whole Company offered to give a performance for nothing. Equity forbade this, to everyone's dismay. We would have liked the Koreans to have a filmed record of our historic visit.

The British Ambassador attended our opening night, coming on stage at the end to congratulate the Company. The next morning he and his wife gave the Company a reception during which we were treated to a performance of diverse and fascinating dance outside in the sun on their lawn. We watched as two masked jugglers danced, then three 'farmers' with ribbons streaming from their heads displaying their celebration of fertility rights. I liked best a beautiful temple dance performed exquisitely by a girl. We were sorry to leave the sunny ambience of the Ambassador's beautiful garden.

I was trying to write my report for the governors when Peter B rang me saying the Reuters correspondent was waiting to talk to me in the theatre. Vass took class, which was followed by rehearsals, but I was not satisfied with Piers' partnering and overhead lifts with Starr in *Swan Lake*. He had trouble managing her gracefully and I was worried for the performance. But in the event all was well and the Company achieved an ovation at the end of our all too short season in Seoul.

13 *Success In Japan*

Next morning we left for Japan – after a delay of over half an hour at Seoul airport: a corps dancer, Paul Waller, had left his passport in the hotel. He returned to retrieve it and, with rain gusting in sheets, it was a chaotic start to the day. We had trouble over our music tapes at the airport and with making the payment in an acceptable currency. On arriving in Japan we were met by the British Council representative, Mr Dukes, with our agent Mr Okayama who got us through health and passport control quickly. It took time loading our cases onto the waiting buses and an hour and a half to drive through heavy traffic to reach our hotels. My room was so tiny that I refused to stay there. Colin suggested we tried the Akasaka, which had one room available for a few days. Tokyo was packed with conference delegates and tourists and every hotel fully booked. I was thankful for the temporary accommodation, optimistic that something would materialise.

Rain was falling heavily next morning and continued during the first of many meetings with Nippon. This one was in their head office on the 31st floor from where I could see the mist closing in. Peter B, Paul, Colin and I met an ageing Mr Band who, together with Okayama and two others, welcomed us with many traditional Japanese bows. However, we soon disagreed over the fee for televising the Company in *Sleeping Beauty*. They began by offering $3,000; we switched to pounds, suggesting £3,500. After a long wrangle we compromised, agreeing to drop just £250. We thought this should have been set out in the contract. We then argued over the payment to local children appearing in *Nutcracker*, but finally agreed to share the costs. We would not consider having different children in Osaka than those we were to teach and train in Tokyo but this was unresolved when we had to leave to attend a big press conference in the Daiichi Centre. Present were thirty members of the press firing questions for one and a half hours. To my surprise Andre actually spoke up on several occasions, which was most helpful. We went on to a guitar recital given by Julian Bream – balm after the hours spent at Nippon. It was a pleasure to meet this great artist at the British Council party afterwards. Prince William, Duke of Gloucester, was also present and impressed me as a fine person. Somewhat exhausted from my first full day in Tokyo, I finally tumbled into bed at 2.30am.

Ongoing wrangles continued with Okayama, mainly about the children. Jack Carter lost his temper and was extremely rude to him and everybody got cross. Carter felt keenly about the standard of his *Swan Lake* and *Nutcracker,* and Joanie had gone ahead from Seoul to teach the children who were slow to learn their parts and needed more work. Like us, Carter would not consider training new children in Osaka. The Japanese would not give in either and I felt concerned at this impasse. Nippon were not abiding by their agreement to provide transport for me so I was paying for taxis to get to the theatre but was cheered by the theatre itself – the Koseinenkin Kaikan. Although modern it did not have a cold impersonal feeling about it and the stage was good. It was large, remarkably wide but with a few slippery patches which had to be avoided. I enjoyed giving class there but the children remained a worry. They had not remembered what they were taught, and I knew it was risky putting them on in the ballet. I resolved never again to use young amateurs when on tour abroad. Gilpin was unwell, and I wondered if he would recover in time for the opening next day.

Arriving at the theatre, Peter B and I almost tripped over the heavy television cables which were trailing everywhere in the auditorium. Although we had not been informed, Nippon had accepted our financial terms and would televise the next evening when the royal family were to attend. The audience for our first night in Tokyo was not particularly smart, and I thought the Company uninspired, possibly still feeling their way on the unusually wide stage. I was disappointed in Gilpin's dancing. He lost his nerve in his final solo, cutting his double tours and having little elevation in his leaps. But despite feeling sick he partnered Dagmar adequately, and there had been no complaints from her husband Jelencic. Margot, meantime, had stomach and chest pains which did not augur well. Because of the traffic I dared not return to the hotel at six o'clock to change after rehearsing, so squeezed into a room in the theatre backstage, two floors down and shared with two conductors, two pianists, two ballet masters, our stage manager, general manager and company manager!

The following evening, Saturday, was the televised gala attended by the Empress of Japan, the Crown Prince and his Princess with their six-year-old son. The audience was well dressed, which somehow communicated itself to the Company who gave a wonderful performance. I met the Empress, with whom I had a long talk and who I found delightful, warm and gentle, reminding me of our own Queen Mother. In the third interval Dagmar Kessler, John Gilpin, David Taylor and Jack Carter were presented to the Royal Family by the British Ambassador, Sir John Pilcher. Conversation flowed: the Crown Prince had already seen the ballet in London so there was much to discuss, and we felt honoured to spend this time in his distinguished company. There was a fine reception at the British Embassy after the performance with plenty of food for the ever-hungry dancers.

I was wondering where I could find another decent hotel like the Akasaka as I was reminded my room was booked for another occupant in two days' time. Sunday morning was therefore spent on the phone but all the good hotels were full. In desperation I rang Mr Duke, the British Council representative, who was most helpful. He called back to say that the British Embassy was happy to house me and would collect my luggage from the hotel next morning. Much relieved, I went to the theatre to rehearse two principal couples in *Swan Lake* but was called away by Kern to listen to our music tapes. We found *Bourrée Fantasque* was poor and *Corsaire* too fast and agreed they would have to be re-recorded. Returning to the theatre in time for the matinee it was heart-warming to see it full of children, there at half price and enthralled by *Swan Lake*. Between the shows Peter B, Colin, Vass and I met to discuss our pending Kuala Lumpur visit. But Vass was in a bad mood – his name had accidentally been omitted from the brochure, and we felt for him. The evening show went well, however, and I returned for the last time to my hotel room and, munching a sandwich, wrote my nightly letter to Sven.

During the free day, *Swan Lake* was transported across Tokyo to a different venue, the Kaswasaki Hall, for Tuesday's one performance there. Early that afternoon the embassy car was instructed by my kind host Sir John to drive me to join the Company at the agreed assembly point, the busy Daiichi hotel. We boarded the waiting coaches for a one-hour drive across town to our new destination, pleasantly situated near a river packed with boats. Peter B had work to complete so could not accompany us, and Colin was meeting our Korean agent. We were hoping the agent could arrange for a re-recording of our tapes in Korea with Taylor conducting, as surprisingly there were no means for this to be done in Japan. The agent agreed to organise this at no further charge – taking a weight off our minds. On the coach I sat next to our company manager, Paul Sarony, who was worried that our contracts, negotiated by Stiff, were too loose. This was Paul's first tour with the Company, and I was beginning to appreciate his perspicacity.

Later a troubled Peter B confided in me that more cases of cholera in Osaka had been reported, which was disturbing, potentially placing the health of the dancers at risk and jeopardising our season there. We were both concerned – should we, could we, cancel? Gilpin was still unwell and had developed a rash but was walking about instead of resting in bed. Mr Band had asked for a medical certificate and I was insisting Gilpin saw a doctor, which he promised to do the next day. Poor Andre had a badly swollen foot but despite this managed to dance, partnering his swan princess, the ever graceful Galina.

In *Swan Lake* the men – with the exception of two principals – do not appear in the last act so are ready to leave the theatre an hour ahead of the rest of the Company. As there were two coaches waiting outside the Kaswasaki Hall the male dancers climbed into one, expecting the driver to ferry them across Tokyo to their hotel. But the driver stubbornly refused to start the engine. His written instructions were to take the dancers an hour later and he would not listen to their request. All transport arrangements, places and times had been worked out and agreed three months previously in London with Japanese representatives and woe betide anyone expecting these to be changed. We were discovering the reluctance of the Japanese to deviate once a course of action was set. So our men just sat there fuming. But it did no good, and they had to wait to the end of the show by when all dancers, stage and wardrobe staff were packed and ready to leave.

We were glad to be back next night at the more central Koseineki theatre for our triple bill programme. The audience liked these three ballets, the classical *Noir et Blanc,* the dramatic *Witch Boy* and the sensual *Schéhérazade*. Despite some of my principals being off sick, their understudies managed well – Dubreuil in *Noir et Blanc* for Gilpin, Salavisa as the *Witch Boy,* one of Gilpin's most renowned roles, and Bestonso as the Golden Slave in *Schéhérazade* for Loggenburg. Mr Band was annoyed over Gilpin's continued absence, but mollified that my ballerinas were not too ill to appear. Our stage staff and crew were under pressure to have the scenery hung and lit in time to allow the dancers to go on stage for the warm-up prior to the 6.30 curtain. Later in the evening I was exasperated when Starr, Hamilton, Mathé and Beaumont came to see me. Starr asked if Beaumont could partner her instead of Hamilton on the provincial tour in England. Hamilton was not as good a dancer as Beaumont so this switch would mean considerable cast changes, but I agreed to look into it with my ballet staff. In the course of the evening I was heartened and touched when Vass gave me a pen with a small torch attached. He knew that during performances in the darkness I always scribbled notes with corrections for the dancers so this was a thoughtful and most useful gift. To my delight I was given the use of an embassy car and driver to take me to the theatre and collect me after the show at 9pm. I greatly appreciated this as it gave me time in which to write letters. I wrote Max an outline of the current tour, which I knew he would be interested to read. In the alien environment of Japan I often felt a long way from England and writing somehow brought home a little closer.

A visit to the Canon factory in Kawasaki had been arranged. Paul, Jean-Pierre Alban (Jippy) and I were collected by car, setting off at ten o'clock next morning for an interesting tour. We were most impressed by everything we were shown and charmed by their hospitality, but unaware of the problems going on in the theatre. Once again our stage staff and crew were under great pressure with the overnight change from the triple bill into *Nutcracker.* They were having difficulties persuading the local stage staff to change their traditional way of operating in order to be ready in time for the performance. This resulted in the dancers being 45 minutes late on stage for the orchestral rehearsal which, in consequence, ran 20 minutes into overtime. Act II was not set and Act I not lit with Carter of course almost hysterical, screaming at everybody. Colin had a big row with the Japanese stage crew, insisting they work harder to make *Nutcracker* presentable for the public by 6.30. It was barely ready, yet everything fell into place and *Nutcracker* received an ovation, even though Dagmar's tutu had apparently not travelled well and was in a dreadful condition – all droopy! Her prince, Alain, danced with fervour despite no rehearsal. The children surprised and pleased us, looking sweet and acting convincingly to the delight of the audience and Jack Carter.

As there were only two more performances of *Nutcracker* in Tokyo and just one in Osaka before the London Christmas season it was important to try out my dancers in different roles. Gilpin was still off ill, in fact rather worse according to Mr Dukes. Both Paul Sarony and I thought he should return to London although Peter B was not in agreement insisting he was over the worst and getting better. Before the matinee I was able to spend a relaxed hour talking with John and Leila Pilcher in their beautiful Embassy. They were kind and hospitable so I was thrilled that they changed their arrangements to attend our closing performance that evening.

Sir John insisted on taking me in his car to the railway station early next morning, certain that I would get lost. The station was buzzing with people concentrating on reaching their destinations; it was utterly bewildering and practically impossible to locate the right platform, so I was thankful for his presence. Everyone from the Company was late arriving and I felt Sir John sensed an atmosphere amongst the dancers for he stayed by my side until the train departed for Osaka.

14 *Osaka*

On arrival in the hotel I found my single room so pokey and depressing that I changed to a marginally bigger double room before leaving for a television interview. This, like the press conference which followed, was pleasant and filled with goodwill. Once in the theatre, as in Tokyo I practised some double work with Beaumont. As well as instructing him it helped me to keep in training in case of an emergency.

A feeling of unease next morning was fuelled by Alun Rhys attacking me rudely when I got to the theatre. Complaining that no cast sheets were yet available, he asked how he could be expected to have the costumes ready for the evening show? The previous evening we had seen Margot Miklosy's tutu looking inexplicably bedraggled. Beaumont then came to tell me he had seen the wardrobe girl deliberately rubbing the corridor floor with Margot's tutu. I despatched Paul to talk to the wardrobe girl. After the show Moya Knox complained to me that the Company were in low spirits because they felt in need of more correction. They wanted less conflicting direction from Jelencic and Vass – why could I not control them? It seemed she was trying to say that they expected more from me. I was puzzled as the Company initially had resented my corrections and teaching so I was careful not to give too much instruction. They apparently hated Carter's *Swan Lake*, but thought it went better in Osaka that evening. During supper Vass said he had heard there was a rumour going around that I was leaving after the tour ended and that perhaps it was time I spoke to Mathé and Starr refuting this. I was not sure if this would be a sensible move and decided to ignore them and the rumour.

Arriving at the theatre to take class, I found my door locked and Alun Rhys unwilling to look for the key or find someone to open it. Starr was close by, already changed for class, but to my surprise did not attend, saying the notice board was unclear about who was to take class. Following this, I rehearsed Bestonso, taking him through some partnering with me, for I felt tongues would wag if I danced only with Beaumont and they both needed to practise their partnering. I had some emergency casting to do with Joanie, after which Peter B showed me a cable from Stiff with the latest figures from the tour. This anticipated a session with Nippon, together with Paul, until late afternoon. We had to pay for our own sandwiches while arguing over payment of three fares out of eighty people we brought on the tour!

An encounter with a terribly upset Vass followed: Hayworth had insulted him in front of the Company during rehearsal of *Night Shadow* – something to do with Margot's performance. He was demanding a public apology from Hayworth with Paul, Peter B, Colin and me present. To my relief Hayworth came to see me a little later to apologise, and I hoped it would calm down. I received a letter from Sven, and two from Ingvar, which helped lift my spirits. I was well aware of Mathé and Starr's evil sway over the Company, but was determined to battle on. With two more *Swan Lakes* and just one *Nutcracker* to close our Osaka season there was also a lot to do in finalising the casting with Peter B for the London Christmas season and our next five-week provincial tour. This was complicated by the uncertainty over Gilpin's condition. A triumphant Terry Kern conducted his first performance of *Nutcracker* with great aplomb, finishing the evening on a high note.

We arrived in Kyoto on Saturday for matinee and evening performances the same day – it was a miracle we got *Swan Lake* on in time for the matinee. Once again I was grateful for the determination and tenacity of my stage staff as well as the professional manner the dancers took to the untested stage even without a placing call or time for a warm-up. This was the start of a demanding three days with the Company giving three performances of the entire *Swan Lake* in three different cities: Okayama, Kobe and Nagoya. Next day we left for Kuala Lumpur.

We had an overnight stop in Hong Kong where, although pre-booked into the President Hotel, to our dismay we found not enough rooms allocated. Something must have gone wrong somewhere and it fell to me to battle with reception. Eventually, after much haggling, more rooms were miraculously found to accommodate us. How elated I felt when three members of the Company came to thank me saying, 'Wow, you've won them all over now'.

15 *A Kuala Lumpur First, And Home Again*

We were the first ballet company to tour to Kuala Lumpur so there was a lot of media interest in our visit. There had been some difficulty in finding sufficient accommodation for the Company, so the British High Commissioner arranged for some of our dancers to stay in private homes. Peter B and I were invited to stay with the High Commissioner and his wife in their beautiful house 'Carcosa' where we were both looked after like royalty. I was completely spoiled and lived a life of luxury for those few days, my cases unpacked and each morning my clothes laid out, freshly laundered, ready to wear. Kuala Lumpur enjoyed a tropical climate – attractive for biting insects – so I would sleep under a huge mosquito net enclosing my four-poster bed. Every morning for an hour from 9am I was given the services of the Commissioner's secretary. We would work sitting by the swimming pool in the glorious sunshine, amidst a sea of papers. Without Geoffrey to clear them, these had accumulated along the tour. Paperwork done, I would dive into the crystal water to cool down. Leaving for the theatre refreshed, I delighted in the paradise of orchids growing in profusion along the sides of the sandy roads.

We opened on Saturday 25th October to a welcoming, finely dressed audience. It was a well contrasted programme with Act II of the ever popular *Swan Lake* and its corps de ballet of classical white swans; next the sinister *Witch Boy* ballet by Jack Carter. Following this, a two-minute beautiful *Spring Waters* pas de deux, always danced sensationally by Galina and Andre. The evening was brought to an exhilarating close with Chabrier's wonderful music uplifting the dancers in *Bourrée Fantasque*. We gave nightly shows and a matinee over each of the three days, giving a different programme each day for an enthusiastic public.

It was only a short flight to Singapore, the last stop on our tour. We had little time to explore the bustling port, full of ships and flanked by a landscape of attractive low-lying houses. I fell in love with the city but today it is different – skyscrapers having replaced the former view. We were to give two triple bill performances at the National Theatre, in which all our principals appeared. A tired but exhilarated Company flew home from

Singapore to London on the last day of October. It was good to be home. The exotic tour had brought the Company new audiences and much acclaim.

The weekend over, the Company were once more in rehearsal at Donmar with a five-week provincial tour starting a week later. It was heavenly to be home, and it was also good having Geoffrey on hand again at the office where nothing much appeared to have changed during our time away.

Sleeping Beauty opened a two-week season at the Pavilion, Bournemouth. I felt the Company had acquired a new confidence from the eastern tour. Mid-week, we switched to *Coppélia* and attracted better houses so that the triple bill – with *Swan Lake Act II, Piège de Lumiere* and *Bourrée Fantasque* – was well attended during the second week, which closed with full houses for *Sleeping Beauty*. At the Alexander Theatre in Birmingham, with even less stage space, we managed to put on *Sleeping Beauty* as well as the more straightforward triple bill. We could not but appreciate the warm intimacy of the 'Alex' and its enthusiastic houses.

The Opera House in Blackpool presented quite a few problems for the dancers. The stage could only be reached by a lift, which slowly carried our artists from their dressing room floors to stage level. *Sleeping Beauty* uses the greatest number of dancers, and the lift, although large, needed to make many journeys to accommodate all the casts, the girls nobly protecting their tutus from being squashed. As it stopped at every floor to pick up corps, soloists and principals, there was always a battle to catch the lift, and the fear of missing it and arriving late at stage level to hear the orchestra already playing. Our tall stage manager, Colin, frantically held the curtain, awaiting the lift's return with the last of the unfortunate panicking stragglers before signalling the conductor to lift his baton and for the curtain to go up. Fortunately, the Opera House had a big flat stage, ideal for the leading ballerina to hold her balances unsupported during the daunting Rose Adagio. We presented *Beauty* for the entire week, giving several casts the opportunity to appear even though it meant extra rehearsals. I believed in giving promising dancers every chance when possible and was often wonderfully rewarded.

I slipped away to Switzerland for the weekend to talk with Papa Beriozoff in Zurich about his staging of Diaghilev's works and to watch certain dancers in full-length productions. Sven came with me and Papa was the perfect host in every way. Back in London there was time for me to pop into the office, grab lunch at home and receive a short treatment from Sven before returning to the airport and flying back to Bradford.

Waiting in a car for me was Paul Sarony with Geoffrey, anxious to take me to the theatre in time for our opening show. They briefed me en route with the news that Gillian Shane, one of my invaluable soloists, had hurt her neck so was wearing a surgical collar and would be off for two weeks. During the Bradford week the Company were already rehearsing *Nutcracker* every day in preparation for the Christmas season. After Saturday's performance I returned to London troubled, having spoken seriously to the Vass and Joanie Trunoff, already the worse for drink – a weakness I found unsettling.

I was fond of them both and relied on them a great deal, but found their spasmodic drinking embarrassing, particularly in front of the Company who were well aware that alcohol contributed to Vass's moods.

16 Nutcrackers And A New Don Q

I love Christmas with the excitement and goodwill it generates, and once home I began hanging decorations. Mid-week, Sven and I collected Ingvar early morning from Eton and, after dropping them home, I began my usual busy day with the Company, now back rehearsing in London. We had only limited hours available at Donmar so some rehearsals were held at The Dance Centre nearby. I always tried to fit in a lesson with de Vos before rehearsals, happy knowing I would share the evenings with Sven and Ingvar. We attended the first night of an intriguing new opera by Malcolm Williamson at the Coliseum, titled *Lucky Peter's Journey* which was quite good, but I think I enjoyed most sitting between my two big boys who afterwards took me to the May Fair Hotel coffee shop for supper. I felt so proud of them, both well dressed and handsome. I began to think I should not worry so much about Festival Ballet, despite the unpleasantness. I had grown to love the Company, for the dancers were hardworking and dedicated, and I felt a bond developing with them.

Festival Ballet traditionally opened on Boxing Day with a three o'clock matinee at the Royal Festival Hall. This always followed a morning orchestral call. The last dress and lighting rehearsal with the dancers on stage was on Christmas Eve, when Christmas cards and presents were exchanged to be taken home and enjoyed. With just one day free in which to relax and celebrate, the dancers would be returning to Festival Hall for twenty-seven performances of *Nutcracker*, twice a day, for the next two and a half weeks: a gruelling schedule. There were numerous daily cast changes for soloists and principals, but the corps were on all the time. To my dismay, by the beginning of the first full week, flu hit some of the Company. That same Monday was press night, but on arrival at Festival Hall I was told Gilpin was off. The day before he had rung me to say he was well and would dance the next day. Alain Dubreuil substituted for Gilpin, giving Kessler great confidence with his sound partnering. But the flu was spreading; I had already sent Geoffrey home and called Vass to take class as Jelencic was not well enough to come to the theatre. Beaumont was not able to finish class and went home before the matinee. Annette May, although unwell, insisted on dancing at the matinee and to the end of the evening performance. This was courageous of her and avoided a last-minute substitution on the press night. To my relief, Gillian Shane returned recovered from her neck injury.

By Wednesday, for the first time in the season, I left the evening performance before the end so I could be home to see in the New Year with my family.

With the start of January 1970 the cold weather brought hard frosts and Hyde Park was white and sparkling in the winter sun. When Sven, Ingvar and I took a walk there, even the Serpentine was frozen over but not thick enough for skating – save for the skidding birds! Despite the flu, the Company were coping, and midweek I received a letter from Leicester University inviting me to accept an honorary Doctorate of Music. I was astounded and absolutely thrilled, as it came out of the blue. I knew nothing about honorary degrees and most touching was to see Sven and Ingvar's joy, which in turn gave me deep happiness.

The second full week of 1970 turned out to be a good one. Some months before, Boosey and Hawkes had sent me a previously undiscovered piece of music by Dvorak suggesting I might like to use it for a ballet. I thought of Ronald Hynd, now a promising choreographer and a former partner of mine in the Royal Ballet, who I believed to have the sensitivity to translate the romantic music into a ballet. Although reluctant at first he was persuaded to study the score again, and I was thrilled when he told me on Thursday that he felt more confident now to go ahead and create a work to this for Festival Ballet. On the last night of our Christmas season I summoned enough courage to go onstage to thank our audience for their loyal support and tell them of the Company's future plans. After visiting the dressing rooms to thank the dancers for their sterling work and wishing them a good week's rest, Sven, Ingvar and I ate supper at the May Fair Hotel café, our favourite hide-away. I was so thankful that my second Christmas season was a success for the Company despite the flu epidemic.

The so-called free week of rest brought good news at home. Ingvar had passed his English GCE O level so we had a mini celebration – ginger wine, bitter lemon and biscuits. I then left for the office where my new secretary, Victoria, was starting her first day. Geoffrey had left for an Arts Council training scheme as the change from assistant stage manager to artistic director's secretary had been too optimistic. We agreed that he needed more training, particularly in speed typing. I was sad to part with him and interviewed several applicants before deciding who was best suited to replace him.

I was busy dictating letters to Vicky when Stiff called me up to his room for a meeting with him, Nigel and Roy. I was booked to fly to Moscow three days later and they suggested I should fly back from there via Warsaw in order to save money. I was due to fly to Warsaw in a few weeks' time to see Witold Borkowski and discuss his *Don Quixote*. I was certainly willing to do this, set about reorganising the arrangements with Borkowski and successfully merged the two trips into one; I knew Roy was fighting hard to keep spending as low as he could.

I took Ingvar to the Science Museum where my long-standing friend GB Wilson, now curator, was waiting for us. It was an instructive and enjoyable three hours, as GB explained the exhibits to my eager fifteen-year-old son. On returning home, I had a big shock: waiting for me was a glorious bouquet of flowers – from Stiff. I was speechless. Were relations getting better at last? I hoped so. To my horror by Thursday morning I learnt that the press had started writing about the trouble in the Company the previous summer. Apparently Carmen Mathé had been talking to the press, saying things against me again. Why she would do this? I was in the office with Peter B looking at possible designs from an Italian for the proposed production of *Don Quixote* when the Evening Standard rang for comments. Stiff had gone to Paris so Peter B told the press to ring Max Rayne. The paper, however, was not satisfied with Max's communiqué and kept ringing. So Peter and I drew up another statement, which we took to Max that afternoon. Max altered it to make no mention of my name or the Equity enquiry result, stating his regret at the absence of Lord Goodman. I was not totally convinced this would appease the newspaper but I had faith in Max, and it worked. A few days later, a report of my imminent Honorary Doctorate from Leicester University appeared.

My Moscow trip was to seek guest artists for Festival Ballet, and I looked forward to meeting my friends at the Bolshoi again. I left on Saturday morning for Moscow, where I succeeded in having promising meetings with Ministry personnel and the Bolshoi hierarchy. Arriving next day in Warsaw, I was met by the choreographer Borkowski whose production of *Don Quixote* I had travelled to see. I liked what I saw and believed it would suit my Company. We had discussions about designers, the music arrangement, suitable artists, his financial expectations and planning available dates for staging the work. I returned to London Tuesday evening, buoyed up and impatient to start this attractive light-hearted three-act ballet first created in Moscow by Petipa in 1869.

With a lot to do at the office on my return, I arrived later than planned at Donmar so missed the pas de deux class which I had introduced and wanted to watch. This was our first rehearsal week after the holiday and I felt the Company were pleased to see me. A corps dancer (Starr Danias) and a soloist (Maria Guerrero) were still unwell with flu; otherwise everyone seemed restored to health. There was a lot to cover – four one-act ballets as well as *Coppélia*, which we would be presenting on the Spring tour. Towards the end of the week Stiff asked me out to lunch and was amiable. To my utter astonishment he apologised for the horridness and unpleasantness we had been through and hoped we could now put it behind us. I said I would be glad to, but there had to be trust between us if we were to work more closely together. He then came with me to the rehearsal, which I felt was a good omen, and I hoped we might enjoy a better working relationship from now on.

The second rehearsal week began disappointingly with more dancers ill. This played havoc with the casting, so Joanie and I were plunged into reorganising the rehearsal and performance schedules we had planned with such care. I interviewed all our dancers during this two-week period in London, discussing their progress and future plans. Together with Stiff, Peter B, Colin and I met Colin Graham for the first time. I liked him and hoped to interest him in producing *Don Quixote*, providing Borkowski agreed.

It was a new idea to have a ballet produced by a theatre director and I was not entirely sure it would be workable, but Peter encouraged us to pursue the possibility. In the end Borkowski was not pleased with the suggestion, and Peter's good idea was shelved.

17 Spring Tour 1970 – Much Ado

Tuesday morning in Norwich: another full call with orchestra for the second programme starting Wednesday matinee – *Les Sylphides, Piège de Lumière, Schéhérazade*, and a new pas de deux: *Soirée Musicale.* I had asked Peter Darrell to create a short work for Gilpin and Miklosy, and he chose music from the Rossini-Britten suite. It was a scintillating piece, exploiting the dancers' respective talents to the full, and became an invaluable addition to our repertoire.

Driving to London after the matinee in Norwich, Peter B and I arrived in time for an evening meeting in Stiff's office. Waiting for us were Stiff, the production crew, Borkowski and Luzzati, the designer. This was our first meeting all together and we were eager to see Luzzati's costumes and set designs for *Don Quixote*, which he brought for us to approve. I could tell Borkowski was as delighted as we were – they were colourful and would add just the right character to the ballet. We had chosen a talented artist. I promised to contact Lanchbery to arrange a further meeting concerning the Minkus score for *Don Quixote.*

Knowing that Friday was to be another busy day of meetings in London I decided not to return to Norwich as Sarony had phoned to tell me all was well there. He had sharp ears and eyes, and I could rely on his judgment. I was not satisfied with our staging of *Schéhérazade* which we had given in Japan and confided in Richard Buckle, an accepted authority on Diaghilev's works. Knowledgeable and helpful, he promised to watch one of our performances in Eastbourne and give me his verdict.

For our one week in Golders Green at the Odeon cinema we were to give just one programme, *Paquita* and *Coppélia*, to the relief of our hard worked stage crew. I gave Vass and Joanie Monday off so that they could attend a ballet gala at Covent Garden. It was the first time I had put on the opening show alone, and it gave me satisfaction to take the rehearsals and cope with everything on my own. I felt I was really in charge of the Company, and the performance went without a hitch. It was an encouraging start to the week. Stiff and I actually worked for the first time together on our papers for the Executive meeting to be held in Max's office on Wednesday morning. Present from the Board were Abernethy, Cruft, Sebag-Montefiore and – in place of Sainsbury – Gerald Weiss, to whom Stiff, Roy and I gave our respective reports and requests. It was agreed the summer London season should open with a gala premiere of *Don Quixote*, and I was gratified that an increase in the number of dancers from sixty-seven to seventy was approved. This would help alleviate the problem of finding suitable replacements when dancers were off ill.

After such a satisfactory morning I went on to another meeting at the ISTD where, although a member of the Board for many years, I had not been free to attend for nearly six months. This also applied to the Sunshine competitions and many other organisations which continued to demand my time and energy. Even so, it was only a brief stay because Kern and I were to listen to Lanchbery's new tapes of *Don Quixote*. It sounded superb, with his unique stamp of wit, humour and drama. Lanchbery had done a splendid job. By the end of the week we had engaged two young male dancers to strengthen the corps – one from the Legat school and one recommended by Jellincic.

Over at Golders Green, four dancers were waiting to see me followed by a sad Bestonso. He was sulking because I could not agree to his dancing in Barcelona a classical pas de deux for his mother to see. William Perrie asked me if he might be a cavalier in *Beauty*, to which I could not agree. I wondered if these requests followed my concession for Starr to dance Swanhilda. The small group of dancers in the choreographic group I had set up were pleasingly full of ideas. I was keen to find some talent in my Company, and felt this was something worth spending time over. After a performance in Eastbourne, Stiff unexpectedly took Peter B, Vivien Wallace (our press officer) and me to dinner. Next morning, to my surprise, Stiff called in to see me before returning to London, and it seemed he was really trying to make up for the past. I prayed so – it would make work so much pleasanter.

Richard Buckle came on Friday to see *Schéhérazade*. Afterwards at dinner he was adamant that the pas de deux between Zobeide and the Golden Slave should not be included and that Diaghilev would never have allowed it in Fokine's ballet. Richard was, however, pleased with the sets and costumes, and we discussed at length the ballet and Diaghilev. John Percival, The Times ballet critic, came to the Saturday matinee and Oleg Kerensky the Daily Express correspondent arrived in time to see the evening show. Meanwhile Sven arrived from London to spend the weekend with me. We always stayed at the same hotel in Eastbourne, one of our favourite places for a short break.

One of the perks of performing at the Congress Theatre was the availability of the Winter Garden next door for rehearsals, so it was a blow on Monday morning to find the floor had been polished over the weekend, making it slippery for the dancers. Subsidy for the Arts was on people's agenda and radio Brighton asked me to take part in a discussion next morning, which I found most stimulating. In Eastbourne the stage crew were busy on the change-over to *Beauty* and on my return I was soon caught up rehearsing the ballet for the evening show, but to our disappointment the Tuesday evening performance was not sold out.

A press conference in Nottingham had been arranged for Thursday so I returned to London late Wednesday. I met Stiff next morning at Swiss Cottage and we drove to

Nottingham through rain and sleet. Further north it turned to snow but nevertheless we arrived on time at the Theatre Royal to find a dozen waiting journalists. They were interested in the Company's forthcoming visit in March. Stiff and I were interviewed on local radio before driving back to London.

Returning to Eastbourne on Friday I found both Galina and Andre off ill and Kessler not wanting to perform two consecutive Princess Auroras. I had to ask Starr and Hamilton to step in, which they did willingly, receiving a good reception at the end of their performance. Friday and Saturday night are generally good ones in the theatre and Eastbourne always had warm, friendly audiences.

Ronald Hynd was hard at work on *Dvorak Variations*, his first creation for the Company. He was getting on well with the dancers, who became an enthusiastic part of the creative process. It was an abstract ballet using four couples and translating into dance the lyrical music.

Our aspiring young choreographers were also busy working with those dancers who volunteered their free time, and we had our first ever Workshop performance on the Sunday. It was quite well attended and we were pleased to see Peter Williams, editor of Dance and Dancers, in the audience. Although there was no outstanding choreographic talent, I knew it was important to continue to encourage and help those with an interest in creating. There are so few truly gifted choreographers and, always on the lookout, I went to Covent Garden to see *The Ropes of Time* by the Dutchman Rudi van Danzig. It was the first time he had worked with the Royal Ballet and he chose Nureyev, Monica Mason and Diana Vere as his principals. It was also the first ballet to use electronic music at Covent Garden and though an interesting, thoughtful work I disliked Jan Boerman's electronic sounds.

Because Festival Ballet was soon to present *Don Quixote* I arranged with Elsa Brunelleschi to give classes to the Company in basic Spanish dancing. To my disappointment, none of my principals or soloists attended and only nine corps took her class. I was puzzled. Were they so tired that they grabbed the time off (the class was not obligatory) or did they believe they could easily adopt a Spanish style?

The usual midweek office meeting was coloured by the news that Gilpin was off for three weeks, thereby missing the rest of the English tour. After a detailed discussion about three top soloist salaries Peter, Terry and I began sorting out the *Don Quixote* music. I eventually left to go to a three-hour ISTD Board meeting before watching the evening show. Between the meetings I took precious time off to search for some new clothes before rushing to Wimbledon for Carol Yule's first performance as the Sugar Plum Fairy. To my delight she managed beautifully. But to my horror, I was stopped by the police for speeding at 45 miles an hour in a 30 mph speed limit area of Roehampton. Fortunately Annette Page was with me and we both stayed calm and apologetic, and in turn the two policemen were charming. Much to my relief, after hearing of our busy week in Wimbledon, they did not book me but, smiling, sent us on our way with just a friendly warning.

Ingvar's Confirmation was looming so on Friday evening I deserted the Company for Eton where Sven and I attended a beautiful service at 9pm in the College Chapel. The confirmands were given an inspiring address and once the service was over we saw Ingvar to his room before this important day. Saturday 14th March was a special one for us as we watched our dear son confirmed by the Bishop of Oxford in the magnificent Eton College Chapel. Also present with us were my father and Ingvar's godparents: Helena Terry and Lord and Lady Wakehurst. It was a most moving occasion and I felt proud of my son, deeply sincere, so upright in his manner and bearing. After the midday ceremony we had a few happy hours with him before I left for the Company's closing performance in Wimbledon.

Off again, this time by train to Wolverhampton. What a depressing town I thought on arrival, but was quickly cheered by the theatre manager's warm welcome. Humphrey Stanbury put his office at my disposal – a boon as it is hard to find quiet office space backstage in theatres. It was the first day for my new secretary, Toni Nelson, nicknamed Petal, so the train journey gave us a chance to get to know each other. The Company were giving *Paquita* and *Coppélia* but we had several dancers off, so our extended run-through meant Ronald Hynd only had a short time to work on his ballet. With *Beauty* coming in on Thursday evening, we had a tight rehearsal schedule and could only offer Hynd limited periods in which to work. He was understanding, never wasting a second of his allotted time and, despite everything, *Dvorak Variations* was beginning to take shape. I had to slip back to London for a midweek Executive meeting at which, apart from Max, only Abernethy and Sebag-Montefiore were present. Petal and I had two more rail trips to Wolverhampton: on Thursday, returning late after the show, and again on Saturday to see how my new casts performed at the matinee of *Beauty*. I had also to listen to some music which Peter B thought might be suitable for the pas de deux which had been especially requested for our Barcelona season. It was specifically to feature Gilpin, with either Miklosy or Kessler alternating as his ballerina. Peter Darrell, director of Scottish Ballet, agreed to choreograph a dazzling show-stopper!

The Company were to have a busy two weeks in Nottingham with four programme changes, including the demanding *Beauty* and the premiere of Hynd's *Dvorak Variations* during the second week. Also needing rehearsal time would be Peter Darrell, working on his new pas de deux. When I arrived in Nottingham, rehearsals were well in hand for that evening's performance of *Paquita* and *Coppélia*. The house was not full and the bookings poor, which was worrying. Over dinner with Stiff we feared that two weeks in Nottingham was perhaps a mistake.

After a press interview early next morning there were non-stop, intensive rehearsals through the day. I caught a late afternoon train for an evening office meeting with Borkowski and Luzzati which turned out to be full of marvellous surprises. Vass had collected Luzzati at Heathrow, who brought from Italy set and costume designs for *Don Quixote:* stunning, full of character and glorious colours. Alun Rhys chose some good sample materials for us to look at – in just the right colours and textures. It was most exciting and encouraging, especially the music tapes to which Kern, Lanchbery, Stiff, Borkowski and I had listened whilst awaiting Luzzati's arrival.

Next morning, following a constructive technical meeting with Borkowski and our stage staff, Vass, Petal and I were back in Nottingham to watch Starr's debut as Swanhilda in *Coppélia* at the matinee. Although not a soubrette dancer she surprised us, as had Svetlana Beriosova some years before in the same role. After class next morning we had the first run through in costume of *Dvorak Variations*. Borkowski arrived at the theatre midday, initially to go through some cuts in the *Don Quixote* music with Kern and then to watch and commence working with the Company. After Easter in London, an early morning train on Monday took me in good time for the full stage piano call of *Dvorak Variations* followed by a full dress orchestral call that I thought foretold a positive future for the ballet. The designer Peter Docherty had done a good job (although I was not entirely happy about the girls' sleeves), and Hynd was pleased with his dancers and their interpretations.

On Tuesday, to my consternation, I had to speak strongly but carefully to our orchestra manager as there had been complaints over the behaviour of two of our trumpet players. The same day Peter Darrell began work on the new pas de deux for Gilpin, who failed to turn up. Nevertheless Darrell went ahead with the two ballerinas, creating to sparkling Auber music. At the Wednesday matinee everyone was delighted with Noleen Nicol's debut as the Princess Aurora in *Beauty*. She had a marvellous reception, and the Company applauded her on stage after the last exciting curtain call. Having picked Noleen out as a young dancer, I was glad that my faith in her ability had been well placed, and felt she would become a valuable addition amongst our top ballerinas.

The week continued with meetings on *Don Quixote* but Borkowski took his time to make up his mind, which irritated Peter B. I feared this meant Peter B would grow critical about the ballet, and I could only hope I had made the best choice of available choreographers for the work. I knew it would be a fantastic vehicle for Galina and Andre providing the choreography in all three acts was good.

I left Nottingham after last-minute rehearsals before the matinee, checking call sheets and finalising the casting for our impending season in Barcelona. I tried to placate poor Sarony: he was upset by Moya Knox who had told him that morning the Company disliked him. How some dancers like to make trouble! He was a lovely person and first class at his post as Company manager, always alert to problems, keeping an eye on everything and everyone's welfare. I was glad I able to see Carol Grant's stylish debut as the lead in *Beauty* Act I on Saturday before catching a train home with Petal to London.

Sven, Ingvar and I had a lovely break in Switzerland, but after the sun and bracing air of Verbier I thought how white and tired the Company still looked and only wished the break could have been longer. We had the use of Sadler's Wells for two weeks in order to see how *Don Quixote* looked on stage. I was glad that it had shaped up well, despite Peter B's forebodings, providing plenty of good dancing and some amusing mime scenes. Seeing the dryads scene on stage I felt certain little changes would be necessary, although there were some beautiful variations for our soloists and leading ballerina. But the Company got rather depressed over their entrances in Act III, which had to be rethought, rather as Peter B had prophesised. I was pleased with the helpful direction of Colin Graham, who began by talking the Company through the story. He gave each dancer a personal involvement in the action, which contributed to the overall scene. The corps were positioned attractively or given moves with a purpose so that they were not just standing staring during the principals' solos.

On my first day back, a crestfallen Carol Grant spoke to me about her future. The sweet girl had fallen for the endearments of Dudley and their brief affair had reached her husband's ears. He was insisting she gave up her career, wanting her to finish after our forthcoming season in Barcelona. This was awful as she was so talented and popular with audiences, and I could only hope that her husband would relent and allow her to continue her career. Inevitably in such a tight knit group as ours liaisons were bound to occur, although there were a number of happily married couples in the Company.

That evening the ISTD gave a dinner at the resplendent Café Royal in Regent Street to present Anita Heyworth with the prestigious Imperial Award. Among the distinguished guests invited by the Chairman, Cyril Beaumont, was Frederick Ashton. Having not met for some time there was much to talk about and I was glad to be seated next to him.

By midweek, Gilpin had still not turned up for rehearsals so, with Stiff away, I rang his wife Sally in desperation. After a long conversation it materialised that Gilpin appeared to have lost his confidence and, fearful that this might be apparent to the public, kept delaying his return. I explained it was vital for the Company that he appear in Barcelona so Sally promised to try and persuade him to take some private classes. She would try to assure him that he was not expected to appear in *Beauty* but just *Night Shadow*, one of his most renowned roles but one which did not demand too much dancing.

There was only a week of rehearsals left before I was to be away with the Company again, this time for a fortnight's season in Barcelona. It was a traditional annual visit by the Company and was greatly anticipated by both the dancers and the Catalan audience. At Sadler's Wells I auditioned Danish dancer Peter Schaufuss who, though not as tall as I had hoped, was a fantastically gifted dancer. I suggested we went to the office with Stiff to discuss the terms of a principal contract to commence in August. I hoped he would not change his mind in the interim.

Unannounced, and to my surprise, Gilpin came to Sadler's Wells on Wednesday afternoon and I rehearsed him carefully in *Night Shadow*. It seemed possible that his confidence was returning and that he would take the stage again in Barcelona. Stiff and

I went together to an executive meeting Friday morning at Max's office when I was able to report this. Stiff's attitude to me had totally changed recently: he consulted me much more, which resulted in a better running of the Company. That afternoon Gilpin came to the Wells again this time to rehearse the *Black Swan* pas de deux, which he said he wanted to dance in Barcelona with Dagmar. I again took their rehearsal and it went smoothly – my feelings a mixture of hope and anxiety. Dagmar was the perfect partner for him, petite, placid and professional.

18 *Barcelona 1970*

The Company gathered together at Victoria station on a pleasant May morning, and I was relieved to see Gilpin there with them. Sven remarked on the pleasanter atmosphere before waving us off to Gatwick for the flight to Spain. We found Boris Trailine waiting anxiously for us at Barcelona airport from where he drove Stiff and me to our hotels. But not before a tedious search for the Company coaches which after a long wait were finally located – they had certainly managed to hide themselves successfully.

The Gran Teatro de Liceu in Barcelona was one of only two privately owned opera houses in Europe, and the Company were welcomed there every year. Stiff, Peter B and I were soon taken to see Mr Masso, the top man at the Liceu, who immediately began suggesting possible programme changes to which we could not agree. Later that evening we were welcomed by the theatre owners – the Pàmias – who, together with the director, took a controlling role in everything presented in the theatre. They asked that we closed our season with *The Sleeping Beauty* but we explained this would not be possible: we could only present it at the start of our season for four days. After that it had to be shipped back to England for refurbishment in time for opening our London season. To my relief this was accepted. I listened to Terry's first rehearsal of the large orchestra, which sounded powerful, and was then taken to enjoy dinner at Trailine's home.

The season in Barcelona was an extraordinary experience: the theatre became the background to a 'coming out' for debutantes. In the front of house, mingling amongst the smartly attired audience, were beautiful young ladies, their charms complemented by lovely white evening gowns, each vying for the attention of enthusiastic young men in tuxedos who escorted them with finesse through the fine foyers.

On Wednesday, much to my amusement, Stiff virtually exploded on Jack Carter who had behaved appallingly throughout the evening's dress rehearsal, shouting and grumbling about Geoffery Guy's work on the scenery. Carter was rude to Ray Dixon (Duff's replacement as production manager), to Stiff, to me – in fact to everybody. It was the first time Stiff had been seen to lose his patience, and I was glad he had put Carter in his place at last. Through the rehearsal the dancers struggled to fill the huge, raked stage. This stage was actually wonderful for *Beauty* and I knew they would make full use of the space once they became accustomed to it. We finished at 1.30am when the orchestra completed their allocated hours after a disappointing rendering of Tchaikovsky's music. It was not until 2am that Stiff and I were free to sit down for supper so it was well after 3am before I could say goodnight and sink exhausted into my bed.

The day of our first performance was not without incident. Peter B and Paul went to the airport to meet our two guest artists: Patrice Bart from the Paris Opera and Sergiu Stefanschi from the Romanian Ballet. Meanwhile I was rehearsing Kessler and Gilpin, who seemed happy with the way the rehearsal was progressing. Helen Starr, while practising, suddenly developed agonising cramps, and I took her to the hospital where it was decided she must stay overnight. I remained as long as I could but eventually had to leave her to change into my evening dress for the opening night. *The Sleeping Beauty* brought the Company a big success, and I was proud of my dancers who performed that Thursday night, better than I had seen them before. They responded to the challenge of a foreign audience, acting and dancing superbly to a most appreciative but talkative crowd. The curtain did not go up until after 10pm, after which latecomers continued to arrive, and in the interval bells were not rung, so some people wandered back with the ballet already underway. But they loved us and calls were even taken in front of the curtain after each act, which greatly encouraged the Company and made for a thrilling night. It was topped off by a celebratory dinner at 2.30am with an ecstatic Galina and satisfied Andre.

I had arranged a night flight back to London after Saturday's show specifically to meet the Master of Sant Mat, the Indian philosophy with which Sven and I were in complete harmony. On meeting the Mystic one knew that this was a holy man, above all others, modest, kind and full of love and understanding. Being with him gave one an inner calm and his power and strength flowed out to those around him. This meeting with our Master has impacted on my life, furthering my faith and belief in God and giving me the strength to overcome the challenges that beset us in this world.

When I returned to Barcelona I found that, despite their free day, Starr was still unfit to perform and Aitken her understudy as the Lilac Fairy was off, too. Our guest artist Stefanschi was disappointing in the evening's performance and to my disbelief was actually booed. I was thankful for the dazzling dancing of Miklosy and the other guest artist, Patrice Bart, in the *Don Quixote* pas de deux, which brought the house down.

As I feared, Masso rang next morning to say that due to his poor reception by the audience Mr Pàmias did not want Stefanschi to dance any more in Barcelona and asked me to attend a midday meeting in the theatre. Paul was with me as we discussed the problem of Stefanschi and another problem Bristow was encountering with the lighting of *Dvorak Variations*. Neither Trailine nor Peter B was present and, as Stiff was back in

London, it fell to me to speak with Stefanschi. He was devastated, threatening to report this to the Romanian Embassy and also to Peter Williams, his friend in London. In Trailine's absence I saw Pàmias to reassure him that we would not present Stefanschi on stage again in his theatre. Meantime, an admiring Dolin was following Stefanschi everywhere, even at the party after the show that night, which didn't help matters. A worrying few hours followed next day with rumours abounding that Stefanschi was contacting the British Council to save his reputation and that Dolin was telling him to talk to the local press. I rang Stiff who advised drawing up a paper for Stefanschi to sign, agreeing not to appear further in Barcelona at the request of the theatre management. This was done, and next morning Stefanschi agreed to sign it.

A worrying evening followed: Margot Miklosy had strained her foot, John Travis was off ill and another soloist, David Picken, fell over his hoop dancing in *Night Shadow*. But to everyone's joy *Dvorak Variations* looked wonderful and saved the evening.

In Barcelona we had a Sunday matinee which began at 6pm, the exact time our evening performances had commenced in Japan. How incredibly adaptable Festival Ballet dancers were and, with the late evening performances in Barcelona, they certainly deserved their free day. After the final curtain there was a big rush to get everything packed and away to the airport where a plane was waiting to take us back to London. It had been a remarkable two weeks. Carol Grant had been to see me to say she might be able to continue with us after all – news that made a happy finale to the Spanish engagement.

Sven was waiting at Victoria station to welcome me back at the absurdly early hour of 6.30 in the morning. I felt cared for and loved as he whisked me home and, after I had unpacked, we breakfasted together before his first patient arrived. I attended our press conference at the Coliseum at midday but went first to the office, where to my surprise I found Stiff leaving already and being, as Peter B said, 'cagey'. A good-natured press conference lasted well over an hour, heralding a splendid week. The big interest was in the imminent *Don Quixote*, the choreographer, the designer and the music arrangement. In every department the Company's concentration was focused on the new production. With just two days in London we were fortunate to have the stage at Sadler's Wells where, with Colin Graham and Borkowski, we were able to assess the ballet from a distance. Fittings were also ongoing and for the first time we caught a glimpse of the costumes, which to everyone's delight looked fabulous.

After going with the Company to Southampton, where at the Gaumont we felt truly welcome, I was back in town for an Executive midweek meeting chaired by Max at which Stiff and I put forward for discussion our future touring schedules. These were accepted without any objections, much to our satisfaction. Back in Southampton next day to rehearse *Don Quixote*, I thought it still required several little changes to strengthen the choreography, but knew I had to tread carefully with Borkowski who I did not want to upset. The *Paquita* evening performance was untidy: an exacting opener, it needed regular careful rehearsal to retain the style and dancers' lines. I returned late to

London, determined to be with Sven for his birthday morning. To celebrate I always took to him in bed a tray laden with coffee, lit candles and little Swedish buns – in the traditional Swedish manner. Presents, cards and celebrations over, it was time to go to our own particular callings. I auditioned dancers at the Dance Centre in Floral Street but they were disappointing. Once again I realised how much skilled, intelligent teachers were needed.

I travelled to the New Theatre in Cardiff on Monday morning determined to ensure any available time be spent on specific scenes from *Don Quixote*. Poor Paul scoured the city for a suitable rehearsal room, which he eventually found. The mid-week matinee was packed with excited children watching a good performance of *Coppélia* with Starr in the lead role of Swanhilda. A London critic watched the evening show, which the Company danced beautifully. I was disappointed that he did not praise their work at all, merely commenting 'they showed great spirit.' Had they been the Royal Ballet dancers I felt sure they would have been highly praised. I was conscious of a seeming bias of the press towards the Royal Ballet and longed for our Company to win some encouragement.

Three days after our Cardiff opening I was pleased to be invited to judge the Cyril Beaumont Award at the Royal Ballet School. The Cecchetti method of ballet is implicit in the Cyril Beaumont Award for it was he who brought Cecchetti training under the aegis of the ISTD. The style places emphasis on epaulement and the placing of the arms and is recognised as teaching neat, brilliant footwork. It is no coincidence that Massine and de Valois were pupils of Cecchetti. It was heart-warming for me to watch the young students giving their all in the difficult challenge that this particular award presented. In complete contrast, with Sven, I later saw a kaleidoscopic display of Laban's work. This was of deep interest to us both. Laban had been a patient of Sven's, and we found his approach to movement meaningful and thought-provoking.

At the beginning of June, rehearsals began in earnest for our London Coliseum season at the end of the month. We were working in different venues across town: at Donmar in Covent Garden, Sadler's Wells in Islington and at Queen Alexandra House close by the Albert Hall. Colin Graham was not free to give us as much time as I hoped, and I knew that we needed his touch in every act if *Don Quixote* was to satisfy the sophisticated London audiences. But he didn't let us down, managing to come to several run-throughs and making invaluable suggestions for me to pass on to Borkowski. The windmills presented a problem at our first attempt on stage, particularly when Don Quixote tried to cling onto them as they whirled around. We had plenty of laughs. Also working with us was a marvellous swordsman, William Hobbs, who was instructing the dancers concerned how to fight with swords. It was quite astonishing to watch the intricacies to be learned and perfected. It took many calls before he would allow real swords to be used – I found it exciting.

The first dress parade at Sadler's Wells was thrilling. Luzzati worked quickly and clearly: any draft design with which we were not satisfied was changed as requested and returned in a couple of weeks which, for a famous Italian designer, was amazing. We were stunned by the number of brightly coloured dresses and character costumes already completed and could imagine the impact they would make on an audience.

As well as *Don Quixote*, our full-length *Beauty* had to be rehearsed and polished for the third night of our month-long London season. *Beauty* was exacting, with its numerous classical solos, each having several casts. I wished to give my promising dancers the opportunity of being seen in London, carefully rehearsed, and not thrown on at the last minute in an emergency, as can so often happen. There was also *Coppélia* and several triple bill programmes to work on – so we were kept busy throughout June.

That month I had a big shock when Audrey de Vos announced that she was shortly to retire due to her continuing poor health. I was still taking early morning lessons with her when in London and knew she had been unwell and struggling over the past year. Now, sadly, she could continue no more. Like many others, I was devastated: she had been my mentor for over twenty years and her sensitive teaching had kept me in good shape. She was still a controversial figure, ahead of her time. Her approach to training was just beginning to be understood and gradually introduced beyond her studio. She was a firm believer not only in the balance of the body but also the balance of life in day-to-day living.

Before the Coliseum opening Sven went ahead to Eastbourne for our relaxing weekend, and we met en route at Glyndebourne for the Saturday evening performance. After Company rehearsals finished at three that afternoon, Keith Maidwell, one of my soloists (nicknamed Kaffe), dressed my hair for the evening. He often undertook this for me before an important performance when there was no time to get to a hairdresser. Keith was multi-talented and when on tour would dress the wigs for our wardrobe and generally be of assistance with styling the dancers' hair. As I did not wish to drive down to Sussex in my evening dress, I decided to change in the car on arrival in the large car park at Glyndebourne. I managed to slide into my sleek evening skirt without interruption but when it came to zipping up my tight-fitting pink and green striped blouse at the back, the zip broke. As I had no other evening dress with me, I improvised: switching the low bodice from front to back and securing my modesty with two safety pins. Fortunately, they held throughout the opera.

After the final day of rehearsals at Donmar, the dancers had the weekend free while scenery, props and costumes were unloaded at the Coliseum. I went in on Sunday morning for the start of the lighting call, overseeing the placing of props and staying until eight in the evening. There was so much to undertake with the new ballet but on seeing the glorious scenery hung I felt optimistic and looked forward to Monday when the dancers would assemble on stage. In the theatre at last, the Company was totally immersed in *Don Quixote* all day and well into the evening, when to my joy Colin Graham arrived. He insisted on improving the lighting, which I had hesitated to suggest, feeling insufficiently experienced in that field. I worked hard all day, urging the cast to cultivate a convincing Spanish posture and to be more abandoned and wilder in the gypsy scene. I felt the choreography remained weak in places but hoped the scenery and costumes would compensate. Lanchbery's orchestration was brilliant, exciting and exhilarating, creating exactly the right touches of humour and romance.

The following evening Terry Kern conducted our final dress rehearsal of *Don Quixote*, at the end of which Galina had a spontaneous ovation from everyone in the theatre. There was insufficient time left, however, to rehearse the curtain calls with the Company so I prayed all would fall into place at the Gala next evening. I had been upset earlier by Borkowski who, annoyed at the changes made in the windmills scene, had complained to Stiff about me, using Andre as his interpreter. Even Colin lost patience with Borkowski, saying: 'Borkowski should be back in Poland'. When a new work is about to be born all nerves are on edge, and I felt certain Borkowski had begun to see that the changes improved the scene. A little later he came to me and apologised profusely, no less than five times. Next day, after taking the dancers through my corrections from the previous night, Colin and I had a final meeting with the stage and lighting crew to ensure smooth running at the Gala.

And what a great evening. To my intense relief everything worked perfectly: the technical devices, the lighting, the orchestra and the dancers, who excelled themselves. At the end the curtain calls went on and on, Galina receiving an ovation whilst flowers showered down on the company from the gallery and bouquets hurtled across the footlights onto the stage – the Company had never had a reception like this before and certainly deserved it. After the weeks of preparation and worry I could hardly believe it had all come together in time so successfully.

We picked up a pretty good press next day, to everyone's delight, with the exception of Fernau Hall in the Telegraph (the critic who had been so negative about *Beauty* in Eastbourne) but he nevertheless praised Galina's brilliant performance. All energies had now to be directed towards *Beauty* which went on at the end of the week. The Governors gave the Company a marvellous party at the Garrick Club after the show, and I was glad that there was a happier atmosphere than at the previous year's gathering.

Coppélia was our next full length to be staged and with three changes of cast it gave the principals the opportunity to be seen by London audiences. The triple bill programmes were presented in the third week, when Hynd's *Dvorak Variations* received its first London viewing. It was a great success with all the press who were full of praise for the ballet and also the dancers, which was most unusual. Meanwhile in the office I had a meeting with Stiff regarding a letter from Carter complaining about my allocating too little rehearsal time for his ballets. It disturbed me that Carter was obviously still trying to stir up trouble with Equity, and I wished he could be replaced as resident choreographer. But that would need careful thought and tact – he was a slippery customer. Stiff did not help me by tabling a letter from Equity at an Executive meeting some days later, which complained of the number of dress rehearsals called during the season. I was able to explain the situation and was fully backed by Max and the other Board members present. The season was going well, with audiences returning for the different programmes.

To my great delight I was made an honorary Doctor of Music on July 10th at Leicester University. I had never dreamt of receiving such an honour and felt quite overwhelmed. It seemed like a dream – the solemnity of the colourfully gowned procession in which I walked through a packed hall to take my place with the dignitaries on the platform. My greatest happiness was to have Sven, Ingvar and my father present at such a time-honoured ceremony. Their look of pride and love touched me deeply. It was a truly wonderful day.

As President, I attended the All England Sunshine Dance Competition the next morning, making short trips in between to the Coliseum to keep an eye on the performances there, too. The Sunshine all-day event included the special Beryl Grey Award for which, under my direction, the competitors took class on stage in leotards and tights. Then they each danced a classical ballet solo on full pointe, arranged by their teacher. To dance on pointe is a challenge for young teenagers: to hold the body correctly without apparent strain, to retain the unnatural turn-out required in ballet to give a beautiful line, while showing personality and musicality. Only advanced pupils could hope to enter for this award after what would have been a lot of hard work.

The ISTD's yearly faculty presentations took place for a week at the Victoria Halls. As a member of their Council, I was expected to make an appearance from time to time during Congress and also attend the Teacher Training College's end-of-year presentations. A select dinner was given by the ISTD Council in honour of Cyril Beaumont. This was to recognise his tremendous contribution to dance, not only as author and critic and his time as chairman of the Imperial Society, but also for the guidance and encouragement he gave to dancers. Over the years, like so many other dancers, I had visited him at his famous bookshop in Charing Cross Road, receiving help and inspiration. I was seated next to Ashton, which was both a privilege and an entertainment.

The London Ballet Circle honoured Frederick Ashton by giving a reception in his honour at the Martini Terrace, which was well attended by his many admirers and friends, all full of good wishes. On July 9th having seen *Don Quixote* well under way I walked across to Covent Garden and slipped in to see Ashton's Farewell Tribute. Afterwards there was a great celebration, and I was able to introduce Princess Margaret to the dancer Peggy van Praagh and the choreographer Ronald Hynd. To my surprise, Rudolf Nureyev sought me out to say he would like to dance with my Company and would be coming to see *Don Quixote.* This was totally unexpected as I hardly knew him, and I found it somewhat disturbing.

Festival Ballet's 1970 summer season at the Coliseum finished with *Don Quixote,* the ballet with which we opened with such trepidation a month earlier. It was a busy time, packed with incident. Ninette asked me to see two dancers from Turkey who were good, the ballerina tall and graceful with a strong well built partner, both full of enthusiasm and promise. Many dancers were auditioned during the season but by the last week we decided to take on two male corps de ballet dancers who we hoped would fit in well as we were desperately short of men.

I was permitted also to engage an extra member of the ballet staff to ease their heavy work-load. Donald Barclay was a former experienced dancer, trained at the Cone-Ripman and Royal Ballet schools, graduating into the Royal Company followed by engagements in several European companies. He had appeared in a few films and acted as ballet master during the making of *The Red Shoes* film, becoming ballet master with the Sadler's Wells Company for three years from where I persuaded him to join Festival: a decision I never regretted. By the end of the season I personally spoke with all the dancers about their new contracts, their progress, promotions and future position in the Company. Although a strain, it proved both informative and encouraging as few wanted to leave – with the exception of Helen Starr. She was looking for a bigger increase in her salary than we were offering and planned to see Stiff after the holidays.

True to his word, Nureyev came to our last matinee accompanied by Sir Robert Helpmann and Konstantin Sergeyev, director of the renowned Kirov company. To my embarrassment it was a poor house but Nureyev was eager to dance in the production, providing he could alter some of the choreography. In the evening there was a full and enthusiastic audience with Lord Goodman and Max out front. At the end of the performance I was taken on stage by a friendly Andre, who kissed my hand as he brought me forward to speak. The audience, together with the Company on stage, gave me a most wonderful reception. Perhaps, I ruminated, I was winning through at last.

19 New Ballets And New Dancers

The Company departed for a well-earned three-week holiday, and I flew to Sweden to join my family who had arrived there two weeks earlier. What a marvellous time I had, relaxing in the sun and sea and visiting Sven's welcoming relatives. The holiday flew by, and I returned for the two-week rehearsal period: the time so essential to get dancers in training and in good shape again.

So that the Company could see I was back with them I felt it important to give their first class. Our new recruits arrived, including a young, talented Royal Ballet boy who was taking a weekly salary drop of £5, even though we placed him quite high as a third-year corps. This underlined the discrepancy between the two Companies' salary scales. As part of my continuing search for the best leading dancers, Peter Schaufuss, the talented Danish star, joined us, despite having recently undergone a foot operation. Also taking Company class were two more outstanding artists: Kenn Wells from the Western Ballet and Kathryn Wade from the Royal Ballet, who both eventually decided to join as soloists.

I was fortunate that the ageless Frederick Franklin was over from America and agreed to give the Company some classes. These were greatly enjoyed: he had such infectious enthusiasm which greatly invigorated the dancers. For the second rehearsal week I managed to engage the Swiss dancer Hans Meister to give the men two classes, as well as René Bon from Paris who gave two classes to the girls. At the office there was a lot of activity with casting and long-term planning foremost on the agenda.

I had spoken some time previously to Mary Skeaping about staging her *Giselle* for us. Possibly because of our long friendship – which went back to the war years – and knowing the Company to be short of money, she generously offered to put it on for a modest fee. Rehearsals of *Giselle* would need to begin soon, as the first performance was scheduled for the 1971 spring Coliseum season. Stiff and I were also in conversation with Massine as I was eager to have one of his ballets to enrich our repertoire. Massine suggested *Le Beau Danube* providing we could offer him sufficient rehearsal time and that Stiff and he could agree a satisfactory fee. Although Massine was known to ask for high sums, in the end some sort of compromise was reached and *Le Beau Danube* was also to be presented in the Coliseum season. Papa Beriozoff agreed to stage *Petrouchka* for us, but fortunately he was never greedy when it came to money.

Faced with a heavy touring schedule, we left London for a return visit to Saint Jean de Luz at the beginning of September 1970. To start our week abroad, we gave just one performance in this pleasant town, followed by two in San Sebastian and finally three in Biarritz – all triple-bill programmes on consecutive nights. They were most successful and the impresario, Bariere, was pleased with every show. Remarkably, we were back in London in time to open next day at Golders Green with the full length *Beauty*! Quite an achievement on everyone's part.

At the end of our first week Peter Schaufuss made a successful debut in *Beauty*, attracting a lot of press attention. We brought in *Don Quixote* at the beginning of the second week, rehearsing the company in sets and costumes from 2pm until 6pm. This was the first time we were to stage *Don Quixote* on tour and the staff found it a nightmare to get on in time. We had several dancers off, so there were cast changes and even Vass had to go on as the Inn Keeper – a role he played with gusto and panache! Thankfully we finished the fortnight with a triple bill familiar to both dancers and stage staff.

Two weeks earlier, on our return from Biarritz, Stiff had rung me at home to say that Helen Starr was leaving as we could not pay her what she demanded. She had spoken with me in those terms, but I had thought it an empty threat. The relief at the thought of her departure! Now perhaps there would be less tension amongst the dancers, and I felt optimistic. Jippy and Vass had warned me midweek that her husband Alun Rhys, the wardrobe master, was spreading venom backstage and also out front. I had seen him before the show conversing with Gerry Weiss, a member of the Board, who was over-familiar with the dancers. I spoke to Rhys alone at once, and then over a drink together with Starr in the interval. I only hoped it would clear the air and herald a more open and loyal future from Rhys.

20 *Stiff Heads For The Door*

For the next five weeks the Company performed across Great Britain, giving *Don Quixote* and triple bills in Newcastle, Edinburgh, Bradford, Manchester and Oxford. A welcome mid-tour rehearsal week in London offered us a happy opportunity to live at home. To our consternation the Arts Council wished the Company to appear in the suburbs of London for one month a year as well as our Golders Green and Wimbledon seasons. So we began the last five weeks of our autumn tour at the Odeon Cinema, Streatham, moving a week later to the Granada Cinema, Sutton.

This presented the stage staff and dancers with colossal problems: the cinemas were ill-equipped for live stage shows. Their stages were tiny and unsuited for dance, lighting rigs had to be brought in, and there were too few dressing rooms. It was a huge contrast to arrive at the magnificent Empire Theatre in Sunderland. We found little interest in ballet amongst the Sunderland citizens: despite the theatre being a reminder of a more prosperous past, with its plush seating and ornate golden decorations (a perfect surround for our *Beauty*) the local community were immune to its magnificence. Quite the reverse in Birmingham, where we had excellent audiences throughout the week. Although it was tricky staging *Don Quixote* at the small Alexandra Theatre, the dancers were always adaptable. We were glad to end the tour in the spacious Bristol Hippodrome. Here our choreographic group spent their days finalising their work before the showing in London at the Collegiate Theatre. Considering the dancers were also performing every night, it amazed me to see the creative variety of works.

During the time away from London, disquieting rumours reached my ears that John Field was pressing to take over Festival Ballet in my place. He was not content with his position as co-director, with Kenneth MacMillan, of the Royal Ballet, and his ambition was playing into Stiff's hands. I was depressed, too, by a meeting in mid October with Max, when Stiff and Roy implied that my choice of *Don Quixote* had caused box office receipts to drop, taking the Company more into the red and possible bankruptcy. This terrified me. It transpired that Stiff had written to Max pressing for a return of the ill-fated *Swan Lake*, which Stiff had not mentioned to me even though we had met that morning.

I was in Oxford in time to catch the end of the matinee and commence casting for *Giselle* with Skeaping, the Trunoffs and Barclay. This had received Board approval and was coming into rehearsal in a fortnight's time. Later that evening, Paul Sarony had a long talk with me: he was fed up with Stiff and his set-up and felt like leaving. In answer to my enquiry about ticket sales he told me that the drop had not been as big as Stiff implied but was around 25%, and that the membership payment we had to make to the Drama and Lyric Theatre Association was responsible for a 75% drop in income. He mentioned he was writing a report on this to Max, Stiff and Roy.

A week later there was another meeting with Max, for which Stiff sent Max a copy of a horrid letter from Equity commenting on the turn-over of dancers and questioning my ability to direct Festival Ballet. Although Stiff brought a copy of his reply to Equity, Max would not discuss this nor Gilpin's present position as guest artist or the Trunoffs' drinking problems. None of this was debated at the Executive meeting next day, where I was thankful to have really good write-ups of our performances to distribute. I was disappointed, however, that no clear decision was reached regarding *Beau Danube* and *Petrouchka*. I just had to be patient. Stiff was still pushing Gilpin's position while I felt that John Cruft, representing the Arts Council, was not exactly a friend of the Company.

Midweek, during a performance, we got the tragic news that the conductor Terry Kern's four-month-old baby had died. We were asked not to tell him, only to make certain that he left for home as soon as possible. We felt for him – he was always such a kind person, full of life and good humour. That same week Joanna Mordaunt, a tall elegant soloist, appeared at short notice as the Lilac Fairy, managing the difficult solo incredibly well, and bringing the charm, grace and benevolence so important to that role.

To my despair a few days later I found I could hardly move: something had happened to my lower back, and I crawled into bed in agony. Sven's careful treatment enabled me to get up for a short time by Wednesday when Joan and Toni came to do letters and casting. Something remarkable happened that day – a huge bouquet of pink flowers arrived from the Company with a card of good wishes signed by every dancer. I was so touched and pleased that I wept. They actually cared. Peter B rang twice, the second time to tell me that Noleen Nicol's mother had suffered a severe heart attack and Noleen wished to fly home to South Africa to see her. This meant Katy Wade going on in *Dvorak Variations* for first time and Shirley Graham in *Études*.

I was glad they had joined the Company from the Royal, but Shirley was shy and nervous when it came to her performances. As Princess Aurora and the Sugar Plum Fairy she needed a lot of encouragement and reassurance. *Études* was a lesser known ballet and I hoped she would be less apprehensive and really enjoy dancing it. She got an ovation on stage from the Company after her first attempt at this spiky tour-de-force role, which she accomplished most successfully. But she was not able to shake off her nervousness and, even after her success, retreated to her dressing room and sobbed. How were we to help this lovely dancer achieve self-confidence?

Friday 27th November turned into a red-letter day. I received a letter from Stiff telling me he was resigning, and he hoped that I could 'remain in complete charge of the Company'. I was stunned; but what wonderful news. At last I was to be rid of this two-faced person who I had so hoped might change his tactics. The letter did not state when he would be leaving, and I wondered if he would blame his exit on me and spread more unkind stories? Only time would tell. As if in celebration, but totally unrelated, Sven chose this day on which to give me the most exquisite diamond brooch and ring. I felt humbled by his love for me and totally unworthy of such an extravagance. It was so unexpected but I knew Sven loved surprises – and so did I when they were as magical as this!

With the autumn tour completed, the Company was home in London working at Alexandra House in preparation for our Christmas commitments. The first date was the Choreographic Evening on the 14th December, which went better than we hoped and proved an invaluable exercise for those concerned. Three days later, we were in Norwich to reopen the Theatre Royal following its refurbishment. Lord Eccles headed the list of distinguished personages present. *The Nutcracker* performance was followed by an exclusive reception in the beautiful Assembly Rooms to which only Terry Kern, Peter B and I were invited, and I was able to have a long talk with Lord Eccles. We discussed the Company, its current finances and touring schedules and I felt this established a helpful relationship, for at this time he was Paymaster General with responsibility for the Arts.

The New Victoria Cinema opposite Victoria station was where Dolin had wished me to dance with him in *Where the Rainbow Ends* several years previously. This had become something of a traditional Christmas entertainment, featuring himself and Alicia Markova. Festival was now to replace this show with two weeks of *Nutcracker* and two of *Beauty*, opening before Christmas. I was unhappy that the Company was returning to the theatre where it had gone bankrupt only four years earlier: it seemed rather macabre. Our first night on the 21st went remarkably well, and the newspapers next morning were all complimentary. This was an encouraging start although two planned cast changes next day were not as good as I hoped and the cinema was not full. By Wednesday Jippy was off ill and the ballet staff wanted to cancel the Arabian pas de deux in Act II. I did not agree to this but instead gave Jorge Salavisa the chance to take on the role. He did well, partnering Christine Hughes with surprising panache, thus enabling David Long to take Salavisa's place as the lead Cavalier in the Flower Waltz to everyone's satisfaction.

How I wished things were going as well in the office. It was a jolt to find that the bottles of wine given to office staff at Christmas were signed only by Stiff and not jointly with me as was customary. Once in the theatre I signed all the dancers' and stage staff bottles of wine as coming from us both. There had been several unsettling incidents lately, and I again felt Stiff was trying to undermine my position, not even inviting me to the office Christmas party that afternoon. Without telling me, Stiff addressed the dancers after class on the Friday of our first rehearsal week and afterwards the staff at the office at midday on the 11th December, advising them of his resignation due to differences over artistic policy and finance. Kern reported to me that he was fed up with Stiff causing trouble amongst his players and the union by not paying the new, basic £5 increase.

Now I could believe he was really going. But since the last talk with Max (after the December Executive meeting) there had been no further information regarding Stiff's date of departure. On Monday there was an interview in the press with Gilpin, who criticised my directorship. He complained that he had not been invited to perform on the last tour. He also spoke of Stiff's resignation and the number of dancers, stage staff, the choreographer and two conductors who had left. I determined not to be fazed, so only after I had taken class and rehearsals did I ring Max's office at 4pm. His secretary, Jean, told me Max was out but read to me a statement Max had written for the press, which was awaiting Board approval. Some two hours later it went out unaltered. I decided to write to Max asking that Stiff and his assistant Leonard be gone by the New Year, which I knew to be unlikely. But I was dogged by this strong feeling that Stiff was trying to turn the Board and Max against me in favour of John Field. Perhaps I was worrying unnecessarily, but although I had tried to work with Stiff it had proved impossible for, as I had discovered, he was not to be trusted.

I prepared the traditional Swedish Christmas Eve food, which Sven so enjoyed. After checking all was well at the theatre I left for home to celebrate. We undid presents from under the tree in front of the fire, later attending the Swedish church midnight service. I was thankful that I had such a wonderful husband and son who were my inspiration and gave me the love and strength I needed. On both Christmas Eve and Christmas Day my father and Ingvar stayed up late with Sven and me, enjoying snatches of television together.

By Boxing Day snow blanketed half the country, and many dancers arrived at the cinema over an hour late, two girls were off with flu and backstage there was a worrying atmosphere of uncertainty. The cinema was cold, and I apologised to the shivering dancers. Andre danced his worst ever. Audience numbers were understandably low for both shows. With trains marooned in Kent, snow remained throughout the weekend and the extreme cold continued through the last week of December. By Wednesday few trains were even running to Victoria, which did not help our season and ticket money had to be refunded. One by one, my dancers were going down with flu, giving understudies opportunities, with many cast changes even amongst my principals.

Shirley Graham took over from ailing Dagmar as the Sugar Plum Fairy, partnered for the first time by Schaufuss. To everyone's surprise they sailed through the performance and a new partnership emerged. By Saturday, Dubreuil was off with flu, Schaufuss unwilling to dance two shows the same day and Prokovsky would only dance with Galina. Peter B suggested Dudley should take on the role of Prince for the first time, partnering Miklosy with apparent ease. Together they gave a splendid performance at the matinee and a new, strong principal was born.

21 New Year 1971, And Field On The Horizon

Although I had not yet received a response to my letter to Max, 1971 began with a heartening meeting in the office with Mary Skeaping and David Walker, designer of her *Giselle.* His designs were beautiful, and I was thrilled with them. The setting for Act I was clearly defined with the requisite two cottages well spaced, offering a good area for dancing, and the costumes for the royal court gloriously rich. The second act was magical: a mysterious woodland setting with the traditional gothic cross in the back corner. He designed the most delicate costumes for the Wilis and Giselle, and his sensitive use of colour – neither brash nor dull – was governed by a fine sense of period. I felt enthusiastic, happy that I had asked Mary to stage this classic for us even though I knew Dolin would be angry and bitter that I was not using his version. I felt it necessary to give the Company a change. Mary's contained some of the original choreography not seen in current productions, and she had spent two years poring over the archives at the Paris Opera and discovering lost sections, such as the Fugue in Act II with its dramatic choreography. I was certain this would enhance the ballet as well as focusing fresh interest in her production.

Meanwhile Peter B and I looked at a rehearsal room in Grays Inn Road. It was an awkward shape and not really suitable for the Company but, being so much in need of more premises, we realised we might have to use it. I phoned our production manager Manasse in Trieste who was most encouraged by what he had seen of the theatre there we were to give *Nutcracker.* He was busy making preparations for our visit in a month's time and finalising hotel bookings.

The Sleeping Beauty made her appearance at the New Victoria Cinema on 11th January, which turned out to be an extraordinary day with a successful evening. The Company danced beautifully to a full and appreciative house with our governors and the Lord Mayor of Westminster amongst the audience. Earlier that afternoon, during the dress rehearsal, an agitated Mary Skeaping rang me saying she must warn me about John Field – 'he is after your job and is busy slandering you'. She added that she had seen Field having lunch with Stiff, and she was going to see Max Rayne immediately to report this to him. Mary was determined to help me, and I only hoped Max would be free to see her. I now knew I needed all the support I could get – and what she had told me confirmed my fears.

At a reception for the critics that evening Peter Williams mentioned having heard that Max was considering handing in his resignation. I was devastated. Would I cope without his counsel and support? I went home depressed and worried. I was thankful there were no press or VIPs in the audience next evening for, as I wrote in my diary, it was a terrible performance. The conductor, Graham Bond, inexplicably went to pieces in the Prologue, which set the tone for the rest of the performance: *Beauty* failed to awaken.

It was a relief to leave London for a couple of days and fly to Sweden to see Ulf Gadd's work in Gothenburg. Skeaping had worked with the ballet company there and was impressed by this young Swede's creativity, suggesting I might favour one of his works for Festival Ballet. She knew how desperately I searched for interesting ballets by choreographers unknown in England. I was impressed by Gadd's *The Miraculous Mandarin* and discussed with him the possibility of his staging this for my Company with Galina and Andre in the leading roles.

Having prepared papers, I had a private discussion with Max before the all-important Board meeting. He assured me I had his 100% backing but made clear that he was 'a servant of the Board,' and he did not know how much lobbying had been done by Field. But I did. I was terribly worried that I might be kicked out in favour of Field. Max had requested I furnish him with all forthcoming programmes for the London season, and the British and foreign tours which, after some intense work, I was able to produce. He confirmed there was to be a special meeting immediately prior to the normal Board meeting at County Hall when Field's application for the post of General Director would be considered. Max would then tell me the outcome before a statement was issued to the Company: vital in view of the rumours circulating.

D-Day arrived. After the special Board meeting, excluding Stiff, Roy and me, Max came out to tell us the result and issue the statement. 'John Field would not be offered a position within Festival Ballet as it would not be in the best interests of the Company'. I'd no idea things had actually got that far. Fortified with renewed confidence, I was able to cope with the strained atmosphere at the three o'clock Board meeting which followed. During the next three hours there were many tricky questions to be answered concerning my report, future plans and programmes. At the close of the long meeting, Max was the first to leave, giving me a wink as he dashed for the door. To my surprise Weiss gave me a lift home and told me that Field had outlined positive, long-term proposals and programmes, suggesting a part time general director could even be contemplated! My old partner wanted my job badly. How grateful I was to Max for his faith in me.

In the light of the Board's questioning, next day with Peter B I reworked some of our programmes and then with Kern, Martin and Roy finalised the Coliseum opening date. Sarony and I visited potential rehearsal premises in Kilburn, but they would have needed a lot of alteration to make suitable rehearsal rooms for the Company. I was still feeling apprehensive about Stiff and Field, wondering what other tactics they might use to get what they wanted.

For the end of our month-long season at the New Victoria, Sarony and I decided I should not go on stage as usual to address the public as it was neither the right setting nor our regular audience. After the final curtain, I went on stage to thank the Company for their hard work, remarking on how well they had done despite the initial appalling weather and limitations of the cinema. Now there was to be a brief respite from performances for a week but we were still rehearsing for the fortnight's tour abroad. Sarony was grumbling at me about the dancers' overtime which, on checking, I found incorrect. Vass had not filled in the overtime sheet correctly, so I handed the task over to Donald Barclay to complete in future.

In the space of a week there was a lot to do before leaving the country, including a pile of office work, a visit to Poplar with Ray to inspect a possible new floor to lay over the Eastbourne stage, while Mary was awaiting detailed technical discussions on *Giselle*. I also invited Madam to lunch near the Royal Ballet School in Hammersmith where she was still tirelessly involved. We had a good talk about the current situation. I found her most helpful and passed on her recommendations to Max. For the first time I did not feel frightened of her. I must have grown up considerably over the past few months.

I made some headway with choreographers: Lander expressed his willingness to restage his *Études* on the Company, Massine was already booked to put on *Beau Danube,* Beriozoff reviving *Petrouchka* – the latter two ballets in readiness for the Spring Coliseum season. I was disappointed, however, that Cranko was unwilling for Festival to have *The Lady and the Fool* as it would have suited our Company well. I was also talking with Anthony Tudor about staging a work for the Company in about two years time. Following Schauffuss' successful pas de deux from the Danish ballet *La Sylphide* I asked his mother, Mona Vangsaa, the former Royal Danish Ballet ballerina, to teach and produce excerpts from a one-act Bournonville ballet. This required a definite Danish style – virtually the style handed on by the French dancer Vestris during the time he was training the Danish company early in the nineteenth century.

Towards the end of quite a tiring week there was an Executive meeting on Friday evening in Max's office, from which I returned home utterly depressed and seriously considering giving in my notice. I felt there was little understanding of the Company, its work and what I was trying so hard to achieve for its future. Stiff was allowed to speak at length, while Max gave me little opportunity to speak and did not even produce the papers I had been asked to submit and had left for him earlier that week. Sven told me to have faith. Perhaps Max was protecting me. The depression continued Saturday, together with my painful sinus, head and neck ache. By Sunday I recovered enough to enjoy and appreciate being with Sven and Ingvar for the day. They were both such a comfort to me. Ingvar fair-haired and now quite tall, kind and gentle and Sven patient and strong. Should I give up Festival Ballet? The thought of the coming tour and not seeing them for a month troubled my conscience, and on Monday I was still unable to throw off the heavy feeling in my heart.

Arriving at Sardinia airport with the Company on Tuesday afternoon, I was pleasantly surprised to be met by Mario Porcile, our Italian agent. Tall and handsome he introduced me to the associate theatre director, and they drove me to my hotel which featured a modern portal, flanked on both sides by ancient houses on a hilly terrain. On leaving the immaculate airport I noticed an abundance of eucalyptus and palm trees which also flourished in the courtyard of the theatre. My overall impression of Cagliari was that of a casual untidiness somewhat reminiscent of certain areas of South America.

I felt apprehensive about Stiff's arrival and wondered what further mischief he would cause. It was unsettling that his successor had not been found before Max left England on business for a short time. I then heard from Jippy that Field was telling people that he was taking over the Company in six months, despite the fact that Weiss had informed Peter Williams all was now well. I walked the twenty-five minutes to the theatre in warm sunshine and in deep thought.

Our three nights were successful, but Porcile told me he was worried that our repertoire was not interesting enough for Italian audiences. This surprised and disturbed me. I was concerned this comment would reach Stiff's ears and puzzled how I could be doing more. I was endeavouring to build up a varied and interesting rep, attractive for all our audiences but, like everything worthwhile, it would take time.

We flew on to Venice, landing at 1.30am to be welcomed at the airport by the manager of the hotel where a few top dancers would stay for a couple of days, while the rest of us would be settling in Trieste. I had a midday meeting with the director of the Teatro Giuseppe Verdi and he posed some tricky questions. In view of Porcile's observations I felt nervous, worried that the Company might not be of a high enough standard and prayed that Galina and Andre would be sufficiently exciting.

Our opening next night with *Nutcracker* went excellently with the Company dancing beautifully. The local pupils – as children, mice and soldiers – did remarkably well after sound training from Joanie who was in Trieste a week ahead of the Company. The difficult scene changes worked without a hitch, including the transformation and the snow scene. I was greatly relieved the director Guerrini and Porcile were thrilled and more than satisfied.

The next hurdle was the Company's appearance in the opera *Faust*. Papa Beriozoff had been busy choreographing the ballet scene on our dancers in London, with a glorious pas de deux for Galina and Andre. He was in Trieste with us preparing for the first performance of the opera at the end of the week. Dance in opera was a new experience for me. I had attended the opera on our arrival and thought the singing superb. The theatre's orchestra was excellent, too, and bolstered our opening *Nutcracker* performance.

Next morning I was away early with Viv Wallace, en route for London, flying via Genoa. Bad weather delayed us, and we arrived very late at Max's office for the Gala meeting and understandably received a frosty welcome. Max appeared irritated and not the least interested in the big success the Company enjoyed in Trieste. After a frustrating day attempting to reach London, and its unsatisfactorily conclusion, I went home disheartened. I flew back to Trieste next day and Sarony greeted me with the news that the Company were in a bad mood because the administration were not giving a party.

Our appearance in *Faust* was a huge success. Guerrini was pleased with the ballet, although I thought the opera production looked ancient. The orchestra and singers were sublime, and it was a pity that the house was not full. After visiting Munich specifically to see Peter Breuer in performance, my last stopover was in Zagreb, where Dagmar was to dance *Giselle* with Schaufuss. I was not impressed with the *Giselle* production, but thought the evening was lifted by the brilliant appearance of Schaufuss and Dagmar in the *Don Quixote* pas de deux. Back in Trieste, Donald, Vass and I finalised the casts for the Coliseum season. Prior to my leaving Trieste, I wanted the Company to have the casting on the notice board as I presumed there would be some queries. Two dancers, Miklosy and Salavisa, were disappointed not having been chosen to star in Massine's *Beau Danube.* I felt for them both, having endured many disappointments myself, but despite her feelings Miklosy danced beautifully that evening with Dubreuil. Both Guerrini and Porcile sought me out to express their delight with the entire season of *Nutcracker.* This was a great relief to hear as I had to return to London next morning before our Italian season finished and could now relax, knowing how pleased they were.

23 Massine, Skeaping And Bournonville

I returned to the office on Friday. Everything was now set for our annual press conference at the Coliseum on Monday. Max began with a few words, introducing Stiff (who had still not finally left the Company) and me for us to make our separate reports. Massine and Skeaping talked about their work with the Company and their productions. This produced much interest and dialogue for what developed into a stimulating hour. I then met Mrs Sebag-Montefiore for the first time, wife of the board member Harold. She showed great interest in the Company, and I warmed to her. I also met her next evening at the Arts Council reception when she introduced me to Reginald Maudling, the Home Secretary, and his wife Beryl, which I greatly appreciated.

Sven and I went to a reception at the Soviet Embassy and I was pleased to find Vinogradov there. He wished me to meet a woman working with Madam Furtsova, the Soviet arts minister, so we could discuss who would be sent to dance at our Gala. She informed me it would be either Baryshnikov or Vasiliev, and that she would soon confirm which. This was encouraging news – planning a gala is a nightmare, trying to persuade famous artists to participate and dealing with last-minute cancellations. I was not surprised to find Lilian and Victor Hochhauser among the guests at the Embassy, as they had worked remarkably successfully with the Soviet authorities over many years bringing the greatest artists and companies to London.

The rest of the week flew by with intense rehearsals of *Beau Danube*. Massine insisted on perfecting every detail, and Mary was intent on instilling the Romantic period style into *Giselle*. After wrestling with the following week's calls with Joanie, Vass and Donald on Thursday, a broken-hearted Toni rang me late that evening to say the Roneo copying machine had gone wrong and ruined all the call sheets. This was not the first time it had broken down and Toni was terribly upset. She had to spend a good part of Friday typing them all out in time to be pinned on the callboard by five o'clock. I insisted that Roy should purchase a new machine to prevent this muddle happening again.

I felt the Board meeting that week went well and in my favour, although Jane Nicolas, Arts Council representative, seemed rather cold and strained. Attending for only the second time was Mrs Peggy Middleton from the GLC, who invited me to tea in her room after the meeting. She asked me if I realised how near I had been to being replaced as Artistic Director? Astonished, I said no. She explained she had been puzzled about the situation after her first Board meeting and enquired about what was going on. Apparently, there had been many letters exchanged between Field and Max. I remembered what Max had said about his being a servant of the Board. Field had applied for both my position and Stiff's, suggesting two people were unnecessary, and he proposed taking over both posts. Bewildered by this, she spoke to Abernethy, who said: 'Yes, it seems that Miss Grey is going'. It was only after analysis of what Field had to contribute that it was seen that nothing was to be gained by this arrangement and the Board turned down Field's application.

I was taken aback and pondered Max's part in the saga. I recalled his insistence that I bring to the previous full Board meeting the repertoire for the London season and my future plans for the Company. I now realised how crucial this must have been to their decision-making; that and my having raised the standard and reputation of the Company over the last two years and a half years. This had secured my position.

After a short lesson with de Vos the next morning, any misgivings I'd had about the future were banished. I was resolute in my determination to build Festival Ballet into a world-class company. Back in Eastbourne it was heartening to see a full house enjoying the performance of *Nutcracker*, and despite the trials and tribulations I found I had come to love the Company, my dancers and their accomplishments. As if rejoicing, too, the sun was shining as I went into the Congress Theatre on Friday. It was thrilling to watch Massine at work with the Company, a great artist, now 76, an experienced man of the theatre. He was always given the stage to himself for an hour early in the morning to exercise before taking his rehearsals.

I ran through my proposals for his future *Beau Danube* calls, the orchestra, full dress rehearsal and first night dates. He was satisfied with the plans and moved on to the wardrobe department to inspect the costumes in the making. He was precise in his instructions, demanding perfection in every detail. It was then time for me to turn my attention to other matters in the Company. One of my most talented corps girls, Judith Rowan, was to be married but assured me she would be continuing her career with us. A less pleasant task was to say to another corps de ballet girl that I was not satisfied with her work nor her lack of concern about being overweight. Most of the girls were conscious of the need to keep a good figure and were careful over their eating habits.

With a further week in Eastbourne, I had a dreadful shock on Tuesday morning when I rang home and the call was answered by our loyal cleaner, Raymond. Sven took ages coming to the phone and I could tell at once that something was wrong: he could hardly speak. He had been terribly sick the previous night and strained his heart which was still fibrillating and not beating regularly. I felt helpless, caught up with the first stage run-through of *Giselle*. As soon as the evening show was over I took a train, arriving home at midnight, where to my relief Sven seemed back to his normal self. Only partly reassured, I commuted for the next two busy days, overseeing photo calls for *Giselle* and watching Loggenburg's first, surprisingly good *Études*. Neither he nor the dancers were helped by Bond's sluggish conducting that afternoon and evening.

Friday was Ingvar's seventeenth birthday, which coincided with an open day at Eton so Sven collected him that morning and took him shopping. I managed to get home after the morning dress rehearsal of *Don Quixote* and spent a happy evening with them both on Ingvar's actual birthday – for the first time in many years.

A meeting to discuss the programme and seat prices for the Gala was held at the Arts Council on Thursday afternoon, and I left it concerned that we might not sell all of the highest priced tickets. But I was heartened after a private meeting with Max, who confided that he believed in me and my work and had fought for me. This was wonderful to hear, and I left feeling on top of the world.

Peter B and I were in talks with John Vernon, the television director, who appeared keen to present the Company – so there was now every possibility that *Petrouchka* and *Beau Danube* would be televised. Meanwhile Doris Barry, Dame Alicia Markova's sister and a television producer, invited two of our dancers to take part in Hughie Green's regular Saturday night television programme *Opportunity Knocks*, which promised to raise the profile of the Company. We were getting a lot more exposure, and I was frequently interviewed on radio, women's programmes, the BBC overseas service as well as local press and TV stations. This was most encouraging especially as we could only afford one PR person – Vivien Wallace – who was doing sterling work. Once again Stiff was causing trouble in the office by trying to get rid of Martin and Ray's secretary which I strongly opposed – so she remained. I asked Max if he thought Peter B might be a suitable successor to Stiff and, although Max sounded him out, Peter had not wished to hold the position of administrator, preferring to remain as general manager.

We moved into the Coliseum for our second rehearsal week, placing and going through the first act of *Giselle*. Mary was ubiquitous, tidying certain sequences, placing the corps during the divertissements, culminating with Giselle's mad scene. She managed a lot before the next morning's orchestra call, followed by the afternoon's dress parade. David Walker's costumes were breathtakingly beautiful and particularly well made. The display of costumes for *Beau Danube*, which followed, seemed dull in comparison, and I hoped the set and lighting might help. I wanted the ballet to achieve success after all the time Massine had taken.

The preview on Tuesday night went better than expected with *Giselle* receiving strong acclamation but *Beau Danube* only polite applause. It obviously needed more rehearsal, but I felt it would go well once the dancers fully understood Massine's particular style. On our opening night on Wednesday I sat in my box with a nervous Mary who suffered every minute throughout her *Giselle*. It was well received, although I thought the orchestra played a little too slowly in places, Andre was not on the music in his mime scenes and Galina was not as moving in the mad scene as at the preview. David Walker kept guard outside the box and was a calming influence for us both! This particular production, new to the Company and different from Dolin's, received an excellent press much to Mary's relief and was a success with both Company and audience.

During the *Coppélia* dress rehearsal next afternoon we had shattering news that Violette Verdy and Edward Villella from New York City Ballet would not be able to dance at our gala on Monday as agreed. Already having lost another guest artist through a serious injury, this was the last straw. After an agonising 24 hours of telephone calls across the continent we heard from Villella that he had made a mistake over dates and that they would, after all, both be with us for the gala. Indeed they were, arriving from the States in good time for the Sunday afternoon dress rehearsal conducted sympathetically by Terry Kern.

Princess Margaret, the most wonderful supporter of the ballet, was our Royal guest for the Monday Gala inspiring everyone by her presence. Her interest and knowledge of our art was well known, and it was a great privilege to have HRH arriving in good time and in good humour. We opened with *Petrouchka* and after the interval our guest artists performed for the second part of the programme; Liliana Cosi from La Scala, Milan, partnered by Patrice Bart from the Paris Opera dancing the famous *Black Swan* pas de deux; Eva Evdokimova from the Berlin Deutsche Oper with Cyril Atanassoff from the Paris Opera in the skilful Danish *Flower Festival at Genzano* pas de deux; and lastly Violette Verdy and Edward Villella in the dazzling *Tchaikovsky* pas de deux.

Le Beau Danube followed the second interval and, after a short pause, we finished with John Gilpin dancing a solo from Dolin's *Variations for Four* and Galina and Andre performing the *Walpurgis Night* pas de deux. The evening of the 19th April ended with a grand défilé by the full Company, after which the Princess went on stage to meet the dancers, the two conductors and our staff. The joyful party that followed was for me a complete blur after the anxiety.

It was down to earth next day with a struggle to get *Piège* rehearsed and staged in time for the evening show. This, with *Petrouchka* and *Beau Danube*, was sold out, much to our satisfaction. The following evening was spent in my dressing room, locked in discussions with John Vernon, his bookings manager, Peter B and Sarony. I could hardly believe that the Company was to be televised by the BBC. We secured the date, time, place and other details. It made everything worthwhile and the day-to-day problems insignificant. For instance when, the following Friday, the *Beauty* dress rehearsal was held up waiting for the courtiers' costumes to be finished so that the dancers could be placed on stage in their spectacular outfits – an important part of the production. It seemed we were always running out of time, working under pressure; nevertheless, *Beauty* went on that night.

The highlight of the five-week season was my meeting with Paul Findlay which Max organised. Providing everything worked out satisfactorily, it was agreed that Paul be released from his BBC contract to work for Festival Ballet. I liked him straight away. His manner was strong and direct, almost fatherly, and with a quick mind, and I could see him fitting in well with the Company and was pleased to see him at the Saturday evening show with his family. Three days later Max arranged a meeting with Findlay, Stiff, Roy, Peter B and me, and it looked as if Findlay was definitely to take over from Stiff – what joy! Afterwards Sarony and I had an informal chat with Findlay, filling him in on some of the Company's activities. On Saturday evening Findlay sat with me in my box together with his wife, a producer at the BBC. I felt we were relaxed and happy together.

The following week the first performance of *Bournonville Divertissement* received a wonderful reception on the same evening that Eva Evdokimova won great applause dancing Giselle with Cyril Attenasoff. I had won a long battle with Eva's mother over the first act dress which she had not allowed her daughter to wear, preferring Eva to have her own costume. Only after calling in David Walker to explain his whole conception of *Giselle* would she give in. The entire evening was a huge success – the beautiful *Bournonville Divertissement* and a deeply moving *Giselle* with its two outstanding artists.

Monday, 3rd May: the day before Max organised the important 'Findlay meeting' I had received a threatening note purporting to come from the IRA. I thought it a hoax, nevertheless I informed Max's secretary, Jean Walker. Max did not like the letter which concerned the Company's forthcoming season in Belfast and after the meeting I handed it to him. On Wednesday I had another threatening letter and rang Jean who immediately told Max and together they went to the police. There had already been a bomb hoax the previous Saturday evening at the Coliseum when everyone – audience and Company – were cleared from the theatre for an entire hour. During the waiting time some of us took refuge in The Lemon Tree, the popular, hospitable pub around the corner, returning to continue the performance once given the 'All Clear'. Tickets were refunded for those members of the public unable to wait for the performance to restart, losing Festival Ballet a tidy sum.

Over the weekend there were worrying developments in Northern Ireland, more killings and three bombs in shops. On Monday the corps de ballet's representative Moya Knox told me that the Company was worried about going to Belfast amidst the escalating violence. I promised to discuss this with the Chairman, who then consulted with government officials and the Irish Home Office. They thought that the current situation did not warrant the cancellation of our season, pointing out that there was an English football team flying out to play in Belfast at the same time. The Company was informed, but a number of dancers were distinctly reluctant to go.

On Thursday Max optimistically addressed the whole Company on stage to reassure them, but this did not quell their fears. On Friday he suggested those who did not wish to go should give their names to the management and could remain behind in London. To my astonishment, when the count was taken, only a few dancers were willing to take the risk – not enough to make an acceptable programme. It was a hopeless mix of corps, soloists, with no principals except Galina and Andre. Despite Stiff's insistence that the Company appear in Belfast, I knew it now to be impossible, and had to explain this to Max. He was obliged to take this news to the Board, who for over an hour opposed the Company's withdrawal – but thanks to Sir Louis Gluckstein at last agreed.

For the first time I actually felt ashamed of Festival Ballet, finding their decision unprofessional and hard to accept. Dancing with Sadler's Wells Ballet through the bombing in the war, we never thought of pulling out from a performance. At a meeting between the shows Saturday Max told the Company of the Board's agreement to the cancellation of the Belfast season. Few really wanted to go and inevitably amongst the dancers there was a feeling of intense relief. I thanked Max on behalf of the Company and Moya Knox, in turn, thanked me, which touched me after the two and a half years of struggle.

The season was drawing to a close, after encouraging press reviews and good houses even for the triple bills. To attract the public we sprinkled in *Graduation Ball, Dvorak Variations* and *Schéhérazade*. Then for the four final performances, together with *Petrouchka*, we added *Night Shadow* and *Études*, which made for a thrilling finale. After so many different programmes, involving numerous scene changes which the Company and staff managed so adroitly, I could not help but feel proud of their achievements. Our final performance that evening in the Coliseum was memorable for the happy atmosphere engendered by their hoped for news and also delight at the prospect of having a comparatively free week ahead.

24 *A New Start – Paul Comes on Board*

Come May we were off on our provincial tour to Liverpool, Wolverhampton and Coventry. Away from the London office it was difficult to obtain a satisfactory telephone line to the continent. I was desperate to engage certain artists for our summer London season. Artists are difficult to track down, and their directors even harder to contact. I was reduced to pouring coins into the call box in the theatre to speak with Evdokimova in Berlin about dancing in our London season. She was happy to confirm that she would be there but I also needed official agreement from the intendant, which after days of abortive attempts I eventually obtained.

At last Paul Findlay arrived at our offices in Welbeck Street during our Wimbledon week. He was a listener at the Finance meeting and the Full Board AGM meeting next day at County Hall with Stiff still the acting Administrator. At the end of the week Stiff failed to turn up for a meeting with an important impresario, but fortunately I was able to call upon Findlay to help me with the discussions. I felt safe with Findlay, on even ground, and that he was there to help the Company and not to promote himself. We got on well together, and Sven and I invited him for a drink with us at home at the weekend.

Vass and I made a satisfactory visit to the Soviet Embassy regarding a future trip we wished to take in order to see recent Bolshoi productions. The writer Duncan Melvin telephoned with the encouraging news that Sol Hurok, the most important American impresario, intended to see the company in Monte Carlo.

It was harder than ever leaving Sven at London airport Sunday morning 27th June at the start of our tour across Europe, knowing it was to be six weeks before we would be together again. The Company flew to Lyon where, waiting to welcome us, were two former Russian dancers from the Diaghilev company. On Monday we gave our first performance in the dramatic setting of a Roman amphitheatre, with three thousand people seated up the steep semi-circle of stone steps which towered above the stage and orchestra. The stage surface was unusually good, there were three wings on both sides, and the dancers were inspired to give a wonderful performance of the triple bill –*Dvorak Variations, Night Shadow* and the demanding *Études*. There were threatening clouds at the beginning but they blew away to leave a star-studded sky and the performance enchanted a rapturous audience. Next day – after a long session with Trailine, our French agent, Peter B and Paul about the forthcoming tour – Galina, Andre and I were interviewed on radio in French. The ballet staff held an audition hoping to find a good

French dancer, but without success. By evening once again clouds covered the sky and we feared the performance might be rained off, but the gods were with us and a lovely performance was enjoyed by an even more enthusiastic audience.

It was just a short flight to Monte Carlo next morning where the Company had the rest of that day and the following one free. I took advantage of this little break to fly from Lyon to Nice. Waiting at Nice airport was Guy Horne with his driver Gabriel who drove us to L'Olivade. Disturbingly, I saw a change in Guy: he was slower, thinner and looking decidedly older, and I was loath to leave him when the time came.

I rejoined the Company in Monte Carlo for midday class and 2 o'clock rehearsal of *Beauty* with which we opened that night, 2nd July. It was an expectant and distinguished audience. The Minister, who sat in the box with me, did not utter a word although the charming lady accompanying him chatted happily with me in French. At the end of the performance, Princess Antoinette went on stage to thank the Company, and this was followed by a splendid reception in the Hotel de Paris. I think the atmosphere of the small but beautiful theatre with its historic links to the Diaghilev company inspired my dancers who performed *Beauty* better than I had ever seen before. The papers next morning had photos of the dancers and a rave notice headed 'TRIOMPHE'. On to Italy. Our Italian agent Mario Porcile was in Monza ahead of us, with Stiff, for our two performances there.

We left Monza on Friday 9th July but the date could have been Friday the thirteenth, as we experienced the most awful journey to Macerata, almost missing our performance there. As we neared Genoa one of the coaches broke down, and we came to a standstill. Always ingenious, Margot Miklosy whipped a spanner out of her handbag and got to work on the ill-fated engine. She eventually got it going again but the coach could only travel at a slow pace. As time was fast running out it was decided to put the dancers appearing in the first ballet onto the robust coach, transferring to the defective one those not on until later in the programme, and thus saving the evening. The second coach drew up as the audience began arriving for the nine o'clock performance. Although they filled the auditorium, they did not appear to be particularly enthusiastic, which disappointed us after the efforts made to get the show on! We were all inspired though by our next appearance – in the beautiful town of Fano, in a vast square flanked on all sides by Medieval and Renaissance houses.

On Sunday I flew Alitalia home to London. My husband met me at 8.30am, waiting patiently and all smiles. Next morning I had an appointment with Hurok at the Savoy Hotel: a happy encounter as Hurok went out of his way to welcome me and make me feel at ease. I couldn't help wondering, however, how he knew about my early battles with the Company. He complimented me on winning, saying: 'courage, you must always stay firm in your beliefs'. Sound advice that has stood me in good stead.

Findlay was at the Executive and Board meetings next afternoon and readily backed me on various matters, including the Board's request that I organise a benefit gala for

John Gilpin. I was not in favour and explained why, but I was overruled. At the close of the meeting Max thanked me for having conceded.

I flew to Athens next morning where I was met by Peter B with two representatives from the British Council – Peter Naylor and Jane Edgeworth. I knew Jane from her time as Ninette's secretary during my Covent Garden days. Driving straightaway to where the Company were waiting – at our impressive venue, the Herod Atticus Theatre – I found a greatly worried group of staff and dancers. The three camions containing our equipment, costumes and scenery had not arrived. We could get no news of their whereabouts or what had happened to them on their long drive from Italy. We decided that the dancers would wear their swim clothes for class and the orchestral rehearsal, due to begin at 7pm. The orchestra was late starting and, with their breaks, we did not finish until midnight – still waiting for the missing camions.

I was in the British Council offices by 9am next day and to my relief learnt of the safe arrival of the vanished transport an hour earlier. One broke down in Yugoslavia where the poor drivers were stranded for several hours, sleeping in their cabs over night. On their arrival Herod Atticus became a hive of activity: unloading and setting up the lighting equipment, while our small wardrobe staff washed and ironed all the badly squashed costumes, which fortunately dried fast in the blazing sunshine. By evening it was still too hot for Company class, so this was changed to a warm-up shortly before the performance. Once again our staff worked miracles and a glittering *Bourrée Fantasque* and an atmospheric *Giselle* won great praise for the opening of the Athens Festival. The ancient amphitheatre, built in 161 AD on the southern slopes of the Acropolis, made a powerful setting. All the diplomatic corps were in the audience, and in the first interval there was a splendid reception given by the Festival organisers.

In the second interval I am afraid I exploded at Findlay and Peter B. There had been a bad slip-up in the programme – the order wrongly printed – which they said they had realised but had been unable to get corrected by the local firm. Our next three performances in the wondrous location went without a hitch except for a short battle with a German opera company who demanded use of the stage whilst we were rehearsing our change of programme! *Études*, with its demanding lighting changes, difficult entrances and exits as the dance builds excitingly into brilliant turns and leaps across the stage, made a breathtaking finale to our season. After everything was cleared and packed, the entire Company and staff were taken to the beach where a long table stood laden with food and drink for us to enjoy in a strange darkness, close to the gently lapping sea. We felt reluctant to leave Athens but were scheduled to appear in Nicosia for the last date of our tour, flying next morning to Cyprus.

A series of disasters struck our opening night in Nicosia. It began marvellously with the dramatic arrival of President Archbishop Makarios. All lights were lowered and a strong spotlight focused on the President as he stepped out of his car to prolonged applause, his progress brightly lit as he ascended to his seat on a wide stone platform halfway up the towering rows of stone seats, his bodyguards surrounding him. We then commenced the programme with *Dvorak Variations*, when the lights started fusing and the music (tapes) kept shutting off. In total darkness, Peter B rushed up the central aisle to the lighting control box at the top of the steps, dashing past President Makarios seated with his bodyguards, their guns at the ready. Mercifully they failed to shoot at the fleeing figure on his way to discover what had happened. Peter B could do nothing to rectify the situation, and the performance continued with periodic disruptions.

As night closed in, dew began to cover the stage, transforming it into an ice rink; the poor dancers, contending with an increasingly dangerous stage surface, found themselves slipping helplessly. Thankfully we had a sympathetic audience, which included the diplomatic corps. I was dreadfully upset by such dangerous conditions, as well as by the unfortunate moments of darkness and sudden silence. My dancers had battled gallantly against the odds and I felt proud of them. Early next morning President Makarios contacted his Navy to send us a large generator to avoid any further failures in the local electricity supply. What a remarkable President, to find time to help a visiting ballet company. We were grateful and relieved as we had three more evening performances to present.

Having decided to stay for the opening night, Stiff flew back to London for a finance meeting which I was also expected to attend, together with Roy and Findlay. With the problems in performance, however, I was reluctant to leave and decided to stay. In an effort to avoid accidents, the girls were permitted to dance on half pointe, save for the principals who were determined to risk their lives by dancing on full pointe.

The evenings brought the expected problems from settling dew and, during our second night's performance, I decided to cut some of *Études* because the dancers were slipping badly and I was growing fearful of them attempting fouetté turns. The leading ballerina, Miklosy, came off in hysterics, sobbing madly as she had slipped many times during her spectacular tour de force sequences. At my urgent demand, Peter B shot up the steep central aisle again to instruct Mandy to stop the tapes at an obvious cut-off point. As soon as the dancers realised the tapes had stopped, they quickly came forward to take their end of performance bows as normal. Our programme changed on the third night to *Giselle* and *Bourrée Fantasque*, when it was agreed that only the principals should struggle to remain upright on full pointe. But it was a losing battle with the wet stage. So, before the last night, an announcement was made across the island to inform people of an unusually early start to our performance – 7.15pm instead of 9.30 – to escape the worst of the all-embracing damp. To our relief, most people came at the earlier time –including the High Commissioner who to our delight brought with him the young Prince Andrew. This made it a Royal finale to our Cypriot season and was celebrated by a party after the show for the entire Company given by the British Council.

It was the end of a year's hard work by the dancers and the Company disbanded for their holiday, a few staying on in Cyprus, but the majority returning to London before going their separate ways. At Heathrow we found Paul Findlay waiting to welcome us home and wish everyone a happy holiday. He kindly drove me home to Park Street and waited while I unpacked and repacked for my Swedish holiday. We had tea together at Grosvenor House where we went through the figures and reports from Friday's finance meeting. Stiff was too busy playing tennis to join us. I made a telephone call to Max regarding Samsova and Prokovsky – the latter still sulking after Stiff had told him in Cyprus that he was not getting a salary raise. We had gone through all the dancers' contracts in Nicosia. Business over, Findlay drove me to the Cromwell Road air terminal where I bade him farewell and began the last stages of my journey to Sweden. I arrived at 10pm in Jönköping, south west of Stockholm, and found my family waiting for me. Enveloped in their love and devotion, a great feeling of gratitude and humility swept over me.

Although my holiday had begun, there were still some outstanding matters to clear before I could mentally shelve Festival Ballet for a short time. Peter B was soon on the phone helpfully going through various items and enquiries. I told him that the new secretary I wanted, Heather Knight, would be able to start soon after the break. The constant work required at all hours of each day and night had proved to be too much for dear Petal. I knew she would be sad to leave; she had a bubbly personality and would, as Peter B said, be much missed by us all.

Waking late in the quiet beauty of our favourite guest house, I was soon up and plunging into the cold refreshing waters of Lake Vättern. My three weeks in Sweden sailing, swimming, sunbathing and visiting Sven's family and friends was a happy and restorative interlude.

25 *Skeaping's Giselle, 1971*

I flew back from Sweden to London in mid August, ahead of my family. There was only one rehearsal week for the Company, and I was busy taking class and rehearsals. *Beauty* was to open the three-week season at the Royal Festival Hall. My new secretary, Heather Knight, arrived early Monday the day before we moved into Festival Hall, already looking the part in a smart black linen dress with her hair cut shorter. I wrote that evening in my diary that 'she was quiet, quick and sympathetic', an accurate observation which forecast our long working relationship. Vass, Joanie, a rather frosty Peter B and I had a casting meeting at the office and left Heather to type out our final decisions. We rehearsed in Donmar for the last time before moving into Festival Hall on Tuesday. There was only the one afternoon dress rehearsal before opening that evening and I was worried, but the dancers gave an exceptionally good performance. Two big receptions were held in the intervals to celebrate the twenty years of Festival Hall. For part of the performance I was seated in the Ceremonial Box with Roland Freeman, Finance Chairman of the GLC. Lord Goodman and Max Rayne and many of our Board were also present for this historic occasion.

Heather was in the office even before me next morning, busy addressing what needed to be done without my asking. A desperate phone call came from Donald Barclay, rehearsing the newly arrived Italian ballerina Liliana Cosi. He asked if there was any news of Peter Breuer who had not appeared for their rehearsal in Studio Centre. As far as we knew, he had not even landed from Germany! That second night in *Blue Bird* Schaufuss replaced Dubreuil, who had sprained his foot leaping off stage, landing awkwardly in the cramped wing space of Festival Hall. Schaufuss was splendid, partnering Miklosy well for the first time ever as Blue Bird. The Company were in good heart and gave great pleasure to our loyal Festival Hall audience. This was always different from the Coliseum audience – each venue had its own followers and neither appeared to cross the river. Galina and Andre led the Company for the press night, our third performance, which received a super review from the Daily Telegraph and an awful one from the Guardian. The rest were good, which pleased the Company and staff.

Sol Hurok came to our Saturday evening performance and arranged to see Findlay and me the following Wednesday. He was keen for us to bring *Beauty* to the States with Galina and Andre as well as Kern and our orchestra, if finances could be raised. I was encouraged that he was impressed. This followed a call I'd received a week before from Sandor Gorlinsky saying Nureyev wanted to dance with the Company in his own production of *Swan Lake*. It seemed the Company's reputation had improved!

Our crew brought *Giselle* into the theatre on Sunday, and I left Mary to take charge of her lighting. She was specific in her directions and the call went on into the evening until she was satisfied. For the first time ever, Festival Ballet Club members were invited to watch Company class and the *Giselle* rehearsal. At the evening's performance Galina dancing Giselle – beautiful and moving as ever – received a rapturous reception, and Mary's *Giselle* was well received despite our misgivings. It was my father's birthday and he and Sven were out front. Afterwards we went to the May Fair to celebrate. *Giselle* was well received in the press next day – but not *Beau Danube*, which I realised still needed a lot more work if we were to achieve Massine's unique style.

The auditions next day began at 10am continuing until 1pm. This time the standard was higher and we saw some outstanding foreign soloists. As these would have required special licences to appear in England, we had to content ourselves with the best of the British dancers. That evening, Stiff's reign as administrator finally came to an end. There were flowers for the Company from him and a small farewell party, which I did not attend.

Wednesday 1st September 1971 was an important day: Paul Findlay took over as administrator and there on my desk first thing I found roses from his garden. A decent, straightforward man, Findlay had a good brain and after half an hour in his office I felt confident that I would enjoy working with him and hoped he would feel likewise. There was a call from Hurok cancelling his appointment that day in favour of seeing *Giselle* Saturday evening, which we hoped confirmed his interest in the Company.

Salavisa told me that Galina and Andre were taking a few dancers to appear with them in Trieste later in the year and had asked him to join them. Neither the management nor I had been informed, which was surprising. This meant they were infringing on the Company's own booking for Trieste. An embarrassing situation for Findlay to tackle and resolve.

Liliana Cosi, partnered by Peter Breuer, made her first appearance with us in *Beauty* during our third week at Festival Hall. After many rehearsals with Donald she gave a beautiful performance despite having little help from the conductor Graham Bond. He played too slowly throughout the evening, making the Nymphs' dancing in the vision scene agonisingly difficult for the corps. Worryingly, we had the press in front and I was dying a few deaths as each act dragged on but that evening the press were glued to Liliana's every move and were charmed by her personality.

Viv Wallace and I lunched next day with Kenneth Pearson from the Sunday Times, which was most useful, and the following week Findlay and I had lunch with James Kennedy from the Guardian. It was always helpful to be at Festival Hall – its fine restaurant so convenient for meeting and entertaining friends and VIPs. I greatly appreciated being able to go from rehearsals directly to the restaurant when it was necessary to entertain.

During the final week Ursula Moreton, my former teacher and icon from my Vic-Wells school days, came to Festival Hall to see the performance. I always felt admiration, gratitude and love for her and was so happy and honoured to be able to give her dinner before the triple bill – to my joy she greatly enjoyed both! As always she was helpful, giving me practical suggestions and advice. The triple bill which closed our last week at Festival Hall had a disastrous dress rehearsal Monday afternoon but a successful show at night with Cosi effective as the beautiful seductress Zobeide in *Schéhérazade*. But we had an awful shock when the *Don Quixote* pas de deux began and we saw for the first time the dreadful costumes designed by Norman McDowell for Galina and Andre. They had not shown them to us previously and had paid for the costumes themselves.

The Company's chief scenic artist Geoffrey Guy asked to speak with Findlay and me in the office one morning. To our surprise it was not to complain but to make some helpful observations and suggestions regarding structure, organisation and communications within the scenic and other departments, which we found useful. I received an unpleasant letter from Norman McDowell complaining about Roy Rosekilly and me. This tricky character, who had been artistic director of the Company for a brief time in 1965, also sent copies to Max and every board member.

Gorlinsky was in touch with Findlay regarding Nureyev possibly staging *Swan Lake*. Hurok's representative, en route through London, also contacted Findlay, which was encouraging. Peter Schaufuss asked me for more money and more leave of absence with his Spanish girlfriend, soloist Maria Guerrero. The answer to both requests was a definite 'no'. Strangely, John Field attended two performances, which was a little unsettling. I had a lovely surprise one morning when I found some red roses in my office from Peter B. He never seemed to show any emotion, always keeping his cards close to his chest, so this unexpected gesture meant a lot to me. Our Festival Hall season finished unusually on a Thursday night after full houses, even for the closing triple bill – *Les Sylphides, Petrouchka,* the *Don Quixote* pas de deux and *Schéhérazade*. Triple bills were always harder to sell as people generally preferred to come to the well-known, full-length classics.

26 Staging Swan Lake

We were soon off on an eleven-week autumn tour of the provinces with four different programmes. We began with a fortnight in Bournmouth, opening with *Nutcracker* and commencing the second week with a triple bill: *Night Shadow, Schéhérazade, Le Corsaire* pas de deux and *Graduation Ball* – such a happy concluding ballet. Midweek we changed to *Beau Danube* and *Giselle*, so the dancers had little chance to get bored with so many changes of style over short periods. I believe Pavlova would change a little of the choreography each evening before a show so that her dancers were kept alert and not complacent through repetition – they were literally kept on their toes!

Over the next nine weeks we performed in Oxford, Cardiff, Bradford, Manchester, Sunderland, Hull, Norwich and Birmingham, finishing in Southampton. We changed our triple bill programme in Bradford to include *Dances from Napoli* which Mona Vangsaa came from Copenhagen to stage for us. This Danish style takes time to achieve no matter how well it is taught. Mona was demanding but patient with our dancers, and I think the result was worth the hard work. The ballet was charming and proved popular with our audiences.

After returning to London on 18th December, we held our choreographic workshop at the Collegiate Theatre two days later. A number of dancers had been busy working hard on their creations. It was an interesting evening but I was somewhat disappointed as a few cuts had been made during the last rehearsal which I thought weakened some of the presentations. Nevertheless it was enjoyed by those present and the young choreographers learned a lot and knew that the effort involved was worthwhile.

In keeping with tradition, the Company opened on Boxing Day at the Royal Festival Hall but received poor reviews, to everyone's dismay and disappointment. We gave thirty-two performances of *Nutcracker* in just over two weeks with matinee and evening shows. The Company soon got familiar with the difficulties of the Festival Hall stage and adapted accordingly, giving some lovely performances which were enjoyed by the many families who returned loyally every year to see the show.

It had been a happy autumn working alongside Findlay for the first time despite the usual ups and downs. To my joy, the ballerina Gaye Fulton rejoined the Company after seven years as principal of the Zurich ballet company. Bournemouth saw Doreen Wells's first appearance with the Company as guest artist in *Nutcracker*, partnered skilfully by Dubreuil. Doreen was a lovely artist, and we enjoyed having her on tour with us. During the third week of the tour, Carol Yule and Keith Maidwell returned from their performances in South Africa. Gillian Shane, another important soloist, was having a baby and the father was also absent prior to the birth as the baby had to be induced. During our week in Bradford, Dubreuil was given a further week's leave to dance in Cork. Two weeks later Galina, Andre and Salavisa left for a month's tour to South Africa, returning in time for the London Christmas season. Whenever possible I tried to give my leading artists the opportunity to guest with other companies – the experience boosted their confidence whilst also publicising our Company.

Rumours circulated in the theatre world that there was a conspiracy afoot involving thefts by employees in which some of our staff appeared to be implicated. This had to be investigated at once as both Ray Dixon and Roy Rosekilly's names were mentioned. Max arranged a meeting where they were interviewed and totally exonerated of any underhand dealings. Poor Ray Dixon, our stage director, was so hurt by the innuendo that he told me he was thinking of resigning. This would have been a blow for me as I trusted him and relied on his judgement for many stage matters.

Swan Lake became an issue: Nureyev decided he could not be free after all to stage this for us at the agreed time, leaving us with the problem of a new *Swan Lake* production planned to have its premiere in Eastbourne in February. As there was little time to find another producer, after much soul-searching I offered to stage *Swan Lake* myself. The Board were happy for me to undertake this, using the existing scenery and costumes to save the Company money. I began rehearsals on tour early October with Donald Barclay as my assistant. There was much to plan, retaining the exact steps in the traditional sections and creating new choreography where necessary, including the whole of Act IV. Mary Skeaping was helpful over this act as she had choreographed it for the Swedish company and brought me the diagrams and notes of her choreographic version, including music suggestions.

I love the music of the Waltz in Act I but found the six-minute piece a challenge and tried hard to do it justice. I enjoyed planning the national dances in Act III, which are so crucial in providing stylistic contrast with the classical dance which dominates the entire ballet. I asked my Spanish soloist, Juan Sanchez, for some authentic Spanish steps, and he helped in the number's final arrangement. He was proud and pleased to do this, and we had a lot of fun working on it together with the dancers.

Tchaikovsky wrote so much music for this ballet – some unfamiliar to ballet lovers – so I decided to go to the specialist museum in Moscow to discover as much as I could. Once Terry Kern and I agreed which music we would then use, and in which act, he got to work rearranging the Company's existing scores.

A fit-up of the existing sets was arranged at Sadler's Wells to view their condition and ascertain any repairs and repainting required. Likewise, the wardrobe got to work, sorting out which costumes were still wearable and which needed replacing. It was an exciting, busy time, Donald and I planning the production, working on it all hours of the day and night before rehearsing with the Company most days. We were under great pressure, with the usual outbreaks of colds and flu. Vass being away ill for over a month put extra strain on Donald, Joanie and me and underlined my concerns about Vass's drinking, all too apparent to the dancers.

Mary Skeaping suggested Ulf Gadd, a dancer in the Gothenburg company, as a choreographer worth considering for a new company piece. It was agreed that he should come in October to create a ballet for Galina and Andre entitled *Salome*. The work did not develop as hoped as the three of them did not get on well together, so the ballet was shelved at Gadd's request. In its place he gave us one of his existing works, *Ebb and Flow* – but without Andre and Galina. Premiered in Eastbourne in February 1972, it was not a success and soon disappeared from the repertoire.

I had more success with the emerging American choreographer Dennis Nahat who came to stage his *Mendelssohn Symphony*, which he had created for American Ballet Theatre, to premiere in our 1972 Coliseum season. I thought an American work would bring an exciting addition to our repertoire.

By the New Year *Swan Lake* was progressing reasonably well although it took a lot of energy and planning. It was wonderful to put in my own touches to the ballet I loved and in which I had danced many different versions. The music always inspired me. Galina and Andre seemed glad that I was to do the staging and were keen to add their own Russian excerpts, which I welcomed. I was determined, however, to retain the original mime scenes where feasible, even though Galina and Andre urged me to use the Russian danced version instead at the point where the Swan Princess first encounters Siegfried. But I was happy to include the Russian version of Odile's brilliant Act III solo, which Galina kindly taught the other three casts: Fulton, Kessler and Nicol.

For some time I had wanted a work by Anthony Tudor. His *Echoing of Trumpets* was created on the Royal Swedish Ballet in 1963 when Tudor was their director. A highly dramatic work, it was inspired by the atrocities carried out during the Second World War in Lodz. The Swedes are good actors, and the ballet was an intensely moving work. I was determined to obtain it if at all possible – I knew it would be an invaluable experience for the dancers to work with a genius like Tudor. I contacted him in America, and to my delight he appeared during our Christmas season at Festival Hall, watching the Company on stage and in class. He said he would require a choreologist to teach the work prior to his taking over. I rang the Swedish choreologist who had worked with him but she had only two free weeks in February which did not fit in with Tudor's commitments, so the work had to be postponed. I had to be patient, knowing that Tudor had agreed to give us this ballet the following spring when it would suit everyone's timetable.

Findlay and I had lunch with Peter Brinson, director of the Calouste Gulbenkian Foundation. He presented his ideas for the Company's future, suggesting that, on retirement, our dancers should teach pupils studying ballet at the Arts Educational Trust schools. These young students, streamed and trained to feed the Company, would give it a specific style, hopefully securing its future. We thought this was an interesting suggestion and Findlay promised to follow this up but found little enthusiasm within the Arts Education management. Years later the Company finally achieved this aim with the foundation of English National Ballet School under the directorship of our dancer, Katy Wade.

Another idea came from Russell Brown: to establish a small breakaway group, touring only modern ballets – an innovative idea for the time but impractical. Extra staff and dancers would be required for which there was no spare money. Our Company was already operating on a shoestring with a skeleton staff and with a minimal number of dancers. We were often hard pushed to cope.

During the short time Findlay had been in charge he had showed a real interest in the dancers' welfare. One of his first innovations was to appoint a doctor for the Company: Dr Fletcher, a splendid person whose wife was also a doctor. Injections against flu for everyone were introduced over the Christmas season and both Findlay and I queued with the dancers to receive our jabs and encourage the unwilling! Findlay was pretty shocked that dancers still lined up to be handed their salaries in a pay packet every Friday. He put into motion plans for their wages to be paid directly into their bank accounts on a monthly basis. This was much appreciated by all, with the exception of Margot Miklosy who, after her shattering experience escaping from Hungary, wanted to see her money safely in her hand, not trusting banks. She took some persuading to accept and trust Findlay's new arrangement.

In the New Year Peter Farmer, wearing his trademark blue glasses, came to the office to discuss his designs for Nahat's ballet. We got on well together during my first meeting with this gifted designer. There was an unexpected visit from the Australian impresario Michael Edgley who was interested in the possibility of the Company performing in Australia in the near future. Disappointingly, it proved impractical for the time being, so plans were left on hold.

Our three weeks at the New Victoria, following directly on the two and a half weeks at Festival Hall, was a strain on an already hard-pressed Company. As always they came up trumps, even when eleven dancers were off unwell for *Beauty*. *Giselle* had picked up remarkably good notices the week before, when both the Guardian and the Daily Mail said it was better than the one at Covent Garden. This proved to be a big boost for us – hitherto we seemed to have been compared unfavourably with Covent Garden. Perhaps opinions were changing, and I hoped the dancers would receive the accolades they so deserved.

27 New Year 1972 – No More Money

At last the much needed holiday week came, which Sven and I spent in Tenerife. We basked in the sun by a luxuriously appointed pool and took trips across the island, but *Swan Lake* was uppermost in my mind – it was to be premiered in Eastbourne later that month.

On our return I was relieved to learn the threatened orchestra strike had been called off and that Kern was able to assemble his players to start work on the new arrangement of *Swan Lake* and also on *Ebb and Flow*. In Eastbourne we had two complete run-throughs of *Swan Lake* for the first time on a stage. Dissatisfied with some sections, I was relieved when Colin Graham arrived and assisted in the placing and general moves of the corps in the big scenes. As a theatre producer he had a quick eye for adjustments, so to have his professional observations and suggestions after each act was invaluable. My relief was short-lived. After ten o'clock Wednesday evening I had a phone call from Sven saying he was in Moorfields Eye hospital in Holborn. I was distraught, being so far away when my Sven had an emergency operation and needed me. I was determined to get to London after our first *Swan Lake* photo call. By a happy coincidence our wardrobe advisor and his assistant had booked a car for 7pm so I returned to London with them. I was able to spend two precious hours with Sven and eventually left him, comforted by his well-being but praying the operation would be successful and restore his eye to normal. I caught a bus to the station and caught the midnight train back to Eastbourne in readiness for Friday's dress rehearsal and premiere of Ulf Gadd's ballet.

I was disappointed in the final result of *Ebb and Flow*, disliking the swirling drapes Gadd had insisted on putting on the costumes, which obliterated the dancers' lines. The ballet received a lukewarm reception from the audience, but at least he used some beautiful Telemann music and it was good for the dancers to work with a keen, young choreographer.

Saturday was nonstop, clearing last-minute queries with the technical staff on the *Swan Lake* scenery and lighting. All three leading couples needed to be rehearsed independently before and after the matinee, but my heart was heavy worrying about Sven. I bade Gadd farewell during his photo call between the shows after watching his change of cast in *Ebb and Flow* and the second casts in *Night Shadow* and *Graduation Ball*. As soon as I was able to leave, GBL Wilson kindly drove me to London. I was with Sven in Moorfields before nine that evening, leaving him after an hour and a half sleeping peacefully.

Sunday was a crucial landmark in our lives. I spoke with Sven's surgeon by phone before, and again after, his operation, which he assured me had gone to plan. I hoped it had and felt somewhat reassured. As I could not do anything to help Sven I realised I had to turn my attention to the challenge of *Swan Lake* over which at least I had some control. At the first dress rehearsal I was still not satisfied with the new additions so later retired to the hotel with Donald and de Vos who kindly came at my request. There we discussed various cuts that could be made at our final dress rehearsal to improve the production.

There was so much to be done. I went to the wardrobe early next morning to have the top-heavy pieces on the girls' headdresses removed, including those for the pas de trois in Act I. This act was improved by having five couples fewer on stage until they entered for the Pollacca towards the end of the act. For Act III, I took a few dancers off stage re-entering them later for the dramatic ending. There was an upset when our technical director, Ray, dismissed our chief electrician Mohr because he wanted to stop before lighting Act IV. Fortunately, with my lighting designer Charles Bristow present, this was not a problem. We had time to light it and then run through with Donald our notes from the rehearsal.

Back briefly to my hotel I made time for a bath before returning to the theatre for the premiere, ready for whatever was to come. I found a rose in my room from Sarony and flowers from Jippy but nothing from Peter B. Whilst I waited apprehensively on stage with the dancers prior to the overture, some of the staff and dancers came to wish me good luck, which I was so happy to receive. Once out front I held my breath throughout the performance. I had never undergone such nerves, terrified it would not go well. Miraculously it did, the audience's vociferous applause confirming its success. Galina and Andre danced superbly, although Andre was disappointing in the mime scenes, which he had wanted to dance instead of miming. Findlay was thrilled with the production, and we went out to celebrate over dinner, which went on well into the night.

I was up before 6am so I could catch the first train for London to see my husband. I found he had come through the operation well but was shaken to see him with his eyes bandaged. I felt deeply grateful that all had apparently gone well for Sven – it was a tremendous relief after the strain of the past few days. I realised I was blessed that my *Swan Lake* had also turned out successfully.

Although Miklosy was not the ideal swan princess she danced brilliantly especially in Act III with Dubreuil making a handsome prince. He made the mime scenes both understandable and convincing, dancing and partnering at his customary high standard. On Wednesday Kessler with Schaufuss were our two principals, dancing to an appreciative full house. But Schaufuss still needed improvements, underlined by Peter B's tight-lipped manner during the performance. It had been a trying day, with Findlay upset at Ray's dismissal of David Mohr during the heat of Monday's dress rehearsal. I tried to explain to him why and how it happened. I went back to visit with Sven in the hospital for a short time that evening, happy his bandages had by then been removed, although his left eye looked very swollen.

Frank Freeman, an ex Royal Ballet soloist who had been with us for a short time, came to tell me he was happy and would be staying, which pleased me – he was a talented, conscientious dancer. Jonathan Kelly, also an ex Royal Ballet soloist, informed me of two tempting offers he had received to become a principal in Germany and also in Johannesburg but said he had decided to remain with us. All the more important, I thought, to retain and work on Schauffus. To my delight Gaye Fulton had agreed to join the Company and, after coaching from Donald and me in *Swan Lake*, gave her first and very touching performance in Eastbourne. She was a pleasure to work with and proved to be a good actress as well as a pure classical ballerina. I could now list nine principals and four senior artists for our London season.

By the end of our second week in Eastbourne I had closely watched all eight performances of my production. I badly wanted to make alterations, but without any spare rehearsal time this was not possible – Denis Nahat required all the time we could give him on his *Mendelssohn Symphony*. He rang Findlay in advance to say he did not wish to use Andre, which disappointed me as I needed to find a new work for him and Galina, who would only dance with Andre. As the week progressed, Andre gave a much better rendering of the mime scenes in *Swan Lake* and was more affable. Perhaps he had been nervous for the premiere, but I found his moods tiring and tiresome. On Friday Graham Bond conducted but did not manage to light up the evening – rather the reverse as had happened when he conducted *Ebb and Flow*. I was worried about him for he was obviously nervous and not in good health. But I thought it more appropriate for Kern to have a word with him.

To my delight Colin Graham returned to see our last two performances on the south coast and was pleased with how *Swan Lake* was looking. He made some valuable observations and between the shows we sat with Donald, who wrote notes of Colin's suggestions – mainly concerning dramatic points, entrances and exits. I was grateful for his suggestions and we were even able to implement some for that evening's show. During this performance Colin sat with Heather, making yet more notes. Colin's help was invaluable and he was such a joy to be with, enthusiastic and precise.

After the show I drove home to London. I could hardly wait to be with Sven again, and I spent most of Sunday morning with him in his hospital room. The few tranquil hours by his bedside were precious, making me reluctant to return home without him. With the exception of Saturday, I rose early each morning in Eastbourne to travel to town and spend a few hours with him before travelling back to the Company, so it was good the week was over. On returning home I found some lovely flowers from Peter B. This kind gesture of sympathy was totally unexpected, boding well for the future.

The Company were due to open at the Coliseum in three weeks so, with a lot to cover and accomplish, the dancers were back in Donmar on Monday. By the end of the week most of the important changes in *Swan Lake* were completed, but I was still working on the final part of Act IV with David Long and Jippy, who shared the role of the evil magician, von Rothbart. David conceived an exciting, dramatic death for the magician which was just right and which we adopted from then on.

Denis Nahat chose Schauffus and Patricia Merrin for his leading dancers and worked well with the Company on *Mendelssohn Symphony*. Technically demanding, it gave the Company plenty to tackle. At the end of the third rehearsal week we gave our ballet club a party in Donmar but it was slightly blighted for me on learning that Kessler was still unwell and likely to be off for three weeks and that Miklosy's sore toe had gone septic. Despite this I was cheered by Fulton and Schaufuss showing real promise in *Swan Lake* at the run-through on our first evening in the Coliseum – although Schaufuss' mime was still weak.

On Tuesday Colin and I were busy in the theatre all day, tidying up loose ends with the stage and lighting staff, dancers and wardrobe. The waltz dresses in Act I had to be sprayed a softer shade of pink in time for the full dress rehearsal that night. Andre was in a good mood, with Galina dancing beautifully, and I began to feel a little more confident for the morrow. On arriving at the Coliseum Wednesday I was told that Andre's back was bad so he could not dance that night – our opening – and that Dubreuil (his understudy) was in Paris. Peter B tried anxiously for an hour and a half before finally contacting him to return immediately. He caught the next plane to London arriving at the Coliseum 5.30pm. By then I had finally managed to persuade a reluctant Galina to dance with Dubreuil. After a brief try-out together, the curtain went up on time for the beginning of our new season.

Not surprisingly Galina was not as magical as in Eastbourne, and Kern unexpectedly conducted the entire performance slower than usual. This did not lift a sticky audience, although people I met were enthusiastic about the new *Swan Lake* – with the exception of Max. He was non-committal, unlike Sir Louis Gluckstein who was full of praise for my *Swan Lake* at the champagne party held later on stage for the Company. Next day Nicholas Dromgoole of the Sunday Telegraph gave the production an excellent review – he had taken the time to travel to Eastbourne and see *Swan Lake* before the London season. The Telegraph wrote a disappointing report, but the Guardian a glowing one, and we also had good reviews in the two evening papers. By Saturday Andre was back on stage partnering Galina and acting better, even though his back was still paining him particularly in the third act solo. Despite it being the Easter weekend the osteopath Papoutsis, in whom Andre – and many of my dancers – had great faith, was present throughout the evening. The show was sold out and the Company looked good. Even Bond conducted the matinee with style and better tempi.

I felt guilty having had to rehearse the dancers on Good Friday, but with two shows on Monday there was only Tuesday left for rehearsals, including a dress rehearsal of Gadd's ballet. That went well but the evening's *Swan Lake* was pretty awful. Bond conducted more slowly than ever, so that Michael Ho and Loma Rogers almost went to pieces in the vivacious Neapolitan Dance in Act III. Fulton as the Swan Princess was equally thrown, giving a performance below her usual high standard, McCubbin went wrong in the four little Swans, while Merrin was disappointing dancing one of the two big swans for the first time. I was dismayed and blamed myself largely for having conceded to two shows on Easter Monday.

Wednesday was another agonising afternoon of mishaps. The last straw was Ho hurting his foot in rehearsal, claiming he could not dance that evening. I got Joanie to take him by taxi to Papoutsis who proclaimed him fit to dance, the ailment being in his mind! When the curtain went up on *Piège de Lumière* Wednesday evening it revealed a Company on top form. This was a press night and also out front were many governors, as well as Lord Goodman with Max. Next morning at 10am I saw Maina Gielgud in the office and suggested we try her out in *Swan Lake* during the Leeds week in a month's time, when two of my ballerinas would be away guesting. At the Coliseum I saw a weeping corps de ballet girl, Monica Langley, breaking her heart because her husband-to-be insisted she stopped dancing, which she said she could not do. Poor girl, she was so torn. Meantime Ho was now having knee trouble and could not dance, which meant extra rehearsal for Freeman to replace him in two ballets.

On my return to the Coliseum after attending a GLC lunch I found a rather too enthusiastic Vass rehearsing *Igor*, which was disturbing for everyone. After two full houses Saturday for *Swan Lake* I was deadbeat but felt pleased with the Company. Sunday was not a day of rest for any of us, rather a *Mendelssohn* day – the early part taken up with lighting, after messing about repositioning the backcloth to everyone's eventual satisfaction. We had a photo call at 7pm going straight on into the dress rehearsal. Nahat was a real professional and did not waste any time so we were finished by 9.30pm. On the first night (Monday) the Company did him proud and picked up some excellent reviews.

Andre was being difficult, ringing me at home on Saturday to say he and Galina would not dance in the Walter Gore ballet I proposed. He was rude to me when I suggested he came to the office on Monday to talk things over, so I rang off. We had commissioned – especially for him and Galina – a ballet by Walter Gore titled *Danscape*, which was to be premiered in a few weeks' time. Findlay arranged a late afternoon meeting on Monday with Andre at Max's office. Andre kept saying he and Galina were stars and should be consulted on programmes and casting. They wanted more money and thought that, as guest artists, they would get more. Andre was promptly told by Findlay this would not be so! I had to leave for Nahat's premiere before the meeting ended, Max having told me he didn't mind if they left. Next day, Galina and Andre turned up for the *Danscape* rehearsal, Max having won the day, but I had Dubreuil and Nicol covering them just in case they pulled out.

I was seriously worried at the dress rehearsal of *Danscape* the following Monday when it went badly, with the costumes and scenery looking poor. Sarony advised me to take it off. I was fearful of repercussions, however, if we cancelled a work by a British choreographer. The ballet went on that night, with improved lighting and strong orchestral support. The reviews were mostly indifferent and indeterminate, but I breathed a sigh of relief that no one had lost face.

We had a tough meeting with Gorlinsky haggling over fees for Bortoluzzi, and eventually got eight performances for the same fee as six. We did not manage, however, to persuade Eva Edvokimova's mother to agree to her becoming a permanent member of the Company. She stated, 'Not until Festival Ballet had its own rehearsal rooms with proper facilities'.

Although I kept rehearsals to the minimum, there were daily classes for the Company through the week. Bejart came to watch classes on Friday and later, over lunch, to my delight agreed to make a ballet and a pas de deux for us. He said, however, he would not want to use either Andre or Galina. Bejart's creations were always fascinating: theatrical, original and completely different from other choreographers. As Bortoluzzi's terms were agreed and Findlay had come to a satisfactory agreement with Schaufuss about his salary, I felt more confident about the future. Findlay and I met Vernon again, who told us he hoped to present either Carter's *Coppélia* or my *Swan Lake* on Christmas Day television. All encouraging.

The Garrick Club opened its doors to the Company again for another fine party given by the Governors. It was Friday evening and went on late, which was marvellous as the Company were completely free until Monday when we were to open in Manchester. *Swan Lake* was to start a five-week tour of the provinces, visiting Newcastle, Leeds, Coventry and Wolverhampton with a week in each city. When *Nutcracker* was to be presented Joanie would go two weeks ahead of the Company, teaching children from a local dance school their roles and moves. They had to be well trained, quick and ready to fit into the ballet on our day of arrival. There would be just the one run-through with the Company before the curtain went up.

The Executive meeting during our Manchester week was a disappointment. I could not persuade either Max or the governors to raise the dancers' salaries by 10%. They did not understand how difficult it was to attract and retain talented dancers, particularly star principals, whilst offering low rates of pay. Max didn't permit me to say much, telling me: 'Don't get upset about this'. But I was, especially as he did not back me on such a vital issue, and I was worried over what was becoming a problem. Without good dancers it was hard to obtain interesting choreographers, yet it was important to have a varied repertoire in order to entice top artists to the Company. A chicken-and-egg scenario, with an audience also to consider. I felt let down and depressed. How could I build a first class Company with insufficient funds and resources?

28 *Home And Away*

Sven and I spent a relaxing weekend at Hever in 'Meade Waldo', the apartment which Gavin had now arranged for us to use. Before the flood we had been in a different area of the castle; now we overlooked the moat, delighting in watching the antics of the ducks. On Monday I flew to Newcastle with Miklosy, Dubreuil and Gareth Forbes, our recently appointed Australian press officer replacing Viv Wallace, who showed great enthusiasm. It appeared that we were already sold out for the week despite Galina and Andre not appearing, as they were away guesting in Italy for two weeks. Maina Gielgud was to make her first appearance with us in *Swan Lake*, and on Tuesday I insisted we gave her a full run-through with the Company. She was a gifted artist, a sweet person and honestly committed to dance. I was sorry to miss her debut as I was booked to fly to Düsseldorf on Wednesday to see Erich Walter's *Romeo and Juliet* at the Deutsche Oper am Rhein, where he was ballet master and choreographer. The ballet had only one interval and, although the story was clearly unveiled, I found it too Germanic in conception with too little dancing.

Next day I enjoyed a comfortable and interesting journey to Wiesbaden through some lovely country with stunning views of the river Rhine. At the station I found Dr Hoffman waiting to welcome me. He drove me directly to the theatre where he introduced me to the staff, the director of opera, the director of ballet, the dancers, and finally took me to meet the theatre Chief of many years standing. On retiring to his office we discussed Festival Ballet's imminent visit, resolving many queries. He was a most charming and kind man and I valued our time together. He took me to lunch in a beautiful restaurant, afterwards guiding me through glorious gardens – the background for our future performances.

I was sorry to bid him farewell when the 3.30pm train took me off to Frankfurt. Already waiting in my nice hotel – a quarter of an hour early – was the Hamburg Ballet company director, John Neumeier. An American by birth, he had trained partly in the States and also in England. I liked him as soon as we sat down together over coffee. After watching a well produced performance of his *Romeo and Juliet*, packed with dancing, he took me to dinner. There was much discussion as we planned his possible staging of this work, times and dates, as always, the major problem.

I was on the first plane out of Frankfurt for London, where I went directly home to see Sven. Fearful that his eye was not improving he had returned for a check-up with Hudson who admitted that, though the operation had gone well, it had failed to correct the problem of the inner eye. Sven would have to suffer just 85% sight. This was a terrible blow to Sven, and I had hated leaving him for the two days in Germany when he was so distressed and disappointed. At the weekend we escaped to the peace and beauty of Hever, returning to London late Sunday night. I had wrapped Sven's presents in readiness for his 65th birthday next day and early on Monday morning I took him a birthday breakfast in bed, with his cards and presents, to enjoy before I flew to Leeds. Once there I found several dancers off either unwell or with minor injuries. Rehearsals completed to my satisfaction I left the theatre to fly back home and was with Sven by 8.30 in the evening to spend the rest of his birthday with him at a small family gathering. I wanted to share this important milestone with Sven and felt entitled to be absent this once from the Company's opening night.

I returned early to Leeds with Heather by train and we arrived in time for the matinee. This was packed and to my delight Nicol and Kelly (dancing together for the first time) gave a sensitive good performance in *Swan Lake*. Even more thrilling was to watch Maina's performance that evening. She had star projection with a strong technique. I was so pleased when Findlay, who had come specifically to see her, told me that she had agreed to join the Company from mid-June.

More good news too from Peter B later the same week: he had managed to track down by phone Patrice Bart, premier danseur at the Paris Opera, somewhere on the continent. Patrice confirmed his appearances with us in Israel on our next tour abroad and also said it might be possible to come to us for six month periods in future, depending on performance dates. This was most encouraging: Patrice was a powerful, exciting dancer who could add colour and light up any production.

Sven and I drove to Eton for our last June 4th day. It was hard to believe Ingvar was eighteen years old and that those past years spent within one of the finest schools in the country were coming to an end. My father accompanied us as usual to this event and with Ingvar and his godmother Helena we had a wonderful day. We glimpsed a little of a cricket match, visited the art exhibition, the carpentry shop where some of Ingvar's work was on display and later watched the colourful high jinks in the rowing boats. Like other parents we picnicked in the fields and wandered around our offspring's various houses later enjoying a drink with his house master. A weak sun struggled to come out but as it was still cold I wore my green woollen dress and coat by the Italian designer Valentino and a large matching hat by Madge Chard of Bond Street.

Wolverhampton was the last city on the Company's provincial tour, and we had a rewarding week there with excellent houses and a most helpful manager, Humphrey Stanbury. As on our previous visit he handed over his office to Heather and me for the entire week. This was invaluable as I was seeing soloists, coryphée and corps about their new contracts. Those seen were happy to stay in the Company, with the exception of a girl and boy in the corps who had little to offer and a soloist, Chris Adams, who I was sorry to lose as he had talent. There was only one week in London to prepare for a month of performances on the continent. I still needed to conclude the soloists' and principals' interviews, which were held in the Shaftesbury Hotel close to Donmar. This saved the dancers travelling to Welbeck Street where in any case there was little free space.

29 *Germany And Israel*

All too soon Sunday came and Sven saw me off at London airport for Frankfurt where Gareth was waiting to take me by taxi to Wetzlar. The Company were to dance in the beautiful Rosengarten and from mid afternoon the staff were busy setting up mock wings, minimal scenery and many lamps which we always had to carry with us to supplement inadequate lighting. With the orchestra we began a full rehearsal of *Beauty*, but it began raining too heavily for the orchestra and dancers to continue. Later, when the rain stopped, we had to make do with a placing run-through for the dancers without the orchestra.

Our outdoor performance that Monday evening 19th June was jinxed by the weather. The audience was eventually seated by 9pm, the show beginning late. There was a short shower during the Prologue when we held our breath, but mercifully the show continued. In Act I another shower arrived but soon blew away without interrupting the performance too much. By Act III our luck ran out – so did the orchestra, when the sky opened at the finish of the renowned *Aurora* pas de deux. We were forced to end the evening's performance, but as this was the highlight of that act the audience applauded and appeared satisfied. This included the all-important Dr Antoine, who complimented me on the superb performance.

The triple bill next evening had no weather interruptions and the only surprise was, on our return at 8pm, to find TV cameras filming the Company preparing for *Swan Lake*. Dr Antoine oversaw this, and Sarony was furious that there had been no notification or permission given. I thought we could not stop the filming and that in any case it was good publicity for us. *Swan Lake* looked beautiful in the leafy setting, but *Mendelssohn Symphony* looked straggly and the girls' leotards appeared colourless amidst the rural surroundings. *Igor* looked fabulous, however, and made a great finale to our short stay in the Rosengarten. The Industrie Festspiele Wetzlar and the British Council gave the Company a farewell dinner which was greatly enjoyed and appreciated. Whilst this was taking place I was told that all our theatre boxes had been thoroughly searched by the authorities prior to our departure for Israel: we were to perform in the Roman Theatre at Caesarea two days later.

In between I had to leave for a meeting in London with Max. I was relieved when he approved salary increases for the dancers, but he expressed reservations over staging the full-length classic *Raymonda*. Although not much seen in the West, it had just been staged in Zurich by Nureyev, and I arranged to see it next day. After an excellent flight I arrived in Zurich in time to check in at the Europe Hotel and change for the evening show at the Oper, just opposite the hotel. Gaye Fulton, the principal ballerina of the Zurich company, sat with me through the performance of *Raymonda* which I enjoyed. Although it was a little long, I thought it could be a good addition to Festival Ballet's repertoire. On stage afterwards I met Nureyev who invited me to dinner but I refused: I had to depart by six next morning for the start of an arduous journey to Tel Aviv which – due to a long wait in Rome – took practically twelve hours.

Findlay arrived from London and, once through customs in Tel Aviv, we left hurriedly for Caesarea, an hour's drive away. Somehow the show went remarkably well that night, although Jane Edgeworth (British Council) was furious that *Igor* had replaced *Études*. This was on Ray's sound advice and with the ready agreement of Mr Desher, the presenter. *Igor* had an enormous effect when seen within the magnificent circle of grey stone arches, overwhelming in their size and structure. It was also a merciful switch as it was less demanding on the lighting crew and dancers than *Études*.

The performance finished well after midnight, so we were already into the next day – the day of our scheduled appearance in Kiryat Bialik and anxious as we had little time in which to travel and set up the evening show. After the performance in Caesarea finished, two vans left at 1.15am: one with Ray, some local crew and me, the other with Vass, Gareth and the remaining crew. The van taking Ray, me and half the crew broke down, the big end broken and, with the others already ahead, we were left stranded. Miraculously we managed to get a lift into the nearest town where we found a large taxi with a cheerful driver willing to take us on to our destination. There we found Vass and Gareth already at work in the theatre with a few staff and able to reassure us that the stage would be all right despite our apprehension. We joined them working until, exhausted, we stopped to eat at 4am. It was already dawn when I got to my hotel at 5.30am, thirty-six hours after leaving the Hotel in Zurich for the evening's performance in Caesarea. This was one of my longest ever excursions, so I had no compunction in sleeping until eleven that morning.

But this day was to be a nightmare for the dancers. There was only one miserable area under the stage – hot as an oven – where everybody had to change and make up. It was airless, and there was no sign of a café nearby. We were giving *Night Shadow,*

Top: With Lord Max Rayne at the announcement of my takeover of Festival Ballet (©UNKNOWN);
Bottom: With Dame Alicia Markova and Anton Dolin, 1977 (©MIKE HUMPHREY)

Top left: With HRH Princess Margaret at the Gala, London Coliseum June 1969 (©UNKNOWN); *Top right:* Office in Athens, Greece (©JOE BANGAY/ARENAPAL); *Bottom:* Sunshine Gala, All England Dance Competition – The Beryl Grey Award, Drury Lane, July 1970 (©KEYSTONE/HULTON ARCHIVE/GETTY IMAGES)

Top: Sleeping Beauty; Galina Samsova and Andre Provkovsky, The London Festival Ballet at the Festival Hall, London, August 1967; (PHOTOGRAPHED BY GBL. WILSON © ROYAL ACADEMY OF DANCE/ARENAPAL); *Bottom left:* Witold Borkowski rehearsing Patrice Bart and Elisabetta Terrabust in *Don Quixote* 1975 (©ANTHONY CRICKMAY/VICTORIA AND ALBERT MUSEUM, LONDON); *Bottom right:* Carmen Mathé as the Coquette and John Gilpin as the Poet in George Balanchine's *Night Shadow* 1967 (©ANTHONY CRICKMAY/VICTORIA AND ALBERT MUSEUM, LONDON)

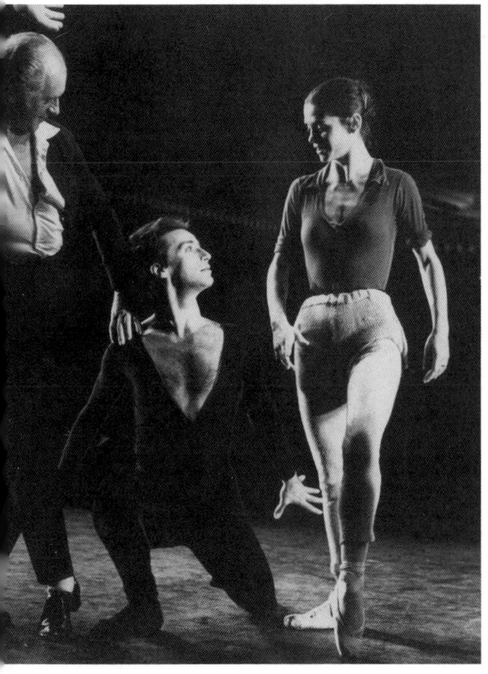

Top: Ballet Mistress, Joan Potter and Ballet Master, Vassilie Trunoff (©ZOË DOMINIC);
Bottom: With Wilfred Stiff (©UNIVERSITY OF DUNDEE THE PETO COLLECTION)

Top left: With Peter Brownlee, General Manager (©Joe Bangay/ArenaPAL); *Top right:* Frano Jelencic, Ballet Master (©Unknown); *Bottom:* With David Rees *(left)* & Paul Findlay *(right)* (©Unknown)

Taking Rehearsal with Galina Samsova & Andre Prokovsky
with Donald Barclay ballet master looking on (©ANTHONY CRICKMAY/VICTORIA AND ALBERT MUSEUM, LONDON)

Top: Sleeping Beauty; with John Gilpin, Noella Pontois, Galina Samsova and Andre Prokovsky; Curtain Call; The London Festival Ballet at the Festival Hall, London, UK; August 1967 (PHOTOGRAPHED BY GBL. WILSON © ROYAL ACADEMY OF DANCE/ARENAPAL); *Bottom:* London Festival Ballet's 21 Anniversary Gala at the London Coliseum with Terrance Kern, John Gilpin, Terry Hayworth, André Prokovsky and Edward Villella, 1971 (©ROSEMARY WINCKLEY)

Top: Ronald Hynd rehearsing Paul Clarke and Patricia Ruanne in his ballet, *The Sanguine Fan* 1976 (©ANTHONY CRICKMAY/VICTORIA AND ALBERT MUSEUM, LONDON); *Bottom:* With Sir Adrian Boult (©UNKNOWN)

Top: Rehearsing *Parade* (©ALAN CUNLIFFE); *Bottom:* With Massine (©UNKNOWN)

Top left: With Dame Margot Fonteyn (©UNKNOWN); *Top right:* Maina Gielgud in Maurice Béjart's *Forme et ligne* 1971 (©ANTHONY CRICKMAY/VICTORIA AND ALBERT MUSEUM, LONDON); *Bottom:* Patricia Ruanne at a rehearsal of *Giselle* (©UNKNOWN)

Top: (left to right) With Paco Pena, Sir Andre Previn and Peter Maxwell Davies (©Steve Wood/Hulton Archive/Getty Images); *Bottom left:* Eva Evdokimova (©Unknown); *Bottom right:* Barry Moreland rehearsing Paul Clarke and Patricia Ruanne *Prodigal Son (in Ragtime)*, 1974; (©Anthony Crickmay/Victoria and Albert Museum, London)

Top: With Nureyev (©THE TIMES/NEWS SYNDICATION); *Bottom:* Rudolf Nureyev and Beryl Grey with President and Mrs Carter at the White House June 1978 (©JIMMY CARTER LIBRARY AND MUSEUM)

Top: With ballerinas from London Festival Ballet, China, 1979 (©UNKNOWN); *Bottom left:* In China (©UNKNOWN); *Bottom right:* With Chinese Embassy Official (©UNKNOWN)

Top right: With Sir John and Anya (Linden) Lord & Lady Sainsbury (©unknown); *Bottom Left:* With Dame Gillian Lynne (©unknown); *Bottom Right:* Receiving London University doctorate from HRH Princess Anne, 1996 (©jeremy makinson)

Top left: Swan Lake Royal Gala; meeting Queen Elizabeth II backstage; Royal Opera House, 1996; (©Keith Saunders/ArenaPAL); *Top right:* Meeting Princess Diana, Pamela Crouch (Sunshine Homes secretary) (©unknown); *Bottom:* With Sven & Ingvar, 1988 with DBE award (©unknown)

Top: Marcela Goicoechea, Irek Mukhamedov, Dr Wayne Sleep, Galina Samsova & Agnes Oaks, A Dance Gala To Celebrate The 75th Birthday Year Of Dame Beryl Grey DBE, At Sadlers Wells, London (©DAVE BENETT/HULTON ARCHIVE/GETTY IMAGES); *Bottom:* With Esteban Berlanga 2006 (©UNKNOWN)

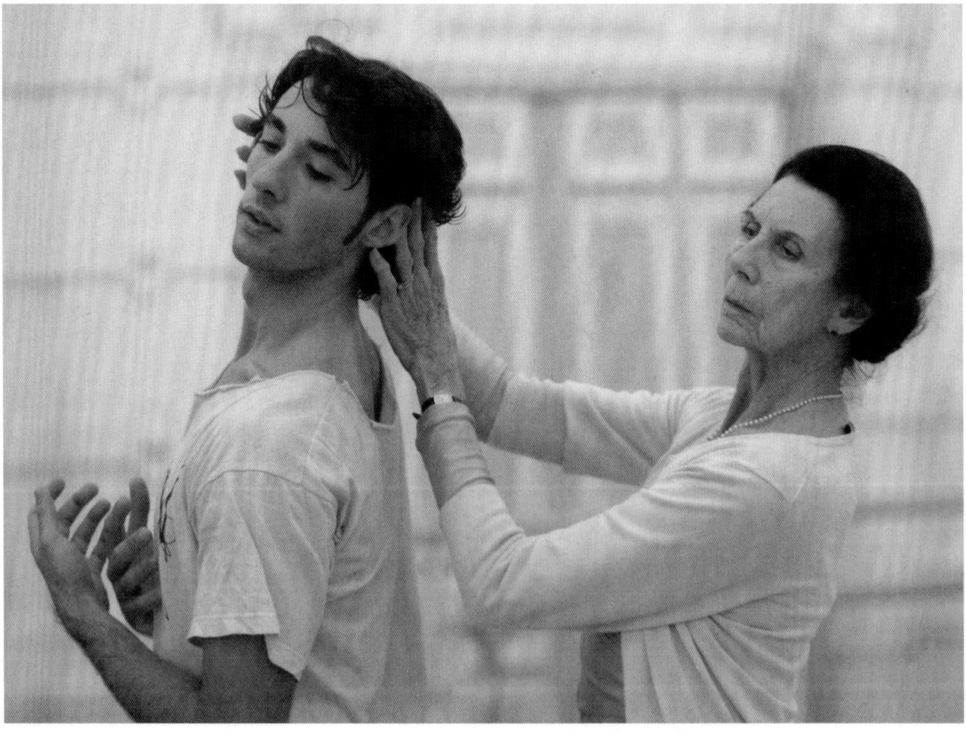

Schéhérazade and *Études* at both the 6pm matinee and the 10pm evening show – a demanding programme at the best of times. I wondered at this engagement, which Stiff had organised in his last year. We were already running late and the dancers needed a stretching warm-up session and a placing call, so it was nearer to seven when the matinee started. We were forced to make cuts in *Études* to allow the audience to depart before the incoming one arrived for a 10pm start. Even so this was behind time commencing, and it was an exhausted Company that crawled into the waiting coaches to take them to their beds in Tel Aviv. I ordered a large taxi to take Mandy, our indefatigable stage manager, Ray her boss, Heather and me with Miklosy and Gielgud to Tel Aviv. Our two ballerinas lay full length on two rows of seats, sleeping all the way to their hotel. Once again the Company had come up trumps, giving their all to enthralled and appreciative audiences.

It was a thrill to be at Tel Aviv's modern concert hall, the Mann Auditorium, where we were to perform that night. However, a recalcitrant local stagehand held up the work of our crew. Arriving on the vast stage for rehearsal we found the backcloth un-hung, still covering the floorboards. This was because the stagehand was on a go-slow, delaying the fit-up – yet he could not be sacked. When the stage was eventually cleared there was no time left to place the dancers. We opened on time at 9.30pm to a most receptive house, which was practically full. Everything was going well until, at midnight, the same stagehand turned off the power, stopping the music tapes. The Company continued dancing unaccompanied as if nothing untoward had happened. Our splendid conductor Kern dashed to the prompt corner where he was able to switch the tapes on again and catch the dancers at the exact moment when they were leaping across the stage – saving the whole evening.

Monday was a free day for us and at 10am I was collected by taxi for a visit to Jerusalem with Findlay and Jane. The driver was a splendid guide, pointing out the new developments, as well as places whose names jumped out at me from my memory of the Bible. He drove us to the Mount of Olives and to the old city where we saw men wearing kippahs standing facing the Wailing Wall. It was almost unbelievable to be there.

I had a meeting the next morning with Findlay and the impresario Desher at 10.30am. There was a problem with the contract, which was ambiguous, and Findlay thought it wise to give in to Desher's reading. Desher was pleased with the Company's performances and suggested a world tour for 1974. This was a surprising proposition and would require careful consideration. I felt thankful that Findlay was proving himself to be a shrewd, practical statesman. He worked wonders with Samsova and Prokovsky, who had finally accepted a lower salary than they had been demanding. I was reluctant to lose Findlay back to London, having appreciated his calm, intelligent presence on the tour.

Next afternoon I received the most thrilling news from Isobel, Max's secretary. She told me that Sven had rung asking her to tell me of an invitation to us both from the

Prime Minister, Edward Heath, to an 'At Home' at Chequers on either the 8th or 9th July, the Saturday or Sunday. On the 9th the Company would be travelling from Nervi to Obitija in Yugoslavia, which meant I could be away and therefore able to accept the invitation for the Sunday. I felt elated, as if on another planet.

30 *Forward Planning*

After our final Israel performances in Jerusalem, I flew to London in the company of the gossiping Jane Edgeworth who had not a kind or good word to say about anybody or anything. It was a relief to part from her at Heathrow and snatch a few minutes with Sven at home before burying myself at the office in a pile of paperwork and forward planning. There was a Sunshine competition meeting at the Lyall Street home of Lady Astor, and it always felt a joy and a privilege to be there with her. Unassuming, wise and cooperative, she had the gift of making meetings pleasant and seemingly effortless. I then went on to County Hall for the AGM and full board meeting, which passed off satisfactorily with Max backing me from the start. Sir Gilbert Inglefield made a good suggestion: that a new ballet be created for the forthcoming Entry into Europe celebration. He proposed music by Peter Maxwell Davies, if he had the time to compose something appropriate. I determined to follow up his idea and contact the young choreographer Barry Moreland, who I thought suitable for this possible commission.

It was hard leaving Sven so soon again when next morning I was off to rejoin the Company in Italy. The plane to Genoa left from Gatwick airport and landing on time I found Heather and Peter B waiting with a taxi for the short drive to Nervi. The park was the centre for the festival and more beautiful than I expected. Mountain-like green hills sloping into the sea surrounded the enclosure where there was a large stage and wooden dressing rooms. I was enchanted by the 'belle époque' Hotel Savoia. A kindly woman took me to my room, which faced the sea and hills on one side and blossoming bougainvillea amongst a host of trees. Waiting to welcome me was Mario Porcile, who had already sent some pink roses to my room, a forerunner of the consideration and courtesy extended to us all.

The evening's orchestral run-through of *Nutcracker* was chaotic. The first scene, bereft of the usual scenery, looked ridiculous on the wide-open stage, so it had to be cut altogether. To our dismay, the children were too small. 'But they were the best dancers,' Joanie said. Despite the orchestral accompaniment, the Company were uninspired, dancing badly and sloppily, so I was only too relieved when the rehearsal had to stop by midnight – it had begun promptly at 9pm with the lighting crew concentrating hard to give the best results. Meanwhile the stage crew were employed working out a way in which to make snow fall onto the open stage! Quite ridiculous really, snow in Italy in the middle of July – but this was our magical world and my staff were miracle-workers. They decided to fix contraptions high up in the surrounding trees from where paper snow, blown through tubes, would shoot out onto the stage. We prayed this would actually work at the performance next evening. It did, adding mystery and even more magic to what was an enchanting event.

The audience was a highly fashionable one – men in tuxedos escorting women in glittering full-length gowns. Their paths were lit by flaming torches held high by bewigged flunkies costumed in 17th-century attire. The audience, however, were not over enthusiastic – perhaps there just to be seen and admired. Porcile was thrilled with the performance and had thoughtfully given seats to the hotel owners. They were overwhelmed by the show and stayed up late to serve us a fine repast. I felt so fortunate to be staying in an adorable hotel with such caring proprietors and staff. They had an old-fashioned dignity, unobtrusive but with a readiness to assist. It was an idyllic place to stay, with extensive elegant gardens in which I worked all day with Heather, Joanie, Vass and Peter B. We were inspired to finish all the casting for the Festival Hall season as well as the more imminent rehearsals. Peter B asked for leave to fly to Australia to see his father who was extremely ill. I could not possibly refuse such a request, though I knew I would miss him.

31 *Farewell Eton, Hello Chequers*

I left Nervi on a high note in the early hours. Already waiting at the airport were Ray and David Mohr also taking a flight out of Genoa – not for London like me, but for Yugoslavia. The Company were due to perform there in four different cities over a one-week period, so they had a lot to prepare and organise. I found Sven at Heathrow waiting to drive us to Eton where we had a 9.30am appointment with Ingvar's housemaster, Mr Parry. For the first time ever he had nothing but good to say about Ingvar, now at the end of his final year. We watched our son win the 50 yard backstroke race and also help his house to win the much sought-after swimming trophy, which he received on their behalf together with his own award. It was wonderful to hear the boys shouting 'Ingvar' and 'Come On Ingvar', willing him to win. A great day for us all.

Sven and I were reluctant to leave everyone next evening at 6.30, but we had this exciting invitation to Chequers. One of Sven's patients had kindly insisted that we were to be driven to Chequers by his own driver. Departing from home in evening dress we drove to Amersham where we were met by the chauffeur. This was a great boon for, as we drew closer to our destination along narrow winding lanes, there was increasing security with police and sniffer dogs patrolling. Our invitations were carefully checked on arrival before we were allowed to drive to the main entrance, arriving together with other guests a quarter of an hour early.

The men were escorted for refreshments whilst the ladies were directed to a first-floor bedroom to 'freshen up'. This was off an open three-sided wooden balcony and looked down onto a square central hall entered from a smaller lobby. The house was furnished tastefully with fine furniture, paintings and tapestries, with bowls and vases of well arrange flowers everywhere. Drinks were served on the terrace at the back of the impressive stone house, looking out across gardens surrounded by high hedges. It was Prime Minister Edward Heath's birthday, and our host was jolly and friendly, totally at ease, going from one person to another making us feel truly welcome. After a while, the Prime Minister escorted us to a beautiful room where we were privileged to enjoy a private piano recital given by the world-renowned Clifford Curzon. Heath himself introduced Curzon, and thanked him profusely at the conclusion of a memorable performance. Shortly after we were ushered to the long gallery for a delectable dinner at which I noted the cheeses served were English. Taking in the colourful scene of well dressed people and glittering jewels, it was strange to remember that it was in this house that Lady Jane Grey was imprisoned before her execution. The evening passed swiftly and by 11.30pm, with expressions of thanks, congratulations and farewells, the birthday party was over. Sven and I were collected by our vigilant chauffeur, who had patiently waited to take us back after the momentous evening.

32 *Southern Slavs To Southern France*

Early the following morning I only just caught the Frankfurt plane. Once there, I was pleased to meet up with the Fergusons – Tom from the Daily Mail accompanied by his wife. Arriving in Ljubljana we waited some time to be collected by a British Council driver for the trip to Opatija. He had been told to look for just one English lady, and as I was with two other people, it took him time to identify me. The countryside was magnificent – isolated hamlets cradled amongst glorious mountains. We were glad to be met by the British Council representative, Dick Lefaune, who swept me off to a hotel, where my room overlooked the sea. He then drove me into the centre of a nearby park where our stage had been built. The dancers had found the surface impossible so it had been covered by some kind of plywood, which proved a lot better. After class and rehearsal I returned to the hotel to change in time for the Lefaunes to accompany me to the performance. Showers of sensational fireworks started the evening and added to the excitement of the three thousand people seated in the open air. This attendance was encouraging for our first performance in Yugoslavia. Although I found the heat oppressive during *Giselle*, it looked perfect in the park and the title role was danced divinely by Galina. It began to rain before the closing moments but nobody minded. An auspicious start to our tour of this beautiful country.

The following day began pleasantly with a swim in the pool but became dramatic after I left the idyllic surrounding for Ljubljana. I met the Festival director at the Park Theatre and inspected the stage and its surroundings. We were anxious that the Company's lunch and dinner arrangements were in place when a furious Paul Sarony called me on the phone from a nearby restaurant. He was with an outraged Company who had not been given any food at their hostel, which they claimed was uninhabitable and unsuitable. I agreed to go at once and hear their complaints before going with Paul and Peter B to inspect the hostel. We found it as bad as the dancers described – everything dirty. The uncarpeted bedrooms' bare wooden floors were badly stained, the lavatories and cupboards filthy, and every lift out of order – it was indeed dreadful.

We went directly to speak to the Festival director and insist that as many of the dancers and staff as possible be moved to decent hotels. I called Sarony who said the Company would not move from the restaurant until I came to confirm their transfer to hotels. I went to reassure the dancers and asked them to report for class in an hour's time at a rehearsal studio close by the Park Theatre. This was in fact an improvised venue, set within a spacious town square bounded on two sides by fine buildings. The main road running through the centre was completely shut off at night, allowing the festival's presentations to take place, with the audience seated on hard, upright chairs. Incredibly that night the Company gave a fantastically moving performance of *Giselle* and, despite the rain, the captivated audience encored Galina and Andre in their ever-popular *Corsaire* pas de deux.

As it was a ten-hour coach drive to the coastal resort of Split, eight principals were booked to fly there, together with Dick's wife. She undertook to ensure the food and hotel arrangements were satisfactory on arrival. Dick, Sarony and I travelled in his car marginally ahead of the Company in order to book food at stops along the way. Three dancers – Nicol, McCubbin and Sanchez – had been ill, and I rang to ensure they were recovered sufficiently to go by road, which thankfully they were. Meantime Heather Birch had lost her passport, which we reported as being British but it transpired that she held an Australian one – green, not navy blue. Only one coach arrived that morning but, after desperate phoning, the lost one was located and directed to the waiting group. Our first stop at 11.30 was at a modern tourist hotel I had noticed on our journey from Opatija. It was good and we left well fed! Our cavalcade travelled across glorious country and passed through Yugoslavia's biggest port, Rijeka, from where we hugged the coast, stopping for a late lunch at the lovely little port of Senje. The meal was served swiftly having been preordered, and we were more than satisfied with both the food and kindness shown. It was then nonstop to Split, drawing up to our hotels shortly before midnight.

I awoke to a breathtaking view of Split over the large bay, its harbour full of bobbing boats, when I was called by a worried Ray to meet him at the theatre by ten o'clock. I decided to walk in the cool breeze, which soon changed to a warmer current, caught in the airless narrow streets of the walled city. I passed the fantastic Diocletian palace and houses built by Venetians over different periods. Coming to our specified site I found the stage only partly erected in the 'Pericles', which was in front of a temple. The surrounding cafes were open until 8.00pm which meant that Company class and rehearsals would be watched by the public. I agreed with Ray that the space was too confined for us to present *Études*, so we hastened to the festival director suggesting we gave *Igor* instead of. If this was not acceptable we would need to be transferred to a larger area. To our joy, he raised no objection to a programme change. We then alerted the dancers in their hotels of the change to *Igor*. They were most relieved at the switch, and the stage was eventually finished ready for them by late afternoon.

The evening passed off well, without further problems, and the audience went mad over *Igor*. Galina and Andre once again scored a big success, too, with *Corsaire*. The director was so delighted with the Company's presentation that he sought me out immediately after the show and showered me with compliments. I was moved and pleased after the initial worries.

Early on Saturday my mind was filled with special memories of my wedding day twenty-two years ago. Having cabled my loving thoughts to Sven, already on holiday in Sweden with Ingvar and my father, I walked for the last time to the picturesque harbour. I watched fishermen busy unloading boxes of fish from their ageing boats and shabbily clad women jostling to buy, whilst others were busy in the waterfront fruit market, picking out the best of the crop.

I bought a ticket for a passenger boat going to Dubrovnik that morning in place of road travel. To my surprise, thirty-four members of the Company chose to do the same, so it was a happy crowd who sat relaxing on deck in hot sun admiring the coastal scene. Once at Dubrovnik, I walked happily to a tower in the walled city near where we were to perform. A stage was being built, but was obviously going to be too small for us to even contemplate staging *Études* there, so once more we had to obtain permission to change the programme to *Igor*. The audience and dancers used the same entrance at this site, which destroyed the magic of performance, so it was a relief for us all to fly off to Nice.

Arriving at 5.40am I was deeply touched to find our friend Guy Horne waiting for me at that early hour with his driver, Gabriel. Guy was so pleased to see me, although he insisted I went to bed upon our reaching L'Olivade. Realising the time with him was precious to us both, I got up at eleven to sit in the garden with him. Unexpectedly Guy insisted on accompanying me later to the Arène de Cimiez, a Roman amphitheatre where the Company were about to take class. I was proud to introduce Guy to Findlay before Gabriel drove Guy back home. Gabriel was totally devoted to Guy, respecting him and looking after him at all times.

Despite the lack of sleep, the Company came up trumps, and the outdoor production was enhanced by a host of fairy lights hanging from trees behind the orchestra. The audience numbers were lower than expected, but those there were enthusiastic and applauded vociferously. The Company were free next day so I was able to spend treasured hours with Guy – I had not realised how much I meant to him.

For our second show on Friday we gave a triple bill programme: *Piège, Igor* and *Études.* This also included a Bejart solo, *Forme et Ligne*, danced – or rather balanced – superbly by Gielgud, and Balanchine's *Tchaikovsky* Pas de Deux which Maina had kindly taught our other principals. The final performance of *Sleeping Beauty* in Nice was sold out, making it a glorious finale to the long European tour. The dancers had more than earned their three weeks' holiday after the heavy demands on their stamina. Some stayed on in France but the majority, like me, returned home to London.

The Sunshine Homes All England competition finals were being held that same weekend, followed by a gala, so I attended the Golders Green Empire Theatre to adjudicate and give the now traditional class. There was a high entry and it was important I was present for this worthwhile event. Eventually the time came to begin my holiday and fly to Sweden, where my dear family were eagerly waiting for me.

The holiday over, *Swan Lake* was back in rehearsal in preparation for a three-week season at Festival Hall. At the office there was a pile of work to clear and it felt good to be back with the Company once more rehearsing at Donmar. We were asked to see a few dancers in Company class from whom we took three: a girl from the Ballet for All group, a soloist girl from Australia (initially as a coryphée), and a talented young Scotsman, Kenneth McCombie. We felt pleased to have found them ahead of the main advertised audition when over a hundred dancers would most likely turn up but few would be of a suitable standard.

Heather had received disappointing news from Bejart: due to lack of time he could not create a work for us in the near future as we had hoped. This was a big blow and I knew how upset Max would be, too – which he was when I told him. He wanted me to contact Bejart and arrange to go to Paris to try to persuade him to make time to fit us into his demanding workload. But Bejart was in Switzerland and unreachable by phone, although I tried and failed several times to contact him.

I was delighted to receive an invitation to take part in the prestigious *Any Questions* radio programme. This dealt with current affairs and was to be aired sometime in the autumn. I had already begun a weekly music programme on the BBC and been fortunate in my producer, Peter Murray. He was exceptionally helpful, coaching me in the art of radio presentation. It was the start of a long friendship which lasted until his death many years later.

For the Festival Hall season, I presented three guest artists to augment our own principals: Peter Martins from American Ballet Theatre partnering Eva Evdokimova, happily back with us again, and Patrice Bart, also returned to partner our own Margot Miklosy. Peter Martins also made a good partner for Maina Gielgud and, with Dubreuil partnering Fulton and Loggenburg dancing with Kessler, we were well covered for our three-week run of *Swan Lake*. Our Festival Ballet club attended several rehearsals and two talks given by Kern and myself in the Waterloo Room.

Life became even busier. Barry Moreland was working with us for the first time and chose Gaye Fulton with Loggenburg and Dubreuil for a sensitive work to music by John Field. Moreland had started his career as a classical dancer with the Australian Ballet but was now attached to London Contemporary Dance Theatre and considered a modern choreographer. For this work Moreland returned, as it were, to his roots, using classical ballet to express deep emotions. Titled *Summer Solstice* it was to be premiered on the forthcoming tour in a few weeks' time, and I was feeling optimistic about its future.

Plans were already taking shape for our contributions to the '*Fanfare for Europe*' programme coming early in the New Year. I was pleased that Moreland would be able to create another ballet for us – this time specially marking this exciting event – and had approached Peter Maxwell Davies who had agreed to write the music. These two artists had been suggested at a recent board meeting so I knew Max would be pleased at the outcome – particularly as Moreland had contacted Nadine Baylis to design his work *In Nomine*.

We were also to give two other new ballets – one by Ronald Hynd and the other by Peter Darrell, former director of Western Theatre Ballet, now Scottish Ballet. He was happy to create a new work for us and chose to use Galina and Andre. This pleased me as they were always asking for new works. Darrell asked Peter Frazer to be his designer for the mythical story *La Peri* to the music of Dukas. Hynd was to use Tchaikovsky's Mozartiana Suite, the composer's homage to Mozart. Taking *Mozartiana* as its title, the ballet would be an echo of the past, with designs by Peter Docherty whose work I knew well. I later heard from Peter Schaufuss that his father Frank proposed creating a new pas de deux to Glazunov music so this, together with the three new ballets, would make for an interesting evening.

Peter Williams continued to take a keen interest in the Company's activities and I greatly valued his comments and advice, offered over many a good meal. I enjoyed my first ever lunch with Lord Harewood, who I found down to earth, reasonable and helpful over future plans for our Coliseum seasons. On the last Saturday of our season Terry Kern and the leader of our orchestra, Donald Weekes, gave a special recital to our ballet club in the Waterloo Room. This midday interlude made a novel end to our season and was much appreciated by our members. Despite lack of praise from some critics, the three weeks of my *Swan Lake* production had not affected the box office takings, which were astonishingly good.

We were immediately off on the road again for a ten-week provincial tour to ten cities, beginning up north in Scarborough. Although the town's summer season was drawing to a close, there was still some entertainment taking place, and I was pleased to see Max Jaffa with his fellow musicians playing there at a popular hotel. He was married to the daughter of Sir Louis Gluckstein, one of my staunchest supporters on the Festival Ballet board. It was in Oxford that *Summer Solstice* received its first showing to a most responsive and appreciative audience. In the early part of the tour I travelled to the BBC Pebble Mill studios in Birmingham to take part in *Any Questions*, which I found rather daunting at first but then actually enjoyed as it went along.

33 *To Russia And Around*

Following the broadcast I flew with my ballet master Donald to Budapest to see their full-length ballet *Spartacus*, given by the Hungarian National Ballet. The choreography was by Laszlo Seregi, whose version I had heard was good, so hoped it might be suitable for our Company. My Hungarian ballerina, Miklosy, was guesting there at this time so had arranged our hotel rooms and theatre seats, being terribly excited at our visiting her home city. On arrival she brought her mother to welcome us and later we met her stepfather and young nephew: a loving family. *Spartacus* was a most thrilling production, but used a larger number of men than we could produce. Highly dramatic and using intricate steps, there was too little dancing overall. This was a disappointment: I wanted a dramatic full-length ballet not given by other British companies.

Arrangements were made in London for Donald and me to continue on to Georgia via Moscow, where we were booked to spend two nights. On the aircraft we got into conversation with a Russian history lecturer and a musical comedy director who had been visiting Italy. At Moscow airport we had trouble with a huge, officious woman over filling in goods declaration forms and were grateful to have our two new friends there to help us. We were eventually rescued by another official, a pleasant man who took us into his office. We were not on the list of arrivals so, as far as the authorities were concerned, we were not officially there, despite having our visas with us from London. As we were not expected, no hotel bookings had been made, and the man told us to wait while he tried to find rooms in a hotel.

After two hours, we were told rooms had been found for Donald and me in a non-Intourist hotel twenty kilometres from Moscow. When we got there, a woman at the desk flew into a rage saying she had no rooms. After a long wrangle she produced a key for a double room which we refused, insisting she found two singles. After exchanges of more unpleasantries, she miraculously found two single rooms. I fell exhausted onto a hard bed in a sparsely furnished room some time after two that morning, worried by not knowing exactly where we were and hoping I would find Donald again in a few hours time. To my relief, we met up safely at a quarter to nine as planned.

We tried to phone Intourist from the desk in the hall as there were no phones in our rooms. But others – Germans, Asians and Americans – were also using the phone and attempting to find other hotels in the city. Whenever we had the phone, Intourist was permanently engaged. We decided to ring a Mr Field at the British Embassy who I was told would have been informed of our visit. He had been trying to locate us and suggested we meet at the Metropole hotel in Moscow as soon as possible and, if there were no taxis (which was the case), to take a bus. On arriving with our luggage we were so glad to see him, especially as after further enquiries Intourist were still unable – or was it unwilling? – to find us accommodation. Mr Field took us to the Embassy and then to his flat where we met his American wife and their son. They kindly gave us lunch, after which Field suggested we went sightseeing while he returned to the Embassy to see what could be done about our accommodation. Intourist were still unhelpful so Field decided that Donald should stay with them while I would stay at the flat of Mr Sculland, a colleague, using their daughter's room, which I found to be warm and cosy.

There was only a brief time in which to change and be driven to the Bolshoi for a performance of *Swan Lake*. We were met at the director's entrance and seated in the box above the directors with an ideal view of the stage. To our surprise a lot of the mime in all four acts was replaced by dance. In the third act there were no longer the exciting Hungarian, Polish and Neapolitan character dances. Instead classical ballet solos were performed to the same music, which meant the contrast which the national dances provided was lost. The dancers were, as always, fantastic, their elegance and beautiful arabesques achieved only through years of hard training. Above all, the total absorption in their roles shone through the performance especially that of Bessmertnova (married to the artistic director Yuri Grigorovitch) and her partner Tikhomirov. They must have been exhausted after the show, having given their all to a packed house, and we had a long wait to congratulate them. We left uplifted and inspired by the performance and wishing that Intourist could have shown the same generosity of spirit.

It seemed unreal awaking in the diplomatic ghetto of Moscow next morning, and I realised how kind it was of Mr Sculland to have taken me in and allowed me to use his daughter's bedroom. I slept soundly not waking much before nine, which was as well – it was to be a full day. We went first to the Bolshoi, to the stage door entrance Number 15 to watch classes and rehearsals. Only after a lot of toing and froing on the doorkeeper's part were we allowed to enter and find Semeyonova taking the corps de ballet girls class. She was strict with them but, on seeing me, rose and embraced me affectionately. She was a wonderful person and a marvellous teacher, and we had to drag ourselves away to see Asaf Messerer taking a class for the principal male dancers. In class working hard were Vassiliev, Fadyechev, Liepa and Levashev, who had been my brilliant evil magician when I danced *Swan Lake* at the Bolshoi. It felt good to be back with them again and to be so affectionately greeted.

Once Messerer's class was over we watched Ulanova coaching Maximova and Vassiliev dancing *Cinderella,* their every movement carefully scrutinised. Then came Timofeyeva, recently returned from having a baby, and with whom Ulanova was equally meticulous. By 3.30pm Donald and I collected our tickets from the box office for the following evening's performance, grabbing a late lunch before contacting Intourist again. Surprisingly they now found two single rooms for us at the new Intourist hotel in Moscow and we hurried to check the rooms. After taking a taxi to collect our luggage from our kind hosts, Mr Sculland insisted on driving us to the Intourist hotel and helped us take the luggage to our rooms. We made a swift departure, running over the bridge to the Kremlin Palace theatre where we were booked to see *The Fountain of Bakhchisarai.* It was most enjoyable, although the dramatic impact was lessened by the vastness of the building and the distance between the artists on stage and the public out front – far away across the other side of the orchestra. I was particularly thrilled to find that my former partner Kondratov was dancing the leading role as Khan Girei, which added extra interest and pleasure to the evening.

Returning to the Bolshoi on our second day I revelled again in the careful tutoring as well as the dedication of the dancers whose love and respect for their art was obvious in their work. We reluctantly left later that afternoon for a cocktail party at the British Embassy, which was most congenial and great fun. I was keen to see Maya Plisetskaya's new ballet *Anna Karenina* that evening, hoping it might be a possible addition to the Festival Ballet repertoire. It was an amazing work, the story unfolding clearly with each act building to a dramatic end. I liked the costumes and the music which had been specially composed by Plisetskaya's husband, Rodion Shchedrin. A life-sized train was brought on stage which, although contributing to the ballet's success, would have made it impossible to stage anywhere in London and certainly impractical for us to tour. It was out of the question, and I was bitterly disappointed – it would have been a wonderful ballet to present to London. It would also have meant a lot to Plisetskaya who had been so remarkably kind and helpful to me during my brief season at the Bolshoi. It was not only the end of my optimistic idea but the end of our visit to Moscow.

The journey to Georgia next day was awful. On landing at Tbilisi there were no taxis, but a kind man who witnessed our plight took us to the other side of the airport and organised with an efficient young girl a car to take us to the Evira hotel. This was just two blocks from the theatre, modern and with fine views. Donald and I immediately reconfirmed our return flights to Moscow for the next day and then dashed to the theatre. I was instantly recognised, and it was explained that that they had been unable to get news of our whereabouts, or even when we would be arriving, until a short time ago.

Chaboukiani had been at the airport the day before waiting for us while we were unable to phone him from Moscow. Working through the Russian authorities was a nightmare.

We arrived in time to see the entire *La Bayadere*, but to our great disappointment found it rather old fashioned. Not only were the costumes, scenery and lighting poor but the presentation was unexciting with long pauses between solos for applause. Obviously out of the question for presentation to sophisticated London audiences. It was terribly embarrassing as Chaboukiani had hoped we would wish to take it into Festival Ballet, and we had to be as tactful as we could. I felt awful about it and slept badly.

At the airport the next morning, after numerous announcements of further delays, I used my limited Russian to complain, and we were transferred at once to another plane which was about to leave for Moscow. Once safely landed there, everybody we approached was vague about departures for London and we could find out nothing at all. Once again we fell back on my Russian, which worked wonders and a porter emerged to carry our luggage and take us out onto the airfield, depositing us at the all-important Intourist hut. It was not long before they sat us in a plane for London where I was more than relieved to land several hours later. Leaving Donald at the station, I took a train to join my husband and son, already at Hever for the weekend.

34 *Home In Britain – Galina And Andre Move On*

Back with the Company in Oxford and to high drama backstage during the evening show. The dress rehearsal of *Summer Solstice* had gone well that afternoon, commencing only marginally late, the lighting of the new work having taken a little longer than planned. But during the performance the hangings got fouled up, and Moreland exploded at our stage crew and Ray, who he blamed for having missed the hanging of the scenery on Sunday. Sarony was deeply shocked by Moreland's outburst, telling him: 'This is a rep company, constantly touring,' and wanted me to tell him off. But I felt for Moreland, having suffered agonies of apprehension myself during first nights when nerves are on edge, so I let it pass. After the performance we went to dinner where Moreland and his designer, Dunlop, lighting designer, John B Read, and our three leading dancers – Fulton, Dubreuil and Loggenburg – were sitting together. We got together over a drink and delicious food: the cloud had burst and the sun was out again.

The autumn tour was a roller-coaster, with Heather and me always at work. Whether on a train to join the Company or back to London, or in a theatre, with Joanie helping Vass, Donald and me with the casting and rehearsal schedules, we were busy. Heather was a wonderful workaholic who I relied on more and more. She managed to organise and fit in my many other commitments outside the Company, as I held numerous other positions – like President of the Association of Ballet Clubs, a post I had held since wartime. These clubs were numerous across the country, an important link for visiting ballet companies encouraging dance enthusiasts to join a ballet club and pass on their interest to others. I tried to visit as many clubs as possible when on tour, giving talks and thereby stimulating audience numbers.

I was a member of the ISTD Council, on the Executive Board of the RAD, there were the Sunshine Homes All England competitions and annual gala to arrange, as well as being a governor of my old school, Dame Alice Owens. The school was heavily supported by the Brewers' Company and was poised to move from the Angel in Islington to the countryside around Potters Bar where the intake was expected to be of a higher standard. I became increasingly aware of the importance of education and was often invited to school prize-giving events as their guest of honour. I tried to accept these unique opportunities to talk with school children and students as I handed them their awards. It was a humbling experience. When I gave a speech I always tried to underline the importance of hard work to achieve success and the happiness that success can bring.

A great highlight came during the autumn of 1972: I was invited to a luncheon at Hampton Court Palace in honour of President Heinemann of the West German Federal Republic. I felt privileged to be at such a distinguished gathering. I could hardly believe I was in Hampton Court, a palace which featured so vividly in my school history lessons. It was a colourful scene with many well dressed women, almost all wearing hats (I wasn't) against the backcloth of beautiful hanging tapestries.

I reluctantly left Hampton Court for the office, where Findlay told me that Andre and Galina were leaving to form their own company. I hoped this would not affect our popularity with foreign impresarios – Galina was an outstandingly gifted ballerina with a big following. Her departure would give my other ballerinas more opportunities to shine and few would miss Andre, but I was sad that they were going, having adjusted to their idiosyncrasies.

Heather and I were not the only ones missing Peter B. I had written to him about our activities to date, and now, with the tour almost finished, he was back after an absence of eight weeks. It was good to have him about again with his observant eyes and acerbic quips.

Swan Lake and *Nutcracker* drew big audiences on the Autumn tour as well as the two triple bill programmes comprising *Noir et Blanc, Petrouchka, Graduation Ball, Summer Solstice, Mendelssohn Symphony* and *Schéhérazade.* The tour finished on December 2nd in Wales at the New Theatre, Cardiff, with the same classic with which we had begun the tour: *Swan La*ke. Our choreographic workshop at the Collegiate Theatre in Holborn took place soon after our return to town, during a three-week rehearsal period allocated primarily for the new *Fanfare for Europe* ballets. These were to be given at a special gala on January 9th 1973 at Festival Hall, at the end of our traditional Christmas *Nutcracker* season.

Some colourful meetings were taking place at the office: the choreographers, their designers and our two electricians – and every department fully stretched preparing costumes, scenery and new music scores for the historic evening. We had the usual tugs of war, but nevertheless things were forging ahead. Docherty was keen for me to see his work for Hynd's *Mozartiana.* The designs for the costumes were lavish but the models for the scenery, though equally rich, were impractical for staging at Festival Hall. This meant changes but Docherty wouldn't budge, other than moving two problematic side steps back a few feet, still on stage where I thought they would hardly be seen anyway! After speaking to Moreland's designer, Nadine Baylis, Ray was asked to try and dissuade Moreland from opening up the rear of the stage. Moreland wanted to reveal the back steps so that the dancers could enter down these in a novel way. Everyone on our staff agreed with Nadine, so this was finally ruled out, despite Moreland's protests. This part of the creative process has always seemed miraculous to me – especially when all the problems are finally overcome.

With Christmas Day 1972 falling on a Monday, our *Nutcracker* dress rehearsal at Festival Hall took place on the Saturday, giving the Company two completely free days before our opening Boxing Day Tuesday. But illness attacked, and Dubreuil gallantly appeared at both the matinee and evening shows. He partnered Miklosy well at the matinee and at the evening press show partnered Fulton beautifully. Breuer and Gielgud flew in from Düsseldorf two days later and were already on next evening. Breuer had greatly improved his overall presentation and was a perfect height for our tall Gielgud.

Sarony and I arranged a morning meeting with Moreland, who turned up late and in aggressive mood. With the gala now much closer, it was worrying that he was working so slowly on his new ballet but, instead of apologising, he grumbled at the lack of rehearsal time. Yet, as I told him, we had given him more time than the other choreographers. With his ballet completed, Hynd had already left for the continent on Christmas Eve. I assured Moreland he would be given as much time as we could fit in for his work but, as we were giving two shows a day, there was little time left for rehearsing anything but emergencies. A partnership I was trying to develop between Noleen Nicol and Jonathan Kelly was beginning to show encouraging results – his height complementing hers.

Jippy meanwhile was being dramatic, telling the Company he was leaving at the end of the year after having been refused an increase in salary by Findlay. Many of the dancers told him not to be so silly and tried to dissuade him. Before the end of the week – and the year – Andre had hurt his back again and was off. Once more Dubreuil came to the rescue and partnered the reluctant Galina most masterfully.

Sven and I celebrated the New Year in Harley Street, at the home of his eye surgeon James Hudson. The evening started at eight thirty with a splendid dinner in Hudson's two consulting rooms, now wondrously transformed: sliding doors opened to allow a large dining table down the centre. Sven had been seeing Hudson regularly since his eyes had begun to give him trouble, and they had struck up a friendship which led Hudson to invite us for New Year's Eve.

With dinner finally over, we withdrew upstairs to watch television and greet the coming year. The Queen's New Year's honours list appeared on the screen and, to my utter astonishment, there was my name with a CBE. This was unbelievable – everyone was congratulating me and saying 'why didn't you tell us you were to have this honour?' How could I when I did not know it was to happen? Early in the autumn I had received a letter stating my name had been put forward for consideration for an award and would I be willing to accept this if approved. My reply had been a yes, but as I heard no more I presumed it was not to be and forgotten about it. What a wonderful surprise. The thrill to be awarded an honour… and a CBE! I was so excited and completely stunned, as were Sven and Ingvar. So after half an hour we said our farewells and Sven whisked us away to celebrate at the Savoy – just we three. I can never forget this time and think it was wonderful to have the honours list only announced at the New Year and not given out well in advance as happens now.

35 *1973 – New Ballets*

The first week into the New Year and the Company were still at Festival Hall busier than ever working on all the new ballets before, and in between, the two shows of *Nutcracker* each day. I had an amusing session on a radio show titled *Petticoat Line* as well as a serious interview on the BBC's French radio service. Clement Crisp delivered a talk on 19th-century ballet to our Festival Ballet Club.

Once the final curtain closed on the Christmas season, frantic activities commenced backstage: the speedy take-down, loading and despatching of *Nutcracker* scenery and its paraphernalia to make way for the rigging of all the new ballets. Any new work at Festival Hall presented a challenge and was time-consuming. This had to be completed and lit ready for the first evening call on Monday and final dress rehearsal on Tuesday, for the gala that night. For me, the Monday was a bit of a nightmare – overseeing everything going on at Festival Hall as well as presiding over the Sunshine Gala matinee at Drury Lane. Lady Astor kindly gave Princess Margaret lunch at the Savoy, then bringing her to Drury Lane in time for me to welcome our Royal guest for the matinee. All went smoothly and Princess Margaret charmed and inspired everyone by her knowledge and genuine interest in the dancers themselves, talking to the young aspirants on stage before leaving.

I then had to hurry back to Festival Hall to see how the new ballets were looking on stage, each within their own specific settings. It was an exciting few hours leading up to the important *Fanfare for Europe Gala.* Many dignitaries were to attend and I felt particularly happy to welcome Prime Minister Edward Heath to see my Company. After the highly successful performance, the GLC had arranged a marvellous sit-down dinner in the Festival Hall restaurant to celebrate the country's partnership with Europe. We had presented four world premieres: three complete ballets and a pas de deux – Hynd's *Mozartiana*, Darrell's *La Péri* and Moreland's *In Nomine* with specially composed music by Maxwell Davies, plus *Glazunov* Pas De Deux, a short creation by Frank Schaufuss for his son. Also new to this country was the solo *Forme et Ligne* created by Maurice Bejart for Gielgud at the time she was in his company. Closing the evening's programme was the ebullient *Bourrée Fantasque.* What a relief to realise that the preparations had not been in vain and that the dancers had excelled themselves. Departing from Festival Hall on such a high note, I felt so proud of the Company.

Two days later we opened with *Swan Lake* at the New Victoria, which was followed by a week's triple bill and then Jack Carter's lively version of *Coppélia* for the final week. The euphoric spirit was suddenly dimmed by a tragedy: Jippy, Jean-Pierre Alban, committed suicide. After swallowing numerous packets of aspirin and bottles of whisky in the middle of the night, he jumped from his upstairs flat in Nell Gwynne House. This was terrible and almost impossible to comprehend. He was depressed that his dancing days were drawing to a close, but his future as a leading character artist in the Company had been secure. Although this was a position of importance and great value to the Company I presumed he did not want it and, being the highly emotional artist he was, decided to end his life while he could still dance. I was dreadfully upset – I was fond of Jippy who had partnered me in the late fifties as Benno in *Swan Lake* when I guested with the Company in London and abroad.

He had always said he was Egyptian and had no relatives other than an obscure uncle who, in the absence of any parent, had brought him up. This was found to have been a figment of Jippy's imagination – he was in fact German. Dear, dear Jippy, he was such a kind, generous person who delighted in giving presents. He was with the Company for many years, and I realised how much I and the Company would miss him. His funeral took place during the Victoria season before we left for a week's much needed holiday, which helped take us away from this great sadness.

There were several new ballets to prepare for the coming Coliseum Spring season, and it was marvellous to welcome Massine back with us again to stage *Le Tricorne* with its stylised Spanish choreography. We were to present it in Eastbourne prior to its showing in London. Massine was also to revive his *Gaîté Parisienne* for our Coliseum gala in April and brought his choreologist Pietra to teach the ballet. *Conservatoire* would also receive its first showing in the Gala, and Mona Vangsaa was already training our dancers in the classic Danish style. This was essential for the delicate Bournonville ballet, first performed in Copenhagen in 1849 by the Royal Danish Ballet.

Another wonderful ballet I managed to obtain for the Company after numerous appeals to Anthony Tudor was his dramatic *Echoes of Trumpets.* For two years Tudor had been director of the Royal Swedish Ballet and whilst there had created this ballet on the company. So before Christmas I went to Stockholm with Ray to see if it would tour. Ray had no doubts, and it was then agreed Tudor would send two people to teach the ballet ahead of his arrival.

Tuesday of our rehearsal period was a propitious one for me. I went to Buckingham Palace at ten in the morning to receive a CBE from Her Majesty the Queen. Entering the palace I was aware of an atmosphere of quiet dignity and restraint. I was shown to an area where, with others, we were told the procedure, what to do and the order expected. The investiture took place at the far end of a long ornate room where many people, including Sven and Ingvar, were seated. There was a band playing and, at the appointed time, I was directed to walk forward and curtsy to Her Majesty. On being handed a medal the Queen pinned it onto my pink coat while congratulating me and speaking encouragingly. After a few more words and a further obeisance I left her Royal presence and was ushered to a nearby passageway. I rejoined Sven and Ingvar after the investiture and press photos were taken outside in the palace courtyard. We walked across to Marlborough House where, in a small cosy gatehouse, William (Billy) Tallon was waiting to congratulate me, welcoming us with champagne and tempting food. He was a great follower of the ballet and a friend of Anton Dolin and John Gilpin. William became one of my most loyal supporters, and I felt most fêted and touched by his kindness and enthusiasm.

The second rehearsal week saw the arrival from Copenhagen of the great mime artist Niels Bjorn Larsen who had come to teach the *Romeo and Juliet* pas de deux from Frederick Ashton's full-length ballet created for the Royal Danish company in 1955. Peter Rice, the designer of that production, had already been to our office to discuss his supervising the making of both costumes, as Ashton wanted. We were running out of space, so these calls were held at Dance Centre. There, after two days learning the pas de deux, it was ready for Frederick Ashton himself to produce. I envied my two principals, Fulton and Schaufuss, having Ashton put his magical touches on their interpretations.

The Company worked full-out rehearsing the repertoire for our forthcoming fortnight in Eastbourne where on the first night – as well as *Mendelssohn Symphony* and *Noir et Blanc* – Massine's *Le Tricorne* was to have its premiere. We arrived in Eastbourne in good time for the Sunday evening piano dress rehearsal of *Le Tricorne.* This followed the hanging and lighting of the fabulous Picasso sets and front cloth – all carefully supervised by Massine. He oversaw every detail and as I sat watching I realised nothing escaped him: every little detail had to be exactly correct. How fortunate we were to have Massine amongst us, a truly great artist in every way. To everybody's delight, the evening's performance was a big success, and *Le Tricorne* received a good reception. To my relief, Sanchez and Nicol as the Miller and his wife were both excellent and even Massine was pleased with them.

After the triple bill premiere the Eastbourne Ballet Club kindly entertained the Company with food and wine, which was thoroughly enjoyed. We were always warmly received in this elegant seaside town, and what pleased me was the interest shown by the local Chelsea College of Physical Education. The college was housed in Eastbourne with fine playing fields on the outskirts, and their principal, Audrey Bambra, always asked for her students to be allowed to watch some of our classes and rehearsals. This was the only college in Britain who came to us with such a request, and I thought it reflected well on its ethos. The students came every year and sat quietly in the circle, absorbing all that was taking place on stage. The college is now named Eastbourne University, a campus of Brighton University, in new buildings with a thriving number of students.

By the weekend Massine, his assistant Pietra and Ray with his stage crew were already in the Coliseum working hard for the opening of our season on Tuesday. We were giving *Le Tricorne* for the first time in London so Massine was on the spot through the day and evening to check on the hanging and lighting of his masterpiece. The ballet is a wonderful example of the value of collaboration between designer, choreographer and composer. Next morning at ten I gave class, with Massine arriving early for his rehearsal of *Gaîté Parisenne*, a new addition for the Company to be given at the gala.

By Monday evening the theatre was buzzing with first-nighters and press eager to see what Festival Ballet could do with *Le Tricorne.* It was well received and Massine, still a striking figure, came on stage at the end to great acclaim.

Our gala was a glittering occasion with the brightest of stars, HRH Princess Margaret, lighting up the entire evening, displaying her enjoyment at the diversity of the programme. It began with the Bournonville ballet *Conservatoire*, followed by a Balanchine pas de deux, *La Source*. After the interval came two more pas de deux – Ashton's *Romeo and Juliet* and Bejart's *Webern Opus 5* – followed by Darrell's short ballet *La Péri.* The second interval over, the Company gave *Gaîté Parisenne* for the first time, bringing the gala to an exhilarating finish. As hoped, the Princess greeted the Company on stage, meeting our three guest artists: Violette Verdy and Helgi Tomasson from New York City Ballet and Peter Breuer from Düsseldorf Opera Ballet. HRH then came to a small informal party given by the recently knighted Sir Max Rayne and his wife Jane in their lovely Hampstead home, making it a happy ending to an exciting but long, nerve-racking day.

Tudor had arrived in time to attend the gala and by the next afternoon was already rehearsing *Echoes* on stage in the set, which was exciting. This followed the morning's run-through of Ben Stevenson's *Three Preludes*, being premiered that evening. To Rachmaninoff's music, he chose Fulton to dance a balletic encounter with Dubreuil across a practice barre. *Petrouchka, La Péri* and *In Nomine* made up the rest of the programme, the latter in the Coliseum for the first time.

Echoing of Trumpets was a highly dramatic work inspired by the brutality and horrors that had taken place in Lodz during its occupation in the Second World War. I knew that working with such a great genius as Tudor on this sensitive subject would be a wonderful experience for my dancers, as well as developing their acting ability. I was thrilled when at the first performance two weeks later, at the end of April, it received an ovation. The repertoire had needed a powerful dramatic ballet and with this, thanks to Tudor, I felt the Company had made a big step forward.

36 *Barcelona*

As soon as the five-and-a-half-week Coliseum season was over we flew to Barcelona, opening in the beautiful Gran Teatro Liceu on Wednesday. We always enjoyed our annual visit which had become a tradition, and I particularly looked forward to renewing my acquaintance with the owners, the Pàmias. They were a delightful, middle-aged couple who were kind, treating me like a daughter throughout our stay. They often took me out for dinner or lunch, dragging me away from rehearsals saying I worked too hard. They were keen for me to accompany them to watch a bull-fight but, not wishing to offend them, I made copious excuses. They wished me to observe the grace and skilful agility of the matadors, of whom, as Catalans, they were justifiably proud. I could not endure watching an animal taunted to its death and was able to avoid this particular experience. During our week of performances we managed to give five different triple bill programmes. *Echoing of Trumpets* scored the greatest triumph despite this work having no famous female leads.

Barcelona was just the start of a fascinating summer. After performances in Venice and Lausanne, returning for a brief rehearsal period in London, we were away again – touring to Istanbul, Izmir, Granada, Carcassonne, Marseilles and Vichy. As well as the triple bill repertoire we carried four full-length classics: *Nutcracker, Swan Lake, Sleeping Beauty* and *Giselle.* The scenery, costumes and skips were transported by camions generally in advance of the Company, who normally travelled in two coaches. This way we saw something of the country and countryside which, though sometimes tiring, was always interesting and enjoyable. When the coaches stopped every so often, dancers could be seen by the roadside, exercising or practising some new pas de deux tricks.

Sven was able to come to Venice during our fortnight of performances there, before the Company left for Lausanne where two performances of *Nutcracker* were programmed. I left Venice a couple of days earlier returning to London for a meeting with Peter Farmer, Ray and Findlay. We talked through Ben Stevenson's forthcoming full-length *Cinderella*, for which he had chosen Peter Farmer as the designer. It was to have a number of magic transformation scenes requiring detailed guidelines, so there was a lot to draw up. Once again, Gorlinsky talked with us about Nureyev putting on his version of *Sleeping Beauty* early in 1975. Though a big coup for Festival, this would mean employing the costly designer Georgiadis who came to see Findlay and me so we could have a realistic idea of the costs involved in order for us to present at our next Executive meeting.

Doreen Wells, ballerina at Covent Garden, was considering guesting with the Company and had an appointment with Findlay and me to discuss this possibility. As the Marchioness of Londonderry she was now related through marriage to Max, who I knew would be pleased if she were to appear with us. Farmer was soon back in the office to show us some designs before I flew to Geneva, where I took a bus to reach the Company in Lausanne in time for our opening night.

On returning to London the Company worked hard with Stevenson, learning his *Cinderella*. He again chose Fulton as his ballerina – it seemed the pair had an affinity, as do so many choreographers with certain dancers. A choreographer is often drawn by a dancer's personality and specific way of moving which inspires their creative process. After two weeks of concentrated rehearsal, Stevenson departed and we too soon left for some exciting venues abroad.

Our first stop was Turkey where we staged *Giselle* in Istanbul at the Open Air Theatre, a magical setting. We also gave a triple bill programme of *Night Shadow, Tchaikovsky* pas de deux, *Webern Opus 5, Le Corsaire* pas de deux and *Études* before going to the port of Izmir (known in the past as Smyrna, a city enshrined in history), to dance the same triple bill in the beautiful Open Air Theatre. But it is Spain, at the Generalife Granada, which stands out most vividly. The dancers appeared in front of the Summer Palace across the moat and, with the reflections in the water, the effect was spellbinding. Carcassonne was also wonderful in a different way. We walked across fields to reach this walled city and it was rather like going back in time, climbing its cobbled narrow streets to the Théâtre du Midi where *Swan Lake* magically materialised. Two more French cities, Marseille and Vichy, brought this incredible trip to an end and the commencement of a well deserved, three-week holiday.

37 *Sardinia Sojourn, New Dancers And Filming*

Edward Seago, the artist whose paintings were so much admired by the Queen Mother, was also a great supporter of both Merle Park and myself. He kindly offered Sven and me the use of his vast apartment in Sardinia where, with Ingvar, we spent a marvellous two weeks. We loved the quiet sandy beaches where one could swim undisturbed, revelling in the peace of the unspoilt countryside. Fragrant wild herbs dotted the landscape, flourishing under the glorious sunshine. We saw a lot of a friend Graham Hill who, with his daughter, was staying in their house a little distance from Porto Cervo. He had a splendid motor-boat and took us on many lovely excursions to the small islands around the coast or to his friends further north. He was a good pianist and took pleasure in accompanying me as I danced in his lounge. His house nestled against a little hill and had a flat roof. Sometimes, after a glass of wine, we would dance up there in the moonlight to the sounds of music from Graham's gramophone.

I welcomed a rested Company back for another year of performances and all that it might entail. During the fortnight rehearsal period Ben Stevenson was totally occupied with his *Cinderella* calls and its staging. This three-act ballet was to open the four-week Festival Hall season and, within a fortnight, we had a costume parade in Donmar – Peter Farmer's work was carefully scrutinised and necessary adjustments made. It was exciting when our stage crew moved into Festival Hall setting up the new scenery, focusing and lighting it through Tuesday night, finishing so the dancers could move in for the piano dress rehearsal on Wednesday afternoon. Our Ballet Club came to the orchestral dress rehearsal next morning from eleven to three o'clock, and I was glad then to slip away to my hairdresser before the premiere that Thursday evening. It was a joy to witness Fulton's success with Stevenson's at the curtain calls, and it was obvious that the Company had acquired another successful, full-length ballet.

It was a successful month which included, amongst many other engagements, lunch with Lord Harewood, Chairman of the Coliseum board, cementing our long-term relationship with the Coliseum. Our link with the Coliseum was crucial for the future of the Company as it was the perfect theatre for ballet, having a good-sized stage with clear views from every seat in the house. Hurok had again been to a performance. Findlay and I dined with him afterwards and affirmed our interest in the Company performing in the United States, providing they did not undertake long tours.

Carole Hill had come to us from the Royal Ballet and been with us for a year, fitting in beautifully as an accomplished, attractive leading ballerina. Now Kerrison Cook, male principal of the Royal Ballet touring company, came to see me about joining Festival. Shortly after, two more principals of the touring Royal Ballet – Patricia Ruanne and Paul Clarke – contacted me, also expressing their wish to join the Company. I liked their enthusiasm and thought Paul Clarke would make a splendid replacement for Andre who was now only appearing as a guest. I was pleased to welcome them as principals into the Company but pointed out that our salary scale was still below that of the Royal. They realised this, and an agreement was reached for them to join. It was gratifying to have an increasing number of leading male dancers, so necessary with our demanding touring and large repertoire. Earlier in the year, an experienced Spanish principal – Luis Fuente – had joined the Company. A strong, expressive dancer, he had performed with success for several years in America and became a suitable partner for Hill. Adam

Luders from Copenhagen, recommended by Schaufuss, had also joined earlier in the year. Young and talented, Luders developed a charismatic partnership with Nicol as well as emerging as an effortless, classical dancer.

Immediately after the London season closed, the Company began a three-month provincial tour, starting in Scarborough on 17th September and ending in Bradford shortly before Christmas. For the first six weeks we brought to our public a big repertoire: three full length ballets – *Sleeping Beauty, Cinderella* and *Nutcracker* – and two triple bill programmes composed of *Le Tricorne, Echoing of Trumpets, Études, Gaîté Parisienne* and several pas de deux for good measure. We also premiered two small works by young would-be choreographers – *Dark Voyage* and *Silver Apples of the Moon* –but neither surfaced again. We found they were not good enough. There were some exquisite performances by the recently recruited Italian ballerina, Elisabetta Terabust, partnered superbly by Schaufuss, which I found exciting. During the final six weeks, solely touring three full-length classics, much was happening. Ruanne, Clarke and Cook danced the classics with us for the first time, strengthening our line-up of principals. In Birmingham the Pebble Mill TV studios took a big interest in the Company, which was encouraging for us. There were interviews with Vass, and with me and some of the dancers, who also demonstrated their work.

My foreign engagements included flights to Düsseldorf, Malmo and Brussels in the continuing search for interesting new ballets and outstanding dancers. Findlay was a joy to work with, and I appreciated his coming out to see the Company on tour from time to time. He even came to Paignton, where the season was creating much interest as far away as Plymouth and Exeter. We both gave interviews there and in Penzance I gave a talk with two of my soloists who also performed some excerpts to the fascinated audience. Between these engagements, I kept in close touch with the Company travelling to and from their different venues across Britain. In mid November, Jack Carter arrived in Cardiff to begin rehearsals of *Coppélia*. The tour finished up north, in Bradford, putting to rest *Sleeping Beauty* with *Cinderella* until the New Year – to awaken at the New Victoria in London.

Nutcracker came to the fore again at Festival Hall as our regular Christmas offering with the Arts Ed children dancing and acting with much fervour. Gielgud and Loggenburg had the first press night midweek and Miklosy and Bart a press night on Saturday. Both couples received good notices and even the Company, too, bringing 1973 to a happy close.

Barry Moreland was working hard on his new ballet, set to Scott Joplin's electrifying music, which was scheduled for Spring 1974. For his leading characters he chose our three recent recruits: Cook, Ruanne and Paul Clark, with whom he had a certain rapport. He used almost all the dancers in the Company who enjoyed his novel movements to the rhythmical ragtime music.

Findlay informed me of a serious problem of 'fiddling the books' that was going on within the production department and was linked to another theatrical management. This was disturbing but he assured me he had it in hand and would be dismissing the miscreant. Meanwhile the choreologist Suzi arrived to commence setting Massine's *Parade*. As before at Festival Hall, we were desperate for rehearsal space. Donmar was taken by another company but Sarony was able to book us for our last Festival Hall week into the Westminster Ballroom in Sutton Ground. During our subsequent three weeks at the New Victoria the dancers worked in a church hall in Pimlico. It was around that time that two bomb explosions occurred – one at the Earls Court Boat show and the other at Madam Tussaud's – but miraculously no one was injured and Suzi did not seem perturbed. We had been interviewing for a stage manager and finally chose David Mogridge, who showed a real interest and knowledge of ballet. Although young he undertook this position with confidence and cheerfulness and came to be a well regarded and popular member of the Company.

After a week's break, class and rehearsals recommenced on Monday morning the 11th February, as Massine was arriving to work on *Parade* and *Gaîté Parisienne*. We were at the Westminster Ballroom which, though spacious, had a dreadful echo – not helpful to our three hard-working choreographers. Moreland struggled to finish his Scott Joplin work, and Hynd was busy creating his *Fairy's Kiss*.

On Monday morning Sven had insisted on driving me to Eastbourne, which was a wonderful surprise, even though he had to return to London almost immediately. Unusually the Company were opening on a Tuesday which released more stage rehearsal time on Monday through into the evening. This extra time was invaluable as Donald was away accompanying Nicol to Varna where she was to guest, which was exciting. I was feeling particularly pleased because Findlay had heard from Michael Edgley that our proposed Australian tour was definitely to go ahead, and I was already working out in my head the programmes and casting. But Tuesday afternoon brought the disappointing news that the tour was strongly opposed by the Australian Ballet as our dates were too close to theirs. Under the circumstances, Edgley felt he could not proceed with our tour as planned, postponing it for the time being. This was a big blow, but the opening performance in Eastbourne that evening did much to lift my spirits. Fuente was terrific, dominating *Echoing of Trumpets*. To my delight Kerrison Cooke was also outstanding in this dramatic ballet, but in *Schéhérazade* he needed to be more commanding. In *Gaîté Parisienne* Paul Clarke danced superbly, much to Massine's approval, although both Clarke and Cooke needed to improve their character make-up which they had never before attempted.

Nicol returned in time to open our second week with *Swan Lake*, partnered by an ever-improving Luders. Much to my relief the swans were better in performance than at rehearsal, but sadly in Act III Nicol fluffed her fouettés, losing control far too early and without attempting to cover this by replacing them with some other turns instead. Luders leapt into the breach completing the remaining music sequence with turns around the stage. After this shambolic display I could not risk Nicol repeating the episode on Friday, the best night of the week, so switched her evening performance to Thursday matinee. She was furious at this change, threatening to walk out, which upset me. I worried that she might leave which would reflect badly on me, but I had a duty to our audiences so had no choice. Happily she stayed, it blew over and Donald worked with her on her fouettés.

As if that wasn't enough excitement for one week, the next night the new assistant stage manager brought down the curtain too early in Act II, before all the swans concluded their dancing and exited. Then he sent the conductor down to the pit after the interval far too early, before the fire safety curtain was raised. The swans in both acts II and IV were straggly – it seemed there was a blight on the show that week. But things improved. Gielgud came back after her successful guest appearances in Australia and was quickly immersed in rehearsals and performances; utterly dedicated to dance she never spared herself. Moreland took almost all the rehearsal time on his new ballet the *Prodigal Son in Ragtime*, soon to be premiered in Oxford.

On March 1st a memorial service for Lydia Sokolova was held in London at St Martin in the Fields church, which I attended along with many distinguished artists of the dance world. Sokolova was the first English ballerina to dance in Diaghilev's Ballets Russes, which she joined in 1913 and, with the exception of one year's absence performing in music halls with her husband, she stayed with Diaghilev until 1929. She was much loved, an engaging generous personality for whom Massine created several roles including the Miller's Wife in the *Le Tricorne*. I was deeply touched when she gave me the blue, shiny earrings she wore in this ballet. Her real name was Hilda Munnings but, as was customary in the early twentieth century, she adopted a Russian name – more acceptable to the general public who considered that only the Russians were capable of becoming true ballerinas. British ballet made such swift headway to become world famous by the mid-twentieth century thanks to the pioneering determination of two great women – Dame Marie Rambert and Dame Ninette de Valois, without whom we would not see the accolades now awarded to British ballet across the world.

38 *Moreland And Scott Joplin*

Prodigal Son worried me as the leading man, Paul Clarke, had gone down with flu towards the end of our time in Bournemouth, so Moreland cancelled Friday's technical run-through. On Sunday, hearing that Clarke was still ill and might be off for a couple of weeks, we rehearsed all day, when I persuaded Moreland to play the lead himself. But the choreologist Bronwen Curry thought Kelvin Coe already knew some of the work and would be a better choice. Moreland was not in favour, until he himself pulled a muscle in his leg, which left him looking for a possible replacement.

By Monday, the morning and afternoon dress and orchestral rehearsals were fairly fraught and the end of the ballet still not finished. I just hoped Moreland would manage to complete it and dance himself for the opening Tuesday night. But it was not satisfactorily finished and even though the ballet had a terrific reception, helped by the brilliant playing of the orchestra, the end was not properly completed and there were too many pauses in both acts. Terrific excitement built before the performance – Moreland's agent, John Perry, was there and scores of Moreland's friends swarming backstage. Despite the hysterical congratulations after the performance, praising it as worthy of showing as a West End musical, the local press next day was dreadful. Coe, after long rehearsals with Bronwen, danced the leading role the second night with much success. After the excitement and strain of *Prodigal Son*, the switch to *Swan Lake* was a welcome change for the last few performances in Oxford.

There was a great deal to rehearse for the 1974 spring Coliseum season opening mid-April, so both Donmar and Dance Centre were booked for the month's rehearsal period. John Taras arrived from the States and Massine came not only to brush up *Gaîté Parisienne* for the opening night but also to stage his famous ballet *Parade*. This had not been seen in London for nearly fifty years. When it had been premiered by the Diaghilev company in Paris, the collaboration between Massine, Picasso, Cocteau and Satie caused a sensation. Under Massine's keen eye we reproduced Picasso's fantastic sets and costumes from his original designs, which was an exciting undertaking for our scenic artists.

While Hynd went ahead with his new mythical ballet, *The Fairy's Kiss,* Moreland still wrestled with the end of *Prodigal Son*. His agent suggested I brought in Betty Anderton from the Royal Ballet, who apparently knew how to motivate him. Anderton was a good teacher and, as I engaged guest teachers from time to time, this was a good moment to invite her before the London season. The final ending for *Prodigal Son* never really fell into place, although the rest of the work was wonderful and enjoyed by audiences everywhere. I had appointed Moreland resident choreographer three years previously because of the originality of his work.

To my surprise, there had been complaints to Findlay about Paul Sarony and, after a long office meeting, it was decided it was best that Sarony leave the Company. This was a blow to me – I had always trusted and relied on him from my earliest days with Festival. I thought all was well within the Company but never really found out what happened. A charming man, Ray Andrews, was appointed Company Manager in his place with whom people got on surprisingly well, but I missed Sarony.

In our third rehearsal week the most thrilling and unexpected surprise of my life occurred. Heather had organised a lunch at Giovanni's with Fernau Hall, the writer and critic. I frequently entertained people from the press, so this was nothing unusual. I left the lunch to take a three o'clock rehearsal of *Swan Lake*, but as I entered Donmar there was a strange silence and most of the dancers were placed on the floor in swan positions. Donald brought forward a man who stepped boldly up to me saying: 'Beryl Grey – This is Your Life', handing me a big red book. I stammered unbelievingly: 'You are Eamonn Andrews.' Everyone laughed and clapped and from that moment on it was absolutely incredible. The expressions on the faces of the dancers was one of such love and pride that I was deeply moved. Before I could take in what was happening I was whisked away in a taxi to a suite in the White House Hotel where I was given champagne and cakes. I was told that my family knew all about everything that was to happen so there was no reason to contact them. Feeling a little more normal but still in a dream I was driven from Great Portland Street to the television studios close by where they were waiting for me in the make-up department.

Then it was happening and the cameras were rolling. A smiling Eamonn Andrews greeted first my Sven, then our son Ingvar, followed by my father, all with little stories to tell. Friends, relatives and dancers appeared, one by one: my earliest teacher Madeleine Sharp on film with some young pupils performing a short dance for me; the ballet mistress Joy Newton; our director the great Dame Ninette de Valois; my present coach Audrey de Vos; my brother-in-law specially flown in from Sweden; a filmed interview with Nureyev from New York; amongst others, the ballerinas Svetlana Beriosova, Merle Park, Maina Gielgud. To my astonishment my last classical partner Philip Chatfield appeared, flown all the way from Australia for the event. This astonishing evening ended with ten of my corps de ballet dancers entering, together with everybody who had taken part surrounding Eamonn Andrews and me. Eamonn Andrews was so courteous, kind and helpful, such an outgoing lovely person and totally professional. How amazing that so much planning had taken place over the last six months without anyone breathing a word. I had absolutely no inkling; even Sven's brother staying near us was kept totally secret.

The next day I found it difficult to come down to earth again and to concentrate on calls and all the other problems. An extra week to our seven-week Coliseum season was proposed and, after a long meeting with Peter B, Evans and Kern, we finally decided to go ahead and drew up a programme for an eighth week. But it was such an effort, my head in the clouds, still reliving the day before. The many other activities which occurred during that same month paled into insignificance: the arrival of the Dutch National Ballet to Sadler's Wells, two weeks later the outstanding Danish Ballet and their marvellous party at the Savoy following their opening night; and Bejart presenting his enthralling dramatic company. There was growing public interest in ballet, which was really heartening.

It was Bank Holiday Easter Monday when, at two o'clock, we were allowed back on stage at the dear old Coliseum. I took the girls' class prior to rehearsals which went surprisingly smoothly, Massine taking the *Gaîté* run-through as well as watching over *Les Sylphides* about which, to my surprise and delight, he was most helpful; Schaufuss had his beady eye on the *Flower Festival* Pas de Deux, and how I would have welcomed Tudor's presence for his *Echoing of Trumpets*. We were finished by ten that evening and back next morning for the orchestral dress call at eleven after which we felt hopeful about a successful opening. That night the Company danced better than I ever saw them perform before, receiving vociferous applause from the audience.

The press, however, was not particularly kind, and only the Telegraph and Guardian were good. It was disappointing particularly for the dancers who worked hard and whose standard had so obviously improved with each Coliseum season. It was most discouraging; there still seemed to be a lingering belittling of London Festival Ballet among some members of the press. I felt more determined than ever that the Company should gain fair recognition.

By Thursday we changed from the triple bill to *The Sleeping Beauty*, but there were a few incidents before the curtain went up. Backstage things were not running as smoothly as planned. A distraught Dudley von Loggenburg arrived, having been thrown out of his home by his wife – our gifted soloist Christine Hughes, and it appeared that the marriage had finally broken up. She was saying she would not be appearing this season now, but she was quite a drama queen and would, I presumed, calm down. Meantime, the production department were having trouble with the lighting technicians while the scene settings were running 20 minutes behind schedule! An overnight change to *Beauty* was always problematical, presenting a huge challenge to the stage and lighting crews, but they never let the public down – though the dancers might have to lose some precious rehearsal time. All our stage crew were professionals, and I never ceased to wonder at their resilience, resourcefulness and determination. The curtain went up on *Beauty* on Thursday evening almost on time, exhibiting some of our most promising soloists to a full and appreciative audience.

I was having trouble persuading Schaufuss to appear as the Blue Bird in a few performances and exchanged words with Fernau Hall, who looked after his interests. I explained that my other principals were willing to take on this iconic piece when not dancing the Prince and, if well danced, the solo could win greater applause from the audience than the main role. How I wished I could be as firm as Ninette and insist but I could not; Schaufuss was not prepared to comply, thus missing the opportunity to outshine the other protagonist. We were getting nearer an agreement for Nureyev to stage staging and dance in his production of *Sleeping Beauty* and I suspected that his agent Gorlinsky was informing Edgley in Australia of this probability, envisaging a tour there. Edgley now came back to us, suggesting a tour of *Sleeping Beauty* with Nureyev at a future date.

I was increasingly worried about the new ballet by Tim Spain, *Silver Apples of the Moon,* to be premiered during our second week. I lay awake all Monday night uncertain what to do. Eventually, having decided I must cancel the ballet, I arrived at the Coliseum early to stop the planned stage rehearsal. I was met at the stage door by sobbing dancers saying they could not go on in the new ballet as Tim had decided they should dance in the nude. Outraged parents were on the phone. I rang Findlay, asking him to come to the theatre as soon as possible. In a meeting at 10am with Peter B, Donald, Vass, Evans and Findlay, it was rapidly agreed to take the ballet off. Each of us had different reasons; Evans was particularly relieved as the set for *Silver Apples of the Moon* was tricky, involving small hanging lights everywhere. The new short ballet had been scheduled for the Wednesday with *Giselle* but would now be replaced with another short work being premiered that Tuesday evening, Bejart's *Rose Variations* performed by Maina Gielgud.

Evans kindly stayed with me while I broke the news to Spain that a decision had been taken to cancel and remove his ballet from the programme. It was horrible having to tell him but he took it surprisingly well; he must surely have realised I would not have allowed nudity. *Les Sylphides* opened the programme that night, prior to the Bejart premiere, for which Gielgud picked up glowing reviews – not surprisingly as *Rose Variations* had been enthusiastically received. The evening continued with *Echoing of Trumpets* and ended with *Igor*, but as it was a press night both of the critics – Fernau Hall and Nicholas Dromgoole – had heard rumours of the forthcoming cancellation. I had to come clean with them and only hoped it would not get blown up in the press.

Next day, following the dress rehearsal of *Giselle*, I arranged a meeting with Spain and his designer Derek Jarman, at which Evans was present. It was a pretty rough hour, and I was thankful that an appointment in the office brought the unpleasant meeting to an end. Both Heather and Evans feared a demonstration by Jarman over the cancellation of *Silver Apples*. The evening, thankfully, passed without incident, no one commenting on the switch to *Rose Variations* and no demonstration by the designer. The evening's performance of *Giselle* was superbly danced by Schaufuss whose partnering of Terabust enhanced her magical interpretation. Somehow Kern lifted the orchestra to new heights, inspiring the Company to some great moments of mimed tragedy within this Romantic ballet.

On Thursday and Friday, *Giselle* was given with two changes of cast. Gielgud danced Giselle with Paul Clarke for the first time: he gave a beautiful interpretation of Albrecht with Maina dancing a surprisingly sensitive Act II. But I thought she still had a way to go to find the right level of acting in Act I. On Friday evening one of our newer recruits, Kelvin Coe from Australia, danced Albrecht with an easy elegance opposite Gaye Fulton as Giselle. I was delighted with this new partnership which promised well for the future.

Immediately before *Giselle* that night Gielgud had given another premiere: the *Webern Op 5*. This was dress rehearsed, with full lighting and an all-important quartet, that same morning, producing an exciting performance to a fascinated audience. Our stage staff then had a difficult overnight change to *Sleeping Beauty* danced brilliantly at the matinee by Miklosy and Luis Fuente and in the evening by Gielgud and Breuer. Theirs was a different interpretation, Breuer had only flown in on Wednesday to prepare for Saturday's *Beauty*; likewise Bart flew in Thursday to prepare for his performance in *Giselle* Monday with Kessler. I felt it was important to present a number of new partnerships now that Galina and Andre were no longer in the Company.

It was a busy time for us – and for Hynd in particular. His new work for the Sadler's Wells Royal Ballet, *The Brontë Sisters*, had its premiere at the Wells on Tuesday 30th April, followed by *The Fairy's Kiss*, which entered our repertoire next night, Wednesday 1st May. The first of two piano dress rehearsals, with lighting and a complicated set, took place on Monday, running from eleven thirty in the morning right up to the last minute at six pm, with only an hour's break for lunch. All things considered it went surprisingly smoothly – although slowly – as the sets were a challenge to erect. Ruanne as the Fairy was patient and unflappable, which was such a help. Peter Docherty's designs were beautiful and were well constructed, whilst our orchestra appeared to enjoy the challenge of the Stravinsky score.

Hynd had everything well under control, working with our splendid staff, and the Wednesday evening's performance went well. A programme of contrasts with the romantic *Fairy's Kiss*, demure Danish *Conservatoire* and exhilarating *Igor* led by a dynamic Patrice Bart contributed to the success of the evening. I was so pleased for Hynd, and to learn that Sir David Webster from the Royal Opera House had been in the audience.

Friday morning came and with it our weekly office meeting when the new finance controller, Peter Morris, along with Peter Evans expressed their concern at the overspend on *Prodigal Son*. But as it was a novel work, with its Scott Joplin music creating much interest, I felt it had been a worthwhile investment. In the afternoon an Executive meeting at Max's office passed smoothly and even the overspend on *Prodigal Son* was accepted. I was relieved that the Board appeared to understand the ambiguities of budgeting. That evening I was able to be in the theatre as Max with his wife Jane, as well as several others from the Board, were in the audience. I was always pleased when Max, now Sir Max, and members of the GLC (our biggest financial supporters) made time to come to some of our performances. It gave the Company encouragement and an added incentive. We also valued the loyal backing of our Festival Ballet Club who appreciated the Saturday morning's forum on Barry Moreland's *Prodigal Son in Ragtime*.

At the end of a staggering week I was interviewed by Eric Johns, editor of *The Stage*. To my astonishment, he expressed his wish to ghost an autobiography for me. Although flattered, I did not think it was yet time for an autobiography, and most certainly I would like to write it myself. I was touched that he should want to do this for me, so promised to think it over and let him know in a few days time.

The next week started badly, with a disastrous dress rehearsal of *Prodigal Son.* Everything that could go wrong did. None of the technical tricks worked; the pianist was new and hopeless with the Scott Joplin music. 'Bertie' Bassett, as we called our pianist, was busily involved at the orchestral rehearsal taking place elsewhere. The dancers were untidy and sloppy and, when two fell over hitting some newly painted scenery, Evans swore at them, which almost brought a man down from Equity. Barry improved Act I but not Act II, which looked under-rehearsed. The newly acquired masks were a disaster and thrown out (shocking waste of money) and the ending was still far from satisfactory. I was terribly worried. It was due on next day for the first time in London, but it was not yet ready to be seen by the public. My nerves were soothed that evening, however, by a particularly fine performance by Fulton and Schaufuss in *Cinderella*, and they deserved a good press. Tuesday morning brought the final dress rehearsal of *Prodigal Son* with orchestra, which seemed to help the dancers find the right stylised movements so that by a miracle the evening's first London showing was a huge success.

40 *Helpful Harewood*

The Festival Ballet Club were excited that Massine was to give them a talk on Saturday morning about the ground-breaking *Parade* – the latest Massine ballet to enter our repertoire. I was fascinated by his thoughts and ideas on choreography, on which he spoke more fully than on *Parade*. Everyone present was thrilled to watch and listen to this great master. The 3pm matinee saw a promising debut by young Judith Rowan in *Summer Solstice*. Donald and I were delighted with her beautiful portrayal and impeccable dancing which strengthened our belief in her future.

Monday 13th May was ghastly: tensions rose all day, up to the end of an eventful evening. It began when Findlay rang me at the theatre during the *Coppélia* dress rehearsal to say Maina had just told him she would not be going on the next foreign tour. I left a message for her to come and see me, which she did. But she stubbornly repeated her decision not to go on our next tour abroad. I did not ask her the reason nor ask her to change her mind, as I believe no one is irreplaceable. Boris Trailine was due to see me at 2.30pm but didn't appear until three hours later, by when I had departed from the theatre with Massine for first fittings of *Parade.* But Massine was dissatisfied with what he found, and we left the maker, poor Jenny Levy, in tears.

On my return, the performance had started: Kelvin Coe was making his debut as the lead in *Prodigal Son*. The Company were excited for him and Max, Keith Jeffery from the Arts Council and the MP Hugh Jenkins were in the audience. Findlay arranged for John Perry, the agent, to come into our box during the second interval to discuss the Maina problem. We continued this out in the foyer when the curtain went up. Donald raced round aghast to tell me Maina had gone on in *Rose Variations* wearing black instead of the usual pink. We couldn't take her off in the middle of her performance but once off stage I told her off soundly. I returned to the inner lobby and the discussion with Perry, and Sir Max came out from the auditorium during the performance complaining at the noise being made by Coliseum staff washing up glasses and crockery from the previous interval. It was unfortunate that I had a commitment to drive Maina to a reception after the show – it was the last thing I felt like doing.

The next day, Tuesday, we had another schools' matinee and again I gave a short introductory talk to the children before the curtain went up on *Coppélia.* It did one's heart good to hear their squeals of delight as the ballet unfolded, and later receiving their little letters with coloured drawings. I felt proud that Festival Ballet had instigated these special performances. Talks continued between Findlay, me and Perry concerning the contracts of a number of dancers he represented, including Barry Moreland, now the Company's resident choreographer. With Perry pressing for improved salaries I just wished the Company had the money to pay them. It transpired that Trailine himself had rung Maina, who finally agreed to dance on his foreign tour after all. But she neglected to notify Findlay or me. She was a strange being, rather like a chameleon, turning on the charm when needed; perhaps it was all a part of her undoubted artistic temperament!

Looming on the horizon at the end of the week was *Swan Lake*, for which rehearsals were well in hand. The Company were in top form and on Friday night the ballet was well received. This helped cheer me; Sven and I were deeply concerned about our close friend David Clayton-Stamm who had undergone a serious operation the previous evening. We felt helpless. He and Eve came frequently to performances at the Coliseum to support and advise me on many factors. Now suddenly they were not there – David was dangerously ill and poor Eve was at the hospital at his bedside, desperate. We could only pray he would come through and recover soon.

At a pre-arranged meeting with Lord Harewood, I found him most gracious and understanding, as at our previous encounter. He listened to my concern over the photographs of the Bolshoi Ballet on display in the foyer of the Coliseum at the same time as we were performing in the theatre. Our seven-week season had been extended for another week and, with a further three weeks to run, he appreciated the situation and kindly agreed to have them removed. This was music to my ears, and I hoped he could see how much I appreciated his co-operation. By the end of the week we had a few mishaps: two dancers off ill and Miklosy hurting her foot badly. She insisted on appearing at the matinee despite being in great pain. She was a real trouper, a true professional, as x-rays taken later showed a broken bone in her foot.

It was some time since Festival Ballet had given Jack Carter's dramatic *Witch Boy*, a ballet based on the American ballad of Barbara Allen. The leading role was closely associated with Gilpin, and it was thought the time had come to revive the work with Bestonso, our French dancer, in the lead. Although he gave an eerie rendering of the role, somehow it did not equate with Gilpin's supernatural interpretation, and to me Ruanne was wrong as Barbara Allen. All the same it was good to have it back in performance, even though it had only a lukewarm reception Tuesday evening.

Next night Massine's cubist ballet *Parade* was much better received, and Massine was satisfied with the way everything worked. The vibrant Picasso sets and costumes, the amusing Satie score, all contributed to a fascinating presentation. At its emergence in Paris in 1917 it had been considered the perfect union of dance, music, painting and scenario, and in 1974 it was still able to spin its unique spell. How greatly I admired Massine, and how proud I felt to have him working with the Company.

Trailine was back on the phone as Maina was now refusing to appear in Barcelona because she wasn't cast to dance Giselle. This after Findlay and I had taken her to dinner where it became clear that she wanted to be the number one star and to my surprise had even criticised our wardrobe and ballet staff. Trailine let slip that Paul Findlay had written into her contract with the Company her appearance in every city (along with my other top stars.) In order to placate her he wondered if we might consider not taking *Giselle* to Barcelona. I nearly exploded down the phone! By the end of the week it appeared that the Maina saga was resolved diplomatically for good, and she would be with the Company throughout the now imminent foreign tour.

Findlay, Morris and I were increasingly anxious about the financial situation of the Company. We were hearing rumours that the GLC were reconsidering our yearly grant in the light of requests from amateur theatrical organisations within the GLC boundaries. We were still in the red and, despite careful budgeting and tight spending controls, there remained £100,000 to recoup. We desperately needed all the financial assistance the GLC could give us. Despite the astronomical costs of a touring classical ballet company the GLC had always backed us and been supportive and proud of our regular seasons at the Festival Hall. We only hoped this support would continue and even produce an increase in our grant.

On a personal level, Sven and I were in constant communication with Eve or her daughter Valerie to hear of David's condition, which was up and down following his emergency operation Thursday. Ten days later, a Saturday, we heard he had died early that morning. We were stunned and deeply saddened at this loss: it was hard to take in.

During the last week of our Coliseum season Findlay and I saw all our leading dancers about new contracts. We held auditions for the corps, which were disappointing and we did not find any suitable dancers. We had good houses and good performances from the dancers and gave another schools matinee mid-week, which I introduced. That same morning Max, Findlay and I had a meeting at County Hall with the director general of the GLC, James Swaffield, to discuss the current position of Festival Ballet. I came away feeling only faintly optimistic. In the evening Sven and I were guests at the Lord Mayor's Banquet at Mansion House where I was to give a speech. The banquet was a glittering affair – men in white tie and tails and ladies in beautiful full length gowns, many sporting decorations. Although apprehensive, I managed to remember almost all the speech I had spent time writing and memorising. I thought one could communicate better with people when not reading from a script.

The final night of our eight-week season at the Coliseum began with the delicate Danish cameo *Conservatoire.* This was followed by Bejart's *Forme et Ligne* solo piece, the mysterious *Witch Boy*, and the evening finished with an exhilarating *Gaîté Parisienne.* I was expected to say a few words at the end of our seasons and, despite feeling totally exhausted, I believe I spoke well: the reception from our audience as well as from my own dancers was marvellous. Sven and I missed Ingvar's presence but he often came to watch performances from my box. Now twenty, he was studying at London University, and had his own friends with whom he was often invited to stay. He was with his sweet girlfriend Maria Noren and her parents that weekend, so we guessed he wouldn't be home until Sunday evening. This gave me all day in which to clean our home as we were without a cleaner. It was a Georgian house with five floors and had to be kept pristine since Sven saw most of his patients there. I was, moreover, off to Wolverhampton with the Company next morning so wanted to leave everything in good order.

Although there are more beautiful cities than Wolverhampton there are not many theatre managers as welcoming and accommodating as Humphrey Stanbury. We were greeted by the warmest of hugs, and found his office cleared for Heather, with coffee cups on a tray – very gratifying after the two-hour drive from London. The week opened with *Cinderella*, the Company finding the stage a little cramped after the Coliseum. Although not full – Mondays are always the most difficult to bring in an audience – it was enthusiastically applauded and enjoyed.

Next day, back in London, I was given some wonderful surprises for my birthday: flowers, little gifts and cards, including one from the wardrobe staff and the stage crew. I was touched at this unexpected start to my birthday, which I celebrated later with Sven, Ingvar and my father at Giovanni's after a long day in the office.

A clash of personalities was taking place between Carole McPhee and Gareth Forbes in the press and public relations department. Findlay and I discussed the situation and agreed that both were wonderful at their work, and we did not wish to lose either. We had disappointing news from Gorlinsky that Nureyev was unlikely to be free to join us on our Australian tour. I was to ring Nureyev about his staging of *Sleeping Beauty* for us, in which it was agreed he would also dance. I had planned to attend the opening night of the Bolshoi Ballet mid-week but on arriving at the Coliseum I found it besieged by angry protesters and press reporters' cameras at the ready, so I turned away, not wishing to be caught up in such a political mêlée. It was disappointing – I was looking forward to watching the beautifully trained dancers, but I had of course seen *Swan Lake* before!

I returned to Wolverhampton with Heather who was, as always, working in the car all the way as I drove, throwing questions at me and organising my day. I do not know how I could have managed to run the Company without her. Letters and queries were always answered promptly, appointments made for me if convenient; she was indeed my right hand. Back in the Grand Theatre we found the Company in good spirits and on good form with the exception of Miklosy. Her foot was still giving her pain, but she insisted on going on even though it meant her falling back occasionally onto half pointe. Our tiny Cheryl Liss was still in trouble with her foot so I would not allow her to go on. I talked to a corps de ballet girl, Tipler, who after weeks of indecision had decided to leave. Joanna Morduant, a fine tall soloist, asked if she could dance the Wili Queen on our foreign tour, which I said I would think about. Providing she had enough stamina she was ideally suited to this commanding role. To my relief Ray Andrews assured me he was happy to stay as our Company Manager, and Gareth told me he was reconciled to working with Carol: cheering news prior to the coming week's break.

Back in London on Friday and work was non-stop. A long session with Findlay, followed by Morris discussing a possible change to the salary structure, whilst I signed cheques. I received a call from the now famous Russian defectors, Galina and Valery Panov, to say they were definitely out of Russia and hoping to dance with us in London. This would be a coup for the Company, and I couldn't wait to tell Max.

Although the dancers had a week free, most took class each day at Sadler's Wells where rehearsals for the principals were taking place. Donald was able to give most classes as his time away filming had been delayed. During the week of our last performances in Coventry I thanked the Company for their wonderful work through the past year and wished them a good, well earned three-week holiday. Sven and I would take ours in Sweden as usual, with Ingvar and my father.

The last week of July, refreshed, we were in Donmar and Dance Centre working once again. After a fortnight of classes and rehearsing the classics and other ballets we had a three-week season at the New Victoria. During *Coppélia* Terry Hayworth as Doctor Coppelius lost his false nose in Act II. Instead of letting it go, he fiddled around trying to stick it back, to everybody's amusement. For the second week *Les Sylphides* with *Prodigal Son* was a sensational success (the Scott Joplin ragtime music was enjoying a revival). The house was sold out on the first night with people turned away, and the following night a 'HOUSE FULL' sign was posted at the box office to our immense satisfaction. The ever loved *Swan Lake* closed our season at the end of August having taken an unprecedented £67,000 at the box office in three weeks. The staff insisted I went on stage at the end to inform the audience of this achievement. It was unbelievable, and the Company departed in high spirits for the foreign tour.

Our itinerary took us to eight European cities, beginning in Belgium at the Ghent Opera House with *Giselle* and *Prince Igor*. Also included for good measure was the *Don Quixote* pas de deux. On the continent these pas de deux were expected and we invariably added them to our programme for the satisfaction of both agent and audience. Ghent was rather a nightmare, with the Opera House's raked and splintery stage. We had to use tapes and the sound system in the theatre was impossible, the music either booming out or dying to a whisper – and we had no Kern in the prompt corner in control. There were too few stage staff and those present were incredibly slow, unused to dealing with requirements on our scale and at our speed. Neither the curtains nor the lights worked properly so *Giselle* looked too dark. Perhaps this was as well: poor Eva was not happy with the tapes, which seemed too slow, so she was not at her best. There followed an embarrassing second interval with unenthusiastic guests. But after an interminable wait for the lights to go down and the curtain to go up, Schaufuss and Terabust gave a dazzling performance in the *Don Quixote* pas de deux. This was followed by a sensational *Prince Igor* with Dudley in wildest action. A reception after the show given at the local bank by the Festival directors proved a happier event.

Next day, however, Peter Evans, our stage director, had an unpleasant scene with the Festival directors about all the problems we had encountered. They claimed Evans had not made clear what was needed on his earlier visit. Unlikely, as Evans – tall, bespectacled, and as meticulous as the pin-striped suits he liked to wear – was usually explicit in his directives. He could be rude and officious, yet even he could not get the staff to light *Petrouchka* in time for the matinee. It had to be cancelled, like the class and run-through with the dancers, as no one could get on the stage. Miklosy arrived in good time with Bart and the tapes for the Balanchine pas de deux to which they were to perform that day. By the evening Vass had succumbed to a large intake of alcohol, and I had to speak firmly to him. It was embarrassing – he and Joanie were a dear couple and lived for the Company. I knew it would do no good: endeavouring to halt the flow of alcohol with a Russian dancer was like asking a duck to live on dry land.

Arriving in Leuven we found the stage small and slippery. One of our young soloists, Forsey, slipped on a wet floor in the hostel, injuring himself quite badly. Donald, now on edge, his dancers again barred from access to the stage for class and rehearsal due to problems lighting *Petrouchka*, vented his anger on Evans for the first time ever. This sent out shock waves – Donald always appeared unfazed and completely in control. He once confided in me, however, that he always felt nervous before taking company class. I could sympathise as I, too, always felt the same apprehension. It was a comfort to know we shared the same sense of responsibility to give the dancers exercises best suited for their imminent performances and the climate.

As we heard nothing from Trailine, the agent responsible for the Spanish and French legs of the tour, I asked our Company Manager, Ray Andrews, to go ahead to Spain after our second show in Leuven to sort out problems and ensure decent accommodation for the Company. We also sent our top lighting man, David Mohr, ahead to San Sebastian, leaving his assistant to light the evening and matinee performances at the Flemish Theatre in Brussels. At the performance, with many VIPs in the audience, I was seated in the middle of a row of these dignitaries, in continual agony as I watched the appalling lighting in *Giselle.* It was too bright for Act I and too dark for most of Act II, where the usual lighting changes failed to work. The theatre had no smoke guns for our woodland mists, so we made do with dry ice. This quickly evaporated into the orchestra pit as the curtain rose on the mysterious woodland scene and failed to work for the rest of the act. Despite all this and the long intervals (extended for stage setting problems), the audience and the distinguished visitors were delighted with the performance and gave the Company a terrific reception. But, trapped out front, I had not enjoyed one minute.

Next morning I awoke in San Sebastian, blissfully unaware that it was to be the worst day of the tour so far. Our stage director, Peter Evans, went to pieces, and it was a miracle that we got the show on at all. Fellen, the theatre director, claimed that Evans had arrived drunk early that morning, dismissing our crew at 10am and leaving the local stage crew to continue without clear instructions. It transpired that Evans had been rude to Fellen when questioned. On arriving at midday I found no one on stage, no crew rigging the scenery, no one lighting, only a frantic Fellen and the local electrician, who asked me for instruction. Finally finding Evans I told him he could be rude to me but never ever to a theatre director. He grumbled that the local crew were 'no good' just like the crews at our other venues. Somewhat abashed, and certainly the worse for drink, he said he would go back to work with them as he 'couldn't lead the Company into disaster'. I told him to pull himself together and lead the Company to success. The dancers' calls had to be cancelled to enable Evans to get the men busy again and set up the show in time for the opening. The curtain was fourteen minutes late going up and the audience began a slow hand clap. As a local critic later remarked to me, it was not a good start to our San Sebastian season.

For the third morning running I coached Gielgud and Clarke for over two hours in *Giselle* and began to see the emergence of an impressive partnership, after which it was time to travel to Biarritz, our next port of call. The Company were taken by coach while I travelled with Trailine and his wife in their car, giving them a late lunch on arrival at our hotel. Checking progress on stage at the theatre, I found more problems. The front gauze and backcloth for *Giselle* had been left behind in San Sebastian, unchecked by Evans, so once again I had to reprimand him. By a stroke of luck the lost equipment arrived in the nick of time; the audience, unaware of the last-minute adjustments, were swept up in the magic of *Giselle* and thrilled with the divertissements that preceded the classic. The Gala performance in aid of the Red Cross was a wonderful success.

I had to leave Biarritz early next morning for the afternoon Board meeting in London. Findlay and I thought it crucial that Evans, as our technical expert, should also attend to explain certain facts concerning new works. Evans travelled with me and despite our recent encounters there were no ill feelings. The meeting was quite a tough one; criticism was raised at the high expenditure for the Coliseum season, including the heavy orchestral costs. I suggested Moreland, as our resident choreographer, should create a much needed new, full-length ballet for the Company. After a busy morning in London I rejoined the Company in Madrid, where I was met by Peter B and Heather. As always my heart was heavy at leaving Sven, who had made time to take me to the airport, sending me off with red roses and a long, loving embrace.

The orchestra were rehearsing as I entered the Teatro de la Zarzuela and to my delight sounded rather good. The theatre director, a tall and imposing Spaniard, met me. He was charming, but I imagined could be a hard man and I hoped our week in his theatre would pass smoothly – which it did. We gave seven performances of two different programmes, which were very popular. The Company benefited from a week in the same city, especially such an interesting one as Madrid. It was a wonderful surprise when Sven joined me on Friday evening for the weekend. After the show, with Heather and Peter B, we enjoyed watching Spanish dancers performing in a nearby café.

I always enjoyed being in Barcelona. My hotel was comfortable, although a good twenty minutes walk from the theatre. I found it relaxing, walking down the Ramblas, its fine trees offering shade from the strong sunshine. The theatre was a joy, too, with its large, well sprung stage. At the Teatro Liceu that afternoon I was greeted warmly by the staff and stage crew waiting for our lorries to arrive with scenery for the next day's opening. They eventually rolled up two hours late, which put our agent Masso into a panic. It made the working schedule difficult and, like our rehearsals the following day, everything had to be rescheduled. Tuesday's performance nevertheless went beautifully with my dear friends the Pàmias delighted with the programme and witnessing the enthusiastic audience. Our press assistant, Tony Barlow, arrived with Noel Goodwin, a London critic who was staying to cover our week's season.

I suggested to Pàmias that we should give *Les Sylphides* with piano accompaniment, but he didn't like the idea, preferring we use the full orchestra. The lighting for *Fairy's Kiss* was appalling that evening, unimproved from the earlier lighting call which, running late, had been obliged to continue during the dancers' stage rehearsals. Next evening, Evans had a meeting with both the local crew and ours to discuss the overnight get out and overtime pay. Within Masso's earshot there was much disagreement and Evans, accused of unclear directives, lost his temper and became extremely rude. The vitriolic altercations led to one of the Spanish stage crew threatening to report Evans to the Ministry: a tragic ending to our stay in Barcelona, the final stop on our continental tour.

Next morning Peter B, Vass and I went back to the Liceu to apologise for Evans's behaviour, hoping there would be no repercussions nor a bad report made to the Ministry. We first apologised to Masso, then found Pàmias who was unaware of the previous evening's unpleasant confrontations and was surprisingly sympathetic. It was important for us to speak with them both to repair our good reputation before leaving Barcelona. But, as we flew to Aberdeen to begin our ten-week autumn tour of Britain, I still felt perturbed. I spoke with Evans and suggested, in the light of the recent debacle, he return to London rather than work with us in Aberdeen, which he accepted quietly.

42 *Nureyev And Bombs*

On landing at Aberdeen, I had a heartwarming surprise: Findlay was there, with the deputy theatre director, to welcome us and present me with some lovely flowers. After a TV interview I dined with Findlay, filling him in on the recent problems, of which he had no inkling. On Tuesday Findlay and I talked with Mohr, our chief electrician, who wanted Evans to return, and with Mogridge, the stage manager, who did not want him back. Mogridge – the brave man – suggested he himself should replace Evans. Findlay could not come to a decision, so it was decided to postpone any further move until Findlay and I saw our Chairman next day in London. In the event Max was more concerned over the sudden death of one of Festival Ballet's Board of Governors, Peggy Middleton (one of my fervent supporters), and the memorial service for her he had just attended in County Hall.

On hearing that Findlay had received a letter from Evans hinting at bringing in his lawyer, Max thought we should reinstate Evans as the Company could not afford any adverse publicity. I thought this wrong, but did not feel in a strong enough position to stand my ground and oppose Max. Findlay was instructed to ring Evans that afternoon, and they agreed for him to return to Edinburgh the next Thursday. He was to supervise the overnight change-over to the triple bill of *Witch Boy, Graduation Ball* and the *Fairy's Kiss* – his problem ballet. I was not happy about Evans return, having suffered so much embarrassment already from his behaviour but, as Sven said to me over dinner, I had to learn to bend with the wind. On Friday, however, Evans turned up at the office in a rage having heard that Hynd had given the choreologist, Bronwen Curry, authority over and above Evans for *Fairy's Kiss*. Findlay for the first time witnessed Evans in one of his appalling moods.

At the end of the week I received a wonderful letter from the City of London University, offering me a Doctorate of Letters, for conferment in December. I was so thrilled, as was Sven, and I almost cried. After the tensions with Evans, it came as balm and gave me renewed encouragement. My father was especially delighted as the honour came from 'his' city of London where he had spent most of his working life.

Monday morning, after appointments at the office, I took the plane to Edinburgh, arriving in time for the *Coppélia* performance that evening. I felt it necessary to see how the staging looked in Evans's absence. I found it properly set up and well lit and the evening's show ran without a hitch, much enjoyed by the audience. I had to return to London early next morning for a meeting with John Tooley, General Administrator of the Royal Opera House, to discuss our respective future plans over a pleasurable lunch. There were some interesting interviews that afternoon with applicants for the technical director's post. After which, to our annoyance, Findlay and I were kept late by a visit from the agent John Perry. He wanted us to get rid of our choreologist, who we suspected must have upset one of his clients. The Arts Council was insistent that we employ a full time choreologist and, as Bronwen Curry was extremely good at her work, losing her was not something we could even contemplate.

By now my sinus was really troubling me, as it so often did after flying. I had arranged to have dinner with de Vos, together with Sven, and did not want to disappoint her. The evening spent with them though was totally refreshing, and de Vos as always was inspiring and encouraging. She was a fine woman: intelligent, warm-hearted and kind, gallant in the face of opposition (from ill-informed and sometimes prejudiced people) to her way of teaching. She was ahead of her time and like a breath of fresh air. Returning to Edinburgh next day I was in time to see 'little' Loma Rogers as Swanhilda in *Coppélia* at the matinee. She enchanted throughout, especially in Act III when she relaxed into the role and undertook the difficult pas de deux without showing any strain.

Thursday was a day full of contrasts. I took rehearsals of the triple bill. Then several dancers came to see me with different requests – Fuente wanted leave of absence to dance in Madrid, Sanchez wanted encouragement, having made up his mind to stay with Festival Ballet, and Gielgud wanted time off next Wednesday matinee to go to London to see her pointe shoe firm. Her regular shoe-maker had left and she claimed she could not dance well in the shoes now being sent to her. There was also another applicant to be seen for the technical director position. I invited Donald to dinner at my hotel, the Carlton, but he was not allowed in the restaurant without a tie so instead we ate in the cafeteria.

I found myself once more flying back to London for a full Board meeting, joining Findlay and Max at his office en route to County Hall. I was disappointed that Max was not in favour of going ahead with a planned gala in view of the seriousness of the current economic situation. His opinion was supported by all present at the meeting, which was a blow. I was immensely heartened by Sir Louis Gluckstein's concern over the Company still having no home. He asked that serious consideration be given to the joint purchase of the Coliseum Theatre by the GLC and the Arts Council, its use thereafter to be shared fairly between Festival Ballet and Sadler's Wells Opera. All the while, plans for our future collaboration with Nureyev were taking shape. By the end of October we sent Ray to Paris for the day to discuss the technicalities he had in mind for *Sleeping Beauty.* Nureyev was quite adamant that he wanted Georgiadis to design the scenery and all the costumes. Georgiadis was a magnificent designer but costly, and Ray was worried that his elaborate sets might be unsuitable for touring. Nureyev insisted Georgiadis would take this into account when working on the decor. Like Ray, I knew that Georgiadis' fees were astronomical, and I could not imagine Max approving such expenditure.

On November 1st, however, the Executive Committee were extremely excited at the prospect of Nureyev dancing and producing his *Sleeping Beauty* for Festival Ballet. Realising the prestige this would give the Company, a green light was given for Nureyev's production and his appearances. This was passed and approved by everyone present, with the exception of a new representative from the GLC, who asked where the money was coming from. I felt both sad and uneasy about Peggy Middleton's successor and wished Mrs Middleton was still with us.

I rang Nureyev in France to tell him the good news but to my disappointment he was unreachable. By Sunday however I heard that he could be free to come with us to Australia for just two weeks with his *Sleeping Beauty* next summer. Obviously he would need to stage the ballet prior to the tour and premiere the production during the coming Coliseum spring season. This meant postponing Moreland's proposed *Romeo and Juliet* for a year which worried me as I did not wish to upset Moreland. In the event, offering *Sleeping Beauty* in the spring season would secure sound box office takings. Gorlinsky also hinted that a season of *Sleeping Beauty* with Nureyev in Paris at the Palais des Sports might be a possibility later in the year.

A few days on, Max invited Nureyev to his home in Hampstead, indicating his approval and interest in the production. I thought perhaps he might give financial support should the need arise. At the end of the month I had a four-hour session with Nureyev and soon discerned how strong-willed and volatile he was. He had many ideas –some good and some totally impractical – for Festival Ballet. He was keen to bring in a ballerina of his choice to guest with him. I pointed out that he would be expected to dance with my top ballerinas also for some performances, which he finally accepted. The number of performances he would give himself had to be agreed with Gorlinsky, and this would be a battle. Nureyev demanded to dance all the performances, which I could not possibly allow. My own leading men had to be given performances, too, else I knew I would lose them.

The ten-week autumn tour continued with Heather and me driving up and down to the different venues. News came through of bombs in Birmingham on Thursday evening November 21st. To our dismay the explosions were close to the Birmingham

Hippodrome where the Company was performing that week. Findlay and I went up immediately next morning and found a jittery Company. For a short time Patrice Bart had been unaccounted for, as were several others who had already left the theatre but been unable to reach their hotels and digs. The news of the bombing was relayed over the world and within a short time Peter Breuer's family were on the phone from Düsseldorf quite distraught and deeply worried about his safety. This call was the first of many from anxious relatives desperate to know of the dancers' welfare and security. The attack unnerved the dancers, and my ballet staff wisely cancelled their classes and rehearsals that day. But they still gave marvellous performances that evening and Saturday and the house was full despite the bombing. Findlay and I stayed on but spent a disagreeable few hours on Friday with Moreland and his agent, furious at the postponement of his *Romeo and Juliet*. Working with Loggenburg Saturday on the *Prodigal Son*, Moreland tried hard to make amends.

As the next week progressed, I began to worry about three imminent challenges: Friday's full Board meeting, tea with Nureyev on Saturday and the City of London University Awards Ceremony on Monday. It was foolish, but I was tired and could not throw off a feeling of dread. I need not have worried. Findlay's board papers and mine were approved by Max without amendments, and the board meeting itself was not a difficult one. All attending approved the forthcoming Nureyev collaboration.

The tea with Nureyev at my home did not materialise because the matinee at Covent Garden ran late. Nureyev greeted me warmly on stage before the show in his most charming manner, confirming our later get together. But there was only time after all for a short talk in his dressing room about his problems with dates, and it seemed there was a diminishing possibility of the Australian tour. I had to leave with nothing resolved as someone arrived wanting to speak with him whilst he needed to get ready for the evening performance. In contrast, the University honorary awards ceremony at the start of a new week was a most glorious occasion with everything going smoothly including the speech I made on behalf of all honorary recipients. I even managed to arrive in Southampton in time to see the Company's opening performance of *Swan Lake* sensitively performed by Fulton and Loggenburg. Back in London I was thrilled to hear that I was to appear in the television shows *Call My Bluff, Whicker's World* and *Petticoat Line*, all of which I was to find great fun.

Michael Edgley rang twice from Australia on Thursday having spoken twice with Nureyev who now might come to Australia immediately following the Coliseum season. To accommodate Nureyev's other commitments, we would have to cut the Company's last few days of performances at the Coliseum. Speaking with Nureyev the same afternoon, however, he still would not completely commit himself. I felt utterly frustrated. What more could be done? Next day, an even more frustrated Edgley rang asking me to talk to Gorlinsky, in an effort to achieve confirmation of Nureyev's appearances with us in Australia.

That evening in Southampton there was a Company party on stage to celebrate the end of the tour. Findlay told the dancers that Moreland's *Romeo and Juliet* might have to be postponed in the event of a tour to Australia with Nureyev and that it was agreed he would stage his *Sleeping Beauty* for the Company's spring season at the Coliseum. This news was met with great exuberance by everyone. It was not until the following Tuesday evening, however, that Findlay and I were given confirmation from Gorlinsky that Nureyev had finally agreed to dance with us for three weeks on the Australian tour.

After two weeks of rehearsals in London, it was Christmas and the annual run of *Nutcracker* opened as usual on Boxing Day. That evening Evdokimova thrilled the audience and inspired everyone by her beautiful dancing.

43 *Enter Nureyev*

The new year held some exciting prospects, but little did I know just how exciting. I visited Georgiadis at his studio where we spent a long time together looking at his designs, which were magnificent. He was a charmer but, oh my!, also tough. I tried to cut costs wherever possible, but he hardly gave in over any costume or décor fees. I left hoping that his knowing the Company's financial stringencies might encourage him to cooperate more as the production proceeded.

January was only into its sixth day when Edgley's representative in Britain came to the office. He had suggested to Findlay a tour of *Sleeping Beauty* for four weeks in Australia with Nureyev dancing most performances. To my embarrassment Findlay told me of this while we were lunching with a person from the Palais des Sports. As I pointed out to Findlay – who had not grasped this important fact – this new suggestion would leave no opportunities for my male leads. It was a proposition I could not possibly accept. The following morning the representative was back in the office and we told him firmly that we wished to take two programmes to Australia for a minimum of five weeks. As we were so adamant, he finally accepted.

Our two-and-a-half-week Christmas season drew to a close with the encouraging information that our box office takings were £25,000 over budget. With Nureyev's *Sleeping Beauty* on the horizon, this came as a welcome windfall.

But it was a big blow when Ray handed in his notice to Findlay: he was finding there was too much pressure as Company Manager. I was surprised – he had been assistant to Sarony before taking over the responsibility, and I thought he was doing a good job. He was popular with the dancers, and I had always got on well with him. The thought of his departure saddened me and I realised we would miss him. Peter Hulme was manager designate and Deborah Weiss, a former corps dancer, assistant to company manager, but I felt sure Hulme had not expected to take over from Ray quite so soon.

I was also beginning to feel uneasy about the Panovs and in which ballets we should present them. Even though they were Soviet dancers they were still an unknown quantity and I had heard they had some pas de deux of their own which they would surely wish to perform. I thought *Petrouchka* and *Giselle* might appeal to them should they chose to dance in any of our repertoire and hoped to speak with them after our traditional week's holiday to which we were looking forward. Sven and I went to Tenerife and enjoyed it there, coming home with attractive suntans.

When the dancers returned it was to commence work on Nureyev's *Sleeping Beauty*, so there was much excitement and anticipation in the air. A capable and delightful woman, Gilda, took the initial *Sleeping Beauty* Monday morning call and by the time Nureyev arrived at 3.30pm she had covered a fair amount of the Prologue and he seemed pleased. I noticed Gielgud hanging about all the morning into early afternoon, leaving only a short time before Nureyev walked in. I later asked him if he wanted to dance with Gielgud? 'Not if she will not do the pas de six,' he said, and it seemed he did not wish to dance with her in Australia, either.

Nureyev was a hard task-master but the dancers loved working with him. He was inspiring and never spared himself. He oversaw the first costume fittings before he left for a three-day engagement abroad, confident in Gilda's good work. The ballet began to take shape surprisingly swiftly but as the Company were to perform for the following two weeks in Eastbourne and Oxford, Nureyev on his return wanted the dancers to work Sunday. This, however, was not permitted. Nureyev told me that Gilda was not entirely happy about her pay, so we worked out a scheme: Festival Ballet would pay her hotel bills and Nureyev himself would add an extra £100 a week to her salary, which I thought generous of him.

The weekend started badly when Terry Kern came to tell me he had been offered the Music Directorship of Scottish Opera, a position he would like to take, as well as remaining with us as Music Director. I could not visualise how this would work and did not know what to say – if I told him I couldn't agree to his doing both he might leave us. I stalled and said we needed time to think it over in detail. Both Donald and Vass thought it a bad idea, yet if we agreed to share him there would always be the possibility of losing him to the Scottish Opera and Ballet. What to do? Then, on arriving in Eastbourne, I had a telephone call from Tooley saying Covent Garden was having a gala and would I mind if they asked the Panovs to appear with them. My answer came easily and swiftly. 'John, I most certainly would mind.' After the time and trouble that had gone into contracting the Panovs for our London season, this could not be allowed. I wrote in my diary 'this is typical of Covent Garden, presuming a right to have first call'.

By midweek Nureyev was on the phone to say he did not wish to dance with our guest artist, Liliana Cosi, and was reconsidering Gielgud as a possibility. Patricia

Ruanne, having been awkward at their first rehearsal, had got on the wrong side of Nureyev. I began to hope that he might agree to dance with Evdokimova who was tolerant, cooperative and also a pure classical ballerina.

Findlay and I were being pressed by Nederlander to arrange for the Company to appear in New York in the autumn with the Panovs, who we were told were available at that time. Personally I felt that it would not happen because we would need a lot of sponsorship to cover the costs. A few days later Gorlinsky showed Sarony and me the prices that Nederlander wanted to charge: £25 a seat for two thirds of the house. We thought it too high in comparison with the Royal Ballet's £17.50 a seat. We were under pressure from the States demanding confirmation but neither Sarony nor I could decide at this stage.

I rang Clive Barnes, who I had known for many years. Now in New York and America's most influential critic, I sought his opinion. He thought the financial terms were satisfactory and that we should accept them and appear in New York – but with the proviso that the Panovs did not appear outside of New York and New Jersey beforehand. I rang Gorlinsky with my doubts and reservations and handed the phone to Sarony, hoping this would see the end of the proposition. What a relief it was when the whole idea was called off.

At the weekend Sven and I were invited to dinner with two long-standing members of the Board: Mr Abernethy, Assessor for the GLC, and Gerry Weiss. Findlay, together with Vass and Joanie, completed the group. For some time I had not felt comfortable about Weiss, who was always backstage talking with the dancers, which seemed inappropriate for a Board member. Two weeks later Max arranged an afternoon meeting with Weiss, Findlay and me to discuss the future. As Chairman of the National Theatre since 1971 Max had overseen their move from the Old Vic to the South Bank and had coped valiantly with the great but demanding Laurence Olivier. It appeared he was beginning to find Festival Ballet increased his work load. I began to feel uneasy.

The Company's two performing weeks passed swiftly and we were once again back in Donmar for a month, rehearsing the new *Sleeping Beauty*. It was difficult planning calls as Nureyev would only make up his mind one day in advance, which made it hard for Heather to get the call sheet typed and up on the notice board by the requisite time. It was satisfying to watch Evdokimova in the ascendency while Nureyev considered partnering Doreen Wells, too. She fitted in well with the Company as a guest artist and was a joy to have around. Nureyev refused to dance with Elisabetta Terabust, which disappointed me – she was a lovely dancer, petite and with an appealing personality. I remained in close touch with Edgley as well as the wily Gorlinsky who I took to Giovanni's for lunch one day. I was beginning to appreciate his shrewdness, and we got on surprisingly well, sharing views and ideas. He even said he would like to be my agent, and for no charge! We discussed the state of the country which was disturbing – strikes taking place, even by NHS doctors.

There were also two family highlights at this time. A dinner party at the Savoy for Ingvar's 21st birthday, followed a few days later by a larger party at home. Both were special and a great success and Ingvar was over the moon. It was wonderful to realise this son of ours had grown into such a strong young man, full of confidence and charm, with many delightful friends. Despite our cleaner being ill we had kept the house spotless and filled the rooms with flowers, which looked lovely. Our cleaner could not continue to work, and it was hard to find another as efficient and trustworthy. This added to my workload – I was already feeling tired with the extra strain of dealing with Nureyev. To my amazement, toward the end of our second rehearsal week, the John Field spectre rose again.

Sir Louis Gluckstein rang to ask me how I would like to work with Field as the administrator in place of Findlay. Apparently Weiss had said he thought Findlay was not of the right calibre – 'the Company needed someone more high powered to reflect and retain their position of importance'. I said at once that I would not be in favour of such an arrangement and did not trust Field. I wondered what was going on? I felt sorry for Findlay: we had developed a good working relationship and I found that people appreciated his gentlemanly manner. Concerned, I contacted Skeaping who told me to be sure to stand firm against any proposition concerning Field. It became obvious that Field had a strong supporter in Weiss. My feeling of mistrust was well founded.

There was a packed, excited audience at Sadler's Wells on the 25th March for the Panovs Sunday gala and they were given a warm, moving reception. I found their choreography old fashioned, but Valery's dancing was fantastic, thrilling the house. I was disappointed in Galina, though: her dancing was indifferent and her feet poor. Despite this she had a refreshing personality. They had a big supporter in George Whyte who threw a huge party in their honour at the Dorchester in the beautiful Oliver Messel suite.

44 *A Royal Surprise*

The storm clouds floated away two days later on March 25th. I was rung by Lord Plunkett to say the Queen would like me to lunch with her on Tuesday 22nd April at Windsor Castle. How wonderful to actually lunch with the Queen, who I had always so admired and respected. I later met with some marketing personnel from BOAC, who we were hoping might help in sponsoring the flight to Australia. Next morning Dudley von Loggenburg, Vivien Loeber and I caught a train to Birmingham. At the television studios we had a rush to be ready for the *Pebble Mill at One* programme. The forthcoming appearances of Nureyev and the Panovs with Festival Ballet were creating a lot of media interest. Following a talk with me about Festival Ballet, my two principals danced well in the limited area allocated, and I felt proud of them.

All was not running smoothly at Donmar. Nureyev and Valery Panov – both dictatorial artists, proud and jealous of their Russian training and heritage – had clashed. I only hoped it would blow over as Nureyev was scheduled to dance with Galina. But their first rehearsal together was not a success. She refused to do his choreography, whereupon Nureyev was extremely insulting to her, as he was to Evdokimova when working with her previously. Evdokimova had somehow displeased him, so he descended into one of his black moods. No one present felt Nureyev was in the right but, being Evdokimova, she let the whole thing pass, and remained cool and unruffled. In contrast, we could see that Galina was intensely upset and out of her depth. Perhaps the Panovs' notoriety as brave defectors from Russia and their widely publicised appearances in Israel had gone to their heads.

We were beginning to find them a handful. Papa Beriozoff had had big problems with them over *Petrouchka*. To his dismay in performance they switched to their own version, disregarding all his careful work with them on our production. Skeaping also found them impossible with her *Giselle*. The careful coaching she had given them was ignored during performance when they reverted to their own choreography.

The National Ballet of Canada opened at the Coliseum with a splendid Royal Gala. Afterwards we passed Princess Margaret on her way out. She stopped and turned back to greet Sven and then came over to me with an affectionate kiss, which delighted me. We had met many times at formal events, but since becoming director of Festival Ballet I had met her informally at Max Rayne's home on several occasions. The Princess always spoke frankly and held definite views on productions and dancers, enjoying coming backstage after performances and talking with my dancers who loved seeing her and appreciated her attention.

Nureyev, although working hard all the week on *Sleeping Beauty*, was becoming uneasy about his forthcoming performances in *Giselle* with the Canadian company, staying late to work on it with Bronwen. By the end of the week he actually allowed me to take the *Sleeping Beauty* rehearsal, together with Donald and Vass. Nureyev seemed happy with what we achieved, though too tired to make any final decision on the casting of all the solo roles. His preferences changed from day to day, and I only hoped that the next week would see a clearer picture and a tighter production. To everyone's excitement we'd had the first dress parade on Tuesday, with Georgiadis and Nureyev avidly scrutinising every costume.

The next week began with a disappointing run-through of the second cast – Nureyev was not satisfied, and neither was I. They needed a lot more work, which we gave them when Nureyev was away Wednesday and Thursday for his two performances of *Giselle* with the Canadians. When Sven and I went to the Thursday performance I was disappointed in the production overall and disliked the orchestration and music cuts. Nureyev seemed to be forcing himself, although Karen Kain as Giselle was lovely. But to me she appeared too big for Nureyev, even though we knew he liked to dance with her.

Marshall, Stephen Dunne's deputy on the technical side, handed in his notice to me because of what he felt was Stephen's increasing incompetence. Marshall felt his head would be on the block if things went wrong with *Sleeping Beauty*, and it took an hour to persuade him to change his mind. He said Stephen was not capable of putting it on: he drank too much and drawing up a programme schedule was just a fantasy as he got others to do his work for him. Terribly worried I spoke with Findlay, and it was agreed to keep a close watch on Stephen over the Coliseum season. I just prayed Stephen would not go to pieces and that the show would be ready in time.

On arriving at Donmar I found it packed with a crowd of onlookers as well as Nureyev's usual coterie – all there at Nureyev's invitation to watch the run-through. Both Miklosy and Loeber were away ill, and the extras ordered for the front cloth scene had not materialised so we had to improvise. Nureyev was displeased that Evdokimova, with whom he had finally been persuaded to dance, could not be there in time for Act I and asked for Kessler to step in for her.

On Saturday morning Mallory, our wardrobe mistress, came to me at Donmar to tell me that her small staff were overwhelmed with the size of the show, the ornate costumes and all the extra pieces. I did my best to reassure her as there were still a few more days to go but once again my heart was in my mouth. On Saturday Donald and Vass were able to give Kessler, Evdokimova and Paul Clarke intensive coaching – we did not see Nureyev because he was on in *Coppélia* that evening with the Canadian company. It was the end of their Coliseum season and my stage staff were all set to move in and begin fitting up *Sleeping Beauty* as soon as they moved out. Sven and I were at the last performance and watched a terrific show from Nureyev – a joy in an otherwise lacklustre production.

Sunday was another full day. I went to the Coliseum in the morning and found to my relief all the stage staff in good spirits with everything going to plan and on time. It was the only day we had in which to build and hang the new scenery in time for the electricians to focus the lamps for each act and scene. Equity had given permission for the Company to rehearse at Donmar on Sunday so they worked with Nureyev from 1pm until 7pm with all the Blue Bird casts staying for a further hour. I then returned to the Coliseum, where the staging was well in hand and running only a little behind schedule. By 7pm next evening (Monday) the stage was clear, ready for the dancers to begin with Nureyev a long rehearsal of *Sleeping Beauty* until 10.30pm. The first stage rehearsal of a new ballet is full of stops and starts, placing and fixing entrances and exits. There are a number of these in *Sleeping Beauty* particularly in the Prologue. We were only halfway through Act I when the soloists began to walk through their number. When one looked at her watch, I realised that we had reached 10.30pm. They must have been exhausted as they had started work midday in Donmar and were called for 9.30 Tuesday morning back in the theatre.

We were on such a tight schedule that I had to persuade Nureyev to continue from where we had stopped the night before and not to go back to the beginning again. The excitement grew for our first dress rehearsal with piano in the afternoon which, although we still lacked a number of costumes, helped give the dancers a feeling of period. The evening dress rehearsal followed, this time with orchestra, which inspired the dancers even more. The orchestra sounded splendid despite the harpist's absence through illness. Worryingly, the production looked messy with too many overdressed people on stage, which in my opinion still appeared under lit. The quick changes had not worked and neither had the Awakening Scene, but we were all too tired at that time of night to do anything more. Next morning first-night nerves were tempered by the final full dress rehearsal with the orchestra, now complete with the all-important harpist, sounding good.

By a miracle this spectacular full-length ballet actually worked, everything falling into place for the opening performance with only one noticeable mishap with the scenery. It was an undoubted success, as too was the marvellous party afterwards given for the Company by Max. I felt dazed, unable to grasp that it had happened at last and that Nureyev was actually happy, too. He partnered Evdokimova superbly, and she responded by giving an exquisite performance as Princess Aurora.

The press had been invited for the next performance: Thursday. I sensed the tension in the Company, all hoping for positive reviews. To my relief the Company were more at home in the production by that second night and, though Evdokimova did not reach the same heights as on the opening night, Nureyev danced better. I spoke with the press in the interval but they were for the most part noncommittal, with the exception of Richard Buckle, who was most enthusiastic and said how much he liked the production. As the final curtain fell the audience gave it a thunderous reception, and I felt sure we had a box office winner. I was glad that Michael Edgley's wife Jane was there to see the Company's success. Nureyev danced even better, but shocked us later by furiously tearing up three of the four black and white photographs she had chosen to take back for advance publicity. Although he passed a few colour shots we were greatly saddened by the outburst and his willful, destructive behaviour.

That evening I was also worried about Kessler. I returned to the theatre, after an interview for *Kaleidoscope* at the BBC, to find her sobbing, saying she did not want to dance any more. I took her to my wonderful Dr Pigott hoping he could help her. She was to give her first Princess Aurora at the Saturday matinee and was obviously terrified. But next morning, on returning to the Coliseum, she broke down again and we realised she would not be able to go on. I rang Ruanne and Clarke who went on that afternoon instead. They gave a splendid performance together and to everyone's delight Patricia managed the difficult balances well. It happened to be a totally full house, our first ever sold-out matinee at the Coliseum.

Together with a few of his friends, Nureyev invited Sven and me to dinner after the show at his house close by Richmond Park. Nureyev always had many waiting to speak to him after a performance, so the dinner party was a late affair. His house was richly furnished, revealing his impeccable taste. Antique furniture, exquisite paintings and tapestries showed he was an avid collector, particularly of uncommon objects. He made a good host, and I thoroughly enjoyed our time there. He talked about his wish for all his choreographic works to be held by one company. Was he hinting at Festival Ballet as custodian? If so, could we possibly afford this? The party did not break up until after 3am so by the time we dropped his friends at the Connaught Hotel Sven and I were not home in bed until 4.30am. After a quiet Sunday, writing the script for my BBC music programme, I found it hard to concentrate on Company activities. I was already contemplating the next day's visit to Windsor Castle for lunch with the Queen.

45 *A Royal Luncheon*

Tuesday dawned, and it was as if I was in a dream. I found the entire occasion so unbelievably wonderful that I could hardly take it all in. On arrival at the castle I was met and courteously escorted down a long, beautifully furnished corridor on the first floor to a smallish drawing room where a few other guests were gathered awaiting the Queen's arrival. Coming up from the staircase opposite, Her Majesty entered the room, smiling warmly and greeting her guests in turn. Her Majesty was so natural that I was able to relax a little as she mingled amongst us. There was a sudden commotion as barking dogs were heard making their way up the stairs. The Queen expressed dismay at the unexpected arrival of her Mother with her corgis, who she remarked did not get on well with her own corgis. The Queen Mother was wearing a lovely blue hat, which perfectly matched her outfit, and there were loving exchanges before we went into the dining room for lunch. I was seated on Prince Philip's right and was overcome when he asked if I would like wine or cider. I chose cider, determined to remain completely sober to relish every minute of the occasion. Returning to the drawing room for coffee we were joined by the two young princes, Andrew and Edward.

The Queen Mother, always so gracious. mixed effortlessly amongst us, so relaxed, even applying her lipstick as she talked with me. She confided that her lipstick refused to stay on, but that her daughter Princess Margaret never had that problem and hers never seemed to wear off. The Queen's lady in waiting was charming and told me how much Her Majesty liked a quiet evening when she could sit and talk about those she met during the day. Driving back to London I could not help thinking how blessed this country is to have such a diligent Royal Family.

From 7pm until 10pm that evening I was at Broadcasting House recording one of ten transmissions about music for the ballet. It was an enriching experience, researching the historical background to my chosen pieces. After such a full, royal day, I went home with music still playing in my ears, exhausted but elated and happy.

Wednesday was a sad day for the Company. Poor Kessler again went to pieces, sobbing her heart out and, on medical advice, it was finally decided she should return home to the States. We were already short of leading ballerinas and Nureyev had agreed to partner her. Trouble was unfolding with the Panovs and the American tour. They refused to accept our programme, insisting on the inclusion of their *The Lady and the Hooligan* ballet – so awful that I could not possibly allow it to be shown with us. Once more I thought the tour should not be undertaken but Findlay did not agree. Meanwhile I had Gorlinsky on the phone and Whyte, who came to see me at the Coliseum – both pressing for the tour to go ahead. I only hoped that Findlay, who had flown to New York, had not signed anything. There was no news from him, which was a little worrying. The next day was no better, Gorlinsky again on the phone, and none too polite, pushing for the Panovs' tour.

The Panovs were being impossible, too, saying everything must go through their agent. They wanted a new ballet created on them, while still insisting on dancing their *Hooligan* and *Harlequinade*. I heard that Galina was extremely rude both to Vass and about Festival Ballet. Nureyev was also being impossible, refusing to dance with any of our three well established guest ballerinas – Carla Fracci, Italy's leading ballerina, Cosi and Terabust. That evening we had the Swedish Ambassador and his press attaché out front and I was pleased that Nureyev danced well with Evdokimova for their fourth consecutive performance together that week.

The next evening, Friday, he was to partner Galina Panov for the first time in *Sleeping Beauty*. It proved a disaster, with him swearing at her on stage during performance. The press next morning was terrible with the Daily Express quoting Nureyev as saying: 'she's not up to it', and the Panovs saying: 'the English are dull and money mad', which was odd coming from them. Nureyev's last performance Saturday had the most amazing reception. At the end there were people in the boxes with armfuls of fragrant narcissi, which were hurled onto the stage at his feet. It was a marvellous sight, especially seeing the look of real happiness on Nureyev's face. I felt we had got on well during the many weeks he had been with us. I was also sure we would miss him and his dramatic outbursts. There would be only two and a half more weeks at the Coliseum before we rejoined him in Australia.

After twelve consecutive *Sleeping Beautys* it made a pleasant change to move into *Swan Lake*. Breuer danced superbly and Maina was a lot better, although still too uncontrolled in Act III. The house was full and the Company were excited to hear that the Duchess of Kent and the ex-Queen of Greece with her children were out front. Findlay met them in the first interval and I was introduced in the second, charmed by the graciousness of the ex-Queen. To my surprise a beautiful bouquet of flowers came for me from Nureyev. His kind gesture delighted me.

A dreadful day of indecision and anxiety followed as news reached us that the Panovs were approaching other companies to tour them, including the Stuttgart Ballet and even the Scottish Ballet. But no company thought them good enough, and I again felt strongly that we should not risk an American tour with them. We had no Kessler, and I had just learnt that Fulton would also be away for some time, having a baby. Findlay informed me that Gielgud had requested a year's leave of absence, wishing to become a guest artist.

Not as surprising, Kern told Findlay he definitely wanted to conduct Scottish Opera for one year which he had already spoken to me about when I had been non-committal. Valery Panov still refused to learn Papa's version of *Petrouchka*, and they appeared to reach an impasse. Donald then reported a disappointing rehearsal with Galina Panov, who he said was not good enough as Giselle. The Panovs arrived one and a quarter hours late at the office to speak to Findlay and me about their programme for America, which they insisted must include the awful *Hooligan* and the slightly less bad *Harlequinade*. After they left I said to Findlay we could not afford to be seen with them in New York, so the tour must be called off. We rang Barnes in New York who said there were now rumours of a tour with the Panovs appearing in Montreal and other cities. The one happy note that day was a phone call from Terabust in Rome saying she would be coming to dance *Sleeping Beauty* on the 8th and 10th of May at the Coliseum and was also able to join us in Australia for the last week in Sydney. This was welcome news indeed.

Wednesday was a better day when, after a hugely successful children's matinee, Findlay came to watch the Panovs in rehearsal and at last agreed to pull out of the American tour. At the end of the week, on Saturday evening, we had a most distinguished guest in my box: the country's Prime Minister, Edward Heath. As an interesting try-out we were giving *Les Sylphides* with piano accompaniment instead of the usual full orchestra. Edward Heath liked this but thought we should engage a concert pianist to play Chopin's beautiful piano music.

The next week I endeavoured to soothe a highly upset Skeaping over the Panovs' insufferable behaviour, insulting her *Giselle* production. A meeting featuring Max, Findlay, Weiss and me was upsetting. Max pushed hard for the Panovs' contract to be renewed, but only after Weiss had left the room. Findlay explained we would upset the Company if we gave them a further contract. Max retorted, saying: 'If I had listened to the Company then you [BG] would not be here today.' I replied simply that I stood for high standards and could not condone the Panovs' contract being renewed. His comment had been so unnecessary and insulting, and I was hurt.

By Saturday evening the *Sleeping Beauty* sets, costumes and other requirements for the Australian tour were packed ready for shipment. Then Monday, three days before our season closed in London, Max brought Princess Margaret, with Evelyn de Rothschild, to our triple bill programme. I was invited to the Royal receiving room for the second interval, leaving Sven with our guest. The Princess, enquiring after Sven, asked for him to join us. I suggested he should bring Papa Beriozoff and his daughter, the ballerina Svetlana Beriosova, with Trunoff to meet the Princess. This delighted her, and she chatted to Papa about his production of *Petrouchka*. The evening finished with a thrilling rendering of *Études*, after which I took Princess Margaret backstage, something she always enjoyed. There we found Bart lying on the stage groaning with agonizing cramp, which the Princess found most amusing. The other two leads in *Études* – Peter Breuer and Margot Miklosy – were still upright on their feet, smiling and talking happily with the conductor Terry Kern. They were overjoyed to see Princess Margaret had come informally on stage and thrilled to talk with her for a short time. On leaving, Max said 'all credit to me' before he swept the Princess away into the night!

Before I could realise it Wednesday came and the closing night of the Coliseum season. Following the final exciting curtain calls for *Études* I gave my traditional thank you speech which Sven helped me write and memorise. It was my best to date, which pleased me as Max was out front prior to his 'farewell to the Company'. We had a drinks party on stage but it was a rather dismal affair. Max had found being chairman of both the National Theatre and Festival Ballet too heavy a load. He said a few words, followed by Gerry Weiss speaking as our new chairman, and Max was given a sketch by Georgiadis. Not all the Company were there as the departure for Australia was next day. I was not happy at losing Max and distinctly uneasy about his successor.

With my Company and a heavy heart we flew to Frankfurt en route for Australia. I was so exhausted I even managed to sleep through the following day as the plane flew over Sofia and Istanbul, touching down for a short time in Bombay and Singapore. At Perth there was no press, nor anyone to greet us. Once inside the airport, however, we were welcomed by Michael Edgley, his sister and his assistant. To my amazement, sky scrapers populated the city's centre which was modern, as was the plush hotel which was to be my home for the next week. In my room I found flowers and fruit from Edgley, and the hotel management had placed an exotic orchid by my bed. As I was finishing my unpacking at 3am the phone rang with Sven and Ingvar at the other end. How that cheered me and helped me to fall into a long, contented slumber.

Perth proved to be a highly successful week for the company artistically and financially. The auditorium was vast, and we were told later that over 46,500 people enjoyed and paid to see our performances of *Sleeping Beauty* with Nureyev. This meant the overheads for the rest of the five-week tour were covered, which was reassuring. Michael Edgley, part owner of the stadium, 'Channel 7 and Edgley Entertainment Centre', invited Donald and me for champagne on the closing night, and dined with us later in our hotel restaurant. This remained open late each evening specially to accommodate my hungry dancers, Perth restaurants closing early.

After the show Nureyev flew to Melbourne on the late plane taking Paul Clarke with him, but not Richard Buckle the critic who was covering the tour for The Observer. Nureyev had invited Buckle and me to dine with him several times in his hotel room after the show. I had begun to see some of the many facets of Nureyev's character and to realise what a responsibility it was touring with him. His swift mood changes and his unaccountable rudeness contrasted with his charm and many kindnesses.

His first two performances of *Sleeping Beauty* were with Evdokimova and had received wondrous applause. The third performance was with Ruanne, to whom he had been particularly supportive, sweet and encouraging. After the performance she cried with overwhelming relief that all had gone well and that Nureyev was pleased. But his dresser had walked out and his masseur was threatening to do the same – both complaining of his truculent, offensive behaviour. Next evening, after another triumphant show, Michael Edgley gave a dinner party for Evdokimova, Ruanne, Clarke, Buckle, me and of course Nureyev, who suddenly became abusive and rude, spoiling the entire celebration. 'What a strange person he is,' I wrote in my diary. On our last evening in Perth he angrily refused to sign Edgley's little son's autograph book, leaving the poor boy in floods of tears. Nureyev later signed the book, however, and all was forgiven but probably never forgotten.

I took away a favourable impression of Perth, my first ever Australian city – the beautifully laid-out grounds surrounding the University, the Swan River and the whole ambience of light and cleanliness delighted me. With more cities to embrace we flew on to Melbourne, leaving us with plenty of time that day to explore the coastal capital of Victoria. It contrasted with Perth, far larger and spread out with 19th-century buildings dominating tree lined boulevards. The theatre, of a more traditional style, was close to the sea in the St Kitts district. Most of the Company were housed nearby in small self-catering flats which they loved, while I was closer to the centre in a cosy old Victorian hotel, The Windsor. They still offered open fires in the bedrooms, which gave it a homely touch, and I had never before experienced such helpful and friendly staff.

Our opening night seemed to have voodoo on it. Transportation was the first major setback: the scenery arrived terribly late at the theatre, two hours after midnight on the day of performance and not, as expected, the previous morning. This gave the stage staff an almost impossible task to get it all unpacked, set up and lit, scene by scene, in time for the opening that evening. There was therefore no time for placing the dancers on the unfamiliar stage. The wardrobe was also badly served – the costumes, wigs, hats and footwear only appearing at two that afternoon. Mallory, the wardrobe mistress, did her best in the limited time available but the ballet looked shoddy and was not helped by the appalling orchestra. Sitting by me was the British High Commissioner with his wife, who kept complaining throughout.

The entire miserable evening was only redeemed by Nureyev's mesmerising appearance with Evdokimova. The press were invited for the following night, which was just as bad. The Company had received a shock towards the end of their rehearsal period when Kenn Wells, one of our most talented character dancers, fell backwards off the stage into the orchestra pit below and lay lifeless for quite a few minutes. We thought he was dead. Frantic I rang for an ambulance but when it arrived Kenn had come to and was up walking about. He was whisked off to hospital for X rays but miraculously was OK and there were no bones broken.

The dreadful sounds coming from the orchestra on the second night must have affected the conductor Graham Bond, who took the whole performance at a snail's pace. Even Edgley, our constant admirer, commented on the slow tempo. The sluggish music had a dampening effect upon the dancers who were equally dull and performed below their animated standard. The corps was ragged and the soloists weaker than usual, and I just hoped that the press would be so enamoured with Nureyev that these Company failings would go unnoticed. Nureyev had demanded that the Canadian dancer Karen Kain be engaged for part of the tour as one of his ballerinas. As she was also staying at the Windsor, we took a taxi there together on her arrival. She was a sweet person and a dancer with whom Nureyev performed well.

I had an urgent call from our technical director asking me to fly down to Sydney to see the theatre in which we were booked to appear. He had been to the Festival Theatre in Adelaide and found it modern and perfect in every way. He was, however, deeply concerned as to whether we could manage at the Capitol Theatre in Sydney, let alone stage *Sleeping Beauty* under such cramped conditions. He was right to be worried. The theatre was old and dilapidated, reminiscent of the poor old Finsbury Park Empire in North London. The stage was small and ill-equipped, there was no orchestra pit, few changing rooms and little wardrobe space. It was thoroughly depressing but back at Edgley's sister's house we were assured it could and would be improved for our forthcoming two-week season. We were back in Melbourne for the evening show, which went much better as Bond had the orchestra more under control. The dancers were back on form, although Ruanne was not as good as before. To my relief we picked up good reviews, although one paper reported the performance was dull (a fair comment). I knew we had been saved by Nureyev.

I was invited to lunch at the Australian Ballet's headquarters, an old tyre factory, which had been completely transformed for the company. It seemed odd to meet there

Robert Helpmann, Margaret Scott and Peggy van Praagh: all former Royal Ballet artists. As in Perth, the resident ballet company entertained our dancers by giving an enjoyable tea party. I had some lovely flowers in my hotel room from their administrator, Noel Pelly, which gave me much pleasure.

By Saturday Nureyev was in one of his black moods. I said hello that evening as I passed him doing his barre work, to which he responded with a growl and a glare. I was surprised – he had always been so polite and charming towards me. Later on stage before Act II, I asked him how he was, to which he replied 'Oh f*** you and the Company… leaving clinic on stage'. I could not fathom what he was talking about until our stage manager said he thought he must be referring to tissues dropped on the stage by Nureyev himself, who was now blaming his Lilac Fairy. Keeping somewhat aloof, I went as usual to his dressing room after the show; he turned to me and said, 'Well haven't you enough energy to f*** everyone in the Company?' which I found dreadfully distasteful, particularly in front of Buckle and van Praagh. She praised the dancing of Manola Asensio, which annoyed Nureyev who said, 'She must never dance my pas de cinq again; if she does I not dance'. I replied that he wasn't running the Company, I was, and soon after, with a wry smile, Nureyev walked out into the night.

47 *Adelaide And Sydney – Rudi Tantrums*

Despite Adelaide's remoteness we found their Festival Theatre extremely modern and a joy to work in. It was equipped with new technology and advanced innovations, which had been implemented by a forward-looking manager after looking at theatres in other countries. The stage was available on time for classes and an unrushed rehearsal. The dancers responded by giving a splendid opening performance that night. Poor Asensio came to me saying Nureyev told her he did not wish her to dance in his pas de cinq anymore, and she was upset. As he had final say on casting of his ballet, he had taken the decision out of my hands and there was nothing I could do.

With others present I just spoke briefly to him before the show, wishing him success but adding: 'I do not love you any more.' He pretended to be surprised in what I took to be a disdainful manner. After the show, when I introduced the South Australian Premier to Nureyev in his dressing room, I noticed Buckle appeared to be jealous. Edgley gave his now traditional dinner for the evening's principals during which both Buckle and Nureyev became embarrassingly drunk.

Barry Moreland's brilliant ballet *The Prodigal Son* was billed for the second week in Sydney but, because of the theatre's limitations, it had to be put on first to avoid a third interval. I had warned Moreland about this on my return from Sydney with Stephen but

Moreland was now terribly upset about its position in the programme. I sympathised with him and tried to explain the technical problems which made this the only solution. Meanwhile Edgley had acquired a free return ticket from London and proposed Findlay use it to come over so they might discuss reducing Festival Ballet's fees. I thought this an outrageous suggestion and assured him Festival Ballet could not possibly afford to change the financial terms already contractually agreed. I added it would be unethical to call Findlay to Australia at this late stage, pointing out that the tour was proving a great success. By Saturday's last *Sleeping Beauty* in Adelaide Karen Kain was exhausted and crying from homesickness. Nureyev sent me some beautiful orchids – a peace offering?

In Sydney, despite the tiresome restrictions within the ancient theatre with its small shallow stage, we finally got on stage for class. Already running late, Nureyev decided to stay for the dress rehearsal, which held us up badly. Evdokimova left after Act I as there was no time left to rehearse the last act, which we paid for later in performance. During the opening polonaise in Act III, Donald (as the majestic king) fell over his cloak onto his knees while Evdokimova got hopelessly caught on Loggenburg's costume. Earlier – after the unexpected arrival of the Governor General of Australia who I hastily welcomed and escorted to his seat – the theatre had been plunged into darkness. We sat without light for what seemed an age, but our distinguished guest was unperturbed and understanding. It took the electricians twenty minutes to repair the fuses and restore all lighting so we could at last begin the performance. As usual, after every show Nureyev had scores of visitors wanting to see him in his dressing room. On this particular evening, Buckle brought a sculptor who wanted to show Nureyev the piece he had sculpted of him in motion. Nureyev took one look and threw it angrily to the ground, smashing it into pieces. Buckle and sculptor made a hasty retreat.

For the first-night dinner Edgley had booked us into a rather opulent Chinese restaurant. Buckle was unusually silent and halfway through the meal Nureyev shouted crossly to him, 'What the f*** is wrong with you?' Buckle replied, 'You know very well; you have destroyed my sculptor friend's work.' A furious Nureyev picked up a jumbo prawn and threw it across the table at Buckle. It missed, landing instead in my bowl of white rice and scattering it all over my black velvet coat and fur collar. At this point Nureyev got up and stormed out, leaving onlookers speechless. This dramatic little scene was reported back by Buckle for printing in The Observer, so readers in London knew of the incident.

Two days later was my birthday and I arranged a small party for after the show, downstairs in our hotel. I checked that the long table was decorated with flowers, leaves strewn across the cloth and a standing candelabra. I was sent a bowl of red roses by an unknown admirer, carnations from Miklosy, champagne from Bart, as well as more from other members of the Company. The table looked lovely. I felt a little nervous but Nureyev could not have been nicer, really going out of his way to be sweet, kind and charming. For once he did not send back any food and ate his way through five courses.

He gave me a most beautiful present, a brightly coloured finely embroidered Japanese shawl. I was deeply touched and have treasured it to this day. At present it graces a chair in my sitting room, a remaining link with this charismatic, egotistical, temperamental artist. At the end of Nureyev's final performance in Australia, the audience went mad, giving him a terrific reception with stamping and slow hand clapping. He loved every minute, bringing me on stage kissing my hand and embracing me warmly. It was a merry farewell dinner which Edgley gave, and again Nureyev could not have been nicer to me.

Nureyev flew to the States next afternoon leaving us in Sydney with just one more week and a change to a triple bill programme. There was a heated discussion between Edgley and me over the lack of publicity for Bart and Breuer and the absence of any of their photographs in the front of the theatre. After an angry exchange, he and Miriam his press assistant agreed to amend this 'so-called' oversight. Photos were eventually displayed in the front of the Capitol, where *Sleeping Beauty* had been so difficult to stage. There was no room for a cross-over behind the back-cloth, so dancers in period hunting costumes had been forced to dash into the street and around the side of the theatre to reach the opposite side of the stage. Now we were faced with putting on the complicated *Prodigal Son* and demanding *Études*. The stage staff worked hard so we just managed to get the curtain up on time, but the lighting in *Études* was not accurately focused on the dancers. Miklosy had a sprained foot so was not quite as sparkling as usual. Bart and Breuer, however, were on top, athletic form – competing against each other in line with the exciting choreography. The Scott Joplin music helped secure *Prodigal Son* an enormous success, while the two classical pas de deux show pieces received a rapturous reception. I was proud that my Company won their laurels without the presence of Nureyev. Before we left, the Australian Ballet gave us a memorable party, where it was so good to meet up again with many dancers from the Royal Ballet days, including my dear partner Bryan Ashbridge, now the company's television expert, and Helpmann, the same as ever, idiosyncratic and a compelling actor. Friends made in Sydney were to be thanked for many kindnesses and bade farewell before leaving Sunday. The Company was given a wonderful reception from the audience, and I went on stage to thank them for all the encouragement and support we had been given during our time in Australia.

In view of Kern's wish to go for a year to Scottish Opera and Ballet, I spoke to John Lanchbery about the possibility of his returning to England as our chief conductor and he promised to write to me with his decision. I bade farewell to Edgley – a strange man, completely tied up in himself – so unlike our French Trailine and Italian Porcile whose first concern was always for the Company. Disappointing weather, cold, wet and windy, dogged our visit not only in Sydney but throughout most of the time in Australia and I was longing for the holiday and some Swedish sun.

To my joy my darling Sven was at Heathrow waiting to welcome me back. He had cancelled his morning's patients to be there and had the car close by to take me home.

There at number 78 was my father with lunch ready and, after a few minutes, an excited Ingvar burst through the front door. It was wonderful to be surrounded by the love of my dear family.

I was soon at the office and an Arts Council meeting. Once clear of those obligations, I was able to go to Potters Bar that evening with Sven. I felt so grateful and blessed to be back in time to listen to a discourse by our spiritual Master, in England for only a short visit. Radiating love, compassion and serenity we came away filled with renewed faith and inner peace.

48 *Changes Afoot And A Company Home*

The next morning there was a long Board meeting – sadly Max Rayne's last with Festival Ballet. To my surprise no one commented on this nor thanked him for his nine years as Chairman, guiding the Company out of its near bankruptcy in 1966 to its present secure position. I thanked him, saying how much he would be missed, but as it was almost 2pm many were already leaving. After much discussion they had decided against Barry Moreland creating a new *Romeo and Juliet* for the Company. Considering the high costs of a full-length ballet they thought it too risky with a relatively unknown choreographer. Although I was relieved in a way not to take on this responsibility, the decision left me in a dilemma, with no new full-length for the Coliseum season in the Spring. The general consensus was to bring back *Don Quixote*, but I pointed out it was not a foregone box office winner.

Suffering agonizing pain in a tooth, I had to go back to my dentist for root canal treatment before returning to the office and tidying up the pile of paperwork with Heather. Sven collected me later that evening and took me home. I was so tired we just had Weetabix for supper and I could not even begin to pack for our holiday until the next morning. Both Donald and Terry Hayworth rang me to wish me a happy holiday. Somehow I managed to be ready when my father arrived, and we shut up the house securely before departing.

Instead of taking the boat directly to Sweden we took an evening ferry to Bremerhaven. The food on board was good but we wished the tablecloths had been clean and the German woman in charge more welcoming. For the first time ever, Ingvar was not with us. Now a young man of twenty-one he was crewing with some friends of Sven's. We missed him greatly, especially my father. Used to having Ingvar share his cabin he now found it difficult to relax and sleep, more aware of the continuous creaking as the boat rocked its way across the sea.

We were eager to get to Vadstena and collect keys to the little house we rented for our stay. The house was right on the water front and ideal in every way, well equipped and having a lovely back garden. With the lake at our doorstep we had all that we wanted and were able to entertain several of Sven's school friends. Sven's parents had died at the end of the sixties, but I still missed his dear mother and father who were always so loving to me, the girl from England. I was pleased they had met my mother in 1951 before she died and had got to know my father over the years.

The holiday passed quickly and happily with trips to see Sven's family and friends in different parts of Sweden. We swam frequently and enjoyed plenty of glorious sun but also experienced some wet and chilly days. The London office sent regular packets of mail so I was kept up to date with everything – Findlay and I had agreed never to take a break at the same time. Heather rang once a week, too, and on my return to the office after the holiday she gave me some good news: Stephen Dunne had decided to take a job on offer in Canada. Now David Mogridge could be offered the position of stage director, which I thought he would manage well, loving the Company as he did.

There was a request from the BBC to take part in an hour-and-a-half radio discussion about the current arts scene with the Arts Minister and Anthony Field from the Arts Council. My initial feeling was not to accept, but Sven and Heather both thought I should. I became so nervous I hardly slept that night but in the end the Arts Minister cancelled, sending a deputy instead. Both men were charming and relaxed, and I found it enjoyable and informative. Bob Holness was a splendid interviewer and the time passed quickly. I felt grateful to Peter Hulme for having looked up facts and figures for me so that I went armed with plenty of current data.

The Company looked so well after their much needed break and were in good form, with the exception of a corps de ballet girl. She had suffered a strained foot which had not improved over the holiday. She was still not right, nor was her toe, and unfortunately she had put on some weight. Her doctor advised a three-month break from dance to allow the foot to fully recover, which I said I would agree to. This she found difficult to accept and was bravely trying to stem her tears as we discussed her whole future and whether or not she should continue with a career in dance. I suggested she should give herself time to see how the foot progressed and warned her it might never be strong enough to stand the strain of pointe work, and she must be prepared for the worst. On a happier note, Ruanne came to tell me she had decided not to go to Sydney and dance the lead in Helpmann's new ballet as he wanted. I was relieved and happy at her decision to stay.

There were great happenings afoot for the Company with the possibility of a permanent home. Sir Louis Gluckstein, a trustee of Festival Ballet was also chairman of the board of governors who looked after Queen Alexandra's House, a hostel for women music students. Before Max left, he and Sir Louis discussed the real chance of acquiring a part of this building. The Queen Alexandra governors needed a certain sum of money and would be willing to lose part of the building to Festival Ballet if we could meet this sum. I accompanied the architect, Bailey, to the site with his detailed plans to see how he proposed dividing the huge hostel into two completely separate buildings, if we were to go ahead. The main loss for the resident students would be the rarely frequented, compact theatre as well as a large gym in the basement. This would give the Company two large studios with plenty of further accommodation for administration, staff and other necessary facilities. I was most impressed with his whole concept, which would provide ideal headquarters for Festival Ballet.

During the rehearsal period, Sven and I had dinner one evening with Gerry Weiss and his wife Ruth. It was a pleasant enough get-together, but my instincts were confirmed: he was full of Company gossip. I thought it wrong for the Chairman to mix with the dancers, as was his habit, and feared it could undermine my position with the Board as well as with the Company. I was always careful not to be close to any of my dancers but to have friendships with my ballet staff – Donald, in whom I had complete trust, Vass and Joanie, and of course Paul Findlay. I steered clear of gossip, which could do so much harm, and was careful not to become involved with the various liaisons which inevitably occurred from time to time in the Company. At the next Executive meeting (held now, since Max's departure, at County Hall), I was astonished to be asked to consider inviting Samsova to rejoin the Company. I did not feel I should ask her back since she had left of her own accord with Prokovsky. After much pressure I had to say I was not prepared to do this and explained my reasoning.

August was the month of contract renewals when I spoke with each dancer about their progress and position in the Company. I was always a little apprehensive about these interviews – some dancers came with high hopes which I sometimes had to dash. I hated disappointing them. To my surprise Asensio brought her husband to her interview, and he expressed his disapproval of her salary and present position. I explained that a higher salary would come when she became a principal, but she needed a few more months to strengthen her technique. As he would not accept this I said perhaps they should return to the States. Paul Findlay echoed this when he joined us, the husband having refused to budge. Thankfully she remained in the Company and worked hard. True to my word, four months later I was able to make her a principal.

Findlay was a good spokesman for the Company and at the Arts Council meeting he managed to get them to agree a 30% increase to the dancers' salaries. He also returned with a letter confirming the Arts Council's financial support towards the purchase of Queen Alexandra House. Things were moving, and I so hoped it would become a reality.

Following rehearsals the Company went into a month of performances in London. It started encouragingly in August at Festival Hall with good press reporting that the Company were dancing well. Even Gilpin and Dolin said the same when I dined with them and their friend Jane Buchanan-Michaelson after a performance of *Noir et Blanc*, *Schéhérazade* and *Gaîté Parisienne*. Towards the end of the week, however, there was an outbreak of terrorist bombs: Thursday evening in Tottenham Court Road, Friday in

Kensington Church Street, and a mid-week explosion out at Caterham. I was fearful it might affect our forthcoming three-week season at the New Victoria cinema, but the bookings continued to be promising. Before the end of our first week of *Coppélia* there was a serious bomb outrage at midday at the Hilton Hotel in Park Lane. Two people were killed and forty injured.

In this nightmare week we also had 16 dancers off with flu, and I was thankful when we emerged from *Swan Lake* into *Dances from Napoli* and *Prodigal Son* for the last week. These were also Kern's last performances with us, and we gave him a little send-off party on stage. Our loyal orchestra leader, Donald Weekes, gave a lovely speech, then introduced me as Miss Grey CBE, as he always insisted on addressing me. Kern gave an inspired performance, lifting the whole evening, and I felt devastated that he was leaving – he had given me such good advice and been a marvellous conductor for the dancers. But, like many of his era, he wanted to conduct opera and not just to be confined to ballet. It is rarely understood that only the best musicians conduct ballet well: Ernest Ansermet, Pierre Monteux, Thomas Beecham, Robert Irving, Constant Lambert, John Lanchbery and Ashley Lawrence being obvious examples.

After the London month, our traditional autumn tour began in Norwich, continuing to Southampton, Oxford, Liverpool and Cardiff, where we presented *Sleeping Beauty,* but not without difficulty. Magnificent as Georgiadis' sets were, they presented great problems for our stage staff during our regional tour. To get the scenery placed, hung and lit in time for Monday's opening performance meant the dancers' placing call had to be curtailed or cancelled. We seriously considered not opening until Tuesday, thus cutting out the Sunday overnight stage work, saving the overtime money and giving the stage staff and dancers more time. No one, however, really wanted to sacrifice the Monday performance and the suggestion was dropped. After the mid-tour rehearsal week in London, with the choreographic evening at the Collegiate Theatre, the Company broke with tradition, staying for the first time for a fortnight in each of the next three major cities: Birmingham, Bristol and Manchester. Finally back in London for a week's break the Company opened its Festival Hall Christmas season of *Nutcracker* and embraced the start of 1976.

I could hardly believe 1975 was over: it had seen so many exciting developments, professional and personal. In late autumn David Gillard, critic and author, began to write my biography. We had already had a couple of sessions together, and I found him easy to talk to, intelligent and patient. I was confident he would write honestly and sympathetically, providing I could give him enough time and information.

Sven and I had for some few years been looking for a hideaway in the country. Our friend the architect Edward Mills helped us in the search, sending us newspaper particulars from time to time. One Saturday we were invited by him and his wife Elsie for lunch and dinner primarily to inspect three totally contrasted properties. All were fascinating but we fell completely for a Scandinavian style house in Ashdown Forest.

Edward and Sven were immediately in touch with the agent and by Monday the price was agreed and the purchase a real possibility. I was blissfully happy. So were Sven and Ingvar with the only dissenting voice Sven's sister, who thought it too isolated and too big. Isolated it was, and that was what appealed to us. We loved it so much that after two years we gave up our London house, making 'Fernhill' our permanent home.

Within the workings of Festival Ballet, amidst the inevitable comings and goings, the greatest loss was the departure of our chairman, Max Rayne; highlights included the Board's approval of a contemporary work by Glen Tetley, the possibility of a home for the Company and, undoubtedly, Nureyev's association with the Company, his glorious production of *Sleeping Beauty* and the triumphant Australian tour.

49 *Nureyev Paris Season 1976*

Shortly after 23 performances of *Nutcracker* in London, Festival Ballet travelled to Paris to appear in the vast Palais des Sports with Nureyev in his *Sleeping Beauty*. My first visit to this unattractive environment had been with Mogridge, Tony Barlow (our press officer), and Georgiadis in mid-October. The great designer grumbled, saying he found the stage too shallow for his sets. Grunwald at the Palais des Sports, however, refused to lose any more seats so it was left to Mogridge to work out how best to achieve the desired results.

The Company flew to Paris on Saturday, three days ahead of our opening: 20th January 1976. After checking in at the Sofitel Hotel, Donald and I went to the Palais des Sports to find things running late. The lighting had not even been started for Act III, and the scenery looked squashed. I was not surprised when next day Nureyev asked Mogridge to bring the legs and borders further forward, which he was loath to do, but I joined Nureyev in the battle to get this done. It certainly improved the whole perspective. Despite the late availability of the stage for a final rehearsal, we managed to open on time. This was a miracle as Nureyev completely lost control and exploded at our chief carpenter, Allan Cleary, who was refusing to amend some scenery. He finally capitulated and eventually everything fell into its appropriate place. On our opening evening I felt proud of my Company who danced well, inspired by Nureyev who received a fantastic ovation which made the whole evening thrilling. There was a champagne reception for the Company afterwards, in a crowded corridor, from which Nureyev soon escaped. The press lady told me where to join him with Heather at Club 27 near the Paris Opéra. I was seated next to Sharon Gold, and Nureyev had Yvette Chauviré on his left and me on his right. After commenting that the soloists needed to be stronger (which was true), Sharon discussed taking the Company with Nureyev to the Metropolitan Opera House in New York, and to Washington and Boston with *Sleeping Beauty* and his proposed *Romeo and Juliet*. Nureyev then said that they and Edgley could pay for the new production!!

I was flying to Moscow next morning so had little sleep. Even as I was leaving the hotel, Loggenburg was waiting to ask me for three weeks leave of absence. I answered I would have to think about it. Once on the plane, Philip Lewis introduced himself as head of BBC Outside Events. I was to be working with him for the BBC coverage of the 200th Anniversary celebration of the Bolshoi Ballet, founded by Empress Anna in 1776. I was met by the BBC's David Gautier and an interpreter who whisked us through customs to be met by a tall woman from Intourist. The shooting next day took place outside in the freezing cold. How grateful I felt to Sven for his recent wonderful gifts to me of a mink hat and coat, specially for this prestigious occasion, because he was so proud for me.

I worried that I might not remember the script accurately but all went well, even though it seemed strange to be left alone without instruction or even told where the cameras were. Only the producer, John Vernon, came up to me. He said to just be happy and smiling, if possible, and not speak too quickly. But on the first take I lost my concentration on taking out a card to read and spoke too slowly. The second take went right through with only a wee stumble at the end. We retook the finish twice more to make sure it was all right and the producer and crew were pleased with the results. Over dinner Vernon congratulated me and said, 'You were just right and smiling happily throughout!' It was such a relief to know they were satisfied.

The following evening at the Bolshoi, as part of the celebrations, I went on stage at the end of the gala performance to give Natalia Bessmertnova a huge bouquet of flowers. It was wonderful to be there amongst these Russian dancers once more, such super people who made me feel so happy. When I see them dance I want to dance again. They give of themselves completely, putting so much energy into their performance, and I knew I would be reliving Lavrovsky's thrilling performance with Bessmertnova for months to come. I saw them at the German Embassy reception next evening when I was able to discuss with a top member of Intourist the possible guest performances of two Bolshoi principals with Festival Ballet. I was pleased that this was met with enthusiasm and we got down to dates and repertoire – all most encouraging.

Much of that last day was spent at the Ballet School, where I watched Golovkina teaching their top students. I also watched the second year girls and later was transfixed by the incredible turn-out already achieved by a class of young boys. The classes were given by superb teachers, and it was inspiring to see such care and discipline. At night we were taken to see *Swan Lake* at the Kremlin Palace, a venue I disliked because of its size and impersonal atmosphere. John Vernon must have overslept next morning, and consequently kept me waiting with an increasingly worried interpreter. When Vernon finally emerged with his luggage she hustled us into a waiting taxi who then drove frantically over snow-covered icy roads to the airport. We were rushed through customs safely with the TV film and out onto the plane awaiting take-off. After such a hair-raising hour it was a comfort to be airborne and a pleasure later to indulge in some delicious caviar.

Leaving Heathrow, I took a train to Victoria where Sven and Ingvar were waiting for me. We went straight to a snow-covered Fernhill. I could not believe that this dream place was now really ours. In my absence they had already done quite a bit of work inside, as well as outside in our two-acre wild, woodland clearing.

Monday and Tuesday I was back in the office before taking off for Paris again where the season was going reasonably well. On Friday Sven joined me in Paris which was lovely as we were able to go together to the British Embassy reception on Saturday. The 'Queen Victoria Party' had been arranged by the Hendersons, the British Ambassador and his wife, whom we had got to know in Chile when I was dancing there nine years previously. They were so kind to us during that visit, and it was good to see them again under such agreeable circumstances.

We left Paris late Sunday, and on Monday, arriving at the London office I found Findlay in a flap having just heard that Nureyev had been taken ill. Being Monday there was no performance that night, which gave me time to try and contact Breuer and Bart. We could find neither until our switchboard girl located Breuer's parents in Munich and they kindly agreed to get in touch with him. At 10pm Breuer was on the phone telling me that he would be arriving in Paris on Tuesday in time to rehearse with Evdokimova and perform with her that night. I rang Paris to give Grunwald and Heather the good news and also rang Findlay at home to put his mind at rest.

I took the early plane to Paris next morning to be met by Grunwald and Joanie who took me straight away to see Nureyev. He was ill with a patch on the lung, but pleased to see me, so I stayed for an hour. Breuer landed at midday, and it was reassuring to watch him rehearsing with Evdokimova. Breuer danced better than ever that night. After such a successful achievement, I took the two stars to dinner with Graham Bond, Donald, Heather and Nicky Johnson, who had already danced the prince's role a few times in England. At the end of the meal Breuer dropped a bombshell – he didn't want to be in our revival of *The Fairy's Kiss* at the Coliseum as agreed because South Africa's major ballet company had offered him an enormous fee to perform with them at the same time. I was horrified by his attitude. His name was already in print but, despite my objections, he was determined to go. Meanwhile, Bart had been contacted and was due to arrive in Paris on Wednesday to dance the evening show. But his plane was delayed and diverted to Genoa, so Johnson went on as the prince and did well indeed. He had been a principal with the Royal Ballet before joining Festival during the past year and was proving invaluable as a classical dancer and a talented actor. He was a jolly person to have around, and I was pleasantly surprised when he came to say he would like to be in

Festival Ballet. However, his wife, Laura Connor, a beautiful ballerina, would be staying with the Royal Ballet.

I had to return to London Thursday afternoon to make a report to the Conservative MP Paul Channon who chaired a small committee, together with the opera singer Geraint Evans, to look into the state of the arts. Paul Findlay was also invited, but I felt somewhat embarrassed by his manner and unwillingness to look at things broadly. I was happy when it was over and I was able to spend the rest of the evening at home with my son.

I went back to Paris next day and was astonished to learn that Nureyev was going on that night for the first time since Sunday. He had spent four days in bed with a temperature and the lung had not yet fully recovered. I thought he showed terrific courage. He enjoyed a great ovation – no-one could perform like Nureyev. After all his admirers left, he seemed to want me to stay and, at his request, I massaged his neck, shoulders and chest. It was strange to find him in such a mellow, relaxed mood. After Saturday's show he was weak and exhausted, but insisted on dancing at both the matinee and evening on Sunday. I saw he needed the excitement of performing to resuscitate him.

Yet another serious worry emerged with the rumour of a new touring classical company being formed with headquarters in London. It was said that De Beers, the big diamond corporation in South Africa, were putting up two million pounds, and it would be run by Ben Stevenson with John Field's involvement. Paul Sarony was approached for the London management and already Trunoff had been asked to stage *Graduation Ball.* Findlay told me they also wanted permission to have *Summer Solstice.* They were offering higher salaries than we could possibly afford, and Stevenson had already talked to some of my dancers. I hoped they would not try to lure Nureyev away from us. Whatever could we do?

I knew I must contact Weiss immediately and began to wonder if we could pay a higher salary to our principals and Betty Anderton. She had joined us recently from the Royal Ballet as ballet mistress and teacher. She was excellent at everything she undertook and got on well with Nureyev, who had confidence in her and her ability to rehearse his *Sleeping Beauty*. I also considered appointing Donald Barclay as my assistant director if finances permitted. Findlay flew to Paris for a long management meeting before which I spoke seriously with Nureyev about his future association with us and whether this also included staging *Romeo and Juliet*? He said he definitely intended creating it on the Company in time for the 1977 Coliseum season and to tour with us to Australia, America and South Africa. This might be the answer to the threatened competition.

Our final week in Paris saw me flying backwards and forwards as usual. I needed to be with Findlay for a meeting with the impresario from South Africa. Gorlinsky was eager to see us appearing there with Nureyev in the summer. Lilian Hochhauser rang saying she had already offered Nureyev a season at the Coliseum in the summer. We met at Gorlinsky's office where he was rude to Lilian because she asked him about letters he had written promising Nureyev for June at the Coliseum. Later at our office I got Findlay to find out from the Coliseum the exact dates Lilian had been given. Findlay had a meeting with Equity about the threat the new company would pose to Festival Ballet. They thought another company would not necessarily be a problem, particularly if backed by sufficient money. Although South Africa was not popular, with apartheid still in place, de Beers finance would provide work and money to more dancers. They were, therefore, not too concerned about the impact on Festival Ballet.

After Tuesday's performance, Nureyev generously gave a fabulous dinner party at Maxim's. Our principals and conductor were present, and we were thrilled to be at this famous restaurant. Next evening I was in London giving a speech on the arts at the Mansion House: rather daunting but wonderful to be a part of so much tradition. I had another long session with Gillard, who happily was making good progress on my biography, before returning to Paris for the last night at the Palais des Sports. All 27 performances were hugely successful, attracting large audiences, pleasing all concerned including the dancers who were now looking forward to a week's holiday.

50 *A Home For Festival*

We were soon back at Donmar deep in rehearsals of *Don Quixote* with the choreographer Borkowski. Ruanne and Breuer were dancing in Hong Kong and Fulton with Loggenburg were soon off to guest in South Africa. This was a big challenge for them and also a good advertisement for Festival Ballet. I encouraged my dancers to accept invitations to guest with other companies even though it generally meant reorganising our casting.

Plans for the acquisition of a part of Queen Alexandra House were moving fast. Weiss and I met our architect on site to make final decisions on its transformation. Findlay and I went to NatWest headquarters in the City, coming away two hours later with a verbal agreement of a £15,000 loan. Nureyev had agreed to the first night of his June Festival Season becoming a gala in aid of our building fund. Lady Astor generously allowed us to launch this gala evening with a press conference at her house in Lyall Street, to which Nureyev came.

I heard from Terabust of the possibility of her dancing part-time with Roland Petit's company. I promptly said we would raise her salary, not even knowing if we could afford this. She was important to us and I could not risk sharing her with Petit. I prayed we could find enough money to retain her. Moreland was working so slowly on his new ballet, *Dancing Space*, that Kern wanted me to withdraw it from our coming Coliseum season. I was loath to do this and felt I must rely on Anderton to help him work faster. Moreland complained that he had too little rehearsal time even though we always gave him as much time as we could spare. Also disturbing was a report from Heather that Ronald Hynd was to ask for heavy royalties for his *Nutcracker*, while Moreland's agent was also seeking higher fees for his clients.

A four-week tour to Eastbourne, Bournemouth, Wolverhampton and Leeds began in Eastbourne with a disastrous dress rehearsal of *Don Quixote*, followed by an awful performance in which the Company appeared sloppy and untidy. It was only saved by the exciting dancing of Bart and Terabust, and some good conducting by Bond. The theatre was not full, confirming my anxiety over audiences' reluctance to see a ballet with an uncommon title. We needed our marketing officer to advertise it better.

Returning late Thursday to Eastbourne I found that Moreland had got temperamental and walked out of his second call with his tapes. We could not continue rehearsing his *Dancing Space* and had no option but to cancel his calls for the remainder of the week. I was furious and rang Findlay to contact Moreland's agent who was full of excuses touching upon royalties still not agreed for the new ballet. A week later, to my relief, Moreland returned to continue work. It would not have looked good if an advertised new ballet was withdrawn from the London programme.

The following Sunday Gorlinsky arranged a press conference at the Royal Lancaster Hotel about the forthcoming Nureyev Festival. The Canadian ballerina Karen Kain was there because, to my surprise, Nureyev had invited her to dance with him on the opening night. I had presumed that it was to be Evdokimova as Nureyev had not told me otherwise.

On Friday morning 2nd April the ballet world was shocked and saddened to hear of the death of David Blair, one of the Royal Ballet's brightest stars. He had suffered a heart attack and his daughter had found him dead in the bath. The previous week I had attended a memorial service at the Russian church for Lubov Tchernicheva. This Russian dancer had become a legend, leaving Russia to dance in Diaghilev's company, in the de Basil and then Ballet Russe company. She and her husband, Grigoriev, went on to teach and produce some of Diaghilev's ballets for many companies, including the Royal Ballet. These deaths shook me into thinking about the unpredictability of life and how fleeting were the dancing years.

There were ongoing complications over our performances with Nureyev. Grunwald told Findlay he was taking Scottish Ballet to Paris and not us, as Nureyev had told him he wanted to appear with us at the London Palladium instead of in Paris. Gorlinsky denied this, saying that Nureyev wished to dance the Bournonville ballet *La Sylphide* with whichever company could obtain it for him. And so it went on, until Gorlinsky admitted it was up to Nureyev to sort it out. Nureyev rang me in the middle of the night and told me to meet him the next day at the Ritz at 1pm. I dressed smartly, arrived in good time but waited in vain for an hour. He never appeared and I never received an explanation.

Another upsetting development was Heather's decision to leave in three months. She was my right hand and a workaholic but, after five years, said she had to have a break. I knew I would miss her terribly, but as I got dreadfully tired myself, at times totally exhausted, I understood. I hoped I had not upset her by being too demanding or impatient. I began looking for a replacement, wondering if Geoffrey McNab might like to return now he had taken his one-year arts administration course. I could not decide what to do but contacted him to find out what he was planning.

I had an interesting evening at the Chinese Embassy for a showing of a Chinese ballet film, *Red Detachment of Women*, and Sven and I were pleased to see Fonteyn there. Over the fine dinner to which we were treated I was able to have, possibly my first ever, totally relaxed conversation with Fonteyn – neither of us was still dancing.

Sven and I had an exciting invitation to dine at No 10 Downing Street with the Prime Minister Edward Heath, who was entertaining the Prime Minister of New Zealand, Robert Muldoon, and his charming wife Thea. Although the invitation clashed with our opening night I could not turn down such an honour. Thea came to watch a full dress rehearsal of *Don Quixote*, which she obviously enjoyed even though it was a stop-and-start affair. In the event I managed to see most of the first act of *Don Quixote* before leaving with Sven by taxi for Downing Street. There were quite a number of people present, including the Liberal Leader Jeremy Thorpe, one of Sven's patients, who greeted Sven as an old friend.

51 *Two Coliseum Seasons And A Royal Patron*

Our April-May Coliseum season passed swiftly, with appreciative audiences. We gave four full-length classics and four different triple bill programmes in an endeavour to attract a wide audience. I worried constantly that there was insufficient rehearsal time to polish each work. With the number of programme changes the stage staff also worked to a tight schedule, frequently running late, which cut into the dancers' class and rehearsals. Towards the end of our fourth week, the Company had its regular meeting at which ensued a big disagreement. The Equity representative, Terry Hayworth, resigned, handing over the leadership to – not one – but eight dancers.

The next day was the first ever performance by the Company of *The Golden Cockerel*, Papa Beriozoff's brilliant and amusing production. The entire triple bill dress rehearsal was running late when I was told by one of the new Equity committee that I now had to ask the dancers if they were willing to go into overtime. I could hardly believe what I was hearing and felt sick at heart. This was not characteristic behaviour from my Company, and I felt uneasy.

A few days later, Weiss and I went to Equity headquarters where we were met by John Cruft for a Policy Committee meeting. We were questioned for almost an hour, which I resented but tried to keep my responses light-hearted with a touch of humour. I wondered if the new group had complained, but I loved my dancers and always considered their welfare. In order to survive, the Company had to rely to a great extent on its box office returns to supplement our GLC and Arts Council grants, always operating on a tight budget. Weiss and I heard no more and the normal routine continued unhindered.

Our last week began dramatically. We were to give *Spectre de la Rose* Monday evening with *Giselle*, but there was no Fulton and no Bart to be seen for the morning rehearsal with orchestra. Kern took his players through a difficult passage in Act II of *Giselle* while the understudies, Johnson and Rowan, quickly prepared to do the first run-through. Fulton's neck trouble was bad so she could not dance that day. To my relief, Bart arrived, his plane having been delayed. He went through *Spectre* with Rowan dancing it for the first time.

I was satisfied with neither the set nor the essential chair and thought Beriozoff's interpretation of the choreography somehow lacking. We tried to make a few improvements when someone came rushing up to me saying Johnson had fainted. To my horror, he was unconscious for over three minutes. There were no medical staff on hand to help, but when he came to it transpired he was on antibiotics for a poisoned tooth, which had become so painful that he had taken some painkillers as well. He recovered and was on next evening in *Spectre* with Rowan, and Bart danced in *Giselle* with a recovered Terabust. We heard that Geoffrey McNab was interested in returning, this time as general manager – to which Findlay was totally opposed – let alone what that would have meant for Peter B; Findlay, Weiss, Geoffrey and I met at the theatre to find a resolution, and it was decided Geoffrey would come as Findlay's assistant.

An amazing evening followed: the curtain went up late as there was trouble with the lighting; the computer went wrong because the air conditioning had broken down and the switchboard overheated; then, in the second interval, there was a fire in the dustbins and everyone in the Coliseum was temporarily evacuated, so we were late finishing the performance of *Giselle*. Our experienced Kern was the conductor that evening. He quickly read the score and cut the beginning of Act II starting with the entrance of the Wili Queen, thereby saving quite a few minutes. In the interval Peter Schaufuss came to see me about returning to the Company at the end of the week – but I could not take him back at such short notice. He was upset and, much to my surprise, became quite offensive. That evening coincided with the final performance of Imre Dozse, an excellent leading dancer from Hungary. We were sorry to see him go, and I was touched when he handed me a lovely bowl as he departed.

Don Quixote closed the season on Friday and Saturday but sadly, despite its humour, colourful sets and costumes enlivening some glorious dancing, it failed to attract full houses. I was feeling terribly tired and realised how touchy I was at home with Sven and Ingvar, the two people I loved most. It was wonderful that we were able now to spend our weekends at Fernhill in the peace and beauty of its surroundings, even though there was much work to do there both in and out of doors. It was magical waking to the singing of birds, looking out of our full-length bedroom windows to see deer and pheasants amongst the untramelled areas of our two-acre clearing in the forest.

Two weeks later the Company was back dancing at the Coliseum for the Nureyev Festival, a three-week season of twenty-seven performances of *Sleeping Beauty*. To my delight I received a letter from Lady Napier, Princess Margaret's lady-in-waiting, confirming the Princess's patronage of London Festival Ballet. This was a great honour, giving the Company prestige and tremendous encouragement. It was timely that Princess Margaret, now our Patron, was present for the launch of the building fund appeal for our first ever home, near the Royal Albert Hall. The Princess was charming and in a relaxed, happy mood despite arriving ten minutes late, after the foyer was cleared for her planned arrival at 7.15pm. The whole evening went beautifully and after Nureyev's final ecstatic applause died down, I took Princess Margaret on stage where she spent a long time talking with the dancers and staff, captivating everyone by her elegance and sincere interest. I then heard that Evdokimova had developed measles so it was fortuitous that Nureyev had invited Karen Kain to dance with him on the first night.

Once HRH had departed, everyone was invited to the Hochhausers' garden for a midnight supper party. They were the presenters of the festival for Nureyev, who I thought seemed a little distant with me, but perhaps I was imagining it. Everyone was thrilled by the evening's performance, and I knew my Company had danced their best. I was concerned that we might encounter illness and injuries over such a prolonged season of one of the most demanding of all classical ballets.

Tuesday 15th June became an extraordinary day. After a full Board meeting at County Hall, Weiss and I were whisked away to the Banqueting Hall in Whitehall for the Queen's Silver Jubilee celebration, and from there were driven to Sadler's Wells to a gala celebrating the Rambert Dance Company's 25th anniversary. We met Sven at the theatre just before the arrival of Princess Margaret, who looked exquisite as always.

The small company danced well under the new direction of Norman Morrice. Marie Rambert had created the first ever British ballet company in 1926. Five years on it became known as The Ballet Club and was linked to the Mercury Theatre, with Alicia Markova as their principal ballerina. In 1935 it took the name Ballet Rambert until it underwent changes in 1966, becoming a modern dance group and discarding its classical repertoire. Classical ballets are expensive to stage and use many dancers, and Madam Rambert always had to run her classical company on a shoe-string. The change to more contemporary work was sad but made sense, making the company more successful and maintaining a high standard which was evident at their gala performance.

June was the month in which our company contracts were discussed and when I spoke with each dancer about work and prospects. Findlay joined me when I saw the principals, as salaries were important to all parties. Inevitably there were leavers every year, which gave me the chance to continue building the standard of the Company. We were always on the lookout for good classical dancers to strengthen Festival Ballet. But although we held regular auditions and would willingly see applicants on tour in Company class, real talent was hard to find.

I was sad to lose one particular dancer for whom I held high hopes: Judith Rowan. Having worked her way up swiftly from corps to senior artist she had been given some interesting roles. She began to get difficult, however, even refusing to go on in Nureyev's pas de cinq one evening when she was not to be the lead dancer. I could see that she was impatient to become a principal but in my opinion she was not quite ready for that responsibility. She left to join the Royal Ballet, though not as a principal.

I was delighted when, towards the end of the season, Weiss brought Markova into my box and I was able to ask her if she would stage *Les Sylphides* for the Company. Her understanding and interpretation of the Fokine ballet was legendary, so I was pleased when she readily agreed to prepare and present this for us. The last matinee was even more exciting than the closing performance of the Nureyev season. He received ecstatic acclaim from the audience from whom flowers and bouquets were showered onto the stage. The evening was less wild and, to my surprise, Nureyev brought me on stage, giving me an enormous embrace.

I was thankful when the final curtain brought the season to a happy conclusion without any major disasters having occurred other than Gorlinsky's mischievous meddling… one day Paris was on, the next it was off, as he said he was inviting Makarova and the Scottish Ballet in our place. I could get no clear answer either from Nureyev, who merely said that even if we were not appearing with him in Paris he could still find six weeks in which to create *Romeo and Juliet* for our Company.

52 *Monte Carlo And Princess Grace*

On the horizon was a week in the glorious setting of Monte Carlo, the last engagement for the dancers before their three-week holiday. Princess Grace of Monaco took a deep interest in visiting companies and for our week requested a new work be premiered. I asked Ronald Hynd if he could create something suitable. He suggested a work using the story and music of *La Chatte,* a ballet Balanchine produced in 1927. But the Princess would not accept this as it had been premiered in Monte Carlo with the Ballets Russes and she wished for a completely original ballet during our season. Boosey and Hawkes had earlier sent me some hitherto unknown music by Elgar titled *L'Eventail*, wondering if I might like to use it for a ballet. Hynd heard it but had dismissed it. We thought if he created a work to this music it would be a first in every sense, and Princess Grace was pleased with the idea of an Edwardian period piece reflecting Elgar's atmospheric music.

An excited Company flew to Monte Carlo a day before our opening in the historic Opera House. It was thrilling to be there and, as the successful week progressed, we were deep into orchestral, stage and dress rehearsals for Hynd's premiere. I felt we were continuing the Diaghilev tradition – his company had been resident for several months in Monte Carlo each year in order to create new works for his company. Happily *L'Eventail* received a good reception at the end of the week when the Princess attended the premiere. When the curtain came down she showed her appreciation by coming on stage to thank and congratulate everyone. The ballet became a valuable addition to our repertoire, but for me it would always be linked to the gracious, beautiful Princess Grace.

The week was a happy one for me as Sven came too and visited his friend Ian Javal who, after a severe illness, lived in Opeo with his wife Joan. They were the owners of an extensive olive grove which came with their fascinating cottage. They looked after Sven handsomely, driving him around the countryside as well as to Monte Carlo for our performances, which they thoroughly enjoyed. It was strange, however, not seeing dear Guy who had recently died. As we passed his house L'Olivade a wave of sadness at his death overcame me. His house looked unchanged but his garden, of which he had taken such care and pride, was not the same, appearing less loved and less nurtured.

The season ended on Sunday and the Company's year was also at an end. In holiday mood the next morning Sven and I flew back to London. My father was waiting to greet us at number 78, patient and smiling as always. We decided to spend the holiday mostly at Fernhill, attempting to tame the wilderness that was our garden. There were also some engagements in town to be carried out but, even so, I knew I could feel free from stress and was looking forward to the holiday. I was still deeply saddened by the recent death of my goddaughter, Alison, who had slipped away from this world while only nine. It was tragic; she was ill for a long time so for Alison it was a merciful release, but heartbreaking for my cousin Rosalie, her mother. It affected all the family; her three brothers and her father loved her dearly. How cruel life can be.

At the office on Tuesday morning, the time came to say adieu to Heather and the staff had laid on a little party. Heather would shortly return as my assistant, and in the meantime I had engaged as my secretary Margaret Kingsnorth who had worked for me during my two years at the Arts Educational Schools.

The next few days at Fernhill were idyllic – that is until the second week brought a letter from Ingvar in Germany where he was working on a farm for a month. To our horror, he had suffered a bad accident and been taken to hospital. He had been high up on a ladder, repairing windows of an old farmhouse, when a passing car hit the ladder throwing Ingvar down onto the street below. The surgeon said it was a miracle he was not killed nor too badly injured, just terribly bruised, with his eyes having taken a nasty blow. He returned the next day with two black and bloodied eyes, and it was a joy to have Ingvar safely home with us.

I had only to go to London once during the third holiday week. This was for an Executive meeting, when I took advantage of being at the office and going through the post and other things with Geoffrey. The Executive was not particularly helpful regarding new works. I had contacted Glen Tetley to see if he would give us one of his ballets and had an enthusiastic reply suggesting his work, *Greening*. My delight was not shared by the governors who were wary of contemporary works. I explained how important it was for our dancers to work with different choreographers, to keep them challenged and stimulated, and also for them to be seen in some contemporary works. Yet it was hard to find talented choreographers whose work was appropriate for the Company.

53 *1976: Company On Television, And Losing Paul*

Returning refreshed and relaxed from the holiday for rehearsals at Donmar and Dance Centre, I was upset by what Donald told me: Betty Anderton had said that the Company had a bad name for overwork and underpay and also lack of discipline, which I could not understand. It gave me a horrid feeling inside and brought back the burning pain of a threatened ulcer for the first time in ages. She said the dancers were not good enough for *Greening*, adding Tetley thought the same, which seemed strange as it was he who had suggested this work for the Company. Donald said he replied that a dancer's life was sheer hard work, to which she retorted that we have to relate to today and existing conditions. Had she forgotten we were soon to acquire our own quarters for the first time? Whatever had got into her? I felt most disturbed. She was obviously unaware of the debts the Company had incurred and which, since I was appointed, we had tried to pay off, so every penny was counted. How thankful I was for Donald's loyalty and support.

We had two weeks before the start of a month's season at Festival Hall where we were putting on three classics and a triple bill – each programme running for a week. The first dress rehearsal was a disaster, and I was frightened how *Giselle* was going to look that evening. The period style so essential in Skeaping's production, marking it out from other ballets, seemed to have gone. It returned, however, and the Company pulled itself together and gave a sensitive rendering of this dramatic ballet. I sat on tenterhooks the entire evening in the Ceremonial Box with Mrs Townsend of the GLC, but Terabust and Bart inspired everyone and *Giselle* had a good reception. But *Giselle* failed to attract full houses at Festival Hall; perhaps placing *Spectre de la Rose* with it as an opener had been a mistake, although *Giselle* was always a difficult ballet to attract a full house. On the second night the audience became impatient at the long interval between *Spectre* and *Giselle* and started slow hand-clapping, which was disconcerting. We were puzzled as it took no longer than our intervals took at the Coliseum with the same change of scenery.

The *Swan Lake* week saw much higher attendance and so did the ever attractive *Coppélia*. Even the triple bill did better than *Giselle* and far better than we expected. All in all it had been a productive month at Festival Hall, its restaurant and other facilities enabling us to entertain a lot of VIPs and hold comfortable press and magazine interviews. I longed for our own place to be ready. Queen Alexandra's House was still undergoing big changes to equip us with studios and offices befitting our Ballet Company's headquarters.

As soon as the Festival Hall season was over, we began our annual autumn tour of the provinces. In six cities we gave either *Swan Lake* or *Coppélia* for the entire week, which certainly brought in the public. After a busy week back in London we were on the road again premiering the new Ronald Hynd *Nutcracker* in Liverpool, which was exciting yet also worrying. *Nutcracker* was a guaranteed Christmas income every year. It had to be a good production with family appeal. The first dress rehearsal on Monday was an hour late starting and ran from 4pm until 10pm, by when I was worn out with worry. I was disappointed in the Act I set and costumes, which appeared rather dull and colourless; the fight scene was messy; the snow scene was not bright enough; the dancers were finding the choreography difficult and to me the story seemed unclear. Should I propose changes, or was I over-reacting? Certainly the end of a long stressful day was no time to have such a discussion with the designer and choreographer, so I decided to wait and see what the morrow would bring, hoping that things would improve.

The premiere arrived – along with a TV crew, press reporters, Findlay, Weiss and other notables. The lighting crew and stage staff spent the morning adjusting the sets, lighting and transformation scenes with the designer Peter Docherty and Ronald Hynd. This concentrated effort was followed by the final dress rehearsal with full orchestra, which proceeded fitfully with many stops and starts, not concluding until after 6pm. It was a packed house, and to my overwhelming relief the audience reaction was good. They applauded the new *Nutcracker* enthusiastically. Nureyev had been in front but left by car as soon as the curtain came down. I joined the *Nutcracker* sponsors, NatWest, who gave a celebratory drinks party front of house and were delighted with the production.

We gave a party on stage for the Company and staff with a happy Docherty and Hynd and a most incredulous me!

As the tour progressed from Liverpool to Leeds and then on to Newcastle we were able to make careful changes and modifications to *Nutcracker.* At the Birmingham Hippodrome we played for two weeks, opening with a triple bill which made a happy interlude from *Nutcracker.* The BBC were to televise the ballet in Birmingham and John Drummond came to see it. Evdokimova and Breuer were not at their best that evening, having both flown in from Germany that day. For the first time ever I was embarrassed by their poor performance and only hoped it had not been obvious.

As soon as our season was over on Saturday night the television people moved into the Hippodrome and had everything set up and ready for our first rehearsal with them on Sunday afternoon. We started at 4.30pm for what I would term a 'walk-through and placing call', stopping at 7.30pm. I was careful to watch the TV crew setting up the cameras as the dancers needed to be aware where they were placed.

There were more rehearsals Monday and Tuesday before the final recording of the ballet Tuesday evening in front of an invited audience. I felt nervous about the recording and was on edge all day. In consequence I made a poor speech before the curtain went up. Outside the theatre in the broadcasting van I sat in suspense throughout the recording, watching every move. I should not have worried. Everyone behaved professionally, working happily under the direction of John Vernon, an experienced producer. Evdokimova and Breuer danced superbly, and our conductor Graham Bond brought out the best from our orchestra. The ballet was screened on BBC1 Boxing Day afternoon, which gave the Company marvellous exposure. It is extraordinary that the fee for the transmission of the entire ballet was £180.

The dancers could hardly wait to return to London for a few days' intermission after such a full tour. There had been the new *Nutcracker* and at the end of the tour the television recording. All had added excitement and extra work as well as new prestige for the Company. As the rehearsal week progressed, we received more coverage when Doris Barry (Markova's sister) arranged for a few dancers to appear on the children's programme, *Blue Peter*. Before the week was out, Nureyev was back with us in Donmar beginning initial work on his *Romeo and Juliet*. But Christmas Eve was soon upon us and we were dress-rehearsing the new *Nutcracker* in Festival Hall. Considering it was hung there for the first time it worked surprisingly well, even the problematic transformation scenes. Docherty was a clever designer and our stage crew were skilled at their work so we were able to depart early evening with our cards and gifts to enrich our Christmas.

Findlay's six-year contract was now coming to an end, and he had written a letter saying he wished to stay on. His future was discussed at the November Executive meeting when it was agreed he stay for a further year. But at the close of the Board meeting at County Hall mid-December the question of Findlay's contract came up again. I was asked to leave the room. I heard later that most Board members were content for him to continue as administrator with the exception of the chairman, Weiss. By pushing for a younger person with more drive he finally won over the majority, who then agreed not to renew Findlay's contract. Weiss told me this and informed me that the Board suggested I take over as the top person with Peter B as administrator under my authority. I said to Weiss this proposal would need careful thought.

Thrilled as I was, I realised this added responsibility would impinge on my time and detract from my work with my dancers. It was a great boost, however, to know the Board had such faith in me, and this gave me renewed confidence. I thanked God for their trust in me and began to ponder the right way forward. In the event, Peter B still did not want to take on the responsibility of administrator, preferring once again to stay in his present position as general manager. After deliberation, it was decided to seek someone externally to take on Findlay's position as administrator and act jointly with me as artistic director as before.

After a good opening Boxing Day matinee we had press out front in the evening. There was a strike next day so we had to wait for the press reports which, when they came out, were good with the exception of an awful one by John Percival in the Times. He was vitriolic about Hynd's changes and had not a good word about any of the dancing. We all expect some criticism but I wished this one had been a little more constructive. It had no bad effect on the box office and we gave 31 successive performances with various casts. Our main protagonists were Evdokimova and Breuer, Ruanne and Bart, with Hill and Johnson appearing regularly. At the end of the first week we gave Nicol and Dubreuil the matinee, and they delivered a most lovely performance together. During the second week Hynd was keen we put on Asensio with Dubreuil, which came over impressively. We also gave Kenneth McCombie some leading performances for the first time in London with Nicol, whose gentle calmness gave him confidence. By his second performance he danced excellently, but still needed more guidance with his partnering. I ensured that each couple received a press night as I felt it important they should be encouraged and be seen in the new production now firmly established.

Ruanne and Bart gave the last performance of our three weeks at Festival Hall. During that time Gareth Forbes, our publicity man, arranged for me to entertain several senior figures from firms and organisations we hoped might sponsor the Company. Gareth had always devised ways in which to promote the Company, so it was rather a blow when he told me he planned to return to Australia for good in six months' time. I knew we would miss him greatly and his enthusiastic loyalty. During his years with us he really cared about the Company, remaining cheerfully positive. He handled so well my *This is Your Life* programme, keeping it a complete secret from me. He was now working on a special fashion show to be held at the Goldsmiths' Hall at the beginning of our third rehearsal week. Our dancers were to take part as mannequins and hopefully also perform in the presence of HRH the Duchess of Gloucester.

Mid-January arrived and the Company had their one-week winter break. On Sunday, at the end of the week of performances, my indefatigable male dancers played a football match at the 'Private Banks Sports Club' at Catford Bridge – what energy! During the coming five weeks of rehearsal we had Papa Beriozoff working on the two-act ballet *The Golden Cockerel* which was scheduled back into the repertoire in the forthcoming three-week season in Manchester. By the end of the second week we saw Enzo Frigerio's designs for *Romeo and Juliet* for the first time, which were closely examined by Kim Baker, our wardrobe supervisor, and Ray Dixon, our technical director, who thought they were dark and macabre. We were rather puzzled and somewhat shaken by the proposed artwork. I saw Gorlinsky, telling him we were disturbed by the designs. He suggested I went to Paris to discuss it with Nureyev in person. I also spoke to the critic Nigel Gosling of our misgivings who, having seen the synopsis, was able to reassure me in some measure about Nureyev's conception, which he was apparently placing in the Renaissance period.

Eventually I was successful in reaching Nureyev and, following Gorlinsky's advice, suggested I went across next day to talk over his ideas on the ballet and our reaction to the costume and set designs. Nureyev resented my questioning his conception, so we had a verbal tussle over the phone. He eventually agreed we should meet in Paris for a good talk, but did not want Findlay to accompany me. It had to be the following week after the third of his first nights was over. This suited me as I was booked to fly midweek to Geneva with Donald to see Jonas Kåge dance and have a discussion.

On arrival in Geneva we were well looked after by Patricia Neary, tall and thin like all Balanchine dancers. She was charming and most helpful, but I sensed a certain nervousness in her. We dined with Kåge and his wife after the performance to discuss his possible appearances with Festival Ballet, and left next morning satisfied the journey had been worthwhile. Despite only an average technique we felt Kåge would produce distinctive performances and give us some added glamour – he was well built and good looking. He was a lovely person, and we hoped to offer him some interesting roles as a guest artist.

That same week the fashion show at the Goldsmiths' Hall took place and was a great success. I welcomed HRH the Duchess of Gloucester. She was relaxed and enhanced the glamour of the whole evening, making my role as escort a happy experience.

At Covent Garden mid week, Sven and I saw the first night of Cranko's *Taming of the Shrew* and loved every minute. I thought how perfectly it would have suited Festival Ballet. Next day I flew to Manchester for a press conference then on to Paris to see Nureyev. He was performing at the Palais des Sports, after which we had a detailed discussion over dinner on his intriguing plans for *Romeo and Juliet.* My fears and reservations about his production now put to rest, I felt impatient for him to start rehearsals. But these could not begin for a further month as we had a fortnight's season in Manchester while Nureyev, likewise, was fully engaged elsewhere.

The Golden Cockerel, back in the repertoire, looked marvellous with Donald Barclay on stage once more as the amusing magician. But not so *Études*. It was a mess at the dress rehearsal, and I had to take some sections again to improve the dancers' work. This was much better at the evening's performance, the start of our second week in Manchester. The stage staff made a mess of the crucial changes of the barres, and the ballet was rather spoiled. I had to have strong words with Mogridge and his assistant Vicky who admitted it had been a fiasco. Paul Findlay was up for the performance, seemingly not unduly disturbed by the muddle.

I determined not to miss Ingvar's degree ceremony at the Royal Albert Hall on March 9th, although it fell in the middle of our Manchester season. The degrees were presented by the Queen Mother and I felt my heart racing as he bowed to HRH with such respect. I was so proud of his having achieved his Bachelor of Science with honours from London University. He had lived at home with us during the three years of study, and we saw how hard he worked. It was a great day and once home we found my father waiting with a bottle of champagne to celebrate Ingvar's success. Sven took us out later to the May Fair where we enjoyed a fine dinner in a haze of happiness.

Once the Manchester season was past and the Company home in London, I flew to New York. My purpose was to meet Jane Hermann, the Artistic Director of Presentations at the Metropolitan Opera House, and then go on to Washington to meet with Martin Feinstein. In planning a visit of Festival Ballet with Nureyev it was necessary to find out their wishes regarding the number of Nureyev's appearances they would expect, versus those of our own principals. From Gorlinsky, it appeared that Nureyev would be doing almost every show, which was worrying – hence my visit to hear their wishes and their point of view. As I suspected, this was not what either Jane or Martin had in mind, so I could foresee a battle ahead with Gorlinsky and Nureyev.

54 *Nureyev's Romeo And Juliet*

The next day, Sunday, Geoffrey welcomed the designer, Frigerio, to London where he planned to remain until the premiere of *Romeo and Juliet*. Nureyev arrived in London next day – the beginning of our second rehearsal week – and began work at 5pm amidst ardent anticipation: the next few weeks would be crucial. *Romeo and Juliet's* gala premiere, scheduled for the latter part of our London season, was two months hence. Nureyev appeared with his Italian masseur and a small entourage of enthusiastic supporters armed with flasks of coffee and food to sustain him. They generally included Nigel Gosling, the art critic, and his wife Maude Lloyd, the former Rambert dancer. They adored Nureyev and seemed to understand his temperamental outbursts which inevitably occurred from time to time. I was thankful that Betty Anderton was able to cope so well with Nureyev at these moments and only wished for more support from her regarding Company matters. For example, she chose not to attend our auditions where her judgement would have been invaluable.

I stayed to the 8.30 finish on numerous evenings, intrigued and captivated by Nureyev's choreography. It was completely original, cleverly fitting the familiar Prokofiev music and totally unlike the choreography seen in other ballets of this story. Highly dramatic, the dancing portrayed a clear story line. By the end of the week he had already staged the banquet scene. Meanwhile Frigerio had organised wig fittings in Fleet Street, and I felt things were moving at last. On a personal level I was to have my portrait painted by Edward Halliday who chose carefully the dress for my sittings. It was proving difficult to find mutually convenient hours but I was determined to make the time – it was an honour that he wished to paint me. A great and highly regarded artist, he had been the President of the Royal Society of Portrait Painters for many years. I found the time spent with him both restful and rewarding; he was such a kind, caring man. Also encouraging was David Gillard, now at the point of putting the final touches to my biography. Sven and I were invited to the publishers W H Allen & Co to see the proposed lay-out, with which we were pleased. Sven made some suggestions, knowing more about printing and publishing than his ballerina wife!

Soon the rehearsal weeks were over, not without the now familiar struggles between Festival Ballet, the Hochhausers, Gorlinsky and Nureyev. The main contention was a leaflet released by the Hochhausers, announcing Nureyev's *Romeo and Juliet* with little reference to Festival Ballet. Findlay and I were incensed and insisted on a meeting with them. Hochhausers agreed to withdraw the leaflet and replace it with one approved by us. This, as they explained, would also have to be passed by Gorlinsky and Nureyev and was finally agreed after a lot of arguments. We also had to insist that Evdokimova gave three performances with Nureyev at the Coliseum.

Nureyev was playing up more and more – even Betty Anderton was saying she could not stand him and his rudeness to everyone for much longer. I was really concerned that she would leave. We all put up with the unpleasant scenes as the ballet emerged as something special, and his rehearsals continued during our Coliseum season. A complicating factor was Nureyev's involvement in Ken Russell's film *Valentino.* He was playing the role of Rudolph Valentino for which he took lessons in the tango from the famous TV ballroom instructor Peggy Spencer (on the board of the ISTD with me). With Nureyev flying in and out of the country to fulfill other engagements – as were my four regular guest artists, Breuer, Bart, Terabust and Evdokimova – it meant careful juggling of dates for performances and rehearsals to meet everyone's requirements.

The dress rehearsal for the opening night for our season at the Coliseum on 26th April went from bad to worse. The lighting switchboard broke down, the dancing in *Études* was awful and *The Golden Cockerel* a total mess. I feared the evening would be a disaster – and certainly *Cockerel* fell rather flat due mainly to Bond's sluggish conducting, erasing the humour from the ballet. But the performance ended with a thrilling exposition of *Études* by all involved – dancers, stage and lighting crews, and with a fully restored switchboard. It was as if all had engaged in a great rejoicing – the two dynamic leading men Breuer and Bart in choreographed competition with one another and Miklosy dazzling with her pirouettes and personality, the ballet brought the house down. We felt this a good omen to our five-week run before Nureyev joined us for four weeks of his *Romeo and Juliet*, finishing with one week of *Giselle*. As expected, during our season Michael Edgley and Noel Pelly flew in from Australia to watch the Company in performance and talk with Gorlinsky.

Findlay and I had a high-level meeting at the Arts Council, together with Lord Harewood and Rupert Rhymes, the Coliseum's General Manager, to work out next year's dates at the Coliseum and make sure they slotted in with Nureyev's availability. There was a definite feeling of goodwill, and we came away relieved that they were willing to give us the dates we requested.

I was glad I had invited Dame Alicia Markova to produce our revival of *Les Sylphides*. Her performances in the Prelude in this Fokine ballet were legendary and, having worked with the creator of this exquisite classic, she was an authority. She had a gentle way of rehearsing the dancers by demonstrating the arms and body movements with an effortless grace and clarity. At the dress rehearsal Monday 9th May she did not overcorrect or overwork them but, by reminding them of the style and quality of movement, she achieved the desired effect from the dancers for the evening's performance, when it was much admired. It is invaluable when an artist conveys to the next generation the content and meaning of the original choreography. All too often one sees attention being given to steps and placing without an understanding of the reason behind moves and movements.

The following Thursday I introduced the children's matinee with a brief history of the Coliseum and an outline of the ballet *Nutcracker*. That afternoon my talented Vivian Loeber and Nicky Johnson gave a terrific first performance in the leading roles, identifying wonderfully with their young audience, who were carried away to a land of make-believe. The applause and shouts of delight by the end were deafening, and it did one good to see the happiness on the children's faces.

On Sunday, Sven's 70th birthday was celebrated at Fernhill with friends and family present. His eldest brother Ruben, with his wife Gunborg and Sven's sister Greta, had arrived in London several days ahead, staying with us in Park Street before the happy event in the country. I hoped my father would stay on at Fernhill with the Swedish relatives, but he wished to return to town on Monday with Sven and me – my father was a true Londoner, born and bred.

A triple bill took over the next week and Sir Adrian Boult came to conduct Elgar's score L'eventail for *The Sanguine Fan*, Hynd's romantic new ballet. I had been warmly welcomed by Sir Adrian and his wife to their home near Regent's Park, and was thrilled that he had accepted this invitation. As well as being prestigious for the Company and an inspiration for the dancers, it was also a challenge for the orchestra to play under such a distinguished conductor. They all stood and applauded him at the end of the final rehearsal and played superbly under his baton at every performance.

Our season finished on the Friday because of the stage preparations necessary for the incoming new production of Nureyev's *Romeo and Juliet.* We had already endured the first dress parade on Thursday, with Nureyev and Frigerio arguing and disagreeing. With so many costumes, wigs and accessories the parade took all day. The period costumes were splendid and those for the ballroom scene glorious. To everyone's delight, Sir Arthur Bliss came to watch our Friday rehearsal of *Romeo and Juliet.*

This was immediately before the last performance of our season for which, to my disappointment, Sven was not in front. When he knew I was to be in the theatre the entire weekend he had taken his Swedish visitors to friends in the West Country. Dear Sven: he was always so patient and understanding, but my absence during his family's visit upset him. It was one of the few times in our marriage that we had fallen out, and I felt sad going home alone to an empty house.

The next few days were a bit of a nightmare. While Nureyev worked with the Company at Donmar on Saturday, things were not going well at the Coliseum. The scenery was delivered late and incomplete, and the staff were having difficulty moving the heavy, wide pieces. Tharon Musser, the American lighting designer who was over at Nureyev's request, said the get-in was poorly directed and the scenery incorrectly hung – I feared she was correct. By Monday, however, the sets were in place for the Company to get on stage in costume but, with a late start, we had only covered two acts by 6.30pm. Nureyev asked the dancers if they would work on another two hours and they agreed. Whenever Nureyev and Frigerio disagreed, Frigerio would walk off the stage saying he would not return. A worried Findlay rang from the office to tell me Frigerio had given in his notice, but I reassured him we were seeing frequent temperamental outbursts and not to worry. Finishing at the agreed hour that evening, Nureyev dashed off to appear in a gala at Covent Garden. To my joy, Sven came to the theatre to take me out for supper, and how glad I was to see him.

At rehearsal next morning Nureyev insisted on running Act I again despite our not having finished Act II the night before. This was foolish: the Act I scenery had been taken out of the theatre for alteration and most of the costumes were being dyed or sprayed under the strict eye of Frigerio's wife. There was also a feeling of despondency amongst the Coliseum stage staff, which I had never encountered before. They could not see the production being ready in time for the Thursday Gala. Everyone worked on determinedly through Tuesday and Wednesday, punctuated by regular clashes between Nureyev and Frigerio, when the designer would 'walk out' and then return!

I was desperately worried, yet by Thursday afternoon the storm clouds cleared and, miraculously, all was going to be ready for the premiere that night.

I felt excited as I slipped home to change into a new white evening dress. On returning to the theatre I found to my dismay that I had forgotten my evening gloves, but the wonderful wardrobe came to my rescue just in time for me to greet Princess Margaret. She arrived on time, wearing a beautiful blue satin dress with glittering shoulder straps. A welcoming group escorted her to the Royal retiring room before the curtain rose at 7.40pm, ten minutes late. The first act went reasonably well but the first interval seemed to go on and on. The Princess asked: 'Were we not starting soon?' I knew the difficulties with which the stage crew were struggling and did my best to appease her. But, after a good second act, the second interval was even longer. The Princess enquired, 'When are we going to see the rest of the ballet?' It was the rest of the ballet that was worrying me. The tomb scene was under-lit and seemed long. I felt Nureyev spent too much time hauling his Juliet off the bed and dragging her across the floor of the sinister crypt. I feared the drab, sober ending would kill the ballet and I would be blamed for wasting so much money on the production and not having controlled Nureyev. Despite my fears, the public loved the ballet and gave Nureyev a great ovation which lasted a long time while I was taking Princess Margaret backstage. The applause finally over, HRH went on stage, congratulating Nureyev and meeting the dancers and staff involved with his dramatic production.

A dinner party at the Savoy followed and, though I lost Sven in the mêlée at the Coliseum, I found him seated at the Savoy patiently awaiting our arrival. Princess Margaret joined the party and Nureyev, deliriously happy with his success, sat next to her for the dinner. At the office next day reviews were read anxiously: the Times and the Financial Times gave the ballet rave notices, while the Telegraph was cautiously lukewarm and the two evening papers downright damning.

Having satisfactorily tied up with Gorlinsky and Findlay a second Nureyev tour in Australia, Edgley had returned satisfied to the southern hemisphere before the gala, having watched many rehearsals. Tharon Musser waited to see the gala and two more performances before leaving for New York. Having embarked on a run of twenty-five performances of *Romeo and Juliet*, Nureyev made sure that other influential people were invited to see the production at the Coliseum. He was keen to perform it in Paris and New York. Although Grunwald was interested in putting it on at the Palais des Sports, he said it would have to be shortened. This point was immediately taken up by Nureyev and John Lanchbery summoned to help Bond make acceptable cuts in the score, to which Nureyev was in accord.

It was already the Glorious Fourth of June celebration at Eton and this year Ingvar took his girlfriend there. He was happily telling us about it, stroking his white guinea pig on his lap, when Snowy suddenly died. Poor Ingvar was terribly upset. In fact we were all saddened by Snowy's unexpected death. I had not realised how fond we had become of this lovely, furry creature. She was mourned for several days – Ingvar's much loved pet left a gap in our lives.

On 7th June, like millions of others, we watched the television coverage of the celebrations for the Queen's Silver Jubilee. It was pouring with rain as the Royal procession wound its way to St Paul's, and, in true English fashion, it continued to rain during the spectacular firework display two evenings later.

The entire next day was spent interviewing for Findlay's replacement, which was tiring and unproductive. On getting to the theatre for the evening show I found that Rik Werner had left rehearsal abruptly on learning he was not to be promoted to principal status in September. He was back in time to appear in the role of Tybalt that evening but in the fight scene Nureyev flung him too forcefully and Werner complained his ribs were broken. Peter Hulme took him straight to the Middlesex Hospital – no real damage had been done. But I said to Nureyev we must put David Long into the role at some performances.

Nureyev's moods were tiresome, and next day was a bad one. Werner announced he could not do the performance as his ribs were too sore, while the orchestra was taken at its slowest pace ever. I was thankful when the performance was finally over and I could go home.

The *Romeo and Juliet* season continued with many stormy meetings, the first with the Hochhausers unable to reach an agreement about future dates. After we had explained how vital the Coliseum seasons were for Festival Ballet, we were able to reach a compromise. But, at a promising get-together with Gorlinsky, neither of us was able to persuade the prima ballerina and defector from the Kirov, Natalia Makarova, to give up her fourth Giselle during the last week of the Nureyev season. I had hoped that Evdokimova could have been given that performance. Nureyev had invited Makarova to dance several performances with him, and she was determined not to give way.

I witnessed a tempestuous Board meeting when Findlay and Peter Morris completely lost their tempers. I was inwardly furious with Peter for stating the number of dancers on the pay roll as 79. This appeared a lot to the Board, who had no conception of the necessity for so many dancers. Illness and injuries took their toll with constant performances, and there was a need for covers. I also encouraged my principals and leading soloists to accept guest artist invitations, all-important publicity for Festival Ballet and a challenge and morale-booster to the artists themselves, but potentially leaving us short of dancers.

I was astonished to receive the Queen's Jubilee Medal. It was a great honour, and I wore it with pride that evening at a dinner where I was speaking. Later that week we went to Ascot, where we met many VIPs including Harold Sebag-Montefiore from our board with his charming American wife Harriet. She had just been elected to the Festival Ballet Board and was to become one of my staunchest supporters.

To my surprise, Jane Hermann from the Metropolitan Opera House in New York arrived at the Coliseum on Saturday evening especially to see *Romeo and Juliet.* Nureyev was delighted and, accompanied by Gorlinsky and Findlay, we had dinner later at Inigo Jones on the corner of Floral Street. It was a productive meeting. Jane was charming and natural but a strong match for Nureyev and his appalling bullying. He demanded she cancel the American Ballet Theatre season in September in order to present his *Romeo and Juliet.* He named his possible Juliets as Ruanne, Evdokimova, and to my relief, Terabust, who he had not chosen for the role until now. Throughout the haranguing from Gorlinsky and Nureyev, who swore at Jane, she kept her composure and managed them well. The outcome – her suggestion – was that we went in the Spring or even July. We said July would not be possible for the Company nor apparently for Nureyev, so it was left to Jane to reorganise and do what she could.

Mary Skeaping was busy preparing *Giselle* for the final week of the Nureyev season. Her first full stage call went well under her strong direction. I had to take the next one on stage as she was away adjudicating and poor Donald was in hospital. I love Skeaping's *Giselle* and was pleased that Nureyev also respected her version. With Makarova as Giselle we witnessed some remarkable performances, but Nureyev decided to dance only three performances with Evdokimova. When telling her this I pointed out they would include the prestigious last night of the season.

The Company had been at the Coliseum for ten weeks and were becoming overtired with several temperamental outbursts. The last straw was when a small delegation of men complained about rehearsals taking place at the Lyceum Theatre. Anderton and I were infuriated. We ended up at loggerheads when she refused to rehearse Terabust in *Giselle* and stated she didn't want to go to Australia with us, either. Nureyev had been suffering a bad foot for some days and by Friday was limping. He insisted on performing, warming up on stage hanging on to a piece of scenery, which delayed everything and we were ten minutes late starting.

Our last week drew to its conclusion with flowers showering down from the gallery and boxes, strewn across the stage transforming it into a sea of colour. A party for the Company was given by the Governors at the Garrick Club and much appreciated by the dancers, who were looking forward to a week's break. To my amazement, Nureyev danced with the Danish company on their opening night on Monday. So once again it was a trip to the Coliseum to watch Nureyev perform, but he appeared thin and tired. I felt anxious about the Australian tour ahead.

A week later, reassembled at the unpopular Lyceum, the dancers endured three days of classes and rehearsals without any lino having being laid as expected. The search for another Chief Executive to replace Paul Findlay finished with two possible candidates under discussion at the Tuesday Executive meeting. There was also the overspend on *Romeo and Juliet* to be presented, and Peter Morris was busy up to the last minute, gathering details from all departments. This information was received with some surprise, and anxiety was expressed about financial control of future productions. I was relieved when it was finally decided that David Rees, General Manager of the Royal Ballet Touring Company and who knew the ballet world, should be appointed as the new Chief Executive. I looked forward to a happy working relationship with him, while feeling sad to be losing Findlay, who had always done his best and given me his loyalty.

55 Australia 1977: Had Rudi Gone Mad?

We were off to Australia again flying BA via Bahrain and Singapore. Having arrived at Perth after midnight, I dragged myself out of bed for a 10.30am press conference that same morning where there was much interest and many questions about *Romeo and Juliet.* The dress rehearsal on Monday evening ran late, and McCombie complained to me that the Company should not continue. I was shocked that this young dancer should be so unprofessional, wanting to stop when there was one more act to complete and the show opening next evening. The orchestra was awful as I said to Edgley, who told me it was due to the playing of twenty music students who, surprisingly, had been with us two years before.

Romeo and Juliet worked remarkably well in the huge stadium and looked good on the first night, receiving great applause. Following this success, on Tuesday night I had to be at the dinner party for the principals and friends given by Edgley. I loathed these dinners because of the worry about Nureyev's possible abominable behaviour but, having declined the party invitation on Sunday, I had to be present this time.

I was fed up with Nureyev who had gone behind my back to Edgley. Nureyev had demanded the dress rehearsal in Melbourne on Monday be in the morning and not the afternoon, even though he knew the stage staff needed the morning time. Nureyev also complained to Edgley about the presentation of his production: he said the lighting was dreadful, which it most certainly was not. He insisted on having a spotlight over himself in Act II, thus destroying the wonderful atmosphere. When I challenged him on this he just shrugged and flounced off. By now Edgley was so exasperated with Nureyev that he asked me to arrange for the latest Russian defector and ballet superstar, Mikhail Baryshnikov, to dance with us on our next Australian tour. Edgley was not prepared to put up with Nureyev in future.

That afternoon Nureyev became ill at the *Giselle* rehearsal with Evdokimova. We had to call in a doctor who prescribed antibiotics and an inhaler. Nureyev insisted on performing at night with Evdokimova who gave a superb performance. By Saturday we had a sulky Nureyev but after the matinee he became amiable. We saw the other side of this troubled soul. He danced with Terabust for the first time on the last night and was kind and helpful to her. Seemingly he was not happy unless causing trouble, then became sad, having gone too far.

We were taken by coach to the airport where, to everyone's astonishment, Nureyev actually arrived in time to board our plane to Melbourne. I noticed he held his head in his hands on take-off and landing. He had taken it into his mind to dance not Romeo but Mercutio at our opening performance on Monday. I did my best to dissuade him, knowing that Nicholas Johnson was no Romeo, but Nureyev was resolute and would not change his mind. This resulted in a disappointing performance for our opening. At his afternoon call he not only altered the lighting but also some choreography for the corps, cutting ten bars from the score, to the consternation of our conductor. I was thankful that Findlay, after extended delays flying from London, was now with us and could see my predicament. I felt sure a certain member of staff would take back to London, Weiss and the Board a picture of my inability to control Nureyev.

The Palais Theatre Melbourne had become dilapidated and run down since our previous visit, and I had a deputation from the male dancers complaining of conditions. They were forced to change in a caravan at the back of the building and were getting wet in the pouring rain when dashing into the theatre. To ease the situation, the caravan was brought round to the front of house. Michael Pink then complained it was too cramped, so Anderton told him to go and change in the wardrobe! At the traditional Edgley dinner after the opening a totally charming Nureyev behaved impeccably without swearing, which was astounding.

Next morning I was off to Sydney and Brisbane with Mogridge on the 9am flight, accompanied by our chief electrician David Mohr and master carpenter Dave Clark. The Company was booked to appear at the Regent Theatre in Sydney, a different venue from last time, and anything but royal. We found the apron already covered the orchestra pit and would only extend two feet more. The restricted height was also to present formidable problems for hanging scenery. We felt shabbily treated. Why were we not in the Opera House? This cinema was a depressing place, dirty and uncomfortable backstage. There was one bright star: the staff were old friends from our last visit to Sydney and drove us to the airport in time to catch the plane to Brisbane where it was pleasantly warm and sunny.

The Festival Hall in Brisbane was unbelievable. It had a raised platform in the middle of the hall, obviously used at times as a boxing ring. It seemed almost impossible to contemplate presenting the Company there. We were told it was the only location and was used for concerts and other entertainments. There was no means of hanging scenery and it would take some imagination to stage. Another problem would be covering the entrances and exits of dancers who would have to cross an open space to the dressing area. Depressed, we flew back to Perth in time for the evening performance. Travelling by air the great distances in Australia is like getting on a train in England! Some of the Australian Ballet came to see the show that night, and I was so glad to see my former partner Bryan Ashbridge amongst them. We sat together with his wife Dorothea Zames throughout the performance, and it was as if the years had melted away.

At the next evening's show Nureyev danced and behaved appallingly on stage. Whatever is wrong with him? I thought he had gone mad. I did not know what to say to him when the curtain came down and was thankful that Donald called me to the waiting taxi. We were perturbed by Nureyev's behaviour and at a loss to know what to do. I was also concerned that one of my principal ballerinas had become pregnant. The local doctor recommended an immediate termination and arranged this for the morning. He assured me she should be back dancing soon with no ill effects and without losing any of her performances. Like us, he only hoped she would not be too sad. Bronwen was the only one in the Company who knew about it and was a true friend to her. No one else ever heard about it, and she was none the worse for the operation.

Accompanied by Donald, I took an evening off to see the mime artist Marcel Marceau also performing in Melbourne. We were both greatly impressed by his extraordinary gift of taking us with him into his make-believe world. We had dinner with him in my hotel room later. It was refreshing to be with such an honest person, an artist of integrity and high ideals with whom it was really inspiring to talk.

Melbourne gave me some wonderful surprises. Towards the end of the week my last regular partner, Philip Chatfield and his wife the ballerina Rowena Jackson arrived from New Zealand to see me. Philip, who was a Christian Scientist, looked radiant and as young as ever, and it did my heart good to be with them again. I had been matron of honour at their wedding during our Royal Ballet days and missed them after they left England. I had another happy reunion with one of my teachers, Peggy van Praagh, ex-ballerina with Sadler's Wells, now living in Australia. After directing the Borovansky Ballet company for several seasons she later became the first Artistic Director of the Australian Ballet. She was now in a wheelchair as a result of a number of unsuccessful hip operations. I had dinner with her before the show and, although I did not realise it then, it was to be our last time together. How precious memories become as the years slip by.

Nureyev was becoming increasingly difficult. I always made a habit of seeing him in his dressing room to wish him well before a performance and had began to dread these encounters. I now took Donald with me for support during the escalating temperamental outbursts staged by Nureyev. Although he would not admit it, his agility and strength were declining, and he needed a scene to get his adrenalin flowing. He revelled in his commanding position. One could see it gave him gleeful satisfaction to upset and worry others. At Findlay's suggestion towards the end of our Melbourne week I told Nureyev how glad I was to see him recovered from his short illness and dancing better again. This was not well received: he resented my reference to his having been below par.

We arrived in Sydney early Sunday morning. On going to the theatre on Monday, the day of our opening, I was shocked and worried. Chaos reigned in the dreadful old Regent Theatre. The track rail was distorted and of no use whatsoever. Nureyev asked Mogridge and me if we could 'fly' the houses in instead, but we had already tried this without success. We had several different attempts following suggestions from the stage crew until they hit upon a temporary solution. We had to cancel the afternoon rehearsals, giving the orchestra and dancers only 45 minutes to prepare, before the stage had to be cleared in a desperate preparation for the opening of *Romeo and Juliet*. Nureyev also needed time to place the 'extras' – girls and boys who mingled in the crowd scenes. They had gone to the wrong studio to be shown their moves and waited in vain until discovered and hastily brought to the theatre. We got the show on somehow, thanks to our imaginative stage workers.

I was seated next to the Governor General and on tenterhooks through the performance, dying a thousand deaths. But the audience was enraptured and by a miracle the performance came together with surprisingly good results. There was the traditional first night Edgley gathering afterwards at which Robert Helpmann was present. It was odd seeing him again after many years, my partner for my earliest debut days. As a young fledgling of fourteen I had been in awe of him, so it was good to meet again, now that we both had experience directing big ballet companies.

Disturbed to see the bandages in which Nureyev was now encased to get through a performance, I spoke in depth with him one evening over a meal. Careful to point out his other gifts as a choreographer, producer, director and conductor, I asked him why he continued dancing in pain when he had these other great talents. He replied he wanted to dance first and foremost and could not visualise a time without performing. He was determined to go on dancing, unwilling to admit his body was in distinct denial. I found this terribly sad, witnessing his ever-declining strength, from performing in one art he could have continued to shine in another. But he was obsessed with dancing on stage for his public.

There was a curious incident that week. At an open-air lunch party I was approached by a vicar who begged me to give a small pendant to Nureyev. He wished Rudi to wear it to protect his soul from the evil within him. Whether or not he wore the talisman I do not know.

To my astonishment and delight another of my earliest Sadler's Wells partners contacted me in Sydney. Tony Burke, a leading soloist during the war, was now an art teacher in one of Australia's top boarding schools. He invited me to his home a little way from Sydney where I met his wife, a highly successful doctor and a lovely woman with a fine figure.

During the Sydney week Nureyev's close friend Charles Murland (a member of our Board) arrived from London. I do not know why but I always felt uneasy when he was about. He lived close to London's Hyde Park and threw many parties for Nureyev, who he had obviously taken under his wing. I was furious when Murland rang me early one morning to say he had contacted a dancer who Nureyev wished us to engage and had rung Weiss regarding his salary. As nicely as I could I asked him to refrain from ringing Weiss and not to become involved with the Company's business. I only hoped I had not offended him, knowing his closeness to Nureyev. I was outraged but, after giving class and taking a *Sylphides* rehearsal (which was looking good), felt calmer again.

Brisbane brought us to the end of the tour and its many challenges. Even here we could not escape them. The Company had been prepared for the open crossing between the changing rooms and the stage in the middle of the hall. Nureyev was in a bad mood all afternoon prior to opening, swearing at me because we couldn't arrange the sets to his liking. On the opening night he insisted on warming up, not behind the changing rooms like the other dancers, but on the stage. There was no way to hang curtains to conceal him on the raised platform. He stubbornly refused to hurry, keeping not only the dancers waiting but also the general public who stood outside waiting for the doors to open. Long after the advertised time, they were ushered into the hall and to their seats. This became a big scandal locally and next day's papers reported that the ballet was half an hour late starting because of Nureyev's behaviour. He enjoyed causing this anxiety and distress, and revelled in the publicity. For once I felt thankful to be leaving the Company next day for London to attend an Executive meeting scheduled for Thursday.

Back at Heathrow I found myself in Sven's arms and thankful to be back safely. My first duty next morning was to visit the office before going to the Palladium with Mogridge to ascertain its potential for a season there – surprisingly promising. Mogridge was in high spirits as he had just become a father. Knowing of the impending event I had agreed for him to fly back early from Sydney and he had returned to London in time to be with Carole Hill for the birth of their son. At the office we were thrilled for them.

Reporting on the tour that afternoon I told the Committee of the decline in Nureyev's dancing and of the request by Michael Edgley that we did not tour with Nureyev again in Australia, suggesting Baryshnikov instead. I was mightily relieved that Charles Murland, Nureyev's staunchest supporter and close friend, was absent from that meeting. It was awkward and embarrassing to have Murland on the Board – I disliked and mistrusted him. It was not an easy meeting, Weiss unexpectedly making a fuss over the outlay of money for the premises that housed our scenery and wardrobe. I reminded him of the size of Nureyev's recent production, which would also need housing. Thankfully it was passed over without further comment.

56 *Nureyev's Machinations*

By Wednesday evening, after only a day's break, the Company was back performing with great spirit at Festival Hall in *Coppélia*. A most enthusiastic audience greeted our return, demonstrating its pleasure on seeing the Company back from Australia, applauding throughout the evening. It made me realise what a remarkable following the Company had built. Terabust, dancing Swanhilda, received a warm reception together with a great ovation for the entire Company, which was both touching and thrilling.

A week later, my biography written by David Gillard was celebrated with a pre-performance reception at Festival Hall at which Dame Alicia and Anton Dolin were present. I was happy that they came as it made it special. A memorable evening followed with Sir Adrian Boult conducting *The Sanguine Fan*. His very presence – authoritative yet benign – gave the performance a great lift and inspired artists and audience alike. How pleased and proud I felt at having such a conductor with the Company for the entire week. *Giselle* barely made the third and last week: three flats had been found missing on the previous Friday and new ones had to be hastily made and painted in time for Monday's performance.

This was the first season without Donald Barclay by my side as ballet master. Diagnosed with lung cancer, he had been getting weaker on the foreign tour. Knowing he would never get better, he visited as many of the nature reserves in Australia that he could fit in, appreciating to the full everything he saw. It was to be his last time with us, for on our return he was admitted to the Royal Marsden Hospital in Chelsea, where Heather and I visited him several times. He wore an oxygen mask as he had difficulty breathing. Three days after the close of the Festival Hall season he died, only 43 years old. I was broken-hearted: he was the only member of my ballet staff who I could completely trust. His funeral took place during the vacation so there were only a few dancers present: most were holidaying abroad. I thought this tragic, as Donald had devoted himself to the Company, caring for and helping every dancer. He was such a good teacher, a kind, enthusiastic ballet master with a keen eye. He watched every performance, often with me. He loved ballet and most of all the Company, and I knew I had suffered a terrible loss.

The holiday started on Friday 16th September, and the next day Nicholas Johnson married Laura Connor, a leading ballerina with the Royal Ballet. Sven and I attended their church wedding early afternoon in Acton – the bride looked radiant. All the guests went back to a party at their house on the patio which Nicky had recently built.

3rd October, the last Monday of the holiday, saw the premiere in Leicester Square of the film which featured Nureyev as Valentino. Sven and I were invited, and it was a high-profile affair with Princess Margaret gracing the evening and looking glamorous in a white ball gown. I did not enjoy the film, which was not to my taste, and although there was a big party afterwards I did not think I should go. I was missed according to Paul Findlay, who was told this by a furious Murland next morning.

A few days later I received a really horrible letter from Weiss: he accused me of failing Festival Ballet, annoying Nureyev, infuriating Gorlinsky and Murland. It upset me terribly. I could not sleep at night and felt like resigning. I made an appointment to see Sir Louis Gluckstein first thing Monday, the day of the Company's return from holiday. He was shocked and apologised for Weiss' letter. He was most sympathetic and eventually thought it best I did not retaliate in the same 'bitchy manner', but write a brief dignified acknowledgement of Weiss' letter, suggesting we meet in person. Sir Louis was right, and I took his advice. I then dashed to see the Company in our new home. I spoke briefly about Donald and his death in the holiday. We were given some money in his memory and a studio was named after him.

For the dancers it was a different return to work as they entered their own premises for the first time. At last Festival Ballet had its own home. The fine Victorian building which had been Queen Alexandra's House had been successfully divided into two separate premises. It was thrilling to be close to the Royal Albert Hall, within the cultural area conceived by Prince Albert. Around us were the Royal College of Art, the Royal College of Music, the Imperial Colleges of Learning and Medicine together with the three magnificent museums: the Science Museum; the Natural History Museum and the Victoria and Albert, all situated close together. We felt privileged and proud to be within this artistic enclave.

My heartfelt thanks went out to Sir Louis Gluckstein for all his efforts in having achieved this dream. It was a miracle. The stage, which had been at the far end of the enormous ground floor room, was gone, demolished, giving us a huge studio now fitted with full-length mirrors fixed to the walls. To our satisfaction we also found more full-length mirrors in the large refurbished basement gym. Both studios had sprung floors, chosen with care specifically for dance. The ballet staff had their own changing rooms, showers had been installed, and I was particularly pleased to have my choice of Amtico tiling the floors. Everybody was thrilled with the work that had been done – with the exception of Betty Anderton, who was like a wet blanket. She even criticised the sprung floors and had not a good word to say, which I found strange.

For the first time each department had its own offices and would soon settle in their new quarters, once we had vacated Welbeck Street, where we had been for nine years. I made sure that Heather's little office was adjacent to mine and that we were directly opposite Findlay and his splendid secretary, Janet Fairweather. It took time to realise that this was truly the Company's permanent home, Festival Ballet's own headquarters, which we christened Markova House in honour of the great ballerina, co-founder of London Festival Ballet.

Following a fortnight of classes and rehearsals, we were off on the road again for eight weeks in the provinces. The autumn always saw some changes amongst the dancers, with newcomers replacing those who had left for various reasons. Although losing one of my top soloists, John Travis, as a dancer, he became our first ever archivist. For this change of career he undertook a full training at Manchester University. This was to be invaluable as there had been no records kept since the Company's beginnings nearly 30 years previously. John looked forward with enthusiasm to the mammoth task ahead.

I took David Long to dinner to discuss his future, hoping he would become ballet master, replacing Donald. I was so pleased when he assured me he would be happy to change his position as a leading soloist to become a teacher, while still retaining his character roles. The two-month tour took us to familiar major cities with *Swan Lake, Nutcracker* and *Romeo and Juliet. Swan Lake* returned to the rep after a two-year absence and, following my endless rehearsals, revived well. This was a relief: I had worried about the production, no longer having Donald to work on it with me. To everyone's expectations the Shakespeare ballet created much interest, and the tour was a big success financially and artistically. Bart was an inspired Romeo, partnering Terabust with care and dancing with abandon.

There were quite a few meetings with Nureyev, Gorlinsky, Findlay and myself, some good, some not so good, but always long and argumentative. I was always apprehensive beforehand, anticipating abuse from Nureyev and his agent. Talks were about future seasons or foreign tours to Australia, America and Paris, with Nureyev dancing the majority of performances. He was so greedy. This did not further my principal male dancers nor my ballerinas either with whom he was reluctant to dance, insisting on inviting guest ballerinas instead. There was always a battle.

I began to wish we had not become so embroiled with Nureyev. I could see he was just using us to his own advantage. Ours was a good classical Company in which he could shine. As a great artist and a fantastic producer he was an inspiration for our dancers, but I detested his foul language, rudeness and unpredictable bad moods. But he could behave rationally and was capable of great kindness. At one of our meetings, when Frigerio was present, money was under discussion and Nureyev was at his most genial, showing patience and an understanding of the Company's financial situation. He even invited me to fly with him on his private jet to Venice following his gala at the London Palladium. As if I could – what would Sven have said?

As America now seemed a real possibility, it was agreed I should fly across to New York and Washington for talks on repertoire with the directors of the Metropolitan Opera House and the Kennedy Center. I was only away for a couple of days but these meetings were invaluable. Nureyev was keen that I saw him dance *Don Quixote* in Vienna. I was happy to visit Vienna again, a city I love. This time I stayed at the Imperial Hotel, very grand, living up to its name. Nureyev arranged my stalls ticket for collection at the stage door, and I found my way round to the front of the magnificent red and gold auditorium. I thoroughly enjoyed the performance and only wished that Festival Ballet had the same production. I went backstage to Nureyev's dressing room afterwards, which as usual was full of admirers. We eventually slipped away with the director and the ballet mistress for dinner in our hotel's café. Nureyev was in a good mood and was entertaining and charismatic.

In December the Company returned to London for their annual Christmas season of the *Nutcracker* at Festival Hall. After 31 performances we proceeded to Paris to give

34 presentations of *Romeo and Juliet* with Nureyev at the Palais des Sports. The dress rehearsal Wednesday was fraught with rude, tempestuous outbursts from Frigerio and temperamental scenes between him and Nureyev. Each one walked out for a time, threatening never to return, with the bewildered French stage manager Dio caught in the crossfire. This bad temper did not upset me so much as usual, and I remained calm. My concern was to get the show lit and ready in time. My dancers were wonderful, working beyond the stipulated time, eager for the ballet's success. We opened only a little late, but I did not think *Romeo and Juliet* worked as well as *Sleeping Beauty* in the enormous stadium. Nureyev danced reasonably well, but I noticed Johnson got as much applause for his endearing performance as Mercutio. Next day the reviews were split – some excellent and others poor.

Later in the season a dramatic situation arose one evening on and off stage. During Act I Nureyev, in a bad mood, attacked one of our leading ballerinas from the Argentine: Liliana Belfiore. He swore at her and kicked her up the backside so hard that she left the stage in great pain. A doctor was called who, after examining her, said that her coccyx had been damaged and was bent. She was in agony, and the doctor advised us that the injury might cause her to act unpredictably and temperamentally. This South American was one of our most outgoing, volatile artists, so this was not good news! In a rage she went to a police station with her boyfriend about Nureyev's attack. This complaint was duly recorded in the police records. A friend of Nureyev's rang the London office informing us of what occurred.

It was agreed we must go to Paris and try to dissuade Belfiore from pursuing a case against Nureyev in the courts. Peter Hulme met our new Chief Executive, David Rees, and me at the airport and after learning more details I went to see Nureyev in his dressing room. We were both icily calm, but Nureyev was not apologetic. He began running down the Company and saying Belfiore had displeased him. I said, 'That didn't give you the right to kick her'. He answered: 'I am the greatest dancer alive and I can do what I want.' To which I unguardedly retorted, 'There are other great dancers too, Rudi.' He was furious at this and menacingly picked up a knife but was restrained by his masseur, Luigi. On hearing raised angry voices someone threw the door open and I was hustled away by David, with Nureyev shouting: 'No more performances!'

Once back in the hotel David and I rang Weiss who we had kept informed from the outset. David and I talked until two in the morning, upset and concerned that the season was in jeopardy – Festival Ballet and the Hochhausers could lose a lot of money. Gorlinsky was in Paris already for a meeting with Grunwald, and the Hochhausers soon learnt of the contretemps. Early next morning David rang Nureyev's friend Nicole saying she must persuade Nureyev to go on that night and continue the season as planned. David and I took Belfiore to the police station at 9.15am having persuaded her not to sue Nureyev. The policeman was disappointed not to proceed with charges against the big star, stipulating that the case remained on the books ready to reopen at any time.

David and I then had a long meeting with Peter Hulme, the company manager, and Heather in our hotel.

I felt sick with worry until Nicole rang at lunchtime to say Nureyev would be dancing that evening and for the rest of the season. What a relief! Gorlinsky rang to say he wanted to meet with David and me to discuss future plans including the American tour. Still feeling the after-effects of all the worry, I was in two minds about this. I was well supported by David who told Gorlinsky it was too soon after the recent drama, and he must wait until we were ready to proceed. Bearing in mind the circumstances surrounding the incident with Nureyev, I thought it wise to stay on in Paris another couple of days to make sure all was running smoothly at the Palais de Sports. Great efforts were made to keep Nureyev and me apart.

57 Across The Channel And The Ocean

Back in London I found a stack of work to address before seeing Weiss late afternoon and bringing him up to date with Paris. Next evening I went to the gala at Covent Garden for the premiere of *Mayerling*. Kenneth MacMillan received an ovation for this highly action-packed three-act ballet. Lynn Seymour, always a fine dramatic dancer, was exceptionally outstanding and brilliantly partnered by David Wall. There was an impressive line up of principals, and I found all the intricate pas de deux thrilling. MacMillan's choreography was more inventive than ever. After directing the Royal Ballet for seven years he had recently been appointed the company's resident choreographer.

Returning to Paris, Gorlinsky was hot on my heels demanding a meeting with David and me to plan the future. I persuaded David to fly over on Saturday for what began as a pleasant meeting with Gorlinsky. On hearing we might not be able to extend the American tour because of our London commitments he became rude and abusive, distorting the true facts. We got up and left with Gorlinsky shouting, 'No more association!' which was exactly what David wished for.

Outside Peter Hulme was waiting to drive us to the Paris Opéra to see a performance of Yuri Grigorovitch's production of *Romeo and Juliet*. It was breathtaking with brilliant crowd scenes, stirring moments of drama and poignant love scenes. This was great theatre, but I preferred Nureyev's own production, which was totally original and included all the dramatic ingredients of this well-known tragedy. I felt pleased and proud that Nureyev had created his masterpiece on my Company and that we had secured the rights to it.

Next day – the final of the eventful Paris season – I had to fly back to London so was not at the last performance party which Nureyev gave the Company. I regretted not being there for two reasons. First, Murland had rung from London to enquire if Nureyev and I were on speaking terms. And second, as Heather pointed out, in my absence Nureyev might try to swing the Company against me. She had a point. One could never underestimate Nureyev's machinations. I could not be there, however, since Jane Hermann had arranged an important meeting in London regarding the New York season and an American tour, which David and I had to attend together with Peter Morris. Since the Company were anxious to know whether or not we were going to America before leaving for London I confirmed that it was now a question of agreeing suitable dates.

Back in London after a dreadful journey I was soon busy at the office with Peter and David before we three left for the Savoy. Jane Hermann was there with Martin Feinstein who came fully cognisant with details, and we got off to a good start. I had met them both when I was a dancer with Sadler's Wells on the early Hurok tours. It was in a fairly relaxed atmosphere that we talked for well over two hours. We discussed the Company's repertoire, our principal artists and a season in both New York and Washington with Nureyev. Martin was also trying to squeeze in a short tour after Washington which could accommodate everyone. He was most helpful, understanding the problems involved, and it was a pleasure to work with them both without rude interruption from Gorlinsky. Afterwards David and I contacted both Weiss and Sir Louis to inform them of everything we had discussed and of our optimism for the American appearances.

The following afternoon we met Jane and Martin again at the Savoy, this time joined by Gorlinsky. Jane handled him well, praising Nureyev and saying how important it was for him to perform with Festival Ballet in the States. We tackled and agreed many points: 'London Festival Ballet' to be in capitals as large as Nureyev's name on posters was one of the big battles. They also finally conceded that London Festival Ballet would appear with Nureyev and no other guest artists, so it was understood that he would dance only with our ballerinas: Ruanne, Evdokimova and Terabust. The conditions appeared satisfactory and David visibly relaxed – arrangements were now to go ahead.

Meanwhile the Company had returned from Paris for a week's well deserved rest. When not required in town, I relaxed in the quietness of Fernhill before the following two weeks of rehearsals. These were special – the famous contemporary American choreographer Glen Tetley came to work with us for the first time. He had agreed to stage *Greening*, a work he had created on the Stuttgart Ballet in 1975. It was thrilling to have this genius amongst us, so modest yet so accomplished and kind. He would talk to the dancers about the ballet, explaining the meaning and reason behind every movement, many of which were quite new and strange for our classically trained dancers. They were mesmerised, never having worked in such a detailed and informative manner. I watched in awe, admiring his unique approach, and we were to become firm friends up to his death in 2007.

During the Company's absence from London, our remaining staff finally left the Welbeck Street premises and we were now all under one roof. David Rees, addressing the Company for the first time since taking over from Findlay, referred to this important move which was to transform and simplify our existence. He spoke well and was able to confirm Festival Ballet's season in New York and Washington in July, which went down well. He had already checked with Gorlinsky that negotiations were sufficiently advanced to inform the Company. Curiously, we received a cable from a Mr Nederlander in Canada stating all arrangements were agreed for a two-week tour following Washington. We wondered if he was acting for Gorlinsky, but we could not consider staying longer in North America and turned down the extra fortnight. Next day came another cable regretting our unavailability. We breathed a sigh of relief as we were now booked into Festival Hall a week after Washington.

David and I had a short meeting at Equity with Peter Plouviez to organise for our four Company Equity representatives – McCombie, Wynne, MacLaurin and Dominic – to get together with the Equity Council and report on any worries or queries the Company might have. It was a happy gathering with no grumbles, after which we were able to outline to the dancers the Company's future plans.

The layout for a new three-act ballet by Ronald Hynd was taking shape with designs by his friend Peter Docherty. It was based on Johann Strauss' operetta *Die Fledermaus* and we tried to find a title other than *Gay Rosalinda* to attract audiences (it was finally presented just as *Rosalinda*). At the beginning of March we met with our technical supervisor, John Berrill, stalwart of the Company, and Kim Baker, our talented young wardrobe supervisor. They began exchanging ideas, and it was fascinating listening to them and watching designs evolve. To take the leading roles in *Rosalinda*, Hynd chose Patricia Ruanne with Paul Clarke and Kenn Wells.

The following Spring – 1979 – was a potential problem as we could not be certain of the Coliseum's availability. David and I went to inspect the Dominion cinema at Tottenham Court Road as a possible venue. We spent an hour and a half there and, to our surprise, it offered an adequate stage and good sight lines, although the back stage space was limited. The auditorium seated a large number of people and it was in a convenient position for transport, so we felt confident about this possibility. We also had an important meeting with a director of a big American insurance firm from which we came away optimistic that they might give financial assistance for our forthcoming season in America. Our second rehearsal week proved productive with Tetley happily at work with my dancers.

The first night of our eight-week provincial tour in Bradford was extraordinary. Ruanne was dancing the Swan Princess when, during the second act, she hurt her foot and could not continue. Hurriedly, Carole Hill put on Ruanne's costume and finished the act for her. Terabust was backstage and, donning the Act III costume, limbered up and danced brilliantly as the scheming seductress Odile. The Prince Siegfried was Bart, her frequent partner, unfazed by the appearance of a third ballerina. Then, for the final act, Carole Hill once again put on the white tutu and reappeared as Odette, the tragic Swan Princess. The audience must have wondered what was happening, or perhaps they thought it was part of the magic!

We were able to book Attilio Labis for some performances to partner Evdokimova. A strong, French dancer from the Paris Opéra, Labis was now freelance, sometimes partnering Fonteyn at Covent Garden. When I was a dancer good tall male partners were scarce. They were still in the minority so it was fortunate he could perform with us.

The spring tour was memorable for the first night in Oxford of Tetley's beautiful ballet *Greening*. The initial stage call had taken place the previous week in Eastbourne with no sets. Much to my annoyance, Mogridge forgot to indicate their positions with markings and also to clad his stage staff in black for the visual scene changes. Tetley was tolerant and seemed pleased with my dancers and their confident approach to his style.

But by the end of that week we were dogged with bad luck: Vass had a thrombosis and needed to be walked back slowly to his nearby hotel. Two of my most helpful dancers, John and Bernie Tyler, undertook to do this and took great care of him. Friday evening was also bad, as one of the rapiers wielded in *Romeo and Juliet* flew offstage during the first act into the orchestra pit and straight into a cello. It narrowly missed the cellist, causing consternation among the players. At the end of the show I found the safety nets had not been well secured, the responsibility of the stage manager. At the same time one of my soloists, Manelle Jaye, was hysterical, crying because Betty Anderton had reprimanded her in front of the whole Company.

I returned to my hotel for a peaceful dinner with Sven and our friend, the widowed Helena Terry, and while waiting for them I reflected on the past few days: an uncomfortable, strained Board meeting when the question of my salary was raised with Murland present, which I disliked. As expected, David and I were asked to withdraw temporarily – so embarrassing. I was collected before the end of the meeting to take part in Anton Dolin's *This is Your Life* programme, which was a happy reunion of many artists. He had enjoyed a wonderful life, internationally recognised as a fine danseur noble as well as an exceptional partner to many famous ballerinas. I felt honoured to be part of the distinguished group, which included his partner of many years, the famous prima ballerina Alicia Markova, and also their close friend John Gilpin.

Moving on to Oxford we were excited about Tetley's ballet, which was to open the triple bill programme with *Schéhérazade* and *The Sanguine Fan*. These two were given in Eastbourne, together with *Études,* now returned to the repertoire after some absence. It was well revived by David Long, who was becoming a first class ballet master. This was fortunate as Vass was still not well, having X-rays and blood tests. Because *Schéhérazade* and *Sanguine Fan* were in performance, *Greening* had the entire three-hour rehearsal with orchestra. Tetley ran the ballet through twice and at the conclusion of both runs gave detailed corrections. A short photo call followed and at 7.30pm the curtain went up on this beautiful ballet. Evdokimova was quite exceptional. Tetley was delighted and pleased with her, as he was with all the dancers.

58 *Markova House And Ups And Downs With Rudi*

It was a cheerful group who gathered for a management meeting next morning when we discussed the official opening of Markova House by Princess Margaret the following week. I had not realised the number of details which had to be covered with all the planning involved. I was just thankful that we were not responsible for giving HRH dinner – she had an evening engagement following on from us. Before the afternoon rehearsal of *Sleeping Beauty* I had a talk with Betty Anderton about finding another good choreologist since Bronwen could no longer stay with us. This was a shame – she was first class and had a strong personality. Anderton was now much more involved with the Company's planning in the light of her request for a stronger position on the staff.

Nicky Johnson came to see me saying he was off with a badly bruised foot – I could not believe it was so bad and told him so. I was sure he was sulking because Tetley had told him he had not danced well enough. We put on the understudy, Jean Louis Cabane, in his place and although a coryphée, he did surprisingly well. I was pleased that Tetley had picked him out as having promise and that he did not disappoint. Mid-week Tetley put Terabust on in the leading role, but she was not in the same league as Evdokimova. To me Terabust played the little girl too much so her performance, though well danced, lacked intensity and was not profound. The Nordheim music was compelling, and we were so pleased that the BBC interviewed Graham Bond about this piece and other scores he conducted for Festival Ballet.

We staged *Sleeping Beauty* for the week in Southampton which was much enjoyed by the public and also my 'up and comings'. It gave opportunities for our young talent to be tried out in solo roles and at the midweek matinee Vivian Loeber danced her first Princess Aurora, a nerve-racking and yet rewarding role, which she managed with aplomb.

Once again Nureyev was giving David and me a worrying time. According to Jane Hermann he planned to dance all 15 performances of *Romeo and Juliet* in New York, to which we would not agree. We talked this over with Weiss and decided to send Jane a cable saying just that. Schaufuss and Bart had arranged to be with us, if needed, during our time in the States, which was important for Festival Ballet's image. After many battles it was agreed we would also present a triple bill programme, as well as Skeaping's *Giselle*. Jane was unhappy that Bart was unknown in the States and suggested we ask Nederlander (who only seemed interested in promoting Nureyev) to send out some publicity about both Bart and Schaufuss. The battle was ongoing and there were more looming, now the programmes had finally been agreed by all parties.

Casting caused problems and a furious Jane was on the phone to us from New York. There were local newspaper reports that Evdokimova was to dance *Giselle* in Berlin with Bart immediately prior to their appearances with us in the States. Jane said they could not be permitted to dance in New York with us so soon after the Berlin engagement and that she would get Makarova instead of Evdokimova. This would be a disaster – we could not possibly afford to lose Evdokimova from our American booking. David and I were immediately on the phone to Evdokimova who confirmed that they were indeed scheduled to appear in Berlin before coming with us to America. Eventually after we had explained to Evdokimova the awkward situation, she promised to do what she could to postpone their engagement in Berlin. After an anxious few days, she rang – she had managed to persuade the management to postpone the Berlin engagement, much to our relief.

Before the week in Southampton was over I flew to Johannesburg. Although it was ten years since I had been there, to my great joy friends made at that time contacted me. Sadly, the Stodels, my good friend the General Manager of South African Consolidated Theatres and his wife, had both now died, but many of their staff took care to see I was well looked after. I felt happy to be back in Johannesburg once again. The purpose of my trip was to see Hynd's South African production of his new ballet *Rosalinda*. I arrived in time to watch the dress rehearsal and appreciate the high standard in South Africa Ballet Company. I met many I knew at the theatre including South Africa's great teacher Dulcie Howes and their outstanding prima ballerina Denise Scholtz. There was a matinee 'try out' next afternoon before the evening's Gala, and I thoroughly enjoyed the ballet which included plenty of humour although I thought there was too little dancing in Act I. This and various other points I raised with Ronnie next day, including the costumes and scenery. The ballet was well received and there were drinks on stage for the company to celebrate after the Gala.

Flying back to London next evening I felt the visit had been most helpful whilst also giving me a welcome break. Now it was to be all stations go to make sure the arrangements were in place for the visit of Princess Margaret on Wednesday April 26th. The great day dawned, and we were feeling excited. The police checked over Markova House with their Alsatian sniffer dogs and kept a discreet low profile throughout the Princess's time with us. People began arriving from 6pm onwards and about 7pm motorbike outriders zoomed into our courtyard, announcing the Princess's imminent arrival in her black limousine, just ten minutes behind schedule. She was gracious even when the newly installed lift stuck for a few moments – understandably she did not then choose to take the truculent machine up to inspect the shining administration offices. The Princess was in a colourful full-length evening dress, as were many others present, myself included. The Royal visit was a great success, and the rehearsal rooms greatly admired. I had worried in advance over my speech which I experienced difficulty in remembering but, when the moment came to say my few words, I remembered it all. The time passed swiftly and all too soon Princess Margaret embraced me before departing. It was a most memorable and happy occasion after which a number of us decided to celebrate with Sven at the Savoy.

After the excitement, the dancers and I were rewarded with a week's holiday, which I spent at Fernhill. The ferns, bracken and briars were gradually disappearing and the forest clearing beginning to have the makings of a garden, but there was still a long way to go.

The Company had just one week to rehearse before opening in Coventry with *Romeo and Juliet.* Waiting in Festival Ballet House to rehearse were four important producers: Mona Vangsaa for *Conservatoire*; Skeaping for *Giselle;* Hynd for *La Chatte*; and last, but certainly the most demanding, Nureyev. I dreaded meeting Nureyev for the first time since our altercation in Paris. I saw he was in class and all seemed well between him and the dancers. Returning when class was over I located Nureyev in the lower studio where, on seeing me, he smiled and waved. I went up and kissed him, after which he remained in a super mood all day. I was so relieved. Why oh why could he not behave always like this? A born producer when he took rehearsals of his own works, he really inspired the dancers.

Having all our work-in-progress under one roof meant that by Saturday afternoon the staff and dancers actually finished and left, thanks to the time saved having our own studios in the same building and not having to travel between Welbeck Street and Donmar. The next two weeks away in Coventry and Bristol gave us the opportunity to break in *Conservatoire* again with *Giselle.* Following this a fortnight of rehearsals ensured each ballet reached as high a standard as possible for our month's season at the Coliseum. Hynd was busy finalising everything for the premiere of *La Chatte.* To our conductor's delight he was using the same Henri Sauguet music chosen 70 years earlier by Balanchine, who created a ballet around the Aesop fable. Disappointingly, Hynd's ballet was short-lived but the dancers involved enjoyed performing in it.

During the Bristol week, David and I took a train to Brighton to look over the big arena, the Brighton Centre, and meet the manager with a view to presenting the Company there. It was extremely attractive to us with a large performing area, massive seating allocation and a keen and helpful management. We hoped that we could have some seasons there – the Brighton Theatre Royal was too small for Festival Ballet and we wanted the Company to be seen in the town. It was not to be – the Arts Council demanded a guaranteed sum, which Brighton was not prepared to give. Disappointing, as we were convinced it would have been a financial success as well as attracting a new public.

It was thought expedient that I go to New York and Washington for a few days to tidy up loose ends. We were still having big problems sorting out the definitive New

York / Washington casting, and I needed to clarify this, particularly in Washington with Martin Feinstein. David and I began to wonder if all the wrangling was worthwhile. Keeping our dancers happy and Nureyev satisfied was no mean feat, but my visit proved productive and somehow casting and programmes were finally resolved to the satisfaction of all parties. I spent two days in each city and, to my surprise, was bombarded for press and radio interviews, which I greatly enjoyed. The Cuban ballet had recently performed in Washington with enormous success, and Martin Feinstein said to me, 'Don't think you will have a walk over,' which was worrying. We would be compared to the sensational Cubans. Despite such strong competition I was determined my dancers would also receive acclaim.

It was good to be back in Markova House with my Company on Monday morning, but I was in for a shock by the afternoon. Kerrison Cooke, one of my principal dancers, came to tell me he had decided to join Ben Stevenson at Houston Ballet, where Ben had been the artistic director for the last two years. I was bitterly disappointed after all we had done for him since he left the Royal Ballet touring company to join us in 1973. But I thought it prudent to let him leave as he was so determined. That same afternoon, to my astonishment, Rik Werner gave David his written notice to leave. David refused to accept it, telling him that an abrupt departure at such a crucial time, before New York, was unacceptable. I hoped we could persuade Werner to change his mind and wondered what had triggered this? He was remarkably tall and had become a valuable character artist, although I had only taken him into the Company because he was the boyfriend of one of my soloists, who begged me to engage him. When we spoke with him in the morning, together with his close friend, leading ballerina Ruanne, we persuaded him to stay. I was glad – he excelled as Tybalt in Nureyev's *Romeo and Julie*t for which his powerful physique was well suited.

By Sunday, Tetley and Skeaping had both arrived in London ahead of our Tuesday opening at the Coliseum, as had Terabust, Schaufuss and Bart. Manola Asensio was back after a successful week guesting in Salzburg. To help our ongoing fund-raising, diplomats' wives were invited to watch the dress rehearsal Monday for a modest charge. I gave a little welcoming talk explaining what they would be watching. They talked during *Les Sylphides* and *Schéhérazade* but also, to my horror, chatted incessantly throughout Tetley's sensitive ballet *Greening*. Tetley took it well – perhaps the music had not appealed to them.

We had a well contrasted programme for the first three nights, changing to *Conservatoire* and *Giselle* for the next three performances. Although the shows went well I was only too aware of our need for better, more mature, male dancers. I was always searching for talent, even auditioning while travelling in Europe. We were completely reliant on my regular guests Bart, Breuer and Schaufuss with whom we had wonderful working relationships, their loyalty to Festival Ballet demonstrated by their willingness to come at short notice whenever we had an emergency. At the close of

Friday's performance the Company gave me a surprise party to celebrate my ten years as director. I had no inkling that this was to happen and was deeply moved. With the ups and downs and constant worries I was getting dreadfully tired and exhausted so this was a much needed boost, like sunshine breaking through dark clouds.

I had not been pleased with David Mohr's lighting of *Études* so sat with him in the lighting box during the ballet Friday. He would not agree that it was incorrect, but guiltily admitted he had trouble with his right eye and had just had a stye treated that day. I felt I could not complain any more, although I felt ashamed by the way the lighting was mis-focused on the important spotlight changes during the ballet and mentioned this to David Rees. Schaufuss was upset, too, because of Bond's slow conducting, so David and I had a little talk with Bond, suggesting he was overworked, which he stubbornly denied. Poor David also suffered a confrontation the same day with the stage staff about their per diem, the daily allowance given to staff while they were on tour, which they were unwilling to accept. On Saturday with Sir Adrian Boult conducting *The Sanguine Fan* in his masterful manner, I was delighted to welcome back the Duke and Duchess of Gloucester for the second time that week. It was Sir Adrian's last evening with us and I was loath to say goodbye to him and Lady Boult – both were a wonderful inspiration to our Company, undemanding and totally committed. We later bid him a warm 'adieu', his modesty and retiring dignity a beacon of eminence.

My incredible stage crew had everything set up and ready in time for the 2pm Monday rehearsal of *Romeo and Juliet*. Nureyev was in a good mood and we got through the whole ballet by 6pm, which was wonderful. The performance that night was a huge success, Nureyev taking numerous curtain calls. I knew the lighting was poor, but Nureyev made no comment about this, seemingly delighted with his ovation.

Mid-week I had a terrible shock when at the end of the Board meeting Murland made a point of attacking me verbally about a press release mistake. Weiss did not come to my rescue, preferring to agree with Murland that: 'I should not pass the buck to Barlow [Festival's press officer].' I was so surprised by his outburst and this horrid accusation that I was still shaking on my return home to change for the evening show. I was cheered that evening by sitting with friends and by Evdokimova dancing Juliet with Nureyev, lifting his ballet to even greater heights. The stage staff were soon busy overseeing the safe 'get-out' of *Romeo and Juliet* for America, the first of our ballets to be on its way there.

On my return home I rang Weiss and had a most unpleasant exchange over the phone. I was careful what I said and Sven was reassuringly by my side. I asked Weiss if he did not have faith in my artistic direction. We got nowhere, and for the first time I felt like giving it all up, particularly if Murland was to remain on the Board. He was obviously gunning for me, and the next morning I received a horrid letter at home from Murland. He was not apologetic, but showed what a nasty person he really was, confirming all I felt about him, this friend of Nureyev. Where would all this lead? Murland tried to speak to me in an interval at the Coliseum but Sven swept me away and into my box.

The dress rehearsal of *Giselle* earlier that Thursday afternoon was embarrassing, with Nureyev in his worst mood, sending up Skeaping's production. But all went well that night. The audience obviously enjoyed and appreciated it.

I was absent for the Saturday performances as I was compère for the Royal Festival Hall BBC concert. I wore a white ball gown made for me in South Africa and was well looked after, with plenty of time to rest after the rehearsal. Knowing both the Festival Hall and the conductor, Ashley Lawrence, I could unwind a little and was able to enjoy every minute of the concert. Being on stage near to the players was wondrous and I felt part of the music itself – so different from being in a recording studio divorced from the musicians. By the end of the concert I felt refreshed and uplifted. That night was the second 'get-out' with *Giselle* and *Conservatoire* commencing passage to New York.

For the last week of our season we presented Nureyev's *Sleeping Beauty.* On the second night Nureyev was unusually charming to me. During one interval he said he intended to appear at the Vienna Opera House next summer in their ballet company's production of *Don Quixote*. This would mean that instead of four weeks with us at the Coliseum he would only dance for two. So much for the agreement between Gorlinsky and the Hochhausers and also with us! Gorlinsky would benefit because Makarova would be dancing with Nureyev in Vienna. This was a disappointment and meant a lot of rearranging; a repeat of what happened in January. We just had to cope with these unreliable characters and be better prepared.

Heather said she was exhausted, so David and I spent half an hour talking to her. She was also feeling nervous about the American tour and thought she might have to give up on our return from the States. This would be an awful loss, and I hoped she would not leave. She had seen her doctor a year previously because she was feeling depressed, caused by overwork, he said.

I understood Heather's exhaustion as every night I felt dead beat when going to bed. There was always so much going on and so much planning to be undertaken, not only the weekly call sheets, the casting and planning repertoire for three years ahead. I liked to give at least one class a week in order to keep close to the dancers, as well as taking rehearsals, and there were always choreographers, composers and many other artists to meet. I found it important to attend most rehearsals and enjoyed spotting and nurturing any potential talent. There were weekly management gatherings as well as numerous other meetings besides the all-important Executive and Board meetings. I have never shirked work, nor a challenge, and enjoyed every facet of being the Artistic Director of the Company I loved.

It was hard to believe the Coliseum season was over and that in a few days the Company would leave for America, with Sven joining me. Ingvar returned mid week from a holiday in Malta with Anna and her parents, which gave us a short time together. Sven and I spent the last but one evening with my dear father, now looking much older but as always cheerful, gentle and kind. It tugged at my heart-strings leaving him alone for a month. But my Company was also important to me. It was exciting to know that Tuesday evening the technical staff had left for New York. By mid-day Friday the Company, Sven and I were en route for the States.

Arrangements had been made in New York for Ruanne, Evdokimova and me to be photographed in the morning at the Met, with press interviews to follow. Out front at the Met was an enormous black and white poster of Ruanne as Juliet, so we knew that the publicity machine was at work. Our staff were busy, side by side with their American counterparts, preparing for our opening Tuesday. Most of Sunday they spent focusing the lights, while in a rehearsal room the extras for *Romeo and Juliet* were being carefully instructed, afterwards going for their fittings in the wardrobe department. Monday the Company had class and a short rehearsal in the afternoon, with an unusually long orchestral dress rehearsal running from 7pm until 11pm. Thankfully Frigerio was not present, but Gorlinsky was prowling about trying to stir up trouble, so I tried to keep out of his way.

The opening night, Tuesday 18th July, was a dressy affair, the performance commencing at 8pm. At the end *Romeo and Juliet* received the greatest possible ovation. The applause went on and on. Murland was there with Gorlinsky and Weiss and, although the stage manager had expected Nureyev to bring me on stage, he did not – much to my relief, as those three were ready to criticise. There was a big party afterwards which was really appreciated and enjoyed by everyone, including an ecstatic Nureyev. Next morning: a superb notice from the influential critic Clive Barnes. How wonderful – it would seem the Company had made it in New York. By Thursday there were more marvellous notices for the Company, the production and of course for Nureyev himself.

On Friday we presented Skeaping's *Giselle* with Nureyev partnering Terabust who, to my disappointment, made less impact than I had hoped. Evdokimova, partnered by Nureyev on Saturday, however received a great reception. After a free day the Company went into the triple bill programme on Monday with Nureyev dancing in three of the four works. At the *Conservatoire* rehearsal he had wanted the corps further back behind him but he had no such request for *Le Spectre de la Rose* pas de deux! In both he made a great impact and was on form, but he didn't seem to know what he was doing in *Schéhérazade*, either at rehearsal or performance. But the audience just loved to see him on stage looking magnificent as the bare-chested Golden Slave. He partnered Asensio who was strikingly sensuous as Zobeide and managed to control his embraces. We were about to give *Romeo and Juliet* when, on Thursday 28th July, we received the news of the death of Nicholas Johnson's baby son. Poor Nicky was inconsolable and could not stop crying through class, rehearsal and even performance. It was heartbreaking to see his distress and unhappiness. We felt for him, so far from his ballerina wife Laura Conner, who must have been suffering terribly.

Always on the lookout for talent I hoped to find some good male dancers in New York. We auditioned quite a few, including a strong dancer from Joffrey's company, Jeffrey Hughes, who it was agreed would guest with us from October. We had also seen a young classical dancer with a beautiful line, Jay Jolley, who agreed to join Festival Ballet on our return to London. We were attracted by an American soloist, Starr Danias, who joined the Company in the autumn. Nureyev suggested I watch him take class with the famous teacher Stanley Williams, a former soloist from the Royal Danish Ballet, who gave a tough class into which he breathed calmness.

David and I had lunch with the former leading ballerina of American Ballet Theatre, Nora Kaye, a fine dramatic dancer, and her husband Herbert Ross, the film director. He was keen that our Company and Nureyev take part in a film about Nijinsky, with the Company performing *Schéhérazade* and *Prince Igor*, but without our principals. Nureyev was to decide in due course who he would partner. This was due to be filmed in England in April on a two-week schedule – one week shooting and one for contingencies. We showed interest pending further information.

During our time in New York we were overwhelmed by hospitality, the rekindling of friendships, as well as meeting many interesting people. Above all the Company with Nureyev had achieved success, which was demonstrated on our amazing last night at the Met – twenty minutes of applause, so thrilling and gratifying. Nureyev brought me on stage and forward to the orchestra, to the audience, along the sides of the dancers and back to the centre to take more calls with him. Nureyev was so happy and pleased as the stage was showered with flowers. All the battles and strains worthwhile. We had now to conquer Washington.

The only cloud on the horizon was my concern about Heather. She had been rather strange and distant during the week, unlike her chatty, bubbly self, and to my surprise wrote me a letter of resignation that day. I did not know what had come over her and decided to ignore the letter for the time being.

The Company travelled by coach to Washington on Sunday with a free day Monday which Sven and I spent relaxing before settling in at our hotel, The Watergate. I was keen to see how our 'get-in' was going at the Kennedy Center, worried that the Company would only get on stage for the first time after 4pm on Tuesday, with the opening four hours later. We were allotted two rooms for classes before the stage call which began a little late but we managed to be finished by 6.15. The curtain went up at 8pm promptly for our opening in Washington but failed to produce the same excitement as our first night in New York. Nureyev had worked with Anderton in the morning, but I thought he was not in such good form as on Saturday. He, however, was pleased with the performance. At a dinner party given afterwards by the Theatre Club Gold Supporters he was in a good mood and amiable to everybody.

For the next two days I felt unwell, but had to keep on going as interviews had been arranged. The evening of the Company's free day we were all invited to the British Embassy for an enjoyable party. To my embarrassment, Nureyev chose not to attend, but spent the day out in the country together with Ruanne, Werner and Johnson. But he did not turn down the invitation to meet President Carter on Wednesday morning, together with Sven and me.

60 The White House, Wednesday August 9th 1978

I was tremendously excited and also nervous as the time drew close for us to be collected and taken to the White House. Our lovely, raven-haired chaperone, Louise, held out the necessary papers to the guard at a small circular gatehouse, and we were allowed through into the grounds. Once inside the house itself, passing along carpeted corridors, all the eyes of the staff were focused on Nureyev, smartly attired in a dark suit, dark shirt and colourful tie. We were ushered into a bright and elegantly furnished room and asked to wait. After a short interval, President Carter entered followed by his wife, both shadowed at a discreet distance by impeccably dressed men. It was extraordinary to be in the same room as the most powerful man in the world, who came up to each of us in turn in the most friendly and relaxed manner. The First Lady was surprisingly modest and charming, putting us at our ease before we were surrounded by photographers.

I was a little disappointed that time did not allow a longer talk with the President before Nureyev captured the President's attention, referring to a letter he had written. In it he had asked for the President's help in obtaining permission from the authorities to return to Russia to see his mother. Carter took Nureyev to one side, calling over his Secretary of State Zbigniew Brzezinski, but it seemed they were unable to help. At the appointed time we were bade farewell and respectfully escorted from the room, Nureyev leaving last. Walking down the corridors I felt I was dreaming, as if floating on air, while staff gazed in wonder at the famous Nureyev, dancer-defector. Louise suggested we wait in the garden a few minutes to see the helicopter land and take the President onto his next assignment. It was like watching a movie, except we were caught in the terrific air-surge swirling from the helicopter.

Next evening I encountered a big problem. Terabust appeared to be having a nervous breakdown, saying she could not dance *Le Spectre de la Rose* that night with Nureyev.

Her boyfriend Kenneth McCombie and I had a long talk with her, but she kept saying she wanted to give up dancing. She cried and cried, but eventually agreed to try to finish the season. Although she danced that evening she came with McCombie next morning to see me. She could not face dancing *Giselle* that night with Nureyev, and McCombie wanted me to let her go home to Marseille. I explained this could not be permitted as she was under contract to us, which she readily accepted and went off bravely to class. Even though she tried, she just could not get herself to dance with Nureyev in *Giselle*, so Evdokimova danced in her place. I felt so sad for Terabust, this sweet lovely artist, much loved and now so bewildered and forlorn.

On Saturday, Ruanne was taken to hospital with suspected appendicitis, which fortunately turned out to be a false alarm; it was nervous tension. Sven gave Evdokimova treatment in the hotel – it was the last *Giselle* of the tour and she had performed the role the previous evening for Terabust. Throughout the month away, Sven had been called upon by dancers for help, and he was happy to give them treatment free of charge. The dancers were used to the osteopath Papoutsis attending them once a week on tour in England. His widow later told me we were the first ballet company to employ an osteopath, and it certainly proved of great benefit to the dancers.

To Nureyev's delight Brzezinski came to the *Giselle* performance with his wife. They both enjoyed it so much that he came again on Sunday to see the triple bill with another member of the White House staff. This was our last performance in Washington, the end of our tour in fact, and it was agreed with Martin Feinstein that Nureyev was to bring me on stage for the final calls. I had the most terrific reception and was also applauded vociferously later on leaving the stage door with Sven. What a precious memory to take back to England.

It was unbelievable that the Company had achieved such a success, and I was feeling so thankful and happy. That was until Murland, over a drink on the plane, unexpectedly accused me of having put my name above Princess Margaret's on the programme, adding: 'You just want to get an honour'. It was such an extraordinary accusation, totally without foundation, but it hurt and upset me. The euphoria was now totally obliterated. Why was he behaving in this way to me? I began to think back to his sly remarks, which I first took as just tittle-tattle, about how Nureyev could be running Festival Ballet. It was common knowledge that Nureyev had wanted to run the Royal Ballet and was looking elsewhere.

How glad I was to get home with Sven safely to Park Street by 10am, finding it spotless and welcoming. We were not expecting to see Ingvar until much later so, after unpacking, we went to bed and had a decent sleep before the phone calls began. Ingvar arrived looking well and dressed smartly I felt so proud of my son. He was chatty and we had such a lot to talk about that I was pleased Sven took us to the May Fair for supper to save me cooking.

Returning to the office next day there was a mass of mail to be dealt with, besides papers to prepare with David and Peter Morris for the Executive meeting that afternoon. To my relief all went well, even though Murland was there. Margaret had managed to get copies made of all our press cuttings from New York and Washington which we were able to hand around to the committee. I was optimistic that Heather would now be staying on with me, despite the letter she had written me in New York. We had a nice chat in the office that evening which cleared the air, so happily could now look forward to getting back to normal.

In less than a week the Company were to open with *Swan Lake* at Festival Hall so the dancers could only have two free days before coming in for class and *Swan Lake* calls. It had been well rehearsed in Washington so it was just a question of polishing certain items for the first night on Monday. I knew putting on the Festival Hall season so soon after returning from America was going to be tight, but America had been slotted into an already busy schedule. Evdokimova look like thistledown in the white acts, partnered by Labis. They performed well together, so we had a beautiful opening to the three-week season at Festival Hall. Some good partnerships developed during the two weeks of the great classic: Ruanne with Schaufuss; Asensio with Jonathan Kelly; Belfiore and Bart or Johnson, who also partnered Carole Hill giving a most promising Odette / Odile at a Saturday matinee. We were pleased to welcome Terabust back again, dancing *Swan Lake* during the second week, tenderly partnered by Bart. A little exhibition opened in the front of house upper terrace before our third evening's performance on Wednesday, paying tribute to Julian Braunsweg, who had headed Festival Ballet for 15 years, and showing the early history of Festival Ballet. This was a big boost for the season and had been carefully planned by Festival Hall to coincide with our appearances there.

I had thrilling news from the Chinese authorities at the beginning of September: our proposed visit to China was a distinct possibility. I rang Sir Louis immediately, also David and then Sven. At a later meeting, the Hochhausers seemed willing to release us from one or more weeks of their Coliseum season if dates should clash. Although this would mean Festival Ballet losing money, going to China was so prestigious that it was thought the loss would be justified. The Hochhausers were now going ahead with the Chinese Embassy, detailing plans for our appearances in Peking and Shanghai the following spring of 1979. It was agreed that Kern should conduct for us in China, which did not please Bond when I told him later that day.

After taking Evdokimova's rehearsal I had a long talk with her about future plans. She was thrilled to hear about China and assured me she would do her best to be free to come with us. I also told her of the planned production of *La Sylphide* in which we had cast her in the title role. She was most enthusiastic about this. I was in time to catch a little of the rehearsal of *Greening*, due to open the triple bill programme the following week, and was thrilled at Long's masterly handling of this unique ballet, so different from our other works. But the dress rehearsal on Monday of the triple bill was a strain – it looked messy despite careful preparation. My diary states: *Flower Festival* 'appalling', *Greening* 'awful', *Corsaire* pas de deux 'a disaster', *Three Preludes* 'backcloth unsatisfactory' and *Bourrée Fantasque* 'untidy'. I went home depressed, realising we expected too much from everyone and should have been given more time to recover from the flight back from the States. There was now only one week left before the holidays and I knew the Company would do their best, even though we rarely seemed to get much encouragement from the British critics, unlike the American press.

By the evening the Company were somewhat recovered, although I could see the dancers were not able to reach their highest standard and the technical staging was also rather shaky. The performances definitely improved as the week continued, which was just as well for we had many important visitors out front including the Gloucesters. David and I had papers to prepare for a midweek Board meeting at County Hall when we spoke frankly and directly. We wanted to give the committee a clear picture of the Company's tremendous hard work and achievements and hoped our outspokenness would do some good for the future. Sir Louis picked up the problem of not having a guaranteed entry to any one theatre and again floated the idea of purchasing the Coliseum. This had been turned down by Sir Max during his time as Chairman and was not taken on board either at this meeting.

The next day, Thursday, we received written confirmation from the Chinese Embassy of our forthcoming appearances in China. I was so pleased, even though they had booked June for the visit. This would clash with the Hochhausers' Nureyev season with us at the Coliseum. The Hochhausers were not too worried about our missing two of the four-week season, although we would be in debt to them. Peter Morris was concerned about his budget and the loss of two weeks income from the summer season, but agreed the Company must dance in China. Meantime the end of the Company's year arrived with our closing performance of the triple bill on Friday at Festival Hall. It was an amazing scene on stage – flowers were thrown across the footlights to the leading ballerinas and also to me. The stage became a sea of flowers as the applause and joyous shouts continued. It was wonderful to realise the audience's love for the Company and its delight at our success in America. This reception was so heartening and, in response, I gave my best ever speech of gratitude.

The three week Company holiday I spent with Sven mostly at Fernhill – working in the garden, visiting friends and swimming at the Mills' in their lovely pool. I returned refreshed, pleased to be with my dancers once more in our own rehearsal rooms and all too soon embroiled in office matters. David, Peter B and I saw Peter Finch from Equity before he spoke to the dancers regarding their future salaries. He explained to them a five per cent rise was the most Festival Ballet could afford and that he had been assured this would be raised should the Arts Council grant be increased next April as hoped. He recommended the dancers accept the five per cent increase and succeeded in securing their rather reluctant acceptance. David and I followed this by informing the Company of future plans for the coming year. They were thrilled by the prospect of dancing in China. Sven and I were invited to a reception at the Chinese Embassy where, to my joy, I was told plans were going ahead for the Company to perform next May in Shanghai as well as Peking.

Anderton was asking for a second choreologist, to free her from teaching new dancers the choreography of our ballets. I explained we could not entertain that idea with finances being so tight. She was such a good teacher, and I hoped she understood the position. I had already asked a freelance teacher, Brian Loftus, to periodically take the men's class, which I believed would reduce a little of her work load. It was the best I could do. How I missed Donald.

On Sunday 15th October 1978 the Company gathered at the Coliseum to attend a special gala performance in memory of one of our most loved and gifted leading dancers, 27-year-old Paul Clarke. He had died, having been taken ill while having treatment at his dentist and never recovered. Many supporters were also present, including my friends Sir Alex and Lady Alexander who insisted on giving me dinner to lighten my mood. They took such an interest in Festival Ballet's progress; a connoisseur of the arts he had raised a huge sum of money for the rebuilding of Glyndebourne Opera House in Sussex. He knew Sven and I had decided to sell our London house, and Sven was keen to hear of any interesting offers. Alex understood that Sven, having long passed retirement age, wished to live in the beauty of Sussex.

Before the start of our two-month tour of the provinces, there was an Executive meeting, prior to which David, Peter Morris and I met Weiss and GLC board members for discussions over lunch. I was asked to prepare a paper – a three-year plan. This was well received by the Executive with the exception of Murland, who did his best to criticise it.

David and I met Nora Kay and Herbert Ross regarding the film they were to make about Nijinsky, featuring Nureyev. They wished the company to dance *Schéhérazade* and *Petrouchka*. We believed this would bring both publicity and money for Festival Ballet, and that the dancers would enjoy the experience of filming for two weeks in the New Year following our time at Festival Hall. It was agreed that we would take part, subject to Board approval.

The next week David and I prepared for a business lunch with senior representatives of IBM, hoping to interest them in supporting our forthcoming tour to China. It was paramount that we tried to find financial help for this tour, specifically to cover the high cost of flights to China and back. David and I were constantly seeking avenues of financial help from possible supporters.

We had a dreadful accident in Birmingham on the Friday night when, in Act III of *Sleeping Beauty*, a chandelier fell on Anthea Neal, one of my corps de ballet. It hit her head, cutting it open and blood poured across the stage. David Long and Betty Anderton came swiftly on stage as the curtain was brought down. Miraculously there was a surgeon in the audience who also rushed to her aid, taking her to hospital for stitches. The poor girl soon recovered, and we breathed a sigh of relief.

Autumn brought fog and with it difficulties for our guest artists who were flying into London from different cities across Europe. Joanie took care when casting ballets to match their availability with our requirements, so flight delays could play havoc with our programming. The week ended with Bart fog-bound in Paris and unable to reach Birmingham. This gave a wonderful opportunity for Tom van Cauwenbergh to take his place and partner Terabust in *Sleeping Beauty*. It turned out to be a surprising success and fans, having made the journey from London, were delighted to be present for Tom's debut, throwing flowers on stage at the end. At the beginning of the new week I received a report of the previous Friday's accident. I sent David Mogridge a stiff memo because it was found to have been entirely the fault of the stage crew, who were his direct responsibility.

Graham Bond guest conducting in Stuttgart and David Coleman likewise in Paris gave Bramwell Tovey the opportunity to conduct *Sleeping Beauty*. He managed this demanding ballet, with all its different soloists, remarkably well. I was pleased he coped so splendidly. He was working closely with Ronald Hynd, now immersed in rehearsals for his new three-act *Rosalinda*. It was lovely to hear the strains of the Strauss operetta drifting through the theatre each day and exciting to see the ballet taking shape, with Kenn Wells acting most amusingly as the drunken jailer in the last act.

John Morgan of the Foreign Office Cultural Relations department was overseeing our visit to China, and David and I had several sessions with him. I now told him of the letter the Hochhausers had received from Gorlinsky, in which he insisted Nureyev should go as guest artist with Festival Ballet to China. John Morgan was plainly horrified to hear this and said the Foreign Office would definitely not approve. He pointed out that the Foreign Office was raising most of the money for the tour – not the Hochhausers. I was so relieved that the Foreign Office did not want us to take Nureyev, thus avoiding any personal clash between him and me.

After our December Board meeting I was depressed because my three-year plan, on which I had worked so thoughtfully with Heather, was turned down. Murland had demonstrated his opposition to my ideas by walking out. It was a disappointment that Weiss, as Chairman, did not show a firmer hand, even though Sir Louis, with Harold and Harriet Sebag-Montefiore were in favour of my proposals. It left me again wondering what the future held, lacking a strong Chairman.

Following Festival Hall's three-week Christmas season, the Company played *Nutcracker* for a week in Leeds, returning to the Hall to give *Sleeping Beauty* for a week. I had several meetings with Herbert Ross before the filming started the next week. With Nureyev taking the lead in all three ballets, *Petrouchka, Schéhérazade* and *Igor*, my principals accepted guest artist engagements abroad.

Princess Margaret came to watch the filming, being so interested in all that was happening. Her visit gave me confidence for what I had decided to say at the Board meeting next day. I had become so disillusioned with my Chairman, Weiss, in whom I had completely lost faith. It worried me that he went around talking to the dancers and more importantly failed to support me at Board meetings and at the unpleasant Gorlinsky encounters. My job was constantly demanding, and I was beginning to get terribly tired. It kept me away from Sven so much, and I think the rejection of my three-year vision had shaken me. It seemed the Board were not with me and without their backing I thought it irresponsible and foolish to continue. Perhaps the time had come for me to step down and make way for a different Artistic Director?

After saying this to the Board at the meeting I was asked to go into an adjoining room together with David Rees and Peter Morris. After a wait of one and a quarter hours we were recalled and told that all the Board were behind me and wanted me to remain as Artistic Director. They read out a statement to this effect, but I replied I was not convinced and truly intended to resign. I would now need to think things over while awaiting their formal letter through the post. As the meeting broke up Miss Morgan kindly gave everyone drinks in her office ,and I was touched that Sir Louis and the other GLC members were hopeful that I would stay on.

The letter from the Board arrived on Tuesday morning and I was so worried about when and how to answer it that Sven arranged for me to obtain advice that afternoon from a solicitor, Johnson Hicks. He asked me many searching questions, and I got the feeling he thought it a pity I had decided to step down. He said if I decided to leave I must offer six months' notice to give time for a replacement to be found, making my departure as pleasant as possible. I spent a good part of the next day writing my letter of resignation, sad and irresolute. I loved the Company, and it was the Chairman's underhandedness that had pushed me to it. I realised how much Sven had gone through with me and how much I owed him. I felt it was time to consider him first instead of the Company. But my heart was heavy. I felt so torn and prayed to God for direction.

As I knew Weiss would not change, it seemed to me I had no option but to leave, so rang Weiss telling him I was resigning, and giving six months notice. He had lunched with Gorlinsky, who had apparently railed against my not taking Nureyev to China; evidently Murland had also been on to Weiss with the same complaint. I rang Sir Louis to tell him of my six-month resignation notice and inform him of the Gorlinsky China situation. He was understanding and helpful, and I knew I had a friend in him. I was feeling as wretched as the weather, so sad at the thought of leaving Festival Ballet.

Snow and ice carpeted many roads and I had difficulty in London driving up the hill from Mount Pleasant to see my father in Lloyd Square. I had to give up and leave the car halfway up the hill and walk the rest of the way. Now that Sven and I had sold our Park Street house I paid my father a visit before going to the country. Our move meant my father was further away from us, and we determined to visit him regularly as well as having him to stay with us from time to time.

62 A Premiere And Preparations For China

The Company's belated holiday week approached: they had enjoyed the two-week filming, a new experience for them, and could now relax for a week before resuming class and rehearsal. On Sunday 18th February 1979 I flew to Canada for a conference of directors of ballet companies and dance personnel at which I was the second speaker. Sven saw me off, both of us happier knowing our separations would soon be a thing of the past.

I was back in London by Wednesday morning having only missed the first two days of Hynd's final rehearsals for *Rosalinda*. It was now only two weeks before its premiere at the Dominion, Tottenham Court Road, the new venue for the Company. He was focused, with everyone working full out to make it a success. There are all too few choreographers today who take on the challenge of a full-length work, and I was fortunate that Hynd was happy to create on my Company. He was such a straightforward, lovely person without temperamental outbursts. It was a pleasure to have him around. Docherty was putting final touches to the many costumes, so well designed in the style fashionable between the wars. Terry Kern was happy with the brilliant arrangement of the Lehar music by John Lanchbery, and our stage crew and Company got into the Dominion on Monday.

All went surprisingly smoothly at the Dominion, no doubt helped by the goodwill of the resident staff. We were ready in good time for the Tuesday evening preview given at lower ticket prices. There were plenty of laughs and good applause from the audience. The next night, Wednesday, was a gala enhanced by the presence of the Prince and Princess Michael of Kent. They were the most lovely guests – relaxed and knowledgeable, entering into the spirit of the evening, which was sponsored by Nat West. After the Royal couple met the dancers and conductor on stage, the bank threw a marvellous party for everyone. Next night was the press night but brought a strange audience who neither laughed nor applauded, unlike the previous two. I felt sorry for Hynd especially as Jonas Kåge and Pattie Ruanne acted and danced fantastically well, despite the restrictions of the Dominion. I remember apologising to our talented handsome guest star Käge for the narrow wings and limited space, but he didn't seem to mind and took it all good heartedly.

Rosalinda played for two weeks and was thoroughly enjoyed by the Company and our ensuing audiences. The Dominion manager, Mr Pacey, even opened his office at the end of the first week to give David and me a glass of champagne to celebrate. I felt we had a winner in *Rosalinda*, despite some disappointing reviews. The title role gave Ruanne a wonderful opportunity to shine in a character created round her talents. After two weeks of *Rosalinda, Sleeping Beauty* followed for a week and a half playing to full houses. We closed our season with five performances of a triple bill – *Les Sylphides, Petrouchka* and *Prince Igor*. We were encouraged at the success of our month's stay at the Dominion and glad to have found another acceptable venue in central London for our nomadic existence.

Meanwhile, Lilian Hochhauser had asked for a meeting with the cultural attaché, Mr Chu, at the Chinese Embassy. David and I met her there for what became a most satisfactory gathering. Lilian enquired if we should go ahead with plans for our tour as she had not heard anything from Peking since her last visit nor received any written confirmation. It was such a relief to hear the definite 'Yes' in answer to her enquiry and also to learn it might be possible for us to have their orchestra accompanying us. We left reassured – it was now a little over five weeks before we were due to leave for China. Before that, however, there were two weeks performing outside London: one in Eastbourne with *Rosalinda* and a triple bill, then on to Oxford presenting *Rosalinda* there for the entire stay. After a few days' rest, rehearsals resumed for many ballets including those going on the all-important Far East venture.

During the Oxford week I had another awful Board meeting, the third since I had resigned. I lunched with David and Peter Morris at County Hall where Councillor Fred Weyer, Chairman of GLC Arts Committee, had said he was in his room if I wanted to talk things over with him. He had rung me earlier asking me to reconsider my resignation. I went for half an hour and tried to make my position clear to him and, after our talk, felt tempted to rescind my resignation. Later to the Board I said, however, I could see no point in remaining unless Gerry Weiss went. The GLC board members tried all they could to induce me to stay, suggesting a one-year contract. Gerry Weiss then said he had heard that eight dancers were leaving that summer, implying this was because of me, and he and Shirley Porter thought the Company should be asked how they felt about me. Weiss asked for a vote on this suggestion of a Company meeting with me present. He got four votes against it and five to go ahead. It seemed the Board were not prepared to lose Weiss. News of this went around the Company like wild fire, and I noted that on the day of this unpleasant meeting Nureyev was not in the building to rehearse. Joanie told me that all the ballet and stage staff were behind me with the exception of Betty Anderton. Joanie felt the dancers were with me, with the notable exceptions of one of my leading ballerinas and two male soloists. It was horrid, but I was deeply touched when Nigel Burgoine got up and spoke on my behalf, praising me and all my work.

I planned for the romantic Danish classic *La Sylphide* to be staged by Mona Vangsaa in time for the Festival Hall season in August. The role of the Sylph was ideal for Evdokimova with its flowing romantic movements while offering Schaufuss the perfect showpiece for his outstanding Danish technique, seemingly effortless ballon and brilliant footwork. My friend in the Arts Council, Keith Jeffery, came to watch some of the rehearsals and was enthusiastic about the Company's style in this Danish ballet. The three weeks sped by, rehearsing many ballets while there was a lot of media interest in our forthcoming engagement in China, and Lilian Hochhauser and I were guests at both the Chinese and Soviet Embassies.

63 *To China*

The BBC, and to my surprise Danish television, televised the Company a few days before our departure for Peking. The second week of May 1979 we flew to Peking. At the request of the Chinese, and despite our discussions, we had to bring our own orchestra. Although this was the right decision musically it changed the budget for the tour, throwing it into deficit. Alighting from the plane in Peking I was disappointed that there was no one to meet us but, when we approached the 'garden slope' at the edge of the tarmac, it was lined with a reception committee of Chinese with Tai Aileen, Director of Peking Ballet Company, photographers and Keith Hunter, First Secretary at the British Embassy in Peking. It was beautifully organised as was everything during our visit.

Now returning as Artistic Director I was enveloped in goodwill. Lilian Hochhauser, as our impresario, and I were each allotted a car and driver; four coaches were booked to take the Company to the theatre as well as on sight-seeing trips when I also joined them. It seem strange yet miraculous to be back in this city after an absence of fifteen years, but I was sorry Sven could not accompany me this time. During that fifteen years since I danced there China had undergone the big Cultural Revolution.

One of the most important events for me on the tour was making a speech on Wednesday 9th May in the large banqueting hall of the Peking Hotel. I was remembered from my previous visit as the ballerina who had danced with their Peking company and was asked through an interpreter to prepare my speech in answer to the Vice Premier's. I suddenly became worried about this in the night and, with heart banging at two o'clock, unable to sleep, I got up and wrote most of it. Later that morning Heather got busy typing it ready to give to the interpreter to be translated.

The Company were invited to the British Embassy for cocktails on the lawn and terrace at noon Wednesday, our first full day in Peking. In China one is expected to be absolutely punctual. We found the Ambassador, Percy Cradock, and the kind Keith Hunter most considerate and helpful, and we enjoyed the hour spent in the beautiful grounds of the Embassy within the diplomatic compound.

An afternoon visit to the famous Summer Palace was also organised for the Company, and it was wonderful to walk in the glorious gardens again, this time shimmering in Spring sunshine. We were a large group of 145, and our interpreters struggled to do their best amidst the milling crowds meandering through the gardens. There was no time to enjoy the incredible collection within the Palace but on reaching the famous Marble Boat we were privileged to be taken home across the water in old style launches.

The Company were keen to see the Theatre of Heavenly Bridges, where Festival Ballet was to perform. It was the same theatre in which I had danced with Wang Shao-Pen in 1964. The building seemed brighter than I remembered it, now sporting bright green rubber runners along the centre of the corridors. The rehearsal room was as dark as ever and still half filled with chairs stacked on boxes ready for the inevitable lectures! The stage appeared to me squarer, wider, yet not as deep – although the orchestra pit was definitely deeper than I remembered. There were only a few hanging bars and I was thankful we had decided against bringing *Sleeping Beauty* which would have presented major problems with its heavy Georgiadis scenery – though I knew the Chinese would have revelled in its richness. The theatre seated only 1600 and looked functional and uninviting from outside. I gave my silver cocktail dress to our wardrobe for repairs, and to my astonishment it was mended immediately and quite perfectly. There seemed to be hundreds of Chinese men and women about in the theatre, all friendly and wanting to help. I had, however, forgotten the awkward 'loos', more suited for wearers of trousers than of skirts and a strain on the knees, rather like those encountered in Japan.

At the hotel David Rees was caught in a discussion with our Musicians Union representative and our orchestra manager. This was about playing for the Friday performance when the Chinese wished to have a television crew filming throughout the performance. It was to be a great occasion with the Leaders of China attending, but it would not involve any extra fee for the artists. David spoke to the dancers that afternoon and by evening their representative was able to tell him the dancers were willing to dance Friday without extra payment. Moreover, if our orchestra did not also agree to this, the dancers were prepared to perform *Giselle* with the Peking Symphony Orchestra. Four of our musicians were not prepared to play Friday without extra pay so their representative contacted London. To our relief the Musicians Union gave us the go-ahead despite no extra payment and sent their good wishes to the Chinese and everyone involved.

Our first night, Thursday, was to an invited audience of artists, critics and those who had earned a special award. Having their own production of *Giselle* they were keen to make comparisons. They did not clap much, except for Schaufuss, who they took to at once. They seemed unimpressed with the first act, even though Evdokimova was moving and convincing in the mad scene. In the second act she and Schaufuss achieved an outstanding performance together. The interpreters and Mr Sing Yi were delighted with the performance saying it was a success and much liked by all present. But we were used to much greater applause, and I wondered if we had made the right decision in bringing *Giselle.* The next evening allayed my fears – it was a great success with the powerful leaders present and the audience applauding loud and long.

It followed a full day: the Company spent the morning at the Peking Dance Academy where the students gave an interesting performance in their theatre. It was here where I had taught and produced them in *Les Sylphides,* in the third act of *Sleeping Beauty* and in *Swan Lake.* Now they gave us a remarkable arrangement of enchaînements somewhat similar to our *Études,* followed by a ballet based on Hans Christian Andersen's fairy tale *The Little Match Seller*, and ending with a display of national dances as well as excerpts from Peking Opera. My dancers were amazed at the range and high standard of their dancing and their fluidity in classical ballet. They had improved since I last saw them, particularly the women, who were more poised and confident and projected well on the stage, dancing under strong lights. It was arranged that we would perform something, too, and so Patrice Bart with Elisabetta Terabust danced a superb *Don Quixote* for them, which was rapturously received. The warm welcome spoken by their principal on our arrival was a forerunner of a wonderful shared experience, and we left with a feeling of mutual understanding and joy. Lilian, David and I were given lunch at the Embassy where I was handed a telegram addressed to me from our Prime Minister, Mrs Thatcher, sending the Company and the Chinese Leaders good wishes.

After rehearsals I barely had time to change before the arrival at 7.20pm of the highly respected Leaders of China. Lilian, David and I were led into a side stage room to await a summons. It was like waiting for royalty – rather exciting. Soon I was signalled to take my seat next to the deputy Prime Minister, television cameras whirling busily on us all the time. I passed on to the Leaders the message from Mrs Thatcher over which they were so delighted that they insisted an interpreter read it out for all in the theatre to hear. The Minister said they were happy to receive her message and reciprocated her good wishes. Later, through our Embassy, I sent a cable of thanks and appreciation to Mrs Thatcher reporting the success of the evening.

Giselle was captured on three cameras and the Company excelled themselves. At the end of the performance, the cameras now on us again, I was abruptly signalled to go backstage. Placed in front of our dancers were seven children kneeling on both sides of gigantic baskets of flowers. At a signal, with the Leaders, Lilian, David and I walked onto the stage amid continuous clapping from the audience, returning to the front of stage to be photographed. The curtains were then drawn across and farewells exchanged. At the Leaders' departure the cameras ceased their coverage and our friends from the British Embassy flocked onto the stage with bottles of champagne for the Company to enjoy. It was a most happy, informal party with press from Reuters and the Daily Telegraph mingling amongst us. Lilian, David and I repaired to the hotel for supper, relieved and glad that it had all gone so well. The television people had done a marvellous job and not intruded in any way. They had not even asked for a special rehearsal, merely watching closely our Thursday performance of *Giselle*. They posed no problem nor demanded any lighting changes which was remarkable. They shot the entire performance from three cameras placed a little way back in the stalls without disturbing people in the audience. They certainly knew what they were doing, and we admired their total dedication and professionalism

Next morning I set off with Heather to give class at 10 o'clock at the Peking Ballet School. With excellent interpreters it was possible to give them explanations for certain exercises, and I taught for two hours. There were many people watching, taking photos and filming, and I hoped it was helpful for them. I promised to return on Monday to give another class and to bring Anderton and Schaufuss also to give the students extra training.

I watched the matinee – Ruanne in Act I danced a most beautiful solo but Loeber and Tom van Cauwenbergh were disappointing in their diverts, which rather let down the build-up of that act. The press turned up early so we commenced at 4.30 instead of 5 o'clock. We had been given five questions in advance, and I spoke for an hour. To my relief we had Sun Yi and smiling Mr Chang as our interpreters so it passed surprisingly easily. Before the performance I had an interview with a Canadian correspondent, in the first interval with an American one, and during the second interval with 'China Reconstructs'. A mad day which showed the interest our visit had created internationally.

Retiring to my room at last, I had within ten minutes a phone connection to Sven on a clear line. It was wonderful to hear his voice and to have a three-sided conversation with him and Ingvar. But I thought Sven sounded less happy to hear me than usual. Perhaps it was because he could not share this visit with me, or was I imagining it? Or perhaps it was because he was paying for the call! Whatever it was, it left me feeling unsettled. If only I could see him. If only he could also have come this time with me to China.

Next Monday morning, as promised, I returned to the Peking Dance Academy this time accompanied by Anderton and Schaufuss. We three gave classes to the intelligent and eager students who, together with those in charge, were so grateful and sent us off to the theatre with affection and a wealth of good wishes. I was pleased with the evening's performance. In *Études* Bart and Schaufuss were sensational. The audience obviously enjoyed all the exciting pyrotechnics. I thought many were somewhat bewildered, however, by the more modern *Greening*.

After breakfast the Company were driven to the headquarters of the Peking Ballet Company where we were welcomed with cymbals clashing and gongs banging. We were touched, as we were by the short performance they had prepared for us. Among their smiling faces I recognised several from my visit fifteen years previously and I had many warm embraces. We climbed the numerous steps to their theatre at the top of the building where, in front of the seats, was placed a long table for the expected discussion. Their director Tai Aileen explained that she and all the dancers and musicians had been sent to work in the fields during the Cultural Revolution. This explained why most of the dancers were now over 30 years of age – they had not been given any newcomers since that time. They were now awaiting young talent from the school to emerge and come into the company. Our dancers were enthralled by the programme then presented by the Chinese dancers for us.

It was a shock when Bart announced that he was unable to dance in *Études* that night. We had to ask Johnson to dance it again, this time opposite Schaufuss who inspired him to dance better than at the matinee. The ballet made a good finish to our season but as usual the applause was muted although the audience began a slow determined hand clapping which we took as a big compliment. We found it hard to say goodbye to everybody in the theatre, their staff, the stewards out front and back, the stage crew and the director himself, who had given massage and acupuncture to the dancers. All had been so friendly, kind and helpful, and we struck a bond between us. It was a wonderful time in Peking, every hour packed with interesting experiences. The only setback was when our property manager, Allan Cleary, developed pneumonia which meant leaving him behind in the Peking hospital.

Owing to some dancers oversleeping, we were half an hour late leaving the hotel and, with horrendous traffic, had to make a detour to reach the airport. Our driver was expert in coping with the seemingly crazy hordes – there were twelve cyclists abreast, meandering pedestrians, overcrowded buses, heavily laden lorries and pedicabs dangerously weaving in and between everything. He got us there in time to board the waiting plane, which was spotlessly clean and brightly decorated. On landing in Shanghai we were met by a long line of people, a well organised welcoming committee, shaking hands with each of us in turn before we were whisked away with David, two interpreters and a woman artist from a special Committee.

What changes I noted on our drive from the new airport, once located in rural surroundings. The little huts built over water were now replaced by compounds of larger huts. We drove through towns eventually reaching the city of Shanghai which reminded me a little of Hong Kong. Western style, two and three-storey houses and many soaring buildings dwarfed the crowded streets. After the French district we came to a gate with two sentries on duty. A horde of onlookers gathered on the pavement outside stared at us as we drove through the hotel gates, where, waiting to greet us, were the entire hotel staff and residents.

Feeling tired with a headache I was thankful to get time for an hour's rest before dressing for a big banquet at the headquarters of the Revolutionary Committee. I had written my speech that morning on the plane so Heather could type and give it to an interpreter in advance. Our host the Vice Mayor and head of the Cultural Department gave a speech before the hot courses, to which I replied before desserts were served. I had broken my glasses so could not see too clearly but my reply was much appreciated and enjoyed. The event was a splendid occasion, each of the round tables exquisitely decorated with flowers and ferns concealing centre-pieces of dancers on pointe. It turned out to be a most happy evening and a much needed earlier night than usual.

The next afternoon's dress rehearsal was encouraging. I then changed for the evening in preparation for the arrival of the leaders of the Revolutionary Committee. When summoned from the long waiting room I was pleased to find they were our friends from the previous evening, accompanied by the head of the Ballet School. Cameras running, I took my place with them as directed in the seventh row of the stalls, with David Rees, G. Whitaker and Keith Hunter. The row in front was kept empty while the row behind was filled with many interpreters and 'lesser fry'. At the end of the ballet the cameras followed us through the audience to steps placed over the side of the orchestra and leading straight up onto the stage. There, as in Peking, swiftly assembled with huge baskets of flowers were seven children kneeling around the baskets, which held beautiful red gladioli and orange and pink peonies. With the audience still clapping, we walked down the lines of dancers congratulating each in turn and returning to the front of the stage again amidst singing from the clapping audience. The Leaders then brought forward the principals and the curtains were drawn. All sound ceased, likewise the cameras. It was another amazing evening but surprisingly a happy one, too. After a light supper in the hotel I went to bed thankful that our first performance in Shanghai had had such a splendid reception.

The next morning the orchestra met with players from the Shanghai Symphony orchestra who gave them a little concert, after which the musicians intermingled with help from numerous interpreters. That afternoon the Company attended a special performance of National Dances including exciting excerpts from the Peking Opera at one of their large theatres. At the end I was asked to go on stage to say a few words – the Chinese always expected speeches. We left for the theatre where Anderton was waiting to give the Company class. For the evening performance Ruanne was dancing Giselle partnered by Schaufuss, but without Evdokimova's inspiration his performance seemed a little below par whilst Ruanne's Act I seemed somewhat forced. Act II was more harmonious, and the audience was obviously enraptured.

Vass came with me to the Shanghai Dance Academy at the start of our last week in China. We both gave classes to eager students, some of whom I had worked with the previous week. They had remembered and worked on my corrections, which made for a wonderful rapport between us. Vass went on to teach them our version of *Études*, and I had to pull him away by 2pm to come to the theatre for our rehearsals

Our last performance in Shanghai that evening was attended by another deputy Mayor with a number of important personages. As on similar occasions their every move was televised, culminating with us on a flower-filled stage. We gave *Études* as our closing ballet but, to my great disappointment, it was poorly danced and I felt upset. But the clapping and singing continued until the curtains were drawn, bringing our final contact with the friendly audience to an end. Farewells spoken through interpreters, the Company returned to the hotel where I had a light snack of scrambled eggs. As ordered, the Company were woken by 6am to be ready to depart at 7am. Down in the lobby, to my surprise, there were no staff to be found. They were outside on the steps of the hotel to wave us goodbye. I felt a lump in my throat: where else in the world would one find such loving loyalty?

Our early morning cavalcade coincided with a hubbub of traffic – lorries, buses, vans, cars, pedicabs, bicycles and a host of coaches. We progressed slowly along the densely crowded streets, eventually leaving the city for the countryside and several sandy roads. These enveloped us and all our belongings in a mist of choking dust: many roads were under repair. Although thankful for the food boxes provided we waited until arrival before eating breakfast from the now dust-covered containers. Despite the bumpy journey on poorly upholstered seats, the countryside was a compensation and a revelation. Trees lined the sides of many roads with tiny poor-looking houses at intervals, some with thatched roofs and others tiled. Every inch of land was cultivated, oxen ploughing, peasants standing knee-deep in water, planting rice in the scores of paddy fields, all at differing stages of growth. The well-arranged irrigation system was a joy to behold, as were the large ponds and farms for geese. These closely guarded birds with their white feathers glistening in the sun were to be spotted standing in groups by the occasional river or canal. The waterways were busy as most goods were transported by water – understandably, with the state of the country roads and the haphazard driving of vans and lorries! Flat-bottomed boats were 'punted' by two people pushing hard forwards and backwards on a stiff upright pole. Other boats were linked together, nine or ten at a time, and pulled by one with an outboard motor.

Waiting for us at the airport was a little group who presented me with a book of photos for the Company and an envelope of photos for me personally to keep, together with shots of the Peking Opera which I had requested. A book of treasures from the past, which I had admired in the Exhibition Hall, and two silk ties for my husband and son were also given to me. We were then introduced to their film actress, Yuan Xu, waiting with the grey-haired head of the school of choreography. There was little time for the customary tea, for which I was longing, before we were taken onto the plane for the flight to Peking. Our last sight was of them waving to us from the airport steps under the hot Shanghai sun.

With the welcoming group in Peking there were tables laid for tea in a large room, which was much appreciated after battling through rain and a gale to reach the airport building. A small committee gave me three envelopes of photos, one for Evdokimova, one for Schaufuss and one for me. We were told a farewell dinner had been arranged in a large airport room with the Minister of Culture Chou Er Fu, the Director of External Affairs from the Ministry, and many others including Tai Aileen. It was a happy and unexpected gathering for the end of our time in China, which I thought remarkably poignant.

Back at Heathrow I found Sven looking tired and older. He also seemed less excited than usual to see me, the same manner I detected on the phone from Peking. I wondered why, unaware that his health and sight had begun to worry him. The Company had only Thursday in which to recover, and Sven and I spent a wonderfully happy time alone at Fernhill.

Allan Cleary, now recovered, flew back from Peking on the same Friday that rehearsals began on *Romeo and Juliet.* This ballet was to open the Hochhauser's Nureyev season at the Coliseum in just over a week, so there was a lot to prepare. I had several press and radio interviews concerning our recent engagement in China, about which there was terrific interest. I was also asked to give a lunchtime talk to bankers and politicians about the China we found.

64 *Disturbing Undercurrents; Nureyev Gets Revenge*

Thank goodness Monday was a bank holiday so we could all have another short break before resuming rehearsals. Nureyev was in Tuesday morning and all day Wednesday when he appeared to be in a good mood – until Tom van Cauwenbergh upset him, and it became tricky. I had to leave with Rees for an extraordinary lunch with Weiss at which there were some embarrassing silences. Rees wanted to hear about applications for my position, and I enquired if I was to receive a financial 'handshake'. On leaving, I had to rush to finish my board papers for Heather to type in time for Weiss before the Thursday meeting.

This Board meeting was ghastly – most unpleasant and nerve-racking, starting at 2.15pm and not ending until 7.15pm by when some members had begun to leave. The GLC did not want to let me go and, as I pointed out, I did not want to leave Festival Ballet either. I knew only too well that with Weiss remaining as Chairman and Murland on the Board my position would become untenable.

At first the GLC members employed delaying tactics, querying the procedure for voting on the three candidates for Artistic Director: John Field, Ronald Hynd and

Andre Prokovsky. Were sufficient numbers present for a vote, and so forth. A subsequent show of hands was not accepted, and I was then asked to stay in the room during a written vote but five cards were discounted and the proceedings thought possibly unconstitutional, some members having been absent from the previous meeting. It went on and on until arbitration by GLC and Arts Council representatives was finally agreed. Weiss then said he thought the Company should be involved and a meeting set up so they could say whether or not they wished me to stay as their Artistic Director. To my horror, he got this agreed.

Next morning Harriet Sebag-Montefiore rang to encourage me to stay and fight. I rang to thank Sir Louis for his support, and he suggested I call Sir James Swaffield, Director General of the GLC, to ensure I got a hearing should a Company meeting go ahead. I rang, but both he and his deputy were out of their office. At midday Joanie told me the news was out, and a Company meeting had been called but I need not worry as everyone, including the staff, was for me – with the exception of three leading artists. By 3.30pm our Equity reps went to see Rees to ask him to speak to the Company. After taking Sir Louis' advice, I said I would speak to them. It did not seem to have resolved my position and I began to doubt my dancers' loyalty in the face of an open debate, even though my stage staff told me the reverse. The stage staff wanted to speak, too, in my defence. I did not want to involve them, but thanked them for offering, which meant a lot to me.

I thought it odd that Nureyev was not in the building at all that day, but he was back on Saturday, working until mid afternoon. I watched much of the call but left before he finished. I signed many letters, including 30 to potential donors. On Sunday on the phone Sir Louis persuaded me to withdraw my resignation, and Sven agreed, too, if I really wanted to stay with the Company. Having withdrawn my resignation, I went in to the office on Monday feeling happier, but that afternoon I had a shock. Rees had been handed a letter by the dancers' Equity committee saying the Company had no faith in my direction. I was shattered. Whatever was going on? Rees seemed pretty negative, not surprising as he had only been with us a comparatively short time. I discussed the letter with the ballet staff and Heather, when David Long told us it was all trumped-up. The dancers had no grievance, but someone was stirring up trouble amongst them. It was disturbing, particularly with the Hochhausers' season opening next day.

On 5th June 1979, Nureyev and Ruanne performed in his *Romeo and Juliet* with great success. David Coleman conducted this and the following press night to everyone's apparent satisfaction. The audiences were good. *Romeo and Juliet* was a winner, and the Company were in good form despite the strange undercurrent. Weiss had been in to speak to David and me about the forthcoming meeting on Friday. I heard from Arnold Haskell that he had sent a letter urging the Board to accept my withdrawal of resignation and be sure to retain me as Artistic Director. At the meeting, however, Murland opposed this in view of the Equity reps' letter, whereupon Sir Louis tore the letter into shreds and a debate ensued. Harvey Hines called for a motion to re-elect me, providing I felt I could work constructively with the Company. I assured him I could, and the vote came out in my favour.

Arriving at the Coliseum on Saturday at midday, my heart fell as Vass told me a Company meeting had taken place at which Hugh Rathbone was shouted down by Pink and Werner. This upset me terribly. How could my dancers behave so badly to one another? I did not stay as Sven and I were due at Westminster Central Hotel where our Master, on a visit from India, was to give a discourse. The room was packed but we managed to find two seats at the back and returned in the evening for an informal gathering. His smile was full of loving compassion and all-embracing, and it was a joy to be in his presence. We returned again next day and this time were seated in the front row so could hear and see him clearly. Those two days with our Master were wonderfully comforting. Revitalised, we realised how fortunate and blessed we both were.

My birthday on Monday was overshadowed by the inexplicable unrest in the Company together with Weiss' antagonistic behaviour. Why were the dancers ganging up on me? They had enjoyed great success, acclaim and kindness in China, so why this behaviour now and what was behind it? Already at 9am Weiss had rung me to say the reps were not satisfied with the Board. Weiss spoke as if he intended to further Murland's suggestion of a Company meeting. I learnt later from Heather that at the dancers' meeting on Saturday Nureyev's name had been mentioned as having suggested a strike by the dancers after his season finished. I then realised that Nureyev must be behind the trouble, as Heather rightly surmised, because I had not taken him to China with us. I recalled Weiss telling me of Nureyev's outburst one evening at not having been included in our Chinese tour: he had said he would never forgive me. This was his retaliation.

Nureyev's *Sleeping Beauty* opened on Tuesday after a late morning's rehearsal with orchestra and Nureyev messing about with the lighting to the annoyance of our electricians. The performance appeared well lit, and the audience enjoyed the engaging partnership of Nureyev with Evdokimova. During the first interval Rees and I spoke with Sir Louis. I showed him Haskell's letter, thanked him for the one he had written to the Board and for persuading Weiss to agree that only four or five dancers should speak to the Board on the 20th June.

For the third and last week we went into a triple bill programme: *Conservatoire, Sanguine Fan,* and *Schéhérazade*, with *Spectre de la Rose* included to feature Nureyev. At the Monday afternoon dress rehearsal he began his tantrums, behaving abominably. He stopped the orchestra and insisted on the lighting being altered. Mohr did what he could and explained that to change it all now would take several hours. Nureyev would not accept this and stormed off shouting 'No performance'. I rang the Hochhausers, and Nureyev returned to the stage and went through the whole of *Spectre* with Ruanne, whose debut in the delicate pas de deux was that evening. Anderton looked pleased at the debacle when Nureyev sat down, centre stage, until the gantry was brought down and all rehearsals ended. There was now insufficient time left to finish the *Sanguine Fan* run-through before the stage crew took over. Everything fell into place for the evening, and the triple bill had a good reception. The week was one of mounting tensions within the Company, with another awful Board meeting midweek – Murland gloating at my discomfort and Weiss his unsupportive self. I was so relieved that Arnold Haskell had come from Bath especially to speak with me over lunch at his London home. I felt a lot calmer afterwards, knowing he was to be present at the meeting.

On Thursday morning Margot Fonteyn was at the Coliseum to rehearse *L'Après-midi d'un Faune* with Nureyev. She was as sweet as always, and I helped her with her costume in which she looked wonderful. During Friday evening's performance a worried Heather and Tony Barlow sought me out to tell me the Guardian newspaper was on the phone with a story to read to me before going to press. My heart sank. Our Equity reps had leaked their story to the Guardian, to be printed if they were dissatisfied with the outcome of their next meeting. Later Rees admitted the reps had told him of this in the first interval, yet neither he nor Weiss had told me before they went to a small drinks party given by Murland, to which l did not go.

On Saturday morning, without waiting for the meeting's outcome, the Guardian reported the Company's disquiet; it was also reported in the Telegraph. I rang Weiss and asked him, in view of the reps' behaviour, to cancel the Company's Wednesday meeting with the Board. He later said he could not do this without the Board's permission and, as he was unable to contact anyone, it would be going ahead. That Saturday evening Margot's presence gave a splendid end to the Nureyev season. I was pleased that she had appeared with us. But I was shaken when she suggested to me that I hand the Company over to Nureyev, or at least ask him to become artistic advisor.

After the taxing Coliseum season, the dancers had the first two days of the next week free, and we had not scheduled any rehearsals. To my complete surprise in Tuesday's Guardian a wonderful letter was printed about me and my achievements, written by Paul Findlay. I was deeply touched that he should have come to my rescue at this terrible time. It gave me fresh hope and confidence for the dreaded meeting next day. Heather put on the notice board a letter stating her full backing for my work with the Company, which was wonderful and brave in the face of the intimidation that we heard was taking place.

Wednesday afternoon came and in the lower studio the Board and dancers sat facing one another with the Equity reps between. They began by objecting to my being there, but the Board said it had been agreed I was to be present. They left the room for discussion, returning with their reluctant agreement. They had their say about wanting a change in Director and were listened to by the Board, who eventually stated it was felt an agreement could now be reached between the dancers and me. After consultation the reps reported 'No agreement possible', so the meeting was closed with a further one having been set for Friday. On Friday a sort of mutual agreement was reached, and a statement drawn up for the press in my favour. To my relief this was reported in the Guardian and Telegraph on Saturday. It had been so embarrassing, worrying and unnecessary. I still could not understand what had happened for the dancers to have behaved in such a way. I thought it was all over but, on Sunday, Heather rang to tell me that yet another meeting had been held on Saturday at the end of rehearsals. I sensed more trouble – they had given up up their free Saturday evening for a meeting – and I felt restless.

In retrospect I wonder if this reflected the general atmosphere of the labour environment at the time, the dissatisfaction erupting across Britain, the three day week and constant labour unrest – just the time as well for Nureyev's revenge. It was such a different world from the one I had grown up in. Poor Sven: he was so patient, kind and supportive, experiencing all my depression and bewilderment.

A three-week tour began with a morning train from Paddington to Cardiff. Graham Bond came and sat with me, saying he was disgusted at the dancers' behaviour and wanted me to know he was totally behind me. I was so heartened, as I had been before the awful meeting when Tony Barlow had given me a big hug. I asked Graham what he thought they were grumbling about, to which he replied 'It is a put-up job by someone to discredit you in the eyes of the public, the Arts Council and the Board'. It was somehow beginning to be frightening – there was little I could do to stop the trouble-makers, other than remain calm, courageous and dignified. I had Heather's loyal support, which helped me through the unpredictable days.

Next evening Hynd's *Rosalinda* with Lanchberry conducting was a huge success. Hynd, Lanchbery, David, Heather and I had an enjoyable time at dinner after the show, and we five returned to London next morning. After a busy time at the office, I went with Sven to the Coliseum for the first night of the wonderful Peking Opera. They were amazing – as was the way the Gorlinskys avoided us at the reception which followed. At a meeting next afternoon with Rees and Peter Morris, Rees said he had heard from the Equity reps that they needed clarification of the Board's statement regarding the Artistic Director's willingness to consider suggestions for improvements. I was back in Cardiff with the Company on Thursday when I heard that the reps had received a letter from the Board at which they just scoffed. On Friday there was yet another meeting: it seemed they would never stop. The one lovely event for me was the exquisite performance Terabust gave at her debut in *Rosalinda*. She received enthusiastic applause: quite justified as she was so appealing in her portrayal of the main role.

With the Company's unsettling behaviour, I arrived at Fernhill on Saturday feeling worn out. I had such kindness from our friends the Jennings and their daughter, a TV producer, who put me on her horse and led me in the woods a short way to cheer me. It was my first ever time on a horse and certainly took my mind off the Company. The Jennings knew the pressure I was under and I so appreciated their warm understanding.

By Monday, fully restored, I rejoined the Company in Southampton where there was always a big following for Festival Ballet. Hynd took the *Rosalinda* run-through which finished in good time, allowing me to rehearse a little of *Coppélia* which was due to go on on Friday. We had already begun work on *La Sylphide,* the romantic Danish classic to be premiered in our forthcoming London season. Rees came for the first night in Southampton as we had NatWest personnel to entertain in the intervals with several other local VIPs. Rees had received more horrible letters from the Company reps saying they did not wish me to remain as Artistic Director, despite the Board's ruling. Rees thought the dancers were just disgruntled so I shouldn't worry about their threat of militant action, but I was terribly worried.

After the Friday meeting I had believed the trouble was all over, but if some of my dancers were going to continue in this way I felt I could not stay to be insulted for no apparent reason. On Tuesday, after much soul-searching in the night, I rang my solicitor, Christopher Hall, and arranged to meet him next day telling him of my decision to leave the Company. We met in the Cavalry Club, dear Guy's long-time home, and I knew if Guy were alive he would have told me to withdraw. Christopher agreed with my decision to go and thought I should stay only until the end of the August London season. He would contact Festival Ballet's solicitors and also draw up a suitable statement for the press, clarifying my position and exonerating me from any wrong-doing. I received a copy of a letter Weiss had sent to the reps, toning them down. It was quite good but came too late.

Heather also gave in her notice to me, wanting to get away from the unpleasantness. She was terribly unhappy about the dancers' behaviour and thought I should also consider leaving. As I was in London on Wednesday I was able to attend the evening performance of the Royal Ballet School at the Royal Opera House. I was impressed by the high standard of the students who took to the large stage with enthusiastic confidence. At the end of the week in Southampton, Sven brought two friends to see *Coppélia.* The charismatic theatre manager Ken Watts (known as Mr Bow Tie) kindly entertained us in his office during the intervals. It was a lovely evening with Carole Hill delightfully amusing as Swanhilda. As we left, Ken Watts thrust into my arms two dozen red roses. He had witnessed the strain I was enduring, and I was almost in tears at this quiet show of sympathy.

In Bristol there was another dancers meeting, but it seemed that the tide was turning at last and a vote decided against any boycotting of my rehearsals, which seemed a good sign. On Friday we had a complete run-through for the choreographic workshop due to be held at the Collegiate Theatre the following Thursday.

On Tuesday of the rehearsal week Christopher Hall met with Weiss and me to confirm my definite retirement and to work on a press statement and an agreement paper for presentation at the Board meeting Thursday morning. I rang Sir Louis to keep him informed. He was incredibly understanding.

At the Thursday meeting it seemed to me that the Board had already been informed of my decision to retire, yet I had only told Morris and Rees as we departed for County Hall, so it could not have come from our office. They were both stunned and dismayed, and I saw Rees wiping his eyes. Heather had guessed already, because of Weiss' Tuesday visit to me in the office. The press statement and the agreement were eventually approved by the Board, but not until Murland's objection to the wording had been dealt with by Weiss and also my solicitor over the phone. Once the meeting finished, Weiss and I saw our press lady, Denise Fiennes, who then rang Kensington Palace to tell them a letter was on its way to Princess Margaret. Denise was told that a Charles Murland had rung the previous day to say a letter would be arriving from Festival Ballet. Denise was so incensed by this that she said she would resign – but not until we had written and dispatched our letter to the Palace.

At lunchtime I managed to go to Alexis Rassine's 60th birthday celebration at the Berkeley Hotel. Michael Wood was there and told me that it was Murland who had got him pushed out as press officer from Covent Garden. I was told that Murland had rung Werner, one of the leading trouble-makers in my Company, every morning, directing his mischievous activities. I saw that Nureyev had been using Murland as his henchman.

The choreographic rehearsal in the Collegiate Theatre was pleasing and the show went well at night. I thought it was more innovative and promising than the previous year and, judging by the response, the audience on the 20th thought the same. On Friday 27th the newspapers printed the announcement of my retirement and it was a mixed press; the Telegraph and Guardian were fine, the Daily Mail unsympathetic, but the Evening News was super. After giving me lunch, GB Wilson drove me to see an unwell Madam in Charing Cross Hospital. We talked a lot about the situation and she was sympathetic. To my surprise she knew all about Murland, warning me of his meddling tactics and wishing she had alerted me sooner.

On Saturday I was pleasantly surprised to see how much Schaufuss had achieved to date with his production of *La Sylphide.* Despite suffering too little rehearsal time it was looking promising. It presented the perfect role for Evdokimova and a wonderful vehicle for Schaufuss himself with his Danish background and superb training. The last two days of July were spent interviewing each dancer about their progress and general prospects. This was an annual event but this year, knowing I would no longer be with them to help and guide in the autumn, it seemed to me ridiculous to discuss their future positions in the Company. We spoke as if nothing had happened and, to my relief, I could detect no malice or hatred in them – with the exception of the three main trouble-makers. Many of the younger dancers broke into tears about my leaving. How sad it had got so out of control. I supposed I should never have been persuaded to return after resigning over Weiss's and Murland's behaviour. That decision had left the door open for doubts to be sown about my allegiance to the Company. I wondered who would take on Festival Ballet now? The Arts Council were keen on Kathryn Wade, who I thought would be excellent, but I rather feared John Field, still loitering in the wings, would get himself elected.

Rehearsals for the Festival Hall three-week season were well underway when we had our routine office meeting. This was a particularly sad one, the staff now knowing I was leaving. Rees said some kind words, and I thanked our departing Heather for her hard work and loyalty. I attended a lovely dinner party at the Chinese Embassy, given in honour of Tai Aileen, where I was seated next to Fonteyn. It was one of the few times that we enjoyed an interesting conversation together. We were both relaxed, no longer dancing at the Garden, and I realised what a charming ambassadress she must have been for Panama alongside her husband Tito (Roberto Arias). We met again at Covent Garden at an opening Gala of the National Canadian ballet led by Karen Kain. I thought Karen Kain's technique had improved significantly since she had danced with us at Nureyev's request, and it was a pleasure to see her in the Crush Bar at the reception given after the performance.

Carole Hill was ill and missed her opportunity to take the lead in *Coppélia* on the opening night of the Festival Hall season. We decided that Terabust should take her place, which she did with wit and humour, scoring a great success. We gave *Coppélia* for the entire week, followed by a week of Hynd's *Rosalinda*, which was proving popular with our audiences. Jonas Kåge was outstanding in this ballet, partnering Ruanne with effortless abandon and Swedish charm.

The stage crew, dancers and musicians were now busy preparing *La Sylphide*, scheduled to enter the repertoire at the end of the season. We held the dress parade on Thursday morning – as Sven was driving to Felixstowe to take the boat to Sweden. I was feeling disconsolate but was soon cheered by the costumes of David Walker, so beautifully designed, well sewn and looking lovely. That same day the orchestra held the first of two rehearsals actually in our Festival Ballet House before Festival Hall became available for them. The following Monday and Tuesday were anxious days. We saw a complete run-through of Act I on stage, in Walker's impressive and cleverly designed baronial hall setting. Seeing it for the first time with all the technical tricks was exciting. The rehearsal ran from 1:30 until late in the evening, when the sculptor Tom Merrifield and his wife collected me for a farewell dinner. They also invited Rees and Heather to join us at a smart restaurant just off Marylebone High Street. In the course of the evening Tom gave me one of his bronzes – a beautiful statuette of me in arabesque. I was overwhelmed by his kindness and generosity. As a friend and fellow artist he understood so well my feelings on leaving my much loved Festival Ballet after more than a decade.

The first dress rehearsal of *La Sylphide* with orchestra was on Tuesday evening. This ran for four hours and the last full dress rehearsal, with orchestra, took place on the afternoon of the premiere. For the first few performances, Schaufuss had invited the famous Danish mime artist Niels Bjorn Larsen to perform the role of the wicked witch Madge. The flying and other technical effects presented problems within the limitations of Festival Hall, but these were finally overcome.

I was concerned that Geoffrey McNab had reservations about the success of the *La Sylphide*. I prayed that my final production would not be a failure. He thought the lighting poor and the dancers' lifts, which replaced the customary technical magic, far less enthralling. By the premiere everything worked fairly well, and the evening of the 22nd was an enormous success. I was so happy for Schaufuss whose meticulous work had produced a sensitive romantic ballet: my last production for Festival. To my joy the reviews were all good – a marvellous boost for him and the Company.

Those last few days were a strain and I appreciated the support of my real friends. Sir Alex and Lady Alexander had been present for the premiere and were so upset by the 'whole disgraceful business'. Later Sir Alex told me he was discontinuing his financial support of the Company. Maurice Edelman, the MP, and his wife Tilly were also outraged and took me out for lunch, boosting my confidence with a lot of helpful suggestions for my future. The bookings were splendid, even for the matinee when Andria Hall made a most successful debut as the Sylph. I was thrilled – she had worked hard from the moment I took her into the corps de ballet at the age of seventeen, and here she was a successful principal. I found it so rewarding to help young dancers blossom, and I knew I was going to miss the opportunity to spot and nurture young talent.

Monday saw the last three days to the close of our season and the end of my directorship. I determined to remain calm, dignified and still in charge to the end. Late on Monday evening I fainted for the first time in my life. I was not at the theatre but with Ingvar and Anna at some friends' when, on leaving, I found myself inexplicably lying on the floor. Dear Ingvar was terribly upset and our hosts rang for their doctor. He pronounced me OK but overtired and advised a few days rest and not to drive myself home. After a good night's sleep I was ready for another full day, during which I took time to watch Tetley rehearsing Terabust and Schaufuss in the *Sphinx*. I had scheduled this arresting pas de deux to Martinu music for inclusion on the autumn tour.

Wednesday 29th August arrived and the dread of my farewell. Terry Kern brought me on stage at the end of the performance and I made a short speech to the audience and brought forward Schaufuss and his ballerina of the night, Evdokimova, kissing them both. With the dancers and audience still clapping and under a strong spotlight Terry whisked me off the stage onto the steps leading down to the audience. He escorted me past the public and out of the hall, the doors closing behind me.

It was over, but strangely I did not feel upset. Somehow, after almost twelve years, it seemed the right time to be going. I was given a heart-warming farewell with little posies from a few dancers and bouquets from well-wishers. I was thankful, though, that Ingvar, Anna and my father were there to support me, particularly in Sven's absence; how I missed him. Many good friends came to see me after the show, including Sir Henry Marking who insisted on taking us out to dinner. This was a wonderful surprise and made an enjoyable finish to the evening and the end of another chapter in my career.

66 *Off And Away*

On Sunday I locked up Fernhill, now our permanent home since selling Park Street. Ingvar had been living in my father's flat until he found his own little mews house behind Barons Court, where he had settled comfortably earlier in the year. Ingvar had studied hard on leaving Eton and, after three years at London University, received his degree in physiology from the Queen Mother at the Royal Albert Hall witnessed proudly by Sven and me. This academic work had not come easily to Ingvar – we had watched him at Fernhill, studying determinedly. He went on to train to be a chartered accountant at Thomson McLintock in the City. It was ironic that, not knowing what career he should follow, we had taken Ingvar to a firm specialising in careers advice who said the one path he should not take was accountancy! Yet, having finally chosen that road, it stood him in good stead. Later he ran his own security business for over twenty years – so successfully that it has now been bought by a respected Japanese security firm.

Flying north to join Sven, I reflected on the years with Festival and how much family life I had sacrificed. Had I chosen the right road? I adored the ballet, although I now wished to divorce myself from that art and determined to be more with my family. I failed to realise how enmeshed I had become in the world of dance. As soon as my idyllic time in Sweden with Sven was over, and we had returned to London together with his sister, Greta, I had to go away for a week. This was for something I had been invited to take on some months earlier.

Having previously agreed to head a group of ballet lovers travelling to Russia, I was away for a week from the last Saturday in September. I knew some of the party assembled at Gatwick airport waiting for our take-off to Moscow: Papa Beriozoff, Harold and Harriet Sebag-Montefiore, 'Irene' head of the Legat branch in Scotland, Brian Loftus the dancer/teacher, who had taken recent classes for me at Festival Ballet, and Austin Richardson, Ingvar's prep school headmaster. Our plane was delayed by almost two hours – not a good omen, I thought, and I was correct. The whole trip was poorly organised, resulting in a lot of complaints and justified grumbling about Intourist.

The expedition became one of delights and disappointments. The first upset occurred on the first morning, when only a few people were permitted to go to the Bolshoi School and watch student classes. Instead, a short sight-seeing tour was offered to those turned away. The afternoon was better – the whole group were allowed into the Bolshoi Theatre to meet a few senior dancers and musicians together with their assistant director. Struchkova was their main spokeswoman, and I felt pleased when she spoke highly of me during a question-and-answer session. We returned to the great theatre for the evening's performance, only to find ourselves relegated to the gallery, high up, a long way from the action, on unyielding hard wooden benches. The Pushkin Museum the next day was shut, so we were quickly re-routed to an old monastery. Expecting to see more ballet that evening we found nothing arranged. We sought a venue which could produce tickets for the evening and were fortunate: we went to the Stanislavsky Theatre, but the performance there proved less than enthralling.

Tuesday morning was thrilling for the lucky few of us who were collected by an interpreter and taken to the Bolshoi. We were met at the stage door, where I was immediately recognised as the English ballerina, and were taken up to the fifth floor. There we watched the company at work in two wonderful classes given by two former dancers in spacious studios. We saw several outstanding young male dancers being carefully trained by Gudansky. After half an hour we were ushered along to watch more senior male dancers, together with Plisetskaya who embraced me in her friendly way. This class was taken by Asaf Messerer, her uncle, and was demanding but thrilling. Plisetskaya looked lovely and worked really hard, perspiration pouring off her. Maximova was also in the same class, but not Struchkova who perhaps was in Semeyonova's class in yet another large studio. There was insufficient time to watch any more classes, which meant we were not to see Semeyonova's. This was a disappointment for me because it was she who had coached me so wonderfully in *Swan Lake* and I would have enjoyed watching her at work again. But there were other visits on the agenda and we rejoined the rest of the group in the bitter cold for photos outside the Kremlin Palace before visiting the Armoury.

We experienced an uncomfortable overnight train journey to Leningrad but, once there, were taken on a marvellous, three-hour sightseeing tour of the city. Papa, Brian and I then slipped off to spend the afternoon at the Hermitage, which was even more fabulous than I remembered. We had booked seats for the Maly Theatre evening performance but it was rather a letdown: an obscure opera, followed by a short ballet which neither Brian nor I liked and thought poorly danced.

Spirits were lifted by the most inspiring visit next day to the Kirov Ballet School. The famous ballerina Dudinskya with her husband, Konstantin Sergeyev, gave us a big personal welcome and were generous with their time. They seemed to enjoy answering the many questions from members of our group, all of whom were allowed in. Although the interpreter stipulated that only a few could go, the group was determined that no one would miss out this time. Outside the hotel, when the interpreter was not near the coach, we hid the extra people under our seats. They were not spotted and, as she failed to count the numbers leaving the coach, she never knew and the entire group were ushered warmly into the school by its two distinguished directors.

We were particularly fortunate to see seven of Dudinskya's graduate girls in class. All had well shaped, long legs and exceptional plasticity and body control. They showed supreme confidence in their enchaînements and we witnessed some beautiful dancing. We were given a little display by a number of small girls and boys, all already remarkably turned-out and advanced in their classical work – a joy to watch. Upstairs in Sergeyev's spacious office we saw photos of past great dancers and teachers, the most famous of all, Agrippina Vaganova, whose method is still taught to this day in a number of schools across the world. There were more photos of her outside in the hall and we were loath to leave the happy, dedicated atmosphere pervading the famous school. On our return to the hotel we were bitterly disappointed to be told there were no tickets for the opera after all, and this our last evening in Russia. Some tickets, though, would be made available an hour before the show, if we wished to queue at the Kirov!

On our flight home there was trouble with a faulty door, which was certainly frightening. We bade each other farewell before separating at Gatwick – what a lovely group of people: stoic in the face of many awkward situations. Dearest Sven was there, his arms outstretched to embrace me. It was a deeply grateful Beryl who walked into Fernhill, where both Ingvar and Greta were agog to hear all about the Russian trip.

67 *A New Era*

Retired from Festival Ballet, I expected to have a lot of free time to follow my other interests. Within a year of leaving, however, I was elected a Vice President of the renowned ballet society, the Royal Academy of Dancing, and shortly afterwards to serve on their Executive Committee, where I felt I could contribute something of value. The much respected ballet historian Ivor Guest was Chairman of the Academy at that time and suggested I flew to Hong Kong to help promote interest in and raise financial support for the Academy. I also agreed to give some classes whilst there. It was a trip I enjoyed, especially meeting with several distinguished teachers whose schools were well attended. I also met a well known benefactor of the arts who it was hoped might support the Academy. During my stay he became an invaluable guide, taking me to places of interest in and around Hong Kong as well as to the border of mainland China. I so appreciated the time and hospitality I received from him and his family.

Since we had moved to Fernhill, Sven commuted daily by train to London to his new consulting rooms in Harley Street. To my astonishment, he had ordered a Blüthner grand piano for me. I could hardly believe my eyes when delivery men drew up and began carefully unloading the precious cargo and manhandling it into our house. What astonishment and elation I felt as I realised how deeply Sven must love me. We both enjoyed music and now I could play for him at home on this fine instrument, besides our trips to concerts and operas.

1981 was a significant year – in July Ingvar married Anna Steel, having courted her for almost six years, and we were overjoyed. The wedding took place in Anna's home village of Lindfield, at the local church from where guests could walk down the high street to her parents' house by the village green. In their garden was a huge marquee where family and friends gathered in celebration. It was a joyous occasion, and I was happy that my father was there to see his grandson married to a lovely young woman. As newlyweds they first lived in London, in Ingvar's mews house, deciding later to move to the country where they planned to start a family. Sven and I were so thrilled when our first grandchild, Charlotte, was born. When she was three, Sven and I took her with Anna to Lanzarote for a fortnight's holiday, which was such a pleasure. On the way to the airport, Anna announced that she was pregnant again and seven months later, in October, Oliver made his entrance into the world.

I imagined my connections with the dance world might diminish after leaving Festival Ballet, but happily this has not happened. In fact, the years have become busier and busier, as I have been appointed to many interesting and responsible positions. Requests continue for guidance and advice, which I am always happy to provide if I can. A South African dancer, Harold King, asked for my help in setting up a responsible governing board for a ballet company he was forming. I asked my friend Graham Hill, a lover of the arts and himself a pianist, to be the chairman, a role he kindly undertook with patient authority and, in 1979, London City Ballet came into being.

As a Vice President of the London Ballet Circle since 2001 I have much enjoyed listening to their interesting speakers. I believe societies such as these are invaluable for dance and music lovers, so I was pleased when, the same year, I was asked to give a talk to the Sussex Opera and Ballet Society (SOBS) and subsequently invited to become their Patron. The seeds of this flourishing society were sown in 1974 by Peter Gellhorn and Douglas Craig who gave talks at Glyndebourne where, at that time, they both worked. The early talks took place in the lovely Organ Room at the kind suggestion of John Christie, Glyndebourne's founder, and were organised by Joan Liddle who, inspired by these talks, formed SOBS. But the society soon outgrew the Glyndebourne setting, moving initially to larger premises in Bexhill for weekend courses. It was then that SOBS became an educational charity, of which Sir George Christie (John Christie's son) continued his link as Founder President for the next 23 years. This combination of music and ballet attracts a wide membership who it is a pleasure to see gathered at regular meetings, generally held now in Eastbourne.

Another interesting invitation came in 2003 from Mike Dixon, Chairman of the Critics' Circle Dance Awards, to become their Patron. I felt this a great honour. In 2002, I had myself received their award for Service to Dance and experienced its prestigious encouragement. The awards took place at Sadler's Wells which, together with the Royal Opera House, collaborated with the society for these annual events. Dame Alicia Markova, doyen of British ballet, and Diaghilev's youngest ever ballerina, had previously graced this organisation with her patronage, so I deemed it a big responsibility to follow in her inspirational footsteps. As Patron I was able to lean on significant sponsors for substantial financial support to help ensure the future of these important occasions. I became impressed by the consummate authority with which Angela Rippon charmed those present, eloquently sweeping us through the many award presentations each year at the Royal Opera House. I was asked to create a special Patron's Award and amongst the gifted artists I chose were: David Nixon director of Northern Ballet, choreographer of full-length narrative ballets; Richard Bonynge distinguished conductor, for his research and recording of rare ballet music; and the much loved Darcy Bussell for raising the public profile of dance. I was sorry when Mike Dixon resigned as chairman after ten years and felt it was then perhaps time for me to step down too and welcome a new regime to undertake the Awards.

68 *Staging The Classics*

Early in January 1984 Barry Moreland had invited me to stage *Giselle* for his company in Perth, Australia. Mary Skeaping had created the most perfect production for my Festival Company in 1972, and Barry asked her for this same work. Mary was unwell, so suggested he invite me to put it on instead. I went to see Mary several times in hospital and there she taught me all she had gathered from her time spent in the Paris Opera archives, explaining to me the reasons behind certain arrangements in the ballet. She was also insistent that the dancers learn to hold themselves in the style of the Romantic period, with gently rounded arm positions, perfecting their posture.

Before February was out I was off to Perth this time with Sven, fully versed in the production, armed with pages of notes, eager to carry out all Mary's invaluable directives. Barry gave me a huge welcome, despite the fact that I had not retained him as the choreographer of Festival Ballet. I found his company well trained and the dancers quick to take instruction, so it was a real pleasure to work with them. The production was hailed as a success much to everyone's delight, and I felt proud and pleased for the company. What a pleasure it was to return to the vibrant city of Perth, free of the responsibility of Festival Ballet and Nureyev's antics.

Sven and I fell in love with Perth and were happy to return there when, two years later, Barry invited me back to restage Mary's timeless *Giselle*. On that visit we met Lucette Aldous, the ballerina who had danced so brilliantly with Nureyev in his version of *Don Quixote*. It so happened that, on my second visit, I saw a lot of Lucette's husband Alan Alder who was helping the Perth company with their productions. I also had a wonderful reunion with two of my most devoted dancers from Festival days: John and Bernie Taylor. They now had two children and their own flourishing school. It was good to find them so happy, and we were touched by their insistence that they take us to dinner at a popular restaurant in the old port of Fremantle.

Perhaps the greatest challenge came in 1985, when I was invited to put on *Sleeping Beauty* for the Royal Swedish Ballet in Stockholm. Although it seemed a daunting task I could not refuse – particularly as it would mean working with one of the earliest established ballet companies in northern Europe, founded in 1773. Rehearsals began mid August with 13 weeks in which to teach and produce the full-length classic. Sven and I took a fortnight's holiday in Sweden beforehand, going straight on to Stockholm without returning home first.

Beginning work on Monday morning 19th September I found Nils-Åke Häggbom had been appointed as my assistant. He was waiting to take me to a nearby hall to begin teaching the first scene: Carabosse with her attendant rats. This was the only piece I had not yet worked out in detail, thinking it would be some time before we reached this episode in the prologue, so my heart missed a beat when I met the expectant dancers. I had to think quickly to remember all the correct moves and also choreograph the rats' gleeful gyrations. The dancers were easy to work with, adaptable to any little changes I found suited them, and my first rehearsal passed happily. From then on, all my calls were to take place in the theatre, in a large studio raked exactly like the stage.

I felt a bond spring up between Nils-Åke and myself. He was patient, had a keen eye and an empathy with the dancers, having been one of their leading artists and now on the teaching staff. We worked alongside the choreologist, Agneta Stjernlof-Valcu, who was kept busy notating my *Sleeping Beauty* as it developed. She was brilliant at her work and most helpful to me with an all-important sense of humour. She, like Nils-Åke, was a pleasure to have at one's side, and I owe them both a big debt of gratitude for their help in staging *Beauty*.

Each day after we worked with such concentration I would return exhausted to the little apartment where Sven would be waiting with a hot meal ready. He was unbelievably understanding during the demanding three months that I was working in the theatre. David Walker was my chosen designer for the ballet, and it was good to see how much Sven enjoyed his company. Walker loved visiting Stockholm where in the Opera House his work was much admired and his presence always warmly welcomed. John Lanchbery also agreed to come to Stockholm to conduct *Sleeping Beauty* for me and to check and adjust the scores as necessary. We became a jolly pas de quatre, often eating in the excellent café conveniently adjacent to the stage door.

Once the ballet began to take shape it was good to have Lanchbery at rehearsals. I taught every step and move myself, with only my notes to supplement my memory of Sergeyev's beautiful production, which I aimed to follow as closely as I could. This was the one he had brought out from Russia and staged for de Valois's company at Sadler's Wells in 1939. When I later saw Kenneth MacMillan's *Sleeping Beauty* I thought he too appeared to have been influenced by Sergeyev's production, as our two versions curiously were quite similar.

As the premiere drew nearer there were many decisions to be made about the casting of principal roles, solos and divertissements. It was hard to choose which ballerina should dance Princess Aurora at the premiere. We had three strong leading couples, each with their own individual personality. We were granted generous lighting and stage time prior to the dress and orchestral rehearsals, so did not feel under too much pressure. Although nervously anxious for the company, I felt a thrill of excitement as the curtain rose on the first night of my production. The dancers were inspired by Lanchbery's dynamic conducting as well as David Walker's beautiful period costumes and ravishing sets. It was a great evening – and what a joy to feel the success of the performance together with the happiness of the dancers, only topped next day by the plaudits of the press. It meant so much to me also that Sven's sister, together with many of his family, were able to be at this first night and all expressed their enjoyment of the performance.

I was pleased when, in 2002, I was asked back to the Swedish Royal Opera House to revive *Sleeping Beauty* prior to the company taking it to Japan. This took four weeks, working once again with Agneta and Nils-Åke, and it was a pleasure to be amongst their talented dancers who gave me a wonderful welcome back. They seemed to be born actors and after a month the ballet was at a high standard for performance. This time I was booked into my favourite Hotel Diplomat, welcomed by the friendly but now aging doorman. It was where I always stayed when dancing with the company, and I felt relaxed in its homely atmosphere and old fashioned rooms. The month flew by and before returning to London, Sven and I spent a couple of days at his childhood home in Vadstena.

69 *Yorkshire Ballet Seminars*

One of my most rewarding engagements since leaving Festival Ballet has been teaching young dancers at the Yorkshire Ballet Seminars (now Yorkshire Ballet Summer School) held for many years in Ilkley, where the local College provided excellent facilities. The summer school was the brainchild of a former Royal Ballet soloist, David Gayle, who with the encouragement of Dame Ninette de Valois and Dame Alicia Markova founded it in 1973. Both de Valois and Markova plus many other distinguished artists came, either to teach or give talks for a week during the month's seminar. Like David, I believe it is important for students to have the opportunity to work under the tuition of professional dancers. I used to look forward to my visits which were always well organised by David with the help of just one local lady. David ran the seminars for thirty-one years and they still continue, now in York, under the direction of the former ballerina Marguerite Porter.

My visit to the annual Yorkshire Ballet Seminars in 1983 coincided with Anton Dolin's – he was giving classes in mime, which I made a point of watching whenever I could. He was a past master in the art of mime, less robust than the Russians but with his own calm dignity, characteristic of the *danse noble:* clear and convincing. Dolin and I travelled back to London together at the end of the week and one of the topics we touched on was his dilemma over whether to go straight on to the south of France to pursue his writing or to stop over in Paris first for a check-up. We heard later that he got a clean bill of health from the clinic but, on leaving it, dropped down dead. Little had I realised on our train journey that this would be the last time I would ever be with this great artist. Having watched his classes, I recognised how fortunate I had been to have experienced Ursula Moreton's teaching of mime during my early years. She was such a gracious performer, handing on to her students the art of mime. Little mime is seen in today's ballets, and I fear this great art is in decline and may well soon be lost.

70 *The Big Honour*

Over my busy years with Festival Ballet I managed to retain my place as a Council member of the ISTD, to which I had been elected in 1962. As one of the big dance societies it embraces not only ballet but also many other dance techniques, including ballroom dancing. The renowned Victor Sylvester was also a Council member and an inspiration to this highly successful branch of the Society. The revered historian Cyril Beaumont, with whom everyone felt it a privilege to serve, was Chairman. I became Chairman in 1984 and even more closely involved with each section of the ISTD. At this time their General Secretary was Peter Pearson, who was the greatest help to me. I had serious reservations about taking on such a responsibility but, thanks to Peter's invaluable encouragement and mentoring, I gained the expertise to undertake the role of chairman, not only of the ISTD but also later of several other dance organisations.

I was asked to join several other charity committees, including the Royal Ballet Benevolent Fund and the Dance Teachers Benevolent Fund. I worked closely with Lord Hastings, an enthusiastic supporter of the ballet since the 1930s. He was the most endearing person, chairman of both funds, who I later followed as chairman of the Royal Ballet Benevolent Fund and as vice chair of the Dance Teachers Benevolent Fund. My work with Lord Hastings led to my being elected to the Governors of the Royal Ballet and subsequently onto the Board of the Royal Opera House itself. These positions I was particularly pleased to hold with the Boards' ongoing responsibilities and decisions to be taken. I was proud to be a part of the Opera House again, my home for many years.

It was during my time as a director that the Royal Opera House was shut for two years undergoing extensive building works with many important improvements. So the ballet and opera Companies had to look elsewhere for London venues in which to perform. No doubt there is much to be written about this period, during which time Sir Colin Southgate was the adroit Chairman of the Board of Governors of the Royal Opera House and Lord Sainsbury Chairman of the Board of Governors of the Royal Ballet company. Lord Sainsbury was deeply concerned about the ballet and its future and, as his Vice Chairman, I shared his concerns. He held frequent meetings with Company representatives to support, guide and encourage the dancers during that time when the Opera House was being transformed, through the generosity of its supporters, into the impressive edifice it is today. In 1999 the Opera House re-opened with both Companies restored to their rightful home. The Royal family attended a momentous gala at which Lord Eatwell and I were detailed to look after the Queen Mother and Princess Margaret throughout the evening.

I cannot conclude these memoirs without referring to the most important honour of my life. In 1988 I was created a Dame. This made me feel very humble, and I realise I could never have been awarded this distinction without the love and encouragement of my family, teachers and true friends. I am highly aware of the opportunities life has offered me through this precious, God-given gift of dance. My belief in God has taken me through the dark days from which my faith has been strengthened and my love of dance deepened.

Index